AMERICAN POLITICAL THOUGHT

Revised Edition

Alan Pendleton Grimes
Michigan State University

UNIVERSITY
PRESS OF
AMERICA

LANHAM • NEW YORK • LONDON

Copyright © 1983 by

University Press of America,™ Inc.

4720 Boston Way
Lanham, MD 20706

3 Henrietta Street
London WC2E 8LU England

Copyright © 1955, 1960 by
Holt, Rinehart and Winston, Inc.

Library of Congress Cataloging in Publication Data

Grimes, Alan Pendleton, 1919-
    American political thought.

    Reprint. Originally published: Rev. ed. New York :
Holt, Rinehart, and Winston, 1960.
    Bibliography: p.
    Includes index.
    1. Political science—United States—History.
I. Title.
JA84.U5G7   1983   320.5'0973   83-16877
ISBN 0-8191-3596-8 (pbk. : alk. paper)

To Peg

Preface to the Revised Edition

The role of America in world politics has made an understanding of its political thought of especial interest and significance. The underlying values of American political thought reflect in large measure the values of the Western cultural heritage; philosophers of the West have always provided much of the intellectual grist for American theoreticians. This assumption, of the relatedness of American political thought to Western political philosophy, which underlay the first edition of this book, is continued in the present revision. Specifically it has seemed appropriate to include the economic individualism of the former Austrian economist, Friedrich A. Hayek, now a professor in America, whose *The Road to Serfdom* so clearly articulates the political economic beliefs of many Americans; democratic socialism as represented in the writings of Norman Thomas; Marxian economics, of such world importance, as represented by the writings of Paul Sweezy, and modern conservatism which has drawn no little of its inspiration from the political thought of Edmund Burke. As previously Americans drew upon the writings of Calvin, John Locke, and John Stuart Mill, so have Americans continued to draw upon the thinkers of the West when it has served their interests to do so.

The material following Chapter 15 has been affected by this revision: two new chapters have been added, two others considerably revised. The text prior to Chapter 16 remains the same as in the previous edition. The entire bibliography has been re-examined in the light of new research and revised where appropriate. I am indebted to Mrs. Joyce Bell and Mrs. Jane Wonch for typing; Jay Weinroth for research assistance; the All-College Research Fund of Michigan State University for financial help for research, consultation and typing; and to my wife who helped, as with the earlier edition, with every phase of this book's preparation.

A. P. G.

East Lansing, Michigan
October 1959

Preface to the First Edition

Political thought does not exist in a vacuum. The drama of politics is played within the setting of a society which is seeking a solution to its problems. At issue are the values, beliefs, and working assumptions by which men live. Political theory is born out of the conflicts in a society or between societies, out of the struggle between the "is" and the "ought to be." It is politics—the contest for authority—distilled and articulated into systematic thought. The inevitable problems inherent in any society, of individual and group superiority and subordination, of the control of man over man, compel thinking men to question, as did political philosophers of old, the "why" and the "how" of it all and to ask "to what purpose?" Political theory is thus concerned with descriptive, causative, and normative issues. It seeks descriptively to know the "is," for without knowledge of the existing political environment causative theory loses its basis in reality and normative theory loses the compulsive appeal which arises from contrast. It seeks to know why we behave and believe the way we do, how our political system came about and what, if any, sound generalizations we may make about political behavior. Finally, it seeks to describe the values by which we ought to live; the goals of society we ought to seek; the means by which we should seek them; and the institutional fabric which would best maintain them. Here one finds such concepts as liberty, equality, democracy, social justice, and others. They are values, however, which require definition and interpretation to be meaningful.

While political theory is concerned with the descriptive, causative, and normative aspect of politics, few political theorists deal fully with each of these aspects, nor is there need to. For a clear statement of any one aspect of the political problem usually implies ideas related to the other two. Men think and write within a wide range of assumed thought, else any high level of communications would be impossible. Words may reveal or obfuscate, depending on the thought—the assumptions and beliefs—of the reader. Thus to understand a political theorist one should understand the climate of opinion, the prevailing belief systems, of his time. Words gain and lose meaning, and this is especially true where political values are concerned. Political thought is a part of the social thought of a time and place, of an intellectual environment. In an intellectual environment in which religious values are paramount, or at the top of the hierarchy of values, political theory will be formulated with a religious frame of reference and will draw heavily upon theological assumptions for its arguments. Political theory in Puritan Massachusetts must therefore be understood within the larger framework of the heritage of the Reformation. In an age of secular yet absolute values, political theory was largely concerned with the assumptions of natural law and the nature of natural rights. The right to private judgment in theology reappeared in secular garb as the right to private judgment in politics. Though rationalism had supplanted the system of Scriptural argument, each as a system of thought was essentially deductive in method and absolute in conclusion.

Seventeenth-century theology gave rise to, and gave way to, eighteenth-century rationalism, which system in turn gave way to the philosophical radicalism of the nineteenth-century. Nineteenth-century liberalism was as much an economic as a political theory. The values and assumptions associated with classical economic theory comprised a large part of the frame of reference of capitalistic political thought. To understand late nineteenth-century political theory in America one must refer to the prevailing economic ideology. The principal reformers of the period were, for instance, interested in achieving economic reforms through the political process. Liberty, in a legal sense, took on a distinctively economic connotation, while the progressive movement for social justice was largely a movement for economic reform in the direction of equality of opportunity and rewards. Economic determinism, whether of the capitalistic or socialistic variety, played a large role in political thought. Finally, pragmatism, distinctively American in its orientation, gathered up the loose ends of progressive thought to emphasize the importance of experimentation, flexibility, and the relationship of means to ends, together with the incessant interaction of the individual with his society. The public interest gained as a normative concept as classical economic individualism declined.

Political thought in America has interacted with the prevailing sense of social values, whether derived immediately from theology, philosophy, or economics. Indeed, so intertwined are these systems of belief that their separation, while producing logical order, introduces artificiality. Yet such surgery is necessary as a step towards understanding.

American political thought is thus an expression of American social thought, conditioned by it, yet in turn conditioning it. Political theory operates from assumptions regarding man's social behavior, and its usual mission is to portray the type of social behavior which either is or is supposed to be authoritatively maintained. That is, social theory becomes political theory when it involves the political process in its speculations, for it is through political action that stability is maintained or change brought about. Society, organized as a political community with authority vested in a government empowered to make compulsory rules of action, maintains itself and orders its changes through enforceable law. Political theory is thus largely concerned with what rules of action in society are, or ought to be, enforced, and the causative theory of human relations which makes such conclusions appear desirable or logically necessary.

It is evident, then, that American political thought draws upon ideas that are neither American in origin nor even explicitly political in conception. It is concerned with ideas which have played an important role in the political ideology of a given period of our history, wherever derived. To a large extent American political thought consists of the articulations and modifications by Americans of the political thought of others. Puritan political thought is largely derived from the Frenchman John Calvin. American Revolutionary thought consists primarily of the reformulation in America of the political thought of the Englishman John Locke. Late nineteenth-century liberalism in America was clearly derived from English theorists such as John Stuart Mill and the classical economists. Social Darwinism came from England to America and became for a time part of our social assumptions, which in turn conditioned our political thought. More recently the thinking of the English economist John Maynard Keynes has found a place in American political thought and practice. Few original contributions to political theory have been made by Americans, despite our distinctive political institutions. We have however interpreted, adopted and modified Western political thought to better suit our circumstances.

Jefferson used Locke, to be sure; but Jefferson used Locke with regard to a particular and relevant situation which gave Jeffersonian thought a distinction of its own. John Adams was more than Blackstone; he was Blackstone reinterpreted in the light of Adams' views of past political theory and experience and particularly the American environment. American political thought has always drawn upon relevant prevailing political theories; but the determination of relevance itself involves causative interpretations, values, and selectivity. Thus the fact of historical antecedence of a theory is not as consequential as its particular assumed relevance and applicability. Where American thought was most distinctively original, as in the controversies over slavery and the nature of the Union, it was also distinctively relevant to a situation peculiar to America. Calhoun arose as probably the most original American political theorist; yet for all his originality he became, in many respects, dated with the issues he sought to resolve. Modern democracies, however, are not so distinctively different either in fundamental values or institutions that the basic problems of one democracy are not similar to those of another. Inevitably considerable cross-fertilization in ideas exists.

American political thought is not something already made or finally formulated. There is no terminal point to the subject. At the time of this writing it would appear that pragmatic liberalism, discussed in the last chapter, was being supplanted by something akin to conservatism. Conservatism, like liberalism, has a rich political heritage in America; recent efforts to reformulate conservatism, however, have been occupied mainly with the rediscovery of the ideas of conservatives of the past, most of whom are treated in this text. There are ample references in the bibliography to the last chapter to contemporary efforts to redefine both liberalism and conservatism.

Political theory is constantly in the making as new situations produce new contests between individuals, groups, and institutions for authority in society. Men's values are always at stake; we believe certain things to be descriptive of our immediate situation; we must act and decide on the basis of causative assumptions regarding our fellow man with little more than hunch for proof of the validity of our causative assumptions. We seek to convince our neighbor of the "rightness" of our political convictions; that the only "moral" course for the government to take is thus and so; that "realistically" if this is permitted, thus and so will follow; that "human nature being what it is" we can't do this, or must do that; that "there ought to be a law against it"; that public policy is or is not "really" determined by "economic power"; that "I have a right" to do thus and so; that, in short, as social animals we live with each other and control each other in some fashion on some things. The desirability of this control, the necessity for it, the manner in which it is exercised and the method of its change will, it is safe to say, always be at issue. And in the course of this issue political theory arises to explain, describe and justify.

I am indebted to many people for their kind assistance during the preparation of this book. My colleagues at Michigan State College who read or discussed portions of the manuscript with me gave me the benefit of their criticisms, while my students in American political thought have been a constant source of intellectual stimulation. I should like to note here, however, my deep appreciation for the efforts of the unsung heroes of the manuscript; William Mitchell, Jay Aronson and Rosalie Casad spent long hours checking bibliography and footnotes; Janet Owen helped with the proofreading; Margaret Hunt patiently checked galleys and furthermore played the major role in preparing and checking the index; and my wife helped me at every stage in the preparation of the book.

A. P. G.

East Lansing, Michigan
November 1954

Contents

1. THE RISE OF PROTESTANTISM   1

2. PURITAN POLITICAL THOUGHT   22

3. ENGLISH REVOLUTIONARY THOUGHT   46

4. THE AMERICAN REVOLUTION   66

5. AMERICAN CONSTITUTIONALISM   98

6. THE FEDERALISTS: POWER, PROPERTY AND LAW   128

7. JEFFERSONIAN DEMOCRACY   150

8. THE CONCEPT OF THE COMMON MAN   174

9. THE NEW SOCIETY: INDIVIDUALISTS AND UTOPIANS   200

10. SLAVERY AND THE RIGHTS OF MAN: ANTISLAVERY THOUGHT   222

11. SLAVERY AND THE RIGHTS OF MAN: PROSLAVERY THOUGHT   244

12. THE NATIONAL CONCEPT OF SOVEREIGNTY   262

13. MANCHESTER LIBERALISM IN AMERICA   287

14. AMERICAN UTOPIAN REFORMERS: GEORGE AND BELLAMY   312

15. THE PROGRESSIVE MOVEMENT   354

16. ECONOMIC INDIVIDUALISM   395

17. PRAGMATIC LIBERALISM   418

CONTENTS

18. PROTEST IDEOLOGIES 443

19. CONSERVATISM 478

   BIBLIOGRAPHY 511

   INDEX 547

AMERICAN POLITICAL THOUGHT

CHAPTER 1

The Rise of Protestantism

THE PROTESTANT REFORMATION

ALTHOUGH American political thought begins with a study of Puritan thinking, an understanding of the Puritan in America requires at least a brief survey of the religious forces which brought forth Puritanism. Socially, politically, and economically, colonial Puritan thinking reflected the heritage of late medieval Europe, tempered somewhat by the humanism of the Renaissance and the nationalism of Elizabethan England. Fundamentally, however, Puritanism was another step in the march of the Protestant Reformation.

The Protestant Reformation marked the culmination of effort over a period of several centuries to alter certain tenets and practices of the Catholic Church. Its immediate sixteenth- and early seventeenth-century consequences were the multiplication of Christian denominations, rabid religious persecution, civil disobedience, and war. Its long-range results were the establishment of a new relationship between church and state, the secularization of political authority, religious toleration and the creation of a core of civil liberties. From the detached view of a secular age, steeped in the principles of religious toleration, and removed by centuries as well as a continent from the conflicts of the period, the Reformation appears almost inconceivably remote. In fact, though many seeds of present thought are found in the Reformation, that age of conflict and intense belief is quite remote. For the period of the Reformation was as much an age of faith, of piety, and of theology as subsequent periods of thought have been characterized by their rational, political, economic, or social emphasis. The fundamental questions were theological ones, and the fundamental answers were in a theological vein. It was thus in the context of theology that struggles initiated, and in the context of theology that conflicts were resolved. To understand the conflicts and the consequences of the Reformation one must delve into theology.

In the early medieval period, Western Christendom had been considered as a unity, one great society presided over by two rulers, pope and emperor, in accordance with the doctrine of the Two Swords. Temporal jurisdiction came finally to rest in the hands of the emperor; spiritual jurisdiction passed from priest to bishop and culminated in the authority of the pope. In theory, this was a happy solution to the vexing relationship of the world of the spirit to the world of the flesh, with each ruler moving within his divinely appointed orb. "Christian emperors," wrote Pope Gelasius I in the fifth century, "need bishops for the sake of eternal life, and bishops make use of imperial regulations to order the course of temporal affairs."[1] Yet at best this solution could be only an approximate one, for inevitably issues would arise which involved equally secular and temporal authority. The border-line claims of the contesting rulers would vary with the aggressiveness of the respective incumbents. Presented in its simplest form, the theory of the Two Swords provided for one state and one church occupying coterminous territory with rulers of the state understood to be faithful members of the church while not officials of it, and the rulers of the church understood to be members of the state while not officials of it. In practice, as the Massachusetts Puritans found centuries later, the spiritual unity of the commonwealth could be preserved only by admitting the supremacy of the spiritual sword. The issue of church and state relationship in early Massachusetts was not unlike that of the medieval period in Europe. The extreme position announced by Pope Boniface VIII in the opening years of the fourteenth century might well have been a statement by a Puritan of the relationship of church and state:

> Both swords, the spiritual and the material, therefore, are in the power of the church; the one, indeed, to be wielded for the church, the other by the church. . . . One sword, moreover, ought to be under the other, and the temporal authority to be subjected to the spiritual. For when the apostle says "there is no power but of God, and the powers that are of God are ordained" they would not be ordained unless sword were under sword and the lesser one, as it were, were led by the other to great deeds.[2]

[1] Cited in George H. Sabine, *A History of Political Theory* (New York: Henry Holt and Co., 1950), p. 195. See also in Sabine Chapters 15, 16 and 18.

[2] *Unam Sanctam*, cited in William Elliott and Neil A. McDonald, *Western Political Heritage* (New York: Prentice-Hall, 1949), pp. 309-310.

With the close of the fourteenth century, the power of the Church waned as the theory of the one great society proved totally incompatible with political conditions in western Europe. Secular authority passed into the hands of provincial princes and the rising national monarchs. These rulers, jealous of competing authority, were eager to hedge the power of the Church when it conflicted with their political designs. The Babylonian Captivity (1309-1377), when the papacy was moved to Avignon at the insistence of Philip the Fair of France, was but a dramatic illustration of the power of the new temporal authority. The Great Schism which followed, in which there were two and for a while three popes, left the claimants of spiritual authority in a precarious position.

In order to restore the dignity and authority of the Church, reform seemed imperative. This reform proceeded along two lines. On the one hand was the peculiarly political and administrative problem of the relationship of the pope to proposed church councils within the Church. The main attempt toward a solution of this problem became known as the Conciliar Movement and took place during the fourteenth and fifteenth centuries. It was during the course of this controversy that many illustrious scholars, among them Marsilio of Padua, William of Occam, and Nicholas of Cusa, spoke up for the supremacy of a council rather than the pope in Church affairs. It was, in effect, a movement to substitute for the absolute monarchy of the pope a representative assembly or council. Although the movement failed to alter the institution of papal supremacy in the Catholic Church, the movement gave voice to fundamental theory concerning the authority of representative bodies as opposed to personal absolutism. To this extent it stands properly in the historic course of the development of democratic thought, and its effect upon church organization may be witnessed in the constitution of the synod, or council device, in many Protestant churches. The Massachusetts Puritans, in adopting the principle of church synods, followed the stream of ideas developed by the Conciliarists.

The other aspect of Church reform struck directly at the heart of Church doctrine and the practices associated with it. Developing along with the Conciliar Movement, the major burden of this effort was to rid the Church of certain practices which were considered corrupt by the reformers and certain ceremonies which were considered unnecessary for salvation. This movement, developing first within the Church itself, later in opposition to it, sought to reduce the role played by the Catholic hierarchy in both religious and secular affairs and to eliminate some of the procedural and substantive requirements heretofore thought necessary for salvation. It marked a trend towards simplification of dogma and ritual and emphasized Scripture as opposed to the heavy tomes of scholastic writers. It sought to reduce the accretions of a thousand years of Church scholarship to a doctrine more comprehensible to less tutored men.

An Englishman, John Wycliffe (1320-1384), was one of the first notable doctrinal reformers. He challenged the doctrine of papal supremacy and popularized the arguments of William of Occam. He emphasized the place of the Bible in religion and anticipated Luther's stand on the priesthood of all believers. Wycliffe, in challenging papal authority, made comfortable room for secular national power. The Church should be reformed by restricting its jurisdiction to purely spiritual affairs, leaving the state to govern all temporal affairs. In his doctrine of *dominium* or lordship, he emphasized a direct personal relationship between God and man which required, theoretically, no intermediate church institution. Wycliffe's followers in England, the Lollards, like the followers of John Hus (1369-1415) in Bohemia, helped prepare a favorable climate of opinion for the more consequential leaders of the Protestant Reformation who came more than a century later.

It was during the first half of the sixteenth century that the Reformation proper broke out in Europe. Starting as a movement of religious reform, it soon became, when challenged, a movement of religious revolt. Though the specific issues were theological, the material stakes as well were of fundamental importance. Monasteries and other church properties, revenue drained from princes and destined for the Holy See, ecclesiastical as well as secular appointments—all these were at stake, and consequently all theological argument promptly assumed a political complexion. If it was to the advantage of secular rulers to be rid of the often-conflicting authority of a foreign pope and his alien retinue, it was doubly to the advantage of such rulers to have a national church which would help keep all loyalties and moneys at home. Even as temporal authority was passing from the hands of an emperor no longer able to maintain effective jurisdiction over his mythical empire into the hands of strong national monarchs, so now did a considerable amount of ecclesiastical jurisdiction pass from the Catholic Church, centered at Rome, to western European and English national churches. The Reformation was, in this respect, a great decentralizing movement which fractionalized the medieval conception of one civilized world and one Christian religion. But when considered in relation to the rising national states it considerably accelerated the tendency towards nationalism and centralization within the state.

The Reformation brought forth, directly, three new religious doctrines: Lutheranism, Calvinism, and Anglicanism. While Catholicism lost ground, it continued to hold its predominant position. Now, however, the effort to maintain a true religion involved no longer an occasional struggle against isolated heretics and infidels, but rather a major and continuous combat against highly organized and equally devout forces. If there could be only one true religion, then it was essential that the true religion be defended, if necessary, by all the power and might of secular authority. As by this reasoning there could be only one legitimate religion in any state, practicing non-conformers were not tolerated. Thus in a sense the medieval doctrine of one church and one state was continued. The very existence of a diversity of religious beliefs, however, presaged a bad future for this doctrine. Lutheranism was the first of the new religious doctrines brought forth in the Reformation.

When Martin Luther (1483-1546) nailed his famous Ninety-Five Theses on the door of the Wittenberg church in 1517, he still looked forward to reforming the Church by ridding it of such practices as the sale of papal indulgences. In the course of subsequent debate with a papal representative, however, Luther revealed a doctrine not dissimilar to the views held by the heretics Wycliffe and Hus. Placed in a position of choosing between recanting or open opposition to the Church, he chose opposition and thereby began the first successful revolt against Catholicism in the Reformation. Luther attacked the Catholic hierarchy by proclaiming his belief in the priesthood of all believers and in justification by faith alone rather than by sacraments and works.

> All Christians are truly of the Spiritual Estate, and there is no difference among them, save of office alone. As St. Paul says . . . we are all one body, though each member does its own work, to serve the others. This is because we have one baptism, one Gospel, one faith, and are all Christians alike; for baptism, Gospel and faith, these alone make Spiritual and Christian people.[3]

[3] Martin Luther, "*Address to the German Nobility Concerning Christian Liberty,*" as found in *The Harvard Classics*, edited by Charles W. Eliot (New York: P. I. Collier and Son, 1909-10), vol. 36, pp. 278-279.

Luther's belief in the priesthood of all believers, coupled with his belief in justification by faith alone, subsequently served the cause of democracy; for central to the democratic conception was the belief in the importance of the individual. Furthermore, Luther felt that ecclesiastical officials could not claim immunity from secular authority.

> Therefore I say, forasmuch as the temporal power has been ordained by God for the punishment of the bad and the protection of the good, therefore we must let it do its duty throughout the whole Christian body, without respect of person, whether it strikes popes, bishops, priests, monks, nuns, or whoever it may be.[4]

In a few decades, Lutheranism spread over the North German principalities. The interesting alliance between the German princes and the new religion was indicated by the Peace of Augsburg, in 1555, which provided, among other things, that Lutheranism was the only permissible form of Protestantism and that each prince would decide for his subjects whether the kingdom would be Catholic or Lutheran. Thus far the Protestant Reformation in Europe had instituted a new doctrine and a new ecclesiastical bureaucracy in the form of a national church, but the fundamental relationship between church and state remained the same. However, the areas in which either Lutheranism or Catholicism were to be permitted were defined by political boundaries and determined in the last analysis by existing political authority. Protestantism was thus linked to the state, to secular authority, in the early course of the Reformation, and the temporal hand clearly helped hold the spiritual sword.

CALVINISM

By far the most important of the religious reformers from the point of view of the Puritan movement was the Frenchman John Calvin (1509-1564). Writing the first edition of his great *Institutes of The Christian Religion* when he was only twenty-seven years old, he made an indelible mark upon the Protestant Reformation. Trained in the law, he brought into his theology the fruits of his rigid formalistic background. To document this endeavor to codify the new theology, Calvin found ample material in the Mosaic code

---

[4] *Ibid.*, p. 281.

and other decrees of the Old Testament. The theology of Calvin thus developed after the pattern of the Old Testament into a logically organized body of injunctions and commands, whose moral codes regulated in detail the minutiae of human problems associated with daily living. Cavinistic doctrine was strict, orderly, and authoritarian.

Calvin agreed with traditional Christian theology that the sinfulness of Adam caused a fall from the grace of the Lord and imposed a penalty upon subsequent mankind. Since the fall, man was but a lowly worm in a world ruled by a glorious God. Basically, where Calvinism departed from both Catholicism and Lutheranism was in the means of man's escape from the full consequences of the fall. In Catholic doctrine, man might escape the wages of sin and attain salvation by faithfully observing the sacraments of the Church and personally evidencing good works. In effect, the choice between redemption and damnation was left largely up to the individual himself, who might in conformance with the creed determine by his own efforts in this world his place in the afterlife. Of course, the Church was the necessary intermediary between God and man and its position in this respect was defended by Scriptural quotation as well as long-continued practice. Lutheranism, on the other hand, denied the role of the Catholic Church as the instrument of salvation. Not only was the necessity of observing the Catholic sacraments attacked, but to Lutheranism as to all Protestantism, the Church was considered an agent of the Anti-Christ. It is essential to understand this point, for it makes all the difference in the issue of religious toleration. In place of sacraments and works, Lutheranism substituted justification by faith alone. Of course, by faith was meant not only faith in the one Christian God, but a firm belief in the essentials of the Lutheran creed. Nevertheless, Lutheranism, like Catholicism, afforded the individual some part in the determination of his fate. That man was intrinsically frail and prone to sin there was no doubt; yet by diligence, self-control and an overwhelming desire, true faith might be achieved and with it its glorious consequences.

At the very outset, Calvinism took a more pessimistic view of man. How could corrupt and sinful man ever attain the purification necessary for salvation? How could man, who so easily succumbed to the wiles of the devil, whose knowledge was as nothing compared to God's wisdom, whose petty life of fears, hates, jealousies and unscrupulous desires condemned him to insecurity and anguish—

how could such a one overcome these things to approach the kingdom of Heaven? If, in other words, man is sinful, how can he overcome sin? How does faith come to such a man? Calvinism rejected the Catholic approach of justification by sacraments and works, as well as the Lutheran approach of justification by faith. Since God had suffered man to fall, only an act of His grace might redeem mankind. The Calvinist means to salvation, therefore, required first the grace of the Lord without which individual effort was to no avail. Those who had received the grace of the Lord, were beneficiaries of His mercy, became thereby the "elect" in the Calvinist system. As only a relative few ever achieved this elevated status and as this achievement was due not to the efforts of the elect, but rather to God's judgment, Calvinism substituted for free will a doctrine of rigid determinism. This principle was called pre-destination, for God had always known who would be saved and who would be damned.

> When we attribute foreknowledge to God, we mean that all things have ever been, and perpetually remain, before his eyes, so that to his knowledge nothing is future or past, but all things are present; and present in such a manner, that he does not merely conceive of them from ideas formed in his mind, as things remembered by us appear present to our minds, but really beholds and sees them as if actually placed before him. And his foreknowledge extends to the whole world, and to all the creatures. Predestination we call the external decree of God, by which he has determined in himself, what he would have to become of every individual of mankind. For they are not all created with a similar destiny; but eternal life is fore-ordained for some, and eternal damnation for others. Every man, therefore, being created for one or the other of these ends, we say, he is predestined either to life or to death.[5]

In seeking to understand subsequent Puritan thought, it is impor-tant to consider Calvinism not from the point of view of the majority who are damned but rather from the point of view of the aristocracy who are saved. In the ranks of the majority one could never be entirely sure of damnation; there was always the hope of some eventual sign of grace. But the minority, the elect, certain of salvation and inspired with the holy zeal implied in their selection by the Lord, must henceforth engage in a militant crusade

---

[5] John Calvin, *Institutes of the Christian Religion,* translated by J. Allen (Philadelphia: Presbyterian Board of Christian Education, 7th American edition, 1936), vol. II, pp. 175-176.

against the Anti-Christ, Protestant heretics, non-conformers, slackers, backsliders and all the multitudinous forms which Satan might take to seduce mankind from the ways of righteousness. It was a ceaseless and exhausting struggle with rewards not readily discernible; but with salvation at stake, how could one fail to exert his efforts to the utmost? The battle of the elect to preserve the ways of the Lord gave Calvinism a militancy which manifested itself in intolerance and persecution where Calvinists were in control of the state, and in an equally belligerent demand to maintain their religion where they were not in political authority.

Because the selection of the chosen few was not an action based on human standards of righteousness, there might be some questions as to how one knew to which category, the saved or the damned, one belonged. This presented, however, no great problem to the devout. For when God offered salvation, Calvin held, He "assigns it in such manner, that the certainty of the effect is liable to no suspense or doubt."[6]

There was a certain psychic element in Calvinism, a religious conversion experienced by those who were chosen. It fell to the Calvinist churches to determine the validity of the individual's claim to salvation and to recognize those who were truly called, as opposed to the imposters and the self-deceived. Inasmuch as salvation itself hung upon this decision, the Calvinist churches exercised for their followers an awesome authority. Those who thought themselves called but were adjudged not to have been, like Mistress Anne Hutchinson, had either to recant or be exiled.

In Calvinist thought the church performed a crucial and all-important function and, of necessity therefore, its position in society was a prominent one. Because of its important role, the church could not risk the possible corruptions that might come with partnership or alliance with the secular state. For such a relationship might, eventually, bring the church within the control of the civil authorities. Thus Calvinist doctrine opposed the idea of an episcopal form of church government with bishops appointed by royal authority. In Calvinism there could be no union of church and state in a single monarch. Calvinism presupposed two societies, one secular, the other ecclesiastical. While these societies in fact might inhabit the same territory, nevertheless they were under separate governmental jurisdictions. In Geneva under Calvin, however, no less than in Massachusetts Bay under the Puritans, it was difficult

[6] *Ibid.*, pp. 179-180.

to see where ecclesiastical jurisdiction ceased and secular authority began, so closely were they interwoven and so harmonious was their accord.

Because the fundamental preoccupation of Calvinism was with things of the spirit—the hoped-for grace of redemption—it might be expected that secular authority would find no major place in the system. If salvation is all-important, if this life on earth is one of sin with no real reward except through grace, what then is the place of secular authority? Are the governors supposed to be less sinful than the governed? Are the rulers presumed to be members of the aristocracy of the elect?

In the last chapter of Book IV of his *Institutes*, Calvin developed his theory as to the place and functions of civil government. It was this theory which became subsequently, with minor variations, Puritan political theory in New England. First, Calvin, in explaining the secular aspect of the "two-fold government in man," attacked the anarchistic view that if the government of God were all-important there was no place for a government of man. It was our corruption, he argued, which necessitated the government of man. Were all men truly pious, devout members of the faith, there would be no need of secular authority. But "while the insolence of the wicked is so great, and their iniquity is so stubborn," the tranquillity of society could only be preserved by an agency capable of exercising the maximum of force against transgressors. This was indeed purely a negative view of the function of government. Beyond this, civil government had a far more important role. It was the duty of government,

> . . . as long as we live in this world, to cherish and support the external worship of God, to preserve the pure doctrine of religion, to defend the constitution of the Church . . . to form our manners to civil justice, to promote our concord with each other, and to establish general peace and tranquillity. . . .[7]

Thus the government was more than a policeman: it was the protector of the faith and promoter of the good society. As a result, there were few limits to the functions of government in the Calvinist state. The object of civil government, Calvin wrote, is not only

> . . . that men may breathe, eat, drink and be sustained in life, though it comprehends all these, while it causes them to live together; yet, I say . . . its objects also are, that idolatry, sacrileges against

[7] *Ibid.*, p. 772.

the name of God, blasphemies against his truth, and other offences against religion, may not openly appear and be disseminated among the people; that the public tranquillity may not be disturbed . . . that there may be a public form of religion among Christians, and that humanity may be maintained among men.[8]

This surely was a sweeping declaration of authority indeed. It becomes now more evident why Calvin rejected the idea of a national church; nothing was lost by the separation of church and state into two societies when the functions of the civil authority included the enforcement of church doctrine. Under such an arrangement there was little danger of the church's succumbing to the state. The reverse, rather, was the intended result—civil government would become the agent of the church.

Having declared the proper purpose of civil government, Calvin then turned to an examination of the office of the magistrate, the governing authority, and the relationship of the people to him. Because of the vast and consequential duties assigned to government, it was apparent that the holders of governmental authority were not of lowly estate in the sight of the Lord. They were, indeed, performing a sacred trust and their office constituted "the most sacred and honorable in human life."[9]

Inasmuch as God created the office of magistrate, the incumbent thereof was properly considered his deputy, or vicegerent. It was due to the magistrate's elevated status in the divine plan that he was responsible for far more than the administration of justice among men. Were the civil magistrate not a vicegerent of the Lord, he might be expected to exert his energies only in matters pertaining to the flesh, leaving to the church the determination of issues pertaining to the spirit. Such an approach would have been in keeping with the traditional doctrine of the Two Swords. However, the divine nature of his office gave him a dual responsibility in both ecclesiastical and secular affairs. His authority extended to both tables of the law, that is, to the first four of the Ten Commandments declaring man's relationship to God, as well as to the last six Commandments declaring man's relationship to man. Thus it was the magistrate's function to guard against blasphemy and violation of the Sabbath as well as to punish for burglary, murder, and covetousness.

The exalted character of the office of magistrate led directly to the doctrine of passive obedience on the part of the subjects.

[8] *Ibid.*, p. 773.
[9] *Ibid.*, p. 775.

The first duty of subjects toward their magistrates, is to entertain the most honorable sentiments of their function which they know to be a jurisdiction delegated to them from God, and on that account to esteem reverence of them as God's ministers and vicegerents.[10]

A proper attitude toward the government required of subjects more than obedience alone. Magistrates were not, Calvin wrote, "a kind of necessary evil," nor should subjects obey magistrates simply out of fear. Subjects should look upon their magistrates with honor and veneration.

Hence follows another duty, that, with minds disposed to honour and reverence magistrates, subjects approve their obedience to them, in submitting to their edicts, in paying taxes, in discharging public duties, and bearing burdens which relate to the common defence, and in fulfilling all their other commands. Paul says to the Romans, "Let every soul be subject unto the higher powers. Whosoever resisteth the power, resisteth the ordinance of God."[11]

Yet Calvin was realistic enough to note that upon occasion magistrates had forsaken their duties as shepherds of the Lord, to become wolves who preyed upon innocent subjects. Did passive obedience still apply to subjects ruled by tyrants? One must obey tyrants as well as benevolent princes, for all magistrates ruled by divine commission. Though it might seem a little difficult to understand why a tyrant should partake of the magistracy of the Lord, Calvin found an explanation and a justification for submission.

Those who govern for the public good are true specimens and mirror of his beneficence . . . those who rule in an unjust and tyrannical manner are raised up by him to punish the iniquity of the people. . . .[12]

Since magistrates were agents of the Lord, whether tyrants or princes, they were not responsible, of course, to their subjects. They were directly responsible to God. Thus, in the face of tyranny, the obedient subject could contemplate either his own past iniquities or the judgment of the Lord when the tyrant reported finally to his Maker. In either event, the proper thing for the subject to do was to pray to the Lord for a speedy deliverance.

In spite of Calvin's insistence on passive obedience, he did permit two exceptions. In the first instance, where a constitutional device

[10] *Ibid.*, p. 795.
[11] *Ibid.*, p. 796.
[12] *Ibid.*, p. 798.

(such as the Spartan Ephors or Athenian Senate) was established, it might properly protect the liberty of the people and exercise its authority as a command of God in opposition to a tyrant. The second exception was more fundamental. In this instance, Calvin came to grips with the basic problems of a possible conflict between the church and the state. On this point Calvin left no doubt as to his position.

> The Lord, therefore, is King of kings; who when he has opened his sacred mouth, is to be heard alone, above all, for all, and before all; in the next place, we are subject to those men who preside over us; but no otherwise than in him. If they command any thing against him, it ought not to have the least attention; nor, in this case, ought we to pay any regard to all that dignity attached to magistrates; to which no injury is done when it is subjected to the unrivalled and supreme power of God.[13]

Calvin's thought thus justified passive resistance as well as passive obedience. While the latter received emphasis wherever Calvinism was in control of the state, as in Geneva and later in Massachusetts, it was the former aspect which received emphasis wherever Calvinists were in the minority. In Catholic France the Calvinists so disregarded the doctrine of passive obedience that, after much conflict, they were granted a large measure of toleration in the Edict of Nantes (1598). In Scotland, under Catholic Mary, John Knox made famous the resistance side of Calvinism. On the surface it would appear that there was an inconsistency in Calvin in his advocacy of both passive obedience and resistance. Yet on reflection it should be evident that this superficial inconsistency gives way to a higher inner consistency. Believing his doctrine to be that of the true faith, he quite properly advocated adherence to it at all times. Thus in countries where Calvinism was recognized as the true faith and the magistrates performed their proper function of maintaining the faith and ridding the country of heretics and non-conformers, it was fitting that passive obedience be the rule. It was, of course, equally proper that Calvinists endeavor to maintain the true faith in countries where it was not recognized as such. Decrees to the contrary would naturally be resisted. It is an interesting paradox that while the major emphasis of Calvinist political thought was on passive obedience, its major indirect contribution to political institutions lay in its stalwart defense of non-conformity.

[13] *Ibid.*, p. 805.

CALVINISM IN ENGLAND

While Lutheranism was spreading in the Northern Germanies and Calvinism in Geneva and France, England too, almost inadvertently, moved away from Catholicism. When the first ripples in the advancing wave of Protestantism reached England, Henry VIII (1509-1547) moved quickly to suppress these heresies. For his part in guarding Catholic England from the onslaught of Lutheranism, Henry VIII gained the title "Defender of the Faith." But in spite of his efforts at suppression, including the burning of heretics at the stake, the reform movement would not be put down, and Lutheran and Zwinglian doctrine continued to have a regenerating effect upon religion. Inevitably, however, the consolidation of royal power by the ambitious Henry led to conflict with a pope jealous of his temporal domain. The specific issue which brought about the break in relations was the desire of Henry to divorce Catherine so that he might marry Anne Boleyn. Because the pope refused the divorce, the erstwhile "Defender of the Faith" led England away from Catholicism.

In lieu of an alien pope, Henry assumed the position of head of the church in England and appointed archbishops and bishops favorable to his views. Parliament subsequently supported him by confirming his position as head of the church in England, by prohibiting the traditional appeals of ecclesiastical issues to the pope and by authorizing the confiscation of monasteries by the state. This was not Protestantism any more than it was Catholicism; rather it was a manifestation of sixteenth-century English nationalism. Protestants continued to be persecuted, only now added to them were Catholics who remained loyal to the pope. Henry VIII made the break with the Church without following through with a change in the doctrine. Thus, in a sense he remained a Defender of the Faith, though he was charged with maintaining "Popery without the Pope."

Following Henry's death and the succession of the child Edward VI, there was hope among the growing number of Protestants that an elimination of Catholic doctrine might be effected. With the assistance of Edward's Protestant regents, the Forty-Two Articles of Anglican faith were written and made the official church doctrine. The publication of the Articles, along with the *Second Book of Common Prayers* in 1553, placed England in the Protestant camp. Essential to the creed, as in Lutheranism and Calvinism, was the belief in justification by faith and the heavy emphasis on the authority of the Scriptures.

England returned officially to Catholicism under Mary Tudor. Mary, however, for all the intensity of her effort to root out Protestantism, failed in that endeavor. Persecution of Protestants did drive many out of England into the arms of John Calvin on the continent. Some of these refugees, returning to England following the succession of Elizabeth, were fortified with Calvin's Protestantism, which became in England Puritanism. It was under Elizabeth that the Reformation was completed in England. The Forty-Two Articles were reduced to Thirty-Nine, and Elizabeth appointed bishops who accepted her position. Thus Anglicanism became Protestant in doctrine and episcopal in organization. It now remained to "purify" the reformed church in accordance with the basic principles of John Calvin.

The Elizabethan settlement had scarcely been established and the Acts of Supremacy and Uniformity (1559) proclaimed when sundry protests were raised condemning this Anglicanism as stopping short of a true reformation. These Protestants, in general, sought to purify the Anglican church by ridding it of its lingering vestiges of Catholic ceremony and by substituting a presbyterian for an episcopalian organization. In Scotland, under the dogmatic leadership of John Knox, a presbyterian church was achieved. Followers of Calvin in England sought to secure eventually the same triumph at home. For under the presbyterian system the Queen would be unable to appoint ecclesiastical officials; these would be selected by the congregations and synods and thus the true faith would be secure from secular intervention. In other words, the Puritans, as they came to be called, were Anglicans who were dissatisfied with the existing settlement. The astute Elizabeth kept this dissatisfaction from flaring up into a major crisis during her reign. Upon her death in 1603, however, an immediate effort was undertaken to persuade James I to call a General Church Assembly which would lead to reform of the church. James I, well acquainted with Presbyterianism while James VI of Scotland, answered his persuaders bluntly and knowingly: "If you aim at the Scottish Presbytery, it agreeth as well with monarchy as God with the devil." The successful maintenance of firm royal authority would be jeopardized by a national church free from the control of the ruler of the national state. Some followers of Calvin, faced with the adamant James, chose to continue as Anglicans while quietly instituting reforms in their own congregations. Others of a more eager stripe, failing to reform the Anglican church from within, chose to separate from it and to institute an independent reformed church. Thus, early in the seventeenth century the followers of Calvin in England were composed of those who remained Anglicans formally though practicing Calvin's creed locally, and those who practiced Calvinism locally without any semblance of union with the Anglican church. It was these two reformist movements which subsequently coalesced to form the New England of the seventeenth century.

SEPARATISM

An Englishman, Robert Browne, in the late sixteenth century supplied the justification for what became the Separatist movement. In *A Treatise of Reformation Without Tarying for Anie* (1582), Browne declared that the sanction of the established church was not essential to the creation and maintenance of churches devoted to the true faith. Browne in effect reasserted the doctrine of the priesthood of all Christian believers as against all existing authorities whether secular or ecclesiastical. Even as the Protestant Reformation sought a means to salvation which did not require the interposition of the Catholic Church, so now in this extension of the spirit of the Reformation, Browne announced a means to establish churches, essential to salvation, without the assistance of and in fact in opposition to the only recognized church in England. Despairing of reform of the Anglican church, Browne declared in favor of any group of believers separating from Anglicanism and establishing their own local church. Inasmuch as such a group of dissenters, once they renounced the Anglican church, were in a position of being cast out of organized religious society, they were forced to create one anew. Hunted and persecuted, they experienced a fundamental problem in survival, especially as they became bolder in their assertions. Yet equally fundamental was the fact that once they departed from organized religious society with its established hierarchy, they were thrown, so to speak, into a religious state of nature as far as organization was concerned. They had a religious creed without an organization to assist them in maintaining it. Thus Browne's solution, while elementary in retrospect, was of great consequence to later development. The local church might be established by a mutual covenant or agreement of the members to join together as a congregation and to elect a pastor to serve them. Hence Congregationalism, as it came later to be called, found a means of establishing a religious society where none had existed before. Local, democratic self-government became that essential means. In contrast to the established system of appointment of ecclesiastical officials from above, Congregationalism offered election from below. At this stage, each congregation was a church, separate unto itself with its own officials consisting usually of pastor, teacher and elders. It required a further step, the creation of the synod, to bring these congregations together into a wider organization. Thus, a more general organization of indefinite authority, a weak confederacy, was established. Because Browne sought to establish a voluntary church society outside of the declared laws of England, it was to be expected that he would be opposed to intervention by the magistrates, or the Anglican church, with the local congregations. His claim was for the autonomy of a minority against the national claims of the majority. Though Browne subsequently departed from his own program to return to the established church, his followers carried out to a large extent the ideas he had propounded. It was such a group who followed John Robinson and William Brewster to Holland and later, in 1620, landed in Plymouth. These men had departed from established religious society to organize their own, claiming direct authority from God for such a project; and by mutual covenant they established a church. As these Pilgrim Separatists aboard the *Mayflower* reached the place of disembarkment, they reaffirmed the principles whereby this religious society might be as well a body politic. Previously, in England and Holland, they had been an autonomous religious group within an established political society. Now they must organize a civil society as they had previously organized a church. The *Mayflower Compact* becomes thus more intelligible and perhaps less extraordinary when considered in the light of the experience in church organization of the members who drew up the *Compact*. For the Pilgrim Separatists had accepted and were now practicing the principles of Robert Browne.

PURITANISM

In Old England, meanwhile, the Puritans, faced with growing royal opposition, were being forced more and more into the same position as the Separatists. While the Puritans did not make a formal break with Anglicanism, the difference between Anglican and Puritan became more distinct and important. James I clearly did not intend to compromise with the Puritans; in Scotland, under their presbyterian government, they had constantly clashed with James, and the first of the Stuart monarchs of England was too shrewd not to see that the Puritans threatened the monarchy. In a speech to Parliament in 1604, James declared that the Puritans

> . . . do not so far differ from us in points of religion as in their confused form of policy and parity; being very discontented with the present government and impatient to suffer any superiority, which maketh their sect unable to be suffered in any well-governed commonwealth.[14]

Nevertheless, the Puritans continued pressing for reform of the Anglican church. They attacked the episcopal hierarchy, the wearing of the surplice, the observance of saint's days, the use of images, the placing of the altar, the ostentatious ceremonialism, the *Book of Common Prayer*—indeed, all those elements of Anglican worship for which the Puritans could not find direct and explicit authorization in the Scripture. Unable to conform in heart to these tenets, the Puritans moved to observe the true doctrine within their own congregations, separate from the jurisdiction of the Anglican hierarchy. They claimed to be still members of the Anglican church. Yet, as John Cotton wrote in Massachusetts some years later, "There were some scores of Godly persons in Boston, in Lincolnshire, whereof some are there still and some are here, who can witness that we entered into a covenant with the Lord and with one-another to follow after the Lord in the purity of his worship."[15] The covenant procedure thus became as essential a device to Puritans as to Separatists.

Whereas Robert Browne became the fundamental spokesman for Separatism, an extremely important influence on Puritan thinking undoubtedly was William Ames. This extraordinary figure cast aside a successful theological career in the Anglican church by his insistence on Puritan doctrine. Fleeing to Leyden, he preached, practiced and wrote on the Puritan creed to a multitude of disciples from all

---

[14] Cited in Ralph B. Perry, *Puritanism and Democracy* (New York: The Vanguard Press, 1944), p. 69.

[15] John Cotton, *The Way of the Congregational Churches Cleared* (1648) p. 17. Cited in Thomas J. Wertenbaker, *The Puritan Oligarchy* (New York: Charles Scribner's Sons, 1947), p. 23.

of Europe.[16] It was Ames, who, like Browne, taught that the church was but a congregation of believers.

> There are so many churches as there are companies, or particular congregations, of those that profess the faith, who are joined together by a special band for the constant exercise of the communion of the Saints.[17]

Although there was only one true faith, there might be from an organizational point of view any number of churches or congregations practicing that faith. The episcopal custom of ordaining a minister without his having been appointed by a particular church or congregation was, Ames wrote, "as ridiculous as if any should be fained to be husband without a wife."[18] The burden of Ames' writing served to strengthen the position of the local Puritan congregations within the Anglican church, and his works were frequently cited in support of Puritanism.

King James I and his bishops were not prepared to accept the Amesian modification of Anglicanism. From the Puritan point of view the situation grew worse when Charles I succeeded to the throne in 1625. With politics and theology closely intertwined, and with religious issues growing in political importance, the deterioration in political affairs under Charles I served to aggravate rather than mend the religious differences. Because many Puritans were represented in Parliament, Charles' opposition to that body was doubly felt, for as titular head of the church and acting head of the state, he opposed the Puritans in both domains. In 1628, the year Charles signed the Petition of Rights, he appointed as Bishop of London William Laud, a man most zealous in his fidelity to the established Anglican church and its existing organization. It was now that some Puritans talked of the impossibility of instituting reforms in the church at home and thought of seeking a haven elsewhere as the Separatists had done before them. Convenient to their purposes was the New England Company, organized by such prominent Puritans as John White and John Winthrop. Early in 1629 this group, now incorporated as the Massachusetts Bay Company, re-

[16] Thomas Hooker, a great Puritan theologian and founder of Connecticut, said that "if a scholar was well studied in Dr. Ames his *Medulla Theologiae* and *Casus Conscientiae* so as to understand them thoroughly, they would make him, supposing him versed in Scriptures, a good divine, though he had no more books in the world." Cited in Wertenbaker, *op. cit.*, p. 24.

[17] William Ames, *The First Book of Divinity*, p. 178, cited by Wertenbaker, *op. cit.*, p. 24.

[18] Cited in Wertenbaker, *op. cit.*, p. 25.

ceived a charter from Charles I which granted considerable authority to the members of the company. The charter granted authority to the company to govern its membership by the enactment of orders and statutes "not contrairie to the Lawes of this our Realme of England." It further provided that the inhabitants of the New World "shall have and enjoy all liberties and Immunities of free and natural Subjects" of the Crown "as if they and everie of them were borne within the Realme of England."[19]

The charter of the Massachusetts Bay Company was to serve as the basic instrument of government for that colony until 1684. Though the powers granted by the charter were broad, nevertheless they were limited by the specific content of English law and the heritage of English liberties. Because of the recognized importance of the charter the stockholders of the Massachusetts Bay Company brought it with them to the New World. They left behind no absentee stockholders who might deliver up the charter or attempt to control their affairs from England. They were thus free to institute in Massachusetts a government, indeed a society, favorable to the growth of Puritanism.

The Puritans, however, were not the first to carry the new doctrine of Protestantism into the New World. Settlers had arrived in Jamestown, Virginia, in 1607, while in 1620 the Separatists had established Plymouth, Massachusetts. The settlement of America, the establishment of the colonies, continued for over a century until, with the founding of Georgia in 1733, England had thirteen colonies in the New World. Many motives were involved in bringing about the settlement of the New World, on England's part in permitting and encouraging the emigration as well as on the part of the colonists, who were the direct participants in the movement. However, from the point of view of subsequent American thought the significant fact is that the settlers brought with them to the new world the social, indeed, the political, economic, and religious values which they had accepted in the Old World. These values thus served as the precursory frame of reference for what developed into the commonplaces of subsequent American thought, and thus they initiated the idea experiences of subsequent Americans. In seventeenth-century English thought lay the distinctive ideologies of Protestantism, democracy, and capitalism. Of these, Protestantism, though varying in creed and church organization, was the theory most

[19] See Francis N. Thorpe, *The Federal and State Constitutions* (Washington: Government Printing Office, 1909), vol. III, p. 1857.

articulated and mature in its development. It provided a cosmic view of man and the universe which inevitably included a view of the nature of man, his virtues and deficiencies, and the possible consequences of his political relationships. It provided a value standard, but, like all such arrangements, it operated from certain causative principles; thus Protestantism at once provided a value scheme for man and a causative theory oriented to its realization. In Massachusettts, due partly to the nature of the settlement, partly to the articulateness of the governing officials and partly to the historical sense of subsequent generations, the theory of Puritan Protestantism is available in its original form. It is in Puritan Massachusetts, then, that one finds the most influential formulations of the beginnings of American political thought.

CHAPTER 2

Puritan
Political Thought

THE PURITAN settlers of Massachusetts left the old world for the new because they had previously given up orthodox Anglicanism with its episcopal organization for the new creed of Calvinism. Unable to reform either church or state, and in England reform of the former required control of the latter, they came to America to establish their own community. It was in all our history the boldest and most energetically sustained effort to put into operation a utopian commonwealth. Primarily they sought an opportunity, unavailable at home, to practice Calvinism untrammeled by a hostile king, unrestrained by a hostile church hierarchy. This reform, to be effective and complete, required the full cooperation of civil government. Thus, while they accepted the principle of church and state as separate societies, they believed that the two must be in full accord as to goals and cooperative in their efforts. This meant, in effect, that the church would cooperate with the state in determining policy, and the state would lend its coercive arm to effect the execution of this policy. It meant a partnership of body and soul, with the soul the superior partner. They sought to establish a closely knit community whose members were in complete agreement on fundamentals, the tenets of Calvinism as interpreted by William Ames and as practiced by the Puritan leaders.

Though the Puritans were Calvinists in a new undeveloped land, they were of course far more than this. They belonged to the early seventeenth century, an era of wars of religion, intolerance, flagrant persecutions, and tortures. They were members of a rigid class system, for the most part of the middle and slightly lower classes. They were of the age of mercantilism, of royal monopolies and trading privileges; in fact, their own charter was such a royal grant. And they were Englishmen, with a legacy of law and rights and concepts of justice that included Magna Carta, the common law, equity, and the very recent Petition of Rights. They were loyal subjects of a state full grown in nationalism and commencing its vast expansion across the globe. They were colonists in a new imperial enterprise. Some of these settlers doubtless came to further their financial status, but they certainly did not intend for themselves *laissez-faire* capitalism. Some may have come to further their social and political position, but they had no intention of establishing democracy. Most of them came, and this was the crucial consideration for the original exodus, so that they might be permitted freely to practice the religion which they believed to be the only true religion; but they never intended that others of opposing views should enjoy this privilege in their jurisdiction. The utopia which they envisaged was designed, like all utopias, only for its originators. There was, of course, a rational justification for this attitude. To remove three thousand miles, to make a perilous voyage of nearly two months in incommodious quarters, to set ashore on an unknown continent with known Indian enemies required a tremendous amount of conviction and courage. Fortified by the assurance of the Lord's will and a minimum of capital, they struck out. Others who felt conditions at home intolerable might well pursue the same course, though if they disagreed with the plans of the Puritans they would be well advised to anchor elsewhere. But the risk involved, the anxiety, the momentous departure from all that was known, even though disliked, gave conviction to the Puritan argument that Massachusetts Bay was all their own, their utopia, their haven for the seekers of God *via* the Calvinist creed. Though it was expected that many trials, famines and misfortunes would be encountered, they knew that the Lord's vineyard would not be barren. This was, they felt, the Promised Land. When considering the specific content of the thought of the Puritan leaders, it is well to bear in mind that this experiment, with its institutional and theoretical expressions, was their consistent approach to a homogeneous, organic society seeking salvation.

THE PURITAN CHURCH IN MASSACHUSETTS

A *Platform of Church Discipline*,[1] proposed by a church synod and adopted by the General Court of Massachusetts Bay in 1649,

[1] The following quotations from A *Platform of Church Discipline* are found in Cotton Mather, *Magnalia Christi Americana* (Hartford, Connecticut: Silas Andrus and Son, 1855), vol. II, 211-236.

reveals the Puritan attitude in regard to the church, its organization, and its relationship to the state. The fact that it was drawn up by the highest ecclesiastical body, the synod, and adopted by the highest secular body, the General Court, is itself evidence of the close harmony of the two distinct societies of church and state. "The parts of church-government," declared this document, "are all of them exactly described in the word of God. . . . So that it is not left in the power of man, officers, churches or any state in the world, to add, or diminish, or alter anything in the least measure therein." In such manner did the church declare its independence from the intermeddling in its government of either state or hostile officials of an alien church. The powers and organization of their church they believed to be the command of God as evidenced in the Scripture or reasonably deduced therefrom. They would therefore deny any credit to human ingenuity for a magnificent bit of organizational improvisation in the establishment of the congregational system.

> A congregational church is by the institution of Christ a part of the militant visible church, consisting of a company of saints by calling, united into one body by a holy covenant, for the public worship of God, and the mutual edification of one another in the fellowship of the Lord Jesus.

It is important to note how the congregational system paralleled town government, for both represented the locality and thus served as a decentralizing force in colonial politics. In the Southern colonies, the stronghold of Anglicanism, the unified hierarchical church structure paralleled the centralized unitary system of county government, but in New England the emphasis was always on the locality. This was no mere accident of geography, or even of economic necessity. The congregational system was intended to maintain and promote the ecclesiastical well-being of a small closely-knit community, and the size of any church was limited by the conviction that it "ought not to be of greater number than may ordinarily meet together conveniently in one place." Were it to grow too large, discipline and essential harmony would be placed in jeopardy. Thus the Puritans did not wish to have a unified national structure, but as many separate Puritan churches as there were separate compact congregations.

Fundamental to Puritan thought was the idea of a covenant. By a covenant, or contract, persons pledged themselves to bend their efforts to accomplish some mutually beneficial end. The promise made before God became a sacred obligation. As such it served as a theoretical bulwark for the close-knit church community. Obviously, a church or any other institution might be established without going through the contract formula, but when building anew the Puritans felt the need for a reassertion of the fundamental principles which made a miscellany of men a congregation, a "plantation religious." The covenant idea is frequently expressed in the Old Testament, and the Puritans drawing heavily upon the Old Testament for their codes of behavior, found it convenient to their purposes. Because the contract idea in political thought is associated with the principle of government only with the consent of those governed, there is the temptation to over-read into the Puritan covenant the vital principle of democracy. There was, to be sure, the idea of consent involved in the covenant, but it was not intended to mean consent of all those subject to the jurisdiction of the church, but only those saints who instituted the church. It recognized the right of the limited members of a closed corporation to enter freely of their own consent into an agreement binding themselves to a mutual obligation for all time hence. Contemporaneously, in England and Connecticut, Puritan leaders were giving the contract idea wider application in the political sphere. As applicable to the establishment of a religious society, however, the contract was limited only to saints and not to the populace. The Puritan church covenant was a mutual pledge to walk faithfully in the ways of the Lord, to submit obediently to His commands. It was a pledge of future good behavior to make themselves worthy in His sight to be constituted as a church, the better to preserve His holy name and fulfill His grace.[2]

[2] Something of the spirit and purpose of the Puritan covenant may be seen in an early Northampton church covenant: "Disclaiming all confidence of, or any worthiness in, ourselves either to be in covenant with God or to partake of the least of His mercies, and also all strength of our own to help covenant with Him . . . by relying upon His tender mercy and gracious assistance of the Lord through Jesus Christ, we do promise and covenant in the presence of the Lord, the searcher of all hearts, and before the holy angels and this company, first and chiefly to cleave forever unto God with our whole hearts as our chief, best, yea and only good, and unto Jesus Christ as our only Savior, husband and Lord and only high priest, prophet and king. . . . We promise and engage to observe and maintain . . . all the holy institutions and ordinances which he hath appointed for His Church. . . . And as for this particular company and society of saints, we promise . . . that we will cleave one unto another in brotherly love and seek the best spiritual good each of other, by frequent exhortation, seasonable admonition and constant watchfulness according to the rules of the Gospel." Quoted in Thomas J. Wertenbaker, *The Puritan Oligarchy* (New York: Charles Scribner's Sons, 1946), p. 58.

After the covenant which created the church had been made, it was necessary to select the officials who would guide and guard the organization. The officers—minister, deacons, and elders—were elected by the church membership and might "in case of manifest unworthiness and delinquency" be deposed by the membership. It should be remembered that this election, while free, was not freely willed. That is, under the Calvinist system such an election really manifested the Lord's will.

> A church being free, cannot become subject to any but by a free election; yet when such a people do choose any to be over them in the Lord, then do they become subject, and most willingly submit to their ministry in the Lord, whom they have chosen.

The powers of the officers were mighty, but from the point of view of church government, or any other type of government of the period, it was the democratic rather than the authoritarian provisions which might be considered extraordinary. The elders, in spite of ample powers, were finally responsible to the church membership.

Finally, the church *Platform* laid down certain rules regarding the relationship of church and state. Church government and civil government, the *Platform* declared, "both stand together and flourish, the one being helpful unto the other, in their distinct and due administrations." Because their powers were positive and promotional, magistrates were to be looked upon as the vicegerents of God.

> Idolatry, blasphemy, heresy, venting corrupt and pernicious opinions, that destroy the foundation, open contempt of the word preached, profanation of the Lord's-Day, disturbing the peaceable administration and exercise of the worship and holy things of God, and the like, are to be restrained and punished by civil authority.

Of course, the church was to be maintained by public contribution, but this contribution was not to consist of free gift alone. A tax was to be levied upon all for the support of the church. A tax, being a secular affair, brought into play the powers of the magistrate.

Indeed, the magistrate might assist but never deter the growth of Calvinism. It was the negative aspect of this, the denial of the authority of the secular society to restrain the operation of the Calvinist religious society which promoted the concept of the separation of church and state from the point of view of political interference in church affairs.

> It is lawful, profitable and necessary for Christians to gather themselves together into church estate, and therein to exercise all the

ordinances of Christ according unto the word, although the consent of the magistrate could not be had thereunto. . . .

The doctrine clearly stated that the magistrates could not declare who was to be a church member and receive of the Lord's Supper. Such action would, of course, be interference with the ecclesiastical domain of the church. On the other hand, in spite of Calvin's separation of church and secular authority, it was the promotional aspect of the magistrate's power which effected religious intolerance in New England for well over half a century.

JOHN WINTHROP

Undoubtedly the most significant spokesman of orthodox Massachusetts Puritan political theory was John Winthrop (1588-1649). Serving in office almost continually for the last twenty years of his life, as lieutenant governor and governor of the Massachusetts Bay colony, he was intimately familiar with all the birth and growing pains of the infant commonwealth. He, being one of the founders, one of that small group who agreed to subscribe to the stock if the charter was brought to America, knew the high mission intended as well as the daily problems of administration that arose in the course of fulfilling those ideals in New England. Fortunately for posterity, he kept a journal of his beliefs, conflicts and undertakings. A man of intense religious belief, he was to those who knew him a man of warmth, generosity and wisdom. He came from a family of rather high social station, education, and economic means. As the country squire of Groton Manor in Suffolk, England, he possessed a respectability which perhaps would have remained unmarred had he not become a devout Puritan at an early age. His popular position in Massachusetts is attested to by his successive annual elections to the office of Governor.

Winthrop's decision to join the Massachusetts Bay Company was no doubt influenced by his declining fortunes in England.[3] Never-

---

[3] Something of the economic condition of England may be seen in Winthrop's complaint of the mother country shortly before his departure for America. "This land grows weary of her inhabitants, so as man, who is the most precious of all creatures, is here more vile and base than the earth we tread upon and of less price among us than a horse or a sheep . . . it has come to pass that children, servants and neighbors, especially if they be poor, are counted the greatest burdens, which, if things were right, would be the chiefest earthly blessings." Cited in Wertenbaker, *op. cit.*, p. 35.

theless it seems evident that Winthrop participated in the venture primarily because he believed it to be the fulfillment of a holy mission. He looked upon the journey into the American wilderness as an expedition by the regenerate, the "fellow members of Christ," to carry out a command of the Lord. That the fundamental purpose of the new community was religious rather than commercial was emphasized in Winthrop's sermon *A Modell of Christian Charity* (1630), written while he was still in passage aboard the *Arabella*.

> Now if the Lord shall please to hear us, and bring us in peace to the place we desire, then hath he ratified this Covenant and sealed our Commission, and will expect a strict performance of the Articles contained in it, but if we shall neglect the observation of these Articles which are the ends we have propounded, and dissembling with our God, shall fall to embrace this present world and prosecute our carnal intentions, seeking great things for ourselves and our posterity, the Lord will surely break out in wrath against us, be revenged of such a perjured people, and make us know the price of the breach of such a Covenant.[4]

The civil society envisaged by Winthrop to carry out the work of the Lord was a cohesive interdependent community in which "every man might have need of other, and from hence they might all knit more nearly together in the Bond of brotherly affection." It was a community of unequals, the high and the low, the rich and the poor, whose interdependence made a harmony of purpose essential. For all the inequality, however, no man stood above the community.

> In such cases as this, the care of the public must overswing all private respects, by which not only conscience, but mean Civil policy doth guide us, for it is a true rule that particular estates cannot subsist in the ruin of the public.

While it was agreed that the public interest was superior to any private interest, nevertheless the inevitable problem arose as to how to determine the public interest. Should any individual be permitted to declare arbitrarily the civil policy, this would offend the dignity of the Lord, the only absolute ruler recognized in Puritan political thought. Should the people themselves be permitted to make this decision, such a form of government would be a "mere democracy,"

[4] This and the following quotations from *A Modell of Christian Charity* are taken from *The Winthrop Papers* (Boston: Massachusetts Historical Society, 1931), vol. II, p. 297.

which Winthrop declared had no Scriptural support and which was "accounted the meanest & worst of all formes of Government." Puritan ingenuity, however, found an escape from this dilemma by devising in theory a modification of the ancient dictum *vox populi, vox dei.* Puritan theory had always emphasized the element of consent, of covenant, as being essential to a well-ordered civil society. Yet, unwilling to be led into democracy, the Puritans limited political authority to the regenerate. This political authority was exercised by the regenerate in the elections of the Governor, his Deputies, and in fact the General Court. Here, however, the political authority of the regenerate populace ceased as the actual power of administering the community passed into the hands of the elected officials. This system was described by Winthrop as a mixed government, as opposed to a tyranny or a democracy, for the regenerate chose the officials who would rule over them. Once elected to office, though, the magistrates ruled by divine decree. "It is yourselves who have called us to this office," Winthrop declared in 1645, "and being called by you, we have our authority from God."[5] Thus the organization of the political society was modelled after that of the church society, in which the regenerate, in accordance with predestination, reflected in their votes the will of God, and for their authority the chosen officials could find a mandate in heaven.

This curious combination of consent and divine right could lead to an unrestrained exercise of authority by the magistrates. Actually, Winthrop believed magisterial authority to be always under what today would be called a constitutional restraint, for the magistrates were subject to laws and rules. At all times the magistrates were subject to the commands and injunctions of the Scriptures as well as to the charter and the rules established by the General Court. As a result it was understood that no man should be deprived of his life, reputation, or property or be in any way punished "unless it be by the virtue or equity of some express Law of the Country, warranting the same, established by a general Court and sufficiently published." Thus Winthrop denied an accusation made in 1644 that the government of Massachusetts Bay was arbitrary.

The Government of the Massachusetts consists of Magistrates and Freemen: in the one is placed the Authority, in the other the Liberty of the Commonwealth: either hath power to Act, both alone, and

[5] *Winthrop's Journal, History of New England (1630-1649),* edited by James K. Hosmer (New York: Charles Scribner's Sons, 1908), vol. II, p. 238.

both together, yet by a distinct power, the one of Liberty, the other of Authority; the Freemen Act of themselves in Electing their Magistrates and Officers: The Magistrates Act alone in all occurrences out of Court; and both Act together in the General Court: yet all limited by certain Rules, both in the greater and smaller affairs: so as the Government is Regular in a mixed Aristocracy, and no ways Arbitrary.[6]

The old oligarchy was losing some of its hold upon the people by 1645. There had been a demand for increasing the number of deputies each town might be allowed in the General Court, as well as a demand for extending the franchise. This movement to broaden the base of political authority, in the name of popular liberty, was interpreted by Winthrop as a direct challenge to the authority of the magistrates. In response to the demand for greater popular control Winthrop gave a "little speech" in which he sought to set the people right as to the true nature of liberty. He declared that there were two kinds of liberty, natural and civil. "The first is common to man with beasts and other creatures. By this, man, as he stands in relation to man simply, hath liberty to do what he lists; it is a liberty to evil as well as to do good." This kind of liberty Winthrop found to be entirely incompatible with political authority, for it called for a removal of all restraints. The other type of liberty was that found in the moral law, in the covenant of the regenerate with God, and in political society. "This liberty is the proper end and object of authority, and cannot subsist without it; and it is a liberty to that only which is good, just, and honest. . . . This liberty is maintained and exercised in a way of subjection to authority; it is of the same kind of liberty wherewith Christ hath made us free."[7] Liberty, to Winthrop, did not call for a removal of restraints, for no society could exist unless certain restraints upon individual behavior were generally recognized. The jungle freedom which characterized the liberty of the beasts of prey would characterize the liberty of men as well did they live "freely" without the restraints of law and morality. This was inevitably so because of man's propensity to evil since the fall of Adam. If regenerate men lived constantly in the shadow of temptation, how much greater the struggle for righteousness of the unregenerate multitude? Civil liberty, on the other hand, presupposed the existence of Calvinistic morality as a guiding force in

[6] Robert C. Winthrop, *Life and Letters of John Winthrop*. . . . (Boston: Little, Brown and Co., 1869), vol. II, p. 454.
[7] *Winthrop's Journal, History of New England (1630-1649)*, vol. II, pp. 238-239.

man's conduct. Natural liberty, or license, was the liberty to do evil; civil liberty, or morality, permitted one only to do good. The very purpose of the Massachusetts settlement was to establish a community whereby men would be free to do good according to the tenets of Calvinism. Had the Puritans been permitted this liberty in England they probably would not have departed from there. They settled New England so that they might henceforth enjoy that "kind of liberty wherewith Christ hath made us free."

Winthrop's approach to liberty was a positive one, since he saw it more as a freedom to act than as a freedom from restraint. He illustrated his concept of freedom by the analogy of a woman becoming a bride. Her husband was freely chosen by her; she took him of her own accord. The marriage was similar to the covenant which established the state, for two were now bound by contract where before only individuals existed. But although the contract was freely entered into, with the marriage the husband became the lord and she his subject. Now, Winthrop inquired, had the bride lost her liberty, forsaken it of her own free will? On the contrary, her subjection to her husband was a way of liberty and not of servitude or bondage. In the same manner did civil liberty supplant the baser license of the beasts. The liberty of the wife was like the liberty enjoyed by individuals who had covenanted into a church community. With Christ the lord and husband of the church, members obeyed His commands without any feeling of sacrifice or restraint because the object was always the ultimate good. The moral of Winthrop's speech was clearly stated.

> If you stand for your natural corrupt liberties, and will do what is good in your own eyes, you will not endure the least weight of authority, but will murmur, and oppose, and be always striving to shake off that yoke; but if you will be satisfied to enjoy such civil and lawful liberties, such as Christ allows you, then will you quietly and cheerfully submit unto that authority which is set over you, in all the administrations of it, for your good.[8]

Thus did Governor Winthrop defend the mixed government of Massachusetts against the charges of arbitrary rule and the claims of the populace for a greater measure of liberty. In his effort to retain a close-knit community dedicated to the continuance of the Puritan belief, he strengthened the aristocratic position of the regenerate and postponed the coming of democracy to the Bay colony.

---

[8] *Ibid.*, p. 239.

JOHN COTTON

As John Winthrop was the most significant secular spokesman for Puritan political theory in the Massachusetts colony, so was John Cotton (1584-1652) the pre-eminent spokesman of that theory in the ranks of the ministry. It was Cotton who preached the farewell sermon to the Massachusetts Bay Company as it prepared to embark for the new world in 1630. A zealous Puritan, he fell into disfavor with the orthodox during the scourge of Bishop Laud. Protected by friends, he went into hiding until he too could escape to the new world in 1633. Cotton's reputation had preceded him across the ocean. A man of extraordinary energy in matters both civil and ecclesiastical, he was soon elected teacher of the Boston church.

As a high ecclesiastical official in the colony, he was of course called upon for much advice in matters both secular and divine. His statements therefore may be considered as the typical views of orthodox Puritanism. An occasion of magisterial supplication for ministerial wisdom arose in 1636 when Lord Saye and Sele, a Puritan noble, wrote to the Massachusetts Bay Company inquiring of their form of government and the peculiar relationship of that government to the church. He and other Puritan gentry were interested in moving to the new community but were concerned lest they lose their high political and social station in a commonwealth where distinctions in rank appeared to be based primarily on theological status. The delicate task of answering this letter of inquiry was assigned primarily to John Cotton.

In reply Cotton made clear the distinct character of the New England community. Although generally churches were obliged to accommodate themselves to the ordinances of the state in which they were located, in Massachusetts the church members were in a position to establish their own commonwealth according to the requirements of the Scripture. Under such circumstances, Cotton noted, "It is better that the commonwealth be fashioned to the setting forth of God's house, which is his church: than to accommodate the church frame to the civil state." Thus the settlers of Massachusetts Bay had an opportunity which was not readily had elsewhere. Yet lest the noble gentry be misled as to the nature of the government, Cotton hastened to explain the conviction of the founding fathers, and himself. "Democracy," he wrote, "I do not conceive that ever God did ordain as a fit government either for church or commonwealth." In his view the Scripture approved of both monarchy and aristocracy, but preferred theocracy as the best form of government. However, the sort of theocracy that Cotton had in mind was not one of a personal identity of ministerial and magisterial office. It involved rather a personal separation of church and state officers while permitting a union of church and state policy.

Lord Saye and Sele had been concerned about the broad grant of authority possessed by the church, for if the church determined its membership, and only church members might vote, would not all secular affairs pass under the ultimate jurisdiction of the church? In answer to this Cotton endeavored to explain the subtle distinction between secular and ecclesiastical jurisdiction. It was true that only church members might vote, but the magistrates themselves held no church office, that is, there was a personal separation of power. Furthermore, the magistrates did not govern by direction of the church (he did not mention consultation), but by the civil law as declared by the General Court and the courts of justice. The only function of the church in such matters was to prepare "fit instruments both to rule, and to choose rulers." As to the church itself, it fully recognized the laws of the commonwealth as binding upon all. Thus it happened that church and state worked to the advantage of each and an ideal arrangement was achieved. This arrangement consisted of "authority in magistrates, liberty in people, purity in church." "Purity, preserved in the church" he argued "will preserve well-ordered liberty in the people, and both of them establish well-balanced authority in the magistrates."[9] Nearly a decade prior to Winthrop's "little speech" on liberty, Cotton, voicing orthodox Puritanism, observed the conformity of magisterial authority with the true liberty of the subjects.

In addition to the letter in reply to the inquiry and proposals of Lord Saye and Sele, a document was added detailing the specific answers to the questions. Here, point by point, Cotton attempted to make clear the nature of the Massachusetts commonwealth. It was demanded, for example, that the governor be chosen always "out of the rank of gentleman." This demand expressed the fear of the gentry that regenerate Calvinists might not always be of acceptable social standing. Cotton's reply sought to placate the gentry with the

[9] Thomas Hutchison, *History of the Colony of Massachusetts-Bay* (London, 1760), vol. I, pp. 496-501.

assertion that such was always the case anyway. But the demands of the gentry represented by Lord Saye and Sele went too far when it was insisted that they be admitted directly and automatically into the upper political hierarchy. The answer was tactful, but to the point.

> Though we receive them with honor and allow them pre-eminence and accommodations according to their condition, yet we do not, ordinarily, call them forth to the power of election, or administration of magistracy, until they be received as members into some of our churches, a privilege, which we doubt not religious gentlemen will willingly desire and christian churches will as readily impart to such desirable persons.[10]

The point was clear; no secular authority would be granted non-church members no matter how high a social station they claimed. The fundamental requirement was still regeneracy as determined by one of the local churches. To fly in the face of accepted social position, even in the case of loyal noble Puritans in England, was indeed a brave effort toward local autonomy. It made clear the claim that regeneracy was official only as determined by the local membership of the church where the individual concerned was applicant. It showed seventeenth-century respect for men of proper social station and religious convictions, but denied a commission of magisterial authority without the basic requirements of local church acceptance and subsequent political election. Cotton's reply sought to substitute religious qualifications for social or financial ones. Religious conviction, in turn, was fundamentally evidenced by things of the spirit and not of the flesh. Were church membership not the qualification, but wealth alone, "then, in case worldly men should prove the major part, as soon they might do, they would as readily set over us magistrates like themselves . . . and turn the edge of all authority and laws against the church and the members thereof. . . ." Such an event would subvert the very maintenance of the peace "which God aimed at in the constitution of Magistracy."[11]

Ministers and magistrates together sought to protect the plantation of religion from degenerating into a colony devoted primarily to the pursuit of worldly gain. Thus they were properly concerned lest worldly men should become the dominating part of the political community and erected the test of regeneracy as a fundamental prerequisite to political activity. They were equally concerned lest the

[10] *Ibid.*, pp. 492-493.
[11] *Ibid.*, p. 495.

desire for personal profit pervert the purpose of the community. As late as 1661 John Higginson wrote in *The cause of God and His People in New England:*

> My fathers and brethren, this is never to be forgotten that New England is originally a plantation of religion not a plantation of trade. Let merchants and such as are increasing cent per cent remember this, that worldly gain was not the end and design of the people of New England.[12]

Because the preservation of the religious community was of such fundamental importance to the Puritans, the ministry frowned upon economic transactions which evidenced an excessive desire for personal profit at the expense of the community of church members. The community standards of wages and prices were sufficiently well established that those who took advantage of the community by exorbitant demands were liable to public censure. Prices and wages were occasionally fixed by law and were always considered proper subjects for community action, for the Puritans believed that everything that affected the community had its moral aspects. Because morality was the proper domain of the theologians, it was not unusual for ministers to instruct their parishioners on matters of economic behavior.

In 1639 one Robert Keaine was accused of overcharging for his goods. At the time there was no law governing prices; nevertheless John Cotton took occasion to lay down some rules governing economic behavior. Inasmuch as his "false principles" of economics as well as his "rules for trading" reveal the Puritan attitude in regard to economic questions, they are worth quoting in full. His "false principles" of economics were:

> 1. That a man might sell as dear as he can, and buy as cheap as he can.
> 2. If a man lose by casualty of sea, etc., in some of his commodities, he may raise the price of the rest.
> 3. That he may sell as he bought, though he paid too dear, etc., and though the commodity be fallen, etc.
> 4. That, as a man may take the advantage of his own skill or ability, so he may of another's ignorance or necessity.

Cotton's proper rules for trading were:

> 1. A man may not sell above the current price, i.e., such a price as is usual in the time and place, and as another (who knows the worth

12 Quoted in Wertenbaker, *op. cit.*, p. 202.

of the commodity) would give for it, if he had occasion to use it; as that is called current money, which every man will take, etc., 2. When a man loseth in his commodity for want of skill, etc., he must look at it as his own fault or cross, and therefore must not lay it upon another.

3. When a man loseth by casualty of sea, or, etc., it is a loss cast upon himself by providence, and he may not ease himself of it by casting it upon another; for so a man should seem to provide against all providences, etc., that he should never lose; but where there is a scarcity of the commodity, there men may raise their price; for now it is a hand of God upon the commodity, and not the person.

4. A man may not ask any more for his commodity than his selling price, as Ephron to Abraham, the land is worth thus much.[13]

While the Puritans, as seventeenth-century Englishmen, were firm believers in class status in society, they would no more admit that financial status of itself gave one an independent place in society than they would allow men of high social rank to escape the controls of the commonwealth. They believed that regeneracy might well coincide with high social and economic position, but forced to choose between regeneracy and social rank, it was the former which was the controlling consideration.

The religious motif in the colony affected political thought in still another respect. It has been noted how church membership qualified a person for political rights, and indeed for the high privilege of being a governor. Election to the magistracy by church members gave such a magistrate a divine calling, so that while elected he really served by divine authority. Because of the divine character of his office, exercised under a broad charter, it might appear that his power was absolute and, in fact, totally irresponsible. Nevertheless, there were in theory fundamental limitations upon the magistrate. There was the usual one attached to the divine-right theory, that the magistrate was always responsible to God, and thus while his rule might be absolute in exercise it was fundamentally conditioned in authorization. There was also the belief that the magistrate was always responsible to those who had called him to office; thus at any time he might be impeached or called to account. For all the Puritan belief in regeneration, the ministry maintained a very healthy respect for the powers of Satan and the temptations of men toward depravity. Man, treading fearsomely on the brink of depravity, must

[13] *Winthrop's Journal, History of New England (1630-1649)*, vol. I, pp. 317-318.

wage a constant struggle to maintain the ways of the Lord in the face of the continuing temptation to succumb to what Winthrop called natural liberty.

John Cotton, in one of his sermons, lectured his parishioners on the necessity of curtailing the powers of all men, high and low in office, secular officials as well as divine, servants, wives, husbands, and monarchs. "Let all the world learn," Cotton admonished, "to give mortal men no greater power than they are content they shall use, for use it they will." The grant of power invariably meant the eventual use of such power. This was one of the fundamental facts of human nature: power once granted would be put to use.

It is therefore most wholesome for Magistrates and Officers in Church and Commonwealth, never to affect more liberty and authority then will do them good and the People good; for whatever transcendent power is given, will certainly overrun those that give it, and those that receive it: There is a strain in a man's heart that will sometime or other run out to excess, unless the Lord restrain it, but it is not good to venture it: It is necessary therefore, that power that is on earth be limited, Church-power or other: If there be power given to speak great things, then look for great blasphemies, look for a licentious abuse of it. It is counted a matter of danger to the State to limit Prerogatives; but it is a further danger, not to have them limited; They will be like a tempest, if they be not limited. . . . It is therefore fit for every man to be studious of the bounds which the Lord hath set; and for the People, in whom fundamentally all power lies, to give as much power as God in his word gives to men: And it is meet that Magistrates in the Commonwealth, and so Officers in Churches should desire to know the utmost bounds of their own power, and it is safe for both. . . . It is wholesome and safe to be dealt withall as God deals with the vast Sea; *Hitherto shalt thou come, but there shalt thou stay thy proud waves.*[14]

There is an important distinction between the doctrine of limitation which Cotton expounded and the concept of limited government subsequently developed in American political thought. Later theorists sought to limit governmental authority, as did Cotton, for fear of its abuse, but these theorists sought to curtail governmental power in order to expand the sphere of individual liberty. Cotton sought no such purpose. It would have been entirely inconsistent with the Puritan conception of an organic society in which prices,

[14] *An Exposition upon the 13th Chapter of the Revelation* (London, 1656), pp. 71-73. Quoted in Perry Miller and Thomas H. Johnson, *The Puritans* (New York: American Book Co., 1938), p. 213. (By permission.)

wages, clothes, manners, public behavior, and religious belief were all subject to official scrutiny and action for Cotton to propose limiting governmental or church authority. He assumed such functions of the state were all legitimate. What he was endeavoring to explain, however, was the inevitable corruption of all mankind which led men to abuse or take advantage of every privilege given. He sought to make clear that all mankind should be restrained, not just the governors. Cotton's sermon was therefore the religious counterpart to Winthrop's speech on natural vs. civil liberty. What Cotton was stressing was the element of human fallibility, even among the regenerate, which tended toward depravity, or as Winthrop called it, the liberty to do evil. Cotton told his congregation to

> . . . go home with this meditation; That certainly here is this distemper in our natures, that we cannot tell how to use liberty, but we shall very readily corrupt ourselves: Oh the bottomless depth of sandy earth! of a corrupt spirit, that breaks over all bounds, and loves inordinate vastness; that is it we ought to be careful of.[15]

ROGER WILLIAMS

The conception of liberty in the Massachusetts colony was basically the liberty to conform with orthodox Puritanism. "All Familists, Antinomians, Anabaptists and other Enthusiasts," wrote Nathaniel Ward, author of the Massachusetts *Body of Liberties*, "shall have free liberty to keep away from us."[16] By and large the Puritan settlers of Massachusetts did not seek to colonize further, or spread their belief beyond their own communities. They sought, rather, primarily to be let alone so that they themselves might practice the true religion as they saw it. Thus Calvinism in Massachusetts was characteristically defensive in nature. The Puritans sought to preserve themselves and their posterity from religious corruption, whether the attack came from Catholics or from the various sects within the Protestant faith. It was the latter which gave the Puritans the more immediate cause for concern, for they encountered Anglicans, Antinomians, Seekers, Quakers, and Baptists. The Puritan effort to maintain religious purity led inevitably to religious persecution and banishment of dissenters. Puritan dogmatism in religious

---

[15] *Ibid.*, p. 214.

[16] Nathaniel Ward, *The Simple Cobbler of Aggawam* (London, 1647). Quoted in Miller and Johnson, *op. cit.*, p. 227.

matters, however, provoked a demand for toleration from the dissenters. Such a dissenter was Roger Williams, one of the earliest exponents of religious toleration in America.

Roger Williams (1604-1683), a protégé of the famous English lawyer Edward Coke, had prepared for the ministry in the Anglican church. This effort was but the first of his many religious excursions. He was an Anglican, subsequently a Puritan. Later he established a Baptist church, and later still broke from it. He was a sincerely religious man who could find no permanent home in any established religion. That he never found a completely satisfactory haven is perhaps a key to his insistence upon the doctrine of religious toleration. A seeker who sought and never really found, he respected the right of other men to do likewise.

Roger Williams came to New England in 1631, early in the history of the colony. As a Puritan, he had known John Cotton and Thomas Hooker in England and in Massachusetts. Yet his stay in Massachusetts was brief and turbulent, for he criticized the policies of the established oligarchy. He criticized the New England churches for not officially separating, as had the Plymouth churches, from the established Anglican system. Massachusetts Bay, while declaring Anglicanism, maintained Puritanism. To Williams, this was a fundamental moral issue; either one was or was not in theory and fact a Puritan. In Massachusetts Bay, the oligarchy, fearful of losing the charter, never officially took the inexpedient route of repudiating the established faith which had permitted the charter.

To add further to his unpopularity with the established order, Williams attacked the very titles under which the settlers, indeed the colony, claimed ownership of land. The land, Williams claimed, was owned originally by the Indians. Legitimate transfer of title could be accomplished only by purchase, or cession, in either event with the consent of both parties. Yet the land had been taken from the Indians by conquest. Surely the king had not the authority to grant land which in fact did not belong to him. To legitimatize the claimed holdings Williams maintained that the colonists must now pay the Indians. Once again Williams' crusade for morality encountered understandable political opposition.

Furthermore, Williams advanced a purist's interpretation of Puritanism—that oaths tendered in the name of the Lord could be binding only upon regenerate souls. If an oath was binding only upon the regenerate, then the majority of the inhabitants were incapable of taking an oath of allegiance, submission, or contract. In theory, only those whom God had recognized by admission into the category of the regenerate could promise a future obligation in the presence of God. The use of the Lord as a sort of collateral was available only to those whom the Lord had recognized. Politically, however, the acceptance of this view would have undermined the entire civil establishment of Massachusetts, which was based on obligation testified to by oath. Again it was a question of moral conviction in conflict with political expediency.

Finally, Williams took the view that there ought to be a distinct separation of church and state and that the latter should not intervene in affairs of the former. Puritanism had heretofore maintained that it was the function of secular authority to root out heresy and assist in the maintenance of the true religion. Williams challenged that basic approach by insisting upon religion as a separate and distinct institution from civil authority. Williams' views were clearly incompatible with those held by the Puritans, and in 1636 he was banished from Massachusetts Bay.

Fleeing southward, Williams purchased land from the Indians and established the colony which became Rhode Island. The society which developed there put into actual practice the principles of the contract theory. While in theory both Massachusetts and Rhode Island were founded on the contract theory, with consent exercised through frequent elections, Rhode Island eliminated the religious qualifications for the suffrage, thus broadening the basis of consent. In Rhode Island there were not only frequent elections, but a unicameral legislature; the initiative, exercised through the concurrence of towns on proposed measures; the referendum, by which a majority of the towns might disapprove acts of the General Court; and the recall, by which elected magistrates might be removed from office. The governor lacked power to veto measures enacted by the towns and General Court. On the whole, Rhode Island was a much more tolerant and generous society than Puritan Massachusetts. Imprisonment for debt was abolished; divorce laws were quite lenient for that age; the criminal code was not as harsh as that of Massachusetts Bay. The method for the settlement of disputes, whether between citizens, between citizens and Indians, or even between colonies, was arbitration. Williams' role as arbitrator of impending disputes was of historic consequence in the growth of the Rhode Island colony, and in fact his efforts were of considerable importance to the peace and security of the northeastern seaboard settlements. It was, in all, Rhode Island which led the way in New England toward democracy, toleration, and a healthy respect for the rights of man as man, and not just as members of an established church. While critics of Williams observe that he was not always consistent, his actions at times failing to measure up to his high ideals, nevertheless it is to his credit that he led Rhode Island along the path eventually taken by the rest of the colonies.

In 1643, Williams went to England to seek a royal charter for Rhode Island, the Providence Plantations. It was a tumultuous time in England, the country torn by civil strife and religious persecution and governed by the faction-ridden Puritan Parliament. As Cavaliers battled Roundheads, the Long Parliament (1640-1660) sought to secure peace without sacrificing control. In such a setting there was much to give one pause to think about the cause of conscience and religious liberty. In 1644, Williams and his friend the English poet, John Milton, each published significant tracts on the subject of freedom of thought and expression. Milton's famous *Areopagitica* has long overshadowed the consequential work by Williams. Whereas Milton's work was primarily concerned with the censorship of ideas and expressions which were not necessarily religious in nature, Williams plunged right into the heart of the issue of religious liberty. His study, *The Bloody Tenet of Persecution, for Cause of Conscience,* was a direct assault upon the principles of the Massachusetts colony, and particularly on the point of view of his former friend, John Cotton. But the attack drove further than Cotton; it reached all the way back to John Calvin himself.

Williams maintained that not only was there no Scriptural authorization for persecution for cause of conscience, but rather that such persecution was directly opposed to the teachings of Christ. Arguing from Scripture, morality and expediency, he attacked persecution as the cause of much civil strife and the endless spilling of innocent blood. The starting place of Williams' theory was his clear-cut distinction between the secular and religious societies. Because the two estates were separate and distinct, the civil magistrate should not intervene in matters respecting religion. By denying to the magistrates the power to coerce persons into religious uniformity, Williams admitted the possibility of a continuing diversification of religious beliefs. But the spreading of the true faith could only be achieved by the "Sword of God's Spirit, the Word of God." Coercion would produce only outward conformity in some, rebellion and civil war in others. Religion, to be meaningful, must penetrate to conscience, and thus Williams maintained that the Lord commanded that "a permission of the most Paganish, Jewish, Turkish, or Anti-christian consciences and worships, be granted to all men in all Nations and Countries." This position was not only divinely authorized, he argued, but it was the only reasonable way in which true conversion might be effected. Furthermore, in view of the bloody conflicts resulting from the efforts to coerce uniformity, toleration was clearly the expedient policy. Williams' position in this matter was quite radical for his age. Whereas it seemed inconceivable to others that the true faith could survive in the face of competition offered by the sects of Satan, it was equally inconceivable to think of two religions settling down side by side in the same civil society. "True civility and Christianity," wrote Williams, "may both flourish in a State or Kingdom, not withstanding the permission of divers and contrary consciences, either of Jew or Gentile."

Once the distinction was made between civil and religious societies, Williams was able to elaborate on this thesis to show that the ends or goals of these societies were separate. The religious society sought the spiritual peace of the Lord. The civil society was framed, however, for a less heavenly end, the human peace and civility of the members of the community here on earth. Thus it was possible to have "glorious and flourishing cities of the world" which maintained civil peace, even though they contained no established church society. "O how lost are the sons of men in this point?" Williams wrote:

> The Church or Company of worshippers (whether true or false) is like unto a Body or College of Physicians in a City; like unto a Corporation, Society, or Company of East-Indies or Turkey Merchants, or any other Society or Company in London: which Companies may hold their Courts, keep their Records, hold disputations; and in matters concerning their Society, may dissent, divide, break into Schisms and Factions, sue and implead each other at the Law, yea wholly break up and dissolve into pieces and nothing, and yet the peace of the City not be in the least measure impaired or disturbed; because the essence or being of the City, and so the well-being and peace thereof is essentially distinct from those particular Societies; the City-Courts, City-Laws, City-punishments distinct from theirs. The City was before them, and stands absolute and entire, when such a Corporation or Society is taken down.[17]

There is in the thought of Roger Williams a secular emphasis where society at large is considered. Religious toleration was justi-

[17] Roger Williams, *The Bloody Tenet* in *Narragansett Club Publications* (Providence, 1866-1870), vol. III, p. 73.

fiable because religion was a personal experience which need not destroy the basic harmony of a society. The state, on the other hand, was clearly a social experience which attended to men's actions as religion attended to men's thoughts. Because of this fundamentally secular and social aspect of the state, Williams added to his concept of toleration a firm belief in democracy. The "Sovereign, original, and foundation of civil power," declared Williams, "lies in the people."

> And if so . . . a People may erect and establish what form of Government seems to them most meet for their civil condition: it is evident that such Governments as are by them erected and established, have no more power, nor for no longer time, than the civil power or people consenting and agreeing shall betrust them with.[18]

The democracy of Roger Williams was not restricted to regenerate men in the Puritan church. It approached modern concepts of democracy in that it reached toward the right of those subject to the jurisdiction of an institution to have a share in its government. By removing the requirement of regeneracy for a voice in the civil government, Williams moved Rhode Island out of the Puritan seventeenth century and into the secular era of the eighteenth century. It was inconceivable to the orthodox Massachusetts Puritan that unregenerate souls should be granted the franchise. Such a move meant, in effect, giving the controlling voice in government to those who might most seriously challenge the views of the established conservative group. Williams, however, was able to make this break because he did not share the views of the inner circle of Puritans, and because of his attitude regarding the relative positions of church and state. An orthodox Puritan could reasonably be reluctant about relinquishing control to non-Puritans. A non-Puritan, who still had doubts about any single true faith, could view politics in a more secular light, and could consider religious issues as irrelevant to politics. Politics concerned the affairs of the state, not the spirit; and the affairs of the state were concerned with matters of action, not personal belief.

There is a point, however, where belief, to be meaningful and consequential, must be translated into action. It is at this point that the claims of religious liberties have traditionally encountered the claims of public authority. Some eleven years after his pleas for religious liberty in *The Bloody Tenet*, Williams was forced to hedge in the liberty he had previously so boldly proclaimed. All liberty of

---

[18] *Ibid.*, pp. 249-250.

conscience, he argued in a *Letter to The Town of Providence* (1655), is a limited sort of thing. To illustrate his point, he drew an analogy between a ship and a state. Many persons of divergent religious views might be safely embarked on such a vessel, and none might be compelled to attend the church service of one church, or forbidden to attend their own. Nevertheless, Williams counselled, even with this liberty,

> . . . the commander of this ship ought to command the ship's course, yea, and also command that justice, peace and sobriety, be kept and practiced both among the seaman and all the passengers. If any of the seamen refuse to perform their services, or passengers to pay their freight; if any refuse to help, in person or purse, towards the common charges or defence; if any refuse to obey the common laws and orders of the ship, concerning their common peace or preservation; if any shall mutiny and rise up against their commanders and officers; if any should preach or write that there ought to be no commanders or officers, because all are equal in Christ, therefore no masters nor officers, no laws nor orders, nor corrections nor punishments;—I say, I never deemed, but in such cases, whatever is pretended, the commander or commanders may judge, resist, compel and punish such transgressors, according to their deserts and merits.[19]

Democracy, if considered as a political system in which the numerical majority of those governed determine the composition and policies of the government, requires no necessary amount of toleration for religious minorities within the state. Toleration, if considered as a form of state policy whereby those dissenting from the majority on religious issues are nevertheless permitted to practice in peace their views as confirmed by conscience, requires no necessary form of political organization, whether monarchy, aristocracy, or democracy. It was the genius of Roger Williams to envision democracy and toleration as mutually fulfilling concepts, each one perfecting the true achievement of the other. Toleration was thus dependent upon the existence of a democratic society, while democracy could be realized only where there was genuine respect for dissenters, as it was based upon the interplay of individuals and groups with opposing points of view.

Within the space of a generation of settlement in New England, heterodoxy of belief had sprouted from religious orthodoxy. In a

[19] *Letters of Roger Williams, 1632-1682,* ed. by John Russell Bartlett in *Publications of the Narragansett Club* (Providence, 1874), vol. VI, pp. 278-279.

sense this development was inevitable, given the logic of the Reformation. For the Reformation had enthroned individual conscience, and thus the right of private judgment in matters of religious belief. True, the claims of conscience in religion, as in other areas of thought, had to risk the judgment of public opinion, the claims of society itself. Religious orthodoxy was still imposed by secular as well as priestly authorities, but since the legitimacy of any religion rested in the final analysis upon its acceptance by believers, religious questions became matters of individual judgment. The fractionalization of religion that had begun formally with Lutheranism thus continued as new religions arose to satisfy the quest for faith of new believers. The early claim of Luther for the priesthood of all believers led to many priesthoods of diverse beliefs.

While the existence of several religious societies made necessary either a war of annihilation or else some measure of toleration, it was Roger Williams in America who first made clear the reasonableness of toleration as a policy of state. Although orthodoxy lingered in Massachusetts throughout the seventeenth century, even this stronghold of Puritanism came to accept religious toleration as a necessary policy in the well-ordered state. Religious toleration, indeed, has remained one of the basic values in American political thought.

CHAPTER 3

English
Revolutionary Thought

DURING the period of militant Puritanism in Massachusetts, the period in which colonization spread and developed along the Atlantic seaboard, the vicissitudes of English politics cast the mother country into civil war. The zealous persecutor of English Puritans, Archbishop Laud, was impeached, sent to the Tower, and finally executed, as a Puritan-dominated House of Commons took control of the government. In 1649 Charles I was executed. When it is remembered that the King's claim to rule at this time was divine authorization, one can appreciate better the tremendous ferment in political, and indeed, social, thought which brought forth this bold challenge to the established order. With the establishment of the Protectorate in 1653, Oliver Cromwell was granted virtually dictatorial powers under a constitutional scheme called the *Instrument of Government*. Radical Puritanism failed, however, to maintain control of English politics, and the death of Cromwell was followed by the Restoration of the Stuarts (1660-1689). Religious and political issues continued to vex England until a settlement was reached in the Glorious Revolution of 1688-1689, in which William and Mary were brought to the throne and Parliament enacted the Bill of Rights.

The American Revolution, following the Glorious Revolution in England by nearly a century, was in many ways the child of this parent event. While the religious issues in the more secular eighteenth century were not present in the American Revolution to the degree they were in the English, nevertheless there are many obvious points of similarity. The struggle in each instance involved the authority of representative institutions. The political rationale of the insurgents called for profound consideration of the very fundamentals of political organization, and in both instances the contract theory was found sufficient for these purposes. In both cases victory lay with the side which maintained rights against the side which defended authority. Indeed, aside from the issue of imperial organization, the political thought of the American Revolution on such crucial points as representation, property, taxation, and personal rights had already been developed in the literature written during the English civil war and its immediate aftermath. As the ideas made current by the Protestant Reformation form the background of American Puritanism, so do the ideas developed in seventeenth-century England have an essential place in the political thought of the American Revolution. Political conflict has a way of breeding political theorists, and England, torn by civil strife in the seventeenth century, produced a galaxy of political thinkers and pamphleteers, a host which made that century the most notable in the history of English political thought. Neither in quality nor quantity could any other European country compare with the political literary output of England. From the vast number of thinkers whose work has been consequential to political thought, the names of Edward Coke, Algernon Sidney, John Milton, Thomas Hobbes, James Harrington, and John Locke stand out as particularly appropriate in a study of American political thought. However, the germinal ideas of the latter three may be sufficient for our purposes.

THOMAS HOBBES

Thomas Hobbes (1588-1679) spoke to all ages with the voice of conservative authoritarianism. When Daniel Leonard, in the last stage of the American Revolution, opposed the severing of ties with England because it would cast the colonies back to a miserable state of nature, he echoed Thomas Hobbes. Those who fear the masses of men unrestrained by police authorities and positive law repeat the fears of Thomas Hobbes. Hobbes feared mankind on the loose—that savage and aggressive beast that was man. Calvin, Luther, and the Catholic theologians distrusted man as prone to evil, but found his saving grace in his moral sense granted by God and governed by the Scriptures. It was Hobbes who put aside God and the Scriptures and talked about man as though he were a mass of substance, unrefined by divine alloy. Hobbes agreed with Calvin on the corruptibility of man; indeed, Hobbes would have been in agreement with Cotton on that lust for power which resides within men. But Hobbes broke with the theologians in finding a materialistic basis for the actions of men, and thereby he set the stage for a more secularistic explanation of political behavior. Hobbes saw man as ruled not by God and Satan, but rather by desires and aversions. His examination of these desires and aversions, together with their political consequences, made him a precursory thinker in the field of political psychology.

The *Leviathan,* written in 1651, after the beheading of Charles and shortly before the Protectorate of Cromwell, was Hobbes' most significant contribution to political theory. In it he drew a picture of the state, the Leviathan, as one vast artificial man, an organism possessing soul, joints, nerves, strength, memory, health, and reason. Within this conceptual image were the ordinary human beings who composed and, in fact, created it. Selfishly aggressive yet timidly reluctant beings, they moved along the path of least resistance toward that which they desired, shunning that which caused them discomfort.

> But whatsoever is the object of any man's Appetite or Desire; that is it, which he for his part calleth *Good:* And the object of his Hate, and Aversion, *Evil;* and of his Contempt, *Vile* and *Inconsiderable.* For these words of Good, Evil, and Contemptible, are ever used with relation to the person that useth them: There being nothing simply and absolutely so; nor any common Rule of Good and Evil, to be taken from the nature of the objects themselves; but from the Person of the man (where there is no Commonwealth;) or, (in a Commonwealth), from the Person that representeth it; or from an Arbitrator or Judge, whom men disagreeing shall by consent set up, and make his sentence the Rule thereof.[1]

Hobbes further denied the effectiveness of any natural laws of morality; for while there were natural desires, these desires were not universally enforced as laws. To Hobbes, what had been previously called natural laws were nothing more than moral precepts which lacked the necessary sanctions to make them truly effective. Because these moral precepts could not be enforced, there was no universally recognized standard of justice.

> To this war of every man against every man, this also is consequent; that nothing can be Unjust . . . Where there is no common Power, there is no law: where no law, no Injustice.[2]

Beastly man, forever in competition with his neighbor, jealous

[1] Thomas Hobbes, *Leviathan* (New York: Everyman's Library, 1914), p. 24.
[2] *Ibid.,* p. 66.

and fearful, could know neither peace nor security without a powerful government which could declare the law and enforce it. In describing the behavior of mankind in a state of nature, Hobbes compared the state of nature to the international scene, in which, lacking a supreme government which might command all nations, countries lived in perpetual antagonism to each other.

> . . . In all times, Kings, and Persons of Sovereign authority, because of their Independency, are in continual jealousies, and in the state and posture of Gladiators; having their weapons pointing, and their eyes fixed on one another; that is, their Forts, Garrisons, and Guns, upon the Frontiers of their Kingdoms; and continual Spies upon their neighbours; which is a posture of War.[3]

It is not strange that Hobbes described man's life without government as "solitary, poor, nasty, brutish, and short." It is notable that the conclusions of the author of the *Leviathan* were in many respects similar to those of the Puritan—and, more generally, Christian—theologians. Hobbes, by way of a materialistic psychology, found the sons of Adam prone to sin and inclined toward "a perpetual and restless desire of Power after power, that ceaseth only in Death."[4] To the theologians, as to Hobbes, the only realistic check upon the evil propensities of the masses of men lay in a strong, energetic government. The means of achieving this government, however, caused Hobbes and the theologians to part company, for the latter believed the office of magistrate to have a touch of divinity in it, while Hobbes believed the office arose out of the grim necessities of mankind. Yet, upon analysis, the Puritan writers and Hobbes were not too far removed, for such figures as Winthrop and Cotton turned to the contract theory for the immediate justification of their strong government. Hobbes, however, arrived at authoritarianism through the contract theory without the least touch of divine ordination or restraint. He gave to the contract theory a purely secular justification, in which form it continued in English and later in American thought.

To remove man from the impasse of the war of all against all, Hobbes credited man with a degree of foresight which would appear to be quite inconsistent with his premises. For he considered the origin of the state to be found in a contract whereby every man divested himself of his right to govern himself so that some man, or assembly of men, might govern for him. In such manner was

---

[3] *Ibid.*, p. 65.
[4] *Ibid.*, p. 49.

formed the great Leviathan, the state, which henceforth would maintain peace and order amongst men. Thus was created the sovereign power of the ruler.

> For by this Authority, given him by every particular man in the Commonwealth, he hath the use of so much Power and Strength conferred on him, that by terror thereof, he is enabled to form the wills of them all, to Peace at home, and mutual aid against their enemies abroad.[5]

Since the sole aim of the commonwealth was to achieve order and security, the burden or privilege of ruling rested with those who could fulfill these purposes. They kept their position only so long as they could in fact maintain order and security. Against the rulers the ruled had only the most primitive right of self-preservation, and even this right rested entirely upon self-enforcement. The government, in other words, was absolute and continued in power so long as it was able to maintain its authority. Without the power to enforce its decrees, the government would be unable to maintain law, and without law there could be no security. It was inconceivable to Hobbes that there might be in an orderly commonwealth large spheres of private activity with which the government could not interfere. Private activity meant private judgment, and private judgment rested on personal desires and aversions. Thus private activity, immune from governmental intervention, would lead inevitably to private conflicts which would soon spread into public disorders. To eliminate such conflicts, there must be some supreme authority which could intercede at any point to prevent disorder. To those who found unattractive the thought of such an authoritarian regime, Hobbes had only to cite the alternative, the state of nature. The overthrow of established government meant a return to that abominable condition of mankind in which life was "solitary, poor, nasty, brutish, and short." This left little choice for unregenerate mankind.

Hobbes, employing materialistic reasoning and a crude psychology, secularized the conclusions of the seventeenth-century theologians regarding the nature of man. And to the reader of any era who professed to be shocked by his pessimism, he said:

> Let him therefore consider with himself, when taking a journey, he arms himself, and seeks to go well accompanied; when going to sleep, he locks his doors; when even in his house he locks his chests; and

[5] *Ibid.*, pp. 89-90.

this when he knows there be Laws, and public Officers, armed, to revenge all injuries shall be done him; what opinion has he of his fellow subjects, when he rides armed; of his fellow Citizens, when he locks his doors; and of his children, and servants, when he locks his chests. Does he not there as much accuse mankind by his actions as I do by my words?[6]

This distrustful view of mankind, so strikingly presented by Hobbes, has often been voiced by conservatives as a check upon those who would upset the established system of law and order and risk by revolution a return to the state of nature. It was this fear of man in a state of nature which led Daniel Leonard to oppose the American Revolution. It was a fear of man's impulse toward chaos that Alexander Hamilton used as a justification for a strong national government. And it was the belief that man's moral faculties were subservient to his immediate desires that constituted such an essential part of the pro-slavery argument against the theory of natural law and the inalienable rights of man.

JAMES HARRINGTON

While the chaos of mid-seventeenth-century England led Hobbes to seek a haven of ordered security in the state, it brought James Harrington (1611-1677) to consider the impetus behind the social forces which were so rapidly transforming the English political scene. In his one great book, *Oceana* (1656), a utopia, Harrington contributed a host of political ideas to the general conceptual pattern which later became American political thought. Harrington and Hobbes both sought to explain the causes of political disruption in England and to seek its cure. But while Hobbes emphasized the individual with his aggressive self-interest as the source of inevitable conflict, Harrington explored the field of economic interests and their relationship to political developments. Hobbes would cure conflict by absolutism, but Harrington looked to an equilibrium of political and economic forces, and a representative commonwealth ruled by laws instead of men.

Ever since men have attempted political theory writers have sought to explain the causes of revolutions. Plato discussed the subject, and Aristotle devoted a whole book of his *Politics* to an examination of revolutions. Harrington, drawing heavily upon Aris-

6 *Ibid.*, p. 65.

totle, observed in modern times the relationship of changing property ownership to changing political power. Hobbes had extolled the might of the sword of political authority; Harrington discovered the owner of the hand which held the sword. Writing of Hobbes he said:

> But as he said of the Law that without this sword it is but paper; so he might have thought of this sword, that without a hand it is but cold iron. The hand which holdeth this sword is the Militia of a Nation; and the Militia of a Nation, is either an Army in the field, or ready for the field upon occasion. But an Army is a beast that hath a great belly and must be fed; wherefore this will come unto what pastures you have, and what pastures you have will come unto the balance of propriety, without which the public sword is but a name or mere spitfrog.[7]

In Harrington's day economic power rested with those who held property in land. Since the great beast, the army, had to be fed, political authority was conditioned by and in fact dependent upon economic power. Or to put the statement into a positive maxim: economic power conditions political power, and fundamental changes in economic power will effect basic changes in political authority. Applying this maxim to English history, Harrington found that the great redistributions of property under Henry VII and Henry VIII had wrought a fundamental change in economic power —away from the nobility and into the hands of the gentry—which, inevitably, had had political repercussions. Only the "perpetual love tricks" of the astute Elizabeth postponed the political readjustment. Now, under the less skilful Stuarts, the gentry were demanding political authority commensurate with their economic power. Thus, long before Karl Marx, Harrington discovered a necessary relationship between political and economic power. John Adams, following Harrington's approach, carried this idea over into the stream of American political thought; and later Daniel Webster recorded his indebtedness to Harrington for this fundamental observation.

With the concept of a condition of disequilibrium between political and economic forces as the basic cause of political disorder and instability, Harrington proposed to apply the lessons of this discovery to the framing of a well-ordered, stable commonwealth. Ideally, he believed a wide distribution of property ownership

---

[7] James Harrington, *Oceana*, edited by S. F. Liljegren (Heidelberg, 1924), p. 49.

more desirable than a tightly restricted system, and thus his utopia would curtail the excessive exploitation of primogeniture, so that property would not fall by inheritance into the hands of the few. The radical innovation by which he proposed to control this was an "Agrarian law" which would prevent the passing of large estates to the eldest son alone if other heirs existed. With property widely distributed among the gentry, the economic basis was secure for the establishment of a republican commonwealth.

The political structure which Harrington created contained many features of significance to democratic thought. He favored a separation of governmental powers into a deliberative senate, a popular assembly to accept or reject senate proposals, and an executive branch. Election of officials would be by secret ballot. Members of the senate and assembly would hold three-year terms of office, with one third of each body retiring each year, while magistrates might hold office for only one year at a time. Indeed, the idea of rotation in office played an important part in Harrington's system. The elaborate edifice detailed in the *Oceana* was to be bound by a written constitution, which constitution was to be superior in legal status to all other enactments. Thus would be established what Harrington called the "equal commonwealth."

> An equal commonwealth . . . is a Government established upon equal Agrarian, arising into the superstructures or three orders, the Senate debating and proposing, the people resolving, and the Magistracy executing by an equal Rotation through the suffrage of the people given by the Ballot.[8]

In this fashion did Harrington seek a solution to the problem, posed by Hobbes and, indeed, by English history of the seventeenth century, of how to maintain a stable and orderly government when there were conflicting interests among men. In place of Hobbes' solution of absolute and irresponsible rule, Harrington sought a responsible government limited in its authority by a written constitution, "an empire of laws and not of men."

JOHN LOCKE

It was John Locke (1632-1704) who, of all seventeenth-century English political theorists, had the most lasting influence upon

[8] *Ibid.,* p. 33.

American political thought. An accomplished writer in diverse fields of interest, he delved into education, religion, philosophy, psychology, and economics, as well as political science. Whatever subject was touched by his thought bore the imprint of that contact for generations. Although Locke in his political thought lacked Hobbes' insight into human behavior and Harrington's understanding of the role of economic forces in politics, nevertheless his lucid reformulation of old truths of political thought made him not only the apologist for the Glorious Revolution in England but the major precursory thinker for the American Revolution.

In 1660 England abandoned its efforts to set up a republican government and returned to monarchy with the restoration of the Stuarts. With a jealous Parliament standing guard, the Stuarts remained in power for nearly thirty years. This political development of a restored monarch checked by an aggressive Parliament made Harrington's republican solution for England as obsolete as Hobbes' absolutism. The shift of economic power away from the nobility gave a new political prestige not alone to the gentry, but also to the rising middle class. While it was Harrington who had observed the relationship of property ownership to political power, it was John Locke who gave to property claims the status of natural and inalienable rights.

Although Locke devoted one of his efforts in political science directly to American conditions, the abortive *Fundamental Constitutions for the Government of Carolina* left no real mark in American political thought. It was the writing devoted to English conditions that left an impress upon both English and American thought. Two of these works deserve notice here, both published after the throne had passed to William and Mary and the Glorious Revolution was a *fait accompli*. His *Letter Concerning Toleration*, published in 1689, indicated the justifications for a public policy of religious toleration, a policy eventually adopted both in England and America, while in the second of his *Two Treatises of Government*, published in 1690, he developed his "true original, extent and end of civil government."

In arguing in favor of toleration, Locke actually added little to the discussion that had not already been indicated by the Rhode Islander, Roger Williams. Yet Locke, by continuing the appeal with the particular persuasiveness of his pen, made a substantial contribution to what became later an essential part of English and American public policy. Like Williams, he defended toleration on the grounds of Christianity and expediency; but where Williams depended heavily upon Scriptural references and Divine allusions in keeping with the form of religious discussions of the times, Locke is quite modern in insisting upon the utter reasonableness of the proposition. Why, Locke inquires, if men may be permitted to meet peaceably in the market place to transact business, may they not meet peaceably together in the church? Certainly there is less likelihood of the state's being endangered by meetings devoted to non-secular affairs than by meetings in the market place devoted to civil affairs. The fear of sedition on the part of religious minorities was a fear without foundation in fact, Locke argued. If diversity of religion is permitted, each religious group will cherish the state which grants it the freedom to enjoy its own form of religious practice and experience. It is religious persecution and oppression, on the other hand, which generate sedition, for there is a common inclination of all mankind to escape oppression and "to shake off the yoke that galls their necks."

Locke maintained, however, that there must of necessity be limits to the degree of religious toleration permitted in the state. That is, freedom could not be permitted if such freedom would destroy the state and society. Thus he would ban such opinions as were opposed to "those moral rules which are necessary to the preservation of civil society."[9] Should a religion teach that men should not keep their promises, or that princes who subscribed to a different religion should be dethroned; or should a religion demand freedom for itself only until it could seize the government so that it could deny freedom to others—such a religion, Locke held, ought not to be tolerated. Further, no religion should be tolerated which was so constituted that its adherents became bound "to the protection and service of another prince."[10] Finally, Locke denied toleration to atheists on the grounds that atheists could not be bound by oaths and promises, and such agreements were essential to all organized society. Aside from these conditions, however, he made a strong plea for religious liberty. "The sum of all we drive at," he wrote, "is that every man may enjoy the same rights that are granted to others."[11] Only through religious toleration was it possible for members of the civil society to enjoy the right of freedom of worship, unmolested by

[9] John Locke, *The Second Treatise of Government and A Letter Concerning Toleration,* edited by J. W. Gough (Oxford: Basil Blackwell, 1946), p. 154.
[10] *Ibid.,* p. 155.
[11] *Ibid.,* p. 159.

the state. Only in such manner could churches and the state live harmoniously together in the same society. Locke, like Roger Williams, separated the affairs of church and state and framed in theory the ideas which were later put into practice in America. If church and state each remained within its separate sphere, "the one attending to the worldly welfare of the commonwealth, the other to the salvation of the souls," then, Locke wrote, "it is impossible that any discord should ever have happened between them."[12]

Locke's *Two Treatises of Government* was published in 1690. The first treatise was devoted to a refutation of the obsolete theory of monarchy held by divine right, as expounded by Sir Robert Filmer in his *Patriarcha* (1680). It was in the second treatise, however, that Locke stated his positive views on the origin of government, its structure, and the rights of man, views which have found a lasting place in the course of political thought. Writing to "justify to the world the People of England," whose Glorious Revolution had established King William on the throne, Locke stated the arguments which were used as a justification for revolution nearly a century later.

Like Hobbes, Locke considered political power to be the authority to make and enforce laws binding upon the political community. This power was conditioned, however, in that it might be exercised "only for the public good."[13] Thus it was far different in kind from that wielded by Hobbes' absolute, irresponsible sovereign. In order to develop this conception of political authority, Locke used the contract theory and its basic assumption, a state of nature. If political society was made by man rather than by God, then there must have been a time when man lived without political organization. It was this logically-prior period that was characterized by the contract theorists as the state of nature. The assumptions regarding the condition of man in this state of nature, however, largely determine the sort of political authority that will be created by man through the contract device. Contract theorists Hobbes, Locke, and Rousseau, assuming different conditions in the state of nature, developed different conceptions of the authority of established government.

Locke believed the state of nature to be one of natural equality among men. This had been the opinion of Thomas Hobbes also. Unlike Hobbes, however, Locke believed that these men, while free,

[12] *Ibid.*, p. 162.
[13] John Locke, *Of Civil Government* (New York: Everyman's Library, 1924), p. 118.

were nevertheless restrained by the law of nature. Thus he assumed a natural morality among men which kept this state of liberty from becoming a state of war of everyman against everyman. By supporting the natural morality of men, derived from natural law, Locke drew to his position the heritage of Christian political thought. Indeed, this line of thought reached back through the Christian writers to the early Stoic philosophers, and was to carry forward into the twentieth century.

> The state of Nature has a law of Nature to govern it, which obliges every one, and reason, which is that law, teaches all mankind who will but consult it, that being all equal and independent, no one ought to harm another in his life, health, liberty or possessions. . . .[14]

From Stoicism on down through Christian thought this basic assumption had been the same. God had created men free and equal and had endowed them with reason. One need only consult one's reason to discover natural law. It was by virtue of reason and natural law that one knew the fundamental laws of morality.

This state of nature obviously had certain serious inconveniences, even though it was a state of liberty rather than one of war. While all might discover natural law, nevertheless there was a complete lack of governmental machinery to proclaim the law, to see that it was properly enforced, and to adjudge cases arising under it. Thus natural law, while always present, was dependent entirely upon the awkward arrangement of self-enforcement.

The assumption of natural law carried with it the further assumption of natural rights. With Hobbes, man's only natural right was the right to preserve himself against destruction. With Locke, however, natural rights had a strong positive connotation, for they included not only life, but liberty and property as well. In developing the right to property as a fundamental personal right, Locke in a sense rationalized the shift in property ownership to the middle class which Harrington had observed before him. In making the ownership of property a valuable right in modern society, Locke developed the theoretical basis for capitalism. However, his labor theory of value was as much a justification for orthodox socialism as for classical economics. Locke developed his theory of property and his labor theory of value in the following manner. Since God had created the universe and man, it must be evident that the fruits of the earth were intended to support mankind. Originally this benefice,

14 *Ibid.*, p. 119.

granted to all mankind, was given to men to hold in common. Thus
the original state of man was a communistic one in which "nobody
has originally a private dominion exclusive of the rest of mankind."[15]
Yet out of this situation private property developed.

> Though the earth and all inferior creatures be common to all men,
> yet every man has a "property" in his own "person." This nobody
> has any right to but himself. The "labour" of his body and the "work"
> of his hands, we may say, are properly his. Whatsoever, then, he
> removes out of the state that Nature hath provided and left it in, he
> hath mixed his labour with it, and joined to it something that is his
> own, and thereby makes it his property.[16]

Thus it is that, out of possessions held in common, man annexes
to himself by virtue of the contribution of his own labor property
that is his personal possession. Out of common property comes
private property. Man, owning himself, owns also his efforts. Where
his efforts touch that which is held in common, the object that is
affected by his efforts becomes annexed to himself as a possession.
The illustration used by Locke was simple but effective. At what
point, he inquired, did apples grown in the wild become the private
possession of man? "When he digested? or when he ate? or when
he boiled? or when he brought them home? or when he picked
them up?"[17] The exertion of individual labor upon common property
commenced from the moment he picked the apples up, and thus at
this stage the annexation of the apple as part of his personal possessions began. Had he not picked up the apple, he might have
starved, and this would have violated the natural law of self-preservation. While the apple lay on the ground it was the possession of
all men in common, and thus no other individual had prior claim
to it. It was not only necessary but legitimate, therefore, that the
individual who exerted his efforts to acquire the apple possess it of
right as well as in fact.

This justification of private property was not intended to mean,
however, that any man might acquire as much property as his
capabilities might make possible and his desires might demand.
"As much as any one can make use of to any advantage of life
before it spoils," declared Locke, "so much he may by his labour
fix a property in. Whatever is beyond this is more than his share,

[15] *Ibid.*, p. 129.
[16] *Ibid.*, p. 130.
[17] *Ibid.*, p. 130.

and belongs to others."[18] Thus, Locke, while defending the establishment of private property, did not seek to defend the insatiable accumulation of property. The Lord gave the earth to men to develop, to cultivate, to make the fruits thereof their own. Men, being born equal, were given the world in common to enjoy for their sustenance. Yet it could hardly have been intended that the earth should always remain in common, for the benefit of the earth lay in cultivation. So, Locke argued, the earth was given to mankind by the Lord to be cultivated for their benefit. "He gave it to the use of the industrious and rational (and labour was to be his title to it); not to the fancy or covetousness of the quarrelsome and contentious."[19] The exertion of effort became thus a positive standard of morality, for the industrious and creative were now morally distinguished from the lazy and incompetent. It would appear that Locke presumed that the possessors of property were in fact those who were industrious, while those who failed to remove property from its common origin were lazy and incompetent. Such a view would certainly have been satisfying to the seventeenth-century property-holders, or the property-holders of any age. The possession of private property became, therefore, not only morally legitimate but socially necessary, for property was the mark of the industrious man.

In order for man to achieve the fullest benefits from the possession of private property, the art of barter or exchange was introduced. Thus a man might accumulate more than he could possibly use or consume, provided that he exchanged the surplus for goods he could use before they spoiled. Exchange of physical goods themselves, however, was a rather cumbersome system, so the substitution of money for goods was introduced. Money, Locke reasoned, represented stored-up goods. It was the introduction of money Locke admitted, which altered the system he had constructed thus far. For, while there was always the limit of the amount which might be used without spoiling set upon the goods which might be accumulated by any man, there was no limit upon his accumulation of money, the value-equivalent of goods.

The illustrations used by Locke to justify the ownership of property would suggest that his theory was most applicable to the instance of a man moving upon virgin territory, who by dint of his own labor transforms the wilderness into an orchard. Here, the

18 *Ibid.*, p. 131.
19 *Ibid.*, pp. 132-133.

labor theory of value had full place, for without the application of labor the wilderness remained, of course, a wilderness. Locke took only the simplest of situations, the case of the man who grew exactly the amount he needed or who was able to exchange entirely the surplus crop. The question may be raised, however, whether all the surplus produce of the orchard was due to the man who had expended his labor on it, or whether such surplus, threatened with spoilation, must be given away to those who had not, for whatever reason, contributed their labor? Locke's concept of property was, like Harrington's, concerned primarily with an agrarian economy. However, the concept of money as unspoilable stored-up goods, which implied expended labor, which further implied virtuous past performances—this concept of money as an unlimited aspect of private property was in keeping with the progressing entrepreneural economy of the period. Private property as a symbol of industry and virtue, and therefore a qualification for political status, was destined to play an important role in all subsequent political thought.

Prior to the organization of political society, Locke assumed that all men lived in a condition of freedom and equality under natural law and possessed certain rights, of which the ownership of private property was one. Assuming this condition of mankind in a state of nature, Locke reasoned that "no one can be put out of this estate and subjected to the political power of another without his own consent. . . ."[20] The social instincts of man impelled him toward political society, and the inconveniences of the state of nature gave further impetus to this desire. However, no man entered this new society except by his own consent. He was not forced into it through the fear of destruction, as Hobbes had argued, but rather entered freely to avoid the annoyances of a state of nature which was unpleasant but not intolerable. This approach is quite important, for it gave men a claim over the political authority which they would create. They were not refugees from an earthly Hell, fleeing in fear into the arms of an irresponsible sovereign; they were, on the contrary, simply establishing institutional devices to protect more securely that which they already possessed. Because of their fundamental equality, no man had a superior claim in respect to another, and thus the consent of all was required.

> For, when any number of men have, by the consent of every individual, made a community, they have thereby made that community

[20] *Ibid.*, p. 164.

one body, with a power to act as one body, which is only by the will and determination of the majority.[21]

Locke's theory, therefore, required unanimous consent to establish a political society which would, thenceforth, be governed by majority rule. By the use of the contract device man transformed his condition from a natural state to a political state. But the whole purpose of this arrangement was to facilitate the enforcement of the rights which man already possessed. He gave up no rights by this arrangement and was bound only in one respect, to abide by the decisions of the majority.[22]

The government which Locke constructed, obligated to preserve the rights of life, liberty, and property of those subject to its control, was in the last analysis itself subject to the control of those it apparently ruled. Paradoxically, those who were ruled were in reality the rulers; in appearance only did the agent rule the principal. All authority rested ultimately with those possessed of natural rights, who were, of course, all the people, since government rules only by the consent of those governed. Even though the government was responsible to the governed, the agent subordinate to the principal, Locke sought a separation of governmental powers as a restraint upon those in authority. He divided the work of government into legislative, executive, and federative powers, the last being those powers affecting the foreign affairs of the country. His major purpose, however, was to keep separate legislative and executive authority, for "it may be too great temptation to human frailty, apt to grasp at power, for the same persons who have the power of making laws to have also in their hands the power to execute them." Locke, like John Cotton in America, accepted as one of the weaknesses of mankind the tendency of those in authority to lust for ever greater power. It is the Frenchman Montesquieu who is given credit for devising the functional separation of powers into executive, legislative, and judicial groupings, in which form the separation of powers became accepted in American practice. Yet Locke clearly anticipated Montesquieu in his fears concerning consolidated power.

Having set down numerous conditions governing the exercise of political authority, Locke reasserted the ultimate political supremacy of the people themselves. Should the government, established by consent, prove punitive, then the people had the latent right to

[21] *Ibid.*, p. 165.
[22] This of course poses a crucial problem itself: What if the majority rule against his rights? See Willmore Kendall, *John Locke and the Doctrine of Majority Rule* (Urbana: The University of Illinois Press, 1941).

revoke their consent. Should the established government abrogate its trust and violate the rights of the people, then the ultimate right of revolution (in which instance "God in heaven is judge") might be exercised. Locke did not believe that the right would be exercised frequently, for people were inclined to accept minor mismanagements and wrongful laws "without mutiny or murmur."

> But if a long train of abuses, prevarications, and artifices, all tending the same way, make the design visible to the people, and they cannot but feel what they lie under, and see whither they are going, it is not to be wondered that they should then rouse themselves, and endeavor to put the rule into such hands which may secure to them the ends for which government was at first erected. . . .[23]

John Locke laid a modern theoretical basis for religious toleration, the right of private property, government by the consent of the governed, and the ultimate right of revolution. His theory, essentially secular in character, was well suited to meet the needs of the triumphant Whigs in England as well as the rapidly rising middle class in America. Here was a theory dependent upon neither crude force nor divine right, a theory which might well appeal to the reasonable faculties as well as the economic experience of society in the late seventeenth century.

In the space of less than a century, English political thought had moved far away from the tight theological context of ideas which characterized the Reformation. The political thought of that extraordinary period of civil unrest in seventeenth-century England thus set the framework for what were later considered to be the guiding principles and arguments for English and American political ideas. As the Reformation had stressed the importance of individual conscience in matters of theology and had paved the way toward religious belief based on the consent of the believers, so now did the political thought of the English civil war elevate the role of individual judgment in political affairs. Orthodoxy and authoritarianism imposed from above gave way to heterodoxy and compromise. The claimed right of private judgment became increasingly accepted in religion and politics, so that toleration of religious and political dissenters became an article of the English—and later American—political creed. It was the right of individual judgment, of conscience, which gave equal dignity to every man, as a man, and justified his claim to life, liberty, property, and happiness. For the assumption of conscience and the capacity to judge was an assump-

[23] *Of Civil Government,* p. 231.

tion which, in effect, proclaimed the rationality and morality of man.

Reason, as this term was used in the seventeenth and eighteenth centuries, generally implied rationality and morality. Thus an appeal to reason was an appeal for a decision that was correct in an action sense and proper in a moral sense. A right judgment was therefore one that was right in fact and right in value.[24] It was the distinctive faculty of man that he was rational. Aristotle had found man to be a social animal; Christianity had long emphasized man's moral nature; late seventeenth- and eighteenth-century thought added another virtue: reason. The reasonable man of John Locke, however, gathered together the virtues of the ages so that he was at once social, moral, and essentially intelligent. Such a reasonable man was truly competent to exercise a political judgment; a majority of reasonable men might legitimately guide the affairs of the state, for their policies would be reasonable; there need be no conflict between majority rule and individual rights, as the social, moral and intellectual faculties subsumed under reason would indicate the limits of action in each instance.

By basing political authority upon the vast aggregate of the people rather than placing it in the hands of a divinely sanctioned king or usurping tyrant, Locke sought to establish the intellectual foundations for a state built on reason rather than on superstition and fear. In the Lockean sense, democracy was a reasonable political system, at once sensible and proper. Government by consent of the majority meant in effect the right to political judgment of all men governed. It is important to note, however, in understanding Locke, that his system was built upon an assumption of reason in man in which strong theological and moral connotations were implicit. Toleration was a reasonable policy in that it was at once efficacious (a practicable means whereby people of diverse beliefs might live together in peace) and right (religious beliefs ought to be immune from governmental control). Locke's defense of private property and the labor theory of value was stated as a reasonable proposition, that is, as a proposition which combined practicality with moral judgment. Under the rubric of reason, man's discernment of natural law, Locke established a system of thought which made bold man's claim to human dignity and equal individual rights

[24] It was not until David Hume published his *Treatise of Human Nature* (1739-40) that the ambiguities and difficulties inherent in a system which united rationality and morality were thoroughly examined. Hume rejected this position in his analysis and in so doing he played intellectual havoc with the accepted interpretation of natural law and the role of reason.

determined by private conscience, yet which limited man in those actions which had social consequences. For in elevating reason, Locke also elevated conscience—self-imposed restraint. The *ought* element in Locke thus at one and the same time authorized intuitively perceived rights and decreed duties and limitations. This conception was to Locke in the nature of a self-evident truth; moral ideas, indeed, were innate to man as a rational animal.[25] Yet the ideas which Locke advanced as self-evident, as reasonable deductions from natural law, were in large measure accepted as the working assumptions of the political theory that prevailed in England and America for more than a century after the conclusion of the Glorious Revolution. It was indeed the underlying theory of the English Bill of Rights of 1689, the Declaration of Independence, and the American Bill of Rights of 1790. By bringing together into one system of thought the major prevailing assumptions of English theology, politics, and economics in defense of the rights and dignity of the individual, Locke bolstered and joined the Anglo-American values of Protestantism, democracy, and capitalism.

Locke, loyal to the established English institutions of church and king, worked within what had become traditional frames of reference. Hobbes and Harrington, however, put aside these accepted institutions and placed their systems of thought on a more secular basis. Hobbes with his authoritarianism and Harrington with his republicanism sought radical solutions to England's problem of civil strife, and the moralistic strain so significant with Locke is absent in their writings. Indeed, Hobbes rejected morality as nothing more than the expressed fears and desires of men found in their sensory reaction to given stimuli. In his animalistic approach to politics, Hobbes put aside the moral values of individual freedom and private judgment and elevated as the major goal of politics the peace, order and security of the state. This dim, distrustful view of man, with its accompanying emphasis upon fear and insecurity and its appeal to a firm authority (a father figure, perhaps), has long found a place in crisis politics. While Hobbes' political theory never received the acceptance that Locke's did in America, he nevertheless anticipated a line of thought which came to be considered as part of American political ideas. For Hobbes' psychology, which was the

[25] Compare this aspect of Locke with his *Essay Concerning Human Understanding* (1690), in which he took the position that the mind was essentially a *tabula rasa* on which were written the experiences of the senses. Such a view was completely contrary to a conception of innate ideas, intuitive knowledge, and in fact the whole theory of natural rights.

basis of his political theory, had lingering effects even though his political system found few adherents. His classification of good and evil into personal desires and personal aversions not only brought into question the whole conception of a natural and absolute moral law, but further paved the way for the hedonism of the nineteenth-century utilitarians in England and America. In an effort toward a scientific understanding of political behavior, Hobbes turned away from the traditional moral premises and turned toward a psychological analysis, which, though crude, nevertheless influenced the movement of political theory away from a theological context.

Where Hobbes had rejected universal morality and used a system of psychology as a distinctive aspect of his political thought, Harrington's republic of *Oceana* was founded upon an economic base. The key to an understanding of politics, Harrington believed, was in the realization that the state is based upon an economic order. Changes in the economic order therefore produce changes in the government of the state. To achieve stability in politics, therefore, one need not turn in submission to Hobbes' absolute ruler but rather to a stable economic arrangement. Thinking primarily in terms of the ownership of land as the basic economic factor, Harrington held that where one man owned more land than all others combined, he was an absolute monarch; where ownership of land was widely distributed, the state was what he called a commonwealth. It was his contention that the most stable economic arrangement, and therefore political system, was one in which land ownership was widely distributed. Thus he argued for his agrarian law. When there was a wide distribution of land ownership, there would follow a wide distribution of political authority; popular government was thus founded upon popular wealth. This relationship of economic to political power, advanced by Harrington in the seventeenth century, was restated in nineteenth- and twentieth-century America in a variety of forms and for a variety of purposes. It became, indeed, a significant aspect of modern political thought.

The political theories of Hobbes, Harrington, and Locke are indicative of the radical change in context of political argument that took place in England in the course of less than a century. Theological arguments and premises became less explicitly stated, and secularism developed as the proper context of subsequent political thought. Rationalism, with its varying interpretations, became the new method of thought, and reason supplanted Scriptural quotation as the means whereby man's political values and propensities might be better understood.

CHAPTER 4

The American Revolution

It was inevitable, of course, that the extraordinary events in England would affect the lives of Englishmen living in colonial America. To what extent the changing political fortunes of King and Parliament, of Anglican, Catholic and Puritan, and the political speculations of Englishmen altered colonial political ideas it is difficult to assess, but it is certain that eighteenth-century America found its working conceptions of political theory vastly different from those accepted in the seventeenth century. Eighteenth-century theorists turned to reason with the same intensity of conviction that the theorists of the early seventeenth century had turned to God. This was true not only in England and America but generally throughout western Europe. Man, after centuries of struggle, seemed to have attained his full stature, to have pierced the barriers of obscurantism, and appeared ready to enter what Carl Becker has so aptly characterized as "the heavenly city of the eighteenth-century philosophers."[1] Increasing religious toleration was but one phase of this movement toward the secularizing of society. God, so ever-present to the Puritans, was now withdrawing into Heaven, and Satan was retreating into Hell. With no other contenders on the field, man was left master of himself and his society.

The absolutism of the period of the Reformation reflected a low conception of the natural proclivities of men. In order to restrain depraved mankind, God had instituted government, and thus it might be said that princes were ordained by God. Rebellion against divinely appointed government thus constituted not only sedition but heresy. But what if there were no divine authorization for a particular government? What if man were after all only a little lower

[1] Carl Becker, *The Heavenly City of the Eighteenth-Century Philosophers* (New Haven: Yale University Press, 1932).

than the angels? Could not such a being, endowed with reason, cognizant of the laws of nature, frame a suitable government for himself? These questions gave a distinctly modern tone to the political speculations of the eighteenth century. As the conception of God became less personal, He became, consequently, less fearful. He became the creator of the universe, under whose beneficial laws all things and beings were governed for the most harmonious of purposes. It became man's duty and responsibility to use his reason in order to discover and obey these laws. Man, as an individual, a rational being, had at last come into his own. Political systems and other institutional arrangements could no longer hope to justify themselves on the basis of divine decree alone, but rather would have to seek the support of rational argument.

This changing basis of fundamental belief had already found expression in the political discussions of the Whig revolution and its antecedent events in England. This new rationalism reached into colonial America, even into the Puritan fortress of Massachusetts. It is indeed rather startling to find early in the eighteenth century a Massachusetts clergyman defending the organizational arrangements of his church on the basis of natural rights and the contract theory, yet such was the impact of the new learning upon many of the thoughtful. It was this rationalism, this new conception of the rights of man, which provided the philosophical underpinnings for the revolutions which took place in America and France later in the eighteenth century. Thus it is important to note the uses of this political theory in colonial America as a conditioning influence upon Revolutionary thought.

JOHN WISE

John Wise (1652-1725), a Congregational minister at Ipswich, was the first American colonist to write fully on the contract theory. A frequent participant in public affairs, he led a protest by the selectmen of Ipswich against a tax levied by Governor Andros on the grounds that it was "against the privilege of English subjects to have money raised without their own consent in an Assembly or Parliament."[2] For his part in this protest Wise suffered fine and imprisonment. In the lamentable feverish days of witchcraft trials

[2] Cited in Thomas J. Wertenbaker, *The Puritan Oligarchy* (New York: Charles Scribner's Sons, 1947), p. 330.

in Salem he entered into the controversy to protest the prosecutions, although by such objections he ran the risk of ministerial disfavor. In this age of superstition, he supported the movement for innoculation against smallpox, the scourge which had hitherto been accepted with fatalistic resignation as part of the curse upon mankind. The specific issue which called forth Wise's systematic study in political thought, however, was the threat against the independence of the New England churches. Presumably this movement toward a centralized church authority was led by Increase and Cotton Mather, and would have carried the churches away from Congregationalism into a Presbyterian structure. Wise, in opposing this move, published the *Churches' Quarrel Espoused* (1710) and the *Vindication of the Government of the New England Churches* (1717). These works were republished in 1772 in the heat of the controversy over the rights of the colonists.

Wise wrote to defend the government of the Congregational churches, yet his generalizations were such that they were applicable to any governing institution; he did not write of the church government as being exclusive or exceptionally different in character from any other type of government, and his justifications for government generally were based upon a secularistic rationale. Surely this is indicative of a remarkable change in the climate of opinion of New England. It had been the practice to justify secular government on the grounds of scriptural references and the scholarship of church authorities, yet in this instance Wise, while employing the Scriptures, chose mainly to defend the organizational arrangements of the church on the basis of pronouncements of secular authorities and the principles drawn deductively from reason. The early Massachusetts Puritans had turned to John Calvin of the sixteenth century to bolster their position, but Wise turned for authority to the seventeenth-century writer on natural law, Samuel Pufendorf.[3] Pufendorf, like Locke and Hobbes, followed the approach of the contract theory.

In *A Vindication of the Government of the New England Churches,* Wise gave detailed attention to the foundations of society and the origins of government. Unlike his Puritan predecessors, he did not believe that God had ordained any particular form of gov-

---

[3] Pufendorf, a Dutchman, wrote *De Jure Naturae et Gentium* (1672), which was published in an English translation in 1710. Although Wise's *Vindication* was composed of five parts, or "demonstrations" as he called them, it is only with the second one that we are concerned here. In all, his justification included Scriptural argument and historical practice as well as the light of reason.

ernment for man, and thus the whole issue was open to discussion and might be examined in the light of reason. Following the contract theory approach, Wise turned first to a state of nature to discover the condition of man without governmental control and direction. In the state of nature, Wise found that man possessed three great "immunities." The first of these was that man was at all times "most properly the subject of the law of nature."[4] As a subject of natural law, man, possessed of reason, was always capable of discovering the basic tenets of this law. It was this immutable law governing mankind which set the standard for just conduct and obliged all men to seek to do right and to avoid that which was wrong. Among the basic inclinations of man were those of self-love and self-interest, but there was also a sociable disposition in his make-up and further "an affection or love to mankind in general."[5] Mankind according to Wise was therefore quite different in character from mankind as described by Hobbes. Here was a man capable of discovering the principles of morality, able to discern the public interest as well as his own, and kindly in his general attitude toward his fellow man. It was a fundamental law of nature, Wise observed, "that every man as far as in him lies, do maintain a sociableness with others, agreeable with the main end and disposition of human nature in general."[6]

Man's second great "immunity" Wise found to be the "original liberty instampt upon his rational nature."[7] This liberty was not the abusive freedom of license, but rather the liberty of rational creatures living under the law of nature to order their own affairs in accordance with the dictates of their own judgment. It was this natural condition of liberty which prevented any man from claiming authority over another in the state of nature. This condition of liberty led then to man's third great "immunity," the equality of men in a state of nature. Since no one man had by nature authority over another, then all men must be considered as equals. All mankind are equally the sons of God, and on this earth "we all owe our existence to the same method of propagation."[8] Even as equality marks the nature of our entrance into this world, equality marks also the nature of our departure from it. "Death observes no ceremony, but

[4] John Wise, A Vindication of the Government of the New England Churches (Boston: John Boyles, 1772), p. 23.
[5] Ibid., p. 24.
[6] Ibid.
[7] Ibid., p. 25.
[8] Ibid., p. 27.

knocks as loud at the barriers of the court, as at the door of the cottage."[9] Yet Wise believed that some aspects of this natural equality are lost when man enters into civil society, for then distinctions as to honor and ability may be recognized, and "many great disproportions appear."[10]

Having posited a state of nature in which men enjoyed liberty and equality under natural law, Wise proceeded to the construction of civil society. Civil society was brought about partly because of man's sociable nature, which impelled him toward association with his fellow man, and partly because of the security from injury which such an association might achieve. "For none so good to man, as man, and yet none a greater enemy."[11] Thus Wise's natural man was more of a social creature than that supposed by Locke, and while capable of inflicting injuries, he was not the morally irresponsible creature supposed by Hobbes. Wise speaks of a state of nature which may well be preferable to certain kinds of governmental authority. Like Locke, Wise held that "the first human subject and original of civil power is the people"[12] and that all political authority must rest upon this popular foundation.

With more detail than most contract theorists were inclined to employ, Wise constructed political authority by building one covenant upon another. The first covenant would bring man out of a state of nature and into society. It was a social contract which made possible future collective decisions. This first contract, evidencing consent, also bound the members to abide by a decision of the majority as to what form of government should be established. The next step was to decide what form of government—democracy, aristocracy, or monarchy—was most desirable for that society. Following this decision a new contract would be required, this time between the governors and those governed, the former pledging to "take care of the common peace, and welfare," and the latter "to yield them faithful obedience."[13] Here then, was the legitimate origin of government.

When Wise considered the various forms of government, he made quite clear his preference for democracy. A democratic government, he argued, was most likely to promote the interests of the people and protect them in their rights. The laws of nature indicated that

[9] *Ibid.*
[10] *Ibid.*, p. 28.
[11] *Ibid.*
[12] *Ibid.*
[13] *Ibid.*, p. 29.

a democracy was most agreeable to the inclinations of mankind. Furthermore, democracy was least likely to fall victim to the machinations of selfish and unscrupulous governors, for the governors, responsible to those governed, would be inclined always to promote the welfare of society and thus achieve the true end of government.

> The end of all good government is to cultivate humanity, and promote the happiness of all, and the good of every man in all his rights, his life, liberty, estate, honour, etc. without injury or abuse done to any.[14]

So firmly did Wise believe in the doctrine of consent as the basis for governmental authority that he not only made provision for it at every step in the establishment of government, but he further declared that should any government depart from this basic principle, then "all power returns again to the people, who are the first owners."[15] Wise therefore assumed an inherent right of revolution.

Having established the case for democracy, it only remained for Wise to transfer this reasoning to the institution of the church to argue that the very cause of the Reformation would be lost unless the people themselves remained the fountain of church power. Thus he concluded that the democratic government of the New England churches was "justified and defended by the law and light of nature."[16]

JONATHAN MAYHEW

Wise had argued in behalf of the independence of the Congregational churches of New England, faced with a threat to their democratic government. Yet the argument, drawn from natural law, was bound to carry further in the eighteenth century, for his defence of natural rights and democracy contained the essential philosophical ingredients for revolutionary speculation. It was Jonathan Mayhew (1720-1766), however, who developed fully the rational justification for revolution. In order to legitimatize revolution, it was first necessary to qualify seriously the Scriptural injunction against disobedience to the magistrates. Mayhew accomplished this undertaking by the simple expedient of construing the Scriptures reasonably, and in

14 *Ibid.*, p. 40.
15 *Ibid.*, p. 43.
16 *Ibid.*, p. 44.

so doing he advanced the cause of rationalism against Biblical authoritarianism. Like Wise, Mayhew was a Massachusetts minister who had been impressed with the reasoning of the secular philosophers. Writing of his background, he observed:

> Having been initiated in youth in the doctrines of civil liberty as they were taught by such men as Plato, Demosthenes, Cicero, and other renowned persons among the ancients, and such as Sydney and Milton, Locke and Hoadley among the moderns, I liked them; they seemed rational.[17]

In 1750, a century after the beheading of Charles I, Mayhew developed the justification for revolution in a sermon entitled *Unlimited Submission and Non-Resistance to the Higher Powers*. This sermon was not written to combat any specific oppression, for it was composed in that happy calm that lay between Walpole's regime of "salutary neglect" and the commencement of the Seven Years' War. Yet the priniciples it espoused were decidedly radical in import and needed only the occasion to make their full effects felt.

The theoretical question which Mayhew raised was whether subjects are bound to submit to their rulers under all conditions and circumstances. He accepted the position taken by Christian writers that rulers of the earth were "ministers of God" and that, generally, disobedience to them constituted an offence against God. But, he inquired, was it reasonable to suppose that the Biblical command to submission was intended to apply to every ruler, even a tyrant, even one who specifically violated the commandments of the Lord and enjoined the fulfilling of His ways by others? In spite of the fact that the Scriptures make no exceptions to the injunction against disobedience, Mayhew took the position that reasonable exceptions might be implied. Thus, he reasoned, the command meant to include submission only to those "who actually perform the duty of rulers by exercising a reasonable and just authority for the good of human society."[18] While such good rulers ought to be obeyed, those rulers who injured their subjects, who violated their rights and failed to fulfill the true duties of government, "they have not the least pretence to be honored, obeyed, and rewarded, according to the apostle's argument."[19] Having breached the walls of Scriptural authority so as to permit revolution, Mayhew proceeded to give a secular justi-

[17] Cited in John Wingate Thornton, *The Pulpit of the American Revolution* (Boston: Gould and Lincoln, 1860), p. 46.
[18] *Ibid.*, p. 69.
[19] *Ibid.*, pp. 72-73.

fication for government. Government existed, he argued, because of its utility to men. It was the function of government to benefit human society, not to despoil it, and where the government failed to fulfill its true purposes it might legitimately be overthrown. Without the barrier of the Scriptural injunction to restrain men, and with reason to defend their actions, it was right and proper that subjects themselves pass judgment upon their governors.

> The only reason of the institution of civil government, and the only rational ground of submission to it, is the common safety and utility. If, therefore, in any case, the common safety and utility would not be promoted by submission to government, but the contrary, there is no ground or motive for obedience and submission, but for the contrary.[20]

Jonathan Mayhew and John Wise, Massachusetts theologians of the eighteenth century, stood in marked contrast to the Puritan divines of the formative period of the commonwealth. Theirs was a rational, secular emphasis that was unknown in the days of John Cotton. The church had receded in worldly importance to become but one of many similar societies within the greater secular society, the state. Full religious toleration was still a long way off, and yet the advance in toleration by the time of Mayhew was quite remarkable. Natural law was in competition with divine law as the supreme governing ordinance of mankind. Government, established by that rational creature, man, for his own preservation and welfare, held only a limited commission to govern, for the subjects of government possessed inalienable natural rights. Thus, by the middle of the eighteenth century the doctrine was available for those who chose to use it that a government which violated the terms of its commission might be overthrown and supplanted by another. Hobbes had employed the contract theory to arrive at an effective political principle of non-resistance. In America, however, the Lockean use of the contract theory was found more congenial, for it led to what the colonists believed to be its natural conclusion: the right of revolution.

NATIONALISM IN THE COLONIES

Shortly after Mayhew wrote against the doctrine of unlimited submission, events in colonial America moved so rapidly that the

[20] *Ibid.*, p. 86.

next generation of Americans saw full scale revolt, the practical applications of Mayhew's theory. In 1756 the Seven Years' War commenced in Europe, and its American counterpart, the French and Indian War, seriously affected the development of England's colonial empire. The French and Indian War, providing the colonists with a common enemy, presented them also with a need for a coordinated defense and fostered a common sense of unity. The defeat of the French at Quebec in 1759 and the fall of Montreal and other French strongholds the following year gave England unchallenged authority over her colonial possessions. In the middle of the Seven Years' War, in 1760, George III came to the throne in England and a new colonial policy was inaugurated. The Navigation Acts, over a century old, were most energetically enforced, and new restrictive measures were added. The Sugar Act (1764), the Stamp Act (1765), the Townshend Acts (1767), the Intolerable Acts (1774)—each of these contributed to the felt oppressions which led to war in 1775.

The series of British restrictions and tax measures came at a most inopportune time from the colonial point of view, and the colonial response of protest and petition accelerated the movement toward American national unity. Britain, seeking to make effective a mercantilist policy which had long lain dormant, encountered unexpected resistance from the colonists. With the elimination of the French and Indians as immediate threats to colonial security, Americans were in a better position to enjoy political self-confidence than any time previously. Economically, the colonists had continually improved their position under previous British policy and these gains as well as the promise of future advancement were placed in jeopardy by the new restrictions. Had the colonists been largely dependent upon England economically they would no doubt have been powerless to make good their political claims against the mother country. Yet had the colonists lacked the political habits and traditions of Englishmen with a century of experience in America, it would seem equally certain that the revolution would not have taken place. The unifying ideology which cemented the colonies and the organizational techniques by which political action was achieved were those inherited from English political traditions. It was this achievement of a considerable amount of political and economic independence, this union of political and economic purpose and ability which elevated these English subjects from colonists to Americans and made any threat to their established rights a vital challenge. It was this national spirit, temporarily elevated in the face of a common danger, which found dramatic expression in Patrick Henry's remark in 1765 that he was no longer a Virginian but an American. It was this fundamental conception of themselves as a nation which made meaningful the various theoretical claims of the colonists against the British and gave them a will to resist even to the point of revolution. It was this commonality of will that led the colonists to subordinate local differences to join in a common purpose. Thus it was, as John Adams noted, that "the revolution was effected before the war commenced. The revolution was in the minds and hearts of the people."

FRANKLIN, OTIS, AND DICKINSON

The political theory of the American Revolution may be considered under two general headings. In the first instance, it may be considered as a problem in imperial organization involving the British constitution and the rights of Englishmen. Secondly, it may be considered as an expression of radical political philosophy involving the contract theory and the natural rights of man. The discussions concerning imperial organization and the rights of the colonists were of consequence for only the two decades preceding the Revolution and were in fact concentrated in the period between the Sugar Act and the First Continental Congress. The basic assumptions of the contract theory, however, were in acceptance in America long prior to the Revolution. When the philosophic argument was joined with the constitutional one, it bolstered the rights of Englishmen, but when considered alone it justified the natural rights of all men, whether under the protection of the English constitution or not. As long as the colonists sought a settlement of the issues within the British system, they used arguments drawn from the English constitution and spoke of the rights of Englishmen. When the constitutional approach proved unavailing, the colonists looked to a solution outside the British system and so emphasized the philosophic arguments of the contract theory and the natural rights of man. There was, of course, an inevitable overlap in the constitutional and philosophic arguments, and some authors used both to bolster their position.

The question of imperial organization was essentially a legal one. It involved the nature of the constitution, the colonial charters, the relationship of Parliament to the colonial legislatures and the traditional rights of Englishmen. Were, for instance, Englishmen in

America inferior in their rights to Englishmen in England? If the colonists possessed equal rights with Englishmen at home could they then be taxed by a legislative body in which they were not represented? Indeed, did it accord with the traditional rights of Englishmen to be subject to any laws not of their own making? These were the questions which arose over the issue of imperial organization, as the colonists sought to remodel the imperial system to give greater protection to their claimed rights. As England endeavored to tighten up its policy of mercantilism, the colonists replied with a claim for a measure of autonomy, an area of jurisdiction free from the control of Parliament. As England sought to make effective the assumed jurisdiction of a mother country, the colonists claimed in return that measure of self-government which they had habitually exercised, which King and Parliament had by long custom permitted.

The conflicting claims of colonists and mother country were given early expression in the discussions surrounding the Albany Plan of union in 1754. The essential issue at this time was the means whereby colonial defence might be achieved against the menace of the French and Indians. The correlative issue of the method of financing the burden of colonial defence became in time, however, of paramount importance. The British proposal called for taxation by Parliament to defray the cost of colonial defence. Benjamin Franklin (1706-1790) objected to this proposal on the grounds that the very nature of the problem made it one most suited for colonial consideration. The colonists should participate in determining what funds were needed for colonial defence; for, knowing what dangers jeopardized their security, they could best determine how to meet them. Furthermore, Franklin argued, it was contrary to the basic rights of Englishmen to be taxed in accordance with the British proposal; the colonists not being represented in Parliament, such a levy would be without their consent. Thus, two decades before the First Continental Congress, Benjamin Franklin was voicing the contention of the colonists that it was "an undoubted right of Englishmen not to be taxed but by their own consent, given through their representatives."[21] To preserve the rights of Englishmen and yet provide for taxation by Parliament, Franklin proposed actual representation of the colonies in Parliament. This would not only bring about a closer union between the colonies and the mother country, but it would give the colonists an opportunity to influence the course of legisla-

[21] *The Works of Benjamin Franklin,* edited by John Bigelow (New York: G. P. Putnam's Sons, 1904), vol. III, p. 50.

tion, especially as it affected them. Such a scheme of imperial organization, as compared with the existing arrangement, would be "more
agreeable to the nature of an English constitution and to English
liberty."[22] While Franklin subsequently abandoned the claim for
actual representation in Parliament, this early statement is indicative of the colonial effort to find a more accommodating position in
the British empire. The discussions in 1754 of taxation and defense
thus raised the fundamental query as to what sort of organizational
arrangements would best protect the claimed rights of Englishmen
in America.

A decade after the Albany Plan discussions, Parliament enacted
the Sugar Act, followed by the Stamp Act and the other tax measures which were to incense colonial opinion. American publicists
responded with petition and pamphlet. James Otis (1725-1783), who
had previously challenged the Writs of Assistance, now published
a pamphlet entitled *The Rights of the British Colonies Asserted and
Proved* (1764). Otis employed both the philosophical and constitutional arguments to establish the rights of the colonists. Philosophically, Otis took the familiar position that government is but a trust
with all ultimate power resting in the people. The function of government is to protect the natural rights of man. "It is above all things
to provide for the security, the quiet, and happy enjoyment of life,
liberty, and property."[23] The colonists, as men, were thus entitled
to the same protection of their rights as subjects of the mother country at home. In essence, this argument was, of course, nothing more
than a restatement of Locke. Otis' more suggestive contribution lay,
however, in his joining of the philosophic argument with the constitutional one to find specific limits upon the jurisdiction of Parliament. Under the constitution the colonists were subject to two governments, the English government abroad and the colonial governments at home. Of necessity Parliament was superior to the colonial
governments, and the latter could not refuse obedience to enactments of the former. Ideally the colonists ought to be represented
not only in their provincial assemblies but in Parliament as well.
However, even if the colonists were represented in the House of
Commons it would not be appropriate for that body to enact tax
measures or trade restrictions, for such matters were best controlled
by the local colonial legislatures. Thus, even though the colonists

[22] *Ibid.*, p. 56.
[23] *The University of Missouri Studies* (Columbia, Missouri: The University
of Missouri, 1929), vol. IV, p. 309.

were represented in Parliament, trade and taxation measures ought to be left to the decision of the locally elected bodies. And without any representation from America, Parliament violated the principle of government by consent when it imposed taxes on the colonists.

Under the constitution, and in accordance with the natural law declared by God, there were set limits upon the authority of Parliament. "Should an act of Parliament be against any of *His* natural laws, which are *immutably* true," Otis noted, "their declaration would be contrary to eternal truth, equity and justice, and consequently void. . . ."[24] Furthermore, should Parliament not repeal such improper enactments, it was the function of the judiciary to declare them void. The English constitution provided for such a check and balance system that the supreme legislature must always confine its jurisdiction within the immutable boundaries fixed by natural law. Under such a constitution the colonists might prosper, secure in their rights as Englishmen. The only feature required to improve the imperial arrangements was the representation of the colonists "in some proportion to their number and estates"[25] in Parliament.

Thus Otis, like Franklin, sought colonial representation in Parliament as a device to improve imperial relations. While Franklin had pressed this on the grounds of expediency, Otis took the more radical position that this would achieve government by the consent of those governed. Yet while Franklin believed in 1754 that given colonial representation Parliament might legitimately legislate on a variety of subjects, Otis took the position that even with colonial representation Parliament was restricted in its jurisdiction. In each instance, however, the central issue was where and how to achieve that measure of representation that would make taxation of the colonies legitimate.

When the Stamp Act Congress met in New York in 1765, delegates from nine colonies drew up a series of resolutions protesting the imposition of a tax on legal papers and documents. They reasserted the principle that taxes could be levied only by representatives of their own choosing and that taxes imposed by other representatives were unconstitutional. However, there was no longer any strong feeling that the colonists ought to be represented in Parliament. As long as there was no colonial representation in Parliament the colonists could argue against taxes imposed by this overseas

[24] *Ibid.*, p. 334.
[25] *Ibid.*, p. 347.

body on the grounds of "no taxation without representation"; but the price of representation might be taxation. The Stamp Act Congress resolved, however: "That the people of the colonies are not and from their local circumstances cannot be represented in the House of Commons in Great Britain." Leaving only one possibility for colonial representation, and that in the local colonial assemblies, they left only one possibility for taxation, that is, as long as they could make good the claim of "no taxation without representation." The earlier thinking in favor of colonial representation in Parliament as a new method of imperial organization was now fairly well put aside.

The problem of being subject to two governments—a continuing problem in American political thought—was not so easily settled. Admitting that the government in England was superior to the governments in America, there was still the basic jurisdictional question as to the amount of authority possessed by the central government. Without a written constitution specifying powers, without a federal system providing for delegated powers, what was the criterion for establishing the limits of the central government's authority? A strong feeling of local autonomy, precursory of later states' rights sentiment, was aroused by the encroachments of Parliament upon what were felt to be matters of purely local jurisdiction. John Dickinson (1732-1808) attempted to draw a line between the authority of Parliament and that of the colonial assemblies in his *Letters from a Farmer in Pennsylvania* (1767-1768). Dickinson, like Otis and Franklin before him, sought a moderate solution within the British system, and his argument is temperate and legalistic. He sought no institutional changes in the organization of the empire, but rather to define the limits of Parliamentary authority under the existing arrangement.

The immediate occasion which prompted his letters was the suspension of legislation in New York due to the failure of that colony to submit to a previous act of Parliament requiring it to raise certain supplies for troops. To coerce New York into line, Parliament temporarily suspended its legislative power. The original statute commanding the raising of supplies was a tax measure, Dickinson argued, and the succeeding statute was a punitive act to enforce the first. If Parliament possessed the power to deprive the colonists of the privilege of levying their own taxes by imposing other taxes upon them, what would prevent Parliament from denying all other privileges? Thus, Dickinson chose to make a legal stand on the question of taxation as a first line of defence against other assaults upon the liberties of the colonists. However, even if Parliament were denied jurisdiction over tax measures, the legalistic mind still needed to distinguish between tax laws and other statutes. For instance, was a custom duty imposed on the colonies a tax measure, and therefore proscribed, or was it merely a trade measure? "The Parliament unquestionably possesses a legal authority to regulate the trade of Great Britain and all her colonies."[26] Tax measures which were incidental to the fundamental purpose of regulating trade generally were therefore permissible. Custom duties, however, which were not imposed generally for the regulation of trade, but imposed specifically upon the colonies for the purpose of raising revenue, were certainly tax measures and therefore illegal. To admit the legality of tax measures disguised as specific custom duties would complete "the tragedy of American liberty."

Dickinson, in his opposition to taxation by Parliament, even refused a technical distinction between external and internal taxes. Some critics of his *Letters* have protested that he failed to distinguish between external taxes, imposed specifically upon the colonies to regulate trade, and internal taxes imposed to raise revenue. Dickinson cut through the entire discussion by arguing that a tax was imposed for the sole purpose of raising revenue. When this purpose was incidental and the primary purpose was to regulate trade, then such measures might be permissible. Nevertheless all tax measures affecting the colonies, internal and external, that is, all measures whose primary purpose was revenue, were forbidden to Parliament.

Dickinson's discussion of taxation as opposed to regulation, even of external versus internal taxes, may seem to modern readers like so much legalistic logic-chopping. Yet the discussion illustrates the search for constitutional limitations on governmental authority in colonial America. The discussion not only revealed the conservative legal point of view at that time, but it set the tone for much of the constitutional scholasticism that developed subsequently in the United States. It was Dickinson's purpose to join the colonists together on this matter in a moderate, non-violent stand. He did not seek a settlement outside the British empire, or even one involving an organizational change. He sought, essentially, to reinstate the situation which had prevailed prior to the passage of the Stamp Act. With the repeal of that act, he sought to resist further aggression. "When an act injurious to freedom has been once done, and

[26] *Memoirs of the Historical Society of Pennsylvania,* edited by P. L. Ford (Philadelphia: The Historical Society of Pennsylvania, 1895), vol. XIV, p. 312.

the people bear it, the repetition of it is most likely to meet with submission."[27] Dickinson sought to preserve colonial liberties by preventing any improper submissions. He sought to support liberty with vigilance. In his twelfth *Letter* he summed up his case.

> Let these truths be indelibly impressed on our minds—that we cannot be happy, without being free—that we cannot be free, without being secure in our property—that we cannot be secure in our property, if, without our consent, others may, as by right, take it away—that taxes imposed on us by parliament, do thus take it away—that duties laid for the sole purpose of raising money, are taxes—that attempts to lay such duties should be instantly and firmly opposed—that this opposition can never be effectual, unless it is the united effort of these provinces—that therefore benevolence of temper towards each other, and unanimity of councils, are essential to the welfare of the whole. . . .[28]

WILSON, HAMILTON, AND JOHN ADAMS

John Dickinson had drawn a legalistic line between the authority of Parliament to tax the colonists and its authority to regulate the trade of the empire. He had found that Parliament lacked the power to tax, while it did possess the power to regulate trade. James Wilson (1742-1798), however, who had studied law under Dickinson, carried this same line of reasoning to the point where all Parliamentary authority over the colonies was denied. In his *Considerations on the Nature and Extent of the Legislative Authority of the British Parliament*, published in 1774, Wilson carried the legalistic defence of colonial jurisdiction to its ultimate conclusion. Citing with judicial precision Blackstone, Coke, and Bacon, he carefully documented his findings that Parliament lacked the authority to regulate colonial affairs "in every instance." Wilson based his reasoning on the natural law assumption that all men in a state of nature were free and equal and that government, founded on consent of the governed, was established to promote the happiness of the governed society. Governments were thus restricted in their authority, for, were they not so, the liberties of the people would be destroyed and the people would reap no advantages from departing from the state of nature. It was the glory of the British constitution that the liberties of British citizens were preserved under it, and the colonists, as

[27] *Ibid.*, p. 389.
[28] *Ibid.*, p. 400.

citizens, were entitled to these same liberties. Under the constitution, laws required the assent of King, Lords, and the House of Commons. It was this mutual check, or restraint, within the legislative branch that protected the rights of the inhabitants of Great Britain. In England this restraint applied to the House of Commons, for this body was responsible to the "collective body of the commons of Great Britain." In what manner, however, could the colonists check the Parliament? Without an effective check upon the government the liberties of the people were placed in jeopardy. "Do those, who embark, freemen, in Great Britain disembark, slaves, in America?"[29] The colonists, lacking a check upon Parliament, could become subject to that body only at the expense of their liberty and happiness, the very principles upon which government was founded.

> What has been already advanced will suffice to show, that it is repugnant to the essential maxims of jurisprudence, to the ultimate end of all governments, to the genius of the British constitution, and to the liberty and happiness of the colonies, that they should be bound by the legislative authority of the parliament of Great Britain.[30]

Denying the jurisdiction of Parliament over the colonies, however, did not mean the renunciation of allegiance to the king. "Allegiance to the king and obedience to the parliament are founded on very different principles. The former is founded on protection; the latter on representation."[31] The colonists were not conquered people and therefore there could be no claim for superiority of Great Britain over them. The dependence of the colonists upon Great Britain should be construed to mean only that measure of loyalty and obedience owed to the kings of Great Britain. The settlement of the colonies was accomplished in the king's name, governments were instituted under his prerogative or charters, and the wars with the Indians were with his authority. This measure of dependence ought to be continued, Wilson maintained, for it was by this common allegiance to the king that British subjects in England and America were commonly united. "They are fellow subjects; they are under the allegiance to the same prince; and this union of allegiance naturally produces a union of hearts."[32]

[29] *The Works of James Wilson,* edited by James De Witt Andrews (Chicago: Callaghan and Co., 1896), vol. II, p. 523.
[30] *Ibid.,* p. 526.
[31] *Ibid.,* pp. 528-529.
[32] *Ibid.,* p. 541.

Thus Wilson anticipated an imperial scheme similar to that later established for the British Dominions. With a common allegiance and loyalty to the king, each unit would nevertheless be autonomous in regard to its legislative powers. Thus had the constitutional argument over the nature of the empire progressed: from representation in Parliament so that that body might tax the colonists, to no representation and no taxation by Parliament, to no legislation at all by Parliament for the colonies. Taxation is but a form of legislation, and the argument of "no taxation without representation" was but a lesser degree of the claim of no legislation without representation. James Wilson carried the argument to the point where the reasoning behind "no taxation without representation" prohibited any legislation at all by Parliament over the colonies.

While Wilson advanced the discussion of the nature of the British system to its outermost constitutional limits, leaving but the slender thread of loyalty to the king as the last tie between the colonies and the mother country, other writers were moving in the same direction. Alexander Hamilton (1757-1804) published in 1774, when he was only seventeen years old, *A Full Vindication* in which he denied the authority of Parliament over the colonies. The following year he developed this position more fully in his rebuttal to the Loyalist Samuel Seabury when he wrote *The Farmer Refuted.* Essentially, Hamilton applied the natural-rights and contract-theory approach to find that the colonists, who neither participated in Parliament nor consented to its authority, could not be under its jurisdiction. While denying the authority of Parliament, Hamilton, like Wilson, maintained that the colonists owed allegiance to the King. "He is king of America by virtue of a compact between us and the kings of Great Britain."[33] This contract was implicit in the grants and protection granted by the English monarchs to the colonists. "We hold our lands in America by virtue of charters from British monarchs; and are under no obligations to the Lords or Commons for them."[34] While pledging loyalty to the king, Hamilton maintained that "The right of colonists, therefore, to exercise a legislative power, is an inherent right."[35] Loyalty to the king, thus, remained the slender strand that held the colonies in the British system.

John Adams (1753-1826), more cautious than Hamilton or Wil-

---

[33] *The Works of Alexander Hamilton,* edited by Henry Cabot Lodge (New York: G. P. Putnam's Sons, 1904), vol. I, p. 67.
[34] *Ibid.*
[35] *Ibid.,* p. 88.

son, developed a strong constitutional case for the colonies in his *Novanglus: or a History of the Dispute With America from Its Origin in 1754 to the Present Time* (1775). Reasoning from the colonial charters and the rights of Englishmen, Adams denied that the English Parliament had any more authority to govern the colonies than did the Scottish Parliament. These two legislative bodies, he observed, governed their respective territories under the same king. In what manner did the English Parliament acquire control over the colonies? If the British constitution called for a supreme legislature for all the British possessions, then surely all of the possessions would have to be represented, proportionate to their number of inhabitants. On the face of it, it would be ridiculous to accomplish this. Yet Adams admitted the necessity for some body to regulate matters of trade and commerce, and this function he granted to Parliament. "And here is a line fairly drawn between the rights of Britain and the rights of the colonies, namely, the banks of the ocean, or low-water mark. . . ."[36] Within the colonies, however, colonial legislatures would be supreme. Should Parliament be the supreme legislature over the colonies as well as the seas, then the British constitution would be violated, for the democratic part of this mixed constitution which provided for representation in the legislature would be ignored. Without representation of those governed, the British government, which was a mixture of monarchy, aristocracy, and democracy, would degenerate into either aristocracy or oligarchy. "That a representation in parliament is impracticable, we all agree; but the consequence is, that we must have a representation in our supreme legislatures here."[37] Thus to preserve the British constitution the authority of the colonial legislatures must be complete and unencumbered within their own jurisdictions.

Like Wilson and Hamilton, Adams maintained that the colonists owed allegiance to the king. Yet by permitting Parliament to regulate the trade though not the money matters of the colonies, Adams did not carry the constitutional argument to its ultimate limits. For all the cogency of his reasoning, Adams carried the claims of the colonists little beyond the position previously taken by John Dickinson. In substance he declared his position as follows:

> We are a part of the British dominions, that is, of the King of Great Britain, and it is our interest and duty to continue so. It is equally

[36] *The Works of John Adams,* edited by C. F. Adams (Boston: Charles C. Little and James Brown, 1851), vol. IV, pp. 105-106.
[37] *Ibid.,* p. 119.

our interest and duty to continue subject to the authority of parliament, in the regulation of our trade, as long as she shall leave us to govern our internal policy, and to give and grant our own money, and no longer.[38]

THOMAS PAINE

The arguments based on the nature of the British system and those based on natural rights were not mutually exclusive, but, on the contrary, mutually supporting bases for the colonial claims. It was common to justify government on the basis of consent and to glorify the British constitution for putting this fundamental principle into practice. It was equally common to assert the natural rights of man and extol the British constitution for guaranteeing these rights to Englishmen. Thus, while the natural-right argument was, by nature, the more radical and was eventually adopted as the accepted theory of the Revolution, yet it should be evident that since the time of Wise the contract theory had been the underlying basis for political thought. Otis had used the contract theory for his inquiry into the nature of the British system, while Dickinson assumed the existence of rights and liberties of those governed. James Wilson also entered into his constitutional discussion with a brief statement of natural rights and the consent principle behind government, and Hamilton's arguments were based almost entirely on the natural-rights philosophy. Yet none of these writers had, by 1775, gone further than to deny the jurisdiction of Parliament, either in whole or in part, over the colonies. Although they pushed the claims of the colonies almost to a point of political autonomy, they still sought a solution within the British system.

Colonial national sentiment had increased quite rapidly, however, in the years of discussion and protest following the Stamp Act. While the theorists developed their arguments against Parliament, political organizations were being developed which would help crystallize the collective will and channel the protests in such a fashion as to give them force. The informal Committees on Correspondence led to the First Continental Congress in 1774. When the Second Continental Congress met the following year, the conflict in ideas had developed into a contest of arms. For several months the war spread along the seaboard without the colonists' clearly

[38] *Ibid.*, pp. 120-121.

defining the ultimate goal for which they fought. Were they making this determined stand so that they might enjoy the privilege of taxing themselves while permitting Parliament to regulate their trade? Were they fighting to be rid of all authority by Parliament, yet remaining loyal subjects of the king? Or were they fighting to place themselves outside the British system?

The issue was resolved in January of 1776 with the publication of Thomas Paine's *Common Sense*, a pamphlet which enjoyed immediate and astonishing success. Paine (1737-1809), an Englishman by birth, a citizen of the world in ideas, was a philosopher of conflict, a fomenter of revolution wherever he felt the sacred rights of man to be endangered. His *Common Sense* abandoned the worshipful approach of other colonial literature toward the British constitution, as he provided the arguments for cutting loose from king, constitution, and all other ties that held Americans to Britain. His arguments returned to the first principles of political obligation. Distinguishing between society and government, Paine found the former produced by our wants, the latter by our wickedness. "Society in every state is a blessing, but Government even in its best state is but a necessary evil,"[39] he wrote. It should be noted that Paine's view of government was generally acceptable to Christian theology, for, since the fall, man's sinful propensities required some restraint. It may be noted further that Paine's negative role of government was later given enthusiastic endorsement by *laissez faire* economists.

Paine illustrated the contract theory by framing a state out of a fictitious society. He supposed a simple state of nature, a primitive territory inhabited by only a few men. These men, of necessity, would be drawn together into society, but this society would lack government. In time, however, men would find it necessary to decide upon public matters and to make regulations. "In this first parliament, every man, by natural right, will have a seat."[40] With the passage of time, an increase in numbers, and the extension of area occupied by this early society, it will be found necessary for the members of this society to elect representatives to appear for them on public matters. Frequent elections, returning those elected to the entire body of electors, would insure "their fidelity to the public will." On this simple arrangement "depends the *strength of*

[39] *The Writings of Thomas Paine, edited by M. D. Conway* (New York: G. P. Putnam's Sons, 1894), vol. I, p. 69.
[40] *Ibid.*, p. 70.

government, and the happiness of the governed."[41] In this fashion were governments formed for the purpose of achieving freedom and security for those governed. With this as the true model and justification of government, Paine then turned to examine "the so much boasted constitution of England." Instead of finding this constitution to be a charter of freedom, he found it to be constructed of "two ancient tyrannies, compounded with some new Republican materials."[42] As the king and House of Lords were hereditary and not dependent upon the people, "in a *constitutional sense* they contribute nothing towards the freedom of the State."[43] The check and balance system in the constitution he found to be "a mere absurdity," for it presumed a greater wisdom was possessed by that power that could check another; and yet in the English constitution commons and king could check each other. It was not the English constitution of king, peers, and commons that had preserved the freedoms traditionally enjoyed by Englishmen. On the contrary, *"it is wholly owing to the constitution of the People, and not the constitution of the Government,* that the crown is not as oppressive in England as in Turkey."[44]

Until 1776, the American colonists had not only expressed reverence for the English constitution, but loyalty to His Majesty, the King. Paine's iconoclasm not only besmirched the constitution, but, further, ridiculed the king. Monarchy was brought into the world by the heathens. "It was the most prosperous invention the Devil ever set on foot for the promotion of idolatry."[45] Monarchy was doubtless first established by force, but its claim to continuance could hardly be justified. Turning to William the Conqueror, Paine observed:

> A French bastard landing with an armed Banditti and establishing himself king of England against the consent of the natives, is in plain terms a very paltry rascally original. It certainly hath no divinity in it.[46]

Having undermined the constitution and the king, Paine pleaded for a united effort in the cause of the colonies. The time for reconciliation was past; the time for independence was at hand. "A gov-

[41] *Ibid.,* p. 71.
[42] *Ibid.,* p. 72.
[43] *Ibid.*
[44] *Ibid.,* p. 74.
[45] *Ibid.,* p. 75.
[46] *Ibid.,* p. 80.

ernment of our own is our natural right," he declared.[47] No advantages could be gained from reconciliation, but many, economic and political, would accrue to an independent America.

Though Paine appealed to the reader's "common sense," the pamphlet radiated the heat of strong feeling, and his impassioned pleas were clearly intended to touch the heart as well as the mind. Turning away from the king, the constitution, and any effort at reconciliation, Paine sounded his call to action and to arms:

> O! ye that love mankind! Ye that dare oppose not only the tyranny, but the tyrant, stand forth! Every spot of the old world is overrun with oppression. Freedom hath been hunted round the Globe. Asia, and Africa, have long expelled her. Europe regards her like a stranger, and England hath given her warning to depart. O! receive the fugitive, and prepare in time an asylum for mankind.[48]

THE DECLARATION OF INDEPENDENCE

Shortly after Paine issued his call to the colonies to unite in their efforts to cast off British authority, sentiment moved rapidly towards independence. In June of 1776 a resolution introduced by Richard Henry Lee was approved by the Second Continental Congress, to declare the colonies independent of Great Britain. A committee, composed of John Adams, Benjamin Franklin, Thomas Jefferson, Robert Livingston, and Roger Sherman, was authorized by Congress to prepare such a declaration. The major burden of the task, however, fell upon Thomas Jefferson. Some fifty years after the drafting of the Declaration, Jefferson made the following observation in regard to it:

> When forced, therefore, to resort to arms for redress, an appeal to the tribunal of the world was deemed proper for our justification. This was the object of the Declaration of Independence. Not to find out new principles, or new arguments, never before thought of, not merely to say things which had never been said before; but to place before mankind the common sense of the subject, in terms so plain and firm as to command their assent, and to justify ourselves in the independent stand we are compelled to take. Neither aiming at originality of principle or sentiment, nor yet copied from any particular and previous writing, it was intended to be an expression

[47] *Ibid.,* p. 99.
[48] *Ibid.,* pp. 100-101.

of the American mind, and to give to that expression the proper tone and the spirit called for by the occasion.[49]

The Declaration of Independence is a single document which may be analyzed in four parts. First, there is a statement as to why it was written; second, the philosophic nature of the case; third, the political situation and the listing of specific grievances; and last, the course of action to be taken. It is, in its entirety, a most extraordinary document, precise in wording, lucid in meaning, and well suited in style to the lofty sentiments expressed. It contains in its few sentences the philosophic conclusions of generations of thinkers.

In the opening paragraph, which is but a sentence, there is a statement as to why the document was written. This statement of itself has considerable significance, for the authors note that "a decent respect to the opinions of mankind requires that they should declare the causes which impel them to the separation." Why, it may be asked, should the opinions of mankind enter into this controversy between the colonies and England? Why should this new-born state wish to justify its existence to the rest of the world? The answers are found in the assumption that the opinions of mankind are of value, are of consequence, that mankind generally may judge right from wrong, and that the righteousness of the cause of the colonies will be clear. This tacit assumption of the Declaration, like so many of its expressed assumptions, goes back to the early Stoic philosophers. It expressed the belief that man and his opinions were worth something, that there was a tribunal that was mankind sitting in judgment upon the actions of men and states. It assumed the validity of a universal moral judgment that was made clear to men when they used their reasonable faculties. It assumed, in fact, the eternal validity of natural law.

Following this simple statement of explanation of why the Declaration was written is the philosophical argument. Here are enunciated the self-evident truths. These truths are self-evident because they need neither empirical proof to substantiate them nor the refined reasoning of deductive logic. They stand, in other words, without explanation or verification, upon their own merits. Yet the very assumption that, first, there are certain truths which must be universal, and, second, that these are not obscurities but on the contrary, self-evident, suggests a view of mankind which would

[49] Letter to Richard Henry Lee, 1825.

lend cause for a decent respect. This view of mankind recognizes a common rationality, at least in fundamental conceptions. Enumerated among the various truths are two. The first of these, the conception of equality, is again a conception which is as ancient as the Stoics. The concept of the brotherhood of men and the fatherhood of God is reinforced by Christianity. In more recent times Hobbes and Locke had assumed the fundamental idea of human equality in a state of nature. This conception of equality should not be confused with equality in physical appearances or mental capabilities, for it merely posited an equality in man's purpose and work. To a theologian, all men were equal in the sight of the Lord; to a lawyer, all men were equal in the eyes of the Court. But, even beyond these specialized fields there was a fundamental equality that made every man's reason of value and every man's feelings worth considering.

The second self-evident truth was the possession by men of certain rights which were unalienable because they were granted to men by God. These rights included, among others not specified, life, liberty, and the pursuit of happiness. With the exception of the last, these were the rights of John Locke and the colonial writers. To deny the right of a created creature to live would be to deny the purpose of his creation. That each man values his own life would not be a fact worth noting were there not a universal sentience regarding all mankind. But it was this common sentience that was itself a universal and justified the existence of all men everywhere. If the right to life is established, then the other rights follow quite naturally. For, if man is entitled to have his opinion respected by other men, then he must be equally entitled to liberty. If man was but an instrument, a means to an end, he could have no value in himself, and his liberty would be of no significance, as he would be a mere tool for some higher fulfillment. If man has, however, value in himself, is possessed of the reasonable faculties that characterize men, then he is entitled to freedom to exercise his powers. As a reasonable creature, he may exercise his reason to solve his problems. To deny him liberty would be to deny the equality of his creation or the very significance of his right to life. Lastly, among the enumerated unalienable rights is the right to pursue happiness. To what purpose is man's life, and his liberty, if not to attain happiness? Individual happiness, this common end, signifies a common element in all mankind. It is ultimately for happiness that men cherish their right to live and so extend themselves as to enjoy liberty. Thus did the Declaration of Independence build up the secular trinity of life, liberty, and happiness. Only in the substitution of happiness was the theory thus far a variation from Locke's established rights of life, liberty, and property. In essence, however, the Declaration went well beyond the physical component, the right of property, in Locke.

Yet, following Locke, the Declaration of Independence states that men possessed of these unalienable rights established government in order to preserve these rights. Since these rights are inalienable, they cannot be bargained away; no government can legitimately usurp them. Furthermore, since governments are established by those possessing these rights, governments must exist for the creatures who established them. Thus, they exist only at the pleasure of those subject to them, for should they exist without the sufferance of those governed they would violate the essential and eternal rights of man. Since the rights of man are the very principles on which governments are founded, and since the preservation of these rights is the sole justification for continuance of governments, it follows that the failure to preserve these rights is sufficient justification for the overthrow of government. Had the Declaration of Independence followed Hobbes, this conclusion would not, of course, have followed. For Hobbes, the essential right was life; and as long as this was preserved no condition of existence could prove so intolerable as to justify the overthrow of government. With Locke, and with Jefferson, however, there was more than mere existence involved; there were those rights which gave men stature, those rights which proclaimed the dignity of men. That the protection of such rights was the proper function of government was proclaimed to all as one of the self-evident truths. Such being the case, the following truth was evident:

That whenever any Form of Government becomes destructive of these ends, it is the Right of the People to alter or abolish it, and to institute new Government, laying its foundation on such principles and organizing its powers in such form, as to them shall seem most likely to effect their safety and Happiness.

Thus was proclaimed the right of revolution, derived from the natural rights of man. Such had been the justification of revolution set forth by Locke after the *fait accompli* in England; such now was the justification set forth by the Declaration of Independence in the course of revolution in America. Neither Jefferson nor Locke supposed that the right of revolution might be a frequent recourse of the people. Both cited the habit of the populace to accept continued maltreatment before a recourse to arms. But without this ultimate remedy, there was no escape from long-standing abuse. The philosophic conclusion of the Declaration of Independence was the right of revolution. It remained but to relate this conclusion to the situation in the colonies to prove that the colonies were justified in exercising this right.

After the philosophic argument, there follows a list of specific charges, or grievances, the long train of abuses which the colonists claimed they had suffered. It is significant that only incidental mention was made of the extension of the authority of Parliament over the colonies, and that the real burden of the attack was brought against the king. Having, in the past, professed loyalty to the king while denying the jurisdiction of Parliament over the colonies, it was necessary for the colonists to cut this last remaining tie in order to achieve independence. Paine had challenged the legitimacy of monarchy as an institution; Jefferson in the Declaration sought to prove that this monarchy had become tyrannical. At the end of the list of charges against the king, it is asserted: "A Prince, whose character is thus marked by every act which may define a Tyrant, is unfit to be the ruler of a free people."

Finally, in the last paragraph, independence is declared, by "the Representatives of the United States of America," absolving the colonies of allegiance to the British Crown and claiming a new status in the world as "Free and Independent States." Thus was concluded this classic statement of the rights of man with its corollary justification for armed resistance.

LOYALISTS: SEABURY, LEONARD, BOUCHER

During the decade of debate preceding the Declaration of Independence, the arguments of the rebellious colonists were met with the rebuttals of the Loyalists. It is to be remembered that these conservatives were equally Englishmen, claiming certain rights under the constitution, who believed that these rights were best preserved under the existing colonial system. As royalists, they were anti-republican; and as constitutional conservatives, they sought to preserve the existing arrangements with England rather than separate and embark on a bold new venture. Three of these Loyalists,

Samuel Seabury, Daniel Leonard, and Jonathan Boucher deserve brief notice.

Samuel Seabury (1729-1796), a New York clergyman, wrote *Letters of a Westchester Farmer* (1774-1775), in which he debated with Hamilton and sought to justify the preservation of the existing colonial system. Seabury took a view similar to that of Hobbes, that a pre-political condition of mankind would have been most unpleasant, for without law and government the strong would have surely oppressed the weak. In such a state, the rights of the weak would have been meaningless. When he considered specific governments, Seabury felt that the English constitutional system of king, lords, and commons was far more likely to preserve rights and liberty than was a republican Congress. Accepting the dependence of the colonies upon the mother country, he insisted that the empire must have some supreme governing authority or else it would split into independent parts. Where else might this supreme authority reside than in that mixed government of king, nobles, and commons? To the argument that under such an arrangement laws were made for the colonies by representatives not of the colonists' own choosing, Seabury replied:

> A great part of the people in England have no vote in the choice of representatives, and therefore are governed by laws to which they never consented either by *themselves* or by *their* representatives.[50]

To the claim that the colonists were bound to the king though not to Parliament, Seabury answered that the king was but the guardian of the laws passed by Parliament. Since it was part of the responsibility of the supreme government to protect the empire, it was logical to assume that authority existed to tax those units so protected. It was essential to the prosperity of all the empire that the supreme government regulate the trade in all its parts. To deny this power to the mother country would throw the colonies into commercial conflict with each other.

> Let it be considered, that no scheme of human policy can be so contrived and guarded, but that something must be left to the integrity, prudence, and wisdom of those who govern. We are apt to think, and I believe justly, that the British constitution is the best scheme of government now subsisting: The rights and liberties of

[50] *Seabury's Letters of a Westchester Farmer,* edited by Charles H. Vance (White Plains, New York: Westchester County Historical Society, 1930), vol. VIII, p. 111.

the people are better secured by it, than any other system now subsisting.[51]

The discussion in New York between Seabury and Hamilton was paralleled in Massachusetts by the exchange of views between Daniel Leonard (1740-1829) and John Adams. In a series of letters signed "Massachusettensis" (1774-1775), Leonard, a lawyer, presented the Loyalist argument which inspired Adams to reply in his *Novanglus*. Like Seabury, Leonard sought to secure the rights of Englishmen rather than to deny them. And he, too, felt that these rights were better preserved under the mixed government in the British constitution than under a provincial Congress. If a mixed form of government with its reciprocal checks was the best form, then it was clearly foolish to deny the authority of Parliament over the colonies, for to do so would be to remove the checks of Lords and Commons from the government. This would result in either an absolute monarchy of king over the colonies, or the anarchical arrangement of independent states, with each state claiming complete political authority. In point of history, the colonies had only such jurisdiction as was granted to them in the charters. Because America was occupied by charter grants, the colonies were subject to the ultimate jurisdiction of those who had made the grants. In point of logic, since a supreme political authority must reside somewhere in an empire, the best place to have this authority was in the English government, mixed in form and controlled by the English constitution. To argue against the authority of Parliament was to argue against the constitution and its bill of rights. Taking a Hobbesian view of humanity, Leonard believed that the purpose of government was to protect the people from the violent turmoil which typified the state of nature. Thus he counselled the colonists against following that path of rebellion which would dissolve government and society and throw man back into a state of nature. "But when government is laid prostrate, a state of war, of all against all commences; might overcomes right; innocence itself has no security, unless the individual sequesters himself from his fellowmen, inhabits his own cave, and seeks his own prey."[52] Only by remaining in the British system could the dire consequences of a return to a state of nature be avoided, and the present liberties maintained.

While Seabury and Leonard defended that constitutional system

[51] *Ibid.*, pp. 121-122.
[52] Daniel Leonard, *Massachusettensis* (London, MDCCLXXVI), Letter 9, February 6, 1775, p. 64.

which they felt preserved the rights of Englishmen, other Loyalists
were more extreme. Jonathan Boucher (1738-1804), who at times
preached his loyalist sermons with a pair of loaded pistols in the
pulpit, was driven from his pulpit and from the colonies in 1775.
Later, however, in 1779, he published under the title *A View of the
Causes and Consequences of the American Revolution,* a collection
of these sermons. Boucher's attack went straight to the roots of the
contract theory. Essentially, his argument was theological rather
than legal in character. He took the Bible rather than the British
constitution for his text, and, in arguments reminiscent of the Puritans in Massachusetts, chose not to entertain his parishioners with
"flowery panegyrics on liberty" but to impress upon them their
obligations according to the Scriptures. The Gospel was not concerned with constitutions of government, mixed or otherwise, but
with ensuring the obedience of Christians to a Christian government, whatever its form or singular characteristics; for "when Christians are disobedient to human ordinances, they are also disobedient
to God."[53] The much-talked-of liberty of mankind was frequently
a misnomer, Boucher maintained, as had the Puritan John Winthrop
before him. "True liberty, then, is a liberty to do everything that
is right, and the being restrained from doing any thing that is
wrong."[54] He attacked the theory of government by consent on the
grounds that it undermined majority rule as well as individual
absolutism, for in either event the minority were ruled without their
approval. The Lockean theory of resistance, he pointed out, was
entirely incompatible with the Lockean theory of majority rule, if
government by consent was to be a meaningful and universal
principle. Furthermore, the principle of equality was undermined
by the contract theory, in that those who willingly subordinated
themselves to others admitted an essential inequality. Boucher
denied the validity of a state of natural equality and freedom and
the principle of government by human consent. Instead he turned
like the seventeenth-century Englishman, Sir Robert Filmer, to the
patriarchal theory of the origin of government. Adam, the first
father, ruled his children like a king. The glory that God gave to
Adam carried down to the rulers of subsequent generations. The
commission of government is from God, not from man, and thus
no man may challenge the authority of government. Boucher sought

[53] Jonathan Boucher, *A View of the Causes and Consequences of the American Revolution* (London, 1779), p. 508.
[54] *Ibid.*, p. 511.

in effect to counter the secular claims of authority in man with the superior claim of authority in God. In so doing, however, he was only more obsolete in his argument than Sir Robert Filmer had been a century earlier.

The political thought leading to and through the American Revolution followed in many respects the thinking developed in England in the previous century. Filmer and Hobbes were echoed in America by those who feared the consequences of democratic home rule and whose view of mankind combined the Calvinistic conception of depravity of man with the amoral Hobbesian view of personal motivation. It was the Lockean thesis, however, that represented the predominant theme. The Puritan view of depravity had given way to the conviction of the eighteenth-century enlightenment that man was more rational than depraved, and basically as concerned with happiness on earth as salvation in an afterlife. Security, in a system of government by consent, depended after all upon the faith that those whose consent counted and who therefore controlled the government were neither depraved nor amoral but were rational beings with a sense of public responsibility. The assumption that certain truths were both truths and self-evident; the assumption that certain rights were moral imperatives and natural rather than conventional; and the assumption that there was a universal standard of political values which was so obvious and certain that it could be called natural law—these were assumptions which were as much a tribute to man's rationality as expressions of it. For though these propositions expressed some of the basic beliefs of the age of reason, they were confidently advanced in the expectation that, man being rational, other men would find themselves in complete agreement with their statements. That is to say, if the standard of moral and political values was fixed by nature or by nature's God and was immutable and universal—and this was an essential "given" behind the belief in natural law—and if man was truly rational—which meant in part that he could find through reason the tenets of natural law—then it was clear that there was a common element of political and moral belief existing among men. Were there no natural law, and were men not generally rational, such agreement on belief would be unlikely.

The theorists who argued in support of the American Revolution drew heavily upon the basic assumptions of the contract theory as advanced by Locke. Fundamental to the entire stream of Revolutionary thought was the belief that man had by nature, and ought to have in fact, certain rights which no government could deny him and remain legitimate. Among these rights, it was clear as the argument developed, was the right to representation in government, especially representation in legislatures where there was authority to impose taxes. Closely associated with this claim was the right to property, which ought not to be taken except through the consent of those governed. Thus not only the fundamental assumptions of the contract theory as stated by Locke found expression in the literature of the Revolution, but Locke's theory of private property and representation found expression as well.

While the philosophical features of Revolutionary thought were both more radical and fundamental, the developing conception of constitutionalism was of considerable importance to subsequent American political thought and practice. The conception of rights, of due process of law, of jurisdictional divisions in the empire, of, in a phrase, limited government carried over into post-revolutionary America with the framing of the state and national constitutions. The legal argument over the substance, or the specific content, of the British constitution could well be generalized into a discussion of the terms of any legitimate constitution. For the rights of Englishmen were generally considered to be in fact the rights of man. Constitutionalism and the contract theory were thus considered to be mutually supporting systems of thought in defense of the American Revolution.

CHAPTER 5

American Constitutionalism

AMERICANS accepted constitutionalism long before they ratified the Constitution of 1787. For all the differences of opinion in the Philadelphia convention, there was nevertheless an underlying fundamental agreement among the delegates upon the desirability of a constitution for the United States. Prior to the framing of the Constitution of 1787, Americans had drawn up the Articles of Confederation and had concurrently framed fundamental laws in their respective states. The conscious and deliberate framing of written constitutions on such a grand scale was, in the eighteenth century, a political innovation and remains one of America's major contributions to political science. Yet the writing of a constitution defining the powers and limitations of the government was but a means of giving tangible and lasting expression to an existing prevailing belief in constitutionalism itself.

The essence of constitutionalism is found in the belief that the powers of government ought to be defined and limited. Thus a constitution, whether written or unwritten, would be superfluous to an absolute system of government. The assumption behind constitutionalism i that there is a law superior to the enactments of the government which in fact restrains the government in the exercise of its powers. The classical distinction made by the Greeks between a legitimate ruler and a tyrant, long before the advent of the written constitution, was that the tyrant ruled without law while the legitimate ruler followed the law. From the time of the Greeks there has been a lasting stream of political thought which has opposed the claims of absolute government in the name of a higher law which stood above all government. Some writers have called this higher law divine law, some have called it natural law, but in either case it set bounds upon the powers of the government.

The belief in limitations on the powers of government carried with it the idea that the state existed for a moral purpose, a purpose which might be thwarted were there no restraints upon governmental activity. The assumption of a moral purpose behind the state found expression in the oft-repeated statement that the state existed to make possible the good life. Government, as the agent of the state, was thus limited in its functions to those which would promote and insure the welfare of the people and was prohibited from engaging in activities which would impair the general welfare. Cicero, St. Thomas Aquinas, and John Locke are but a few of the figures in a long stream of thought which found the justification for political authority in the welfare of the people and maintained that public power might be exercised only for the public good. Thus the constitutional concept of limitation was associated directly with the belief that the powers of government were limited to those which promoted the public good.

Eighteenth-century constitutionalism gave institutional expression to the belief that a higher law existed which restricted the powers of government in behalf of the general welfare. In England the gradual acceptance of certain governmental practices, together with such formal documents as Magna Carta, the Petition of Rights, and the Bill of Rights, gave to that country by the close of the seventeenth century an established constitution. Only in certain instances were the limitations upon the government and any of its branches spelled out; in many instances the constitutional limitations would have to be found by an examination of long-continued practices. Behind both practices and documents, however, was the higher law, discernible by reason, which made legitimate the restrictions upon governmental authority, for it was felt that the constitution merely gave tangible expression to the more fundamental ordinances of mankind. Thus in a well-ordered state the rights which man might claim by nature were also the rights guaranteed to him in the constitution. In the political thought of the American Revolution there appeared to be general agreement that the rights of man and the rights of Englishmen were in content identical. After the separation, the former colonists claimed as Americans the rights they had previously claimed as Englishmen, rights which were once again based upon a belief in a higher law above all government. By identifying the constitution with the higher law, Coke in the seventeenth century, Otis in the eighteenth, and John Marshall in the nineteenth could each endorse with solemn assurance the principle that laws contrary to the constitution were void.

The unique contribution of American constitutionalism lay in its joining of the accepted belief in a higher law to the contract theory of the state. It was this conjunction of two historic streams of thought which found institutional expression in the popularly-ratified, written constitution. The belief in a higher law need not be associated with the contract theory of the origin of the state; but the contract theory, implemented by the written constitution, popularly ratified, made possible a thoroughly reasonable way of arriving at the higher law. The belief in a law above the government led to the institutionalizing of this law in the constitution, while the belief in the contract theory led to popular ratification of the constitution as a method of arriving at government based on the consent of those governed.

COLONIAL CHARTERS

Historically, Americans had ample precedent for written constitutions. Experience with written constitutions came in the colonial period when the colonists lived under grants or charters which authorized governmental power and fixed certain limits to its exercise. While these charters were legally inferior to the enactments of the mother country, they were superior to the colonial governments which were instituted under them.

With the Mayflower Compact and the Puritan church covenants, practical experiments in the contract theory were undertaken. While these efforts were on a limited scale, still attempts were made to spell out the terms of obligation and secure the assent of those most directly affected. A more ambitious effort to frame a written constitution, and this one of civil government, was undertaken in 1639 when the towns of Windsor, Wethersfield, and Hartford drew up the "Fundamental Orders of Connecticut." In this early written constitution it was provided that freemen, by majority vote, would annually elect their governor, magistrates and deputies, whose broad powers were to be exercised for the "public good." Soon afterward, written constitutions incorporating the principle of popular consent were drawn up by the colonies of Rhode Island and Connecticut, whose charters were to serve as their fundamental laws until well into the nineteenth century.

The development of the fundamental law in Rhode Island is an especially interesting illustration of the concept of constitutionalism based upon the consent of the people. Roger Williams and his followers were eager to protect the practice of freedom of conscience in the new community as well as to promote arbitration as the proper method for the settling of disputes. In an early "Plantation Agreement at Providence" (1640), a simple governmental system was vested in the town meeting. The town was to choose five "disposers" to handle the affairs of the town in between general town meetings. Every three months a new election was to be held for the town "disposers," although at any intervening time an injured party might have the clerk (at his discretion) call the town together for a "trial" of the "disposers." Beyond this rather rudimentary though democratic frame of government, the "Plantation Agreement" provided for an elaborate system for the settlement of disputes by arbitration. It further provided: "We agree, as formerly hath been the liberties of the town, so still, to hold forth liberty of Conscience."[1] As evidence of a form of approval or ratification of the compact, some thirty-nine signatures were attached to the document. While this compact was a step forward in the path of democracy, and the provision for liberties in Rhode Island was the most generous of any of the colonies, it should be noted that the political townsmen were only those who held stock in the town.

In 1641 the General Court in Rhode Island made further provision for the government of that colony. It declared the government of Rhode Island to be:

> a Democracy, or Popular Government; that is to say, it is in the Power of the Body of Freemen orderly assembled, or the major part of them, to make or constitute Just Laws, by which they will be regulated, and to depute from among themselves such Ministers as shall see them faithfully executed between Man and Man.[2]

Rhode Island received a patent from Parliament in 1643 which, while reserving residual powers to a Governor and Commissioners in England, nevertheless granted to the settlers authority to set up such a government as the majority of them should choose. Thus Rhode Island practiced self-government with the authorization of Parliament. The patent did contain the usual limitation, however, that the constitution and laws of the colony must be conformable

[1] Francis N. Thorpe, *The Federal and State Constitutions, Colonial Charters,* etc. (Washington: Government Printing Office, 1909), vol. VI, pp. 3205-3207.
[2] *Ibid.,* pp. 3207-3208.

to the laws of England, "so far as the Nature and Constitution of the place will admit."[3]

Finally, in 1663, King Charles II granted to Rhode Island the charter authorization for self-government that was to last throughout the colonial period. In this charter, Rhode Island's claims for religious liberty were guaranteed by royal authority. In some detail the charter described the organization of the government—the Governor, the ten Assistants and the representatives from the towns. The powers of the government were enumerated, again with the provision that the actions of the government must be conformable as far as possible with the laws of England. In effect, the charter permitted the settlers of Rhode Island to continue governing themselves as they had in the past.

Because of the ample self-governing provisions of the charter, Rhode Island was able to continue to use this authorization as its constitution until Dorr's Rebellion called attention to the need for its revision in 1842. The course of constitutional development in Rhode Island during the colonial period calls attention to the uses of a written constitution as a means of authorizing governmental powers while prescribing limitations upon them. Furthermore the provisions regarding religious liberty in the Rhode Island charter are suggestive of the later development in state constitutions whereby a bill of rights was incorporated in the basic frames of government.

THE HIERARCHY OF LAW

Implicit in the idea of constitutionalism is the concept of a hierarchy of law in which the enactments of any particular government can never claim a supreme status but must always be considered as inferior to the law above the government. Above the colonists, even the self-governing colonists of Rhode Island and Connecticut, was an extraordinary hierarchy of law. The individual settler was presumably subject at this time to the natural laws of the universe prescribed by God for the government of man as well as nature; the British constitution, developed by generations of Englishmen, which defined the powers and limits of the English government; the patents and charters declared by the King in exercise of his prerogative powers; the statutes of Parliament governing the empire

[3] *Ibid.*, pp. 3210-3211.

as well as England; the final decisions of the Privy Council and in some instances the Board of Trade; and finally, the laws, judicial decisions and executive orders issued by the colonial government. It is no wonder that the colonists believed that there was a law above the government.

The existence of the English government, prior to the Revolutionary period, with recognized authority in the general fields of trade, finance and defence accustomed the colonists to living under a dual system of government. There was a government at home in the locality to regulate their internal affairs and a government elsewhere to control external affairs and matters of general concern. That this dual system of government was comprehended within the British constitution was a generally agreed-upon proposition. Under the British constitution, and conformable to it, were the written frames of law governing the individual colonies. The dual system of government was thus strengthened by a dual constitutional system whereby each government was under a fundamental law but the lesser colonial units and their charters were subordinate to the government of the realm and its constitution. The question of the degree of subordination, even to the point of whether there should be any subordination at all, became a fundamental political question during the Revolution. It was a central political issue in the discussions concerning the Constitution of 1787. In fact, the problem of subordination of political units, of the locality to the generality, of the city to the state and the state to the nation, of the nation to any international organization, has always been a hotly contested question in American politics.

STATE CONSTITUTIONS

With the severing of ties with England in 1776, the dual constitutional system, and with it the dual system of government, was cast aside. Americans moved rapidly, however, to reinstate a dual constitutional and governmental system, this time of their own choosing. Within the space of fifteen years, some twenty written constitutions were drawn up, two of which, the Articles of Confederation and the Constitution of the United States, provided for a general national government. In May of 1776 the Continental Congress resolved that the states should draw up constitutions for themselves and also that a constitution should be drawn up for the national government. In response to the first resolution, as well as to an immediate need now that the authority of England was no longer recognized, the states turned to writing their own frames of government. Only the self-governing colonies of Rhode Island and Connecticut continued to operate under their colonial charters. While there was a considerable change of content between the old charters and the new written frames of government, still there was a continuation of the established principle that there ought to be behind all government a fundamental code of law.

Although there were minor differences between the state constitutions drawn up during this period, nevertheless the similarity of colonial institutions of government, together with the colonial heritage of English liberties, led the constitution makers to arrive at basically the same results. Nearly all of these early state constitutions were drawn up by legislatures or conventions and were not submitted to the people for ratification. Nearly all provided for a bicameral legislature which in most instances selected the governor. The qualifications for members of the senate were higher than for those of the lower house and the terms of office longer. The senate was intended to be the conservative equivalent of the colonial Governor's council, or the English House of Lords. In most of the state constitutions judges were appointed either by the governor, by the legislatures, or by the governor with the approval of the senate. In all cases the suffrage was restricted, the major liberality being that the same people could now vote for more officers than they could have voted for prior to the Revolution.

Beyond the organizational arrangements for government, however, the state constitutions reflected certain fundamental political conceptions of lasting value. Theory and institutions are interacting; they are cross-fertilizing agents. The early state constitutions in part reflected and in part shaped the political theory of eighteenth-century America. They expressed the belief that government was subject to a higher law or constitution which ought in fact to be spelled out and not left to mere conjecture. Although most of these constitutions were framed by the legislatures, or by persons appointed by the legislature, nevertheless there is little doubt that the legislatures intended to enact a fundamental law which would be binding upon all, themselves included. These fundamental laws usually provided for a functional separation of the powers of government so that no one group might monopolize all the duties of government. It was feared that power would be used for tyrannical purposes if it were concentrated in the hands of any irresponsible person or persons. In other words it was assumed that power, unless adequately checked, would be abused. This belief was fortified not only by the recent experience of the colonists with their colonial governors, but also by the teachings of political theorists and many theologians. The fear of power was based primarily upon the accepted theological belief in the corruptions of the flesh and the general corruptibility of man. Accepting this pessimistic view of human nature the state constitution-makers were, like John Cotton, believers in granting no more authority to a person or agency than the circumstances absolutely required. Thus while they considered power in government essential they also believed in so distributing the exercise of power among human beings that no one person or group of persons could directly control all governmental activities. For precedent in political theory they could cite John Locke, who had advocated a separation of power in the government, or Baron Montesquieu, who had praised the British constitution for achieving such a separation. Montesquieu, who in 1748 had written the *Spirit of the Laws*, had observed that in England there was political liberty and that this liberty was the result of the constitutional arrangement. The English constitutional system had achieved political liberty because power had been separated into functional divisions. Speaking of a division of governmental work into three branches, the legislative, the executive, and the judicial, he wrote:

> There would be an end of everything, were the same man, or the same body, whether of the nobles or of the people, to exercise those powers, that of enacting laws, that of executing the public resolutions, and of trying the causes of individuals.[4]

Power was necessary to all government, but considering the fallibility of human beings it was better to distribute this power than concentrate it. The state constitution makers were impressed by the necessity for dividing the necessary powers of government so that no one person or persons had complete control over the governed.

In the colonies generally there had been a governor who was the chief executive but responsible neither to the people nor to the legislature. By and large the upper council, the political protégés of the governor, combined executive, legislative and judicial functions and by their acquiescence to the wishes of the chief executive

---

[4] Baron Charles-Louis De Secondat De Montesquieu, *Spirit of the Laws,* tr. by Thomas Nugent, rev. by J. B. Pritchard (London: George Bell and Sons, 1878), vol. I, bk. xi, ch. 6.

illustrated Montesquieu's thesis. The problem was thus to achieve a personal separation of the powers of government while retaining the crucial element of popular control. In most of the states this problem was resolved by making a personal separation of powers according to the functions of government, while providing for the ultimate supremacy of the legislative branch. Here again the constitution framers followed the principles of John Locke and the practices of English government. In most of the states the legislature appointed the governor as well as the judiciary, controlled in the main the affairs of the state, and was not checked by an executive veto. All branches of the government were limited by the constitution, yet even beyond these limitations the executive office was impaired in that the governor was made largely an administrative officer of the legislature rather than an independent executive. This belief in legislative supremacy under a constitution was carried beyond the realm of state government and applied to the Articles of Confederation as well.

While the executive and judiciary were responsible to the legislature which appointed and might remove them, the legislature on the other hand was in most cases the only branch of government that the people could get at directly. In accordance with Locke and the contract theorists generally, government was based upon the consent of those governed; yet the only direct provision for consent was the election of the legislature. The new state legislatures thus became very nearly the American equivalent in their authority to Parliament in England. Furthermore, in most instances bicameralism was retained even though both houses of the legislature now fell under popular control. That in point of actual suffrage this was not democracy full grown is not to be wondered at considering the extent of the suffrage in England and Europe at that time. Certainly the franchise in the American states was greater than anywhere else in the world in the eighteenth century. While the suffrage was limited in practice, in political theory, political authority was vested in all the people, not just property-holders, taxpayers, or persons of acceptable religious beliefs. In time the practice approximated the theory. According to the contract theory, it was the right of the people to institute government; yet in the drafting of the new state constitutions there was very little opportunity in most states for express consent by the voters. This difficulty was overcome in later constitutions by the device of popular ratification.

Underlying the state constitution was the belief in certain natural and inalienable rights, and the conviction that government was established to protect these rights. Over half of the states followed the example of Virginia, which in 1776 drew up a detailed bill of rights to be incorporated into its constitution. The idea of a bill of rights is a natural corollary to the belief in limited government. Limited government is justified on the grounds that the welfare of society is best preserved when the powers of the government are defined in such a manner as to prevent the government from becoming omnipotent in all affairs over all its subjects. The conception of limited government assumes that in certain matters the government may not act at all, while in other affairs it may act only in accordance with specified procedures. Governmental authority is thus restricted to those activities and those procedures in which governmental intervention is conducive to the good of the community. There is a social or community emphasis behind the concept of limited government, for the major concern is the welfare of the whole community. A bill of rights, however, further defines the concept of limited government by emphasizing the individual in the community. The rights enumerated in the various early state constitutions are the rights of individual human beings. The constitutional aspect of limited government thus served to protect society, while the bill of rights sought to protect still further the individual.

In the Virginia Bill of Rights of 1776, it is declared that all men are equally free and independent and are possessed of certain rights: "the enjoyment of life and liberty, with the means of acquiring and possessing property, and pursuing and obtaining happiness and safety." The contract theory is stated in essence to indicate the fundamental political right of the people to form, alter or even abolish their government. So basic and inherent are the individual rights that they cannot be bartered or contracted away by the people. Thus even in the formation of a new state the natural rights cannot be given up, not even voted away voluntarily, for they are inalienable. Enumerated among the basic rights are freedom of religion, of the press, of trial by jury—substantive and procedural rights which were later incorporated in other state constitutions as well as in the Constitution of the United States. It may be noted that while it was acknowledged that constitutions were framed, indeed governments instituted, to protect the natural rights of man, the state constitutions advanced the area of rights into the realm of social and political institutions when they declared such rights as trial by jury and freedom of the press, rights which could hardly have been claimed to have existed in a state of nature.

The early state constitutions set a pattern of political ideas and institutions which profoundly influenced the thinking of those who were called upon to consider the Constitution of the United States a little over a decade later. In this early period the general temper of the states was to establish a limited government under a written constitution, a scheme of separated powers which retained the primacy of the legislative branch, a bill of rights to protect the individual, all of which found its theoretical justification in the contract theory of the state. The contract theory, whose disruptive aspects had been utilized during the Revolution, had now been turned to constructive purposes.

JOHN ADAMS AND THE MIXED CONSTITUTION

The early experiments in framing state constitutions reflected the colonial distrust of executive powers as previously wielded by King George III and his appointed governors in the colonies. The state legislatures gained at the expense of the chief executive. In nine of the states the governor was elected by the legislature, usually for a one-year term, while in all of the states his appointive power was subjected to some form of legislative approval. In no state, prior to 1780, did the governor possess the exclusive power of vetoing laws passed by the legislature.

In 1780, Massachusetts, the last state to accept a constitution, was the first to provide for popular ratification of its basic instrument of government. So enduring were the efforts of the framers of this constitution that, amended, it survives as the only original state constitution in operation today. It enumerated a long list of rights and provided for a separation of the powers of government into legislative, executive and judicial branches, "to the end it may be a government of laws and not of men." It reflected, however, a change in attitude on behalf of its framers and the people who ratified it, for the governor was reinstated as a chief executive, elected by the people and possessed of an independent veto which might be overridden by two-thirds of each house of the legislature. As in the other states, the franchise was restricted to those who possessed adequate property qualifications. Eligibility for office was also restricted by property qualifications, with the requirements highest for governor and lowest for members of the house of representatives. In point of view of the different property qualifications, it was evident that different economic and social interests were intended to be represented in the government. In place of a functional separation of powers which nevertheless admitted of the supremacy of the legislature, Massachusetts elevated the governor to a coordinate position in the government. The separated powers were each provided with a check upon the actions of the other branches. Behind the Massachusetts constitution was the principle of the mixed government. It fell to John Adams to explain and defend this ancient principle of government to his countrymen.

In 1785 John Adams was sent to England to work out a commercial treaty with the English. During the following three years in England he applied himself to a study of English government in operation as well as to numerous classics in political science. The results of his efforts are found in a rather tedious and rambling three volume work entitled *A Defence of the Constitutions of Government of the United States of America.* The first volume, published in London in 1787, was made available to delegates meeting at the Philadelphia convention in that year. The remaining two volumes appeared the following year, while prior to the turn of the century the entire work went into two English, two American and one French editions.

The immediate cause for writing the *Defence* of the state constitutions was to answer a criticism made of them by the Frenchman Turgot in 1778. Among the various criticisms of the state constitutions Turgot observed an "unreasonable imitation" of the English system in that the states had established bicameral legislatures, and executives, instead of concentrating all governmental power in one body. In opposing this Turgot wrote:

> They undertake to balance these different authorities, as if the same equilibrium of powers which has been thought necessary to balance the enormous preponderance of royalty, could be of any use in republics, formed upon the equality of all citizens; and as if every article which constitutes different bodies, was not a source of divisions.[5]

In his effort to refute M. Turgot, Adams was led to explore the writings of previous political thinkers, from whom he quoted extensively,

[5] Extract of a letter of M. Turgot to Dr. Richard Price, March 22, 1778, quoted in *The Works of John Adams,* edited by Charles Francis Adams (Boston: Charles C. Little and James Brown, 1851), vol. IV, p. 270.

as well as the experience of various governments throughout history. Adams' defence of the principle of mixed government as being essential to an orderly constitutional system, a system which does in fact protect liberty, was based upon his belief that people in any society had unequal talents, abilities and possessions. Every man was entitled to protection by government in his unequal holdings. Recognizing a fundamental natural cleavage in society, Adams sought a governmental system which would protect as well as promote the interests of each major class or group. He did not believe that his views were in any way at variance with the doctrine that all men were created equal and were equally entitled to the rights of life, liberty and property. He did maintain, however, that while all men were equal in their rights, they soon developed physical, intellectual and economic distinctions which gave them an unequal status in society. Unequals as well as equals merited the protection of government.

Adams believed that each man selfishly pursued his own interests, tempered in his conduct only by morality and the force of law. Since the interests of men were frequently in conflict, how could a government be framed which would protect the rights of the conflicting individuals or groups? If all the conflicting interests were to be thrown into one body, representing all the interests of the state, then the majority would prevail at the expense of the minority, or else the minority would corrupt the majority into agreement. In either case the rights of one group would be sacrificed to the ambitions of the other.

Fundamentally Adams' concern for the rights of the minority was based upon his fear that the property of the few would be despoiled by the many. "In every society where property exists, there will ever be a struggle between rich and poor."[6] Furthermore the poor will always greatly outnumber the rich. The self-interest of the many poor, if not checked by some constitutional device, would soon lead the majority to plunder the possessions of the few who were rich.

> The idle, the vicious, the intemperate, would rush into the utmost extravagance of debauchery, sell and spend all their share, and then demand a new division of those who purchased from them.[7]

Under any system of simple majority rule, the minority, no matter how slight, would lose to the majority, and so losing, those rights

[6] *The Works of John Adams,* edited by Charles Francis Adams (Boston: Charles C. Little and James Brown, 1851), vol. VI, p. 68.
[7] *Ibid.,* p. 9.

would be destroyed for the protection of which they instituted government.

Although Adams was fearful of the power and inclinations of the majority of men, he was unwilling to give government over to the aristocracy of the rich and noble families, for the curse of selfishness fell upon the rich and poor alike. Aristocrats, whether through riches, intelligence, or leadership, inevitably acquired an enormous influence over the masses. Should the powers of the state be concentrated in the hands of the aristocracy, should the aristocrats be given control over the legislative, executive and judicial functions of government, then such a system would eventuate into "the nobility of a few families, and a tyrannical oligarchy." The aristocracy was just as likely to abuse power as the masses, and government by the aristocrats would doubtless result in a denial of rights to the poor. By what means could the rich be protected in their rights, and the poor protected in theirs? The natural divisions within society would give rise to natural divisions in the government, with each side seeking to gain powers and privileges at the expense of its opponent. The only solution was to establish a unit of the government to represent each of the two major groupings of society. Under such an arrangement the people would be represented in an assembly or house of representatives, while the aristocrats would be represented in the senate. In order to protect the liberties of its constituents, each branch would possess a check or negative on the motions of the other.

To perfect this mixed arrangement of government, Adams provided for a single executive to be elected by the people at large, but whose qualifications placed him in the upper class. Were the legislature to appoint him it would give rise to intrigue on the part of the legislature and dependency on the part of the governor. The governor would be empowered with a veto that would complete the system of checks begun with the divided arrangement of classes in the legislature. Thus the chief executive, armed with a negative upon the actions of either branch of the legislature, would hold the balance of power between them. Yet should the governor succumb to the lust for power, he in turn could be checked by the legislature. "Self-interest, private avidity, ambition, and avarice, will exist in every state of society, and under every form of government."[8] The selfish passions of the separate classes of men, of senators, represen-

[8] *Ibid.*, p. 57.

tatives, or even the governor, could not be checked by frequent elections within the very classes which called them to office.

> The only remedy is to take away the power, by controlling the
> selfish avidity of the governor, by the senate and house; of the
> senate, by the governor and house; and of the house, by the gov-
> ernor and senate.[9]

The mixed arrangement of government was founded primarily
upon the division of classes in the legislature. It was here that the
check and balance would operate most effectively. Beyond this,
however, Adams advocated a functional separation of powers along
the lines established by Montesquieu. A functional separation of
powers into legislative, executive and judicial branches, with each
branch concerned primarily with its own type of work, was equally
essential to the preservation of liberty. For like Montesquieu he
believed that should the executive succeed in taking over legislative
and judicial duties, or the legislature gather in the executive and
judicial powers, the liberty of the people would be lost.

In developing the theory of the separation of powers superimposed upon a mixed system of government, Adams followed
what he believed to be the principles, although not the practice, of
the English constitution. That this view of the English constitution
was accepted by others is indicated in the work of Sir William
Blackstone whose *Commentaries on the Laws of England* appeared
in 1765. Published in an American edition in 1771, this work was to
exercise considerable influence upon the course of American jurisprudence. In explaining the English constitution, Blackstone noted
that the executive power was centered in the king, who possessed
a check upon the legislature and was checked in turn by it. The
bicameral legislature was divided into lords, chosen for "their piety,
their birth, their wisdom, their valor, or their property," and the
commons, *"freely chosen by the people from among themselves."*
Under this arrangement no one branch could attempt to harm the
others, "each branch being armed with a negative power, sufficient
to repel any innovation which it shall think inexpedient or dangerous."[10] Blackstone further noted in his *Commentaries:*

> In the legislature, the people are a check upon the nobility, and
> the nobility a check upon the people; by the mutual privilege of

[9] *Ibid.,* pp. 57-58.
[10] Sir William Blackstone, *Commentaries on the Laws of England* (Dublin:
L. White, P. Byrne, and J. Rice, 1796), p. 51.

rejecting what the other has resolved; while the king is a check upon both, which preserves the executive power from encroachments, and this very executive power is again checked and kept within due bounds by the two houses. . . ."[11]

As Blackstone explained the English constitution, it combined a check-and-balance system between branches of government with a check-and-balance system within the legislature. It was essentially this conception of the English constitution which Adams sought to have established in America. It was this system, Adams believed, which had preserved English liberties and, properly adapted to American conditions, might preserve American liberties as well.

THE CONSTITUTION OF THE UNITED STATES

For a dozen years prior to the Philadelphia convention of 1787, Americans maintained a national unit of government. While the transformation from former English colonies into independent American states took place rapidly during this period, the establishment of a genuine union of these states was a more gradual process. The exigencies of the Revolution had given to the *ad hoc* Continental Congresses a national character adequate only for the immediate purpose of carrying the war to a successful conclusion. In 1776, when it was proposed that the states draw up constitutions to replace their former charters, it was also proposed in Congress that a constitution be drawn up for the United States. In 1781, by which time all the states were under a written constitution (Rhode Island and Connecticut using their colonial charters), the first constitution for the United States went into effect. The Articles of Confederation were short-lived, however, and were supplanted by the present Constitution after eight years. Yet the Articles of Confederation, like the Constitution, reflected a strong sense of constitutionalism, a desire for union, and a need for a national institution of government.

Throughout most of the colonial period, Americans had accepted a dual system of government—a government in the colony to attend to internal matters and a government elsewhere to attend to affairs of the realm. Much of the constitutional controversy preceding the Revolution centered on the respective powers of these two governments. It was not without precedent, therefore, that Americans es-

[11] *Ibid.*, pp. 156-157.

tablished a dual system of government following the Revolution. Again a vital issue was the amount and kind of power that should be granted the central government. With the previous experience of what the people considered to be an abuse of power by the central government still fresh in their minds it is no wonder that they were reluctant to grant many consequential powers to the national government. In view of the recent issue with Parliament, trade and finance were considered to be especially delicate political subjects which were best left to the control of the states. Lacking independent powers in the vital fields of trade and finance, the central government established by the Articles was doomed from the start. It could be no more than what in fact it was intended to be—a confederation of sovereign states. The central government was but an agent of the states which sent delegates to it, and while it maintained a secretariat, so to speak, to handle foreign affairs and matters of defense, it did not bear directly upon the people. Deficient in authorization and organization, the mere confederation was inadequate for the broader national purposes of the United States, and when this became evident, a convention was called to meet in Philadelphia (1787) to revise the fundamental framework of government.

The Philadelphia convention, like the Stamp Act Congress and the first Continental Congress, was born of a desire on behalf of many influential people along the eastern seaboard to utilize political power to achieve economic ends which they felt were being jeopardized under the existing system. Prior to the establishment of the Constitution several notable political successes were accomplished by the various Congresses—the War of Independence was won, a favorable treaty of peace was made with England, embryonic executive departments were established, and the Northwest Ordinance of 1787 was enacted. These were major political achievements for any national government. The major grievances under the Articles were primarily of an economic rather than a political nature. For all the political achievements under the Articles, the nation was imperilled by economic dislocation and the jealous rivalries of states. State trade barriers met with retaliation in kind by neighboring states. The variety of trade restrictions together with the variety of fluctuating currencies used in the states made difficult, where not impossible, the growth of a national economic system. This economic dislocation was felt to be aggravated in some states by legislative enactments which released debtors from the full obligations of their debts. The credit standing of the national as well as state governments was in jeopardy. Economic disunity fomented political disunity, and under the Articles Congress was unable to take effective action.

The framers of the Constitution were men of an economic class which was vitally interested in removing the deficiences of the Articles of Confederation.[12] The ratification of the Constitution in the conventions in the various states, however, should make clear that a majority of those voting in the conventions also believed that the national government should be clothed with greater powers in the economic field.[13] And it is significant that the major proposals before the Philadelphia convention were all in agreement that the national government should possess greatly strengthened powers in trade and finances.

Beyond the problem of establishing a frame of government conducive to the growth of a national system of economics there was the even more complex problem of reconciling the many political differences between sections, states, and groups within the various states. Indeed the fundamental issue before the framers was how to achieve a political system that would not only reconcile their own immediate differences but also serve in the future as an instrument for reconciliation. Born of compromise, the completed Constitution also provided the machinery for future compromises. The interests of the North, the South, the large states, the small states, the manufacturers, the planters, the aristocrats and the republicans all went into the making of the Constitution. It was the problem of the framers to build unity upon this diversity, a diversity which they believed would be a continuing one in American politics. That the framers were largely successful in their effort to build a union in spite of diversity may be credited to their own basic differences as well as to their political wisdom.

The major plans presented before the convention reveal something of the basic differences in approach to a national constitution.[14] Hamilton sought to establish the aristocracy in a position of

[12] See Charles A. Beard, *An Economic Interpretation of the Constitution of the United States* (New York: The Macmillan Co., 1939 edition), pp. 149-151.

[13] See Jonathan Eliot, *Debates in the Several State Conventions on the Adoption of the Federal Constitution* (Washington: printed by the editor), 5 vols., 1836-1845.

[14] The proposals and arguments before the convention may be found in Max Farrand (ed.), *The Records of the Federal Convention of 1787* (New Haven: Yale University Press, 1911), 3 vols.

perpetual power with political appointments made for life. Madison, Randolph, and the Virginia delegation sought a strong federal system which would govern states as well as individuals. Paterson of New Jersey offered some modifications to the Articles of Confederation while maintaining its basic spirit. Political ideas ran the gamut from aristocratic nationalism to modified confederation. Fortunately, adroit compromises reconciled these and many other differences. Yet these compromises would not have been possible had there not been a firm core of agreement on fundamentals. There was agreement on the desirability of union and therefore on the necessity of providing for a national government. The framers were generally agreed that such a national establishment should not supplant the state governments and that, while its powers ought to be commensurate with its responsibilities, these powers should be delegated and limited. Even in the process of enlarging the powers of the national government the framers retained a belief in the constitutional concept of limitation. There seemed to be general agreement that government rested upon the people, who were indeed the original source of political power. Yet the framers completely rejected the notion of establishing democracy on a national scale, for they had little faith in the very people who were admittedly the source of political authority. Thus they declared in favor of government based on the people, while establishing a system which, they felt, would avoid the evil consequences of popular rule. Government based upon the people, whose power was carefully limited in exercise, they termed republican government. While the framers were distrustful of democracy they had, generally, strong misgivings about either monarchy or aristocracy. They sought, like John Adams, some sort of balanced system which would recognize the competing claims of divergent interest groups without falling exclusively into the control of any.

In a letter to Jefferson, then in France, Madison noted what he considered to be the major problems before the convention. These were, he wrote, the major issues of debate:

1. To unite a proper energy in the Executive, and a proper stability in the Legislative departments, with the essential character of Republican Government. 2. To draw a line of demarkation which would give to the General Government every power requisite for general purposes and leave to the States every power which might be most beneficially administered by them. 3. To provide for the

different interests of different parts of the Union. 4. To adjust the clashing pretensions of the large and small States.[15]

The resultant compromises made possible a strong national government with separate executive, legislative and judicial branches, resting upon the people as well as upon the states, and with appropriate powers over both. In the hierarchy of law there were now above the state constitutions national laws, treaties, and the United States Constitution. While the traditionally popular branch of government, the lower house, was given a popular national character, the electoral college and the Senate depended directly upon the states. Given independent authority in the essential fields of finance and commerce, the national government was armed with sufficient power to maintain itself and the national economy. With its own executive and judicial branches, the national government was legally equipped to enforce these powers. Although the national government was limited in its delegated powers, the Constitution also imposed limitations on the states. In establishing federalism, the framers achieved a major triumph in the development of constitutionalism, for under this written instrument was a dual system of government—national and state—with each government possessed of sufficient but limited powers.

Shortly after the work of the convention was completed, the Constitution was submitted, by direction of Congress, to the various states for their consideration. The Constitution itself provided that it would become effective when ratified by conventions in nine of the states. Of the thirteen states which subsequently ratified the Constitution, the vote was unanimous in three;[16] ratification by an overwhelming majority occurred in five;[17] and the vote was quite close in the remaining five.[18]

In order for the new government to be a truly effective political organization, it was necessary that the large states, Massachusetts, Virginia, and New York, give it their support. The conventions in

[15] Madison to Jefferson, New York, October 24, 1787. Quoted in *The Writings of James Madison*, published by order of Congress (Philadelphia: J. B. Lippincott and Co., 1865), vol. I, p. 344.

[16] Delaware, New Jersey, Georgia.

[17] Pennsylvania 42-23, Connecticut 128-40, Maryland 63-11, South Carolina 149-73, North Carolina 184-77. North Carolina did not ratify the Constitution until 1790.

[18] Massachusetts 187-168, New Hampshire 57-46, Virginia 89-79, New York 30-27, Rhode Island 34-32. Rhode Island did not ratify the Constitution until 1791.

these states might largely determine the success of the new political venture, and their debates left no aspect of the Constitution unexamined. Aside from differences of opinion on technicalities, the two major criticisms of the Constitution were that it omitted a bill of rights to protect popular liberty and that the national government might in the future impair the proper authority of the states. The first ten amendments were enacted in response to these criticisms, for the first nine amendments were intended to supply the deficiency of a bill of rights, while the tenth amendment sought to clarify the relationship of the national government to the states. The demand for a bill of rights was, in fact, fairly well satisfied by the addition of the first nine amendments, but the issue of state powers as opposed to national powers has remained a fundamental political question ever since. Although some of the criticisms of the new Constitution centered upon the indefinite elegibility of the President and what was felt to be a faulty separation of powers, the substance of the reservations about the Constitution was a fear of extensive national power.

Those who sought strong national government, as well as those who opposed it, tended to argue from a conviction of the corruptibility of man. Opponents of strong government, whether that government was state or national, pointed to that frailty in man which lured those who possessed power to exploit it for their own advantage. Because of this unfortunate tendency in mankind, no person or group ought to be granted any more power than the requirements of peace at home and abroad necessitated. Such governmental power as was not needed to meet these simple requirements was, it was felt, more likely to be utilized for oppression than for the extension of freedom. This, after all, was the reasoning behind the accepted concept of limited government. The problem became essentially a question of degree, a determination of the point in the powers of government where the limitations should be set. Furthermore, opponents of a strong national government were inclined to the view that distant government was more likely to abuse power than local government. Their experience with Parliament suggested a theory of political abuse which found a direct relationship between the misuses of power and the distance of the seat of the government from those governed. Thus, opposed to strong government at home, they were even more anxious to avoid strong government in some distant capitol.

The advocates of strong government were more fearful of the

corruptibility of the masses of men governed than they were of the corruptibility of the governors. Essentially Hobbesian in their view of mankind, they believed that man, if unchecked by government, would engage in a war of all against all. As a little government was preferable to none, since it would prevent the evils of anarchy, so strong government was better than weak government, for it would safeguard and promote civilized society. Only a strong government could adequately protect the rights of man, among which was the Lockean right to property, the heart of the existing economic system. This system, with its demand for the validity of contracts and an established currency, could not be protected by a weak government, for the corrupt masses of men would refuse to honor their obligations when it was not convenient to do so and would either capture the government or refuse obedience to its laws. The political situation in Rhode Island and Shays' Rebellion in Massachusetts in 1786 illustrated their worst fears. Only a strong national government, they believed, could preserve the inviolability of contracts, of currency and the rights of property. While they admitted the possibility that the possession of power might corrupt the governors, they believed that the constitutional system they had established would prevent any abuse of power. The debate over the ratification of the Constitution was thus centered largely on the issue of the possession of power by the national government and the possibilities of its abuse.

THE FEDERALIST

The most consequential campaign literature in favor of the Constitution was a series of articles published in the New York press from October, 1787, until August, 1788, under the signature "Publius." *The Federalist,* written by Hamilton, Madison, and John Jay, was not only persuasive political literature, but is recognized today as the classic statement of the political principles behind the Constitution.[19] The primary thesis of *The Federalist* papers was that the Articles of Confederation were deficient for national security, popular liberty, and the protection of property, and that the Constitution

[19] Of the eighty-five essays, it appears that Hamilton wrote fifty-one and Madison twenty-six, and that they collaborated on three while Jay did five. See Douglass Adair, "The Authorship of the Disputed Federalist Papers," *William and Mary Quarterly,* Third series, vol. I, 1944, pp. 97-122, 235-264.

remedied these deficiencies and ought therefore to be adopted. Throughout the essays is a thorough explanation of the organization of the national government and its powers as well as a vigorous justification for this system.

It was argued in *The Federalist* that the Constitution had incorporated the proven principles of political science as well as adopting more recent discoveries in the field. In an early essay, Hamilton noted the recent improvements in the science of politics which had been incorporated in the Constitution. These included:

> The regular distribution of power into distinct departments; the introduction of legislative balances and checks; the institution of courts composed of judges holding their offices during good behavior; the representation of the people in the legislature by deputies of their own election. . . .[20]

In the course of the arguments in *The Federalist,* each of these propositions was examined and defended.

The authors of *The Federalist* sought to state the case for a strong national government without at the same time creating anxieties on the part of the strong-state sympathizers that the states would be swallowed up in the larger unit. This was a delicate task, for the type of government which they were defending had no clear precedent in history, and what had been arrived at by expediency had nevertheless to be justified on principle. Hamilton, stressing the necessity for national power, observed that a strong national government was required to counteract the separatist tendencies of the states. The danger was not that the central government was likely to prove too strong but, on the contrary, that over a period of time it would become too weak. In *The Federalist,* Number 15, he noted that

> in every political association which is formed upon the principle of uniting in a common interest a number of lesser sovereignties, there will be found a kind of eccentric tendency in the subordinate or inferior orbs, by the operation of which there will be a perpetual effort in each to fly off from the common center.

Madison likewise laid down this tendency as a historical rule of associations especially liable to disturb the arrangement under the Constitution. Madison believed that it was necessary under our system of government to divide power between the national and state

[20] *The Federalist* (New York: Tudor Publishing Co., 1937), Number 9.

governments, and he attacked those states' righters who were fearful of this grant of power to the national government.

> Was, then, the American Revolution effected, was the American Confederacy formed, was the precious blood of thousands spilt, and the hard-earned substance of millions lavished, not that the people of America should enjoy peace, liberty, and safety, but that the government of the individual states, that particular municipal establishments, might enjoy a certain extent of power, and be arrayed with certain dignities and attributes of sovereignty? As far as the sovereignty of the States cannot be reconciled to the happiness of the people, the voice of every good citizen must be, Let the former be sacrificed to the latter.[21]

Yet *The Federalist* carefully observed that while the national government operated directly upon individuals, it depended equally upon the states. The Senate check was essentially a state check upon the national government and might operate against actions taken by the House of Representatives or against the President in his appointive and treaty-making power, or even against the judiciary in trying cases of impeachment. The Constitution in fact provided for a composite system of government, one which was in part national and in part followed what Madison described as a federal plan. In Number 39 of *The Federalist* Madison attempted to describe the nature of this constitutional system.

> In its foundation it is federal, not national; in the sources from which the ordinary powers of the government are drawn, it is partly federal and partly national; in the operation of these powers, it is national, not federal; in the extent of them, again, it is federal, not national; and, finally, in the authoritative mode of introducing amendments, it is neither wholly federal nor wholly national. . . .

In explaining and defending the national establishment, *The Federalist* examined the separation-of-powers theory and defined the work of each of the branches of government. It had been argued in opposition to ratification of the Constitution that the new system violated the separation-of-powers theory. In creating separate branches of government fully clothed with national powers, the framers had thought to give sufficient power to the central government. Yet they had recognized a tendency in all governments and human beings alike to aggrandize given powers. "In framing a government which is to be administered by men over men," noted Madi-

---

[21] *Ibid.*, Number 45.

son, "the great difficulty lies in this: you must first enable the government to control the governed; and in the next place oblige it to control itself."[22] Madison fully recognized the necessity for restraints upon the improper use of power. One of these restraints was the ultimate dependence of the national government upon the people themselves, who would be sensitive to any abuse of governmental authority. Yet this dependency was insufficient as a check in itself, and additional devices were required. The most effective way to check power was to counter power with power and interest with interest. This was achieved, Madison felt, under the separation-of-powers system incorporated in the Constitution.

> The accumulation of all powers, legislative, executive, and judiciary, in the same hands, whether of one, a few, or many, and whether hereditary, self-appointive, or elective, may justly be pronounced the very definition of tyranny.[23]

The Constitution avoided this, however, by distributing powers into separate branches. That the Constitution did not absolutely separate powers but in fact provided for a system of checks in the legislative and executive process was no substantial criticism of the document, for all that was required under the separation-of-powers theory was that no one branch of government exercise the consequential powers of another branch. Inevitably the processes of government required a mixture of these powers.

The Federalist papers indicated a strong belief that in a republican government the legislature would of necessity be the predominant branch. It was essential therefore to the efficacy of the separation-of-powers system that the executive and judicial branches be given adequate powers to check the legislature, and, furthermore, that they be constituted in such a manner that they would be beyond the immediate reach of the Congress. Thus the Constitution had provided for election of the President by the electoral college rather than by Congress and for the appointment of judges for terms of good behavior. The silence of the Constitution on the President's re-eligibility to office, however, had aroused considerable criticism. Jefferson, for instance, had attacked the Constitution for permitting the chief executive to be indefinitely eligible to succeed himself. Hamilton, in defending the arrangement, employed arguments later used in connection with the Twenty-second Amendment.

---

[22] *Ibid.*, Number 51.
[23] *Ibid.*, Number 47.

He argued that re-eligibility of the executive would be a strong incentive to good behavior while in office and would increase his sense of duty to the public rather than his selfish interest in private advantage. Indefinite eligibility would make the office more attractive to able men. Were the eligibility of the chief executive restricted, the community would lose the benefit of experience gained in office. This would be especially unfortunate in time of national emergency, such as war, when the continuance of an experienced executive in office might be essential to the national security. It should be remembered, however, that Hamilton had proposed a plan in the Philadelphia convention whereby the President would hold office during good behavior.

In describing the judicial branch of the national government, Hamilton made quite clear that this branch was expected to exercise the powers of judicial review. Indeed, his statements on this subject directly anticipated the reasoning of John Marshall in the famous American constitutional law case of *Marbury vs. Madison.* Believing that the judicial branch, possessed of neither "the sword nor the purse," was the weakest of the three branches of government, he argued that "the general liberty of the people can never be endangered from that quarter. . . ." Judicial review, he wrote, did not imply a superiority of power in the judiciary to the derogation of the legislature, but rather the superiority of the people who authorized the Constitution. The doctrine of judicial review has become such an important part of the American political system that Hamilton's justification of the principle bears quoting at length.

> There is no position which depends on clearer principles, than that every act of a delegated authority, contrary to the tenor of the commission under which it is exercised, is void. No legislative act, therefore, contrary to the Constitution, can be valid. To deny this, would be to affirm, that the deputy is greater than his principal; that the servant is above his master; that the representatives of the people are superior to the people themselves; that men acting by virtue of powers, may do not only what their powers do not authorize, but what they forbid.
>
> If it be said that the legislative body are themselves the constitutional judges of their own powers, and that the construction they put upon them is conclusive upon the other departments, it may be answered, that this cannot be the natural presumption, where it is not to be collected from any particular provisions in the Constitution. It is not otherwise to be supposed, that the Constitution could intend to enable the representatives of the people to substitute their

will to that of their constituents. It is far more rational to suppose, that the courts were designed to be an intermediate body between the people and the legislature, in order, among other things, to keep the latter within the limits assigned to their authority. The interpretation of the laws is the proper and peculiar province of the courts. A constitution is, in fact, and must be regarded by the judges, as a fundamental law. It therefore belongs to them to ascertain its meaning, as well as the meaning of any particular act proceeding from the legislative body. If there should happen to be an irreconcilable variance between the two, that which has the superior obligation and validity ought, of course, to be preferred; or, in other words, the Constitution ought to be preferred to the statute, the intention of the people to the intention of their agents.[24]

It was with considerable candor that *The Federalist* disclosed the intentions of the framers of the Constitution. While the national government would bear upon people and states alike, it was established upon such principles that the states and national government might check each other, and furthermore, within the national government the functional branches might also check each other. It was an ambitious and novel effort to establish republican government on a federal basis in such a manner that adequate power would be delegated yet adequate checks retained.

Many of the features of the Constitution were the result of compromises made necessary at the convention between persons of different political persuasions and states with conflicting interests. Yet one of the most significant features of the Constitution is that it institutionalizes the method of compromise as a political process of orderly government. The framers of the Constitution were not especially interested in developing a democratic government, but they were vitally concerned with establishing a balanced government. They believed that all political power rested ultimately upon the people, but they did not believe that the people made up a homogeneous group of like political persuasions. The people were a composite mixture of different economic interests, social ties, religious views and regional loyalties. Political action was made possible by alignments of these various interest groups. Yet it was these various alignments which the authors of *The Federalist* dreaded, and throughout the papers there recurs the fear of factions, of selfish alignments that would exploit the community in the name of the public interest. Predominantly the fear of faction

[24] *Ibid.*, Number 78.

was associated with the concern that the lower-income classes would achieve political control at the expense of the merchants and property holders. Shays' Rebellion in Massachusetts had given considerable alarm to the conservatives. Yet the experience of the framers in the convention pointed realistically to the uses of sectional factions to achieve immediate gains of dubious merit to the minority. In the often-quoted essay Number 10 Madison gave special attention to the problem of factions.

> By a faction, I understand a number of citizens, whether amounting to a majority or a minority of the whole, who are united and actuated by some common impulse of passion, or of interest, adversed to the rights of other citizens, or to the permanent and aggregate interests of the community.

In a republic, a government based upon the people, factions were inevitable. The only way factions could be destroyed would be to impose a tyranny over men so that they could not hold divergent opinions or espouse divergent interests. Such a cure for factions, however, would result in the destruction of liberty and thus be worse than the disease. In a free political system, factions would arise because men with different faculties and attainments would have different political interests and aspirations. Indeed, Madison observed, "The protection of these faculties is the first object of government."

Madison believed that the major source of factions was the unequal distribution of property. A continuous conflict thus existed between those with and those without property, between debtors and creditors.

> A landed interest, a manufacturing interest, a mercantile interest, a moneyed interest, with many lesser interests, grow up of necessity in civilized nations, and divide them into different classes, actuated by different sentiments and views.

While economic interests were the primary source of political factions they were by no means the only cause of political divisions.[25] Different opinions regarding religion, government, and public figures were also listed by Madison as sources of factions.

> The latent causes of faction are thus sown in the nature of man;

[25] For an interesting analysis of Number 10 of *The Federalist*, see Douglass Adair, "The Tenth Federalist Revisited," *The William and Mary Quarterly*, Third series, vol. VIII, no. 1, January, 1951, pp. 48-67.

and we see them everywhere brought into different degrees of activity, according to the different circumstances of civil society.

Since faction was inevitable in a free society, the resultant problem was how to prevent it from perverting public power to private advantage. Madison believed that faction was more likely to injure a small state than a large one, more likely to damage a pure democracy than a large republic such as was established under the Constitution. In a republic in which the people acted through representatives rather than directly, there was opportunity for refining the various views on political questions. There was an opportunity, in other words, for the representatives to distill the sentiments of various factions rather than succumb directly to any one group or special interest. Furthermore, the size of the republic helped check the abuses of local factions, as minor groups would be unable to organize on a national basis and, while they might succeed in controlling a state, they would have difficulty in controlling the national government. In a large republic the number of factions would be greater than in a small one, and this very diversity of interest groups would make it difficult to achieve effective blocs of power. So spread out over the entire area of the United States, any one faction or small group of factions would find its political power diminished.

Madison's essay on factions is in many respects similar to John Adams' statement of the case for the mixed constitution. Both men believed that human nature was such that men would continually seek their private advantage at the expense of the rest of the community whenever opportunity permitted. This strain in mankind permeated all classes of society and was characteristic of the rich as well as the poor, the merchant, the farmer, the laborer, the South as well as the North. While Adams believed that the public good could be achieved by balancing these competing interests in the legislature, Madison believed that competing interests would tend to check each other's machinations on a national scale. Neither man believed that under a system of simple majority rule the rights of the minority would be protected.

The Constitution, together with the defending essays in *The Federalist*, provided the fundamental matrix for subsequent American political thought. A major triumph for constitutionalism had been achieved. With the early addition of a bill of rights, the brief but extraordinary period of creative constitutionalism closed. Out of this period, however, came the lasting political principles of a federal government based on the people, defined and limited by a written constitution which incorporated a check and balance system as well as a separation of powers. This written document, ratified in conventions in the states by the people who were acknowledged to be its source of authority, carried a provision for its own amendment. While the national government was granted only the powers essential for national purposes, the people were protected by a bill of rights from an abuse of these powers. The accomplishment of the Constitution was a victory for those who favored a national political and economic system; it marked the first major victory for the nationalists over the extreme champions of state sovereignty and states' rights. The Constitution, indeed, provided a means whereby unity, though not necessarily uniformity, might be built upon a diversity of interests, of states, and sections of the country. As the tangible expression of the law in the United States, it soon acquired symbolic as well as legal importance. Like all higher law, however, it became subjected to interpretations which varied with the beliefs and interests of its interpreters. The meaning of the Constitution thus became a highly political question early in American history and has remained a controversial subject ever since.

CHAPTER 6

The Federalists:
Power, Property, and Law

THE RATIFICATION of the Constitution in 1789 by nine states made that document legally effective; it remained to be seen whether this Constitution on paper would become the higher law of a people, a nation—a Constitution in fact. It fell to the Federalists to be the first in office under the new Constitution, and the life they gave to this instrument of government decidedly affected subsequent political developments. Practice and precedent became effective influences on public policy just as surely as did theoretical political principles, and the Federalists, conscious of exerting a guiding hand on history, combined practice and principle to full advantage. Each major decision set a precedent, and during these formative years of the republic, when there were no established guideposts for policy, each course of action left landmarks in constitutional law and political values.

As the questions raised were basic to the course of the republic, so were the answers vital in importance. What was a federal system of government and how ought it to operate? How broad were national powers and, in each instance, what were their limitations? How should a separation-of-powers system operate in conjunction with a check-and-balance system? What were the rights of the citizen against the national government? Against the state government? Assuming the existence of strong national powers, how ought these powers to be exercised, that is, who should benefit from governmental policies and why? These were some of the major questions which arose directly upon the formation of the new government under the Constitution; the answers to these questions helped make the Constitution, but caused a basic schism in American politics. For the effort to establish a government under the Constitution required an interpretation of the Constitution which in turn involved the most fundamental political values. Thus the interpretation of the Constitution as the higher law for the United States brought out into public view the political values of those who did the interpreting.

Conflicts in constitutional construction were, at root, conflicts in political beliefs concerning the nature of the public good and how it might best be achieved. The conflict between the Federalists and the Jeffersonian Democrats was a conflict between the followers of Hobbes and the followers of Locke, between those whose greatest fear was anarchy and those who feared tyranny as man's most terrifying political fate. Such a conflict in fears had as its counterpart a conflict in political desires, so that those who were fearful of anarchy sought a strong government, while those who feared tyranny sought a weak one. The issue over the extent of powers which government ought to exercise thus involved a judgment regarding the nature of man and how man would behave in the absence of strong governmental restraints. In a sense this took the judgment back to the state of nature, for it brought into question man's basic motivations as well as general moral capacity. In the post-Revolutionary era, the political schism generally found those who challenged the fitness of the common man to rule in favor of a strong national government, and those who inclined toward a broader democracy in favor of a strictly limited national government. Those who feared the masses usually feared that their property would be placed in jeopardy should the masses gain political control. They feared, like the arch-Federalist, Fisher Ames, that democracy would become eventually a debtors' government led by demagogues. Indeed Fisher Ames, in his uncompleted *Dangers of American Liberty* (1805), gave extreme expression to this deep-rooted fear of the masses of mankind.

> The truth is, and let it humble our pride, the most ferocious of all animals, when his passions are roused to fury and are uncontrolled, is man; and of all government, the worst is that which never fails to excite, but was never found to restrain those passions, that is, democracy. It is an illuminated hell, that in the midst of remorse, horror, and torture, rings with festivity; for experience shows, that one joy remains to this most malignant description of the damned, the power to make others wretched.[1]

These were the fears of Thomas Hobbes, echoed by the Federalists in America a century and a half after the publication of the

[1] Seth Ames, ed., *Works of Fisher Ames* (Boston: Little, Brown, and Co., 1854), vol. II, p. 393.

Leviathan. And, like Hobbes, the Federalists turned to a strong authority, a government of power, as the political solution.

ALEXANDER HAMILTON

Alexander Hamilton (1757-1804), probably the most significant of the Federalists, stands throughout American history as a statesman whose political and economic policies, while often attacked, have never been abandoned. More than any other figure in his time, Hamilton recognized the necessity for a firm economic foundation for the infant nation, and his ideas formed the basis for Federalist political ideology. While Jefferson and the Republican-Democrats looked to the French physiocrats and an agrarian economy, Hamilton foresaw a powerful industrial America. To achieve this he sought a close alliance of business and government.

Hamilton, having spent his early years abroad, had no sentimental attachment to any particular state and little understanding of the state loyalty felt by others. He was a nationalist, an aristocrat, and a conservative who had little sympathy with popular government and whose nationalism was based on an economic rather than a popular foundation. A follower of Hobbes, Hamilton believed self-interest and fear to be the fundamental forces in human behavior.[2] Self-interest, he believed, would lead the major financial groups to support the national government, as their activities would be best protected by a powerful government. It was, in turn, through the support of these interests that the national government would acquire power. At the same time he thought that fear of the force of the national government would keep the dissenters in check. The importance of power to government was to Hamilton, as to Hobbes, a most elementary principle of political science; his consistent approach, therefore, was to strengthen the national government.

From the time of the Revolution to the end of the period of Federalist supremacy, Hamilton devoted his attention to the building of national political institutions. Examining the governmental system of the Continental Congress, he noted that "The fundamental defect is a want of power in Congress."[3] Always more fearful of

[2] In *The Farmer Refuted,* Hamilton attacked Samuel Seabury for taking a Hobbesian view of human nature. After the Revolution, however, Hamilton gave little attention to natural-rights doctrine, and his basic political theory closely paralleled the reasoning of Hobbes.

[3] *The Works of Alexander Hamilton,* edited by Henry Cabot Lodge (New York: G. P. Putnam and Sons, 1885, 1886), vol. I, p. 203.

anarchy and disunion than of despotism, he criticized the Congress for not exercising to the full its powers. In order to fully exercise power, Congress would have to assume that undefined powers were discretionary in nature, "limited only by the object for which they are given."[4] In 1780 he advocated the calling of a constitutional convention which would grant broad powers to the Congress, especially in matters affecting commerce and finance. Without these, he felt, no national government could long survive; for the states would bicker with each other and the confederation would break apart. "Political societies in close neighborhood must either be strongly united under one government, or there will infallibly exist emulations and quarrels; this is in human nature. . . ."[5] In order to make possible a strong national government, Hamilton proposed a plan at the Philadelphia convention which was modelled after the British system. Under this plan the executive, senators and judges would hold office during good behavior, and the only popular check would be a lower house elected for three years. The national government's prerogative to appoint the state governors would clearly indicate the unitary structure Hamilton envisaged. Further to assure national supremacy, this plan provided that all state laws contrary to the laws or Constitution of the United States would be "utterly void."

As a delegate from New York at the Philadelphia convention, Hamilton had pressed for a constitution that would strengthen considerably the powers of the national government; as prime counsellor of the Federalists in power he advised in favor of an energetic exercise of these powers. Whenever an issue arose involving the scope of national executive, legislative or judicial power, Hamilton was found on the side of those in favor of the exercise of that power.

"Energy in the Executive," Hamilton had written in *The Federalist*, Number 70, "is a leading character in the definition of good government." As Secretary of the Treasury in Washington's cabinet, he sought to enhance the executive powers of the President by attaching certain prerogatives to that office. During the hot political controversy aroused by Washington's Neutrality Proclamation in 1793, Hamilton gave a reasoned defence of this executive action in a series of political articles signed *Pacificus*. The fundamental constitutional issue concerned the authority of the President to issue a proclamation; that is, whether this power was within his juris-

[4] *Ibid.*, p. 204.
[5] *Ibid.*, p. 241.

diction under the Constitution. In the course of his defence, Hamilton was led to consider the nature and scope of executive powers generally, as well as the specific power in regard to foreign relations. The constitutional authorizations for executive power, he noted, contained among others two general grants of authority: the statement that "The executive power shall be vested in a President" and the provision that the President "take care that the laws be faithfully executed." These two clauses should be construed, he maintained, as granting a broad prerogative to the President, far greater than the specific delegations of power in the Constitution. The specific delegations—the enumerated powers—were but a partial listing of the President's full authority. Hamilton's interpretation of executive power was so broad, in fact, that it would appear he intended to give to the President all powers which were not otherwise denied to him. "The general doctrine of our Constitution, then, is that the *executive power* of the nation is vested in the President; subject only to the *exceptions* and *qualifications* which are expressed in the instrument."[6]

JUDICIAL REVIEW AND POPULAR GOVERNMENT

Hamilton construed national judicial power as broadly as he did executive power. At the Philadelphia convention he had declared that acts by state legislatures contrary to the Constitution or laws of the United States ought to be void. This was the accepted view of the Federalists who passed the Judiciary Act of 1789, which authorized the Supreme Court to review cases in which a state law challenged as repugnant to the United States Constitution had been upheld in a state court. This limited provision for judicial review, however, only partially incorporated Hamilton's ideas, for he assumed a complete power of judicial review over both state and congressional enactments. In fact, his discussion of judicial review in *The Federalist*, Number 78, directly anticipated the reasoning of John Marshall in *Marbury vs. Madison*. Judicial review, when coupled with the provision that the judges should enjoy office during good behavior, gave to the Constitution that aristocratic touch which Hamilton so greatly desired. Aloof from politics, the federal judges would interpret the higher law in such a manner as to make the judiciary an aristocratic bulwark against the popular

[6] *Ibid.*, vol. II, pp. 141-142.

passions. Hamilton had lost in his effort in the convention to have the President and Senate elected for terms of good behavior; judicial review by appointed judges holding office during good behavior kept this loss from being too consequential, for the judges could review the actions of those popularly elected.

The practice of judicial review is a distinctively American contribution to politics. So ingrained has this practice and its underlying assumptions become in American thought that it is difficult for students to conceive of a constitutional system without it, or even to realize that a constitutional, democratic system might oper· ate without it. Yet it should be remembered that Locke in his defense of natural rights and popular, legislative supremacy did not feel that the two conceptions were incompatible; on the contrary he based his argument on the contention that man so highly regarded rights that a majority of men would not normally permit their abridgment or denial. No further check was thus needed upon the legislature beyond that check which Locke assumed all men possessed—a sense of reasonable decency guided by conscience. English political growth, following Locke, practiced legislative supremacy; American political growth departed from Locke to the extent that it placed a check upon the legislature in the form of judicial review.

It was the explicit contention in American constitutional law that the written Constitution was the supreme law of the land. Furthermore it was assumed, in accordance with the contract theory of the eighteenth century, that a constitution was an enactment by the people which established a government, defined its powers, and prescribed limitations on the exercise of these powers. The Constitution thus early acquired a symbolic content as being a supreme enactment of the people. In effect the Constitution became the symbolic representative of natural law in America, and to appeal to the Constitution was to appeal to the highest statement of moral principle. The ambiguities inherent in a system of natural law, however, were directly transferred to the Constitutional system. For even though it be granted that the Constitution had superior validity to statutory law, still how was one to know the specific limits or authorizations of the Constitution where the meaning was not clearly stated? It was at this point that the practice of judicial review played a crucial role, for it was left to the judiciary to determine the specific content of the Constitution. It would appear that such consequential authority in the hands of one branch of the government would make that branch the superior department. Yet Hamilton argued in Number 78 of *The Federalist* that judicial review did not elevate the judiciary over the legislature. "It only supposes that the power of the people is superior to both; and that where the will of the legislature, declared in its statutes, stands in opposition to that of the people, declared in the Constitution, the judges ought to be governed by the latter rather than the former."[7] It became thus a distinctive function of the judiciary to protect the people from themselves, that is, to protect the people in the name of the Constitution from popular legislation in the form of statutes where there was an apparent conflict between the two.

Alexander Hamilton, who confessed little sympathy with popular government, was the first major spokesman for the people's constitution and judicial review as an efficient method of protecting it. "It is not otherwise to be supposed," Hamilton noted in the *Federalist*, "that the Constitution could intend to enable the representatives of the people to substitute their WILL to that of their constituents."[8] By a curious use of logic, Hamilton arrived at the conclusion that since elected representatives of the people might misconstrue their mandate, the people's intentions in the Constitution could best be guarded by non-elected officials. Since the Constitution was considered to possess the honorific connotation of representing the people's supreme will, and of expressing in effect the political content of natural law, it was inevitable that the true construction of this document would necessitate the utmost in human wisdom. Furthermore, the accretions of precedent in constitutional law, defining the scope and interpretation of the Constitution, would require an uncommon degree of learning. Thus Hamilton continued in Number 78 of *The Federalist:*

> Hence it is, that there can be but few men in society who will have sufficient skill in the laws to qualify them for the stations of judges. And making the proper deductions for the ordinary depravity of human nature, the number must be still smaller of those who unite the requisite integrity with the requisite knowledge.[9]

Only a few men were qualified to judge the specific content of this higher law. As natural law was once held to be found through reason removed from passion, so constitutional law was held to be found through independent thought removed from partisan politics.

[7] *The Federalist* (New York: Tudor Publishing Co., 1937), p. 102.
[8] *Ibid.*, p. 101.
[9] *Ibid.*, p. 106.

Such independency, it was maintained, was best achieved through an appointed judiciary holding office during good behavior. Since it was assumed that the greatest threat to the Constitution would come from elected officials, it was natural to assume that the Constitution would be best protected by non-elected ones. The equating of independency of thought with non-dependency upon popular support for holding office was clearly a gratuitous assumption, as later events indicated. Nevertheless, as the principle of judicial review was established in our political system, it was clearly associated with an appointed judiciary holding office during good behavior, which judiciary, it was claimed, was independent by virtue of being removed from popular control. Judicial review, so conceived, was thus by intention an undemocratic aspect of our political structure. So ingrained, however, was the concept of judicial review in American jurisprudence that the assumption was made by Hamilton and continued in our political thought that the Constitution could not be preserved without judicial review. The concept of constitutional self-restraint thus early became identified with the judicial branch of government in derogation of the legislatures.

In summary, it may be noted that the Federalist view of judicial review as articulated by Hamilton and practiced by John Marshall—and continued by the Supreme Court for a century more—contained the following beliefs. First, the Constitution was the supreme law in the United States. Second, the Constitution was established by the people—it was a popular document, the people's Constitution. Third, popularly elected legislatures were those most likely to subvert or contravene the Constitution. Fourth, appointed judges removed from the control of popular majorities were those best fitted to determine the true meaning of the Constitution. Fifth, the Constitution imposed restraints as well as authorized power; while such restraints were needed to curb public officials, the only public body in the United States which could not in fact act unconstitutionally was the Supreme Court. Sixth, as the people's Constitution, the Constitution could be changed only by the people through the amending process. The courts did not therefore alter the Constitution through their decisions but only declared what the Constitution really meant. This position was successively weakened by the Court's overruling of previous decisions and the popular recognition that the court did in fact follow the drift of popular political sentiment.

NATIONAL ECONOMIC POWER

It was Hamilton's contention—as it was Harrington's before him—that political power flowed from economic sources and that a firm political union of the states required an underlying and unifying economic system. Thus, recognizing the importance of economic power to politics, he sought to strengthen the national government by identifying it with the interests of the major economic groups. In the Hamiltonian view, what was good for the major economic forces was good for the public as well. The predominant business of government was indeed business. For the national government to act contrary to the interests of the major business groups would disrupt the political system, for the national government, like all government, was dependent upon the support of these same groups. In a class sense this meant that the national government ought to represent and reflect the views, predominantly, of the rich and well-born. Economically, this meant a public policy which was essentially promotional, and would foster rapid economic growth. This policy, however, while working to the advantage of northern commercial and financial interests, brought no direct advantage to the southern planter, whose antagonism was expressed in the demand for a strict construction of the Constitution. Far closer in design to English mercantilism than *laissez-faire* capitalism, the Hamiltonian program laid down the basic constitutional precedents which a century and a half later were brought into the service of the New Deal. Hamilton was indeed the first American spokesman for national economic planning.

The Hamiltonian plan called for a broad construction of the economic powers of Congress, particularly as these powers affected credit, finance, and trade. In his *First Report on the Public Credit* (1790) Hamilton proposed not only that the debts of the United States be refunded at par, but also that the national government pay off the Revolutionary debts incurred by the states. These proposals caused considerable political opposition because several of the states had made a good deal of progress toward paying off their own debts and were therefore reluctant to see other states so relieved of their burdens; and also because the refunding of the national debt at par would give a great profit to speculators who had bought up these securities when their market value had been extremely low. Hamilton argued, however, that in order for the United States to maintain its credit it would have to fulfill its obligations to the letter. By refunding the national and state debts at par, the Federalists not only assured the credit standing of the national government, but they made it, rather than the state governments, the immediate ally of the financiers.

Further to establish the national government in the field of credit and finance Hamilton proposed that it incorporate a Bank of the United States. When this proposal was challenged directly on the grounds that it called for an unconstitutional assumption of power by the Congress, President Washington asked Secretary of State Jefferson, Attorney-General Randolph and Secretary of Treasury Hamilton for opinions on the matter. The first two held the power beyond the scope of the Constitution, while Hamilton, in his *Opinion on the Constitutionality of the Bank of the United States* (1791), laid down the argument which subsequently became part of our constitutional law. Writing in defence of his own project, he declared as a fundamental axiom of government:

> That every power vested in a government is in its nature *sovereign* and includes, by *force* of the *term*, a right to employ all the *means* requisite and fairly applicable to the attainment of the *ends* of such power, and which are not precluded by restrictions and exceptions specified in the Constitution, or not immoral, or not contrary to the *essential ends* of political society.[10]

Thus each government, state and national, possessed sovereign powers "as to *certain things*." Each government had certain objects entrusted to its care, and with regard to these objects its powers were sovereign or complete. Putting aside the Tenth Amendment as being merely a maxim of republican government, "that all government is a delegation of power," he turned to the scope of national power. National power was not limited to delegated powers alone, for "there are *implied* as well as *express powers*," and in addition there are "*resulting* powers." Suppose, he inquired, the United States were to conquer some territory; would not the national government possess sovereign jurisdiction over such territory? Such jurisdiction would result "from the whole mass of the powers of the government, and from the nature of political society. . . ." The basic question in regard to national power must be whether there is a "natural relation" between the means employed and the "lawful ends of the government."

[10] *The Works of Alexander Hamilton,* vol. III, p. 181.

Jefferson, in his opinion, had contended that not all means might be employed by the national government in the exercise of its powers, but only those means which were "necessary and proper" to the execution of the delegated powers—means which were so essential that without them the grant of power could not be exercised. In other words, the Jeffersonian construction would interpret the "necessary and proper" clause as meaning "absolutely" necessary. Such an interpretation, Hamilton countered, would lead to considerable uncertainty and political dispute.

> The *degree* in which a measure is necessary, can never be a *test* of the legal right to adopt it; that must be a matter of opinion, and can only be a *test* of expediency. The *relation* between the *measure* and the *end;* between the *nature* of the *mean* employed toward the execution of a power, must be the criterion of constitutionality, not the more or less of *necessity* or *utility*.[11]

A liberal construction of the powers of the national government was especially important in the fields of finance, commerce, and defence, while a strict interpretation in these fields would restrict the consequential choice of means for coping with national emergencies or promoting prosperity. To observe the Constitution in its literal meaning only would be to "arrest the motions of government"; yet to depart from the literal meaning might lead to grave problems of constitutional construction. Of these dangers, Hamilton believed the latter course to lead to fewer difficulties, and in words that were closely followed by John Marshall, Hamilton laid down the criterion for judging implied powers:

> If the *end* be clearly comprehended within any of the specified powers, and if the measure have an obvious relation to that *end,* and is not forbidden by any particular provision of the Constitution, it may safely be deemed to come within the compass of national authority.[12]

To secure the position of the national government, Hamilton's program called for a revenue system which included not only a tariff on certain imported goods but excise taxes on certain goods produced at home. The payment of the national debt and the other expenses of the new government might have been met by custom duties alone. Hamilton, however, anxious to flex the muscles of national power, chose to push an excise program at home that

11 *Ibid.*, p. 189.
12 *Ibid.*, p. 192.

brought the national government directly to the door of the taxpayer. These excise measures, though they provoked considerable opposition, nevertheless set a precedent for national taxation which considerably augmented the financial strength of the national government.

In 1791 Congress passed an excise measure which placed a tax on whiskey distilled in the United States or imported from abroad. This tax hit directly the farmers in the Appalachian mountain belt, and these backwoods distillers had little inclination to cooperate with the revenue officers. A group of western farmers, never overly sympathetic with the aims of the Federalists, chose to make a stand on the issue and instigated what became known as the Whiskey Rebellion. Claiming that they were fighting the battle for freedom against unjust taxation, the farmers defied the power of the national government. Hamilton, seeing the issue as a fundamental test of national authority, urged that the full power of the national government be employed if necessary to put down the rebellion. Treating the issue as though the fate of the government hung upon it, he wrote that "a sacred respect for the constitutional law is the vital principle, the sustaining energy, of a free government." This respect for the law was being violated by the farmers, for the rebellion represented the challenge of anarchy. More fearful of anarchy than tyranny, he observed "that a large and well-organized republic can scarcely lose its liberty from any other cause than that of anarchy, to which a contempt of the laws is the highroad."[13] The rebellion was put down by the militia which Washington called out for that purpose. This action strengthened the authority of the national government, although Hamilton's critics charged that he had exploited the situation to display national power.

Finally, Hamilton's program called for the direct implementation of certain economic activities by the national government. He desired a strong self-sufficient nation, but he did not believe that the economic prerequisites for such a nation would be fulfilled automatically. It was his contention that the government should intervene in the economy in order to achieve its desired ends, and he believed that the Constitution permitted such intervention. Hamilton's system of economics permitted no more anarchy than did his system of politics. He thought in terms of law and order, economic self-sufficiency and prosperity, and he did not propose to leave the accomplishment of these desired ends to chance. On

[13] *Ibid.*, vol. VI, pp. 27, 26.

the contrary, he proposed in his *Report on Manufactures* (1791), a measure of governmental planning and direction to achieve desirable economic ends. Essentially his recommendations amounted to a strong brief for a protective tariff. A protective tariff would encourage manufacturing in the United States, and manufacturing, in turn, would bring about many desirable economic effects. Manufacturing would promote a division of labor which would then increase the skill and efficiency of productive effort. This would cause an increase in national productivity as well as an increase in the national revenue. Since manufacturing rather than agriculture made greater use of machinery, the promotion of manufacturing would extend the uses of machinery and also increase productivity. Manufacturing afforded employment to persons not ordinarily engaged in business and thus reached beyond the normal sources of employment to tap the resources of women and children. "It is worthy of particular remark," Hamilton noted, "that, in general, women and children are rendered more useful, and the latter more early useful, by manufacturing establishments, than they would otherwise be."[14] Furthermore the promotion of manufacturing would promote immigration from abroad, for foreign manufacturers would be enticed to this country by the prospect of better prices, cheaper raw materials, less stringent taxation, "a more equal government" and "a perfect equality of religious privileges." Only with a diversified economy could full scope be offered for the expression of individual talents.

> If there be any thing in a remark often to be met with, namely, that there is, in the genius of the people of this country, a peculiar aptitude for mechanic improvements, it would operate as a forcible reason for giving opportunities to the exercise of that species of talent, by the propagation of manufactures.[15]

By encouraging manufacturing, the objects of enterprise would be increased and the activity of the human mind stimulated. Finally, the establishment of manufactures would create a constant and secure market for the produce of domestic farms and mines, as well as give a measure of self-sufficiency to the nation in times of international peril. Thus did Hamilton construct his elaborate arguments for promoting manufacturing in America by protecting infant industries. These arguments, it may be added, have been the traditional justifications for a protective tariff ever since.

[14] *Ibid.*, vol. III, p. 314.
[15] *Ibid.*, p. 317.

In addition to the protective tariff, Hamilton further suggested a system of bounties to be paid out of surplus revenue. These bounties, to be appropriated by Congress, would be disbursed by a board of commissioners "for promoting arts, agriculture, manufactures, and commerce." The government would thus directly intervene in the economic sphere by allocating out of the public treasury funds to be granted by the commissioners "to defray the expenses of the emigration of artists and manufacturers in particular branches of extraordinary importance," to promote useful discoveries, inventions and improvements, as well as for other purposes.

That such an ambitious program of governmental activity would be subject to constitutional scrutiny was anticipated by Hamilton. The power of Congress over duties and imposts clearly provided for the tariff schedule. Nevertheless some constitutional doubt might exist concerning the power of Congress to appropriate funds to cover the extensive program of promotion through bounties. Once again he turned to a broad construction of the Constitution. The objects for which money might be appropriated by Congress were the payment of public debts and the providing for the common defense and general welfare. Clearly the spending power of Congress under the general welfare clause was a wide grant of authority.

> The phrase is as comprehensive as any that could have been used, because it was not fit that the constitutional authority of the Union to appropriate its revenues should have been restricted within narrower limits than the "general welfare," and because this necessarily embraces a vast variety of particulars, which are susceptible neither of specification nor of definition. . . .There seems to be no room for a doubt that whatever concerns the general interests of learning, of agriculture, of manufactures, and of commerce, are within the sphere of the national councils, as far as regards an application of money. . . .[16]

This interpretation of the spending power, opposed by Madison, was subsequently supported by Justice Story in his *Commentaries on the Constitution*, and by the Supreme Court in the controversial New Deal cases of *United States vs. Butler* (207 U. S. 1, 1935) and *Steward Machine Co. vs. Davis* (301 U. S. 548, 1937).

Hamilton was more of a political economist than a political philosopher, and his place in American political theory rests primarily on the emphasis he gave to economic affairs as a consequential concomitant to political development. The fundamentals of his

[16] *Ibid.*, pp. 371-372.

political thought were those inherited from the English tradition. These included a staunch belief in the higher law, which, translated into constitutional usage, became the law of the Constitution. His early opposition, in the colonial period, to the enactments of Parliament was grounded on the belief that their measures were contrary to the constitution and therefore void. In his early years he had also spoken forcibly in favor of the natural rights of man. His predilection for a political system closely akin to that of the English, together with the palpable deficiencies of the early American efforts at achieving a national government, left him with a heavy bias in favor of a strong central system of authority. Failing to achieve in the convention the aristocratic government he desired, he concentrated his subsequent political efforts on assuring sufficient national power under the republican form. Yet he always maintained doubts as to whether republican government could really succeed, "whether it be consistent with that stability and order in government which are essential to public strength and private security and happiness."[17] He feared that the people themselves would subvert the principles of republican government and, if left to themselves, would substitute, eventually, anarchy. He seemed to assume the existence of a powerful centrifugal force operating in society, moving always in the direction of dispersion and disruption. The dissolution of society therefore appeared inevitable unless men, motivated by their own self-interest, were held in check by law and force. This assumption of the inevitable dissolution of society under a weak government—fundamentally a Hobbesian assumption —brought with it a corresponding fear in regard to the fate of the union. No state partisan, Hamilton considered as two points in his political creed: "first, the necessity of Union to the respectability and happiness of this country, and second, the necessity of an efficient general government to maintain the Union. . . ."[18] The major threat to the Union he considered to be the jealous competitive rivalry of the states. He saw the states primarily as rival political units whose partisan interests threatened to jeopardize the union. Writing in 1792 of the *power of the states,* he noted, "As the thing now is . . . I acknowledge the most serious apprehensions, that the government of the United States will not be able to maintain itself against their influence."[19]

[17] *Ibid.,* vol. VIII, p. 264.
[18] *Ibid.,* p. 248.
[19] *Ibid.,* p. 263.

In order to build up the national government so that it might preserve the union and counterbalance, if not overcome, the power of the states, he advocated the broadest possible construction of national executive, judicial, and legislative powers. He sought to induce finance capital to support the national government; he saw the possibilities of a diversified economy and the political as well as economic benefits accruing to a nation possessed of industry as well as agriculture. Hamilton, indeed, saw the necessity of national power, political and economic, to preserve union at home and to gain rank among nations abroad.

JOHN ADAMS

John Adams, while never the nationalist that Hamilton was, was equally a Federalist in his political principles. A staunch supporter of the rights of property and the aristocratic element in society, he believed that strong government was necessary to the preservation of these rights. It was during his administration as President that the Alien and Sedition laws were enacted in 1798.

Adams had clearly established his political position in his *Defense of the Constitutions of the United States*, in which he had indicated his leanings toward the British constitution with its mixed government of monarchy, aristocracy, and democracy. In his *Discourses on Davila* (1790), Adams continued to attack a pure republican form of government as being contrary to the natural order and likely to abuse the rights of man. In an age of rising republicanism this position neither enhanced Adams' popularity nor strengthened the cause of the Federalists, for it made quite clear that the program of Hamilton and Adams was basically contrary to a democratic system of government. There was, however, a difference between the views of Hamilton and Adams. Hamilton preferred the rich and well-born because he believed that they were the only people fit to rule a state. Adams sought to defend the position of the aristocracy because he believed their existence in any society to be inevitable, and felt that unless institutional checks were developed to protect them they would be denied their natural rights. Both men agreed, however, on the inequality of men. Thus the assumption of inequality became as basic a tenet of the Federalists as the assumption of equality became of the Jeffersonian Democrats.

Both the Federalists and the Republican-Democrats believed that their political theories were based upon the immutable laws of nature. Both believed that the laws of nature were created by God. But the Republican-Democrats were inclined to find the world a more harmonious place and the Deity a more benevolent Being than did the Federalists. The Federalists, with a touch of Puritan conviction, saw man more prone to sin and the universe more inclined toward damnation than did their opponents. As a result, the observations of the Federalists from nature and from nature's laws emphasized discord over harmony. The theorists of both parties claimed to be realistic; but the one inclined toward what may be called optimistic realism, while the realism of the other was tinged with pessimism.

The principles of political science which John Adams drew from nature were reinforced by his observations of Shays' Rebellion and the French Revolution. Selfish man seeks his own gain at the expense of his neighbor unless there is power in the government to restrain him; but the selfish men in government would abuse their powers also unless they too were checked. The system of checks which he advocated, putting class against class, would, he felt, tend to equalize the pressures of selfish interests, and stability would result. His system was founded, however, upon a belief in a class struggle between the aristocrats and the rest of the people. Unless there was a class of aristocrats, there was no need to represent them in a separate portion of the government. It was this first assumption of the inevitability of an aristocracy which brought Adams under considerable attack from his Republican-Democrat opponents. Indeed, the program of Hamilton was attacked for attempting to create the very sort of aristocracy which Adams believed would come into existence by a natural process.

It was not until after the heat of the conflict had passed, when the administrations of both Adams and Jefferson were over, that a correspondence between Adams and Jefferson and Adams and John Taylor brought out the full meaning that Adams attached to the word aristocracy. It was also in the course of this correspondence that he had an opportunity to point up the main elements of his political theory and defend his system, now that the balance of power had shifted.

"By an aristocrat," John Adams wrote in 1814, "I mean every man who can command or influence Two Votes; One Besides His Own."[20]

20 *The Works of John Adams,* edited by C. F. Adams (Boston: Charles C. Little and James Brown, 1850-1856), vol. VI, p. 455.

One need only observe society to note that there were always leaders and always followers. The aristocrats were the leaders and the democrats the followers. There were, inevitably, inequalities among mankind. If there was a moral equality of individuals at birth, an equality of innocence, it was overcome as soon as a child learned to move and speak. Beyond this stage of equality in innocence there developed physical, intellectual, and moral inequalities which made for recognized inequalities in talents and reputation. Birth in the proper family was certainly a cause of inequality, and, therefore, of aristocracy. Property certainly was a cause of inequality, and, therefore, of aristocracy. "There are many more persons in the world who have no property, than there are who have any; and, therefore, the democracy is, and will be, more numerous than the aristocracy." Knowledge was a cause of inequality, and, therefore, of aristocracy. "The moment you give knowledge to a democrat, you make him an aristocrat." Any attribute which caused the respect, the envy, or the fear of others, which tended to separate society into the few and the many, was an attribute of the aristocrat. This was decreed by nature just as surely as Malthus' law that population tended to multiply faster than the means of its subsistence, and that nine-tenths of the earth's population would have to labor to support all mankind. "Make all men Newtons, or if you will, Jeffersons, or Taylors, or Randolphs, and they would all perish in a heap!"[21]

It made very little difference to Adams what one considered to be the major sources of the inequalities among men. The point was that inequality had always been recognized from Aristotle down through history and no effort at a republican society could ever eliminate it. Suppose, he suggested to John Taylor, that one were to pick the first one hundred men one found on the street, or on a plantation, or anywhere else, and bring them together into a republic. It would immediately appear that there were leaders and followers, and the aristocrats would take over.

Your democratical republic picked in the streets, and your democratical African republic, or domestic republic, call it which you will, in its first session, will become an aristocratical republic. In the second session, it will become an oligarchical republic; because the seventy-four democrats and the twenty-six aristocrats will, by this time, discover that thirteen of the aristocrats can command four votes each; these thirteen will now command the majority, and, conse-

21 *Ibid.,* pp. 516-517.

quently, will be sovereign. The thirteen will then be an oligarchy. In the third session, it will be found that among these are seven, each of whom can command eight votes, equal in all to fifty-six, a decided majority. In the fourth session, it will be found that there are among these seven oligarchs four who can command thirteen votes apiece. The republic then becomes an oligarchy, whose sovereignty is in four individuals. In the fifth session, it will be discovered that two of the four can command six-and-twenty votes each. Then two will have the command of the sovereign oligarchy. In the sixth session, there will be a sharp contention between the two which shall have the command of the fifty-two votes. Here will commence the squabble of Danton and Robespierre, of Julius and Pompey, of Anthony and Augustus, of the white rose and the red rose, of Jefferson and Adams, of Burr and Jefferson, of Clinton and Madison, or, if you will, of Napoleon and Alexander.

This, my dear sir, is the history of mankind, past, present, and to come.[22]

Since these inequalities in the condition and behavior of men were inherent in human nature, a realistic political system must take account of them. There was no way in which society might be levelled even if such an end were desirable. But by so constructing the political system that a distinct place was given to the aristocratic element, that is, in the senate in the states and the Senate in the national government, their actions might be observed and checked if necessary by the democratic branches of the government. Neither the aristocrats nor the democrats could be trusted with unlimited power. "My opinion is, and always has been," Adams wrote to Taylor, "that absolute power intoxicates alike despots, monarchs, aristocrats, and democrats, and jacobins, and *sans culottes*."[23]

Thus did John Adams in his declining years reaffirm his belief in the Federalist program with its frank recognition of the place of an elite in society. Because of his attack upon complete democracy, or pure republicanism, he aroused the political enmity of those who cherished a more generous view of man and his moral capabilities. Yet he was not a believer in either hereditary monarchy or hereditary aristocracy in spite of the support he gave to the British system. His major writings were in support of the American system which, as he understood it, was not and ought not to be a pure republican system. He feared the despotism of the democrats and aristocrats alike. In a letter to Jefferson, written in 1815, he said:

[22] *Ibid.*, pp. 457-458.
[23] *Ibid.*, p. 477.

The fundamental article of my political creed is, that despotism, or unlimited sovereignty, or absolute power, is the same in a majority of a popular assembly, an aristocratical council, an oligarchical junto, and a single emperor. Equally arbitrary, cruel, bloody, and in every respect diabolical.[24]

It should be noted, however, that Adams introduced a confusion into the traditional conception of aristocracy which in effect vitiated his system of mixed government. The traditional belief in inequality, and as its concomitant aristocracy, was a class and not a personal conception. Inequality associated with birth, property, or even education was a class conception; and a man attained status only as he entered a group which already possessed status. The reasoning behind the mixed system of government was that there were in fact two major classes in society which ought, in the interest of stability and justice, to be represented in the government. This was a crude form of functional representation. Aristocrats were to be represented in the upper house of the legislature because aristocrats would seek to further the interests of the aristocrats in the state; the common people were to be represented so that they might further their interests; together, aristocrats and common people might check each other's purely selfish class interest and through compromise and selective policy arrive at a program in the public interest. It was this basic approach which Adams developed at length in his *Defense of the Constitutions of the United States.*

By removing the class aspect of the aristocracy, as he did in his letters to Taylor, Adams destroyed the basis for the mixed government. If aristocracy was nothing more than leadership, and aristocrats (leaders) were to be found among any collection of men, then aristocracy was not a function of class but of personality. No use then to establish a chamber for the leaders (aristocrats), for leaders would inevitably control every chamber. The House would thus be as aristocratic as the Senate. If every man who could influence or control one vote beside his own was an aristocrat, then the greater number of votes one could control or influence the greater the degree of his aristocracy. If the test of aristocracy was leadership, then the most popular leader was the greatest aristocrat. Thus one could best discover the aristocrats in a fully democratic system, for the greater the degree of democracy, the truer the test of aristocracy. Such a conclusion would have been abhorrent to John Adams. Nevertheless, by equating aristocracy with leadership

[24] *Ibid.*, vol. X, p. 174.

he took away the justification for a mixed government, though, of course, not the argument for a separation of powers. For the separation of powers was the last barrier to concentrated or absolute power which he felt to be "inevitably arbitrary, cruel, bloody, and in every respect diabolical." That political power, by his reasoning, would always be wielded by leaders did not of course make such power any whit less dangerous.

In summary: The Federalists conceived the management of political society to be the distinct responsibility of the upper class, who represented the major propertied and financial interests. They distrusted the political and economic wisdom of the common man. They sought a strong, industrialized America by furthering the interests of those who managed industry and finance, and identifying these interests with the national government. Hamilton's vision of the future of economic enterprise in America—the vast spread of the new industrial system, the permeating influence of finance capital whether public or private, the diversification of economic life— proved to be essentially correct. It was perhaps the supreme achievement of the Federalists that they established a national economic system as a basis for a national political system.

The union of political and economic power which overran state barriers in time gave to Constitutional interpretation a nationalistic and capitalistic bias, evidenced by the decisions of the Federalist John Marshall. It became the function of the national government to foster economic development and protect private property. Such a construction of the Constitution brought the national government directly into the economic sphere to use its economic powers as those in control of the government should best see fit. A gradual association of Constitutionalism and capitalism developed in the nineteenth century as this economic system attained the status of an ideology. "Natural" economic law and "natural" moral law tended to coalesce under the rubric of the Constitution. Since the Constitution, as the tangible expression of the higher law, depended upon authoritative interpretation, and since the appointed judiciary early laid claim to this important function, the Supreme Court decided in specific cases what the content of this higher law really was. In practice it appeared that legislation which interfered with the laws of trade, or with property rights, or with economic contracts, were held void as contrary to the Constitution. Thus the economic and political systems were drawn still closer together. Though the Federalists established national powers on a semi-aristocratic basis for a limited economic group, they established the principle that within and according to the Constitution the national government possessed vital powers over the economy. They thus encountered the opposition of the Jeffersonian Democrats, who sought a system of limited governmental powers founded on a broadly democratic base.

CHAPTER 7

Jeffersonian Democracy

Wʜɪʟᴇ Alexander Hamilton and his fellow Federalists were engaged in building up the power of the national government and with it national economic institutions, a movement of dissent developed which manifested itself in the rising party of Republican-Democrats. The unifying ideas of this party were the various political principles which characterized what has come to be known as Jeffersonian democracy. To distill the thought of Thomas Jefferson (1743-1826), the intellectual leader and spokesman for this movement, into any succinct statement is a difficult task, for, although a voluminous writer, he did not leave a full and systematic presentation of his political philosophy. The greatest bulk of his writings is found in his personal correspondence, an extraordinary correspondence reaching across oceans and continents and touching upon the greatest variety of subjects from astronomy to zoology.[1] It is from these miscellaneous writings that we draw the principles of Jeffersonian political thought.

In his vast correspondence, Jefferson made clear the difference in his values and beliefs and those of the Federalists. In a letter written to Doctor Benjamin Rush, for instance, Jefferson described a conversation between John Adams and Alexander Hamilton concerning the merits of the British constitution. In this discussion Adams maintained, as in his *Defence of the Constitutions of the United States,* that if certain defects in the British constitution were removed, it would be the "most perfect constitution of government ever devised by man." Hamilton felt that to alter the British constitution would be to make it an "impracticable government" and

[1] Most of this correspondence has not as yet been published. Fortunately, Princeton University Press is now in the process of publishing a complete fifty-volume edition of all Jefferson's writings.

150

that as it stood it was "the most perfect model of government that could be formed."[2] This heavy bias of Hamilton and Adams in favor of the English constitution of the eighteenth century, with its royalist emphasis upon king and nobility, was in marked contrast to the Jeffersonian demand for an extension of democracy. Hamilton, ever distrustful of the masses of men, sought to balance their political powers. Jefferson, more distrustful of the nobility than of the people, sought to check if not eliminate any element in government not responsible to the people.

Some insight into the beliefs of men may be gained by knowing whom they admired in history, for a man's conception of greatness is often an indication of his framework of values. It is interesting to note in this respect that Jefferson, in a discussion with Hamilton, declared Bacon, Newton, and Locke to be the greatest men in history. Here was the humanist philosopher paying tribute to previous philosophers who also had striven to unshackle the mind of man. Hamilton, on the contrary, maintained that Julius Caesar was the greatest name in history. At bottom, the difference between Hamilton and Jefferson lay in the fact that the former followed in the school of Hobbes, the latter in the school of Locke. Hamilton, impressed with the selfish motivations of men, found government to rest upon fear and favor. Power was thus the prerequisite of government, and a successful national government was dependent upon strong national power supported by strong national economic institutions. Jefferson, believing in the innate goodness of men, cognizant of the common laws of morality, saw power as a threat to freedom. The thinking of Hamilton led to the creation of American institutions of power; the thinking of Jefferson led to the formulation of the American democratic ideas of human liberty.

MORALITY AND RATIONALITY

Jefferson's political ideas sprang from his belief in the integrity of the individual and man's capacity for learning and understanding. Inherent in individuals was a moral sense and a social disposition. "The want or imperfection of the moral sense in some men, like the want or imperfection of the senses of sight and hearing in others,

2 Philip S. Foner, ed., *Basic Writings of Thomas Jefferson* (New York: Willey Book Co., 1944), p. 686.

is no proof that it is a general characteristic of the species."[3] That this basic sense of morality was a part of man's being, implanted in him by his Creator, was an obvious truth to Jefferson. It was because of this fundamental moral sense that it was possible for men to live together in society.

Like Locke, Jefferson believed that man was both a moral and a rational creature. Because man was both moral and rational he had the capacity to learn and to understand. Jefferson, therefore, espoused a broad system of public education, a public library, and the establishment of the University of Virginia. If the people were truly informed, thought Jefferson, they would not be often misled. This was to assume, in effect, that educated people equally possessed of the facts of a case and in fundamental agreement on the laws of morality would not differ widely in their opinions. The successful operation of democracy therefore depended to a large extent upon the education of the populace. In proposing a bill for an extensive system of public education in Virginia, Jefferson noted that not only would such a system train leaders who might later serve as useful instruments of the public, but further that the people generally would also be better informed of tyranny in all its guises and thus be the fitter to defeat it.

> But of all the views of this law none is more important, none more legitimate, than that of rendering the people the safe as they are the ultimate, guardians of their own liberty. . . . And to render even them safe, their minds must be improved to a certain degree.[4]

In this age of reason great credence was given to the possibilities of education as a means of guiding man out of his difficulties. Jefferson saw in education not only a means whereby democracy might be preserved but also a means by which each man might be led to his own happiness. Education in morality would teach people

> how to work out their own greatest happiness by showing them that it does not depend on the condition of life in which chance has placed them, but is always the result of a good conscience, good health, occupation, and freedom in all just pursuits.[5]

It was education which could remedy the defects of an improper understanding of the moral law. For, Jefferson believed, men might

[3] Letter of June 13, 1814, from Jefferson to Thomas Law. *The Writings of Thomas Jefferson*, edited by H. A. Washington (New York: Riker, Thorne and Co., 1855), vol. VI, p. 350.
[4] *Basic Writings*, p. 151.
[5] *Ibid.*, pp. 150-151:

be taught to see that it was to their self-interest to obey the laws of morality.[6]

Education, furthermore, could guide men to an understanding of their true interests. It was this understanding, in conformity with the laws of morality, which would in turn make possible for the individual a fuller realization of happiness. Ignorance was thus not only a barrier to the effective operation of democracy but was equally a barrier to the individual's pursuit of happiness. If an individual knew and understood the laws of morality, he would practice them; if an individual practiced the laws of morality, he would advance considerably in his pursuit of happiness. Though man possessed innately a moral sense, education advanced him in an understanding of his rights and responsibilities.

Happiness was to Jefferson, as to many French thinkers of the late eighteenth century, the goal of every individual. His conception of happiness was not, however, to be equated with mere hedonism; every man sought happiness, but one only approached this goal as he observed the laws of morality and enjoyed personal freedom. The greatest utility of freedom was that it enabled moral man to attain happiness. This conception of the relationship of morality and education served as a basis for Jefferson's political ideas.

THE RIGHTS OF MAN

Jefferson's political thought was built upon his conception of the nature of man, of those who composed political society. To Jefferson, men were not the amoral selfish creatures posited by Hobbes, but the rational and moral individuals assumed by Locke. Endowed by their Creator with a sense of morality and a capacity for learning, they were also endowed with certain inalienable rights that existed as well out of society as in it. Following in the natural rights school,

[6] While Jefferson believed in a universal moral sense, he did not believe that the actions dictated by this moral sense need be always the same. The action might be considered virtuous in one country and vicious elsewhere: "The answer is, that nature has constituted *utility* to man, the standard and test of virtue. Men living in different countries under different circumstances, different habits and regimens, may have different utilities; the same act, therefore, may be useful, and consequently virtuous in one country which is injurious and vicious in another differently circumstanced." Letter of June 13, 1814, from Jefferson to Thomas Law. *The Writings of Thomas Jefferson*, edited by H. A. Washington, vol. VI, p. 351.

Jefferson attacked the notion that these basic rights were the product either of society or of the state. In the course of the debate with England during the Revolutionary period, Jefferson wrote *A Summary View of the Rights of British America* (1774). Here he laid down the grievances of the colonists with "that freedom of language and sentiment which becomes a free people, claiming their rights as derived from the laws of nature, and not as the gift of their Chief Magistrate."[7] Some three years later in the Declaration of Independence he further defined these natural rights as including, among others, life, liberty, and the pursuit of happiness. The substitution of happiness for the Lockean right of property has always been a matter for discussion, for neither Jefferson nor the other signers of the Declaration were in any way opposed to the right of property. It would seem, however, that three explanations consistent with Jefferson's ideas might be given for this substitution of terms. First, the right to property was not as fundamental as the right to happiness. Jefferson's entire philosophy emphasized the goal of human happiness. The acquisition of property might be instrumental in achieving this goal, but the possession of property was not an end in itself. Second, the right to property was not, to Jefferson, a natural right, but a right dependent upon and conditioned by civil society. In this he would depart from Locke, who claimed the ownership of property as a natural right. Third, the claim to happiness was a more comprehensive claim than the right to property. Not directly susceptible of definition, it encompassed in its phrasing a greater variety of objects.[8]

In Jefferson's thinking, the right to pursue happiness was closely associated with the right of liberty. Only free men could pursue happiness as he used the term. As a result, Jefferson opposed monopolistic or authoritarian control in any form and sought always to keep open the channels of ideas as well as trade. To help preserve liberty, Jefferson sought three basic changes in the laws of Virginia. He sought to eliminate laws restricting the transmission of property; he wished to prevent the further importation of slaves; and he opposed the laws which restricted the scope of religious freedom. He was successful in achieving the abolition of the ancient practice of primogeniture for intestate estates in Virginia. In its place was

---

[7] *Basic Writings*, p. 24.

[8] Jefferson was probably influenced by the late eighteenth-century French philosophers, particularly Helvetius, who emphasized happiness as the goal of man's existence.

substituted a system of equal partition which Jefferson described as "the best of all Agrarian laws."

In the Declaration of Independence Jefferson had attacked George III for permitting a continuation of the slave trade.

> He has waged cruel war against human nature itself, violating its most sacred rights of life and liberty in the persons of a distant people who never offended him, captivating and carrying them into slavery in another hemisphere, or to incur miserable death in their transportation thither.[9]

This passage was subsequently eliminated by Congress. Jefferson, however, continued in his struggle against slavery by drafting a bill in 1779 which would have prevented the further importation of slaves to Virginia. Although he believed slavery to be an offense against man's moral nature, he felt that a gradual deportation of Negroes was the only solution to the problem of slavery. In his *Autobiography*, written in 1821, he noted:

> Nothing is more certainly written in the book of fate, than that these people are to be free; nor is it less certain that the two races, equally free, cannot live in the same government. Nature, habit, opinion have drawn indelible lines of distinction between them. It is still in our power to direct the process of emancipation and deportation, peaceably, and in such slow degree, as that the evil will wear off insensibly, and their place be, *pari passu*, filled up by free white laborers. If, on the contrary, it is left to force itself on, human nature must shudder at the prospect held up.[10]

A further aspect of Jefferson's struggle against obstacles in the path of individual liberty was his successful effort to have enacted in Virgina a bill, which he drafted in 1779, for establishing religious freedom. He included this measure, along with the Declaration of Independence and the founding of the University of Virginia as the greatest achievements of his life. In this bill, which prohibited any compulsory contributions of money to any religious establishment or the placing of any burdens on a man for his religious beliefs, he noted that "our civil rights have no dependence on our religious opinions, any more than our opinions in physics or geometry. . . ."[11] His reasoning, as given in this bill, is an extension of that used a century and a half earlier by Roger Williams. The bill declared in part:

[9] *Basic Writings*, p. 24.
[10] *Ibid.*, pp. 439-440.
[11] *Ibid.*, p. 48.

that the opinions of men are not the object of civil government, nor
under its jurisdiction; that to suffer the civil magistrate to intrude
his powers into the field of opinion and to restrain the profession
or propagation of principles on supposition of their ill tendency
is a dangerous fallacy, which at once destroys all religious liberty,
because he being of course judge of that tendency will make his
opinions the rule of judgment, and approve or condemn the sentiments of others only as they shall square with or differ from his
own; that it is time enough for the rightful purposes of civil government for its officers to interfere when principles break out into overt
acts against peace and good order; and finally, that truth is great
and will prevail if left to herself; that she is the proper and sufficient
antagonist to error, and has nothing to fear from the conflict unless
by human interposition disarmed of her natural weapons, free argument and debate; errors ceasing to be dangerous when it is permitted freely to contradict them.[12]

Elsewhere, in his *Notes on Virginia*, Jefferson continued his argument in favor of a separation of state authority from religion. Maintaining that the powers of government could legitimately extend
only to such acts of individuals which injured others, he declared
that one's religious opinions could not hurt another. "It neither
picks my pocket nor breaks my leg," he noted. Furthermore, in
defense of free competition of religious beliefs he wrote:

Reason and free inquiry are the only effectual agents against error.
Give a loose to them, they will support the true religion by bringing
every false one to their tribunal, to the test of their investigation.
They are the natural enemies of error, and of error only.[13]

Jefferson's thinking, leaning always in the direction of expanding
the individual's freedom of thought and action, rested ultimately
on his faith that free inquiry would indeed conquer error; that man
was basically moral; and that educated people would come to agreement on fundamentals. It was this faith in reason, indeed in man,
which made it possible for Jefferson to be such a staunch defender
of the rights of man against any form of oppression by any form of
government. Jefferson's major objection to the Constitution of the
United States had been that in its original form it lacked a bill of
rights.

Many followers of the natural-rights theory tended to group all
the rights of man into a natural-rights category. Jefferson, however,

[12] *Ibid.*, p. 49.
[13] *Ibid.*, p. 158.

was more discerning and distinguished between natural and civil rights. In the first category he placed the rights of "Thinking, speaking, forming and giving opinions, and perhaps all those which can be fully exercised by the individual without the aid of exterior assistance—or, in other words, rights of personal competency." These were rights which man might enjoy even though removed from political society. In the second category, or civil rights, he found "Those of personal protection, of acquiring and possessing property, in the exercise of which the individual natural power is less than the natural right."[14] Natural rights were of course the more fundamental, but it became the proper function of the government to see that individuals were protected in the enjoyment of both classes of rights. It was, in fact, primarily for the protection of rights that governments, under the compact theory, were instituted among men. Even though a government was democratic in character and operated according to the principle of majority rule, it still could not take actions which would violate the rights of man held by the minority. In his first Inaugural Address (March 4, 1801) Jefferson declared:

> This sacred principle, that though the will of the majority is in all cases to prevail, that will, to be rightful, must be reasonable; that the minority possess their equal rights, which equal laws must protect, and to violate which would be oppression.[15]

It was because Jefferson believed that the majority will would be reasonable and would not seek to trample on the rights of others that he believed that democracy was that form of government most likely to preserve and protect the rights of man.

LOCAL GOVERNMENT

Jefferson's faith in the wisdom and conscience of an educated people was in marked contrast to his distrust of all those who exercised the powers of government. Like John Adams and James Madison, indeed like John Cotton, he felt that there was a natural tendency for those who possessed power to abuse it. As a result he believed that government ought always to be kept close to the people, since government inclined to abuse power as it became

[14] The above quotations are from G. Chinard, *Thomas Jefferson: The Apostle of Americanism* (Boston: Little, Brown, and Co., 1929), pp. 80-82.
[15] *Basic Writings*, p. 332.

further removed from those it governed. "Every government de-
generates when trusted to the rulers of the people alone. The people
themselves, therefore, are its only safe depositories."[16] This belief led
him to place local government first, state government next, and the
national government last in terms of scope of powers which should
be granted to them. Where the government was close to the people
they would be quick to check its abuses, for the people were, after
all, the best guardians of their liberties. He sought therefore both to
strengthen in powers and to make more democratic the offices of
local self-government.

Closely associated with his belief in strong institutions of local
self-government was Jefferson's agrarian emphasis. His own agrarian
background, together with his experience in the crowded cities of
Europe, inclined him to the view that the farmer was the best
subject for self-government. "Those who labor in the earth," he
wrote in his *Notes on Virginia*, "are the chosen people of God, if
ever He had a chosen people, whose breasts He has made His
peculiar deposit for substantial and genuine virtue." Farmers came
close to achieving personal independence, he felt, while those who
lived by manufacturing and trade were always dependent upon
their customers. "Dependence begets subservience and venality,
suffocates the germ of virtue, and prepares fit tools for the designs
of ambition."[17] While there was plenty of land in America Jefferson
hoped to see the population spread out, living in small democratic
communities rather than piled upon each other in cities, and engaging in agricultural pursuits rather than trade and manufacturing.
In time he modified his views on the primacy of agriculture so as to
give equal status to manufacturing. His ideas on local government,
however, were always put in terms of small communities composed
of educated yeomen rather than large cities with their teeming and
dependent populace. It was these local cells of liberty-conscious
people which were the essential units for democracy practiced on a
broader scale.

STATE GOVERNMENT

Jefferson's political experience encompassed all levels of government. A county lieutenant and surveyor, member of the Colonial

[16] *Ibid.*, p. 151.
[17] *Ibid.*, p. 161.

House of Burgesses, the Continental Congress, the House of Delegates in the state government of Virginia, Governor of Virginia, and President of the United States, he had experience not only in county, state and national government but in various legislative and executive capacities as well. It was with this wide experience in the exercise of governmental authority in his background that he wrote of the dangerous inclination of governors to abuse their powers and the need for ceaseless vigilance on the part of the governed. In the Kentucky Resolutions (1798), which he drafted, he noted—

> That it would be a dangerous delusion were a confidence in the men of our choice to silence our fears for the safety of our rights: that confidence is everywhere the parent of despotism—free government is founded in jealousy, and not in confidence; it is jealousy and not confidence which prescribes limited constitutions, to bind down those whom we are obliged to trust with power. . . .[18]

A government founded not upon trust, but upon distrust, required constitutional restraints at every turn to keep it within its prescribed authority. Thus a written constitution was necessary to define the powers of government and spell out their limitations. Even though the constitution limited the powers of government, it was a wise precaution to attach a bill or rights so there would be no doubt as to the nature of the liberties of the people. It was indeed for the preservation of these rights that government was instituted among men. Although Jefferson sought to base the government upon the principle of majority rule, he did not believe that the majority would necessarily always be right. He believed that the majority was more likely to be right than the minority, but that even the majority acting in accordance with constitutional process ought not to be able to violate the basic rights of man.

In describing the first constitution of the state of Virginia in his *Notes on Virginia,* Jefferson laid down some six basic criticisms of that document which reveal his basic approach to government. In the first place, he noted, the suffrage was too restricted, so that over half the men in the state were not represented in the legislature. Secondly, the districting of the state was so unequal that the tidewater region of the state controlled the entire government, even though in population it represented only two-fifths of the state. These two criticisms of the suffrage and the districting went to the heart of the undemocratic character of the constitution. His third criticism was leveled against the legislative arrangements.

[18] *Ibid.,* p. 330.

The senate is, by its constitution, too homogenous with the house of delegates. Being chosen by the same electors, at the same time, and out of the same subjects, the choice falls of course on men of the same description. The purpose of establishing different houses of legislation is to introduce the influence of different interests or different principles.[19]

This was, of course, the position later taken by John Adams when he argued in favor of the balanced constitution. Adams wished to have the senate represent wealth and property while the house would represent the people. Jefferson, while criticizing the constitution of Virginia on the grounds that "wealth and wisdom have equal chance for admission into both houses," did not make clear what specific arrangement or alteration in this respect he desired. His fourth criticism was an attack upon the faulty separation of powers. Under the Virginia constitution the executive and judicial branches were dependent upon the legislature, which body appointed the governor and his council, the major executive officers of the state as well as the judges of the superior courts. Thus, executive, legislative and judicial power fell ultimately under the control of the legislature. "The concentrating of these in the same hands is precisely the definition of despotic government," wrote Jefferson, following John Locke and Montesquieu.

An *elective despotism* was not the government we fought for, but one which should not only be founded on free principles, but in which the powers of government should be so divided and balanced among several bodies of magistracy, as that no one could transcend their legal limits, without being effectually checked and restrained by the others.[20]

Although Jefferson had faith that the majority of the people, as voters, would choose their representatives wisely, he did not believe that the majority of representatives, as governors, would rule wisely without personal favor, ambition or prejudice. He had, of course, even less faith in the governors who were not chosen by the people. But the point is that although he trusted the people as voters, he trusted no government, not even a democratically elected one that could exercise fully the powers of the state. It was always necessary to have institutional checks upon the branches of government, so that persons exercising authority could be checked by other persons

19 *Ibid.*, p. 131.
20 *Ibid.*, p. 132.

exercising authority. Power was thus pitted against power in order to help preserve popular liberty.

His fifth criticism of the constitution was that it could be amended by ordinary legislative enactment, which situation could destroy the constitution as a check upon the legislature itself. Finally, he criticized the constitution in that the legislature was able to set its own quorum, under which authority it was possible for a small number to capture control of the legislature, the predominant branch of the government.

In considering these crticisms it is important to note that while two of them sought to extend the democratic base of the government by making the suffrage and districting provisions more liberal, the remaining four sought restrictions or modifications in the legislature or its powers, although this was the most democratic branch of the government. It was, however, not because the legislature was democratic that Jefferson sought to restrict its power, but rather because the powers of government were largely concentrated in its hands. The demand for an extension of the suffrage and for redistricting reflected Jefferson's trust in the people as the proper base for political authority; the demands for restrictions on the predominant branch of the government reflected his distrust of any political system in which power was concentrated in the hands of one group or body.

Some thirty years later, in 1816, Jefferson recorded in a letter his criticism of the Virginia constitution. In general his criticisms remained the same as those he had stated in his *Notes on Virginia*. Now, however, he sought amendments to the constitution which would provide for a general suffrage for "every man who fights or pays," equality of representation through redistricting in the legislature; an elective governor; an elective judiciary; periodical amendments to the constitution; and the division of counties into wards for the better ordering of local affairs. Once again he stated his faith in popular government and his faith in the abilities of each generation to overcome custom and revise constitutions so as to keep the government of man in the care of the living rather than the dead. In his letter of 1816 he noted:

> Some men look at constitutions with sanctimonious reverence, and deem them like the arc of the covenant, too sacred to be touched . . . I am certainly not an advocate for frequent and untried changes in laws and constitutions. . . . But I know also, that laws and institutions must go hand in hand with the progress of the human mind. As

that becomes more developed, more enlightened, as new discoveries are made, new truths are disclosed, and manner and opinions change with the change of circumstances, institutions must advance also, and keep pace with the times. We might as well require a man to wear still the coat which fitted him when a boy, as civilized society to remain under the regimen of their barbarous ancestors.[21]

The state governments, limited by the constitutions yet founded upon the will of the people, were essential guardians of liberty. The states were separate and distinct republics independent in their domestic affairs yet amalgamated for their foreign concerns, and jealous of their own rights, would prevent any consolidation of power elsewhere. Jefferson's belief in states' rights was but another illustration of his antipathy towards concentrated power wherever lodged. Just as he had opposed concentrating public power in any one functional branch of the government, so did he oppose the consolidation of all power into either the state or the national government. "It is a fatal heresy to suppose that either our State governments are superior to the federal, or the federal to the States," Jefferson wrote in a letter in 1821.

> The people, to whom all authority belongs, have divided the powers of government into two distinct departments, the leading characters of which are *foreign* and *domestic*; and they have appointed for each a distinct set of functionaries. These they have made coordinate, checking and balancing each other, like the three cardinal departments in the individual States; each equally supreme as to the powers delegated to itself, and neither authorized ultimately to decide what belongs to itself, or to its coparcener in government.[22]

THE NATIONAL GOVERNMENT

Jefferson was in France at the time that the Constitution of the United States was framed. However, he followed the reports of the Convention with great interest through his correspondence with James Madison. Basically pleased with the results of the convention, he supported most of the important features of the new Constitution. His criticism of the document was primarily on two points. He did not like the provision for the President, under which any

---

[21] *Ibid.*, p. 750.
[22] *The Writings of Thomas Jefferson*, edited by H. A. Washington, vol. VII, pp. 213-214.

man might be eligible indefinitely for the office, for he would have preferred ineligibility for that office after a four-year term.[23]

His other major objection to the Constitution was that it omitted a bill of rights. In a letter to James Madison reviewing his opinions in regard to the Constitution, Jefferson noted his preference for a bill of rights,

> providing clearly, and without the aid of sophism, for freedom of religion, freedom of the press, protection against standing armies, restriction of monopolies, the eternal and unremitting force of the habeas corpus laws, and trials by jury in all matters of fact triable by the laws of the land, and not by the laws of nations.[24]

Aside from these two reservations he was quite willing to see the Constitution have a fair trial, even though he noted to Madison: "I own I am not a friend to a very energetic government. It is always oppressive."[25]

Soon after the Constitution went into effect, Jefferson, as Secretary of State in Washington's Cabinet, found himself in conflict with Secretary of Treasury Hamilton. Hamilton, seeking an energetic national government without too much regard to the states, sought a debt system, a national banking system and governmental assistance to the manufacturing industries. Such a broad program of governmental activity was entirely opposed to Jefferson's views on the functions of the national government. To Jefferson's thinking it was not the Constitution alone that was endangered but, more important still, the liberty of the people. The contest was thus quite basic, involving two opposing philosophies of government. Hamilton, fearful of popular rule, sought an aggressive national government which would overshadow the states and work closely with the merchants and manufacturing interests. Jefferson, proponent of *laissez faire* and agrarian democracy, sought strong state governments as checks upon national power.

Jefferson believed that no generation should impose a public debt upon the next, for the earth belonged to the living and not to

[23] He later approved two four-year terms, encouraging Washington to run for a second term and serving a second term himself. In regard to a limit of eight years for the President he wrote (to John Taylor, 1805): "I shall follow it, and a few more precedents will oppose the obstacle of habit to any one after a while who shall endeavor to extend his term." *The Writings of Thomas Jefferson*, edited by P. L. Ford (New York: G. P. Putnam's Sons, 1897), vol. VIII, p. 339.

[24] *Basic Writings*, p. 564.

[25] *Ibid.*, p. 565.

the dead. Could the dead leave debts, then they would be controlling, to the extent of the debt, the next generation. Hamilton, on the contrary, had seen the public debt as a means of wooing the financial interests of the country to the national government as well as a justification for further taxation. In a letter to Samuel Kercheval in 1816 Jefferson wrote:

> I am not among those who fear the people. They, and not the rich, are our dependence for continued freedom. And to preserve their independence, we must not let our rulers load us with perpetual debt. We must make our election between *economy and liberty*, or *profusion and servitude*. If we run into such debts, as that we must be taxed in our meat and in our drink, in our necessaries and our comforts, in our labors and our amusements, for our callings and our creeds, as the people of England are, our people, like them, must come to labor sixteen hours in the tweny-four, give the earnings of fifteen of these to the government for their debts and daily expenses; and the sixteenth being insufficient to afford us bread, we must live, as they now do, on oatmeal and potatoes; have no time to think, no means of calling the mis-managers to account; but be glad to obtain subsistence by hiring ourselves to rivet their chains on the necks of our fellow-sufferers.[26]

In opposition to Hamilton's plan for a national bank Jefferson gave it as his opinion that the bank bill was not only unconstitutional but a dangerous invasion of the powers of the states. It was unconstitutional in that no delegated power provided for such a bank, nor could such a power be reasonably implied from the Constitution. The "necessary and proper" clause in the Constitution should be construed as admitting all those "*necessary* means, that is to say, to those means without which the grant of power would be nugatory."[27] The bank might be a convenient means of exercising national powers, but certainly not a necessary one.

Although Jefferson was opposed to Hamilton's tariff system for encouraging manufacturing in the United States, his opposition was not entirely due to his preference for an agrarian economy. Here was, again, what was to him another unnecessary intervention by the national government into the affairs of men. A believer in *laissez faire,* he was for general acceptance of this principle of political economy. He was opposed to monopoly in any form; he

[26] *Ibid.*, pp. 749-750.
[27] *Ibid.*, p. 313.

was opposed to restraints on trade as he was opposed to restraints on ideas.

His belief in freedom was, however, most sensitive when it came to issues of ideas and opinions. Man, to pursue happiness, must be free to elect representatives of his own choosing and to engage in an occupation of his own choosing. But behind choice lay reason and argument. Only through discussion and debate could an individual learn the basic issues which would make his choice of representatives, of occupations, of religions, indeed his choice on any consequential subject, meaningful. Thus it was essential that there be freedom of speech, of opinion, and of the press.

In 1798 the Federalists passed the ill-famed Alien and Sedition Acts, which seriously restricted freedom of political opinion. Jefferson immediately challenged this extension of national power as beyond the scope of national authority, contrary to the First Amendment to the Constitution as well as contrary to the spirit of a free people. In the Kentucky Resolutions of 1798, which he drafted, Jefferson stated that the Constitution was but a compact between the states, which could not be altered without the consent of the parties to the contract. Thus the national government could not be the sole judge of the powers delegated to it, for then it and not the Constitution would determine the extent of its powers. He noted that in this issue, "as in all other cases of compact among powers having no common judge, each party has an equal right to judge for itself, as well of infractions as of the mode and measure of redress."[28]

After stating the constitutional objections to the Alien laws, the Kentucky Resolutions went on to announce the principle of nullification.

> . . . this commonwealth is determined, as it doubts not its co-States are, to submit to undelegated, and consequently unlimited powers in no man, or body of men on earth: that in cases of an abuse of the delegated powers, the members of the general government, being chosen by the people, a change by the people would be the constitutional remedy; but, where powers are assumed which have not been delegated, a nullification of the act is the rightful remedy: that every State has a natural right in cases not within the compact, (*casus non foederis*) to nullify of their own authority all assumptions of power by others within their limits: that without this right,

28 *Ibid.*, p. 326.

they would be under the domination, absolute and unlimited, of whosoever might exercise this right of judgment for them. . . .[29]

It was the contention of the Federalists that constitutional issues should be decided by the judicial branch of the national government. Jefferson, although originally pleased with the provisions in the Constitution regarding the judiciary, when faced with a Federalist tribunal headed by John Marshall, came to change his opinion regarding that branch of government. In 1820 Jefferson wrote:

> The judiciary of the United States is the subtle corps of sappers and miners constantly working underground to undermine the foundations of our confederated fabric. They are construing our constitution from a coordination of a general and special government to a general and supreme one alone.[30]

To check this power, Jefferson advocated appointment of judges for terms of four or six years rather than for good behavior. Furthermore, he continued to emphasize that it was up to the states and the representatives of the people, and not the judicial branch of the national government, to decide the delicate jurisdictional questions arising under the Constitution.

Jefferson's political system thus rested upon a belief in the rights of man and the faith that the people themselves were the best guardians of these rights. Since those governments were best which were most responsive to the popular will, he wished to keep government close to the people by innovating wards and stressing the importance of local and state governments. The greater distance between a government and the people it governed, the more likely was it to abuse its powers. Thus a distant government should be delegated only a minimum of powers and be strictly restricted in the exercise of these. Jefferson's strong feelings in favor of *laissez faire*, in ideas as well as trade, led him to oppose any assumption of power by the national government which would foster monopoly or create any unnecessary tax or burden upon the people. The happiness of the people was indeed the true object of government. It was Jefferson's lifetime contention that this object was best achieved by a minimum government, founded upon democratic principles, which respected the basic rights of man.

[29] *Ibid.*, p. 329.
[30] *The Writings of Thomas Jefferson*, edited by H. A. Washington, vol. VII, p. 192.

JOHN TAYLOR

While the underlying thought of Jeffersonian democracy may be found in the scattered speeches and writings of the man from whom it drew its name, Jeffersonian democracy is equally represented in a more collected form in the writings of John Taylor (1753-1824), of Caroline County, Virginia. A wealthy planter with some experience both in the government of his state and the United States Senate, he was a firm believer in states' rights, free trade, and popular government. Perhaps more than any other apostle of the Republican-Democrat policy, he saw in the system of Hamilton, Adams and Marshall a fearful challenge to democracy. He saw in the program of the Federalist a constant endeavor to take government out of the hands of the people and deliver it over to the business leaders of the community. He saw in the schemes of a funded debt, a national bank, and a protective tariff a sinister design whereby the northern capitalist under the guise of necessity and economic wisdom would capture control of the economy and politics of the entire country. This alliance of business and government was producing a new aristocracy which was quietly gaining power at the expense of the common people. Distorting the Constitution by means of broad judicial construction, the Federalists were sure to destroy democracy unless the people were to awaken to their rights and to how they were losing them. John Taylor took it upon himself to warn the people so that they would understand what he considered to be the real threat in the encroachment of the Federalists. His major writings were not published, however, until more than a decade after the Federalists had fallen from power and the policies established by them were firmly entrenched in our political system.

His attack upon the Federalists' interpretation of the Constitution followed along conventional states' rights lines. The Constitution was a compact between sovereign states. The national government thus possessed only delegated powers and, possessing no sovereignty in itself, could not expand these powers without the consent of the states concerned. In one of his earliest writings, published in 1794, he attacked the Hamiltonian expansion of the Constitution. "Usurpations upon constitutional principles," he warned, "if suffered to acquire maturity, will only yield to the dreadful remedy of a civil war. . . ."[31] It was John Taylor who drafted the Virginia Resolutions of 1798, companion to the Kentucky Resolutions drafted by Jefferson. Considering any form of consolidated government to jeopardize the liberty of the people, he opposed the extensions of national powers as tending toward such a consolidated system. The fundamental distribution of governmental powers was between the national government and the states. It was this decision which was guaranteed by the Constitution. As a result of this decision the dual constitutional system was developed, whereby the state constitutions were created by the people and the federal Constitution was created by the States.

> As state constitutions are subject to the supremacy of the people of each state, and the federal constitution to three-fourths of the states, neither are subject to laws or judgments state or federal, or to a consolidated American nation. A supremacy in a federal court to construe the articles of the Declaration of Independence, and of the federal state constitutions, united with a power to enforce its constructions, would as effectually destroy the supremacy of the people, and of three-fourths of the states, as the same species of supreme power in state legislatures would destroy the supremacy of state constitutions, and of the people of each state.[32]

Thus did Taylor in his last work, *New Views of the Constitution of the United States* (1823), attack the claimed supremacy of the Marshall court to construe state and national constitutions and thereby give legal sanctions to the encroaching Federalist policies of centralization.

Although Taylor attacked the policies of the Federalists by seeking to undermine the constitutional props which supported them, he did not rest his case upon a legal argument alone. Indeed he went far beyond the law in question to challenge the legitimacy of these policies as well as the fundamental assumptions beneath them. In the first of his major writings, *An Inquiry Into the Principles and Policy of the Government of the United States* (1814), which is also his most important contribution to the literature of American political theory, Taylor attacked the assumptions of John Adams as well as the policies of Hamilton.

The basic assumption of Adams, that of a natural inequality

[31] John Taylor, *A Definition of Parties* (Philadelphia: Francis Bailey, 1794), p. 3.
[32] John Taylor, *New Views of the Constitution of the United States* (Washington: Way and Gideon, 1823), p. 164.

among men, Taylor found unsound on the grounds that aristocracies are artificial and are not the product of nature. Aristocracies arose through political favors and, once grown, continued through the power of their position to maintain their hold upon society. The Federalist policies of paper money, national banks and tariffs was tending to develop an aristocratic class of capitalists, who, wedded to the national government, were retaining a preferred position in society. Such an aristocracy was clearly an artificial one without the slightest justification in nature.

Not only was aristocracy an artificial growth in society, but furthermore Adams' assumption of the constancy of human nature throughout all ages was false. Beneath the physical appearance of men was their inner sense of morality, and behind the forms of government were the prevailing moral concepts of the community. It was as futile to analyze government by studying its outward forms as it was to know men by observing only their appearance. What Taylor was reaching for was an understanding of the underlying moral concepts which made some governments good, no matter what their form or classification happened to be, and some governments bad. Forms of government, or numerical classifications into monarchy, aristocracy and democracy, did not determine the policies of such governments; and it was the policies of governments which determined whether they were good or bad governments. Yet behind the policies were the underlying moral considerations, the ethic of the community, which motivated the governed and the governors alike.

Morally, man was not everywhere and at all times the same. "If man is not always morally the same, it is not true that he requires the same political regimen."[33] Thus no fixed system of mixed government or any other was necessarily the ideal form for a government to take. The only constancy in man was the originality, diversity, and variations between men of one time and place and those of another time and place. "Out of this intellectual variety, arises the impossibility of contriving one form of government, suitable for every nation; and also the fact that human nature, instead of begetting one form constantly, demonstrates its moral capacity, in the vast variety of its political productions."[34] Thus, although Adams had been led to the conclusion that one form of government is by

[33] John Taylor, *An Inquiry into the Principles and Policy of the Government of the United States* (New Haven: Yale University Press, 1950), p. 39.
[34] *Ibid.*

nature the supreme form, Taylor pushed aside any such conclusions and concentrated less on forms than on policies. It then became the burden of his work to prove "that the policy of the United States is rooted in moral or intellectual principles, and not in orders, clans or castes, natural or factitious. . . ."[35]

Having attacked Adams' system of mixed government, Taylor turned to Adams' division of society into classes or orders. The natural aristocracy which Adams had recognized was founded upon superior knowledge, virtue, or wealth. Yet, Taylor countered, neither knowledge nor virtue, if the English model was to be accepted, were necessarily inheritable entities. And so for an aristocracy based on wealth: "Alienation is the remedy for an aristocracy founded on landed wealth; inhibitions upon monopoly and incorporation, for one founded on paper wealth."[36] Indeed it was knowledge, one source of aristocracy, which had invented alienation and restrictions on monopolies as methods of destroying another source of aristocracy. Furthermore the extension of knowledge has always led to attacks upon claims of a natural aristocracy. "An opposition to aristocratical power seems to have been constantly coeval with an advance of national information."[37] Any society which fostered the spread of education worked in opposition to any scheme for the retention of an aristocracy.

> Knowledge and commerce, by a division of virtue, of talents, and of wealth among multitudes, have annihilated that order of men, who in past ages constituted "a natural aristocracy," (as Mr. Adams thinks) by exclusive virtue, talents and wealth.[38]

Taylor was quite ready to concede that where a superiority in virtue, talents, and wealth was combined in a body of men, they would govern, and in fact such men ought to be the governors. But his point was that in contemporary society there was no distinct class or order of men who possessed such combined superiority. These exclusive possessions in a distinct body of men were vestiges of the past and were not to be found in an educated, free society. The danger was that unscrupulous men might and, in fact, were attempting to use the instruments of government to give themselves the preferred positions of aristocrats.

35 *Ibid.*
36 *Ibid.*, p. 42.
37 *Ibid.*, p. 45.
38 *Ibid.*

Talents and virtue are now so widely distributed, as to have rendered a monopoly of either, equivalent to that of antiquity, impracticable; and if an aristocracy ought to have existed whilst it possessed such a monopoly, it ought not also to exist, because this monopoly is irretrievably lost. The distribution of wealth produced by commerce and alienation, is equal to that of knowledge and virtue, produced by printing; but as the first distribution might be artificially counteracted with a better prospect of success than the latter, aristocracy has abandoned a reliance on a monopoly of virtue, renown and abilities, and resorted wholly to a monopoly of wealth, by the system of paper and patronage. Modern taxes and frauds to collect money, and not ancient authors will therefore afford the best evidence of its present character.[39]

Having thus attacked the class division of society assumed by Adams, as well as the governmental system built upon such divisions, Taylor explained what he considered to be the true foundation for government. Government was based upon moral, not natural or physical causes. Morality in turn varied from society to society and from age to age.

Now the moral qualities of man, being only good and evil, every form of government must be founded in that principle of the two, which prevails, like every other human action of a moral nature. This analysis is anterior to that of monarchy, aristocracy and democracy, and is capable of displaying the true character of every government, of each of its sections, and of all its measures; objects to which the numerical analysis is utterly incompetent.[40]

It was thus possible to evaluate any government by examining its character in the same manner in which one would study the character of an individual. A government founded upon the principles of fraud, deceit or avarice would produce evil effects, while a government based upon "good" moral principles "such as honesty, self-government, justice, and knowledge" would produce good effects.[41] The policies of a government were thus indicative of its true character.

Now the true moral principles upon which the government of the United States was founded were the "good" ones given above. In fact, this nation was the first republic to be established upon "good" moral principles. Furthermore the form of government was

[39] *Ibid.*, p. 57.
[40] *Ibid.*, p. 62.
[41] *Ibid.*

conducive to maintaining these principles because a fundamental division of power was set up between the national and state governments and another equally fundamental division of authority was made between the voters and their governments. A minimum of power was given to each government with the citizens retaining control over all governments. As a result, Taylor believed, the morality of the governments would normally follow that of the citizenry. That is, it would if evil persons in government did not pervert the system away from its true character. Such regrettable perversion was actually taking place, Taylor believed, because the Federalists and their retinue had grossly distorted the original constitutional system, had sought deceitfully to establish an exclusive class in society through the grants of special charters and monopolies and had entrenched their system by means of judicial review. Not until the people themselves were made fully aware of how their liberties had been taken away could the system be brought back to its true moral principles. It was Taylor's hope "that a common sentinel may awaken an army"[42] and that his writings would inspire all democrats to return the government of the United States to its "good" moral principles.

In his subsequent works, *Constitutions Construed and Constitutions Vindicated* (1820), *New Views of the Constitution of the United States* (1823), and *Tyranny Unmasked* (1822), he continued to attack the growing power of the national government. Legislative intervention in the economy was redistributing property and fostering monopoly. Equating *laissez-faire* economics with "good" moral principles, he saw in the Federalists' economic system a threat to the national welfare. The factory capitalists were the dreaded aristocracy who would in time upset the natural agrarian economy. As an antidote to this development Taylor pleaded for *laissez faire* and states' rights. "To define the nature of a government truly," he wrote in *Constitutions Construed and Constitutions Vindicated* (1820), "I would say, that a power of distributing property, able to gratify avarice and monopoly, designated a bad one; and that the absence of every such power, designated a good one."[43]

John Taylor and Thomas Jefferson expressed a conception of democracy that stood in marked contrast to the political theory of the Federalists. The followers of Hamilton sought the firm establish-

[42] *Ibid.*, p. 34.
[43] John Taylor, *Construction Construed and Constitutions Vindicated* (Richmond: Shepherd and Pollard, 1820), p. 15.

ment of national governmental powers; Jeffersonians sought to curtail and restrict national power. Hamiltonians sought a close alliance
between capitalism and the political system, between leaders in
industry and finance and the national government; Jeffersonians
saw in this alliance the creation of a new form of favoritism and
a new kind of aristocracy. Hamiltonians were primarily industrially-
minded, where Jeffersonians were basically agrarian-conscious. The
Federalists of New England inclined toward an elitism founded
on property and commercial wealth, while the Jeffersonians in the
South spoke up for a natural equality of men even in the midst of
Negro slavery. Nationalism, elitism, and power characterized the
theory of the Federalists; limited government, democracy, and
human rights characterized the theory of the Jeffersonians. Taken
together, these basic concepts were the major continuing issues
in American politics. Indeed, it may be said that the distinctive
achievement of the Federalists was the establishment of power on
a national basis, while the Jeffersonians established the premises
which in time put national power on a democratic foundation.

CHAPTER 8

The Concept of the Common Man

THAT period usually known as the "era of good feeling" was but a lull before the storm that broke out in American politics. The old issues of nationalism *vs.* states' rights, of the propertied aristocracy *vs.* popular government, were raised again but the conflict was made more bitter by the rapid institutional changes that took place. Between 1820 and 1840 the suffrage was rapidly extended throughout many of the states; the ballot was lengthened and the terms of public office shortened. These devolpments were a manifest departure from the conservatism of the Federalists. The seeds of Jeffersonian theory finally came to life in the Jacksonian period, and their varied bloom made the age of Jackson one of the most interesting and bewildering epochs in American politics. Yet for all its varied manifestations—the utopian communities, the intellectual individualists, the workers and the frontiersman in the political arena—the fact remains that the essence of this period was a resurgence of democratic theory and practice, and extension of the democratic faith.

To the extent that there was an underlying and unifying theme to the Jacksonian movement, it existed in an emphasis upon equality. Certainly it was this emphasis that impressed the Frenchman, Alexis De Tocqueville, when he observed the democracy of the Jacksonian period.[1] Equality did not mean that men were or ought to be equal in talents or possessions, but rather that men were by nature and should be by law equal in their rights. The Jacksonians did not feel that this emphasis on equality added anything new in political theory; on the contrary, what they intended was a return to the principles of the Declaration of Independence. What was asserted, therefore, was that all men were indeed equally possessed of

[1] See Alexis De Tocqueville, *Democracy In America* (New York and London: Oxford University Press, 1947), pp. 3-7.

174

rights. The Federalists and their followers had developed a program of national banks and tariffs which the Jacksonians found to be basically in conflict with the philosophy of equal rights. The Jacksonian impetus was thus to correct this political pattern so that a fundamental equality might be realized. The struggle of the Jacksonian democrats was directed against special favors and privileges and waged on behalf of the common man. It opposed the prerogatives of property—special charters, monopolies, the exclusive benefits of the few—with the demands of rights and benefits for all. It was during this era that the woman's rights and abolitionist movements began. Believing in the equal rights of all men, Jacksonianism countered political privilege with a demand for the abolition of property qualifications for voting or for holding public office. Opposed to economic privilege, it attacked the Bank of the United States as well as various state-granted monopoly charters. In contrast to Federalist economics it offered *laissez faire,* which it construed to mean economic opportunity for all without governmental favor to any. The system of Hamilton and Marshall had led to special favors to the few, with monopoly charters of banks and bridges. Fearful of a moneyed aristocracy promoted and protected by government, Jacksonian democracy called for free competition as the true economic expression of an equal-rights system. Assuming a harmonious universe, it posited an essential harmony of economic interests among free men. Once the special privileges of the few were removed, this essential harmony might be realized. The Jacksonian program thus sought, in economics and politics, to open wider the doors of opportunity for all men by removing the restrictions and prerequisites which heretofore had favored property holders and men of wealth.

PROPERTY AND POLITICAL POWER

That men possessed a right to property as well as to life and liberty was as much a part of the belief of the Jacksonian democrats as it had been of the Federalists. Yet to the conservative propertied interests the pattern of events appeared to represent a Jacobinical assault on property in the name of the common people. The issue between popular power and property rights was pointed up in the extensive discussions over the qualifications for voting. Between 1820 and 1830, Massachusetts, New York and Virginia held constitutional conventions in which suffrage and popular representation were debated at some length. Essentially at issue in each of the conventions was the question of whether all freemen, regardless of property holdings, might control the representation in the state senate as well as in the lower house. Each of these states under its old constitution had provided for a senate so constituted that it would serve as a check by the propertied classes upon the lower house representing the people. The discussions in regard to altering this arrangement thus involved the questions of the purpose of the separation of powers, and the rights or interests of property in the community.

Those who sought to reform the state constitutions argued that the denial of the right of all freemen to vote for their senators as well as their representatives was a denial of the principles of popular liberty. They maintained that an elimination of property qualifications for voting in no way jeopardized the right to possess property, for they acknowledged the validity of property rights. The attack upon property qualifications for voting, they pointed out, was not an attack upon property in any sense but merely an attack upon a barrier which stood in the path of democracy. Were the masses really in conflict with the rich as the conservatives feared, then, the reformers observed, the niceties of political and legal behavior would hardly serve as adequate restraints upon the majority of men. Thus they denied the existence of a class struggle between those who possessed and those who did not possess property. They further argued that the reform of the senate would in no way impair the operation of the separation of powers system, for one branch of the legislature would still be able to check the ill-considered enactments of the other. Essentially the movement to achieve suffrage reform was, as at later times in our history, an effort to realize a system whereby government actually rested upon the consent of those governed.

There were many distinguished political figures in the conservative camp. Here were found Daniel Webster, Joseph Story, James Kent and John Marshall. Of the various spokesmen for the propertied interests, Daniel Webster (1782-1852) may be selected as having given one of the most systematic defenses of the established order. Speaking before the Massachusetts Convention, he argued in favor of the old constitutional provision whereby the senators were apportioned according to the taxable property in each district rather than in accordance with population. If the propertied interests were not to have a distinct representation in the legislature, he pointed out, it was meaningless to have a bicameral arrangement. Understanding the separation-of-powers system to mean the mixed or balanced government of John Adams, he held that the removal of the propertied element would in fact destroy the separation of powers. In other words, it was his contention that only by having separately represented interests could there be a genuine separation of powers. The reform proposal would thus destroy this separation, for should the members of both houses be "chosen at the same time, by the same electors, in the same districts, and for the same term of office," then it would follow that they would "all be actuated by the same feelings and interests." Thus, though the legislature met in separate chambers, it would be essentially a unicameral body from the point of view of representation. "If all Legislative power be in one popular body," he warned, "all other power, sooner or later, will be there also."[2]

Webster took the position previously taken by John Marshall in *Marbury vs. Madison* that the popular branch of government was merely the agent of the sovereign people. Although the lower house represented the people, it was nevertheless not the people themselves. Thus he argued that "The Senate is not to be a check on the People, but on the House of Representatives." The senate, representing the taxpayers, would thereby protect the people from the improper actions of the popularly elected representatives. Senators, like representatives, were merely agents of the people, so that when one house checked the other it was in effect one agent of the people restraining another agent of the people.

> This does not limit the power of the people, but only the authority of their agents. It is not a restraint on their rights, but a restraint on that power which they have delegated. It limits the authority of agents, in making laws to bind their principals.[3]

Finally, Webster opposed the reform on the ground that unless military force intervened "political power naturally and necessarily goes into the hands which hold the property." Citing with approval Harrington's *Oceana*, Webster noted that it was the laws governing the transmission of property which determined the character of political institutions. Since our governmental institutions were in large measure founded on our property system, "it is entirely just that

---

[2] *Journal of Debates and Proceedings in the Convention of Delegates Chosen to Revise the Constitution of Massachusetts, 1820* (Boston: 1853), pp. 305, 307.
[3] *Ibid.*, p. 307.

property should have its due weight and consideration, in political arrangements."[4] The property system could best be preserved by maintaining the senate check upon popular power; and since the property system was directly related to the political system, it could be said that the maintenance of our political system rested upon the continuance of the senate check.

In spite of the protests of Webster and other conservatives, constitutional reforms in favor of greater popular control took place in Massachusetts, New York, and Virginia.[5] The contest over the extension of democracy in the states revealed a fundamental conflict in attitude regarding the institution of property. Those who sought, as well as those who opposed, the extension of democracy were in basic agreement upon the desirability of maintaining the institution of private property. They were equally in agreement that the right to possess property carried with it the right to have property protected by the government. Here, however, the parties diverged in their thinking. The conservatives maintained that since the many held little property in comparison with the holdings of the few, and since everyone desired to hold private property, then the many would seek to acquire the property of the few. If private property was not desired by all, then no problem would exist, for property would fall only into the hands of those who desired it. But since the possession of property was indeed a universal desire, then there was an inevitable conflict, in fact a class struggle, between those who possessed property and those who were without property. In the New York constitutional convention Chancellor James Kent observed:

> There is a constant tendency in human society, and the history of every age proves it; there is a tendency in the poor to covet and to share the plunder of the rich; in the debtor to relax or avoid the obligation of contracts; in the majority to tyrannize over the minority, and trample down their rights; in the indolent and the profligate, to

---

[4] *Ibid.*, p. 312.

[5] The suffrage movement during this period led De Tocqueville to the following observation: "When a nation modifies the elective qualification, it may easily be foreseen that sooner or later that qualification will be entirely abolished. There is no more invariable rule in the history of society: the further electoral rights are extended, the greater is the need of extending them; for after each concession the strength of the democracy increases, and its demands increase with its strength. The ambition of those who are below the appointed rate is irritated in exact proportion to the great number of those who are above it. The exception at last becomes the rule, concession follows concession, and no stop can be made short of universal suffrage." *Democracy in America*, p. 49.

cast the whole burdens of society upon the industrious and the virtuous. . . .[6]

Were the "poor," the "debtor," the "indolent and the profligate" not in the majority, then the "industrious and virtuous" few would have nothing to fear from majority rule. By making an invidious camparison between the morality of the few and that of the many and further equating the propertied, taxpaying citizens with the virtuous minority, it was not difficult to give to the issue of property against popular rule the proportions of a contest between good and evil.

Futhermore, the conservatives pointed out that they had a vested interest in the government which the majority lacked. All men were concerned that the government properly protect them in their life and liberty. However, the basic rights generally agreed upon were life, liberty, and property. Those who held property were concerned to see that all three of their basic rights were protected, while those without property were only concerned with being protected in the rights of life and liberty. Those who held property had more at stake and therefore had a greater interest in adequate government than those without property. As Chancellor Kent noted:

> Society is an association for the protection of property as well as of life, and the individual who contributes only one per cent to the common stock, ought not to have the same power and influence in directing the property concerns of the partnership, as he who contributes his thousands.[7]

It was, after all, the property owners who paid the taxes which made it possible for government to protect people in all their rights. Government was therefore not only a social necessity but also an investment made by those who paid the taxes. To argue, therefore, that political power should reside in the hands of the majority of the people unchecked by the property interests would be to argue that the stockholders should not control the policies of the corporation. The conservatives thought of the government as one vast public corporation whose policies should be subject to the control of those who had made the greatest financial investments in it.

Those who sought to extend democracy argued in return that the association of poverty and vice was unjustified, for the rich were as

[6] *Reports of the Proceedings and Debates of the Convention of 1821, Assembled for the Purpose of Amending the Constitution of the State of New York,* Albany, 1821, p. 221.
[7] *Ibid.,* p. 221.

guilty of vice as the poor. Furthermore, if the poor were eligible to fill the ranks of the army in time of war, then they ought to be considered eligible to control the destinies of the country in time of peace.[8] As to the argument that the property holders had a greater stake in society than the propertyless, it was observed that people and not property were the basic concern of society; that the equality of humanity took precedence over the inequality of personal possessions. Thomas Lincoln emphasized this point in the Massachusetts convention.

> Our government is one of the people, not a government of property. Representation is founded on the interests of the people. It is because they have rights that they have assumed the power of self government. Property is incompetent to sustain a free government. Intelligence alone can uphold any free government. In a government of freemen property is valuable only as the people are intelligent. Were it not for a government of the people, the people would be without property.[9]

The theory that there should be no taxation without representation was not intended to mean that representation should be based upon the degree of taxation. Furthermore, in one form or another, all men paid taxes.

JAMES FENIMORE COOPER

Additional support for the elimination of property qualifications for voting and for a general extension of democracy came from the novelist James Fenimore Cooper (1789-1851). This wealthy landed aristocrat, squire of Cooperstown, might well have been expected to bolster the ranks of the propertied interests. Indeed, Cooper is usually associated with conservative political thought, for in his later writings especially he was highly critical of his fellow countrymen. *The American Democrat* (1838), for instance, shows Cooper to be a scathing aristocratic critic of Jacksonian democracy. At the same time, like John Taylor of Caroline, Cooper was a member of the landed gentry who saw in America the rise to political power of the

[8] The curious relationship of fighting and voting, interpreted to mean that if one is old enough to fight he is therefore old enough to vote, has often been discussed in America. It came up again during and following World War II.

[9] *Journal of Debates and Proceedings in the Convention of Delegates Chosen to Revise the Constitution of Massachusetts, 1820*, new edition, revised and corrected (Boston, 1853), p. 265.

entrepreneur. And like Taylor he feared the consequences of bourgeois control. Thus for all his aristocratic leanings as one of the landed class, or perhaps because of them, Cooper was sympathetic to the Democratic claims of equality in rights rather than to the Whig tendencies toward an aristocracy of the capitalist merchants and traders.

From 1826-1833 Cooper visited in Europe, where he found little understanding of the American conception of democracy. In his effort to enlighten Europe on the American system, he wrote *Notions of the Americans Picked Up By a Travelling Bachelor* (1828). It was in this work that he made his defense of the growing American system of universal manhood suffrage. First he took issue with those who attributed the prosperity of America to its geographical situation. Its prosperity was rather due, he believed, to the intelligence of the people, which in turn was due to American institutions. Popular education was such an essential American institution; so also was popular control of the government. Ideally, of course, political control would be better if the ignorant and profligate were not allowed to vote. "It is just as true that if all the rogues and corrupt politicians, even including those who read Latin and have well-lined pockets, could be refused the right of voting, honest men would fare all the better." Clearly this could not be achieved without the substitution of a despotism, so that Americans had concluded "that it is scarcely worth while to do so much violence to natural justice, without sufficient reason, as to disfranchise a man merely because he is poor." While under certain conditions of society it might be expedient to have a small amount of property serve as a qualification for voting, it should never be understood that property ought to be represented in government. Against the principle of property-representation in government, Cooper wrote:

A man may be a voluntary associate in a joint-stock company and justly have a right to a participation in its management in proportion to his pecuniary interest, but life is not a chartered institution. Men are born with all their wants and passions, their means of enjoyment, and their sources of misery, without any agency of their own, and frequently to their great discomfort. Now, though government is, beyond a doubt, a sort of compact, it would seem that those who prescribe its conditions are under a natural obligation to consult the rights of the whole.[10]

[10] James Fenimore Cooper, *Notions of the Americans Picked Up By a Travelling Bachelor* (Philadelphia: Carey, Lea, and Carey, 1828), vol. I, pp. 264-265. The two quotations from Cooper that follow are from *ibid.*, p. 268 and pp. 269-270, respectively.

Were men a little closer to the angels, then government might rea-sonably be entrusted to the intelligent few. "But the experience of the world goes to prove that there is a tendency to monopoly wherever power is reposed in the hands of a minority." Such a monopoly of power would inevitably lead to uncontrolled abuse. To prevent such a monopolization of power, it was therefore necessary to diffuse it widely.

Such a wide diffusion of political power would have certain decided advantages. First, impecunious men preferred frugal government. The most profligate governments in the world, observed Cooper, were the governments controlled by the rich. "We find that our government is cheaper and even stronger for being popular." Second, popular control of the government carried with it the necessity for frequent elections. Opponents of democracy had charged that the frequency of political contests would produce an instability in government which would lead to its collapse. On the contrary, Cooper argued, the frequency of elections had been a major factor in producing stability in society, for frequency bred familiarity which often resulted in political indifference. The basic political questions in America were not questions regarding the form of government but rather in connection with "the ordinary immaterial question of a choice between men." Thirdly, by having frequent elections in which the masses were entitled to vote it was made more difficult for either party to corrupt the voters in order to win their support. "No man can buy a state, a county, or even a town."

> If the question be one likely to unite the interests and the prejudices of the humbler classes, nine times in ten it is both more humane and wiser that they should prevail. That sort of splendid and treacherous policy which gives a fallacious luster to a nation by oppressing those who have the most need of support is manifestly as unwise as it is unjust.

Though Cooper did not share the tastes and culture of the common man, he had nevertheless sufficient faith that the political judgment of the common man would not be in general inferior to that of any other group of men. The American system of government, with its wide franchise, was clearly justified by experience. Should subsequent experience prove differently, Americans would no doubt quietly reform their system accordingly. "We have ever been reformers rather that revolutionists," he noted.

> Now it is the distinguishing feature of our policy that we consider man a reasonable being, and that we rather court than avoid the

struggle between ignorance and intelligence. We find that this policy rarely fails to assure the victory of the latter while it keeps down its baneful monopolies.

Cooper's justification of a broad system of suffrage was primarily a pragmatic one, built not so much upon any principles of right but on experience and in fact expediency. Experience had proven that it had worked satisfactorily and that the policies advocated by the more popular party were reasonable and proper. The extension of the suffrage had not in any real sense altered the American system of government. It had brought about no revolution, but only encouraged persistent reform. From the time of the Revolution, Americans had moved daily in the direction of democracy. The extension of the suffrage was but one aspect of this movement. "We are perfectly aware that, while the votes of a few thousand scattered individuals can make no great or lasting impression on the prosperity or policy of the country, their disaffection at being excluded might give a great deal of trouble." It was therefore expedient to extend the franchise, especially in view of the fact that experience had shown that no great harm resulted generally from such an extension.

While Cooper could in no sense be considered an equalitarian, for he was opposed to any leveling tendencies in society, he nevertheless bolstered the popular movement of the day. A defender of the rights of property, he nevertheless attacked property's undue influence in government and thus opposed those who would balance the political power of the people with property. A decade later, in *The American Democrat, or Hints on the Social and Civic Relations of the United States of America* (1838), he noted of the Whig claims to the "stake in society" principle: "Every man who has wants, feelings, affections and character has a stake in society." Property, therefore, gave one no exclusive claims upon the government. Indeed, a society was better off if property was not represented in the government at all.

A government founded on the representation of property, however direct or indirect, is radically vicious, since it is a union of two of the most corrupting influences to which man is subject. It is the proper business of government to resist the corruptions of money, and not to depend on them.[11]

[11] James Fenimore Cooper, *The American Democrat* (New York: Alfred A. Knopf, 1931), pp. 130, 133.

Cooper thus expressed much of the growing democratic sentiment of his day. Though property ought to be respected, it ought not to control government; and finally humanity was a more vital concern of society than wealth.

In general, the Democrats of the Jacksonian period sought a return to the principles of what they considered to be Jeffersonian democracy. They denied that any person or group of persons had a right to control the government because of a pecuniary interest in its maintenance. They sought a return to the natural-law principle that in the possession of rights all were equal. A government founded upon consent and intended to protect the equal rights of all men could not admit of the excessive influence of property. Their emphasis upon the equal rights of human beings was in no way a disparagement of either the value or importance of property. They opposed rather the view, as John Cramer caustically remarked, "that the *turf* is of all things the most sacred."[12] What they sought in effect was an extension of democracy according to the belief in a fundamental equality of men as men, rather than as property holders or taxpayers.

LAISSEZ FAIRE

The Jacksonian democrats followed in the Jeffersonian tradition of states' rights, and their political and economic policies were a repudiation of the Hamiltonian system. Jackson assumed an essential or natural harmony of interests in society where Hamilton had assumed a basic conflict in interests. To Hamilton, planning and control by the national government were necessary in order to bring about a prosperous and healthy economic system; to Jackson, a natural harmony existed which could only be impaired by governmental tampering. Where Jackson looked upon government as an agency to protect the equal rights of all, Hamilton had looked upon government as a promotional enterprise which would wed the moneyed interests to the Union. Thus where Hamilton had sought to augment the powers of the national government to benefit those in economic control, Jackson sought to curtail national power to benefit the common man. Indeed, Jackson opposed the promotional activities of the

[12] *Reports of the Proceedings and Debates of the Convention of 1821, Assembled for the Purpose of Amending the Constitution of the State of New York,* Albany, 1821, p. 238.

national government as an unwarranted and unconstitutional abuse of power. He opposed high tariffs, the use of national revenue for internal improvements, and taxes beyond the minimum required for the operation of the government. The national government, he felt, was strictly limited in its taxing and spending powers "It has no power to raise a revenue or impose taxes except for the purposes enumerated in the Constitution. . . ." With this limited view of national power, Jackson believed the Second Bank of the United States to be unconstitutional as well as unwise. For he believed that the Bank was one vast monopoly whose control rested in the hands of a few, although its monetary policies affected many. He wished in banking, as in other activities, a return to free competition. Opposed to a national banking monopoly, he was also opposed to the creation of state banking monopolies, for these too would concentrate excessive powers in the hands of the few.

> The agricultural, the mechanical, and the laboring classes have little or no share in the direction of the great moneyed corporations; and from their habits and nature of their pursuits, they are incapable of forming extensive combinations to act together with united force.[13]

Thus in place of special privileges, Jackson championed the inauguration of a *laissez-faire* policy in order to re-establish in America a system of equal rights and opportunity for all.

The Democratic position in favor of equal rights under a *laissez-faire* policy was given strong support in the editorials of the *New York Evening Post*. The editorials of William Cullen Bryant (1794-1878), who was one of its editors from 1826 until his death, and of William Leggett (1801-1839), an editor from 1829-1836, put that journal in the forefront of the democratic movement. Both Leggett and Bryant were staunch free traders, followers of Jeremy Bentham and the rising school of English liberals. Both men believed strongly in the cause of labor, the poor and the underprivileged. They believed, however, that this cause might be best promoted not by the passing of special legislation, but rather by the repealing of existing statutes which worked to the benefit of the few. They believed that if the government did not interfere with the economic system, labor would be able to rise through its own merits. Every man was equally entitled to stand upon his own feet, to sink or swim accord-

---

[13] See *Farewell Address of Andrew Jackson to the People of the United States: and the Inaugural Address of Martin Van Buren, President of the United States* (Washington, 1837), pp. 13-14.

ing to his abilities. With equal rights to all and privileges to none, they felt that both the prosperity of the country and the happiness of all the people would be advanced. In view of the later shift in liberal doctrine whereby *laissez faire* came to be considered the policy most hostile to labor, it is important to emphasize this Jacksonian association of *laissez faire* with the cause of labor. So extreme an advocate of *laissez faire* was Bryant that he even opposed laws restricting usury as arbitrary interferences with the exchange of money. Yet Bryant, unlike many later free traders, favored the right of labor to associate and to strike. In commenting upon a sentence passed in New York against twenty workmen who had refused to work at the wages offered by their employer, Bryant wrote:

> If this is not SLAVERY, we have forgotten the definition. Strike the right of associating for the sale of labour from the privileges of a freeman, and you may as well bind him to a master, or ascribe him to the soil. . . . Punish by human laws a "determination not to work," make it penal by any other penalty than idleness inflicts, and it matters little whether the task-masters be one or many, an individual or an order, the hateful scheme of slavery will have gained a foothold in the land.[14]

It was a spirited battle that the *Evening Post* waged in behalf of equal rights, a battle which carried on John Taylor's fight against the artificial aristocracy. But only through such a struggle, it was felt, could the rights of all be maintained, and only in this manner could free government survive. In an election editorial (Nov. 4, 1834), William Leggett stated the Democratic case against the Bank of the United States as an unconstitutional usurpation of public power. He raised again the cry of limited government, and viewed our federal system as one which granted to the national government only necessary, not convenient, powers. Then, launching into the Jacksonian theme he wrote:

> The privilege of self-government is one which the people will never be permitted to enjoy unmolested. Power and wealth are continually stealing from the many to the few. There is a class continually gaining ground in the community who desire to monopolize the advantage of the Government, to hedge themselves round with exclusive privileges and elevate themselves at the expense of the great

[14] From "The Right of Workmen to Strike" (1836), in Tremaine McDowell ed., *William Cullen Bryant, Representative Selections* (New York: American Book Co., 1935), p. 306.

body of the people. These, in our society, are emphatically the aristocracy. . . .[15]

The Jacksonian remedy for this evil was, essentially, the remedy proposed by the Jeffersonian writers. Confine the governments, both national and state, to their true functions of protecting person and property. This would destroy the paper aristocracy; this would achieve equal rights by permitting each man to acquire, through free competition with his neighbor, his proper place in society. No class would be favored nor any restricted, and no man could claim privileges against another. It was this faith in the ability of all men to make their way in this world which prompted the Jacksonians to espouse free competition. They believed equally that interference with this natural process led to privilege; from privilege to prescriptive claims; and from prescriptive claims to political inequality and political abuse. The prescriptive claims of any to hold public office, an idea attacked by Jackson in his first annual message, was felt to be contrary to a fundamental belief in equal rights. Special status or special legislation were found equally opposed to this basic belief. Without privilege or protection beyond that of a most elementary kind, the rich and the poor, the landowner and the tenant, the worker and his employer were to be equally placed outside the scope of governmental interference and left to their own resources.

ORESTES BROWNSON

Not all of the supporters of the Jacksonian movement, however, believed in that basic harmony of interests so essential to the legitimacy of *laissez faire*. A prominent dissenter was Orestes A. Brownson (1803-1876), one of the most interesting figures of the period. Like Roger Williams, he was a religious seeker, and his political ideas were heavily colored by his immediate theological convictions. In the course of his religious wanderings he moved from Presbyterianism to Unitarianism and finally found a haven in Catholicism. A man of strong social conscience, he was in his early years a political radical who sought to improve the condition of labor and who founded, in 1836, a church for workers in Boston called The Society for Christian Union and Progress. As editor of the *Boston*

[15] Cited in Joseph L. Blau, *Social Theories of Jacksonian Democracy* (New York: Hafner Publishing Co., 1947), p. 68.

Quarterly Review, later known as *Brownson's Quarterly Review,* he had an organ for his opinions and made full use of it.

In 1840 Brownson published in the *Boston Quarterly Review* a review of Thomas Carlyle's *Chartism* which indicated without equivocation his dissatisfaction with the existing economic system. This review, entitled "The Laboring Classes," some eight years prior to the *Manifesto* of Marx and Engels stated a theory of class struggle, of the political values of the middle class and the practitioners of organized religion, and of the inevitability of the revolution in which the proletariat would achieve control. The Chartist movement in England, for all the worthiness of its cause, was doomed to failure as an effort toward ameliorating the condition of the working class, Brownson maintained. No movement of the laboring class which was in any way dependent upon the support of the middle class could ever achieve success, because the interests of the latter were inevitably opposed to those of the former. In England, wrote Brownson, it was not the nobility who were the worst enemies of the worker, but rather the middle class. "The middle class is always a firm champion of equality when it concerns humbling a class above it, but it is its inveterate foe when it concerns elevating a class below it."[16]

Although the English commoners had brought down the old aristocracy, they had never done anything to raise up the workers, "the real *proletarii.*"

> Our despair for the poor Chartists arises from the number and power of the middle class. We dread for them neither monarchy nor nobility. Nor should they. Their only real enemy is in the employer. In all countries is it the same. The only enemy of the laborer is your employer, whether appearing in the shape of the master mechanic, or in the owner of a factory.

Throughout the world labor was oppressed by the employers of labor. Indeed the general law of remuneration for work was "that men are rewarded in an inverse ratio to the amount of actual service they perform." Thus the worker exhausted his efforts for a pittance, while his employer reaped the benefits of his labor. The great mass of workers exhausted "Their health, spirits, and morals without becoming one whit better off than when they commenced labor." Even in the United States, where capitalism had existed under most favorable circumstances, the situation was the same. In fact, in this

---

[16] The following quotations from "The Laboring Classes" are found in Blau, *op. cit.,* pp. 302-319; also in Joseph L. Blau, *American Philosophical Addresses, 1700-1900* (New York: Columbia University Press, 1946), pp. 174-204.

country workers were not as well off as they had been fifty years earlier when a worker might aspire to independence. The frontier having receded, new lands were now beyond the reach of the common laborer, who was thus confined and at the mercy of his employer.

So desperate did Brownson find the plight of labor that he found chattel slavery itself no more oppressive than the wage system of slavery. The amount of freedom possessed by a worker under either system was about equal. "The laborer at wages has all the disadvantages of freedom and none of its blessings, while the slave, if denied the blessings, is freed from the disadvantages."

> One thing is certain: That, of the amount actually produced by the operative, he retains a less proportion than it costs the master to feed, clothe, and lodge his slave. Wages is a cunning device of the devil for the benefit of tender consciences who would retain all the advantages of the slave system without the expense, trouble, and odium of being slaveholders.

Such was the condition of labor under the wage system, Brownson felt, that it could not be genuinely alleviated by any temporizing expedients. The remedy for such an inequitable situation would only be found through "war and bloodshed."

> It will be found only at the end of one of the longest and severest struggles the human race has ever been engaged in, only by that most dreaded of all wars, the war of the poor against the rich, a war which, however long it may be delayed, will come, and come with all its horrors. The day of vengeance is sure; for the world after all is under the dominion of a just Providence.

The struggle between wealth and labor was thus the just and inevitable result of the developing crisis. This was the new phase of that conflict which had run throughout history between king and barons, barons and merchants, landed capital and commercial capital. Because of its cataclysmic proportions it was of little use to head off this event by the traditionally proposed reforms of more education and religion. Education, so often heralded by the early nineteenth-century democrats as the panacea for most evils, provided no cure to Brownson. Carlyle had recommended further education to raise the laboring classes in England. Yet, Brownson questioned, suppose you educate the laborers? "Will they require less food and less clothing when educated than they do now?"

If you will doom them to the external condition of brutes, do in common charity keep their minds and hearts brutish. Render them as insensible as possible, that they may feel the less acutely their degradation and see the less clearly the monstrous injustice which is done them.

Nor would it be of any help to turn for real reform to the teachers of religion. The priests, as he called all teachers of organized religion, have had their day. They were the first civilizers of mankind, having substituted for man's savage freedom the "iron despotism of the theocrat." The priests, like the pedagogues, were on the side of the employers. "In a word they always league with the people's masters, and seek to reform without disturbing the social arrangements which render reform necessary." Because any real remedy for the existing inequalities would be opposed by the priestly class, a first step toward genuine reform would be found in the elimination of the priest. "The priest is universally a tyrant, universally the enslaver of his brethren, and therefore it is Christianity condemns him."

It should be noted that Brownson attacked the priestly class and not religion, that he attacked the Christian priests and preachers and not Christianity. His genuinely moralistic attack was made in the name of Christianity; in fact, to achieve the Christian relations of equality and the brotherhood of man he opposed all those who stood in the way of this accomplishment. "Priests are," he wrote, "in their capacity of priests, necessarily enemies of freedom and equality." Christianity itself, however, was essential to reform; only through a genuine belief in Christian values and a sincere concern to achieve them could social progress be accomplished.

Yet Christian belief alone was insufficient, for the evil was not individual but was inherent in the social system, and only when the existing social system was destroyed would the evil be removed. It was not the men but the system that was at fault.

Continue our present system of trade, and all its present evil consequences will follow, whether it be carried on by your best men or your worst. Put your best men, your wisest, most moral, and most religious men, at the head of your paper-money banks, and the evils of the present banking system will remain scarcely diminished. The only way to get rid of its evils is to change the system, not its managers.

Having thus attacked the usual approaches to the labor problem as being entirely inadequate, Brownson advanced his own solution.

Admittedly it was not a complete answer. However, he did go beyond the usual *laissez faire* of the period. "We have no faith," he noted, "in those systems of elevating the working classes which propose to elevate them without calling in the aid of government." The government ought to repeal all laws which operated against labor and substitute in place thereof laws beneficial to labor. Specifically, the government ought to be divorced from the control of the banks, and this was true at both the national and state levels of government. Like John Taylor before him, Brownson saw in the banking system an inexorable opponent of the people.

> The banks represent the interest of the employer, and therefore of necessity interests adverse to those of the employed; that is, they represent the interests of the business community in opposition to the laboring community.

Not only must the power of the banks be destroyed, but the government must be placed "in the hands of the laboring classes themselves or in the hands of those, if such there be, who have an identity of interest with them." Once the banking interests had become separate from the control of the government, the next step would be the eradication of all monopolies and special privileges. One such privilege especially that ought to be destroyed was the privilege of inheriting property. In this respect Brownson followed Jefferson's thesis that the earth belongs to the living, and not to the dead, even though he carried this principle to its furthest extreme. "A man shall have all he honestly acquires," Brownson advocated, "so long as he himself belongs to the world in which he acquires it. But his power over his property must cease with his life, and his property must then become the property of the State, to be disposed of by some equitable law for the use of the generation which takes his place."

Beyond these immediate remedies Brownson offered no general program. And even in the instance of these remedies he reasoned that the business community would never consent to them unless overpowered by force. Nevertheless, he was clearly sincere though often unpopular.

"Now the great work of our age," he wrote, "and that coming is to raise up the laborer, and to realize in our own social arrangements and in the actual condition of all men that equality between man and man which God has established between the rights of one and those of another."

THE DEMOCRATIC FAITH

Jacksonian democracy marked a resurgence of the democratic faith, a faith which found expression in the assault upon those institutions which were believed to place excessive power in the hands of the few at the expense of the majority of the people. In economic affairs this faith was generally expressed in the creed of strict construction of the Constitution and *laissez faire* practiced at all levels of government. The experience of more than a generation under a democratic form of government had proven, it was felt, that the experiment in democracy was clearly a success and all that was now needed was more democracy.

George Bancroft (1800-1891), scholar, minister, historian and statesman, was a major spokesman of this faith in American democracy and indeed in the common man everywhere. Born and educated in the New England stronghold of Federalism, Bancroft rebelled to join the ranks of the Democrats, and throughout his long life he retained his faith in the mission of democracy. His *History of the United States,* the labor of a lifetime, was a glowing account of the progressive fulfillment of the democratic ideal. His political speeches and writings described with missionary enthusiasm the course of democracy, a course which he believed to be a necessity of history; for he saw as surely as the early Puritans a Divine spirit manifested in earthly events. The era of the common man was not only a desirable event, but an inevitable one; and this was the mission of America, ordained by God.

In 1835 Bancroft revealed his faith in the mission of democracy in a speech entitled "The Office of the People In Art, Government, and Religion." He spoke of the *"spirit in man,"* in all men, not just in the "privileged few," a spirit or intuitive sense which led all men to truth. This spirit, implanted in man by God, was conscience, the common possession of all mankind. "Conscience, like reason and judgment, is universal."[17] In this was a fundamental equality of all men. "The Barbarian who roams our Western prairies," he wrote, contrary to the prevalent theory of racial superiority, "has like passions and like endowments with ourselves."[18] Since reason and

---

[17] George Bancroft, *Literary and Historical Miscellanies* (New York: Harper & Brothers, 1855), p. 411.
[18] *Ibid.,* p. 414.

conscience were possessed by all, then to find truth it was well to look to the common judgment of mankind. "The common mind winnows opinion; it is the sieve which separates error from certainty."[19] Thus, in opposition to the doctrine of the elite, that the masses were too ignorant or corrupt to render a reasonable judgment, Bancroft offered the doctrine of the common man and the universal judgment. Truth was a "bond of union" which drew men together, the high and the low, the scholar and the illiterate. Whereas the Federalists had lamented the rise of faction, Bancroft welcomed it, for he believed that within every party, every faction, though there might be much error, there was also some element of truth. He believed that in time the elements of error would be discarded while the elements of truth would survive to the benefit of subsequent mankind. He defended this view by returning to his original assumption of equal basic endowments. Though men might be temporarily swayed by passion or personal interests, in the long run the exercise of many minds on the same subjects would eventuate in similar conclusions. The free competition of ideas would lead to the certain knowledge of truth. It was the democratic system, he believed, which made possible the discovery of truth in politics.

> In like manner the best government rests on the people and not on the few, on persons and not on property, on the free development of public opinion and not on authority; because the munificent Author of our being has conferred the gifts of mind upon every member of the human race without distinction of outward circumstances. . . . A government of equal rights must, therefore, rest upon mind; not wealth, not brute force, the sum of moral intelligence of the community should rule the State.[20]

Hamilton had sought a government resting essentially on those with major economic interests and possessing the power to coerce, if necessary, the rest of the community into obedience. Bancroft's state was based essentially upon the intelligence of all mankind and the moral sense of the community. Thus the object of government was to promote the "public happiness." Such a government, based on the people, would not lead to anarchy as Hamilton had supposed, but on the contrary would be the strongest possible government resting on the firmest of foundations. A government based on the people generally would be a secure government, "for the multitude is neither rash nor fickle." It was the common man, Ban-

19 *Ibid.*, p. 415.
20 *Ibid.*, pp. 421-422.

croft believed, who had found and sought to have applied the "truths" of "Freedom of mind and conscience, freedom of the seas, freedom of industry, equality of franchises. . . ." In fact, he declared, the "Spirit of God breathes through the combined intelligence of the people."[21]

Because he believed in the indestructability of truth discerned by the common conscience of mankind, Bancroft was able to apply this conviction to arrive at a further belief in the inevitability of progress. Though dynasties, cities, and nations passed away or succumbed to error, nevertheless "humanity has always been on the advance, gaining maturity, universality, and power." Progress resulted from the acquisition of new truth by the masses of men and was therefore the inevitable handmaiden of democracy. The path of progress thus led to the further extension of democracy, an extension which was not only desirable in itself but a historical necessity. Bancroft's faith in the common man, in universal reason and conscience, when coupled with his belief in progress and historical necessity thus gave to American democracy a manifest destiny ordained by God.

WALT WHITMAN

It was Walt Whitman (1819-1892) who gathered together the humanitarian sentiment of this period and restated the values of Jacksonian democracy in such a compelling fashion as to deserve the title "poet of American democracy." It was indeed Whitman who first used the term "democratic faith."[22] Intensely democratic and intensely partisan (he identified the cause of democracy with that of the Democratic party in his early years), his editorship of the *Brooklyn Daily Eagle* (1846-1847) did yeoman service for the disciples of Andrew Jackson and William Leggett. Here was a poet whose robust lines proclaimed the dignity of all men, who spoke in favor of the common man. The man who in his verse declared, "Whoever degrades another degrades me," proclaimed in his prose the dignity of immigrants, mechanics, frontiersmen, the seamstress, the slave, paupers, and the sick. In his writings Whitman reveals the

[21] *Ibid.*, p. 425.
[22] Ralph Henry Gabriel, *The Course of American Democratic Thought* (New York: The Ronald Press, 1940), p. 123.

varied impulses that characterized the liberal aspects of this period of social ferment.

Though conservatives opposed an extension of the suffrage, Whitman defended the continued admittance of low-income workers to the ballot. This would spread democracy—and the fortunes of the Democratic party. In America was a chosen people, Whitman felt, whose mission was to prove the practicality of a political system founded upon a firm belief in the dignity of man. And, like Bancroft, Whitman saw and delighted in, though he abhorred war, the vision of the American eagle sweeping across the continent, up into Canada, down into Mexico. This was to Whitman the age of the common man, of progress, of manifest destiny. Behind was the age of aristocracy, of restriction, the tight little world of men in small clothes with smaller ideas; ahead lay the era of liberality, the age of the democratic triumph.

In Whitman, as with other Jacksonian democrats, was the curious combination of a zealous humanitarianism and classical economics. To promote freedom, one must remove restrictions. Reasoning from the past, from aristocratic authoritarianism, it was believed that restrictions were found primarily in governmental policy and not in social institutions. Thus, to promote freedom one must remove governmental restrictions. Such a program, it was believed, would promote the cause of the worker, the mechanic and the dispossessed for each would be free from governmental restrictions to pursue his own interests.

Whitman assumed a close relationship between free enterprise—in the classical-economics sense—and the democratic impulse. Thus he found the followers of Hamilton, the Whigs in his day, on the side of the upper economic class, and in favor of governmental intervention in the economic sphere. Like John Taylor before him, he decried class legislation and class control. The more popular the democracy, he thought, the closer would governmental policy approximate *laissez-faire*. "We must be constantly pressing onward—every year throwing the doors wider and wider—and carrying our experiment of democratic freedom to the very verge of the limit," he noted in 1846.[23] In the same editorial he continued, "We will see whether the law of happiness and preservation upon each individual, acting directly upon himself, be not a safer dependence than

[23] Walt Whitman, *The Gathering of the Forces*, edited by Cleveland Rodgers and John Black (New York: G. P. Putnam's Sons, 1920), vol. I, p. 10.

musty charters and time-worn prerogatives of tyrants."[24] Whitman thus saw popular government as a means of making possible a heightened degree of individualism. Conservatives, fearing popular government, feared also the lifting of governmental restraints. It was the liberals, then, who sought less government even as the conservatives sought more. It was the conservatives who feared this novel experiment. But, Whitman noted, "All that we enjoy of freedom was in the beginning but an experiment."[25] The experiment was thus in the direction of self-government considered in a personal sense, and away from the traditional form of politically-organized social control. Where a century later "experiment" took on a social and political connotation generally signifying a new form of governmental direction and control, in the Whitman sense the term meant the absence or diminution of political authority. "There must be continual additions to our great experiment of how much liberty society will bear. . . ."[26] In Whitman, as in Emerson, democracy was associated with individualism and a keen sense of self-reliance.

> In plain truth, "the people expect too much of the government." Under a proper organization (and even to a great extent as things are), the wealth and happiness of the citizens could hardly be touched by the government—could neither be retarded nor advanced. *Men* must be "masters unto themselves," and not look to Presidents and legislative bodies for aid. In this wide and naturally rich country, the best government indeed is "that which governs least."
>
> One point, however, must not be forgotten—ought to be put before the eyes of the people every day; and that is, although government can do little *positive* good to the people, it may do an *immense deal of harm.* . . .
>
> Really, however, the principles that lie at the root of true government, are not hard of comprehension. The error lies in the desire after *management,* the great curse of our Legislation: everything is to be regulated and made straight by force of statute. . . . The true office of government, is simply to preserve the rights of each citizen from spoliation: when it attempts to go beyond this, it is intrusive and does more harm than good.[27]

It should be clear that the concept of governmental function is conditioned by the prior concept of social goals, of individual rights, and by opinion concerning the degree to which they are subject to

---

[24] *Ibid.,* p. 11.
[25] *Ibid.*
[26] *Ibid.,* p. 12.
[27] *Ibid.,* pp. 52, 54.

spoliation. Continuing the Jeffersonian tradition, Whitman saw rights as threatened primarily by the government, not by private institutions. He deplored the tariff as an instance of class legislation which jeopardized the economic rights of the poor. But the conception of economic rights was itself not clearly established at this time. Every man was obliged to work, but no one had such a right to a job that the government ought to protect him in this regard from spoliation. Whitman lamented the poor pay of factory women and insisted that there was a close connection between women's wages and crime. Yet he saw no remedy beyond an "awakened public opinion," which would inspire the populace to a greater benevolence.

Individualism and self-reliance, coupled with benevolent humanitarianism, marked the progress of social and political reform.

> And, it is to this progressive spirit that we look for the ultimate attainment of the perfectest possible form of government—that will be where there is the *least* possible *government,* so called—when monopolies shall be things that *were,* but are not—when the barbarism of restrictions on trade shall have passed away—when . . . the plague spot of slavery, with all its taint to freemen's principles and prosperity, shall be allowed to spread no *further.* . . .[28]

This was Whitman's dream of the fulfillment of liberal democracy.

Though Whitman broke with the Democratic party for its espousal of slavery (he had little use for abolitionists either), he never lost his faith in individualism and popular government. Following the Civil War, in his *Democratic Vistas* (1871) he asserted again his belief in the people, for all their faults; in the common man, for all his ill-manners and illiteracy. He appealed for a higher taste in morality, in literature, in politics, and trusted in more and better education to bring these goals about. And he never doubted that, for all the unpleasant features of democracy, individuals could succeed in personal fulfillment. And this was of vital consequence to Whitman. "This idea of perfect individualism it is indeed that deepest tinges and gives character to the idea of the aggregate."[29] Though he spoke for Union, he spoke also for the States, for the diversity that gives meaning to association whether among men or among political units.

[28] *Ibid.,* p. 219.
[29] Walt Whitman, *The Complete Prose of Walt Whitman* (New York: Pellegrini and Cudahy, 1948), vol. II, p. 218.

To be a voter with the rest is not so much; and this, like every institute, will have its imperfections. But to become an enfranchised man, and now, impediments removed, to stand and start without humiliation, and equal with the rest; to commence, or have the road cleared to commence, the grand experiment of development, whose end (perhaps requiring several generations) may be the forming of a full-grown man or woman—that *is* something.[30]

Whitman thus maintained his sense of the development of the individual, of society, toward some far-off perfect goal. This idea of progress, of individual and social progress, overbalanced his concern with the disruptive and degrading tendencies in society. He saw a middle-class America emerging, and saw in this a safe, enduring state. "The true gravitation-hold of liberalism in the United States will be a more universal ownership of property, general homesteads, general comfort—a vast intertwining reticulation of wealth."[31] Yet though he looked toward a middle-class America of employed, home-owning men and women, he attacked the impulse toward conformity so often associated with the politics of the middle class. He attacked the "inertness and fossilism" of human institutions. "As circulation to air, so is agitation and a plentiful degree of speculative license to political and moral sanity."[32] Like Jefferson before him, he sought goodness and virtue following in the path of freedom. Thus he gave encouragement to "freedom's athletes."

Vive, the attack—the perennial assault! Vive, the unpopular cause —the spirit that audaciously aims—the never-abandoned efforts, pursued the same amid opposing proofs and precedents. . . .[33]

Thus did Walt Whitman, no longer editor, but aspiring poet and employee of the Department of the Interior—until dismissed on the charge that *Leaves of Grass* (1855) was immoral—carry the gospel of the common man, democracy and liberty into a new generation.

The Jacksonian faith in the common man, the reassertion of the democratic values of equality and freedom, marked the acceptance by a later generation of the basic tenets of Jeffersonian democracy. This faith in the many and not just the few, in common conscience, in the capacity for all mankind for knowledge, was essentially the faith of Jefferson as it had been the faith of John Locke. The deep humanitarianism of the period—the obvious con-

30 *Ibid.*, p. 222.
31 *Ibid.*, p. 225.
32 *Ibid.*, p. 224.
33 *Ibid.*, p. 226.

cern for the poor, the lowly and the dispossessed—gave impetus to the demand for social, economic, and political reform. Jefferson and John Taylor had formulated the basic theories which the Jacksonians attempted to put into practice; beyond this, however, the age of Jackson made its own distinctive contribution, for it initiated the concept of humanitarian democracy. It was this characteristic of Jacksonian democracy which made it one of the truly remarkable epochs in the history of American reform movements.

CHAPTER 9

The New Society: Individualists and Utopians

THE JACKSONIAN movement was but a part, although an integral part, of a ferment that was taking place in America during the 1830's and 40's. Abroad, in Europe, reaction had followed close on the heels of the age of reason, aided in large measure by the rise and fall of Napoleon Bonaparte. The revolutions in 1830 and 1848 were expressed manifestations of repressed reform movements that refused to remain repressed. In America, however, reform and progress were the guiding spirits of the age, needing no revolutions to achieve their effects. The reforms proposed were not only reasonable, but were not dependent upon reason alone; for they appealed to sentiment and instinct as well as to the mind. Romanticism thus invaded the sphere of politics, and cold reason was warmed by conscience.

This was the age in which Lucretia Mott and Elizabeth Cady Stanton wrote a *Declaration of Sentiments* (1848) in behalf of the rights of women, and the brilliant, educated feminist Margaret Fuller wrote *Woman in the Nineteenth Century* (1844). All men were created equal, but so indeed were women. Furthermore, in point of fundamental rights, men and women were created equal and entitled to the same basic privileges in society. These were the times in which Frances Wright shocked her contemporaries by delivering public lectures and by advocating a system of public education, and Dorothea Dix sought more humane treatment for those in mental institutions and wrote a *Memorial to the Legislature of Massachusetts* (1843) to justify her argument. That women could and did enter into the controversies over reform was itself an aspect of the age. But the issue of reform went further and deeper still; it sought to alleviate on the grounds of humanity the suffering of all those oppressed, down-trodden members of society who were controlled without their consent and who were exploited contrary to the common conscience of mankind. Oppressive institutions were the illegitimate offspring of an indecent past. Since reason and sentiment were contrary to oppression in any form, progress consisted in the elimination of such oppressions. Women's rights, the rights of labor, the eradication of slavery, prison reform, the extension of the suffrage, temperance, the abolition of war, popular education— these were the causes of the day, and each cause had its hosts of adherents. This new age was also the age of William Cullen Bryant, Walt Whitman, Nathaniel Hawthorne, James Fenimore Cooper, and Herman Melville, as well as the historians W. H. Prescott, J. L. Motley, Francis Parkman, George Bancroft and others. There were many commentators and many critics of American society, and this fact was in itself important, for Americans had become indeed self-conscious. They looked upon American society, its institutions, and its government with pride and protest. They looked with pride upon its achievements, with enthusiasm on the things still to be achieved and with protest upon all the barriers to these achievements.

America was experiencing a reaffirming of an earlier revolutionary faith in man, in America, indeed in all mankind. It was a faith that transcended immediate political experience, a faith that transcended as well the recorded experience of mankind. Nevertheless the essential point was that man was more than a political being; that the real man was not just a voter, a member of the caucus, a worker, a farmer, a capitalist, but someone who lived above and beyond the standard categorizations of society, someone who was at once separate from but yet a part of the conventional institutions of society and essentially in harmony with nature. This new hope, full of promise, full of eternals beyond the obviously limited experience of birth and death, offered mankind a heaven still attainable on earth. Old reason was conservative, offering the past as testimony against the present, offering facts against intuition. Intuition was the spark that came to each man born anew, while facts were the inheritance of the past. It was again the war of science against theology, only now science was reduced to accepted institutions and theology was called the noblest sentiments of mankind. Eighteenth-century rationalism had merged in America with nineteenth-century romanticism to form an optimistic and democratic romantic rationalism, full of faith and promise, with the future offered as testimony against the present. Here was a new resurrection, a new life, offered in terms understandable to the deistic mind, which was not accustomed to bow the knee to any priest or catechism, but sought fulfillment in a belief that merged the individual with the grandeur of the universe. There was a religious impulse to this new romanticism, but it went beyond religion. It encompassed an entire philosophy of life, which certainly included religion, but which also included every aspect of man's relationship with man as well. The intended result was not political philosophy, but the resulting doctrine inevitably included this subject. Thus it was that Emerson and Thoreau wrote in a vein which swept into the mainstream of American political thought without intending such a result.

EMERSON

Ralph Waldo Emerson (1803-1882), lecturer, essayist, was the major prophet and philosopher of the movement known as American transcendentalism. Transcendentalism itself was derived from the thinking of many nations; from Kant in Germany, Coleridge in England, Fourier in France, as well as Buddhist literature. In America, Unitarianism paved the way for transcendentalism by its demand, reminiscent of the early Protestant revolt, for a more direct relationship between man and God, between man and universal Truth, not dependent upon the established ecclesiastical hierarchies. It sought in effect a new priesthood of all believers which was not even dependent upon belief in the Bible as a source of faith and understanding. William Ellery Channing (1780-1842), in his sermons and writings, fostered the Unitarian idea of the divinity of man made manifest by his noble sentiments and intuition. Transcendentalist literature thus superimposed upon the findings of science and the deductions of reason a romantic faith in the integrity of the individual human being as well as the general benevolence of the Deity and the universe. It was romantic, mystical, and inspirational and seemed in the 1840's well suited to the expansive temperament of America. Primarily, however, its importance lay in its emphasis upon the individual who might, by developing his own potentialities, achieve heaven, or its equivalent, here on earth.

Although Emerson had published a little book entitled *Nature* in 1836, it was not until the following year when he delivered his Phi Beta Kappa address at Harvard that he received public recognition. This address, *The American Scholar,* was a call upon all men to exert their own intellectual powers and to cast off their traditional dependence upon others. The scholar he pictured was not a bookworm laboring in a private chamber but rather, as he simply put it, "Man Thinking." And Emerson called upon all men to be as scholars, to think again and to think anew. The scholar, the thinking man drawing upon nature with its magnificent manifestation of unity and purpose, upon the past in whatever form portrayed, and upon his own action and experience, was fit to cope with the best minds and the best theories. It was a message of youthful hope and inspiration which called upon each new age to write its own books and prepare its own rules. It was in a sense a paraphrase of Jefferson's contention that the earth belongs to the living and not to the dead. "The one thing in the world, of value, is the active soul," declared Emerson.[1] Looking out to nature, and inward to himself, the scholar was not dependent upon the genius of others. "Books are for the scholar's idle times. When he can read God directly, the hour is too precious to be wasted in other men's transcripts of their readings."[2] Educated by nature, by books and by action, it was the scholar's noble duty to trust himself, his judgments, and his insights. With such an education and such a trust the scholar would then know—

> The world is nothing, the man is all; in yourself is the law of all nature, and you know not yet how a globule of sap ascends; in yourself slumbers the whole of Reason; it is for you to know all; it is for you to dare all.[3]

This was indeed a declaration of intellectual independence, a firm statement of individualism.

Emerson's emphasis upon the individual and his own potential capacities was further bolstered in his often-quoted essay *Self-Reliance* (1841). Here again he counselled man, "Trust thyself." Self-reliance ran counter to the grain of custom, to the habits of society, and was thus not an easy precept to follow. Yet Emerson declared, "Nothing is at last sacred but the integrity of your own mind."[4] All institutions in society were the products of the men who

---

[1] *The Complete Essays and Other Writings of Ralph Waldo Emerson,* edited by Brooks Atkinson (New York: Modern Library, 1940), pp. 49-50.

[2] *Ibid.,* p. 50.

[3] *Ibid.,* p. 62.

[4] *Ibid.,* p. 148.

made them. They were the products of self-reliant men who struck out a new path counter to the prejudices of orthodoxy. Man communing with the universe required no institutional mediaries to guide his soul. And through greater self-reliance, a revolution might be achieved in all the institutional affairs of men. Self-reliance thus became in Emerson's phrases an intellectual form of rugged individualism.

Behind Emerson's emphasis upon self-reliance and individualism were his transcendentalist beliefs.[5] Transcendentalism, as Emerson explained in *The Transcendentalist,* was idealism, as opposed to materialism. An idealist was not dependent upon the evidence of the senses alone, nor on facts or circumstances, but upon inner beliefs, conscious thoughts, and intuitions. The emphasis was thus always upon the conscious self rather than upon the external world. "The idealist takes his departure from his consciousness, and reckons the world an appearance."[6] As a result, the idealist could write, "Mind is the only reality, of which men and all other natures are better or worse reflectors. Nature, literature, history, are only subjective phenomena."[7] It was the individual mind of man, his consciousness, his soul—under whatever name—that was the consequential thing. Transcendentalism drew heavily upon faith—this new priesthood of all believers—and was thus likened by Emerson to that earlier conflict of the "preachers of Faith against the preachers of Works." The self-reliant and trusting man with his sights upon the universe about him was the natural epitome of Emerson's philosophical convictions.

> All that you call the world is the shadow of that substance which you are, the perpetual creation of the powers of thought, of those that are dependent and of those that are independent of your will. Do not cumber yourself with fruitless pains to mend and remedy remote effects; let the soul be erect, and all things will go well.[8]

This belief, carried to an extreme, could lead to a doctrine of individual perfection and political passivity and indifference. Indeed, Emerson himself was slow in recognizing the validity and efficacy of political reform; some of his sharpest criticisms were

[5] For Emerson's conception of transcendentalism, see his *Nature* (1836) and *The Transcendentalist,* printed in *The Dial,* January, 1843. Both are included in the Modern Library edition. See pp. 3-42, 87-103.

[6] *Ibid.,* p. 89.

[7] *Ibid.,* p. 89.

[8] *Ibid.,* p. 90.

levelled against the social reformers, for his emphasis was always upon the individual rather than society. If individuals were reformed, the reform of society would follow automatically. In his essay on *Politics* (1844) he noted that while the end of government was the culture of men, nevertheless "the State must follow and not lead the character and progress of the citizen."[9] Laws were but the memoranda of an age, and their record marked the progress of the age. But, he noted, things as well as men were governed by laws, and these were not to be upset by the ambition of governors or the power of numbers. Should, for instance, the law deny to property political influence, or to property holders the right to vote, "Nevertheless, by a higher law, the property will, year after year, write every statute that respects property. The non-proprietor will be the scribe of the proprietor."[10]

Behind all government was the moral identity of men, which reflected the constancy and universality of human nature. And, in accordance with the order of nature, governments of force occurred where men were selfish. When men were wise and unselfish, this counteraction, force, would not be required. Thus the prime political requirement of the times was the cultivation and purification of men. Even the term *politics* carried, in the popular mind, a sinister connotation. And Emerson noted, "Of all debts men are least willing to pay the taxes. . . ."[11]

> Hence the less government we have the better—the fewer laws, and the less confided power. The antidote to this abuse of formal government is the influence of private character, the growth of the Individual; the appearance of the principal to supersede the proxy; the appearance of the wise man; of whom the existing government is, it must be owned, but a shabby imitation. . . . To educate the wise man the State exists and with the appearance of the wise man the State expires. The appearance of character makes the State unnecessary. The wise man is the State.[12]

Thus did Emerson, seeking the cultivation of individuals to the point of perfection, aim for heaven here on earth, a state of innocence and wisdom in the future which would not require the awkward government of man. The absence of government, it should

[9] *Ibid.*, p. 423.
[10] *Ibid.*, p. 426.
[11] *Ibid.*, p. 431.
[12] *Ibid.*, p. 431.

be emphasized, however, hinged upon the attainment of perfection in men.

THOREAU

On the fringes of the transcendental movement was Henry David Thoreau (1817-1862), a strange and indeed singular figure among American men of letters. In part a recluse, and certainly an individualist, he preferred the marvels of nature to the material symbols and standards of prosperity brought about by his fellow men. There appears a streak of Rousseau in his works when he considers the pure and righteous man who has not been corrupted by the gross standards of a civilization concerned with the getting of wealth and when he considers the righteous will that is superior to a majority of numbers. In Thoreau lies the fullest appeal to individuality and non-conformity in a civilization which was increasingly giving way to orthodoxy and social compulsion.

Thoreau, like Emerson, was only incidentally interested in politics. However, like many of his Concord friends, he became greatly agitated over the slavery issue. A peaceable man, opposed to slavery, he became doubly incensed over the course of politics which led to war with Mexico in 1848. His protest against these twin evils is found in "Civil Disobedience" (1849), his most important political writing, in which he stated his case for the refusal of moral men to obey the edicts of an immoral society. His basic approach and his similarity to Emerson's position is indicated in the opening sentences of his work.

> I heartily accept the motto, "That government is best which governs least;" and I should like to see it acted up to more rapidly and systematically. Carried out, it finally amounts to this, which also I believe,—"That Government is best which governs not at all;" and when men are prepared for it, that will be the kind of government which they will have.[13]

It should be clear that Thoreau was not, as he is sometimes considered to be, an anarchist. He did not wish to abolish government even though he did advocate resistance to what he believed to be bad government. He wished to eliminate force as an instrument of

[13] The Concord Edition, *Thoreau's Complete Works* (Boston and New York: Houghton Mifflin Co., 1929), vol. 4, p. 356.

government, but to do this he realized the prior necessity of eliminating those conditions which made the use of force necessary. He wished to help prepare man for that happy society in which each man would be fully governed by his own will and not that of another; governed by that conscience that would operate equally and effectively in all men. This was, perhaps, utopia reserved for the future, a time in which all men were virtuous; but, for the here and now, reform of character and reform of government rather than its abolition held the consequential priorities. Thus he stated, "Unlike those who call themselves no-government men, I ask for, not at once no government, but at once a better government."[14]

The country's achievements, so often attributed to the government, were achievements due solely to the character of the American people, whose achievements might have been greater still if the government had not interfered. "For government is an expedient by which men would fain succeed in letting one another alone; and, as has been said, when it is most expedient, the governed are most let alone by it."[15] The good society, as Thoreau saw it, was one in which each man might go his own way according to the dictates of a universal conscience without any let or hindrance from an external power.

Conscience rather than statute was the important standard of behavior to Thoreau; for government founded on expediency was frequently given to inexpedient actions. The fact that a statute had the sanction of the majority of the community behind it did not make that statute a just one. The sanction behind majority rule was force of numbers, and sheer power had no correlation with justice. "It is not desirable to cultivate a respect for the law," he wrote, "so much as for the right. The only obligation which I have a right to assume is to do at any time what I think right."[16]

Thoreau was not troubled by the humbling notion that two rights might make two wrongs, that political questions are many-sided issues of claimed rights in conflict. For, he held, beneath the claims of numbers, of interests, of expediency, the basic issues revealed themselves, and these were moral issues. As such, under his conception of absolute morality, there could be only one right side of the question. Thus he felt that one need not wait for the sanction of a statute to take an action, or even for the support of a simple

14 *Ibid.*, p. 357.
15 *Ibid.*, p. 357.
16 *Ibid.*, p. 358.

majority, for where God was on his side a man did not need the support of men. "Moreover, any man more right than his neighbors constitutes a majority of one already."[17]

Nothing should stand in the way of a man's acting in accordance with the compulsions of his own conscience. No considerations of social position, no considerations of life or property, not even the national existence of a state should stand in the way of the dictates of morality. Referring specifically to what he considered the current abuses, Thoreau declared, "This people must cease to hold slaves, and to make war on Mexico, though it cost them their existence as a people."[18]

In order to bring about the end of slavery and the war with Mexico Thoreau proposed his technique for political action. He called upon the men of Massachusetts to throw their whole weight, and not merely their vote, in favor of the eradication of these twin evils. A vote was merely the expression of a desire for a given course of action and thus was a relatively ineffectual political device unless one were in the majority. But since righteousness was the important factor, the technique had to be one which the virtuous few could use in spite of and against the less conscientious many. This technique by which the right could bring the wrong into line, the few control the many, he called "civil disobedience." It amounted to nothing more than non-support to the government. It was, he admitted, a form of rebellion, but it was a passive sort of revolution. Refuse to pay taxes or in any manner give support to the government while it condones these iniquities. Go to jail, indeed clog the jails if necessary, for in an unjust state the only place for a just man is in jail. Superior morality would thus overcome superior number.

> I know this well, that if one thousand, if one hundred, if ten men whom I could name,—if then honest men only,—aye, if one Honest man, in this State of Massachusetts, ceasing to hold slaves, were actually to withdraw from this copartnership, and be locked up in the county jail, therefore, it would be the abolition of slavery in America.[19]

To those who might find this political technique a little naive and unrealistic, and inclined to overrate the place of morality in politics, or to those who might find such a prisoner's influence on the state negligible, Thoreau answered that such persons "do not

[17] *Ibid.*, p. 369.
[18] *Ibid.*, p. 362.
[19] *Ibid.*, p. 370.

know how much truth is stronger than error."[20] Yet it would seem that Thoreau looked beyond the lone martyr suffering imprisonment because of moral indignation. He envisaged a wider scope of civil disobedience, with more participants included. For the solitary imprisonment of a single righteous person might be followed by the nonparticipation, and perhaps imprisonment, of all just men.

A minority is powerless while it conforms to the majority; it is not even a minority then; but it is irresistible when it clogs by its whole weight. If the alternative is to keep all just men in prison, or give up war and slavery, the State [Massachusetts] will not hesitate which to choose.[21]

Civil disobedience thus amounted to passive resistance on the part of individuals who could no longer tolerate the decisions of their government. It would appear to put private claims above social claims, private rights above social duties. Thoreau, however, saw no conflict between private rights and public duties unless one side be in error. For in his utopian view of the universe, harmonious relations existed where all people acted rightly. Disharmony and conflict occurred only with the admittance of evil, or bad conscience, onto the scene. Thus his plea for individual conscience was at once a plea for such a public conscience that evil and ignorance might be banished and public duty would agree with private rights. Furthermore, he assumed, all individuals would agree on the specific requirements of their moral obligations. Thoreau, in his opposition to social conformity, thus clearly assumed an essential conformity of private conscience. He spoke for the minority of one, as others in American thought voiced the claims of class and sectional minorities. He emphasized the importance of the individual in society; he disdained the use of overt force and sought, like Mahatma Gandhi in India years later, civil disobedience as a means to give effect to moral values. Nevertheless, it does not appear that it ever occurred to Thoreau that men might disagree on moral values without someone being actually in the wrong.

Civil disobedience, a modified form of the right of revolution, raises certain questions as to expediency and morality. For with the just men non-cooperative and in the jails, and the unjust men on the outside running the government, it might be questionable how much clogging of the machinery of government this minority could do.

[20] *Ibid.*, p. 371.
[21] *Ibid.*, p. 371.

And, it might be further observed, the clogging technique introduces an element of compulsion into political affairs which puts force behind the lever of morality, or, in fact, any other cause. Essentially therefore Thoreau, opposed to compulsions, returned to this method as a means of political action. Such was, however, the necessary recourse until men were properly prepared for that stage in which an absolute morality governed all men and that government existed which governed not at all.

Thoreau and Emerson were alike critics of a new culture which they believed to be essentially materialistic; and they sought to penetrate beyond the outward appearances of things and reach into the common conscience of mankind. That there was such a conscience common to all men they had no doubt, for it was this conscience which set the proper standards in accordance with a universal system of morality. All things and persons were governed inexorably by laws beyond the reach of men; it was the fundamental ordinances that demanded adherence in spite of the fancies of society or the decrees of majority rule. Fundamentally, man's being was in harmony with nature and his fellow man, and one need only trust to conscience as an infallible guide to right and harmonious conduct. Because the individual was of paramount concern, and the precepts of right and wrong were perceptible to all men, man's basic right was to trust and obey the dictates of his conscience. If his conscience ruled contrary to the compulsions of society, then so much the error of society. This high conception of the dignity of the individual carried with it a rather low or at least indifferent attitude toward the government and all other social institutions. No man could bury himself in society, nor could the honest man be true to the state if it meant that he must also be false to himself. The pathway to social or political reform therefore led through the individuals who composed society and the state, for the statutes of men only reflected the character and morality of the age. As the character of individuals improved and came closer to approximating the just and moral man created by God, then society would be reformed accordingly. Only the most obvious and flagrant abuse demanded remedy by political action, for such remedies could never have a permanent effect as long as expedient men controlled expedient governments. The final triumph would come in time when individuals themselves, and not just their governments, refused to tolerate abuses.

UTOPIANS

There were many individuals who sought social reform during this period via a different route than through the character of individuals alone. These chose a method of self-help to be sure; but they cooperated in helping themselves. Whereas Emerson and Thoreau had emphasized the importance of trusting one's self and of going the long hard path to righteousness and reform alone as a self-competent and self-sufficient individual, others found in the spirit of cooperative endeavor a more satisfying and expedient solution. Between the years 1825 and 1860, nearly 100 communities or little utopian settlements were founded.[22] From the days of the early Puritans in Massachusetts, Americans have been given to utopian schemes—the promise of peace and plenty and brotherly love—but at no other time did they crop up as they did in this period. Here, it seemed, was the land in which dreams could come to life and fancy could be fact. One need not resort to the hurly-burly of political action or precipitate a revolution to bring this happy condition about; one needed only to demonstrate by experiment and example how society might be improved. The claims of most of the utopians, while high in ambition, were generally modest in expectation, for they did not seek to impose their systems upon others not desiring such schemes. They sought rather through self-help and cooperation to build communities only for themselves and others who might care to join. A man entered such a community voluntarily and was free to depart at any time. These were schemes of local self-government, independent of the state. While the contests of the tariff, of slavery, of the Mexican war waged without, the little islands of cooperative communities sought to achieve a basic self-sufficiency within. The consequential demands of man were those of his spirit and those of his body, and these could be met in a congenial neighborhood where labor had dignity, the mind was cultivated, and man's higher sense of self-interest found satisfying recognition in cooperation. Elsewhere competition was the iron discipline which, catering to the selfish instincts, led to suspicion, jealous rivalry, and greed; and by its very nature always pitted man against man in spite of his altruistic urges. By substi-

---

[22] See Arthur Eugene Bestor, Jr., *Backwoods Utopias* (Philadelphia: University of Pennsylvania Press, 1950), p. 243.

tuting cooperation for competition, however, the better instincts of man would be rewarded and virtue and brotherly love would characterize the community given over to the good life. These were indeed noble and generous ambitions which inspired the makers of utopias to reorganize society and establish cooperative communities. Many of these settlements were by-products of church organizations which looked to God, the Bible, and church doctrine for inspiration. Such sectarian settlements were founded by the Shakers and the Rappists among others. Others were of a secular cast, finding inspiration in the teachings of Christianity but not affiliated with any church and using the programs drawn up by secular writers. In this period of community settlements the two most influential utopian socialist writers in America were not Americans, but an Englishman, Robert Owen, and a Frenchman, Charles Fourier. Owen's plans and capital established the cooperative community of New Harmony, Indiana, in 1825, while Fourier's influence led to the conversion of Brook Farm to a "phalanx" in 1844. However, many other communities were founded along the lines conceived of by these two men, and their influence extended beyond the settlements; so they may be properly considered as contributors to our political thought.

Robert Owen (1771-1858) was an English manufacturer who sensed the social impact of the rising factory system and sought to ameliorate its effects. While still quite young he had worked his way up in the textile system to become a factory manager and owner possessed of a small fortune. Instead of resting smugly upon his achievements he became a critic of the existing factory system and a propagandist for social reform. The fact that he was a social reformer and a capitalist gave far more respectability to his views than they would have gained if he had been merely a worker protecting himself against exploitation. Once he felt that he had discovered the true principles of human nature and the proper mode of social organization, he spared no expense or effort to see his reforms put into effect. He petitioned Parliament in England; he spoke before Congress in America; he converted a factory town in Scotland into a model community; and he sought in New Harmony, Indiana, to establish an ideal settlement in this country. Yet the rather astonishing thing is that Owen appeared to have no clear-cut plan of social organization, and where he was called upon for specific details he was inclined to contradict himself.[23] His

---

[23] See Bestor, *op. cit.*, for a critical study of the Owenite movement in America.

remarkable appeal is thus not attributable to any social blueprinting, but rather to the exemplary life he led and the high ideals he popularized. For in contrast to the drudgery and poverty and crime so intimately associated with the factory system, Owen offered their opposites: a system of peace on earth and good will toward men. Clearly the appeal of Owen was not specifically an economic one, although he argued that his system would be more profitable to the employer and beneficial to the worker than the system then existing. The appeal was rather to the social than to the pecuniary instincts of men, an appeal that reached to the mind and heart as well as to the pocketbook. The secondary place of economics in his thinking is attested to by the fact that his views on economic questions—the place of private property, equality of recompense— fluctuated, thereby resulting in contradictory statements. Likewise his position on the place of the state varied, for at times he appealed for legislative reform and at other times he sought direct reform of society through voluntary action. He appears to have chosen whatever instrument of reform expediency offered.

Of all Owen's writings, his *A New View of Society* was probably his most influential work. Published in part as essays as early as 1812 and circulated among people of political influence both in England and abroad, the completed collection of four essays appeared in 1816. It was not, however, until 1825 when the Owenite community of New Harmony was founded that this little work was published in America. In his first essay Owen stated several of the fundamental tenets of his belief. Contrary to the common conception that character and basic traits were born with the individual, Owen postulated the principles:

> Any general character, from the best to the worst, from the most ignorant to the most enlightened, may be given to any community, even to the world at large, by the application of proper means; which means are to a great extent at the command and under the control of those who have influence in the affairs of men.[24]

Whereas Emerson and Thoreau had sought to reform society and government by looking to the reformation of character among individuals, Owen looked upon character as the resultant of social conditions. Emerson and Thoreau approached society through individuals, while Owen approached individuals through society. Beyond the essential core that constituted human nature, there were atti-

[24] Robert Owen, *A New View of Society*, third edition, 1817 (Glencoe, Illinois: Free Press, 1948), p. 19.

tudes, opinions, manners, and habits which were imposed upon the individual by society. The primary responsibility for human character thus rested not upon the individual, who was but a victim of the circumstances surrounding him, but rather upon society itself. It was folly, for instance, for society so to circumstance man that he became subject to crimes for which he was later punished by society. The fault here lay not with the individual who committed the crime, but with the society that directly or indirectly molded his character into that of a criminal. The difference between the judge who convicts and the felon who is hanged is essentially one of training and circumstance and not intrinsic character. What mankind needed was instruction in those virtues which benefited all mankind, which taught a man that his "individual happiness can be increased and extended only in proportion as he actively endeavors to increase and extend the happiness of all around him."[25] Clearly what Owen aimed at was a thoroughgoing reconstruction of society with all its accepted beliefs. Yet what gave credence to Owen's beliefs was the fact that many of them had been put into practice in his mill town of New Lanark, Scotland, and there given a trial for over sixteen years. In his second essay he explained how he had withdrawn children under ten from the standard thirteen hours of labor, had set up schools for them, remodeled the village and worked out a contributory sickness and pension system. Settling as an Englishman among the suspicious and often hostile Scots, he had tested his benevolent system and found that it worked. Thus, he reasoned, if so much could be done in spite of prevailing social habits and opinions among mature adults, what greater prospects were in store for those who started a reconstruction of society with the very young! Education was therefore the primary key to reform.

> On the experience of a life devoted to this subject I hesitate not to say, that the members of any community may by degrees be trained to live *without idleness, without poverty, without crime, and without punishment.* . . .[26]

It was with this buoyant optimism that he attacked the conservatives who found sin and poverty part of the curse on mankind, and who took a pessimistic view of human nature. Inevitably he was in conflict with the theologians who called upon men to redeem

[25] *Ibid.,* p. 23.
[26] *Ibid.,* p. 65.

themselves, a redemption which to Owen's view was clearly impossible given the present organization of society. For the much-vaunted will of man was inextricably bound into the existing social fabric with all its prevailing misconceptions. It was folly to call upon man to speak truly and act righteously in a society that did not genuinely cherish and reward such behavior. In his third essay, in which he attacked the "false" doctrines of sectarians, he wrote:

> The will of man has no power whatever over his opinions; he must, and ever did, and ever will, believe what has been, is, or may be impressed on his mind by his predecessors, and the circumstances which surround him.[27]

Since the best government was one "which in practice produces the greatest happiness to the greatest number," and since the community formed the character of its inhabitants, it was imperative that governments undertake to promote happiness by improving the character of their subjects. This could be done through a broad system of public education in which children were instructed in the virtues of doing good to their fellow man. A broad system of public works to alleviate the distress of the poor and unemployed would also be desirable. But the Owen gospel did not rest on any fixed or rigid formula. Any number of variations might be employed as long as the essential cooperative and humane spirit remained.

Transplanted to America, Owen's gospel and much of his money was put to use in experimental communities such as New Harmony, Indiana, Yellow Springs, Ohio, and the Franklin Community in New York. Although Owen saw communities modeled after his ideas rise and collapse tragically soon after their founding, he never lost faith in the cause of cooperation; and for the rest of his life he continued to preach his gospel.

At the time that Robert Owen was expounding the gospel of the new society in England and America, Charles Fourier (1772-1837) was at work in France drawing up plans for a utopian system. Fourier, who in his extraordinary conceit considered himself to be one of the world's greatest social philosophers, sought to discover the laws which governed the behavior of men through an understanding of their basic impulses and aspirations. His work, however, reached out in cosmic proportions as he touched upon an endless variety of subjects from domestic relations and general economics to politics, religion, and the realm of the after-life. In 1808 Fourier published

[27] *Ibid.*, p. 108 (capitalized in original).

his *Quatre Mouvements*, which was followed by a work on *Domestic and Agricultural Association* in 1822. Fourier, unlike Owen, was not known directly in America, but through a disciple, Albert Brisbane. Indeed it was largely through the efforts of Brisbane that Fourier's system came to America when it did, and, having come, surpassed Owen's in the number of collective community efforts to which it gave rise.

Albert Brisbane (1809-1890), born of rather wealthy parents in upstate New York, was singularly fortunate in being able to travel and study extensively in Europe in his youth. In France, at the Sorbonne, he listened to the lectures of Victor Cousin and Guizot and read the writings of Saint-Simon; in Germany he studied under Hegel. His travels took him to Vienna, Athens, Rome, Constantinople. During his six years abroad, 1828-1834, Brisbane, by travel and by study under what were considered to be the best minds in Europe, had a rare opportunity to decide the question which had started him on his journeys: what is the destiny of man? Yet wherever he turned he felt no closer to the solution until he came upon *Domestic and Agricultural Association* by Fourier. From then on for the rest of his life, he dedicated himself to further study of Fourier's system and to spreading these ideas in America. In 1840 Brisbane published *The Social Destiny of Man*, which was a combination of quotations from Fourier and commentaries on them. The book proved an immediate success, and soon Brisbane was doing newspaper and magazine articles to spread the doctrine of what became known as "Association." His list of converts is impressive, for it included for a time Horace Greeley, editor of the New York *Tribune*; Parke Godwin, associate editor of the New York *Post*; Charles A. Dana, later editor of the New York *Sun*; George Ripley, and William Ellery Channing. In 1840 George Ripley established Brook Farm, outside of Boston, as an experiment in community living. So successful was Brisbane in his efforts in behalf of Fourier's Association that in 1844 Brook Farm became a phalanx modeled somewhat along the lines conceived of by the French theorist. For two brief years the community prospered and attracted the attention of the illustrious group of New England writers—Emerson, Thoreau, Hawthorne, Lowell, and Whittier. Then a fire destroyed the main building, which was under construction, and the settlement broke up. While Brook Farm was the most famous of the phalanx experiments, nevertheless many such efforts were made in the decade of the 1840's to realize Fourier's ideal.

So devoted a follower of Fourier was Albert Brisbane that it is difficult to separate the ideas of the two men. In America, however, for all practical purposes Brisbane served as Fourier, and when he spoke it was assumed that he represented the ideas of the man who had died some years previously. Brisbane, like Owen, was troubled by the apparent disharmony in human relations, a disharmony which seemed quite incompatible with the normal generous impulses of men. He believed that at bottom the laws governing human relations were laws conducive to harmony, and that a life without social discord might be had by all mankind if only these basic laws were discovered and applied. In music, man had discovered basic laws which proved that a proper arrangement of notes brought about harmony while an improper arrangement produced discord; and Brisbane and Fourier believed that this principle could be applied to human relations as well. When there was discord in human affairs—and observation showed this condition to be far too prevalent—then what was needed was a new arrangement of parts, a new institutional framework that would bring about a metamorphosis in society. Men are not, then, necessarily impelled to do evil; they do only what the circumstances under existing institutions require of them. With a few radical changes in society, men might be equally disposed to do good, to act in harmony with their neighbors.

> Establish true social institutions—institutions in harmony with the laws of organization in creation (and consequently in harmony with the spiritual forces which are in harmony with the creation); and we shall see them producing as high a degree of harmony as they now produce in discord.[28]

Thus the inquiry of Fourier was led into the recesses of the soul of man to discover his basic nature so that institutions might be framed in harmony with it. Fourier's analysis of man brought forth a psychology which centered around the passions or attractions of men. Included among these attractions was the desire of man for society. Actually Fourier reduced all desires into twelve basic categories which by various combinations would produce all the varieties in character known to men. Curiously, he believed that a group of about eight hundred persons would possess all the possible varieties and characteristics. A careful assortment of some eight hundred

---

[28] Redelia Brisbane, *Albert Brisbane, A Mental Biography* (Boston: Arena Publishing Co., 1893), p. 181.

people could produce, therefore, the perfect community. Twice this number, however, would provide a safe margin for a complete variety of types. It was Fourier's plan that such a community of some sixteen hundred persons be organized into what he called a "phalanx." It was Brisbane's hope that in time these phalanxes would come to replace the townships in America. The phalanx would constitute an essential self-sufficient economic and social unit, and the members would live in a large building called the "palace," with many separate quarters and workshops. Here the individual interests and the social interests might be joined, and cooperation would take the place of competition.

Fundamental to Fourier was his emphasis upon attraction as the essential form of human motivation. It was indeed this aspect of Fourier that first caused Brisbane to become interested in Association. For man need not be driven by fear, or hunger, or punishment, but could be attracted by those objects which were naturally pleasing to him. Only in such a manner, only through the circumstances of attraction rather than repulsion, could the human personality develop properly; and only with fully developed personalities could society be truly a congenial and harmonious unit. Every man had his skills, which with proper training and incentive could be employed to the advantage of society; yet a worker who labored at his skill for excessively long and monotonous hours would find his task disagreeable. To attend a concert for two hours, Brisbane noted, is a very pleasant experience; yet to attend the same concert daily for twelve hours would be well nigh intolerable. Man should therefore labor as he plays, for short and interspersed periods of time, so that rest and variety might break the monotony of what might be otherwise a disagreeable chore. By making industry attractive to all, society would be benefited by having willing, efficient and happy workers. And those who labored at the psychically unrewarding and generally unpleasant tasks that were necessary in all societies should be given shorter hours and higher compensation than those who worked in the pleasanter fields of their own choosing. Thus the spirit of Fourierism was to elevate and ennoble all humanity. "In our actual societies every man has his solitary profession in which he lives and dies, and in the monotonous pursuit of which he becomes in a few years a kind of automaton."[29] In the new society, however, the individual would be received into the inspiring companionship of all the members of the community.

[29] *Ibid.*, p. 250.

The human mind, to comprehend this new system of society, must conceive clearly that the individual man is but a part, a fragment, a molecule, in what is called collective man. As well suppose that a finger, or even a fiber of the physical organism, constitutes a body, as to suppose that the individual man with his limited talents and capacities constitutes a complete social organism. According to Fourier, the collective man is the association of two thousand persons; men, women, and children of all ages. Such association will embrace all the varieties of human character and talent. In it will be found artists, men and women of science, men and women of industrial tastes; in short every variety of talent and capacity—all those shades of character which combine to form what we may call an integral man.[30]

In time, it was hoped, the township, which was but an agglomeration of isolated families leading solitary lives, would give way to phalanxes in which the families living in one great palace would work and play together. The county would give way to about a dozen phalanxes, and so it was dreamed the phalanxes would spread "until they embrace the globe."[31] Yet this movement, purely voluntary, was to be achieved without political action or intervention. It was a movement which seemed prompted by historical necessity, as each generation sought to correct the degrading and ignoble conditions of its age. Civilization as it then existed would give way to the next stage in this historical evolution, "Guarantism," which Brisbane defined as "a system of society in which the general incoherence and conflict of individual interests will tend to disappear in a spirit of collectivity which will lead to an understanding among men for the proper adjustment of all interests both public and personal."[32] Under Guarantism the phalanxes would lose some of their autonomy, for centralized planning and decisions would be required. Under Guarantism, "The commercial operations and relations of a nation will be carried on under the supervision of its government—the *Collective Mind,* and economy and order will be established therein."[33] But Guarantism was a transitional stage itself, for though it would provide organization, it would not provide for that essential harmony which was a prerequisite for the good society. Yet "following on the incoherence of the preceding societies, it will constitute a transition to the final and normal order based on

[30] *Ibid.,* pp. 248-249.
[31] *Ibid.,* p. 248.
[32] *Ibid.,* pp. 253-254.
[33] *Ibid.,* p. 245.

scientific organization, and resulting in social harmony."[34] Presumably then, the evolutionary system would reach a point of perfection at which, happily, it would cease evolving. The nature of this final state, however, was merely suggested and not fully developed.

The America of the 1840's was clearly a nation of intellectual and political ferment. The extraordinary economic development during its fifty years of independence had permitted social attitudes and conditions to become established which now, during this period of ferment, were subjected to the closest scrutiny. The broad humanitarianism of the reformers was but one aspect of this effort to reconstitute the social order along lines more acceptable to a strict sense of conscience and morality. Yet the efforts at social and economic reform were not all politically inspired, although all eventually had their political aspects. The works of Emerson and Thoreau, as well as of the utopians, were on but the periphery of the main political currents of the day; yet they too led in the same direction. For the effort of the period was to ennoble and free man from the degrading tyranny of the circumstances and opinions amidst which he labored. The demand for reform without political intervention is not without its political implications and suggests a theory of social action which clearly has political consequences.

The writings of the individualists and the utopians reflected two aspects of what was coming to be the American tradition. The emphasis upon the individual, his dignity, will, and responsibility, carried on an attitude in secular guise which had heretofore been an essential lesson of the theologians. The individualism of the frontiersman who lived on the fringes of civilized America could be experienced by the men and women still on the seaboard if they would follow their consciences as infallible guides. Viewed in this sense, individualism would call forth the fine characteristics of man and so strengthen them that no man would recognize another as his master unless he be more nearly in the right. It was a call to every man to be moral at all times as a duty to himself and his fellow man. Such moral men would then carry society with them. This appeal continued to have its importance in American politics and, given an economic interpretation, became a component of the theory of *laissez faire;* still later it formed a part of the doctrine of the elite as expressed by Paul Elmer More and Irving Babbitt.

The utopian approach to character was from the opposite direction. Character was developed primarily by circumstance, and cir-

[34] *Ibid.,* p. 254.

cumstance was the product of social conditions. Individuals were the victims or beneficiaries of the circumstances made for them by society. Gradual amelioration could not break the iron chains of circumstance and the prejudicial opinion which developed from it. What was needed was a new start, a new community, a new education which would produce a new generation with moral standards that were practiced as well as preached. While the plans of the Owenites and the Fourierists were vaguely conceived and poorly executed and only of temporary importance, they offered at least the promise that social planning was preferable to haphazard development and that utopia was possible in America. Utopian literature continued to be written sporadically during the nineteenth century, culminating in Bellamy's *Looking Backward*. But community experimentation never again achieved the appeal that it possessed during this period. Yet the possibility of planning, of endeavoring to make a science out of social organization, was revived many years later and found limited expression in community and economic planning. The efforts to reconstruct society that developed at this time, based on individualism and on planning, were thus forerunners of opposing political movements that came a century later.

CHAPTER 10

Slavery and the Rights of Man

ANTISLAVERY THOUGHT

THE LIBERAL ferment that issued forth in the age of Jackson was directed toward a multiplicity of economic, social and political reforms. A greater range of economic rights was sought for the factory worker; a wider expanse of social opportunity was espoused for women; and a more extensive democratic base was demanded for the American institutions of government. In all, this extraordinary ferment which flourished during the two decades from 1830-1850 sought a radical reconstruction of society so that a closer institutional approximation to the ideals declared in the Declaration of Independence might be realized. Specifically it sought to improve democracy by emphasizing the importance of liberty and equality. It sought, in the long run, to make man the master of the institutions which controlled him by reasserting his rights as a human being to be governed only in those affairs in which he had previously granted his consent. It sought equality for all the dispossessed persons in society, arguing that only with the lever of equality could men pry open the doors that blocked the pathways to freedom. What was sought politically, therefore, was not primarily new legislation to elevate the underprivileged, but a repeal of such existing legislation as discriminated against them.

Such a movement was by its nature radical, as it attacked the claimed rights of those whom the social and economic system had elevated to power and who now exercised their claims to stem the undercurrent of unrest. For inevitably the claim of equality ran counter to the claims of those who enjoyed the privileges of their inequality; and the appeal to liberty was hardly meaningful to those whose liberty, already realized, might now be placed in jeopardy. The demand for a reconstruction of society was thus a demand that ran counter to the existing constitutions, statutes and judicial interpretations. Such a demand could not draw upon existing institutions for evidence or support, but could only drive to the very roots of civil society itself into an analysis and examination of the fundamental human rights that belonged to all men by virtue of their being men. It was this fundamental inquiry that was at the heart of the discussions over the suffrage restrictions in some of the state constitutions in the decade from 1820 to 1830. It was but one aspect of the human rights discussion that led to the demand by Bryant and Leggett that the economic rights of the workers be realized through acceptance of the workers' right to strike. The demand for a closer and more consistent adherence to *laissez faire* was at that time but an application in the economic sphere of the principle of equal rights for all. It was the contention of the individualists, Emerson and Thoreau, and the utopian followers of Owen and Fourier, that the dignity and perfection of the individual was the ultimate purpose of the state, and that this could be achieved only when the full human rights of the individual were recognized. It was, finally, this insistence upon human rights in their most obvious and elementary form which ran counter to the established and accepted institution of slavery in the South and led ultimately to the greatest schism that has yet taken place in American politics.

Slavery, which many had thought to be a declining institution in America, came sharply into focus as a political issue in the three decades preceding the Civil War. The conflict was aggravated by the opposing claims of those desiring an agrarian economy supported by extensive trade, and those advocating a manufacturing economy protected by trade barriers. Furthermore, the expansion of the country westward brought the free-soilers and slavery advocates into conflict anew with each question of admission into the Union of additional states. Yet, basic as the economic issues were, the fundamental cleavage was between two value systems, two opposing conceptions of morality. The issues raised by the abolitionists brought forth a re-examination by Northern and Southern thinkers alike of the underlying basis for political authority, which led not only to a discussion of the nature of man but to the equally delicate issue of the nature of the Union itself.

Inasmuch as the demands of the extreme abolitionists were at first contrary to the conservative prevailing tendencies of society at

large, this highly articulate minority of radical reformers often encountered organized suppression of their views and physical violence to their persons. In the South, for all practical purposes, they
were prohibited from appearing in public; in the North, in the
beginning, they were hardly more welcome. As a result the peaceful
machinery of democracy, free discussion and debate, was temporarily put aside in favor of silence, suppression and intolerant vin-
dicativeness. Thus the issue of human rights was inflamed by the
flagrant denial of the civil rights of freedom of speech, of the press,
of assembly, and even of petition. Indeed, so extreme a position was
taken by the United States House of Representatives from 1840-
1844 as to refuse even to receive petitions requesting the abolition
of slavery in the District of Columbia, any state or territory, or of
the slave trade existing between such states and territories.[1] Essentially, therefore, the slavery issue was an issue over civil rights, or
more broadly speaking, human rights with all their ramifications;
and the arguments over the issue of rights necessarily involved the
nature and attributes of man himself.

WILLIAM LLOYD GARRISON

The position arrived at by Henry Thoreau in his contempt for a
government that waged war on Mexico, passed fugitive slave laws,
and protected slavery was anticipated in its militancy of belief by
William Lloyd Garrison (1805-1879), one of the most influential
propagandists in the history of American letters. A founder of the
American Anti-Slavery Society (1833) and editor of the inflammable
organ *The Liberator,* established in 1831, Garrison brought to the
abolitionist movement a crusading zeal that brooked no compromise
on moral principles and coupled righteousness with vindictiveness.
In the initial issue of *The Liberator* Garrison announced:

> I am aware, that many object to the severity of my language; but
> is there not cause for severity? I will be as harsh as truth, and as
> uncompromising as justice. On this subject, I do not wish to think,
> or speak, or write, with moderation. . . . I am in earnest. I will not
> equivocate—I will not excuse—I will not retreat a single inch—And
> I Will Be Heard. . . .[2]

[1] See Dwight Lovell Dumond, *Antislavery Origins of the Civil War in the
United States* (Ann Arbor: The University of Michigan Press, 1939), Chap. 4.
[2] *Selections from the Writings and Speeches of William Lloyd Garrison* (Boston: R. F. Wallcut, 1852), p. 63.

The testimony of history gives ample proof that Garrison was heard. He was a crusader for an immediate application in practice of the natural rights of man in the tradition of revolt reminiscent of Tom Paine, while his intensity of conviction and singleness of purpose is suggestive of the Puritan assurance of salvation. To Garrison the first step toward salvation was the eradication of slavery, for no true Christian, he argued, could either hold men in bondage or tolerate slaveholding by others. Untroubled by the political, economic or social ramifications of the slavery question, he dedicated his energies, in spite of imprisonment, social ostracism, and vilification to the cause in which he soon became justly known as a fanatic. In the *Declaration of Sentiments of the American Antislavery Convention* (1833), which he was largely responsible for drafting, the Garrison program was outlined. Drawing upon the Declaration of Independence as the basis for argument and as a model for the *Declaration of Sentiments,* it was declared that the methods of the abolitionists were not to include force and physical compulsion.

> Ours shall be such only as the opposition of moral purity to political corruption—the destruction of error by the potency of truth—the overthrow of prejudice by the power of love—and the abolition of slavery by the spirit of repentence.[3]

Yet the program of the abolitionists was such that unless one assumed fundamental agreement on the moral question of slavery, the moral argument alone could be of little avail. For moral suasion could only set the climate of opinion which would make appropriate political action practicable. Opposed to gradualism on the grounds that "gradualism in theory is perpetuity in practice," Garrison sought an immediate rather than distant achievement of his objectives.

The *Declaration of Sentiments* stated anew the Lockean concept of natural rights, including the legitimacy of the ownership of the products of one's own labor.

> The right to enjoy liberty is inalienable. To invade it is to usurp the prerogative of Jehovah. Every man has a right to his own body— to the products of his own labor—to the protection of law—and to the common advantages of society.[4]

Because slavery was contrary to natural rights it was an institution contrary to the fundamental moral principles of humanity. It was but a retreat into barbarism. Here was an instance in which prescrip-

[3] *Ibid.,* p. 67.
[4] *Ibid.,* p. 68.

tion could make no claim, in which long-continued practice could only mean long-continued abuse. For the *Declaration of Sentiments* declared:

> That if they [slaves] had lived from the time of Pharaoh down to the present period, and had been entailed through successive generations, their right to be free could never have been alienated, but their claims would have constantly risen in solemnity.[5]

Because there was no moral foundation for slavery, not only ought all slaves to be set free immediately, but there ought to be no compensation granted to their former owners. Indeed all the privileges of society ought to be available to all men without regard to race. Appealing to a higher law of righteousness against the edicts of men the *Declaration* announced:

> That all those laws which are now in force, admitting the right of slavery, are therefore, before God, utterly null and void; being an audacious usurpation of the Divine prerogative, a daring infringement on the law of nature, a base overthrow of the very foundations of the social compact, a complete extinction of all the relations, endearments and obligations of mankind, and a presumptuous transgression of all the holy commandments; and that therefore they ought instantly to be abrogated.[6]

It was recognized in the *Declaration* that under the Constitution slavery could not be eradicated by act of Congress, that each state was sovereign on this question. But it was maintained that the national government was competent to act within its special sphere of jurisdiction, that is, in the interstate slave trade and the territories under its control. Beyond this, however, it was felt that a great moral crusade would make itself felt throughout all the land and thereby bring an end to the slavery system.

Garrison however was not content to rely upon the program of patience and enlightenment espoused in the *Declaration of Sentiments*. A doctrinaire, he would tolerate no compromise with a constitutional system that tolerated, indeed protected, slavery. Thus he was drawn by his own logic to the extreme of anarchy. A government which protected slavery was no proper government for a moral man, and he voluntarily disfranchised himself rather than support it. If the Union was dependent upon slavery, he would destroy the Union. The Constitution he denounced as a "covenant with death,"

---

[5] *Ibid.*
[6] *Ibid.*, pp. 68-69.

an "agreement with hell," a "refuge of lies"; and he publicly burned a copy of it to ashes to dramatize his disapproval of a compact with slavery.

Garrison's place in the slavery issue was primarily that of a propagandist, a dramatic and fanatical personality, rather than that of a thinker. There is little philosophical speculation in his writings. He took his stand upon certain moral assumptions and upon the Declaration of Independence, and led a crusade against all public enactments that ran counter to the inalienable right of man to be free in his own person. He was, like Thoreau, a man who placed his conception of the higher law above all temporal enactments and chose to follow the latter only as he found them in agreement with the dictates of the former. That other men in other circumstances might arrive at other conclusions as to the specific requirements of the higher law did not concern him. By the intensity of his convictions, his untiring zeal, he led the more extreme wing of the abolitionist movement, which eventually gained sufficient support so that the Northern climate of opinion looked upon the antislavery crusade as an imperative political issue. In his militancy, confident righteousness, and anarchical inclinations, however, he was far closer to the antislavery martyr John Brown than to the more pragmatic Abraham Lincoln.

WILLIAM ELLERY CHANNING

While Garrison provided the incendiary element which kept alive the flame of antislavery sentiment during the two decades (1830-1850) of transition in public opinion, others less extreme and more profound developed a more philosophical basis for the discussion. Such a thinker was William Ellery Channing (1780-1842), transcendentalist and Unitarian minister. A friend of Emerson, his idealism was considerably influenced by the perfectionist literature of Rousseau in France and Mary Wollstonecraft and William Godwin in England. His benevolent view of God and man was a product of eighteenth-century enlightenment, and a kindly humaneness characterized all his views on social questions. At a time when abolitionism was highly unpopular among most respectable people in New England, Channing rose to its defense in his speeches and publications. His *Essay on Slavery* (1835), *The Abolitionist* (1836), *Emancipation* (1840), and *The Duty of the Free States* (1842) gave ample ethical support to the cause of abolition and presented the movement with a sobriety of tone which was considerably in contrast to the dramatic pronouncements of Garrison. Basically, Channing was concerned over the moral issue of human rights, which were affected not only by slavery, but by the public militancy and often public violence associated with discussions of slavery. For the abolitionists were a minority, a vocal and insistent minority who disturbed the public tranquility by their demands for immediate reform. Arson, threats of lynching and imprisonment accompanied the abolitionists as they sought to make their views known, and many who were opposed to abolitionism, or were at best only lukewarm supporters of the movement, felt incensed at the flagrant denial of the civil rights of its supporters. The right to speak freely, print freely and petition freely in opposition to the political views of the majority thus became associated with the cause of freedom from bondage for the Negro.

At a time when the abolitionists were encountering persecution and censure for their extremist views, Channing rose to their defense, not as abolitionists, but as champions of the civil rights of man. In one of the most lucid and candid statements in American letters on behalf of free speech, free press, and free discussion, Channing paid tribute to the abolitionists. The abolitionists were not only crusaders for the Negro slaves. "In their persons," he noted, "the most sacred rights of the white man and the free man have been assailed."

> The defenders of freedom are not those who claim and exercise rights which no one assails, or who win shouts of applause by well-turned compliments to liberty in the days of her triumph. They are those who stand up for rights which mobs, conspiracies, or single tyrants put in jeopardy, who contend for liberty in that particular form which is threatened at the moment by the many or the few.[7]

The abolitionists, as a highly vocal and militant minority, had inevitably alienated many in their search for converts. There were instances of excesses of zeal on the part of the reformers as there were instances of excesses of disapproval on the part of those who disagreed with them. Yet to deny reform because of the zeal of the reformers would be to check all movements to improve society. The generous spirit of humanity, when embarked on a crusade, was in-

[7] *The Works of William E. Channing* (Boston: James Munroe and Co., 1848), vol. II, p. 159.

clined to excessive zeal, and only through such zeal was the "iron front" of the "established evils" broken. Social progress was thus dependent upon those who were not faint in heart and weak in spirit but were courageous enough to hold and propagate their beliefs in the face of unpopularity and even persecution. In one of his most striking passages, Channing defended free speech and discussion as a necessity of social progress.

Of all powers, the last to be intrusted to the multitude of men is that of determining what questions shall be discussed. The greatest truths are often the most unpopular and exasperating; and were they to be denied discussion, till the many should be ready to accept them, they would never establish themselves in the general mind. The progress of society depends on nothing more than on the exposure of time-sanctioned abuses, which cannot be touched without offending multitudes, than on the promulgation of principles, which are in advance of public sentiment and practice and which are consequently at war with the habits, prejudices, and immediate interests of large classes of the community. Of consequence, the multitude, if once allowed to dictate or proscribe subjects of discussion, would strike society with spiritual blindness and death. The world is to be carried forward by truth, which at first offends, which wins its way by degrees, which the many hate, and would rejoice to crush. The right of free discussions is, therefore, to be guarded by the friends of mankind with peculiar jealousy. It is at once the most sacred and most endangered of all our rights. He who would rob his neighbor of it should have a mark set on him as the worst enemy of freedom. . . .[8]

Channing's position in regard to the freedom of the unpopular minority to speak, publish, and discuss views found hostile by the rest of the community was in the American liberal tradition of Jefferson and Roger Williams and followed the English position of Milton and Locke. Yet while Milton believed suppression of opinion to be futile because truth would triumph in the end, Channing appeared to doubt that such would be the case. To the contrary, Channing argued that truth, if suppressed, might not be heard and therefore not prevail. Suppression, far from futile, was highly effective and therefore undesirable.

It was not in the area of civil rights as such that Channing's position was best known, but in the broader and more fundamental area of human rights. His *Essay on Slavery,* couched in moderate language, drew up a philosophical basis for emancipation. "The

8 *Ibid.,* p. 161.

eternal law binds us to take the side of the injured,"[9] wrote Channing, as he launched upon his attack of the slavery system. In the opening chapter of this work he took issue with the Southern position, supported by the Southern codes of law, that the slave was property and as such was fully subject to his owner, the master. The slave was in effect a possession, not a man, and as such he had no legal rights of his own. It was this claim to man as property with which Channing took direct issue, for he held that "A human being cannot be justly owned."[10] Yet to prove his contention Channing recognized certain inherent difficulties, for he maintained his proposition was so obvious, so self-evident that no reasoned proof could be clearer or more convincing than the original proposition. The moral contention that no man could be claimed as property by another was therefore a self-evident truth. Channing, however, did not rely on this argument alone, for to those who did not find this proposition self-evident, further persuasion was necessary. Thus he undertook a seven-fold attack upon the assumption that a human being could be held in slavery as a property of his master.

First, he argued that if one man might be held as property, the claim, once conceded as valid, could be extended to any other man.

If there is nothing in human nature, in our common nature, which excludes and forbids the conversion of him who possesses it into an article of property; if the right of the free to liberty is founded, not on their essential attributes as rational and moral beings, but on certain adventitious, accidental circumstances, into which they have been thrown; then every human being, by a change of circumstances, may justly be held and treated by another as property.[11]

It was this inward repulsion to the prospect of being considered as property, as a slave, which any man would experience that demonstrated the moral claim against slavery. Putting aside the issue of slavery as a civil punishment for criminals, Channing based his case for innocent men upon a conception of absolute morality. This conception of morality was applicable to all races, to all places, and in all times, regardless of power or wealth. No circumstance could therefore justify the enslavement of innocent men. This position led to Channing's second proposition: that a man cannot be held as property because he has rights. Regardless of the disagreements among men as to whether these rights were few or many, the

[9] *Ibid.*, p. 11.
[10] *Ibid.*, p. 18.
[11] *Ibid.*, p. 18.

same for all men, it could be assumed that every human being possessed some rights. "This truth cannot be denied," he noted, "but by denying to a portion of the race that moral nature which is the sure and only foundation of rights."[12] The fundamental morality that was the mark of all humanity brought to every man some rights. Yet to subject a man to slavery was both to deny him all his rights and the power to assert them as well.

Channing's third argument was based upon his assumption of the essential equality of men, which he asserted in spite of the protestations of those he called "verbal logicians" who denied equality because men were obviously not equal in any measurable dimension or capacity. Diversities among men Channing freely acknowledged; but, he insisted, "these diversities among men are as nothing in comparison with the attributes in which they agree; and it is this which constitutes their essential equality."[13]

> All men have the same rational nature and the same power of conscience, and all are equally made for indefinite improvement of these divine faculties, and for the happiness to be found in their virtuous use.[14]

Although there were diversities among men, inequalities among men, and even within the same individual an inequality of talents and abilities, these diversities only served to promote the mutual advantage of all mankind. But by what standard, asked Channing, could one make claim to such superiority over others as to hold them in total subjugation.

> Among these partakers of the same rational and moral nature, who can make good a right over others, which others may not establish over himself?[15]

To Channing there could be no such right, and therefore no such claim. His fourth argument against the property status of slaves rested on an analysis of the nature of property. This was in essence a continuation of the case built up previously that slavery was contrary to the contention of rights possessed by all human beings. For property was an exclusive right which belonged entirely to the owner of such property. Property has no claims against its possessor. Yet Channing observed, in the tradition of John Locke, "If

12 *Ibid.*, p. 20.
13 *Ibid.*, p. 21.
14 *Ibid.*, p. 21.
15 *Ibid.*, p. 22.

there be property in any thing, it is that of a man in his own person, mind, and strength."[16] Such "property" might be contracted for, such might be forfeited by the commission of a crime. But in either case the assumption of the original right of a person to property in himself, his mind and strength, was clear and acknowledged. For one could not contract away nor forfeit any part of that which he did not by right possess.

In his fifth argument Channing cited the "universal indignation" that arose against slavery. Not only had a moral judgment been passed against the international slave trade, but in addition Congress had declared it piracy to bring further slaves from Africa. How can that which is acknowledged to be wrong in origin be admitted to be right in perpetuation? How can practice make legitimate that which is accepted as wrong from the start? "Can that very use, which makes the original seizure an enormous wrong, become gradually innocent? . . . Does the duration of wrong, the increase of it by continuance, convert it into right?"[17] Clearly the objection to the slave trade rested upon the objection to slavery itself and the immorality of one was directly associated with the immorality of the other. The slave trade was immoral because no man could be legitimately seized or purchased to be the property of another. The continuance of slavery was thus a continuance of this basic wrong.

Further evidence of the wrong of slavery was advanced by his next proposition that rights and obligations were co-existent. Where there was a right there was also a corresponding obligation. If slavery was right, there was a moral obligation for subservience on the part of those held in slavery. Yet, Channing asked the reader, did one really feel that the slaves were duty-bound, morally obligated to serve their masters, and not to desire an escape from such bondage? No such obligation existed, and thus "the absence of obligation proves the want of the right."[18]

Finally, in his seventh argument against using a man as property, Channing developed what he considered the most important argument of all. Here he combined his theology and morality to explain the dignity of the individual human being.

He cannot be property in the sight of God and justice, because he is a Rational, Moral, Immortal Being; because created in God's

[16] *Ibid.*, p. 23.
[17] *Ibid.*, pp. 23-24.
[18] *Ibid.*, p. 26.

image, and therefore in the highest sense his child, because created to unfold godlike faculties, and to govern himself by a Divine Law written on his heart, and republished in God's word.[19]

All men contained within themselves an element of the Divine. Such beings could not be considered as instruments or means to another person's fulfillment but were destined to be ends in themselves. It was indeed the purpose of education and discipline "to make a man Master of Himself, to excite him to act from a principle in his own mind, to lead him to propose his own perfection as his supreme law and end."[20] This could never be achieved while men were subjected to the mind, the will, the force of another. There could be no development of the intellectual and moral powers of an individual where there was no free exertion of these powers. Thus it was the Divinity, the morality that was an ingrained part of man that repudiated the claim of one human being to hold others as property.

In the remainder of his *Essay on Slavery* Channing developed more fully the ideas presented in his attack on the basic conception of one human being as the property of another. Throughout his essay is the recurring theme of the intrinsic morality, the innateness of conscience, which is the possession of all men and the justification of their claim to rights. All rights rest ultimately upon some conception of morality; Channing assumed a universal morality, common to all men, which made rights the bounty of the Creator and not of society. Rights, therefore, took on an absolute rather than a relative validity.

> In the order of things, they precede society, lie at its foundation, constitute man's capacity for it, and are the great objects of social institutions. The consciousness of rights is not a creation of human art, a conventional sentiment, but essential to and inseparable from the human soul.[21]

Conscience revealed the moral law to man. It was this moral law that was the higher law, above all civil enactments which restrained governments, social institutions as well as individuals in their conduct. It was this "intuitive conviction" in men that gave primacy to the moral law and this deep sense of conscience that protested not alone the wrongs done to one's self, but also the wrongs done to

[19] *Ibid.*
[20] *Ibid.*, p. 28.
[21] *Ibid.*, p. 32.

others. It was this consciousness of wrongs inflicted on others that was such a salient characteristic of man that spurred man's desire for freedom, not for himself alone but for all men. It was conscience that inspired the cause of freedom and led the way to social action. Government in turn was instituted by men to promote the desires of men inspired by moral sentiment. "The great end of government," wrote Channing, "is to repress *all wrong*."[22]

For all his sustained and reasoned attack upon slavery, Channing was quite conservative in his proposals for its abolishment. He was not an abolitionist of the Garrison school; indeed he attacked this camp for being too narrow and fanatical in their views and, through their agitation, of alienating the friends of abolition. For he believed that the success of abolition rested in the hands of the masters of slaves. Abolition would have to come about through voluntary adoption by the Southern states. "They alone can do it safely. They alone can determine and apply the true and sure means of emancipation."[23] Whereas Garrison was willing to alienate the South to achieve abolition, through continued agitation and demonstration, Channing believed that the hope for abolition lay in the adoption in the South of the belief that man could not be held as property and that all men have certain rights by virtue of being men.

Furthermore Channing was opposed to granting, immediately, freedom to those held in slavery. It would be cruelty, not kindness, he argued, to free slaves into a situation that they could neither understand nor enjoy.

> It would be cruelty to strike the fetters from a man, whose first steps would infallibly lead him to a precipice. . . . The Slave should not have an owner, but he should have a guardian. He needs authority, to supply the lack of that discretion which he has not yet attained; but it should be the authority of a friend; an official authority, conferred by the state, and for which there should be responsibilities to the state; an authority especially designed to prepare its subjects for personal freedom. . . .[24]

Thus Channing sought a moderate solution to the problem of slavery to be achieved by appealing to the moral sentiments of the South, where there was legal power to enact his recommendations. Like Garrison, his views rested upon the philosophical assumptions stated in the Declaration of Independence. But unlike Garrison, he

22 *Ibid.*, p. 36.
23 *Ibid.*, pp. 107-108.
24 *Ibid.*, p. 109.

devoted his efforts to a systematic presentation, a logical development, of these beliefs. Both, however, carried on the natural rights tradition in American thought.

ABRAHAM LINCOLN

The antislavery discussions of the 1830's, as conducted by the abolitionist Garrison or the philosopher Channing, were centered on the moral aspects of the "peculiar institution" and inquired as to whether such an institution was in keeping with that higher law that ought to govern the thoughts and actions of all men. The Scriptures were quoted and economic arguments were introduced only to bolster the previously affirmed moral position that slavery was contrary to the conscience of mankind. In this early phase of the discussion the outspoken critics of slavery did not have the support of public opinion in the North; indeed they ran counter to it.

By the middle 1850's, however, Northern sentiment had undergone a decided change, and opinion had clearly crystalized against slavery. The moral issue had been complicated by the continued struggle for power between the slave and free states. In the early 1830's, as a result of the Missouri Compromise of 1820, there were twelve slave states and twelve free states, and the remaining area of the Louisiana Territory north of 36° 30′ was "forever prohibited" from establishing slavery. By 1845, following the annexation of Texas, the balance of power had shifted to the slave states (15 to 13), while antislavery sentiment developed with increasing rapidity in the North. In five years, and with the admission of California as a free state, the balance of power had shifted to the North (16 to 15). Since the days of the founding of the Antislavery Society, the number of slave states had actually increased and each state seeking admission to the Union posed a crucial issue in this struggle for power. Thus the early issue of the abolition of slavery was now compounded by the spread of the institution. Whether slavery ought to exist at all was one question; whether it should be allowed to spread was distinctly another. Yet these two questions were brought together when Congress passed a drastic Fugitive Slave Law in 1850, which not only gave national sanction to slavery where it existed but furthermore jeopardized the civil rights of free Negroes everywhere. State "personal liberty" laws, the Underground Railroad, and the enthusiastic reception of Harriet Beecher Stowe's *Uncle Tom's Cabin* (1852) indicated that Northern opinion was not entirely in accord with the national policy. The Kansas-Nebraska Act of 1854, which repealed the Missouri Compromise, reopened the slavery question in that area in which slavery had been "forever prohibited" by the earlier statute. Three years later the Supreme Court decided the famous Dred Scott case (19 Howard 393) and found that Dred Scott, as a Negro, was not a citizen of the United States and therefore could not bring suit in a federal court. Furthermore a slave was property, and Congress could not restrict slavery in the territories, as it would deprive citizens of their property without "due process of law."

It is in the light of these political developments that Lincoln's position on slavery is considered. Slavery was not a dying institution but a spreading one, and the political balance of power between the slave and free states was sufficiently precarious as to threaten momentarily the existence of the Union. Lincoln's primary orientation and interest was the preservation of the Union, and especially at first, his interest in the eradication of slavery was subservient to the political issue of the maintenance of the Union itself. In his Peoria speech in 1854, following the Kansas-Nebraska Act, which repealed the Missouri Compromise, Lincoln declared that "Much as I hate slavery, I would consent to any great evil to avoid a greater one."[25] But it was this possible extension of slavery that Lincoln thought most jeopardized the existence of the Union. Lincoln opposed slavery, because of the "monstrous injustice of slavery itself," because it brought so many men into "an open war with the very fundamental principles of civil liberty, criticizing the Declaration of Independence, and insisting that there is no right principle of action but self-interest."[26] Yet Lincoln's major argument was against the extension of slavery rather than the continued existence of it. He doubted the practicability of the various proposed solutions of slavery, such as the returning of slaves to Liberia. As to freeing the slaves so that they could be considered politically and socially as equals, he declared:

> My own feelings will not admit of this, and if mine would, we well know that those of the great mass of whites will not. Whether this feeling accords with justice and sound judgment is not the sole ques-

[25] John G. Nicolay and John Hay, eds., *Complete Works of Abraham Lincoln* (Lincoln Memorial Library, 1894), vol. II, p. 236.
[26] *Ibid.*, p. 205.

tion, if indeed it is any part of it. A universal feeling, whether well or ill founded, cannot be safely disregarded. We cannot then make them equals.[27]

He preferred to see a system of gradual emancipation carried out by the South.

It was the likelihood of the extension of slavery through the repeal of the Missouri Compromise that brought forth Lincoln's argument for a policy of containment of a recognized evil. Morally, he maintained, it was as improper to extend slavery to new territory as to bring additional slaves from Africa. To argue that there was no difference in property between a beast and a slave was to deny the humanity of the Negro. Furthermore, to argue that the issue of slavery should be determined in each state as a matter of self-government was fallacious, for it turned again upon the question of whether the Negro was or was not considered a man. If he was a man then he too should have a right to govern himself.

When the white man governs himself, that is self-government; but when he governs himself and also governs another man, that is more than self-government—that is despotism. If the Negro is a man, why then my ancient faith teaches me that "all men are created equal," and that there can be no moral right in connection with one man's making a slave of another.[28]

It was Lincoln's hope that by confining slavery to the states where it already existed, and where, under the Constitution, there was no immediate national way of removing it, that the institution of slavery would gradually decline to the point of extinction. However, the course of political history ran clearly counter to this approach, and in 1857 the United States Supreme Court rendered the explosively controversial Dred Scott decision. This decision, which denied Congress authority to prohibit slavery in the territories of the United States, was directly opposed to Lincoln's policy of containment of slavery through the restoration of the Missouri Compromise. The interpretation of the Declaration of Independence in the case by Chief Justice Taney,—an interpretation supported by Lincoln's rival, Stephen Douglas—that the instrument was not intended to include Negroes was directly counter to the universal hypothesis of natural-rights theory. In his opposition to the Dred Scott decision Lincoln entered into an examination of the Declara-

[27] *Ibid.*, p. 206.
[28] *Ibid.*, pp. 227-228.

tion of Independence and its assertion that all men were created equal. It was manifest, he argued, that this assertion of equality was not intended to mean that men were created equal *"in all respects."* It did mean, however, that men were created equal with respect to their inalienable rights. Obviously it did not mean that all men in 1776 were enjoying the equal exercise of these rights, but rather, the goal being stated, the realization of these rights would follow "as fast as circumstances should permit." While the rights declared and the actual rights realized and enforced might be quite separate, the former rights were the goal to guide in the development of the latter. This, Lincoln maintained, was the intention of the authors of the Declaration of Independence.

> They meant to set up a standard maxim for free society, which should be familiar to all, and revered by all; constantly looked to, constantly labored for, and even though never perfectly attained, constantly approximated, and thereby constantly spreading and deepening its influence and augmenting the happiness and value of life to all people of all colors everywhere. . . . Its authors meant it to be —as, thank God, it is now proving itself—a stumbling-block to all those who in after times might seek to turn a free people back into the hateful paths of despotism.[29]

Lincoln's attack upon slavery drew essentially from the same sources used by Garrison, Channing and other critics of the institution. Slavery was contrary to natural law, which was the law of conscience, implanted by God in all men. It was contrary to the principles of self-government which were such an important part of the American democratic conception. But where Garrison had taken an extreme stand for immediate abolition, Lincoln, like Channing, looked to a system of gradual emancipation. Fully conscious of the inflammatory nature of the slavery discussion and its threat to the existence of the nation as a union of sovereign states, Lincoln's major emphasis was not upon the destruction of slavery but upon the preservation of the Union. He took, therefore, a compromise position. He denounced slavery as an evil institution and sought to prevent its further spread. And while, under the Constitution, he saw no means whereby the national government could eradicate slavery, he, like Channing, hoped that the good conscience of men in the South would set the institution on a decline so that in time the evil would entirely disappear.

[29] *Ibid.*, p. 331.

HINTON R. HELPER

Not all, although the preponderant amount, of antislavery thought was written by Northerners. Indeed one of the most thorough attacks upon the slave system was written in 1857 by a North Carolinian, Hinton R. Helper (1829-1909). *The Impending Crisis of the South: How to Meet It* is a most comprehensive criticism of slavery and a belligerent attack upon what he termed the "oligarchy of slave holders." Writing as a Southerner who sought the restoration of the South to its former pre-eminent position in politics, economics and cultural attainments, he was viewed by his compatriots as a renegade and his book was fairly well suppressed in the South. When the book was reprinted in 1859, and endorsed by various Republican leaders, sufficient controversy was aroused concerning it that it was proposed in the U. S. House of Representatives during a political contest for Speaker of the House that no one who had endorsed this work was qualified to be Speaker of that body.

There was nothing moderate about Helper; he wrote with gusto and vindictiveness to eliminate an intolerable evil. He took his stand for complete abolition, and complete Union, even though he realized that these twin goals were hardly to come about without open conflict. "Each revolving year brings nearer the inevitable crisis," he wrote. "The sooner it comes the better; may heaven, through our humble efforts, hasten its advent."[30] Writing late in the course of the slavery debate, Helper was able to marshall argument against argument and authority against authority in an effort to achieve a complete rebuttal of the proslavery position. Where Biblical allusions to slavery and the beneficence and necessity of this system had been used by its proponents, Helper countered with selected sayings and precepts of the Old and New Testaments to prove his position. He devoted one chapter to Bible testimony and another to the testimony of the churches in his favor. Political philosophers throughout the ages had been cited by the proponents of slavery; Helper replied with three chapters of quotations and references to the political theorists from the Greeks on through civilization, including one chapter of attacks on slavery by the early Southern political leaders. The real significance of Helper's

[30] *The Impending Crisis of The South: How to Meet It* (New York: A. B. Bendick, 1860), p. 27.

work, however, was in its detailed statistical analysis of Southern society, its commerce, its agriculture, its politics, and its literature, and a comparable analysis of life in the free states.[31] It was, in all, a stupendous project, utilizing nearly sixty tables of statistical comparisons and countless miscellaneous figures intended to prove that slavery had sapped the strength, culture, and initiative of the South. At bottom, slavery was an uneconomical system which impoverished the South, and the impoverishment had many dire consequences.

> Indeed, the *unprofitableness* of slavery is a monstrous evil, when considered in all its bearings; it makes us poor; poverty makes us ignorant; ignorance makes us wretched; wretchedness makes us wicked, and wickedness leads to the devil![32]

A slave-oriented society tends toward illiteracy, for it provides fewer common schools, fewer books and periodicals, fewer publishing houses, and finally fewer people who could read literature were it published. This thesis was supported by a variety of statistics comparing the sixteen free states with the fifteen slave states in literacy and sample periodical circulations. "Disguise the unwelcome truth as we may, slavery is the parent of ignorance, and ignorance begets a whole brood of follies and of vices, and every one of these is inevitably hostile to literary culture."[33] Not only were there fewer white persons in proportion to the total white population who could read in the slave states as compared with the free states, but such a society inhibited mental freedom. "A free press is an institution almost unknown in the South. Free speech is considered as treason against slavery: and when people dare neither speak nor print their thoughts, free thought itself is well nigh extinguished."[34] Slavery produced a closed and oligarchical society in which the opinions and habits of the slaveholders alone were respected. It was this oligarchy of some quarter million slaveholders which Helper wished to overthrow. "The liberation of five millions

31 *Ibid.*, pp. 28-32. Helper justified his use of the statistical method to lay the factual basis for his argument. He saw in "the science of statistics" a means of achieving a true understanding of man's political and economic behavior, and quoted with approval a Wm. C. Taylor, who noted that "the great object of this new science is to lead to the knowledge of human nature; that is, to ascertain the general course of operation of man's mental and moral faculties, and to furnish us with a correct standard of judgment, by enabling us to determine the average amount of the past as a guide to the average probabilities of the future."
32 *Ibid.*, pp. 81-82.
33 *Ibid.*, p. 406.
34 *Ibid.*, p. 409.

of 'poor white trash' from the second degree of slavery, and of three millions of miserable kidnapped negroes from the first degree, cannot be acomplished too soon."[35] In order to rally the nonslaveholding white yeomanry to his side, Helper attempted to show "that free labor is far more respectable, profitable, and productive, than slave labor."[36] Yet in the slave states, he argued, all labor was looked upon as menial, and nonslaveholders were viewed contemptuously by the upper classes. These slaveholders, however, had a stranglehold upon the social, political and economic life of the region. Abolition would accomplish a revolution in all departments so that a majority of whites would regain the various Southern states from the abusive hands of the few. He sought a revolution of the yeomanry against the entrenched oligarchy.

Essentially, Helper's thesis was that the slave states and the free states had started off on approximately an equal footing at the time the first census was taken in 1790. If anything, the South held a statistical advantage over the North. But some sixty years later, with the number of free and slave states nearly equal (sixteen free, fifteen slave), the advantage had turned overwhelmingly to the North. For all the physical advantages of climate, soil, and accessible harbors in the South, it was the North that welcomed the immigrants, developed ports and railways, encouraged education and enjoyed an extraordinary development in farms and factories. Drawing heavily upon the census figures and other available statistics he drew comparison after comparison between free and slave states to show the advantages of production in a free society. The North, with less territory, was well ahead in patents and population. Even in the much-vaunted field of agriculture, the South lagged behind, taking totals of all agricultural products. The validity of the moral arguments for freedom were proved in the statistics of production and exchange, schools, ports, and publishing houses.

> Southern divines give us elaborate "Bible Arguments"; Southern statists heap treatise upon treatise through which the Federal Constitution is tortured into all monstrous shapes; Southern novelists bore us *ad infinitum* with pictures of the beatitudes of plantation life and the negro-quarters; Southern verse-wrights drone out their drowsy dactyls or grow ventricous with their turgid heroics all in defense of slavery,—priest, politician, novelist, bardling, severally ringing the changes upon "the Biblical institution," "the conservative

[35] *Ibid.*, pp. 32-33.
[36] *Ibid.*, p. 41.

institution," "the humanizing institution," "the patriarchal institution,"
—and then—have their books printed on Northern paper, with Northern types, by Northern artizans, stitched, bound and made ready for
the market by Northern industry; and yet fail to see in all this, as a
true philosophical mind *must* see, an overwhelming refutation of their
miserable sophisms in behalf of a system against which humanity
in all its impulses and aspiration, and civilization in all its activities
and triumph, utter their perpetual protest.[37]

Helper's plan for abolition was in reality a call to the nonslave-
owning whites of the South for political action. He called for complete—political, economic, and social—ostracism of slaveholders by
the nonslaveholding whites. If a complete boycott were laid against
the slaveholders through the united action of all other whites, then
Helper thought this economic and social lever would help pry
open the doors to politics so that nonslaveholding whites could
either gain office or control the political scene. Once in command
of politics the nonslaveholding whites would place a heavy tax for
each slave against each slaveholder for a six-year period. The re-
ceipts from this tax were then to be used to ship Negroes to Liberia,
South America, or elsewhere in the United States. Where there
were still slaves beyond the six-year period of grace, then the
owners would have to pay an additional tax, to go directly to the
slaves themselves. In this way Helper hoped to tax slavery out of
existence.

The work of Helper, "the voice of the nonslaveholding whites of
the South," was a voice that was little heard in that area on the eve
of the great conflict. Yet his economic analysis of slavery, and the
impact of that system on a society, was indeed penetrating and has
been in many respects supported by subsequent thinkers.

Helper's attack upon slavery, based upon social statistics, was
thus quite a different kind of argument from that employed by
Garrison and Channing. Helper was primarily concerned with the
social consequences of a slave system, while Channing and Garrison
were directly concerned with the legitimacy of slavery as an institution. Helper thought of slavery as a means to an undesirable social
end; the unfavorable judgment on the social end thus carried back
as a criticism on the means. Slavery was not necessarily an evil in
itself, but was an evil because it contributed to the making of a
society which was inferior when judged by the social standards
of a free society. Helper, as a Southerner, thus argued against slavery

[37] *Ibid.,* pp. 391-392.

within the framework of ideas employed by other Southerners to defend that institution. He paid little attention to the moralistic, natural-rights approach and emphasized slavery as a social institution which must be judged in the light of its social consequences. Society, not the individual slave or free man, was his frame of reference for judging slavery, and his standard was clearly not an abstract conception of morality but rather a utilitarian view of social consequences.

Garrison and Channing, however, voiced the predominant Northern criticism of slavery which echoed the assumptions, indeed the phrases, of the Declaration of Independence. Slavery was an evil because it was offensive to the dignity of man—slave and free man alike. They assumed man to be born with natural rights which could not be alienated despite the practices of society. Since these rights were innate and inalienable, the crucial issue was to bring about their realization in the South. That these rights were not realized by the slave in the South was no argument against their existence, for if rights were assumed to be natural, their actual social acceptance was irrelevant. Only socially determined rights required social acceptance; rights acquired from God or nature required only the birth of man for their existence. Thus the issue was fairly drawn between antislavery and proslavery theorists over the nature and source of the rights of man and the obligations of social organizations.

CHAPTER 11

Slavery and the Rights of Man (continued)

PROSLAVERY THOUGHT

SLAVERY was instituted in the South during the Colonial period; there were many, however, who hoped that the movement for American independence would bring an end to this institution. Jefferson, among other Southern statesmen, looked forward to the end of the slave trade and indeed the end of slavery itself. Yet it was generally assumed by these writers that with the end of slavery something would have to be done with the Negroes, as the two races would be unable to live together in peace and harmony. Negro slaves, brought out of the wilds of a primitive and indeed slave society in Africa, were looked upon as an inferior breed of humanity who could not be readily elevated to the standards of western civilization. Thus the early discussions for an end to slavery in the South were coupled with a desire for the deportation to Africa of manumitted Negroes. The American Society for the Colonization of the Free People of Color in the United States was established in 1816 to solve the race problem by deporting, with their consent, free Negroes. The American Colonization Society, which drew its meager support from slaveholders and nonslaveholders alike, was not primarily interested in emancipation, but in deporting those previously emancipated. This organization was supplanted by the sectional Antislavery Society in the 1830's, which was not primarily concerned for the free Negroes, but for those still held in slavery.

The Antislavery Society arose at a time when the cotton industry was making slavery a profitable and, some felt, a necessary institu-

tion, and a considerable change in tone is found in Southern literature on the subject. Slavery, instead of being looked upon as an unfortunate institution which must in time be eliminated, now became
defended openly as a positive good, an institution that ought not to
be restricted but extended. No longer did Southern writers feel
obliged to apologize for slavery on the grounds that if it were an
evil, the original sin lay with the British who established the system
in the colonies, aided by the New England shippers who profited
from the slave trade; on the contrary they now proclaimed that
slavery was not an evil but a blessing which benefited slave and
slaveholder alike. Slavery was not a vestigial remnant of barbarism
but a necessary component of progress and civilization.

The arguments which arrived at this "positive good" conclusion
concerning slavery during the thirty years preceding the Civil War
were designed to meet every conceivable criticism of the institution.
To the argument that slavery was contrary to Christianity it was
answered by Albert Bledsoe, Thornton Stringfellow, and Charles
Hodge, quoting chapter and verse, that the Bible specifically con-
doned slavery. Political philosophers from Aristotle onward were
called upon and quoted in support of slavery. To the charge that
slavery was immoral it was argued by Calhoun, Fitzhugh, and
Harper that only through slavery could morality be promoted. To
the statistical argument that slavery was economically ruinous, it was
answered by David Christy, Thornton Stringfellow, and George
Fitzhugh, with a vast battery of figures, that slavery promoted
wealth, morality, and religion. And finally, to the argument that all
men were created equal, it was answered that in fact nothing could
be further from the truth; and Dr. Josiah Clark Nott, Dr. S. A. Cartwright, and others sought to prove on ethnological grounds that the
Negro was a naturally inferior race.[1]

Indeed, many of the conclusions of Southern defenders of slavery
were summed up in a speech of South Carolina's Governor J. H.
Hammond when he enunciated the "mud-sill" theory of society as a
basis for slavery in 1858.

> In all social systems there must be a class to do the menial duties, to
> perform the drudgery of life. That is, a class requiring but a low
> order of intellect and but little skill. Its requisites are vigor, docility,
> fidelity. Such a class you must have or you would not have that other

[1] See William Sumner Jenkins, *Pro-Slavery Thought in the Old South* (Chapel
Hill: The University of North Carolina Press, 1935), for the development and
content of these various arguments.

class which leads progress, civilization, and refinement. It constitutes the very mud-sill of society and of political government; and you might as well attempt to build a house in the air, as to build either the one or the other, except on this mud-sill. Fortunately for the South, she found a race adapted to that purpose to her hand. . . . We use them for our purpose and call them slaves.[2]

The Southern defense of slavery reached out to attack the free society of the North and, in fact, England and Western Europe. All free society was seething with unrest, a discontent that gave rise to radical notions of reform, to a multitude of "isms." The South, it was maintained, was the great conservative force in civilization which, because of its peculiar arrangement of society, was able to be free of the various "isms." This freedom from "isms" was looked upon as a "positive good" and indicative of the peaceful complacency of Southern society and politics. "Shakers, Rappists, Dunkers, Socialists, Fourierists, and the like, keep themselves afar off," Hammond noted,[3] while George Fitzhugh devoted a short chapter in his *Cannibals All* to "The Philosophy of the Isms—Shewing Why They Abound At The North, And Are Unknown At The South." The South stood for conservatism, and only conservatism, it was argued, carried civilization forward. Thus in substance the Southern social theory held that slavery was morally justifiable, economically desirable, and politically necessary.

JOHN C. CALHOUN

The greatest Southern spokesman for the social theory of slavery was John C. Calhoun (1782-1851) of South Carolina, who gave in his Senate speeches and various writings an elaborate defense of the South's "peculiar institution" together with a detailed statement of the position of the South in the Union. Indeed, the Southern defense of states' rights and the Southern defense of slavery are joined in the work of Calhoun, for he saw in a slave society a fundamentally conservative disposition which could make itself felt only through a national recognition of the validity of states' rights.

[2] Quoted in Jenkins, *op. cit.,* p. 286; reprinted by permission; from Speech in Senate, March 4, 1858, *Congressional Globe,* 35th Congress, 1st Session, Appendix, p. 71.

[3] "Slavery in the Light of Political Science" in *Cotton Is King, and Pro-Slavery Arguments,* edited by E. N. Elliot (Augusta, Ga.: Pritchard, Abbott, and Loomis, 1860), p. 643.

States' rights was thus an institutional means of protecting slavery in the South, and might properly serve as a conservative device for checking any national movements for reform which endangered the status quo in any state.

Calhoun, like most of the Southern writers on slavery, was far closer to Thomas Hobbes than he was to John Locke, as he saw in society an endless struggle between individuals for power and control of their fellow man. Thus, as between the twin desires of man—liberty and security—he felt the more fundamental need was the latter. Liberty was a blessing, a luxury; but security or order was a fundamental prerequisite for survival. Calhoun's political orientation was in favor of protecting the blessings that existed, to conserve the present rather than risk the future, and his attitude in regard to slavery reflects this basic conservatism. Opposed to Calhoun's ideas was the radical philosophy of natural rights stated in the Declaration of Independence and frequently reiterated by the abolitionists: If all men were created equal and brought with them from a state of nature the inalienable right to liberty, what could make legitimate this disregard of liberty through the practice of Negro slavery? As answer to this traditional query of the abolitionists, Calhoun attacked the entire natural rights philosophy.

The state of nature as the logical starting place for natural-rights philosophy, Calhoun found, never did nor could exist, for it was contrary to the very nature of man, who was designed by his Creator for a social and political life.

> As, then, there never was such a state as the so-called state of nature, and never can be, it follows, that men, instead of being born in it, are born in the social and political state; and of course, instead of being born free and equal, are born subject, not only to parental authority, but to the laws and institutions of the country where born, and under whose protection they draw their first breath.[4]

There having been no state of nature, man of course could not have contracted himself out of it. Thus the contract theory of society and government was pushed aside, and with it the arguments that were derived from it. Man, a social and political being, had experienced no other condition of life and could claim no rights antecedent to those granted by society. Had there been a state of nature such as the contract theorists supposed, then it might have

---

[4] "A Disquisition on Government," in *The Works of John C. Calhoun,* edited by Richard K. Crallé (New York: D. Appleton and Co., 1854), vol. I, pp. 58-59.

been said that all men were equal in it; for by definition each man would have been fully independent in this pre-social and pre-political situation. But there having been none, no argument for equality could be derived from it. Furthermore, the opinion that all men were born free and equal was completely fallacious. "It rests," Calhoun wrote, "upon the assumption of a fact, which is contrary to universal observation, in whatever light it may be regarded." There was no such thing as equality of men, and this was indeed fortunate for the future of the human race. For life was a competitive struggle between unequal individuals each seeking to better his condition. "It is, indeed, this inequality of condition between the front and rear ranks, in the march of progress, which gives so strong an impulse to the former to maintain their position, and to the latter to press forward into their files. This gives to progress its greatest impulse."[5] Calhoun thus saw in the course of conflict the path of progress, and stated it in terms anticipating the American social Darwinists later in the century.

There being neither a state of nature nor a condition of equality among men, it was to be expected that man could make no innate claim to freedom as a right. If freedom were given to those unready for it the result would be anarchy. As all men were not equal, so all men were not prepared for freedom. Freedom was not a natural right but rather a social reward.

> It is a reward to be earned, not a blessing to be gratuitously lavished on all alike;—a reward reserved for the intelligent, the patriotic, the virtuous and deserving;—and not a boon to be bestowed on a people too ignorant, degraded and vicious, to be capable either of appreciating or of enjoying it. . . . A reward more appropriate than liberty could not be conferred on the deserving;—nor a punishment inflicted on the undeserving more just, than to be subject to lawless and despotic rule.[6]

With this theory of the nature of society and the well-springs of human motivation, Calhoun was able to proclaim the institution of slavery in the South a positive good to the immediate parties concerned and to the United States at large. The slaves themselves were seen to be directly benefited when their condition was compared either with that of their ancestors in Africa or their free contemporaries in a factory society. The South, it was argued, was civilizing

[5] *Ibid.*, p. 57.
[6] *Ibid.*, p. 55.

the savage. Furthermore, given the existence in society of two separate and distinct races, slavery was the only means by which the two
races could live together without open discord. Even were there not
racial differences in the society, there would be a genuine class problem of antagonisms between the rich and the poor, and this relationship would be aggravated by the racial factor. "There never has yet
existed a wealthy and civilized society," Calhoun declared in a
Senate speech, "in which one portion of the community did not, in
point of fact, live on the labor of the other."[7] As a result of the class
conflict the laborer received but a meager remnant from his productivity, and this was true no matter how this conflict was disguised or
under what system it operated. Yet, Calhoun argued, the slave
laborer received a greater tangible reward for his work than the
wage worker elsewhere, for he was granted by his master food,
shelter, and clothing.

Given this great conflict between labor and capital, which existed
in all civilized countries, it was evident that there would always be
tendencies toward disorder. This tendency toward disorder, aggravated by the racial factor, was brought under control, however, by
slavery. For by keeping the workers slaves the likelihood of agitation
and disorder was diminished, which, reasoned Calhoun, was why
the South was so much more "stable and quiet" than the North.
Because slavery was conducive to this peaceful condition of society,
Calhoun argued that it formed "the most solid and durable foundation on which to rear free and stable political institutions." The
South, removed from the unrest that was disturbing the rest of the
nation, was thus a great force for conservatism. It was this aspect
of the South's political life that Calhoun thought could be turned
to national advantage. For he believed that in all political systems
it was necessary that there be some powerful conservative force to
check the aggressions of the less stable parts. "In this tendency to
conflict in the North, between labor and capital, which is constantly
on the increase, the weight of the South has and will ever be found
on the conservative side; against the aggression of one or the other
side, whichever may tend to disturb the equilibrium of our political
system."[8]

Calhoun thus evolved an elaborate defense of slavery by constructing a theory of society which found the course of progress in the
inequalities of men and the exploitation of the many by the few. He

---

[7] *Works,* Vol. II, p. 631.
[8] *Ibid.,* vol. III, p. 180.

denied the validity of the natural-rights philosophy, and his economics was frankly based upon the assumption of a class struggle. All of the essential arguments in favor of slavery are found in Calhoun's work. While many of these arguments were not original with him, nevertheless his favorable position as a statesman of national repute, together with his ability to think incisively and express himself clearly, made him the pre-eminent spokesman for the Southern cause.

THE SOCIAL PHILOSOPHY OF WILLIAM HARPER

The basic assumption of the antislavery writers was the equality of all men in their inalienable right to liberty. It was equally fundamental to the proslavery writers to prove that this assumption was totally in error, and that a political philosophy built upon it was clearly unsound and incapable of being put into practice. The Southern writers thus offered a challenge in the name of realism to the airy speculations of the natural rights thinkers. No two men were equal; no man was born free; no rights existed without the sanction of society, a sanction which was dependent upon the felt conception of the public good. Rights were thus not anterior to society but derived from it. And, consequently, as Albert Bledsoe noted, "the rights of the individual are subordinate to those of the community."[9] Furthermore, Bledsoe wrote, "The truth is, that all men are born not equally free and independent, but equally without freedom and without independence."[10] This contrary position in regard to the nature of man in relation to society led inevitably to a contrary philosophy of human rights and the organization of political society.

It was William Harper (1790-1847), a South Carolina jurist and a member of the constitutional convention of that state which voted for nullifying the Tariff Act of 1832, who made one of the earliest explicit defenses of the South's social philosophy as a justification of slavery. His *Slavery in the Light of Social Ethics*, written in 1837, is one of the fullest philosophical expositions devoted to a defense of slavery and contains the essential arguments used by other Southern writers in the same cause.

Throughout the course of human history, Harper observed,

[9] "Liberty and Slavery," in *Cotton Is King*, p. 287.
[10] *Ibid.*, p. 334.

slavery was generally found wherever there was a high point in civilization. It was therefore not a peculiar institution but a natural one that was indeed "founded in the nature of man and the exigencies of human society."[11] As a normal institution in human affairs it existed because it satisfied certain basic social necessities. Slavery thus made an essential contribution to the course of man's destiny. It was the destiny of man to achieve civilization; and the institution of slavery Harper found to be "the sole cause" of man's becoming civilized. Without slavery there would be no civilization.

In order to prove this thesis Harper argued that most men were averse to labor and that this aversion could be overcome only through coercion. "The coercion of slavery alone is adequate to form man to habits of labor."[12] Yet without labor there would be no property, and without property there could be no civilization. "Property —the accumulation of capital, as it is commonly called—is the first element of civilization."[13] What slavery provided was that combination of labor necessary to the accumulation of property, which in turn was the starting place of civilization. As property and civilization were found together, so indeed were property and the institution of slavery. Thus slavery, property, and civilization marked the progress of the human race.

> He who has obtained the command of another's labor, first begins to accumulate and provide for the future, and the foundations of civilization are laid. . . . Since the existence of man upon the earth, with no exception whatever, either of ancient or modern times, every society which has attained civilization, has advanced to it through this process.[14]

In the syllogism of Harper, slavery was necessary to property and property necessary to civilization; therefore slavery was necessary to civilization. Conversely, when man ceased to labor, property would cease to accumulate and civilization would decline. In every civilized society, therefore, man was dependent upon his fellow man, and there were unequal consequences from the accumulations of labor and the accumulations of property. "*Servitude* is the condition of civilization," Harper declared.[15] It only remained for him to argue

[11] "Slavery in the Light of Social Ethics," in *Cotton Is King*, p. 549.
[12] *Ibid.*, p. 552.
[13] *Ibid.*, p. 564.
[14] *Ibid.*, p. 552.
[15] *Ibid.*, p. 570.

that among the races the Negro was peculiarly suited to this servitude.

Labor, Harper had stated, was repugnant to some people. "Labor is pain to those who are unaccustomed to it, and the nature of man is averse to pain."[16] For those who found labor repugnant, slavery was the proper answer. Furthermore, every civilized society called for a multitude of diverse occupations and professions. Some of these employments required intellect and training; some were monotonous drudgery requiring no special fitness. It was the latter category of occupations which were peculiarly fitted for slavery, where employment was encouraged by compulsion. It was Harper's contention that the Negro slaves in the South, "from their temperament and capacity, are peculiarly suited to the situation which they occupy, and not less happy in it than any corresponding class to be found in the world."[17] Furthermore, likening the difference between the slave and the slaveholder to the difference between a savage and a civilized man, Harper wrote:

> It is the order of nature and of God, that the being of superior faculties and knowledge, and therefore of superior power, should control and dispose of those who are inferior. It is as much in the order of nature, that men should enslave each other, as that other animals should prey upon each other.[18]

The South had not originated slavery, but was accepting it as a necessity of civilization. The slaves were not being initiated into slavery in the South, but were rather being trained in a higher form of slave society than the African one from which they had come originally. Slavery not only solved the problem of how to have society's most menial and obnoxious labor performed, but it saved such laborers from the frustrations that would accompany their efforts in a free society. For all societies had menial and servile work performed; yet in a free society the lower class laborers who performed this work maintained vain aspirations and bitter jealousies. Of such free laborers Harper wrote:

> That they are called free, undoubtedly aggravates the sufferings of the slaves of other regions. They see the enormous inequality which exists, and feel their own misery, and can hardly conceive otherwise, than that there is some injustice in the institutions of society to occa-

16 *Ibid.*, p. 551.
17 *Ibid.*, p. 553.
18 *Ibid.*, pp. 559-560.

sion these. They regard the apparently more fortunate class as oppressors, and it adds bitterness that they should be of the same name and race. . . . Men do not so much hate and envy those who are separated from them by a wide distance, and some apparently impassable barrier, as those who approach nearer to their own condition, and with whom they habitually bring themselves into comparison.[19]

No such problem existed in a slave society, for the slaves, considered to be of an inferior race of men, performed the menial labor; and with a fixed barrier between themselves and their white masters, they were spared the aspirations and enmities of the free white laborer. Thus Harper joined the necessity of slavery to labor, with a special fitness of the Negro race to slavery, to argue that in the South's slave society there was more harmony and less anxiety and political disturbance than in a free society.

Harper's political theory was, of course, directly counter to the fundamental precepts of the Declaration of Independence. The Declaration of Independence and the institution of slavery, it was generally recognized, were simply not compatible, for if one was morally acceptable, the other was clearly not. Harper, like most Southern writers, thus found it necessary to attack the famous self-evident truths. He found it contrary to the facts of life to declare that all men were born free and equal. "Is it not palpably nearer the truth to say that no man was ever born free, and that no two men were ever born equal?"[20] Inequality and dependence were better descriptions of man's life on earth.

Wealth and poverty, fame or obscurity, strength or weakness, knowledge or ignorance, ease or labor, power or subjection, mark the endless diversity in the condition of men.[21]

Yet it was part of man's nature "That the strong and the wise should control the weak and the ignorant."[22] Governments, or lesser authorities, were based not upon consent but upon strength and wisdom. For all the talk about the natural rights of man, it appeared to Harper that with but one exception rights resulted from the conventions of society. This one exception he found to be a natural right to happiness, for happiness was "The great end of existence, the sole

19 *Ibid.*, p. 592.
20 *Ibid.*, p. 553.
21 *Ibid.*, p. 554.
22 *Ibid.*, p. 555.

object of all animated and sentient beings."[23] Although he conceded this to be a natural right, he nevertheless believed that society might interfere even with it for the protection of the society. "Why all the laws of society," he wrote, "are intended for nothing else but to restrain men from the pursuit of happiness, according to their own ideas of happiness or advantage—which the phrase must mean if it means anything."[24]

Chancellor William Harper sought to gain general approval for slavery as practiced in the South by arguing that slavery was a natural and necessary institution and quite in keeping with the nature of man. In fact, he maintained, civilization itself was dependent upon the practice of slavery. Slavery simply acknowledged and put to use the principle that men were unequal and had varying talents and abilities. According to Harper's ethnological beliefs the Negro race was inferior to the white and should therefore be put to menial labor. Not only did civilization benefit from this slave labor, but the slaves themselves were better off in slavery, for they were spared the tantalizing aspirations of their fellow slaves in the free society. All in all, Harper felt his social theory was a more accurate portrayal of man's behavior than the vague generalities found in the Declaration of Independence.

THE SOCIOLOGY OF GEORGE FITZHUGH

Abolitionism was but one of the many reform movements that arose in America in the second quarter of the nineteenth century. Owenism, Fourierism, Saint-Simonism, Socialism, along with women's rights, prison and poor law reforms, a rapid proliferation of religious sects—all were indications that in the free society the conservative orthodoxy was under attack. It was clearly evident that the burgeoning factory system in England and America was creating acute social and economic problems, and political discontent was its immediate by-product. Nevertheless this radicalism, though it washed against the South, did not penetrate it; and the South remained an island of conservatism in a sea of social unrest. The defenders of slavery were well aware that the movement for emancipation was but a part of a broader social and economic criticism that was taking place, and they attempted to turn this criticism to their

[23] *Ibid.*, pp. 558-559.
[24] *Ibid.*, p. 557.

advantage. The great discontent came out of the North, out of the free society. Was not this unrest, this radicalism, but a symptom of the chronic illness of all free societies, they inquired? A comparison of Southern conservatism and Northern radicalism would show the stability of the former and the precarious political volatility of the latter. While the South looked with horror upon the Northern reform movements, it was quite willing to accept the radical criticism of the free society as proof of the inevitable maladjustments such a social system offered. Thus no little of proslavery thought was composed of an attack on the Northern economic system which led to the rise of the social heresies which the South abhorred.

George Fitzhugh (1806-81), a Virginia lawyer and a prolific propagandist for slavery, carried the war into the enemy's camp in his *Sociology for the South, or the Failure of Free Society* (1854), and *Cannibals All; or Slaves Without Masters*. (1856). His writings, highly personal in style, rambling, digressive and not always consistent, nevertheless present the most thorough criticism of the free competitive system to come out of the South. There is much of Hobbes' approach in Fitzhugh, and considerable criticism of Locke, for like most Southern writers he was more concerned with order and security than with liberty. He attacked the contract theorists' conception that man had once existed as an independent individual in a state of nature. There is in Fitzhugh a continual emphasis on the associative aspect of man. Associations through long and successful usage became institutions; and the history of civilized man is read in his accretions of institutions. It is to institutions and not the vacuous *a priori* speculations of philosophers that man should look for guidance, for institutions are the records of man's experience, and this experience is largely dictated by man's nature. "Institutions are what men can see, feel, venerate and understand,"[25] Fitzhugh wrote in his *Sociology For The South*, and it was to institutions that he claimed to turn in formulating his own ideas.

The institution of slavery was such a tangible association which had existed throughout the ages, and was thus indicative of a basic trait in human nature. As one should look to the working institutions of government to understand political behavior rather than to paper constitutions, so one should look to man's actual social and economic behavior to understand human nature rather than to the vague generalizations of political philosophy.

[25] George Fitzhugh, *Sociology for the South* (Richmond, Virginia: A. Morris, 1854), p. 187.

With an approach that emphasized the associative aspect of man, Fitzhugh was not only at war with the contract theorists and their presupposed state of nature, but with the teachings of classical economics as well. He believed classical economics to stem ultimately from the Lockean contract theory, for it assumed an atomized and individualized concept of man. His attack upon classical economics thus led him further to attack Locke's contract theory. "We believe no heresy in moral science has been more pregnant of mischief than this theory of Locke. It lies at the bottom of all moral speculations, and, if false, must infect with falsehood all theories built on it." In building his own sociology, Fitzhugh thus dismissed the idea of the free individual and laid heavy emphasis upon a conception of man as but a creature and servant of society.

> Some animals are by nature gregarious and associative. Of this class are men, ants, and bees. An isolated man is almost as helpless and ridiculous as a bee setting up for himself. Man is born a member of society, and does not form society. Nature, as in the cases of bees and ants, has it ready formed for him. He and society are congenital. Society is the being—he one of the members of that being. He has no rights, whatever, as opposed to the interests of society; and society may very properly make any use of him that will redound to the public good. Whatever rights he has are subordinate to the good of the whole; and he has never ceded rights to it, for he was born its slave, and had no rights to cede.[26]

No man then could claim private rights against the wishes of society and what society considered to be the public good. No man had a right to liberty if society did not recognize and approve of his claim. Above all private considerations was the public interest, the public good, as determined by society itself. Thus Fitzhugh dismissed the *a priori* claims of the natural-rights philosophers as contrary to the actual societal practice of mankind.

Society developed through a natural process and an individual man's volition had little to do with it. Association and cooperation were fundamental laws of man's nature and it was futile for man to attempt to act on contrary principles. Fitzhugh therefore found the *laissez-faire* system of political economy, characterized by Thomas Carlyle as "anarchy plus a street constable," totally out of keeping with the requirements of man's nature. The free societies were thus based upon principles that emphasized conflict and strife, whereas the slave society was based on man's associative impulses toward

26 *Ibid.*, pp. 25-26.

harmony and cooperation. According to Fitzhugh's sociology, society was intended to be a "band of brothers, working for the common good, instead of a bag of cats biting and worrying each other."[27] The free competitive system emphasized the individual; the slave system emphasized the public good. Socialism criticized the free competitive system for its disregard of the lot of the impoverished laborer, who was often discarded as though he were no more than a surplus piece of machinery. Fitzhugh joined in the criticism and declared that slavery was the "very best form of socialism." Socialism emphasized the need for more government control over man, and in this Fitzhugh also concurred. For, he agreed, as man becomes more civilized, his desires for law and order increase.

> The love of personal liberty and freedom from all restraint, are distinguishing traits of wild men and wild beasts. Our Anglo-Saxon ancestors loved personal liberty because they were barbarians, but they did not love it half so much as North American Indians or Bengal tigers, because they were not half so savage. As civilization advances, liberty recedes: and it is fortunate for man that he loses his love of liberty just as fast as he becomes moral and intellectual.[28]

Thus the movement toward personal liberty was a movement counter to the course of all civilized societies. The pathway of civilization led to more and better government, to more stringent legislation than had prevailed in the past. A policy of *laissez faire* led to retrogression for civilization.

Fitzhugh saw about him in the free societies a genuine effort being made to achieve that degree of order and security which he maintained was present in the slave states. The Chartists in England, the Fourierists in America, the trade unions, the socialists were all seeking ways to exchange some degree of liberty for an equivalent amount of security. Yet, Fitzhugh noted, "Slavery to an association is not always better than slavery to a single master."[29] This demand for what he called slavery, in one form or another, was indicative of the inevitable breakdown of free society because it was based upon principles that were contrary to man's basic inclinations.

> Universal liberty has disintegrated and dissolved society, and placed men in isolated, selfish, and antagonistic positions—in which each man is compelled to wrong others, in order to be just to himself.

[27] *Ibid.*, p. 25.
[28] *Ibid.*, pp. 29–30.
[29] *Ibid.*, p. 44.

But man's nature is social, not selfish, and he longs and yearns to return to parental, fraternal and associative relations. All the isms concur in promising closer and more associative relations, in establishing at least a qualified community of property, and in insuring the weak and unfortunate the necessaries and comforts of life. Indeed, they all promise to establish slavery—minus the master and the overseer.[30]

Slavery, under one guise or another, was thus not only the hope but the final destiny of civilized man, whose nature was such that he could not tolerate the liberty of a free competitive society. It was thus sheer hypocrisy for Northerners to criticize the South for its practice of slavery, for all societies, as they progressed, moved in the direction of increasing slavery and increasing law and order. What the South had achieved, and what was lacking elsewhere, was a personal relationship in slavery which ameliorated its unpleasant features. Impersonal slavery, as in an association, could be cold and heartless; but when personal relationships existed, the slave system was softened by humanitarianism.

Slavery was a universal condition of mankind, and men were *cannibals all*. The Northern wage-slave system—the "white slave trade," as he called it—was much harsher in its effects than the Southern, for it imposed an impersonal system of slavery and thus deprived slaves of the benefits of having masters. The Northern laborers were thus slaves without masters. Now all men, Fitzhugh argued, sought to become successful cannibals, that is to live off the labor of others without laboring themselves. It was a general aspiration to obtain property in one's fellow man, to possess his services and the fruits of his labor. In a free society, however, the capitalist was a successful slaveholder who received the benefits of the labor of others, yet avoided the responsibilities and expenses of their care. In fact, free labor was introduced because it was a cheaper labor system than slavery. Would any capitalist, Fitzhugh inquired, accept the financial guardianship of his workers? The wages paid workers were but a pittance of the amount required to maintain slaves; and the responsibility for the maintenance of slaves in sickness and old age fell upon the masters as well. Slaves could not be laid off when it was uneconomical to maintain them, as could workers in a free society. In a free society, Fitzhugh observed, "Every month brings forth its millionaire, and every day its thousands of new paupers."[31]

[30] George Fitzhugh, *Cannibals All* (Richmond, Va.: A. Morris, 1857), p. 332.
[31] *Ibid.*, pp. 86-87.

There was no problem of pauperism in a slave society, for every master was charged with the upkeep of his slaves.

In Fitzhugh's elitist conception of society, the masses of mankind required slavery and should be accorded it. Furthermore, slavery kept down mediocrity and rewarded genius with the unfettered advantages of liberty. Thus slavery, though intended for most, was not intended for all, for some would have to be the masters of the slaves. "Liberty for the few—Slavery, in every form, for the mass!" Fitzhugh proclaimed.[32] Society, divided into guardians and slaves, would thus conform to nature's plan, in which the higher controlled the lower, the few commanded and the many obeyed. "A very little individuality is useful and necessary to society,—much of it begets discord, chaos and anarchy."[33]

Fitzhugh, accepting the theory of the racial superiority of the whites, found his system at work in the South. With the few in command there was the law, order, and general stability that was lacking in the societies which made such a fetish of liberty. "Liberty of the press, liberty of speech, freedom of religion, or rather freedom from religion, and the unlimited right of private judgment, have borne no good fruits, and many bad ones."[34] It was the virtue of a slave society that these evils were avoided, and the right of private judgment was restricted to the few who knew what was the public good. It was inane to talk of individual appeals to a higher law or some supreme moral standard, "because no two men are agreed as to what the higher law, alias 'fundamental principles,' is."[35] It was hardly reasonable to talk of "self-evident truths" when such so-called eternal truths were discovered late in the course of history and were furthermore not self-evident at all. All governments rested not upon consent but upon force, for it was force and not consent that kept the masses in check. As a result all governments were necessarily conservative in nature, and particularly governments of old societies. "There never was and never can be an old society, in which the immediate interests of a majority of human souls do not conflict with all established order, all right of property, and all existing institutions."[36] A conservative, strong government thus aided in promoting the stability of Southern society.

Fitzhugh's position, especially in his attack upon *laissez faire*,

[32] *Ibid.*, p. 94.
[33] *Ibid.*, p. 103.
[34] *Ibid.*, p. 195.
[35] *Ibid.*, p. 200.
[36] *Ibid.*, p. 335.

was unusual in the proslavery thought of the South, for an opposition to Northern tariffs had wedded the South to *laissez-faire* political economy. However, Fitzhugh saw in *laissez faire* a crucial weapon of assault that could be used against the North. *Laissez faire* condemned Northern workers to wage slavery with all its insecurities; as it approached anarchy, it was contrary to the employers' desire for protection of property and the enforcement of law and order. He thus stressed the anarchical aspects of *laissez faire* to argue that such a policy was contrary to the social dispositions of man, which made for a peaceful society. Indeed, all claims to liberty were associated by him with this policy.

> The doctrines so prevalent with Abolitionists and socialists, of Free Love and Free Lands, Free Churches, Free Women and Free Negroes—of No-Marriage, No-Religion, No-Private Property, No-Law and No-Government, are legitimate deductions, if not obvious corollaries from the leading and distinctive axiom of political economy—*Laissez faire*, or let alone.[37]

As the alternative, Fitzhugh offered chattel slavery, in which the elite would control the many. His attack upon the principles of human liberty reached far beyond the immediate question of slavery in the South, however, and stands as the most blatant attack upon freedom in nineteenth-century American political literature.

The slavery controversy marked the high point of American political speculation in the nineteenth century. Not since the discussions surrounding the framing of the Constitution had fundamental political principles been so searchingly examined or so exhaustively debated. The issue was clear and the various arguments on both sides were pointedly relevant: Was it legitimate to enslave human beings? The issue called for a re-examination of man's political propensities, social conduct and economic institutions. While the political alignment was sectional, nevertheless in point of political theory the issue was largely one of Hobbesian conservatism against Lockean liberalism. In a sense it was again a conflict between Hamilton and Jefferson, with the South, curiously enough, following Hamilton's insistence on security, order, and social organization, and the Northern abolitionists calling for a reassertion of the natural rights of man. Yet, in another sense, it brought forth an issue as old as political thought itself, for in fundamentals it reached back to

[37] *Ibid.*, p. 315.

antiquity and the Greek discussions of the compulsions of "nature" as opposed to the compulsions of "convention."

Though slavery was abolished, the philosophy of abolitionism passed away as well. For the natural-rights philosophy, which for two hundred years had occupied such a predominant position in American political thought, gave way in the twentieth century to a new frame of reference, a new political sociology. Abolitionism marked the last great successful crusade of the rationalistic assumptions of the Declaration of Independence. A new ideology, more accommodating to industrial capitalism, supplanted the old, which had been oriented to the more primitive institutional fabric of Jeffersonian democracy. Indeed, in the decades immediately following the Civil War, Lockean liberalism, with its emphasis on moral values, gave way to Manchester liberalism, which emphasized economic values. Consequently the concept of "right" took on a distinctively economic connotation. Even the Fourteenth Amendment, designed to protect the newly emancipated slaves, was little used for this purpose, but under the new ideology proved to be an effective barrier to social reform legislation in the states.

While natural-rights philosophy declined, Southern political thought continued to have an impact on the American mind. Curiously, aspects of proslavery thought reappeared in late nineteenth-century America in two opposed camps. Social Darwinists restated the Calhoun conception of progress as resulting from the competition of unequals, supported now by the theory of biological evolution. And their political opponents at the turn of the century, the progressives, started from society rather than from natural law in their search for an understanding of social and political values. Indeed it is not too much to say that, barring slavery, twentieth-century American thought found the social theory of Calhoun far more congenial than the rationalism of Garrison and Channing. Thus, while slavery was abolished, much of the social theory associated with it remained.

CHAPTER 12

The National
Concept of Sovereignty

THE SLAVERY controversy in the United States developed along with, and indeed aggravated to the point of war, the persistent and recurring conflict over the nature of the American Union. So intertwined were the discussions of slavery and the nature of the Union in mid-nineteenth-century American thought that spokesmen for one of the issues invariably expressed views on the other. But while the slavery issue emphasized the nature of man and his rights, the discussions on the American Union emphasized the nature of the political community and its prerogatives.

States' rights is at once a theory of political organization and a defensive poltical technique whereby a state may act, or prevent action, contrary to the desires of the national community. A firm adherence to states' rights as a political principle was thus well in accord with the Southern defense of slavery against the rising national sentiment for freedom. Unionism, on the other hand, while not directly threatening the immediate existence of slavery, was well in accord with the nationalistic and majoritarian view of increasing the scope and application of the powers of the national government. Thus the desirability, or undesirability, of national political, economic, and social programs figured then, as now, in the controversy over states' rights. Crucial political and economic issues, such as tariffs, taxes, and internal improvements, inevitably raised the question of the competency and legitimacy of a large political group to act contrary to the interests of the smaller political unit, where in fact the larger unit was the nation and the smaller unit was the state. The question in its immediate and tangible form was a constitutional issue over the extent of delegated powers to the national government and the proper scope of the reserved authority of the states. In its more lasting and theoretical aspects, however, the question involved the principles of majority rule, sovereignty, the contract theory of government, consent of the governed, assumptions of the political behavior of men in power and ultimately the right of revolution. Nationalism, as opposed to states' rights, was at once a jurisdictional issue involving the legal exercise of power and, because of its deeper assumptions and implications, an issue that went to the very heart of political allegiance.

In a sense it may be said that the jurisdictional problem commenced with the first colonial settlements in America. For with the first settlements came the early charters which provided in fact for a certain degree of local autonomy. The colonists were thus from the beginning subjected to the authority of two governments with the charters suggesting the lines of demarcation between jurisdictions. Local matters were subject to the jurisdiction of the particular colonial governments, while general questions were setttled by the authority of the King and Parliament. The distribution of authority was a matter of convenience rather than of right, for the seventeenth-century colonists were not troubled by speculative questions of sovereignty. Late eighteenth-century Americans found the claims of local allegiance of major consequence and the jurisdictional question of the authority of the general government as compared to the authority of the particular colonial governments all important. Common allegiance to the King under a system of divided political authority led to the view that the Crown was omnipotent in certain matters while the colonial governments were omnipotent in others—a view suggestive of the divided sovereignty conception of the *Federalist*. The failure to resolve the jurisdictional question surrounding the exact lines of demarcation led to the exclusive claim of the colonies for complete local autonomy as a right. It was this claim to autonomy which was in fact realized by the Revolution.

In the political system established by the Articles of Confederation the jurisdictional problem of the respective authority of the state and national governments was clarified by Article II of that document. "Each state retains its sovereignty, freedom, and independence, and every Power, Jurisdiction and right, which is not by this confederation expressly delegated to the United States, in Congress assembled." In the short period under the Articles of Confederation this legal division of power between national and state governments proved sufficiently clear to be generally acceptable. The basic political questions of this period were not concerned with whether the national government had exceeded its delegated powers, but whether in fact more power ought to be delegated to it. It was not until the establishment of the national government under the Constitution that the question of the construction and interpretation of clauses granting national power became a basic political issue. Then the constitutional scholasticism which played such an important part in the pre-Civil War political discussions was indicative of the basic struggle between those inclined to states' rights and those inclined to the nationalist view, between the Jeffersonians and the Hamiltonians.

Yet beyond the conflicting interests of the Jeffersonians and the Hamiltonians were the theoretical confusions inherent in the endeavor to construct a complex federal state upon the simple and logical propositions of Locke. Lockean logic was well adapted to a unitary political system such as was found in England. With home rule of the locality admittedly inferior to the national authority of Parliament, one talked of majority rule and minority rights within the relatively simple framework of a single political unit. Furthermore, there was only one compact or constitution, so to speak, between politically organized man and the state of nature. But did the Lockean theory hold true when applied to a complex federal system with a diversity of political units, each with its compact or constitution, and when applied to a multiple situation of rights reserved and powers delegated to coordinate governments?

In the Lockean conception of the contract theory the organized community established government to better protect the rights of the individual members of the community. Of necessity the awarding of authority to the government diminished some of the rights of the members of society, while other rights were so basic, so natural, that they could never be delegated or contracted away. All rights originated in the individual rather than in society. It was the function of the government, as the agent of the people, to see that the rights of the people were carefully protected. By entering into the body politic man gave up certain rights possessed in the state of nature to better protect other rights. In effect, by entering into political society the sovereign individual delegated away certain rights and prerogatives and reserved others. The entrance of the individual into the body politic thus initially posed the problem of the individual interest and the group interest, or the particular interest and the general or public interest. To Locke, this problem was resolved by the simple expedient of majority rule limited to the objects of the public good.

The construction of the federal state in America made the problem infinitely more complex. While the colonists had followed the course of revolution as justified by the Lockean theory to better secure the rights of man and achieve the consent of the governed, the construction of a state on this theory raised difficulties. How was majority rule to be achieved along with the consent of the governed minority? The construction of the various state constitutions was a practical application of the contract theory. The sovereignty of the politically recognized people was demonstrated, especially in Massachusetts, where there was popular ratification of the constitution, as powers were delegated and rights reserved in keeping with the contract theory. But with the framing of the federal constitution, did sovereignty pass to the people of the United States considered collectively or was it parcelled out among the people of each state? Was there an analogy between the political claims surrendered and reserved by the states in the federal constitution, and the political claims surrendered and reserved by the people in framing the state constitutions? Where did political authority ultimately rest in this compact built upon compacts? Were the people of an individual state sovereign to the point that there was no government by consent, if in the Congress their authorized spokesmen were in the minority on such a basic matter as the interpretation of the contract itself, that is, the Constitution? Finally, did the people of a state possess that ultimate right of revolution which they had successfully exercised against Great Britain in the American Revolution?

STATES' RIGHTS

To a large extent these very fundamental questions were argued in a historical and legal context, so that much of the discussion was occupied with discovering who had originally contracted with whom and for what purposes. The political conflict emphasized rights largely as flowing from past compacts, implicit or expressed. And there was abundant historical and legal material at hand for each side to illustrate and document its original intent. Every constitutional treatise, judicial decision, and legislative enactment that had bearing on the issue was exploited in the scholasticism of the mid-

nineteenth century to prove either that the superior political authority lay with the states or, to the contrary, with the national Union.
In the intense political struggle, federalism stood in precarious balance as it was pulled by the states' righters in one direction and
by the nationalists in another.

The *Federalist* papers had assumed that sovereignty was divided
between the nation and the states, or, as a practical matter, that
the sovereign power of the people was divided in application between the national government and the state governments. This
distribution of power was delineated in the Constitution. "Every
thing beyond this must be left to the prudence and firmness of the
people; who, as they will hold the scales in their own hands, it is
to be hoped, will always take care to preserve the constitutional
equilibrium between the general and the state governments."[1] Yet
the problem of deciding in practice just what this equilibrium was
proved infinitely complex, for it hung upon the determination as
to whether the states should pass this judgment, as the Kentucky
Resolutions had declared, or whether the federal courts should render the decision, as John Marshall had argued. Furthermore there
was precedent on each side. Kentucky and Virginia in 1798, Massachusetts, Connecticut, and Rhode Island in 1814, Georgia in 1827,
and South Carolina in 1832 had declared the sovereignty of the
state to determine the extent and obligations of the national compact. On the other hand, there was the long tradition of acquiescence
to the determinations of the national government.

The conception of divided power resting upon the people of the
states was ably supported in the South by John Taylor.[2] The powers
of government were divided, he maintained, but the ultimate political authority lay in the people of the states, separately considered.
The people of a state, through their constitution, created the state
as a political entity. The states, through the federal Constitution,
created the national Union. The national government was thus an
agent of the state, and the latter was in turn a direct agent of the
people. As a mere agent, the national government thus lacked authority to determine the extent of its delegated powers. Turning to
the origins of the Constitution, Taylor defended the argument of
state sovereignty in his *Construction Construed and Constitutions
Vindicated.*

[1] *The Federalist* (New York: The Modern Library, 1941), Number 31.
[2] See Chapter VII.

The members of the convention which formed it [the Constitution], were chosen by states, and voted by states, without any regard to the number of people in each state. It was adopted by thirteen votes, without respecting the same principles. Now what was represented by these voters; the territory of each state, or the people of each state?[3]

In his *New Views of the Constitution,* Taylor boldly asserted his conviction of the complete sovereignty of the individual states. "The states could not have reserved any rights by the articles of their union, if they had not been sovereign, because they could have no rights, unless they flowed from that source. In the creation of the federal government, the states exercised the highest act of sovereignty, and they may, if they please, repeat the proof of their sovereignty, by its annihilation."[4]

It was the belief of the Jeffersonian democrats not only that the states were originally sovereign entities but that on entering the Union they had not given up this sovereignty. The powers of the federal government were, after all, only delegated powers granted by an authority with the capacity to delegate. Not only, it was argued, was this in fact the historical situation, but it should remain so. Government tended to remain responsible insofar as it was close to the people; and the federal government, more removed from the people, was therefore more inclined toward irresponsibility. The doctrine of states' rights was thus thought of as an institutional device for better preserving the rights of the people of a state. Popular sovereignty was thus considered in terms of the people of a state rather than in terms of a national political unit. Thus with each national controversial issue, the question was raised anew as to whether the national majority or the local state majority would in fact and ought in theory to prevail.

JOHN C. CALHOUN

While most of the controversial literature on the nature of the Union was concerned with the historical origins of the Constitution and the semantics of its terminology, one outstanding figure emerged

---

[3] John Taylor, *Construction Construed and Constitutions Vindicated* (Richmond: Shepherd and Pollard, 1820), pp. 43-44.

[4] John Taylor, *New Views of the Constitution of the United States* (Washington: Way and Gideon, 1823), pp. 36-37.

who made a systematic contribution to the political theory of the period. John C. Calhoun[5] brought into his political theory a realism grounded on his long experience in state and national politics. He saw behind the law itself the political forces that made the law and gave it life. Thus while he drew upon law, as he drew upon history, he realized that the struggle over the nature of the Union was more than a lesson in logic or a study in legal history. His theory, logically constructed and legally documented, used history not so much to prove the existing nature of the Union as to illustrate his theory of the political behavior of the American society. Thus his discussion of the nature of the Union took place within the larger framework of his conception of the fundamentals of political theory. *A Discourse on the Constitution and Government of the United States* (1851), concerned basically with the nature of the Union, is largely the documentary evidence for the principles of politics developed in *A Disquisition on Government* (1850). Calhoun's defense of states' rights was therefore not dependent exclusively on the intentions of the framers of the Constitution some generations previously, but upon an understanding of what he considered to be the principles of political science.

As the starting point of his political theory Calhoun stated two basic assumptions. First, that man is by nature a social animal and has never existed in any other than a social state. Second, that society itself has never existed without government of some kind. Given these two fundamental assumptions, Calhoun inquired, "What is that constitution of our nature, which, while it impels man to associate with his kind, renders it impossible for society to exist without government?"[6] He found the answer to this inquiry in the constitution of man himself, which caused each individual to find his own interest of more particular and immediate concern than the interests of his fellow man. This law of man, that "his direct or individual affections are stronger than his sympathetic or social feelings," was as unquestionable, Calhoun wrote, as the law of gravitation. Thus, though man was a social animal, his primary concerns were those affecting himself. The desire for self-preservation was but an instance of this self-regarding and self-protecting urge of man. Inevitably the association of individuals in society, each most directly concerned with his own interests, brought on

---

[5] See Chapter XI.

[6] "A Disquisition on Government," in Richard K. Crallé, ed., *The Works of John C. Calhoun* (New York: D. Appleton and Co., 1854-57), vol. I, p. 2.

conflicts between men which, if not properly checked by a controlling power, would disrupt society. "This controlling power," Calhoun wrote, "wherever vested, or by whomsoever exercised, is Government."[7] As a consequence of this line of argument Calhoun thus stated:

It follows, then, that man is so constituted, that government is necessary to the existence of society, and society to his existence, and the perfection of his faculties. It follows, also, that government has its origin in this twofold constitution of his nature; the sympathetic or social feelings constituting the remote,—and the individual or direct, the proximate cause.[8]

If the social or sympathetic feelings of man were stronger, there would be no need of government; if the individual and self-regarding inclinations of man were stronger, society itself would not be possible. But given the nature of man, both society and government were necessary consequences. Society existed "to preserve and perfect our race," while government existed "to preserve and protect our society."[9]

Calhoun, however, in his statement of the nature of man, stated also the nature of man's dilemma, for he noted that the government, so necessary to the preservation of society, "must be administered by men in whom, like others, the individual are stronger than the social feelings." Here was then a fundamental problem: how reconcile the public and the private interests of the governors? Government must have power: yet how prevent the abuse of power? "That, by which this is prevented, by whatever name called, is what is meant by Constitution, in its most comprehensive sense, when applied to Government."[10] Thus, as the government was necessary to society, so was the constitution to government, because of the same inclinations of men. It was clear to Calhoun that inasmuch as government existed to protect society, nothing would be accomplished by so curtailing the powers of government that society, in any forseeable emergency, could not be protected. To deprive government of power would be to defeat the essential purposes of government, for government existed because organized power was essential to the preservation and development of society. Thus the

7 *Ibid.*, p. 4.
8 *Ibid.*, pp. 4-5.
9 *Ibid.*, p. 5.
10 *Ibid.*, p. 7.

constitutional system that Calhoun was concerned with was one related to a government that was fully capable of exercising such comprehensive powers as might be necessary for the adequate preservation of that society. Such a constitutional system, properly constructed, would provide a government which contained through its internal structure adequate checks upon adequate powers. "Power can only be resisted by power," wrote Calhoun.[11] The ruled, therefore, must always have powers commensurate with the powers granted the rulers.

The first basic constitutional check which armed the ruled against the rulers was the right of suffrage. This right was the "indispensable and primary principle in the *foundation* of a constitutional government," for through the proper exercise of this right the governors could always be brought to account. Although the right of suffrage was indispensable to constitutional government, it was, argued Calhoun, by no means a sufficient check upon the rulers. For at best the right of suffrage placed the ultimate political power in the community of voters rather than in the government. But the community of voters was not a society of like individuals with identical interests; and, even were such the case, there would still be divisions among men as to who occupied the high offices of government and who in turn paid the taxes to support them. The interests of men were not the same, and the right of suffrage, intended to keep the government responsible, in actuality kept the government responsible only to the numerical majority of voters.

Madison had found in *The Federalist,* Number 10, that the expanse of the republic would help check the influence of factions; Calhoun found, to the contrary, that the greater size of the country, the greater would be the diversity of interests among men and consequently the less likelihood of the government serving equally the interests of all society. Factions invariably would unite to form majorities, and majorities would control the government.

> Such being the case it necessarily results, that the right of suffrage, by placing the control of the government in the community must, from the same constitution of our nature which makes government necessary to preserve society, lead to conflict among its different interests,—each striving to obtain possession of its powers, as the means of protecting itself against the others;—or of advancing its respective interests, regardless of the interests of others.[12]

[11] *Ibid.,* p. 12.
[12] *Ibid.,* p. 16.

Government, intended to protect all of society, thus with no further constitutional check than the suffrage, protected only the more dominant interests and in effect promoted the very discord which the institution of government was designed to prevent. The usual restrictions, such as a written constitution providing for limited governmental powers, or even a division of power into separate branches of the government, were inadequate checks upon the government. For since the majority would control the government, it would also determine the powers of the government. The majority party and the minority party would thus be in conflict over constitutional construction and in such a struggle the majority interests would prevail, for the point of attaining office was to utilize power.

> Being the party in possession of the government, they will, from the same constitution of man which makes government necessary to protect society, be in favor of the powers granted by the constitution, and opposed to the restrictions intended to limit them.[13]

Calhoun thus argued that it was a natural inclination for government responsible to the majority of the people to expand the powers of the government in the interest of the majority and to so interpret the constitution as best suited this interest. A written constitution was in itself no protection against the majority, as in the final analysis the majority determined what was in fact the constitution. By the same reasoning, Calhoun was able to argue that a mere distribution of the powers of government into separate branches or departments was an insufficient check upon the abuse of governmental power, for the branches were but separate agents of the same majority. All the branches of government eventually fell subject to the interests of the majority.

A system of popular constitutional government, with its popular suffrage, written constitution, and separation of powers, could not prevent the absolute rule of the numerical majority, for there was no adequate negative power upon the actions of the majority's government. Furthermore, Calhoun argued, unless there was an adequate negative power upon the government there was indeed no constitution. "It is, indeed, the negative power which makes the constitution,—and the positive which makes the government. The one has the power of acting;—and the other the power of preventing or arresting action. The two, combined, make constitutional governments."[14]

---

[13] *Ibid.*, p. 32.
[14] *Ibid.*, p. 36.

The means whereby Calhoun sought a negative check upon the government, and thus a constitutional system, was in the device which he called the "concurrent majority." Men were united, as well as divided, by a variety of interests. If any one interest, or group of interests, were able to control government completely, they would seek to exploit society to their advantage. On the other hand, the way to check such abuse of power was to establish such a constitutional system that those interests which might be adversely affected by government action should have an opportunity to prevent such action from taking place.

> There is, again, but one mode in which this can be effected; and that is, by taking the sense of each interest or portion of the community, which may be unequally and injuriously affected by the action of the government, separately, through its own majority, or in some other way by which its voice may be fairly expressed; and to require the consent of each interest, either to put or to keep the government in action. This, too, can be accomplished only in one way,—and that is, by such an organism of the government,—and if necessary, for the purpose, of the community also,—as will, by dividing and distributing the powers of government, give to each division or interest, through its appropriate organ, either a concurrent voice in making and executing the laws, or a veto on their execution.[15]

Only in this way, by pitting interest against interest and power against power, could an effectual constitutional restraint be established on government. On matters of common interest Calhoun assumed there would be genuine concurrence. On matters of special interests, advantageous to some groups but not to others, an effective veto would be interposed. By balancing interests, sectional, economic or class, against number, Calhoun believed that the concurrent majority would check the actions of the numerical majority. The constitution would thus institutionalize a veto system whereby each major interest group would be able to protect itself against the aggressive actions of others. As a result governmental action would be the end product of adjustment and compromise between the numerical majority and the various groups affected by the proposed action. In application, Calhoun's concurrent majority was an euphemistic expression for unanimous consent. His trial jury example, where the consent of all twelve jurors is required for a verdict, illustrates this. The use of the "veto power" in the Security Council

---

15 *Ibid.*, pp. 24-25.

of the United Nations is a contemporary illustration of the difficulties of arriving at a concurrent majority.

It was basically this system of a concurrent majority which Calhoun believed to have been the intention of the framers of the Constitution, for liberty and order could be reconciled only through a balance of power which, in the last analysis, meant a balance of control between aggregations of interest groups. In *A Discourse on the Constitution and Government of the United States,* Calhoun undertook to apply his theory of the concurrent majority to the actual political developments in the United States. The framers intended and achieved in the Constitution a government of the United States that was at once democratic, federal, and republican in form. This government, he wrote, was—

> . . . democratic in contradistinction to aristocratic, and monarchical; —federal, in contradistinction to national, on the one hand,—and to a confederacy, on the other; and a Republic—a contradistinction to an absolute democracy—or a government of the numerical majority.[16]

It was democratic by virtue of its provisions for popular election of representatives in Congress; federal because of its division of powers between the states and the national government; and republican, in Calhoun's conception, in that it drew upon the concurring majorities of people and states for positive action. The United States House of Representatives represented the numerical majority of people acting in their federal capacity; the United States Senate represented the separate and special interests of the states acting in their equal capacity without regard to differences in population between them. The government of the United States was circumscribed to the extent that in order for it to act it was first necessary for it to acquire a concurrence of the two diverse majorities. In effect, what Calhoun did was to elevate John Adams' theory of the mixed constitution to a federal basis by giving to the states in the Senate the status Adams had reserved for the aristocracy.

The framers had assumed that the major political struggles would take place between the national government with its delegated powers, and the separate states with their reserved powers. Experience had proven this assumption false, Calhoun declared.

> Instead of a contest for power between the government of the United States, on the one side, and the separate governments of the several

16 *Ibid.,* p. 187.

States, on the other,—the real struggle has been to obtain the control of the former;—a struggle in which both States and people have united: And the result has shown that, instead of depending on the relative force of the delegated and reserved powers, the latter, in all contests, have been brought in aid of the former, by the States on the side of the party in the possession and control of the government of the United States,—and by the States on the side of the party in the opposition, in their efforts to expel those in possession, and to take their place.[17]

In consequence, the assumed antagonism between delegated and reserve powers was unfounded, and a system of balance of powers dependent upon this antagonism was unrealistic. The tendency, since the Constitution was put into effect, was for reserved and delegated powers to be consolidated into the hands of the majority party, which so armed was able to overpower the minority party at every turn.

The breakdown of the balance of power between the states, separately considered, and the numerical majority, federally considered, was best evidenced by the use of political parties. The same diversities among men which necessitated government led to the rise of political parties to control government in the interests of their members. Government, which was intended to prevent the strong from oppressing the weak, was itself controlled by the strongest political party. Of all the factors that facilitated the organization and effective operation of a political party which cut through all levels of government, none was so strong in America as contiguity. As man favored his private interest over his social feelings, so did he favor his local and particular interests over the general interest. As a result, political parties in the United States were bound to be geographically oriented. Geographic interests, combined with similarity of institutions and economic activity, made for intensity of conviction and political cohesiveness in the major political sections. In other words, the political party had broken through the barrier between national and state units of government, and made the struggle for power of the diverse political interests a geographical one with the possession of the national government and its broad powers the high stakes at issue. Inevitably the advantage in this contest went to that party which appealed to the greatest number of people and the greatest number of states and sought the greatest consolidation of national power to further advance the interests of its ad-

[17] *Ibid.*, p. 299.

herents. Yet this process led to absolute government, for the minority was left without a check upon the majority. Were the interests of all sections of the country similar, the majority would always run the risk, through the elective process, of finding itself in the minority. But the geographic alignment of parties, and the special interest representation of each, doomed the minority party to remain in the minority. In any political contest between the two geographically oriented parties—whether concerning tariffs, slavery or internal improvements—the majority party's construction of the Constitution would prevail. And where the Constitution was unable to check the government, there was in effect no constitution at all, and the government could be considered absolute.

To restore the constitutional system as he conceived it, with a concurrence of power between states and people, Calhoun turned to his theory of nullification and secession. Sovereignty resided in the people of the several states separately considered. This sovereign power created the respective state governments and authorized the establishment of the federal government. The sovereign people did not, however, divest themselves of the sovereignty that originally resided in them. What they formed in the federal Constitution was but a contract, an agreement between one sovereign people and another.

The interpretation of this contract in subsequent conflicts must, therefore, depend upon subsequent agreement between the respective parties. Certainly, he argued, it was not meant to be unilaterally interpreted. It was in this right to interpret the contract that Calhoun found an effective negative check on behalf of a state against an action taken by the national government. It was indeed, reasoned Calhoun, this power to negate which in fact made the Constitution an effective instrument. On a political issue which hinged upon a construction of the contract, the majority party, acting through the national government, would doubtless exercise the questioned power. The states in the minority would then have a choice between acceding to the wishes of the majority or interposing a negative by declaring the statute null and void. If an overwhelming majority of the states and people were in favor of the claimed power for the national government, then the Constitution should be formally altered by amendment to clarify the issue. Were the majority able to put through the amendment, then the minority states would have a choice between acceding to the claimed power under the amended contract or seceding from the Union. Calhoun believed that if these alternatives of action for states in the minority were clearly established and understood, a large part of the sectional conflict between the divergent interests of the Union would disappear, for the natural desire to preserve the Union would inevitably promote a course of compromise and adjustment on all major issues. Policies that vitally concerned a minority of the states would not become the objects of legislation by the majority if it was known that the minority, rather than submit, would withdraw from the compact. And Calhoun assumed of course that, each state being sovereign, it could rightfully secede from the Union in the same manner in which it once ratified the Constitution.

Thus, Calhoun argued, the intentions of the framers of the Constitution—that power be utilized to check power so liberty and order might exist together—would be reestablished in the light of America's political experience. The framers had not intended to turn the government over to the numerical majority, but rather to provide at all times for a concurrence of diverse majorities. Since political parties had developed in such a fashion as to combine the interests of states and people, the only effective check upon this combined majority lay in the erection of a barrier beyond the reach of the majority. This check Calhoun found in the state negative, which he related not only to his theory of the nature of the Union, but more broadly to his general theory of the political nature of man. Along with John Adams, with whom he had much in common, Calhoun used the Hobbesian view of man as the basic conception around which to build his political theory; and his system of the concurrent majority ranks as one of the major American contributions to the literature of political thought.

NATIONALISM

While the South became increasingly oriented to the extreme states' rights position of state sovereignty, nullification, and eventually secession, Northern political sentiment turned to a conception of sovereignty located in the people nationally considered, and a theory of the perpetuity of the constitutional Union. Thus the early theory of divided sovereignty was put aside as Northern and Southern publicists alike found sovereignty to be indivisible. Both sides found this sovereignty to be located in the people. But the basic political issue centered around the question as to which people possessed this indivisible sovereignty: Were they the people of the states separately considered, or were they the people of the states considered collectively on a national basis. The United States Senate was conceded to be representative of the people of the states considered as separate political units. The House of Representatives was conceded to represent the people considered nationally. Yet behind these questions of organization lurked the fundamental political issue as to where, in case of conflict between a sectional minority and a national majority, sovereignty resided. This was the central question behind the controversial issue concerning the nature of the Union.

The issue of the nature of the Union was pointed up dramatically in 1830 in a debate in the Senate, perhaps the most classic debate in that chamber's long history. With the North and South opposed to each other on the issue of the tariff, each side sought to bring the West to its support. The specific instance that called forth the debate was a resolution offered by Senator Foote of Connecticut inquiring into the expediency of limiting the sale of public lands to such lands as were already on the market. But the issue of public-land policy soon broadened into a debate on the nature of the Constitution itself and for nearly two weeks the Senate was occupied with a discussion of the Constitution and the nature of the Union. Presiding over the Senate was Vice-President Calhoun. South Carolina's views were ably advanced by Senator Hayne, who formally presented to the Senate the theory of state sovereignty and state nullification of acts of Congress deemed by a particular state to be unconstitutional. Hayne in turn was answered by Senator Daniel Webster, the recognized spokesman of the Northern mercantile interests. It was in his second reply to Haynes, presented on January 26, 1830, that Webster, drawing fully upon his considerable oratorical talents, presented the Northern doctrine of the nature of the Union. It was this presentation, a skillful blending of constitutional theory and nationalism, that was accepted as the official statement of the Northern position in the controversial years that followed and culminated in the Civil War.

Webster, in the course of his presentation, argued that there was no constitutional means whereby a state might interfere with or oppose the operation of federal laws. There was an extra-legal or extra-constitutional right of a people to oppose unjust government; but this was the right of revolution, a right which he willingly acknowledged existed at all times. But to resort to such a right, he argued, put one outside the bounds of the Constitution, even as it put one outside the bounds of the law. Within the Constitution, no such right of opposition existed. Nullification was therefore revolution undertaken by a state and clearly outside the constitutional framework. Senator Hayne countered with the argument that he was not merely contending for the right of revolution but for the "right of constitutional resistance" on behalf of a state to unconstitutional legislation. Thus, as Webster replied, "The great question is, Whose prerogative is it to decide on the constitutionality or unconstitutionality of the laws?"[18] To answer this question Webster entered into a discussion of the origin of the general government, and of the Constitution itself. The general government, he maintained, was not an agent of the state governments individually considered, for the presence of twenty-four separate states would make it subject to twenty-four separate wills. If thirteen original states had made the general government, it was nevertheless true that the general government had made the eleven additional states. "It is, Sir," Webster proclaimed, "the people's Constitution, the people's government, made for the people, made by the people, and answerable to the people."[19] National and state governments alike were merely agents of the people.

The people had declared, however, that the Constitution was the supreme law of the land; both national and state governments were limited by this supreme law. Thus the claims to state sovereignty were always subordinate to the superior authorizations and limitations declared in the supreme law of the land. The specific limitations on the states found in the Constitution itself—prohibitions on such sovereign powers as making war, coining money or entering into treaties—were sufficient proof that the states lacked such sovereignty as would justify the doctrine of nullification. The states, like the national government, were under the Constitution and could not legitimately act apart from it. Could the states choose which laws to obey and which not, the Union would become a mere "rope of sand" and the states would be thrown back into the old Confederation which had been deliberately set aside to form a more perfect Union.

"It is too plain to be argued," Webster declared. "Four-and-twenty interpreters of constitutional law, each with a power to decide for

---

[18] *The Great Speeches and Orations of Daniel Webster* (Boston: Little, Brown, and Co., 1889), p. 256.
[19] *Ibid.*, p. 257.

itself, and none with authority to bind anybody else, and this constitutional law the only bond of their union!"[20]

Who then might determine the constitutionality of laws in cases of conflict? The Supreme Court, Webster answered, following the reasoning of John Marshall. The Constitution itself was clear on this matter, for it provided that "the Constitution, and the laws of the United States which shall be made in pursuance thereof . . . shall be the supreme law of the land . . . anything in the Constitution or laws of any State to the contrary notwithstanding." Furthermore, the Constitution declared that "The judicial power shall extend to all cases . . . arising under this constitution [and] the laws of the United States. . . ." It was these two provisions of the Constitution which made for a government, for "without them it is a confederation."

Such was the nature of the Union, Webster argued, based upon the plain language of the Constitution. It was the people's Constitution and if it was construed unfairly or improperly there was a simple and constitutional method by which this construction could be corrected; for at their own sovereign pleasure the people could amend the Constitution. In summary, Webster attacked the doctrine of nullification and justified his theory of the people's Constitution on five counts. First, the plain language of the Constitution supported his contention; second, frequent elections were the popular check on public power; third, an impartial judicial power was authorized by the people to settle such controversies; fourth, the people could amend the Constitution to remove defects; finally there was clearly no authorization by "the people of the United States" for the states to interpret or construe the Constitution.

Interspersed with the constitutional argument, Webster utilized a mystical appeal to the rising national sentiment which proved as lasting as his legalistic theory. It was the Constitution that held the Union together, but the Union in turn was far more than a legalistic arrangement.

It is to that Union we owe our safety at home, and our consideration and dignity abroad. It is to that Union that we are chiefly indebted for whatever makes us proud of our country. That Union we reached only by the discipline of our virtues in the severe school of adversity. It had its origin in the necessities of disordered finance, prostrate commerce, and ruined credit. Under its benign influences, these great interests immediately awoke as from the dead, and sprang forth with

[20] *Ibid.,* p. 258.

newness of life. Every year of its duration has teemed with fresh proofs of its utility and its blessings; and although our territory has stretched out wider and wider, and our population spread farther and farther, they have not outrun its protection or its benefits. It has been to us all a copious fountain of national, social, and personal happiness.[21]

With a flourish, in his peroration, Webster turned his oratorical fulness upon the catastrophe of disunion and concluded with a plea to patriotism, for "Liberty and Union, now and forever, one and inseparable!" It was thus the people of the United States bound together by national sentiment who were the sovereign authority behind the Constitution. The Constitution in turn was the supreme law over the national government and states alike. The Union was one of flesh and blood as well as law, and no part thereof, lacking a revolution, could legitimately declare its autonomy. Thus Webster, a former New England particularist, laid down the classic argument for nationalism in the pre-Civil War period, as Calhoun, the former nationalist, laid down the classic argument for states' rights, nullification, and secession. Neither Webster nor Calhoun lived to witness the Civil War, the awful consequences of their theories in conflict, that catastrophic schism in America which each so greatly feared would eventually take place.

THE DEMISE OF THE CONTRACT THEORY

There is a paradox that runs through the discussions on slavery and the nature of the Union. In attacking slavery, Northern writers turned to natural law, natural rights and the fundamental concepts implicit in the contract theory of government. In defending slavery Southern writers put aside the contract theory of the state and looked to historic origins and institutional development as justification for and explanation of their form of society. It was society, conditioned by history, which determined a man's rights and obligations; and no one might claim rights against his society. The private interest was subject to the public interest as determined by society. No man could claim inherent or natural rights against the conditions of existence which society imposed upon him. The historic forces which made for civilized society were always greater than the individual; thus it was folly and indeed destructive for an individual to claim

[21] *Ibid.*, p. 269.

rights against society. Outside of the individual unit there was a mystical social unit which demanded a basic conformity from its members not only to preserve social existence but to advance the course of civilization and progress. Society and government were not therefore the result of voluntary contractual relationships, but were rather the inevitable products of human necessity and historical development.

In the controversy over the nature of the Union, however, the positions of North and South were reversed. The South looked upon the institution of government as a practical application of the contract theory, and, indeed, thought of the Union itself as simply a contractual relationship between states. A contract so made could thus be revoked in the same manner in which the Constitution had once been ratified. The rights of the states were to be determined by the states themselves. The Constitution did not create, therefore, a larger organic society but only a contractual relationship of separate societies. There was a legalistic rather than an organic union of separate parts, and the separate parts retained individually their inherent rights. The rights of the respective states did not flow from the larger society, the nation, but were antecedent to the formation of the Union and in fact independent of the Union. The rights of the states were original and inherent and could not be modified by the larger society without each state's consent. Having renounced the contract theory of government and the inherent rights of all individuals in the discussions over slavery, the South took up the contract theory of government and the inherent rights of all states in the issue over the nature of the Union. This inconsistency is of course quite apparent in the writings of Calhoun.

The North also altered its position when it shifted from slavery to the nature of the Union. Where it had refused the organic conception of society and a societal interpretation of rights when the issue was slavery, it turned to the organic conception of society when it considered the nature of the Union. The Union was thus more than a mere contract between separate entities, separate states. It was rather a union of early history and future promise, of generations past and generations still to come, of agriculture and industry, of plains and seaboard, of the vast hosts of mystical and emotional forces which give to man a greater sense of belonging, a greater sense of community. This was indeed a far cry from the early contract theorists with their emphasis upon self-conscious parts rather than the whole. Here the larger community was emphasized against the smaller, the greater majority against the local or particular majority, the nation as opposed to the state.

By the middle of the nineteenth century, America had indeed caught the spirit of nationalism that was characteristic of the times. Nineteenth-century nationalism was a unifying movement which drew upon the deep emotional wellsprings of cultural similarity for its mystical appeal. If the eighteenth century was the age of rationalism, the nineteenth was characterized by historicism. Men looked to their past in order to understand the present and anticipate the future. But the eighteenth century idea of progress carried over into the nineteenth century, and history was given thereby a purpose, a plan, a direction. History, given a purpose, led the German philosopher George Hegel to see in man's development the unfolding of the Divine Idea of the state. History, given a purpose, led Karl Marx to the conclusion that man's development would culminate in the triumph of the communist society. In England, Charles Darwin saw in historical purpose the law of evolution in animal life, the theory of natural selection. In politics, the purpose in history was often interpreted as being national destiny, manifest destiny, or national fulfillment. Nationalism was sometimes thought of as a divinely sanctioned movement; it was sometimes given historical necessity; and sometimes thought of as a political manifestation of the natural laws of evolution. In any event patriotism was usually blended with history in such a beguiling way as would prove commonality of purpose and design in political unification.

The reasoning behind nationalism was historical rather than analytical. It appealed to the rich traditions of the past rather than to the legal engagements of the present. This historical and cultural approach to politics was lucidly and eloquently expressed by the Englishman Edmund Burke in his *Reflections on the Revolution in France* (1790). In attacking the contract theory of society and the state he wrote:

> Society is indeed a contract. Subordinate contracts for objects of mere occasional interest may be dissolved at pleasure—but the state ought not to be considered nothing better than a partnership agreement in a trade of pepper and coffee, calico or tobacco, or some other such low concern, to be taken up for a little temporary interest, and to be dissolved by the fancy of the parties. It is to be looked on with other reverence; because it is not a partnership in things subservient only to the gross animal existence of a temporary and perishable nature. It is a partnership in all science; a partnership in all art; a

partnership in every virtue, and in all perfection. As the ends of such a partnership cannot be obtained in many generations, it becomes a partnership not only between those who are living, but between those who are living, those who are dead, and those who are to be born.[22]

It was this mystical sense of commonality, of past purpose and future design that gave to nineteenth-century nationalism its semi-religious appeal. It was this historical-sociological conception of the state that laid to rest the contract theory together with the analytic and legalistic discussions over the exact location of sovereignty. In the United States it was sufficient to say that sovereignty lay in the hands of the people without being at all precise as to which people in fact possessed this sovereignty. Sovereignty thus, like the nation, became a mystical rather than a legalistic conception.

THE NATION

The decline of the constitutional and legal approach to an understanding of the nature of the American Union, and the rise of the organic concept of the nation is well illustrated in the writings of Francis Lieber. An immigrant from Germany, Lieber skilfully synthesized the English emphasis on civil liberty and the importance of local political institutions, with the German emphasis on nationalism. Thus Lieber's nationalism was built upon decentralized institutions which in turn helped protect the civil rights of the citizens. It was, Lieber believed, the happy combination of local institutions and national purpose which protected and fostered civil liberty in a modern nation state. This institutional and evolutionary emphasis in Lieber led him to discard the contract theory of the state, holding that the state arose from the social necessities of man's being. The nation, in Lieber's conception, was a homogeneous population, in a coherent territory, with a common language, common literature and institutions, possessed of a consciousness of a common destiny.[23] It was this aspect of commonality of culture, of history, of political institutions and of destiny which made a given people in a given

[22] Hoffman and Levach, ed., *Burke's Politics* (New York: Alfred A. Knopf, 1949), p. 318.

[23] See Francis Lieber, *The Miscellaneous Writings of Francis Lieber* (Philadelphia: J. B. Lippincott and Co., 1881), vol. II, pp. 227-28; C. E. Merriam, *History of the Theory of Sovereignty since Rousseau* (New York, 1900), p. 175; C. B. Robson, "Francis Lieber's Nationalism," *Journal of Politics*, February, 1946.

place a nation. This organic concept of the nation was certainly far closer to Burke than it was to the contract theorists in America.

It was this organic concept of the nation which, accepted by the North, gave rise to the claim of perpetuity of the Union. A mere contract might be broken; but an historic past cannot be erased, nor the evolutionary growth forgotten. In his first *Inaugural Address,* Lincoln touched upon this concept of the nation.

> The Union is much older than the Constitution. It was formed, in fact, by the Articles of Association in 1774. It was matured and continued by the Declaration of Independence in 1776. It was further matured, and the faith of all the then thirteen States expressly plighted and engaged that it should be perpetual, by the Articles of Confederation in 1778. And finally, in 1787 one of the declared objects for ordaining and establishing the Constitution was to form a more perfect Union![24]

It was this view of the Union that was given legal sanction in 1869 when the Supreme Court, in *Texas vs. White,* was called upon to decide whether the Union had been broken by the secession of Texas. In this historic decision, Chief Justice Salmon P. Chase noted that the Union was not an artificial or arbitrary one.

> It began among the Colonies, and grew out of common origin, mutual sympathies, kindred principles, similar interests, and geographical relations. It was confirmed and strengthened by the necessities of war, and received definite form, and character, and sanction from the Articles of Confederation. By these the Union was solemnly declared to be "perpetual." And when these Articles were found to be inadequate to the exigencies of the country, the Constitution was ordained "to form a more perfect Union." It is difficult to convey the idea of indissoluble unity more clearly than by these words. What can be indissoluble if a perpetual Union, made more perfect, is not?[25]

So firmly entrenched was the concept of the perpetual Union, the product of uninterrupted evolutionary growth, that the Supreme Court refused to give any separate legal status outside of the Union to the former Confederate states. In America, as in Germany and Italy at approximately the same time, the forces of nationalism and union were victorious.

Following the Civil War, there were many efforts to reconstruct

[24] Roy P. Basler, ed., *Abraham Lincoln: His Speeches and Writings* (Cleveland and New York: The World Publishing Co., 1946), p. 582.
[25] *Texas vs. White* (1869) 7 Wallace 700.

the theory of the Union. In the South, Alexander H. Stephens, Vice-President of the Confederacy, brought out *A Constitutional View of the Late War Between the States* (1881), in which he reaffirmed the right of the sovereign states to secede from the Union. In the North there were various efforts to describe the new concept of the nation. Sovereignty was to be found in the nation, and not to be sought for in the formal phrases of the written Constitution. This point of view was generally supported by John A. Jameson in *A Treatise on Constitutional Conventions* (1866), by Orestes A. Brownson in *The American Republic* (1866), by J. N. Pomeroy in *Constitutional Law* (1868), by Elisha Mulford in *The Nation* (1870), and by John C. Hurd in *The Theory of Our National Existence* (1881). The organic aspect of the nation was particularly emphasized by Brownson and Mulford. Orestes Brownson, writing from a Catholic point of view, found Divine sanction behind the nation. Elisha Mulford, acknowledging his indebtedness to Hegel, found the nation to be a conscious moral organism. Finally, nationalism received its fullest and most systematic treatment in America through a political scientist, John W. Burgess. In his two-volume study, *Political Science and Comparative Constitutional Law* (1891), Burgess rejected the contract theory of the state and found the nation-state to be the product of political evolution. The modern nation was the peculiar political contribution of the Teutonic peoples, which to Burgess included Americans. With consuming nationalism Burgess wrote:

> The national state is thus the most modern and the most complete solution of the whole problem of political organization which the world has as yet produced; and the fact that it is the creation of Teutonic political genius stamps the Teutonic nations as the political nations *par excellence*, and authorizes them, in the economy of the world, to assume the leadership in the establishment and administration of states.[26]

With Burgess, American nineteenth-century nationalism passed beyond the range of its more limiting conceptions into the realm of Teutonic imperialism. In post-Civil War America it was clearly evident that the nation concept was victorious in theory as it had been on the field. The Union was composed of something less than sovereign states, while sovereignty lay in the people of the United States.

[26] John W. Burgess, *Political Science and Comparative Constitutional Law* (Boston: Ginn and Co., 1891), vol. I, p. 39.

The Constitution, it developed, was as much unwritten as written, for past practice, experience, was the evidence of the national character of the United States. And in time the term *Union,* shibboleth of the war period, slipped out of common usage and was supplanted by the term *nation* as final testimony of the victory of the nationalist concept.

CHAPTER 13

Manchester Liberalism in America

THE CIVIL WAR in the United States marked the end of a distinct era in American political thought. From the time of the Revolution until the Civil War the common frame of reference for political thought had been the natural-rights philosophy of Locke, Jefferson, and Paine, with its emphasis upon equality, individual volition, commonly assumed principles of morality, government by contract as an expression of consent, and the right of revolution for those who found that the government had violated its charter and transgressed upon the rights of individuals. Rights, it was thought, were derived from nature rather than from society, and the state was considered to be an institution of convenience rather than one of necessity.

The elaborate bills of rights in early American constitutions reflected the impact of this natural-rights philosophy. It is significant that the rights which developed in the late eighteenth century as a product of natural-rights thinking remained as the basic core of rights in subsequent American thought. For all the varied subsequent legal interpretations of these rights, the moral imperatives developed in Jeffersonian thought continued as the essential personal rights in American political and legal thought. With the passage of the natural-rights era, the era which saw the American Revolution and the eradication of slavery, Americans witnessed the passage of the revolutionary spirit.

Reconstruction of the South, inevitably, was the major political concern following the Civil War. Yet throughout the postwar period, immigration from Europe and migration to the West marked a minor revolution in American demography. It was only a coincidence and yet symbolic that in 1869, the year in which the Supreme Court settled the issue of the Union in *Texas vs. White,* the East and West would be linked by rail with the driving of the golden spike at Promontory Point in Utah. With ever-increasing rapidity, America was becoming settled and industrialized, and the nation that had been composed of farmers became predominantly a nation of workers. The frontier, which now reached the Pacific Ocean, would soon reach beyond the ocean; and the changes in centers of population and in economic conditions were reflected in the struggles for political power. The extraordinary change in economic setting which witnessed the rise of the modern corporation, of the modern labor movement, and of the modern farm guild had inevitably decided repercussions on American politics. There is no galaxy of thinkers comparable to John Adams, Thomas Jefferson, James Madison, Alexander Hamilton, John C. Calhoun, or Abraham Lincoln occupying public office in this period. The distinctive formulations of political thought came primarily from nonparticipants, from college professors, editors, and literary men.

The political literature of the decades immediately following the Civil War, while yielding little in the way of a systematic analysis of social organization, was indicative of a changing ethic in American life. Public policy occupied the position of primary concern in political thought. But policy in turn was considered within the framework of an economic context. The rapid industrialization of America following the Civil War quite naturally made economic issues politically imperative. The mode of thinking about economic questions, however, was different from that which had existed earlier in American thought, for previously economic questions were dealt with in the realm of an assumed context of morality which made the economic issues subsidiary to moral issues. The economics of the slavery system, for example, were subordinated to the larger issue of the moral legitimacy of slavery. The Jacksonian attack on special privilege was not basically dependent on the declared economic deficiencies of such a system. The pleas for reform in the pre-Civil War period usually emphasized the humanitarian aspects of reform, which in turn rested upon certain theological premises regarding the equal moral worth and dignity of each individual as an end in himself. A basic shift in values away from the theological context took place in the post-Civil War period, which produced a shift in emphasis in political thought generally.

American thought, closely allied with English thought, had from the earliest settlements reflected and expressed three modern ideological viewpoints: democracy, Protestantism, and capitalism. These major political, economic, and theological beliefs in seventeenth- and eighteenth-century English and American thought were often inextricably interwoven. Furthermore, it was often assumed that they were mutually supporting and dependent ideologies. From theology came the assumptions regarding the nature of man, upon which the political and economic systems were based. From theology as well came the value system, with its natural and inalienable rights. Politics and economics became methods of implementing and making more meaningful the dignity and worth of the individual. As a result, the social system was of consequence only as it affected the individual, for the individual and not society was the focal point in the value system. This view, implicit in all the discussions of individual rights, reached its high point of expression in the nineteenth century in the writings of Emerson, Thoreau, and William Ellery Channing. The shift from the individual to society as the major concern of political thought was clearly anticipated, however, by the Southern defenders of slavery. The shift from "moral philosophy" at the beginning of the century to "social theory" at the end of the century evidenced as well the shift from natural rights to social needs.

This change in approach to social problems was associated with the rise of utilitarianism in English and, subsequently, American thought. For as America had borrowed from England the philosophical premises for its political revolution, so it borrowed the basic theories for the industrial revolution. Thus the ideas of Bentham, James and John Stuart Mill, Adam Smith, and Ricardo found their way into American thought as had the ideas of Blackstone, Harrington, and John Locke at an earlier epoch. The English liberalism of the early nineteenth century, which brought the word *liberal* into popular political usage, provided to a large extent the creed of Jacksonian democracy. The English liberalism of Bentham, Cobden, and John Bright was essentially the same doctrine as that espoused in America by Jackson, Bryant, and Leggett. At this time— the first half of the nineteenth century—Manchester liberalism waged war against traditional abuses in the name of a rising middle class. In America, as in England, the combination of Bentham utilitarianism and classical economics proved to be admirably compatible with an expanding capitalistic and democratic society. It was indeed thought that utilitarianism had laid to rest the rationalistic philosophy of Locke. It was thought that by substituting the standard of utility for the intuitive assumptions of natural law, an objective criterion for action had been found. The test of an action was its determinable consequences. If it promoted pleasure it was good; if it promoted pain it was bad. Morality thus became a simple problem in hedonistic psychology, vaguely reminiscent of the work of Thomas Hobbes. But since utility as a test required determinable and therefore measurable consequences, the tendency of the utilitarian calculus was to utilize quantifiable evidence.

Thus what started off as a simple hedonistic calculus in which pleasure was good and pain was bad, became in fact something quite different, especially as interpreted in late nineteenth-century American thought. For classical economics, as developed in England by Adam Smith and David Ricardo, was transmitted to America as a part of the utilitarian system. In fact the classical economics of early capitalism found its justification in its utility. As a theory, classical economics was purportedly based on observations of man in his economic life. Its conclusions presumed to have the status of objective truth whose natural laws operated without regard to man's desires or intentions. Its utility was thus demonstrable, its adherents maintained. But the demonstrable proof of capitalism in action was the quantifiable evidence of iron-ore production, net tonnage, capital assets, wage rates, wheat harvests, farm implements, and the like. These materialistic symbols, while testimony of the productive achievements of capitalism, were amoral, in a humanitarian sense, unless related to the hedonistic psychology upon which the system was based. Even then the case was not entirely clear as to the relationship between increased productivity and increased pleasure.

Utility, of course, is not a standard in itself. To say that a thing is useful is to say that it has meaning or value when applied to a standard. It was the assumption of Bentham and his followers that man was motivated by his desire to pursue pleasure and avoid pain, and the utility of an action was thus judged by its tendency to promote pleasure and minimize pain. The avowed quest for the "greatest good for the greatest number" was thus a search for the greatest *pleasure* of the greatest number. It was soon evident, as John Stuart Mill observed in England, that pleasure as a standard of goodness raised in turn the question as to what was the standard of pleasure. Pleasure, as a normative conception, thus led directly into the ideological context of the period in which the term was used.

What was the prevailing social conception of that pleasure, that value, which the unimpeded individual would seek to attain? Pleasurable activity, it seemed to be assumed, was the fulfilling of self-interest. But then again, what were the goals of self-interest? With the increasing materialization of values in the late nineteenth century it would appear that by and large the goals of self-interest were essentially those which could be equated with the term *success* used in an economic sense. The values of capitalism thus came to be substituted for the earlier system of theologically derived values. Indeed, in many instances, theology came to the support of the new value system, the new ideology. In other words, the materialization of values ennobled success as a goal within the framework of the capitalistic ethic. That which had utility, therefore, became that which was conducive to achieving success as determined by the possession of wealth. Value, in effect, acquired a distinctively pecuniary connotation. The greatest good of the greatest number was, therefore, interpreted to mean the greatest acquisition of wealth by the greatest number of people. Economic prosperity thus became equated with pleasure, so that the good society was indeed a wealthy society. Furthermore, the conception of equality of men underwent a corresponding change. The natural law assumptions regarding man as an end in himself and, as such, possessed of a fundamental equality with his fellow man gave way to an emphasis upon equality of opportunity alone. Equal opportunity gave to each man an equal chance to prove the extent of his inequality. In a pecuniary value scheme, it was evident that not all men were worth the same. Old concepts thus acquired new meanings as the frame of reference changed.

The changes in the frame of reference, from theology to economics, from an emphasis on individuals to an emphasis on society, from intuitively perceived values to material objectives that could be quantitatively described, from a natural law of morality to a natural law of economics within a utilitarian framework, set a new context for American political thought. As a result, the fundamental issues in post-Civil War thought were basically economic issues; the fundamental assumptions regarding man were those accepted by capitalism; and the basic policy questions involved the operational validity and desirability of classical economics. Industrial capitalism, with its associated values, was in one form or another the central "given" of the new frame of reference. The basic problem of the generation following the Civil War was to find a system of thought which happily reconciled and related the accepted social norms of popular government and industrial capitalism.

GODKIN AND THE NATION

It was against this changing background of thought that the doctrine which was known as nineteenth-century liberalism came into importance. The men most clearly associated with nineteenth-century liberalism in America were editors, authors, and college professors rather than practicing politicians. Representative liberals of this camp were Edwin Lawrence Godkin, James Russell Lowell, George William Curtis, William Graham Sumner, Francis Lieber, and Wendell Phillips Garrison. As Bentham and his followers in England had an outlet for their ideas in the *Westminster Review,* so the American liberals had an outlet in the New York *Nation.* The *Nation,* founded in 1865 and edited from that date until the turn of the century by E. L. Godkin, was the representative organ of late nineteenth-century liberalism in the United States, and its pronouncements on public issues had far-reaching influence.

Godkin, of English parentage, came to the United States shortly after the Civil War. As he noted later in life, the college influence of his liberal teachers was enormous: "John Stuart Mill was our prophet, and Grote and Bentham were our daily food."[1] As J. S. Mill was the prophet to the young liberals—in England, Liberals—of Godkin's acquaintance, so was America the "promised land." "To the scoffs of the Tories that our schemes were impracticable, our answer was that in America, barring slavery, they were actually at work."[2] Slavery was the great barrier to the achievement of liberal democratic reform. It is significant that to the American liberal mind of this period, no less than to many English liberals, slavery was, as J. R. Lowell noted, the "single disturbing element" in the achievement of democracy.[3] It was no doubt because of the importance attached to slavery that the *Nation* was able to proclaim in its first issue at the conclusion of the Civil War:

> We utter no idle boast when we say that if the conflict of ages, the great strife between the few and the many, between privilege and equality, between law and power, between opinion and the sword,

[1] Rollo Ogden, *Life and Letters of Edwin Lawrence Godkin* (New York: The Macmillan Co., 1907), vol. I, p. 11.

[2] *Ibid.,* p. 12.

[3] James Russell Lowell, *Works* (Boston: Houghton Mifflin & Co., 1888), vol. V, p. 217.

was not closed on the day on which Lee threw down his arms, the issue was placed beyond doubt.[4]

It was thus with the highest optimism that liberalism faced the future in America. These same liberals, however, as they neared the end of their careers, viewed America's future with deep pessimism and they became indeed conservatives.

Basically, these liberals were literary men, journalists, conveyors of ideas rather than original thinkers. They took what had been thought elsewhere and applied it to the American scene. As a result, their ideas often have the nostalgic ring of outworn dogma rather than meaningful expression. They accepted Bentham and utilitarianism without, however, clearly departing from natural rights. They retained the substance of the old liberalism while affirming the method of the new. To the extent that a reconciliation was made between utilitarianism and natural rights, it was in their belief that utility should govern the means of attaining the values derived from the natural-rights school; but even here this result seems to have been more accidental than intended. It is perhaps true that they adhered more to Bentham's conclusions than to his method. Legal reform, reform in representation, and suffrage reform were endorsed, in theory, by them. They accepted the Bentham view that the essence of law was coercion and that law existed to compel men to behave in a fashion in which they might not otherwise behave. Thus they accepted the view that liberty starts where coercive law leaves off; and therefore they sought to keep the functions of government to a minimum. Furthermore, they tended to accept the view that man was basically rational, and that his self-interest was desire compounded with reason. It was to education that they looked as the means whereby man might become enlightened as to his true self-interest. It was this enlightening of the self-interest through education which not only improved man's rationality but his sense of responsibility as well. The assumption therefore continued that there could be no basic conflict between enlightened self-interest and the public interest, that in fact the latter was simply the total expression of the former in the community. Thus the pursuit of enlightened self-interest by members of the community achieved in fact the greatest good of the greatest number. The emphasis upon mass education and the peculiar fitness of the

[4] *Nation,* I (1865), p. 5.

educated man was a distinctive and important aspect of nineteenth-century liberalism.

Finally, this liberalism made a distinction between politics and economics, between the area of government and the area of business. The Bentham emphasis on jurisprudence, representation, and suffrage, and the position of John Stuart Mill on education, civil service reform, and proportional representation, became the political tenets of this liberalism in America as well. From Smith, Ricardo, and the early political economy of John Stuart Mill came the essential ideas used in the economic sphere. Both areas of concern, however, indicated the importance of keeping the state's functions to a minimum; for in a juristic sense, freedom was diminished by an extension of coercive law, while in economic theory, state intervention upset the balanced calculus of *laissez faire*. It was, indeed, the tendency of the late nineteenth century to unite the assumed separate spheres of politics and economics that most distressed this school of liberals. In America, the *Nation* school of liberalism accepted this compartmentalization of politics and economics, and accordingly these frameworks will be useful for discussion here.

POLITICAL ORGANIZATION

With the elimination of slavery, America appeared to English and American liberals the promised land of democracy. Opposed to artificial, legal, and class distinctions in society, liberals opposed slavery in America as they struggled against aristocratic privilege in England; for slavery denied the basic working assumption of equality of men before the law. The eradication of slavery posed, however, the question as to how to implement the concept of equality as it applied to the freedmen. Specifically this involved the education of the Negro and the extension of the franchise.

Public education and an extended franchise were both major tenets of the liberal faith; for education gave a man knowledge so that he might cast his vote intelligently, and the wide distribution of the franchise set democratic government upon a broad democratic base. In colonial America some of the major political struggles centered around the extension of public education, while at all times in America liberalism has been closely related to the franchise question. In the colonial period, liberals sought to remove the religious qualifications for voting, and later, in the Jacksonian period, liberals sought to eliminate the property qualifications.

It was to be expected, therefore, that the *Nation* would endorse education for the emancipated Negro and the extension to him of the suffrage. It did both—not, to be sure, as a matter of natural rights, but as a matter of desirable state policy. Yet, as the prime prerequisite for the suffrage, the *Nation* demanded an educational qualification. It was soon apparent, however, that education for the Negro required federal aid if it was to be an effective program. This in turn would involve an extension of the national government's activities in this field, which the *Nation* opposed under the old adage that to govern well one must govern little.[5] Thus while the liberal political creed called for an educated citizenry, the liberal economic creed called for minimum government, and in the contest between the two the latter triumphed! The Bentham objective of a minimum of government supported by the American theory of states' rights overcame the objective of educating newly emancipated Negroes through federal assistance to education. Furthermore, when it became apparent that an educational test would not be required of the Negro, Godkin and the *Nation* drew away from the suffrage movement. Indeed, when the Fifteenth Amendment was up for consideration, the *Nation* advised that the Negro be taught self-reliance and given fewer "gaseous lectures about his political rights."[6]

Within the space of two decades the *Nation* reversed its position on Negro suffrage and, indeed, the suffrage question generally. With the influx of illiterate immigrants in the North, and the appalling results of carpetbag rule in the South, the *Nation* and its coterie of supporters grew increasingly fearful for the educated minority. By 1880 the *Nation* was defending the disfranchisement of the Negro in the South because it kept political power in the hands of the educated property owners rather than permitting it to "pass into the hands of a class without property, without education, and without a single political habit or tradition."[7] By 1886 the *Nation* noted that although the Negro still suffered from injustice, the country "no longer has a Negro problem to settle."[8]

It is clear that the group which identified itself as liberals of the

[5] *Nation*, II (1866), p. 745.
[6] *Nation*, VIII (1869), p. 125.
[7] *Nation*, XXXI (1880), p. 126.
[8] *Nation*, XXXIII (1886), p. 26.

Bentham-Mill school found some of its basic concepts changing in postwar America. Quality in the suffrage, as evidenced by property and education, became more important than quantity, and faith in the intrinsic intelligence of the common man generally began to wane. The pattern of the *Nation's* ideas on Negro suffrage were repeated when the issue of woman's suffrage arose. In England, John Stuart Mill had endorsed woman's suffrage. In America, the *Nation* at first supported, then opposed this movement. In what is now an amusing Victorian comment, the *Nation* protested that since "every female politician knows that she holds her male colleagues or opponents at her mercy," woman's suffrage offered only a new source of corruption in politics.[9] In effect, the American disciples of English liberalism were far more conservative than their tutors.

The mood of buoyant optimism of liberals in 1865 rapidly declined. The promise of democracy, as they understood it, was not being fulfilled. Indeed, the criticism of the American liberals was such that they tended to make democracy the scapegoat for all the evils of society. James Russell Lowell inquired, "Is Democracy doomed by its very nature to a dead level of commonplace?"[10] Charles Eliot Norton, another *Nation* contributor, wrote his liberal friend in England, Leslie Stephen:

> The rise of the democracy to power in America and Europe is not, as has been hoped, to be a safeguard of peace and civilization. It is the rise of the uncivilized, whom no school education can suffice to provide with intelligence and reason.[11]

The attacks of English conservatives upon democracy were well received in the *Nation's* reviews. The criticism of nineteenth-century American liberals turned basically on an ethic that exalted materialism, and on the ignorant and corruptible populace that supported this ethic and demanded of government functions which a wise government ought not to perform. The limits of the agenda of the state were those fixed basically by Bentham and the classical economists. If these limits were sound, according to the opinion of the educated critics, then voters who sought from government action beyond these limits were either ignorant or corrupted. Defining

[9] *Nation*, XVII (1874), p. 312.
[10] C. E. Norton, ed. *The Letters of James Russell Lowell* (New York: Harper & Brothers, 1894), vol. II, p. 173.
[11] C. E. Norton, *Letters of Charles Eliot Norton* (Boston and New York: Houghton Mifflin Co., 1913), vol. II, pp. 236-37.

freedom as the area not pre-empted by legislation, they saw that area recede as, in their opinion, ignorant men voted away their rights. This age, the age of Jim Fiske, Jay Gould, Commodore Vanderbilt, and other millionaires, Mark Twain called the "Gilded Age." The *Nation* called it a "Chromo-Civilization." "We are so set upon material ends," the *Nation* lamented, "that we exaggerate the importance of attaining them; and come to think little of success that does not 'materialize.' "[12] At another time it observed:

> The popular hero today . . . is neither the saint, the sage, the scholar, the soldier, nor the statesman, but the successful stock-gambler. . . . And—what is worst of all—there is a growing tendency to believe that everybody is entitled to whatever he can buy, from the Presidency down to a street-railroad franchise.[13]

This basic discontent with the social and political standards of the age led the liberal camp into a crusade for reform. Their reform measures, however, were not intended to promote and extend democracy, but rather to "purify" it. Their greatest crusade and achievement was civil-service reform through the passage of the Pendleton Act in 1883. Yet in spirit that was simply Bentham's goal of having an honest, efficient, and qualified bureaucracy to administer the affairs of the state. They advocated Mugwumpism, independency in politics, so that the educated minority might achieve a pivotal balance of power; they advocated proportional representation to give greater weight to minority views; they sought an executive budget for the President and an item veto on Congressional extravagance; they proposed restrictions on the legislative branch, as "they constitute a part of the Government which we can best afford to abridge in its prerogative without at the same time striking at the root of popular liberty,"[14] and they supported direct election of the United States Senate only because they did not possibly see how the results could be any worse. It was to the courts, however, that these liberals looked for their champions of their way of life, and especially to the Supreme Court where sat Stephen J. Field. They opposed an elective judiciary on the grounds that it introduced politics into justice. To the *Nation,* the justice decreed by the courts in the late nineteenth century was impartial. "The courts and the law are on the side of both the poor and the

---

12 *Nation,* XLV (1887), p. 432.
13 *Nation,* XLII (1886), p. 419.
14 *Nation,* XX (1875), p. 342.

rich so long as they obey the laws," it noted in the week of the Haymarket Riot.[15]

The courts, by the turn of the century, were developing the concept of substantive due process whereby certain interpretations of the Constitution were rationalized as conclusions of natural law. Constitutional law was, in the conception of Stephen J. Field, natural law. It was, therefore, the judicial function to determine the essential principles of morality which made liberty possible in the modern state. Bentham's departure from natural law had been largely motivated by his desire to bring about reform in the field of jurisprudence. He had found the legal profession as it existed in his time the enemy of reform based on utilitarian principles. His American disciples in the late nineteenth century, however, turned to the legal profession and the courts as the champions of the *status quo*. The early Bentham motivation was lost and the result was that late nineteenth-century liberalism in America proved to be neither liberal nor democratic.

LIBERAL POLITICAL ECONOMY

The questions over the degree of state interference in the sphere of economic activity had been a matter of political dispute in America since the colonial period. The issue played an important part in the discussions leading to the Revolution. The attributed deficiencies of the Articles of Confederation were basically economic in character. The conflict over Hamiltonian and Jeffersonian policy raised again this basic issue. It was certainly evident to early American thinkers that economic issues led to political issues and that questions of economic policy became eventually questions of public policy involving the full play of politics.

Early nineteenth-century liberalism, however, attempted a separation of politics from economics. It is somewhat ironic that at the height of the prestige of classical economics the subject was called "political economy," and that when the intertwining nature of the subject matter was realized, the disciplines were separated into politics and economics. Classical economics, arising in the late eighteenth and early nineteenth centuries, was a protest against various traditional modes of state intervention in the economic sphere. Like Bentham's jurisprudence, it sought to introduce the

15 *Nation*, XLII (1886), p. 356.

principle of utility into legislation, so that arbitrary and inherited forms of state intervention would be revised in accordance with more liberal principles. Adam Smith sought to promote liberty in economics, as had Bentham in jurisprudence, by reducing or eliminating the irrational harassments of the law. Viewing law as coercion, it was assumed that liberty existed in the absence of law. Therefore, in economics as in any other field of activity, the prejudice was in favor of a minimum agenda for the state.

The enlightenment of the late eighteenth century not only whetted man's appetite for freedom but gave him a rational framework to justify this condition as well. For it was assumed that the various principles governing human behavior had been discovered, and that social control was largely a matter of orienting legislation to these basic principles. That all men desired freedom had long been an assumption of liberal political theory; but that economic freedom for individuals was also the best social policy was the distinctive contribution of the classical economists. *Laissez faire* was the economic counterpart of Bentham's theory of legislation. It too was built upon the simple assumption that man would seek to maximize pleasure and minimize pain. Furthermore, each individual following his own selfish interest was best judge of his own advantage. The more individuals who pursued this policy the more advantages would accrue to a greater number of people. Thus the greatest good, in the economic sphere, of the greatest number of people would result from a public policy that minimized state interference with private economic activity. Each individual, by seeking to promote only his own good, would in reality promote the public good.

It was the assumption that the public good was best achieved through the competition of individuals to promote only their own good that provided the ethical basis for *laissez faire*. It resolved, in a sense, the eternal conflict between the selfish and the altruistic motives in man by giving to selfish motives an altruistic justification. Through competition, conflict was resolved into social harmony. By approaching what the classical economists considered a system of natural liberty, man approached the harmonious scheme of nature. The hand of man was prone to error, but the invisible hand that guided the universe was infallible. By deducing what they conceived to be the laws governing the economic relations of man, the classical economists believed they had arrived at the immutable course directed by the invisible hand. Man could not change these laws, as they were considered to have the validity of objective truth. By tampering with the laws, man could only upset the results, which meant, in effect, upsetting the balance of nature. Since it was assumed that the system of natural liberty promoted the greatest good of the greatest number, there was no ethical basis for legislative interference with this system.[16]

While American political economy in practice developed along the lines of Hamiltonian theory, classical economics became deeply embedded in the schools and colleges. The economics textbooks of the post-Civil War period were largely restatements of the economic theory of Smith, Ricardo, and Mill. In the name of liberalism, *laissez faire* was emphasized as the only economic theory fit for a free society. "Political economy," the *Nation* noted in 1867, "has demonstrated that human legislation has its sphere, in attempting to transcend which, no matter how worthy the motive may be, it only works the more injury as it strives to attain an ideal good."[17] Because, it was argued, no greater good was really possible there was no adequate ethical case against *laissez faire*. Furthermore, classical economics had the honorific distinction of being acclaimed a science, which made its attackers adjudged as mere sentimentalists who had not adequately disciplined their minds to the stern edicts of reason. One economist of this period recounts in his autobiography that economics was then considered a "finished product."

> It was held that natural laws established certain fundamental principles for all times and places. It was only necessary that we should study these natural laws and follow them to attain the highest state of economic felicity possible to mankind.[18]

[16] This line of reasoning, leading to *laissez faire,* led equally to philosophical anarchism. The general acceptance of capitalism, together with the long tradition of property rights, precluded the wide consideration of anarchism in America. Individualist anarchism denied the necessity of any government by force—indeed, of any coercive power in society—and placed its faith in the free and equal association of men and women. Opposed to force, individualist anarchists were opposed to revolution and political action; they relied upon education and persuasion to achieve the completely *laissez-faire* society: anarchy. The most important American exponents of philosophical, individualist anarchism were Josiah Warren (1798?-1874), Stephen Pearl Andrews (1812-1886) and Benjamin R. Tucker (1854-1939). See Josiah Warren, *True Civilization* (Boston: J. Warren, 1863); Stephen P. Andrews, *The True Constitution of Government in the Sovereignty of the Individual* (New York: T. L. Nichols, 1854); Benjamin R. Tucker, *Instead of a Book; A Fragmentary Exposition of Philosophical Anarchism* (Boston: B. R. Tucker, 1893).

[17] *Nation,* IV (1867), p. 394.

[18] Richard T. Ely, *Ground Under Our Feet* (New York: The Macmillan Co., 1938), p. 126.

Thus, in a utilitarian sense, the science of economics revealed the pathway to the greatest good that was possible to man. There was therefore no greater utility to be had in state intervention. But there was still another important appeal of this economic theory. As these laws were natural, so also were they judged to be divinely sanctioned. To attempt to alter these laws or their consequences was thus to revolt against science, nature, and indeed the Deity. It was thus not only futile but blasphemous. Francis Bowen, Harvard professor and author of the economics text *American Political Economy*, noted that the principles of economics "manifest the contrivance, the wisdom and beneficence of the Deity, just as clearly as do the marvellous arrangements of the material universe. . . ."[19] Further, he noted:

> Man cannot interfere with His work without marring it. The attempts of legislators to turn the industry of society in one direction or another, out of its natural and self-chosen channels—here to encourage it by bounties, and there to load it with penalties,—to increase or diminish the supply of the market, to establish a *maximum* of price, to keep specie in the country—are almost invariably productive of harm. *Laissez faire;* "these things regulate themselves," in common phrase; which means, of course, that God regulates them by His general laws, which always, in the long run, work to good.[20]

Liberal economics, with its emphasis on *laissez faire*, became the bulwark of the defenders of the status quo against the many social reform programs advanced in America in the late nineteenth century. In the early days of classical economics, both in England and America, *laissez faire* was a theory of reform in behalf of the rising class of tradesmen and entrepreneurs. It was to be used in America in the Jacksonian revolt against those who held privileged charters and grants from the government. It was then used to open the area of freedom by restricting the area of privilege. In the late nineteenth century it became the conservative weapon against the new generation of reformers. Nineteenth-century liberals, clinging to a legalistic conception of freedom, clung to *laissez faire* as its only method of implementation. Cleveland was their hero, as he stood firmly against government intervention in the economic sphere. The record of the *Nation* during this period is revealing. It opposed tariff raising, state "rate fixing," and the Interstate Commerce Commission

[19] Francis Bowen, *American Political Economy* (New York: Charles Scribner's Sons, 1870), p. 21.
[20] *Ibid.*, p. 18.

d the Sherman Anti-Trust Act; was anti-union in its
and had the utmost contempt for the agrarian reformed in *laissez faire,* hard money, and the sanctity of
property. Thus liberals of this school, while turning to such
respectable political reforms as the civil-service movement, opposed
every reform movement that extended the base or the scope of
democracy. For it was patent in the late nineteenth century that
the new reform movements led to increasing the sphere of the
state in the activities of men. Social-reform movements meant restricting some of the accepted rights of property, and this was
anathema to the liberal economists. In defense, these liberals turned
to the courts, which had now become the guardians of classical
economics in America. In economics as in politics, and for basically
the same reasons, the Manchester or nineteenth-century liberals in
America opposed the movements which were both liberal and democratic. Indeed, the school of thought that was best represented in
the articles and editorials of the *Nation* was far closer to the anti-
democratic spirit of Paul Elmer More and Irving Babbitt in the
twentieth century than it was to any genuinely democratic movement of the nineteenth century. For with the change in social and
economic institutions, the unchanging doctrine of Manchester liberalism, so admirably suited to the circumstances of the age of
Jackson, benefited the most conservative forces in society in the
era of Grover Cleveland.

WILLIAM GRAHAM SUMNER

The American liberalism which had drawn so heavily upon Smith,
Bentham, Ricardo, and Mill was bolstered by the work of still
another Englishman, Herbert Spencer. Spencer, who was at once
a philosopher, sociologist and biologist, had a truly astonishing influence on American thought. Certainly no visiting philosopher
before or since has received such a reception as was accorded
Spencer in his triumphant visit to America in 1882. The only plausible explanation seems to be that his writings told many Americans
the very sort of thing which they wished to hear. For bringing his
ideas to America, his disciple, William Graham Sumner, deserves a
large amount of credit.

Americans had turned increasingly to a materialistic standard
of value in the late nineteenth century. Though the liberals had

frequently deplored this standard, they were nevertheless uncritical of the unrestricted capitalism that flourished under it. Natural law, originally a moral conception, took on an increasingly economic content. Liberalism in turn moved further away from its utilitarian base and adopted as absolutes the rights of private property and the immutable laws of trade, and even gave absolute character to the Constitution. So great was the motivation to riches and success along materialistic lines and in accordance with the natural laws of trade, that a Baptist minister, Russell H. Conwell (1843-1925), found over six thousand audiences for his "Acres of Diamonds" lecture. There were acres of diamonds all around, the minister proclaimed, and it was man's duty to discover them in his own home town. "I say that you ought to get rich, and it is your duty to get rich," he declared. With riches a man could do more good than he could were he poor. It was a mistake to associate piety with poverty. Poverty was a sign of shortcomings—one's own or someone else's—not of virtue. "Arise, ye millions . . . trust in God and man, and believe in the great opportunities that are right here . . . for business, for everything that is worth living for on earth."[21]

While legally the doors of opportunity were open to all men, it was quite evident that not all men achieved the same station in society. In early Puritan thought the distinction was made between the regenerate and the unregenerate. Aristocratic thought since the earliest days of America had tended to associate social and economic station with regeneracy, thus making poverty the consequence of original sin. In Locke, it was assumed that the virtuous would accumulate and the lazy and contentious would receive few rewards. In the American heritage the doctrine of equality was in constant battle with the economic ethic which associated poverty with indolence and vice. Neither Malthus in his study of population nor Ricardo in his study of wages gave any promise that mankind could ever banish poverty. That poverty was a deplorable condition and a social evil was generally acknowledged in the nineteenth century. It was even conceded by some that the iron law of wages, which legislation ought not to obstruct, was as regrettable as it was basically unalterable. But the ultimate "why" of the system was not solved by early nineteenth-century economics, which only noted the existence of the system. There had always been the suspicion, under capitalism, that poverty indicated some basic fault

21 Russell H. Conwell, *Acres of Diamonds* (New York: Harper & Brothers, 1915), pp. 18, 50.

with the character of an individual; it remained for biology, as interpreted by a sociologist, to confirm this suspicion and to explain the reason why. The key concept which provided this explanation was social Darwinism.

Actually, John C. Calhoun had anticipated much of the theory of social evolution. In his rejection of the natural rights philosophy he had rejected as well the belief in an intrinsic equality of men. Man's rights and duties were prescribed by the society of which he was a part. Society, however, was composed of unequals, competing for a high station in life. "It is, indeed, this inequality of condition between the front and rear ranks, in the march of progress, which gives so strong an impulse to the former to maintain their position, and to the latter to press forward into their files. This gives to progress its greatest impulse."[22] Calhoun thus saw progress resulting from the conflicts between men who were basically unequal in every sense of the word. His theory, however, was meant essentially to apply to a condition of racial rather than personal inequality. Yet he had related the concept of competition to the concept of inequality, and then related both to social advancement and civilization.

It was two Englishmen who gave to the concept of evolution the scientific cast which gave it the appearance of final truth. Charles Darwin, in his *Origin of Species* (1859), found through his biological studies that the process of growth and development of a species involved a struggle for existence out of which only those organisms adapted to their environment survived. Thus, for all the remarkable fecundity of nature, only a limited number of cells and organisms survived—those which had become adapted to their environment. This was nature's process of natural selection. The possibility for drawing an analogy in human affairs to this biological theory was indeed compelling. It was not Darwin, however, but Herbert Spencer who brought the survival-of-the-fittest doctrine into the social sciences.

Herbert Spencer, a confirmed *laissez-fairist*, had published the first of his many influential works, *Social Statics* (1850), when he was only thirty. He had, indeed, already hit upon the phrase "survival of the fittest" before Darwin had published the results of his research. Subsequently Spencer, in a series of essays, and most notably in his *Man Versus the State* (1884), applied this biological theory to social development. Nature's process of winnowing out

[22] *The Works of John C. Calhoun,* edited by Richard K. Cralle (New York: Appleton and Co., 1854), vol. I, p. 57.

the weak and shiftless, he argued, was a necessary consequence of the laws which governed the development of the human species. Only by eliminating the unfit could the species improve. Life was a ruthless competitive struggle for survival in which some were crushed and some were elevated to the top of the heap; but one always had the consolation that the breed was improving as each generation eliminated the unfit. Late nineteenth-century social legislation was designed to help the weak; but in so doing it could only perpetuate the existence of an inferior stock.

Laissez faire had been justified originally on the grounds that man's liberty was best realized where the state did not interfere with his activities. Each individual, in applying his productive and creative energies, made the best bargain with his fellow man that an unregulated market permitted. The state was obligated to see that each individual lived up to his commitments, that, in other words, contracts were enforced. Property, in the Lockean conception, represented accumulated labor, and therefore property as the reward for labor ought to be protected by the state. The obligations of contract and the rights of property provided the setting of the conditions within which the individual was free to follow his own self-interest provided he did not contravene the existing statutes. Such a system, in this conception, maximized freedom and justified the claim of this school to the title of liberalism. Bolstering this viewpoint, however, was the claim of the classical economists that a policy of *laissez faire* maximized productivity and achieved in fact the greatest good of the greatest number. The social unrest of the late nineteenth century, however, indicated that the greatest number were not entirely convinced that their greatest good was being realized. At this juncture, however, Spencer's theory of evolution, or social Darwinism, as it is sometimes called, entered the breach. *Laissez faire* was now not only the policy that maximized freedom and accorded with the natural laws of economics; it was at once sound economics and good eugenics. Social legislation not only upset the natural laws of economics, but impeded the natural laws of selection. Ricardo's iron law of wages, which declared that wages would inevitably stay at a mere subsistence level, was indeed nature's method of keeping down the unfit. The rich man, who had not only survived but had drastically improved his position in society, was best entitled to sire a new generation.

In America the most significant spokesman for this point of view was a professor of sociology at Yale, William Graham Sumner

(1840-1910). Sumner, in his many articles and books, joined evolution to *laissez faire* to attack all forms of social legislation. *Laissez faire*, he reasoned, left every man free to compete for survival with his fellow man without state favor or privilege. The fit would survive, the weak would be crushed, and the race would improve with each passing generation. Admittedly it was a cruel, ruthless system, but it was nature's plan, not man's. It was thus the whip hand of dire necessity which drove man to work; but society was the beneficiary of this fierce competition. In the last two decades of the nineteenth century, Sumner's views of social, political, and economic life received considerable attention. In "The Challenge of Facts," written in the 1880's, he attacked socialism and efforts at legislative amelioration of the hardships of life.

> The struggle for existence is aimed against nature. It is from her niggardly hand that we have to wrest the satisfactions for our needs, but our fellow-men are our competitors for the meager supply. Competition, therefore, is a law of nature. Nature is entirely neutral; she submits to him who most energetically and resolutely assails her. She grants her rewards to the fittest, therefore, without regard to other considerations of any kind. If, then, there be liberty, men get from her just in proportion to their works, and their having and enjoying are just in proportion to their being, and their doing. Such is the system of nature. If we do not like it, and if we try to amend it, there is only one way in which we can do it. We can take from the better and give to the worse. We can deflect the penalties of those who have done ill and throw them on those who have done better. We can take the rewards from those who have done better and give them to those who have done worse. We shall thus lessen the inequalities. We shall favor the survival of the unfitted, and we shall accomplish this by destroying liberty. Let it be understood that we cannot go outside of this alternative: liberty, inequality, survival of the fittest; non-liberty, equality, survival of the unfittest. The former carries society forward and favors all its best members; the latter carries society downwards and favors all its worst members.[23]

In his often-cited *What Social Classes Owe to Each Other* (1883), Sumner made clear that the rich owed nothing to the poor and ought not to be taxed for their benefit. Social legislation curtailed freedom; was immoral because it benefited the unfit at the expense of the working and deserving; and finally led to the de-

---

[23] A. G. Keller and M. R. Davie, eds., *Essays of William Graham Sumner* (New Haven: Yale University Press, 1934), vol. II, p. 95. By permission.

generation of society. "Here we are, then," wrote Sumner, "once more back at the old doctrine—*Laissez faire*. Let us translate it into blunt English, and it will read, mind your own business. It is nothing but the doctrine of liberty. Let every man be happy in his own way."[24]

It was evident that such a doctrine of liberty supported the claims of the strong against the weak, of the few against the many. Such a doctrine clearly worked to the advantage of those in positions of power against the claims of those who would use the machinery of government to modify or curtail the exercise of this power. The survival-of-the-fittest doctrine gave the honorific and distinctive claim to each person in economic power that he was a product of thousands of years of struggle for survival, and, due to evolutionary growth, superior not only to his ancestors but to most of his contemporaries. In the late nineteenth-century America of trusts, combinations, and enormous aggregations of wealth in the hands of relatively few people, survival-of-the-fittest theory was easily accepted by the barons of industry. Andrew Carnegie defended industrial concentration on the grounds that progress resulted from this survival of the fittest.

> We accept and welcome, therefore, as conditions to which we must accommodate ourselves, great inequality of environment, the concentration of business, industrial and commercial, in the hands of a few, and the law of competition between these, as being not only beneficial, but essential for the future progress of the race.[25]

Now that poverty was clearly associated with vice, laziness, or other forms of weakness, radicalism could be seen as a menace not only to the existing order but to posterity as well.

> The Socialist or Anarchist who seeks to overturn present conditions is to be regarded as attacking the foundation upon which civilization itself rests, for civilization took its start from the day that the capable, industrious workman said to his incompetent and lazy fellow, "If thou dost not sow, thou shalt not reap," and thus ended primitive Communism by separating the drones from the bees.[26]

This same analogy was used by another industrial magnate, John D. Rockefeller, when he explained the rise of Standard Oil as

---

[24] William Graham Sumner, *What Social Classes Owe to Each Other* (New York: Hayser and Bros., 1883), p. 120.
[25] *North American Review*, CXLVIII (1889), p. 655.
[26] *Ibid.*, p. 656.

an illustration of the survival of the fittest, and observed: "The American beauty rose can be produced in the splendor and fragrance which bring cheer to its beholder only by sacrificing the early buds which grow up around it. This is not an evil tendency in business. It is merely the working out of a law of nature and a law of God."[27]

The logic of the survival-of-the-fittest doctrine led inevitably to a justification of the prescriptive claims of the dominant economic forces in society. Furthermore, it carried on the Benthamite confusion which equated freedom with lack of governmental interference. Thus it was assumed that the competitive struggle was a free struggle as long as the government did not interfere, though, it was argued, the government ought to see that the struggle took place within the framework of the traditional rules of the rights of private property. While the rules of the struggle were themselves the product of evolutionary development, it was argued that the rules ought not to evolve further. Thus the rules, as expressed in judicial interpretations of the Constitution and the rights of property, took on a final and absolute character. It was this aspect of the law which led Justice Holmes to protest that "The Fourteenth Amendment does not enact Mr. Herbert Spencer's Social Statics."[28]

While change was but the manifestation of the evolutionary process, it was also clear that not all change was either evolutionary or in the direction of progress. The rise of a group structure, in the form of trusts, mergers, labor unions, Granges, and farm bureaus could be explained in terms of evolutionary development. Yet within the framework of evolution their consequences were evaluated differently. Industrial combinations, it was maintained, were leading to a higher form of capitalism and were producing a higher type of industrial leadership. Labor unions and farm bureaus, however, were held to be forms of retrogression towards a more primitive society, and their leaders were considered to be mere demagogues without any special fitness whatsoever. This value judgment presented a logical difficulty for the advocates of evolution; for once they had conceded that not all change was progress, they revealed an inner standard for evaluating change. Morality was thus introduced into what was claimed to be an amoral observation. Furthermore, since not all change was progress, it was evident that not all

[27] Quoted in Richard Hofstadter, *Social Darwinism in American Thought* (Philadelphia: University of Pennsylvania Press, 1944), p. 31.

[28] *Lochner vs. New York*, 198 U. S. 45 (1905).

who survived were fittest in accordance with the same value stand-ard. The test for fitness, therefore, was not survival alone but some-thing that went beyond mere survival. Fitness, it would appear, was survival plus the acquisition of wealth. Thus the possession of property became, as it had been assumed to be by many previous thinkers in America, the tangible evidence of fitness, the mark of a "good" man.

ANTI-IMPERIALISM

The peace, retrenchment and reform goals of English liberalism were accepted by American nineteenth-century liberals. Retrench-ment meant *laissez faire;* reform meant purifying politics through the increased participation of educated citizens. The civil-service program was a major step toward this goal of reform. Such a high faith was placed upon the understanding of educated men that it was generally assumed that most of the conflicts in politics could be resolved through an increased application of education to the voters. It was assumed that intelligent, educated men would not find them-selves in serious political disagreement. There was thus a tendency of nineteenth-century liberals to talk down to their opponents, for political opposition was but an indication of ignorance. It was fre-quently argued, for example, that if men would only apply them-selves to a study of classical economics, they would understand that the existing wage scale was the necessary wage scale and would cease to agitate for minimum wage laws. Surely, it was argued, if men would devote themselves to a study of political economy they would see the folly of any other public policy than traditional *laissez faire.* Therefore, the more educated the men who entered politics, the less likelihood of serious political differences.

Laissez faire, however, was not a doctrine for domestic policy alone but applied with equal force to the international field. If the state did not interfere with international trade, nations would be-come bound together in an international web. The free-market concept, used in the domestic field, was equally applicable to the international area. In fact, the title of Smith's book, *The Wealth of Nations,* was indicative of the international character of *laissez faire.* If nations and individuals bought cheaply and sold dearly, all would profit alike. If each exporter and importer concentrated his business on his area of special advantage, all would profit. This involved, of course, a major assumption: the harmony of interests among nations. The law of comparative advantage worked to the interests of all because there was an assumed balance between the world's needs and resources and such a distribution of these that all nations would profit through exchange. That classical economics recognized the subsistence level of existence for the worker in the domestic area makes it the more astonishing that it did not recognize this iron law of rewards in the international sphere. At any rate, nineteenth-century liberals sought a universal application of *laissez faire* on the grounds that a free international trade would make for international profit and thus be a compulsion toward international peace. War, it was believed, was the result of the machinations of statesmen who had departed from the basic principles of enlightened understanding and free trade.

The late nineteenth century, however, proved to be an era of petty wars and armament races, the direct antithesis of the international program of this liberalism. Furthermore, the justifications for aggression were often in terms of the liberal dogma of protecting private property, teaching a respect for the law, and advancing civilization through an extension of capitalism and democracy. Finally, social Darwinism crept into the international field as well, so that imperialism was justified as proving to the world which nations were the fittest to survive. In 1885, Josiah Strong wrote of America's mission,

> If I read not amiss, this powerful race will move down upon Mexico, down upon Central and South America, out upon the islands of the sea, over upon Africa and beyond. And can any one doubt that the result of this competition of races will be the "survival of the fittest"?[29]

Imperialism, however, was anathema to the nineteenth-century liberals. Not since the Civil War had the liberals rallied in such a crusade as they did at the turn of the century to attempt to quench the fires of imperialism. Godkin, Sumner, Grover Cleveland, and C. E. Norton among others enlisted in anti-imperialist leagues reminiscent of the early days of the anti-slavery movement. Though they fought a losing cause, they reasserted the doctrine of political freedom and *laissez faire* in a new setting. War led to political jobbing, meddling, and interference, on a grand scale. War was an evil which

[29] Josiah Strong, *Our Country: Its Possible Future and Its Present Crisis* (New York: Baker and Taylor, 1885), p. 175.

an intelligent statesman would always seek to avoid; war inflamed the passions and thus took the throne away from reason. Such, they argued, were the inevitable products of an imperialistic policy. Imperialism meant militarism, high taxes, waste, an increased bureaucracy, and the sacrifice of life and property. Should the goal of the expansionists be achieved, the *Nation* counselled, "it will indeed be in accordance with evolution; but if it is defeated, it will just as much be in accordance with evolution, and evolution of a much more satisfactory kind."[30] Once again the Declaration of Independence took a prominent place in political discussions, as the right of a people to govern themselves was acclaimed as one of the cornerstones of liberalism. Thus it was not alone the dread of state intervention that caused the liberals to attack imperialism, for they felt that such intervention would in the long run deny the values of freedom as they understood this concept.

By the turn of the century it was evident that Manchester liberalism was on the wane as a vital force in American politics. In 1900 the *Nation* sadly observed, "In the politics of the world, Liberalism is a declining, almost a defunct, force. Only a remnant, old men for the most part, still uphold the Liberal doctrine, and when they are gone, it will have no champions."[31] Indeed, by the turn of the century, the use of the term liberal by this group of thinkers was only perpetuating a confusion over the nature of liberalism in American thought. On most issues these men opposed reform and were, in effect, arch-conservatives. A new liberalism had already arisen, but because of the nineteenth-century liberals' prescriptive use of the term, had had to adopt another label. Nineteenth-century Manchester liberalism thus gave way as a reform movement to twentieth-century progressivism.

30 *Nation*, LXVI (1898), p. 455.
31 *Nation*, LXI (1900), p. 105.

CHAPTER 14

American Utopian Reformers: George and Bellamy

AMERICAN political thought was basically conservative in the years following the Civil War. Manchester liberalism in action appeared to be primarily concerned with defending the existing economic system against the humanitarian pleas of reformers. In spite of the claims of Godkin and Sumner as spokesmen for liberalism, their most fundamental crusade in politics was civil-service reform, while in economics the only basic change they sought was to get government out of business, in keeping with the assumptions of classical economics. As remedy for other evils they offered only patience, self-restraint, and a more rigid separation of the spheres of politics and economics. Manchester liberalism thus became far removed from the humanitarian liberalism which characterized Jeffersonian and Jacksonian democracy. American political thought had indeed adopted conservatism under the label of liberalism when it accepted the inevitability and desirability of the existing economic order and denied on grounds of philosophy as well as politics the possibility of improving man's lot through collective or political action. Such a system of political philosophy condemned man to the status quo and made his hope for the future rest upon the gradual mutation of the genes of his progeny. The inexorable laws of economics and biology offered the prolific poor man little hope in the present or future, for he was as clearly outside the approved social status as the unregenerate man in Puritan Massachusetts.

Inevitably, critics arose to challenge this deterministic order. These critics were radical enough to go to the roots of prevailing American conceptions and constructive enough to offer solutions

312

designed for the entire society. They were utopians in that they offered the promise of perfection but a short tomorrow away; they were utopians, as were the Massachusetts Puritans, the Owenites, and the Fourierists, in that they believed that a regenerate and well regulated society would discourage the baser compulsions of men and thus make possible such peace, prosperity and brotherly love as had not existed heretofore in human history; and they were utopians in that they believed man's reason could overcome his conservative obstacles of habit, tradition, and received systems of thought and value. In a land devoted to practical thought, whether in business or politics, these utopians had a wholesome and regenerating effect upon American ideas, as they sharpened the criticism of the existing order, suggested possible solutions, and inspired further discussion by indicating clearly that conditions as they were did not have to be. In an age still paying homage to natural laws in economics, biology and sociology, Henry George and Edward Bellamy came as a fresh breeze across arid land, bringing hope and promise to a people condemned to awaiting the inevitable. Once again the humanitarian sentiment, banished by the Manchester liberals and the social Darwinists, found its appeal in American thought. Once again the claim was made that although man builds his own prison he may with his reason unlock the doors. Not since the age of Jackson had such a general feeling of unrest and social ferment come to American politics. For the intellectual aspects of this ferment, a large measure of credit is due to the work of George and Bellamy, writers whose wide appeal helped formulate the demand for basic social reform.

There were numerous evidences of a growing demand for economic reform in post-Civil War America. Such evidences are found in the rise of farm and labor organizations which were dedicated to improving the social and economic position of their members. In 1867 the Patrons of Husbandry was founded; and by 1875 the Granger movement claimed over a million and a half farm members. It was the Granger movement that spearheaded what has become popularly known as the Agrarian Crusade which, among other political results, led to state regulation of railroads and warehouses.[1] Labor attempted to organize on a national basis after the

---

[1] A reaction of the Manchester liberals to this political intervention in economic life may be found in an article in the *Nation* in 1876: "When the Grangers had once proclaimed that their object was to 'fix rates,' or, in other words, to declare by law what proportion of the market value of services they themselves should pay, and that they would not be bound by the terms of their

Civil War, although neither the short-lived National Labor Union nor the utopian Knights of Labor achieved any lasting political or economic benefits. The Knights of Labor, under the leadership of Uriah S. Stephens and Terence V. Powderly, did succeed, however, in focusing attention on the increasing problems of labor in an era of industrial expansion and no doubt helped set the stage for its successful rival organization, the American Federation of Labor.[2] It was against the background of growing self-consciousness on the part of labor and farmer, together with the economic dislocations of the times—a five-year depression following the Panic of '73, another depression in 1884—that Henry George and Edward Bellamy offered their promises of prosperity and reform, their assurances of the possibility of utopia in America.

HENRY GEORGE

The prevailing political and economic theory in America in the post-Civil War period was Manchester liberalism, modified by the acceptance of social Darwinism, interpreted and expounded by academicians, such as Sumner, and writers with university training, such as E. L. Godkin. Henry George (1839-1897) lacked this formal academic training, and it is possible that the originality of his insight into economic and social problems was partly due to his education having been undertaken outside the received and respected categories of thought. His insight into the relation of progress and poverty was the result of personal observation, after much travel and experience, rather than reading. Born in Philadelphia in 1839, the second of ten children, he had no more than ten years of schooling before he went to work at a seemingly endless variety of occupations. In the space of three years he sailed before the mast to

---

contracts, it was perfectly clear that the Granger movement was rank communism. . . ." (*Nation*, XXII, 1876, p. 58.) Indeed, the *Nation* found that railroad management had come "by a sort of process of natural selection, to be committed to the hands of what is perhaps the ablest body of men in the United States." *Nation*, XVI, 1873, p. 249.

[2] The *Nation* viewed the growing labor movement with considerable alarm. In 1886, the year in which the American Federation of Labor was founded, the *Nation* observed of labor unions: "They seek to overthrow in the moral world the law of the survival of the fittest. . . . They insist that all shall survive, both the fit and the unfit; that virtue shall not have even the reward of achievement, and that the qualities which most distinguish man from the brutes shall not profit any individual man materially." (*Nation*, XLIII, 1886, p. 305.)

Australia, to India, to Boston; then for a time he served as a type-setter in Philadelphia; next to sea again via the Straits of Magellan to Oregon; gold-placing in Canada followed; finally he settled down at twenty-one years of age to typographical work in San Francisco. In the course of his travels he read promiscuously but observed much. It was when he settled in San Francisco, however, that he undertook in earnest to educate himself through disciplined study.

As a young man George had experienced unemployment and a rather incoherent sense of dissatisfaction with the existing economic arrangements. This dissatisfaction, indeed general restlessness, was coupled with a tinge of missionary zeal to right existing wrongs, to bring a little more of the perfect into the present. Some indication of the turn of his thoughts is found in his youthful letters from San Francisco to a sister in Philadelphia. "What a constant reaching this life is, a constant stretching forth, and longing after something . . . and so it will be until we reach the perfect. . . ."[3] This reaching outward is further expressed as he observed:

How I long for the Golden Age, for the promised Millennium, when each one will be free to follow his best and noblest impulses, un-fettered by the restrictions and necessities which our present state of society imposes upon him; when the poorest and the meanest will have a chance to use all his God-given faculties and not be forced to drudge away the best part of his time in order to supply wants but little above those of the animal. . . .[4]

As George became more aware of the pervasiveness of squalor and poverty, whether in backward India or advanced New York, in old Philadelphia or new San Francisco, his thoughts turned increasingly to the causes and possible cures of this basic social ill. His own experiences in attempting to raise a family on a precarious income undoubtedly intensified his desire for a solution to the problem of poverty.[5]

[3] Quoted in George Raymond Geiger, *The Philosophy of Henry George* (New York: The Macmillan Co., 1933), p. 33.

[4] *Ibid.*, pp. 33-34.

[5] Once he was reduced to such financial straits that he later recounted: "I walked along the street and made up my mind to get money from the first man whose appearance might indicate that he had it to give. I stopped a man—a stranger—and told him I wanted $5. He asked what I wanted it for. I told him that my wife was confined and that I had nothing to give her to eat. He gave me the money. If he had not, I think I was desperate enough to have killed him." Geiger, *op. cit.*, p. 36.

By 1868 George, now doing occasional writing for local periodicals, had come to the conclusion that material progress did not
guarantee prosperity. This was the beginning of his basic insight
into the nature of poverty. For instead of assuming that with an
increase in population, in capital, in business enterprise, in all the
material evidences of a progressing culture would come a greater
prosperity for all, George reasoned that without a basic change in
the distribution of wealth the increased production of wealth would
be but a mixed blessing. Writing on "What the Railroad Will Bring
Us" (1868), in anticipation of the completion of the transcontinental
railroad linking the frontier West with the urban East, George
argued,

> The truth is, that the completion of the railroad and the consequent
> great increase of business and population, will not be a benefit to all
> of us, but only to a portion. . . . Those who have, it will make
> wealthier; for those who have not it will make it more difficult to
> get. . . .[6]

Already George had discovered the impact of advancing civ̄iliza-
tion upon land values and business generally. With the coming of
the railroad and the increase in population, it would take more capital to buy land or to go into business. Yet, at the same time, the
increase in population would increase the competition in the labor
market, which would tend to drive wages down. As a result, venture
capital would be harder for the laborer to acquire at the very time
that land and business prices were tending to rise. Thus those who
"had" could enjoy the rise in values, while those who "had not"
would find it more difficult to improve their positions. Here was the
kernel of George's basic idea that material progress did not alleviate poverty.

A year or so after he had arrived at this basic idea as to the
inability of progress to do away with poverty, George was riding
through the California countryside at a point where a land boom
was taking place. He had been to this place before the speculative
boom had materially affected land prices. Now he was startled by
the change that had occurred in land values. Later, recounting this
experience, George noted:

> Like a flash it came upon me that here was the reason of advancing
> poverty with advancing wealth. With the growth of population, land
> grows in value, and the men who work it must pay more for the

[6] Geiger, *op. cit.*, p. 40.

privilege. I turned back amidst quiet thought, to the perception that then came to me and has been with me ever since.[7]

Possessed of this insight George turned in earnest to a study of political economy to understand why such a condition should be. And with consummate zeal he turned to political participation, lecturing, and publishing to point up this condition and its possible remedies. Again and again in lectures and in newspaper articles he emphasized the problem of poverty in modern society, its full social implications, and its relationship to land values. While others talked of individualism and the survival of the fittest, George attacked a social system that would push the weak and helpless to the wall. In 1871 he brought out a pamphlet which brought together his ideas at that time on the land question. It was entitled *Our Land and Land Policy, National and State.* Here he pointed up the desirability of a tax on the unearned increment of land as a means of bringing to society the benefits of a social product whose value was created by society itself. Here he first elaborated on his idea that land, like air, was intended for all mankind to enjoy and could not rightfully be monopolized for the benefit of the few. And here he developed his idea of the relationship of land to labor, of rent to wages.

> The value of land and the value of labour must bear to each other an inverse ratio. These two are the "terms" of production, and while production remains the same, to give more to the one is to give less to the other. The wealth of a community depends upon the product of the community. But the productive powers of land are precisely the same whether its price is low or high. . . . The value of land is the power which its ownership gives to appropriate the product of labour, and so a sequence, where rents (the share of the land-owner) are high, wages (the share of the labourer) are low. . . . The higher land and lower wages, the more difficult is it for the man who starts with nothing but his labour to become his own employer, and the more he is at the mercy of the land-owner and the capitalist.[8]

Even as George developed and reiterated this basic theme, this economic theory, his fundamental concern was with the ethical problem of eliminating or at least alleviating poverty because of its degenerating effect upon society. To a large degree the success of Henry George rested not merely upon his economic ideas but upon

[7] *Ibid.,* pp. 42-43.
[8] Quoted in Henry George, Jr., *Life of Henry George* (Toronto: The Poole Publishing Co., 1900), pp. 222-223.

his larger views of social organization, and the place and rights of the individual. He combined in effect an understanding of what he considered to be the way in which society was organized—the personal motivations involved—with a belief in a value concept of how society ought to be. He wrote in causative terms within a clear and discernible framework of normative ideas. As a political campaigner as well as a writer, he insisted upon associating political, economic, and social questions. For instance, while campaigning for Tilden in 1876 he declared:

> Food, raiment and lodging are essential not merely to animal existence but to mental development, to moral growth, to the life of the affections. Personal independence, the ability to get a living without trembling in fear of any man, is the basis of all manly virtues. Ignorance is the companion of poverty; want is the parent of crime. These are the grand questions . . . yet these are the questions to which we have been paying least attention.[9]

George looked far beyond subsistence living to the good life, for it was his contention that mere subsistence living, inevitably accompanied by anxiety and insecurity, denied a man his true sense of humanity, which indeed separated man from the beasts.

Although George did not begin the writing of *Progress and Poverty* until 1877, the basic fabric of the work had already been developed and expressed by him in his various speeches and articles. He felt, however, the urge to appeal to a wider audience and to state his arguments in as systematic a fashion as possible, and with a full awareness of orthodox thinking in political economy. He therefore set about a systematic presentation of the subject, tediously studying and countering conventional political economy where it interfered with the noble purpose he endeavored to achieve. The resulting work was far more than a treatise on political economy, even though it has surpassed in sales any other work in that field; it was a glowing work in the humanitarian tradition.

PROGRESS AND POVERTY

Progress and Poverty, an Inquiry into the Cause of Industrial Depressions and of Increase of Want with Increase of Wealth, the Remedy (1879) was the imposing title of Henry George's ambitious

[9] Quoted in Geiger, *op. cit.*, pp. 46-47.

work. The nature of his inquiry, timely in the nineteenth century, had not entirely lost its appeal some three quarters of a century later, for George stated what appears to be a perennial problem in social organization. His initial statement of this inquiry is indeed suggestive: In the nineteenth century, a century of progress, in which steam replaced sail and supplanted human labor in factories, in which the railroad replaced the wagon, in which the extraordinary energies released by modern science had removed so much of the drudgery from human labor, might not an observer from an earlier age expect something akin to utopia in mankind's condition of living? Yet utopia was as far away in the nineteenth century as it had been a century earlier.

> From all parts of the civilized world come complaints of industrial depression; of labor condemned to involuntary idleness; of capital massed and wasting; of pecuniary distress among business men; of want and suffering and anxiety among the working classes.[10]

Material progress under existing social organization clearly did not eradicate depressions, want, anxiety, and suffering. Indeed, with civilization, with progress, came poverty as an unfortunate by-product. If San Francisco in the late nineteenth century was less subject to acute poverty than New York, it was only because it was less civilized, had less of progress to boast of. "When San Francisco reaches the point where New York now is, who can doubt that there will also be ragged and barefooted children on her streets?"[11] Thus George posed as the "great enigma" of the times the association of progress and poverty.

While George dealt with this enigma in numerous subsequent publications, it was in *Progress and Poverty* that he first formulated the broad social philosophy for which he became famous. This book was indeed his major work, comprehending in its scope economic, political and social theory, and throughout his life he remained faithful to the ideas expounded in it. Thus to understand Henry George's thought it is necessary to comprehend in some detail the depth and scope of *Progress and Poverty*. Such comprehension requires in turn some familiarity with the prevailing economic theory at the time of George's writing.

In his inquiry into the association of progress and poverty, George

[10] Henry George, *Progress and Poverty* (New York: The Modern Library, 1938), p. 5.
[11] *Ibid.*, p. 10.

was himself led into an examination of existing economic theory and its inner assumptions. For under conventional theory this lamentable condition was inevitable and therefore could not be altered. It was George's argument that poverty and depression were not inevitable and that they could be eradicated by thoughtful changes in the organization of society. Thus George struck at some of the central assumptions of existing social theory. To do this he felt it necessary to rewrite economic theory.

Under existing theory there were two main lines of argument which served as explanations for the inevitability of poverty: the wages-fund theory, and Malthus' theory of population. Either of these theories condemned the masses of mankind to a subsistence level of existence; taken together they served as an apparently insurmountable barrier to any well-intentioned effort to improve the living conditions of labor. Under classical economics, wages were fixed by the ratio between the amount of capital set aside for the payment of labor and the number of workers seeking employment. That is, it was assumed that an employer set aside, or advanced, a fixed fund to be applied as wages of labor; workers, competing for employment were paid out of this fund. Since the competition for employment was assumed, under normal conditions, to be rather intense, the share or wages each worker would receive would inevitably tend downward to the subsistence level.

Thus, under the wages-fund theory, the competition of workers for employment would cause wages to hover close to the subsistence level, or that maximum of poverty in which a man might still be able to live. Accepting the basic features of this theory of wages, the Manchester liberals decried artificial efforts to raise wages through trade unionism or minimum wage laws. For the amount which went into the wages-fund was necessarily fixed by the money market while the number of workers who sought employment was determined by the existing labor supply. To the Manchester liberal, nothing short of a genuine scarcity of labor could effect a rise in wages without upsetting the entire economic system. There was thus no salvation for labor, no hope for more than a subsistence level of wages, and poverty was assumed to be a necessary fact of economic life.

The Malthusian theory of population was equally grim in its condemnation of the masses of labor to poverty. "For poverty, want, and starvation are by this theory not chargeable either to individual greed or to social maladjustments; they are the inevitable results of universal laws, with which, if it were not impious, it were as hope-less to quarrel as with the law of gravitation."[12] Malthus' "Essay on Population" held, in effect, that the constant tendency of population to increase, unless held in check by war, disease or prudence, would inevitably cause it to press against the limits of the food supply, making food more difficult to procure and causing famine to set the outer limits to the increase of population. Assuming that population increased at a geometrical ratio and food supply only at an arith-metical ratio, poverty and famine were inevitable and were nature's check upon the growth of population. This theory, basically ac-cepted in America and strongly fortified by the survival-of-the-fittest doctrine which was built upon it, made efforts to alleviate the dis-tress of the poor not only futile but imprudent. Some inevitably had to starve and many had to barely manage to survive in order to keep population growth within bounds.

The wages-fund theory and the Malthusian theory of population being the two major obstacles to any reasoned effort to eradicate poverty, George in his argument devoted Books I and II of his *Progress and Poverty* to their attack. Essentially George's refutation of the wages-fund theory consisted of his argument that wages are not derived from advanced capital, but are payment for work al-ready performed. That is, he maintained that wages are not drawn from capital, but "drawn from the product of the labor for which they are paid."[13] Labor, in other words, created a product of value and it was from this product that wages were paid. "Production is always the mother of wages. Without production, wages would not and could not be. It is from the produce of labor, not from the advances of capital, that wages come."[14] As a result, he argued, the fixed limits of wages under existing theory were invalid, for wages were not dependent upon a static capital-labor relationship, but were payments deriving from the dynamics of production in which there were no foreseeable limits.

In his attack upon the pessimistic expectations of Malthus, George countered essentially with the argument that poverty and increasing population were not necessarily related at all; that indeed the fun-damental enigma was that poverty came with an advance in pro-ductive power, though Malthus had attributed it to a decrease in productive power. With every mouth, argued George, came two

[12] *Ibid.*, p. 99.
[13] *Ibid.*, p. 23.
[14] *Ibid.*, p. 56.

hands able to provide more goods in any accelerating and progressive society. Indeed, he argued, the greater the population, under
an equitable distribution of wealth, the greater the comfort each
might enjoy.

> I assert that in any given state of civilization a greater number of
> people can collectively be better provided for than a smaller. I assert
> that the injustice of society, not the niggardliness of nature, is the
> cause of the want and misery which the current theory attributes to
> over-population.[15]

The attack George made upon the wages-fund theory and the conclusions of Malthus were only preliminary discussions to the advancement of his own thesis. If continued poverty was not related
either to the prevailing theories of wages and population growth,
how did one account for its existence? Furthermore, how might one
draw up a theory of economics which would explain the current
existence of poverty on the one hand, but on the other would clearly
indicate the path of reform which would lead to its eradication? In
answering these questions, George was led into a major undertaking: the reconstruction of economic and social theory.

Under accepted economic theory there were three major factors
involved in production: land, labor, and capital. Each received rewards for, or returns on, production. Thus land received rent, labor
received wages, and capital received interest. However, under classical doctrine, the laws governing the distribution of returns or
rewards for production were not directly interrelated or synthesized.
Thus in classical theory rent was determined by the margin of cultivation of a given piece of land as compared with the poorest land
then in use. In other words, given an equal application of labor and
capital to land, the difference between the produce of one piece of
land and the produce of the poorest land in cultivation was the
amount which went to the landowner in the form of rent. This was
the law of rent formulated by Ricardo. Labor, under the laws of
classical economics, received wages which were determined by the
ratio between the fund of capital set aside to pay wages and the
number of laborers seeking employment. Finally, interest under the
prevailing theory was determined by the equation between the demands of the borrowers and the supply of capital made available by
lenders. Such was the classical economic theory of the laws of distribution. It should be observed, however, that these laws had no

[15] *Ibid.*, p. 141.

unifying principle; that is, they were separate unrelated laws. The law of rent, for example, was independent of the law of interest.

Having recapitulated these basic laws, George set out to modify them and bring them into an interdependent relationship. His starting place, and the key to his system, was the Ricardian law of rent.

"The rent of land," George wrote, following Ricardo, "is determined by the excess of its produce over that which the same application can secure from the least productive land in use."[16] This concept of rent George applied to all land in use, rather than merely to agricultural land as had Ricardo. Thus, George argued, that return for production which is greater than that which an application of labor and capital could have received for themselves from the poorest land in use will go to the landowner in the form of rent. While this reasoning had always been present in economic theory, George's emphasis, together with his modification of the law of wages, gave it a new importance and turned it in a new direction. In classical theory it was mildly suggested that the owner of land who contributed neither capital nor labor to its improvement received a reward greater than was commensurate with his efforts. For classical theory was concerned primarily with the rewards due to the capitalist, the entrepreneur, who was engaged in manufacturing and trade and risked capital to hire labor to produce and exchange goods. Meritorious effort under such a theory thus took the form of making capital available for productive or exchange use, rather than land. In the writings of Malthus, as well as Ricardo, the landowner contributed least to the productive process and the rewards he received were at the expense of labor and capital. It was this line of reasoning which George developed and emphasized to the point where the landowner was a highwayman who deprived, unjustifiably, the laborer and the capitalist from the full returns for their efforts.

Labor and capital, George argued, are instruments of production, for they require use to bring about benefits. Land has use only as labor and capital are applied to it. Thus the rewards in the distributive process for labor expended or capital invested are socially desirable, while rent is the tribute paid for the mere permission of labor and capital to produce. If this theory was sound, George reasoned, then the laws of rent, wages, and interest were directly related and dependent, for the laws of wages and interest were dependent on the law of rent. Putting this argument in another form, George held

[16] *Ibid.*, p. 168.

that land, in all its forms, was the basic factor in production; there could be no production without land. Since, however, landownership brought as rent the margin between the cultivation possibilities of a given piece of land compared to the poorest land in use, the basic return to labor and capital would always approximate that return that would come from the cultivation of the poorest land. In other words, labor and capital could expect as their share in the distributive process only that amount which they would receive if they were applied to the poorest land in cultivation, for substantially the difference in return between good land and poor land would go to the landowner as rent. The surplus increment of good land over poor land was the tribute extorted by the landowner. Thus George's explanation of the economic laws found that under the existing system, labor and capital could receive in effect only that return which would come from an application of their productive powers to the poorest land in cultivation. Putting his theory into a simple formula, he wrote:

As Produce = Rent + Wages + Interest
Therefore, Produce — Rent = Wages + Interest.[17]

Land was the first essential of production. Land, however, is of limited supply and faced with an increasing demand. After land came labor, for to George, it was labor applied to land that created capital. Capital, created by labor, assisted labor in further production. There was therefore no antagonism between labor and capital; the real conflict was between the landowner on one side and labor and capital on the other. Thus, by reconstructing economic theory, George was able to explain why poverty continued in spite of increased productivity. "If, with an increase of production the laborer gets no more and the capitalist no more, it is a necessary inference that the landowner reaps the whole gain."[18] Rent, wages and interest were each related to the margin of cultivation of land. However, as poor lands were forced into cultivation, the margin between good land and poor land increased and rents rose accordingly. But as rents increased, wages and interest were forced down. As material progress increased, poorer land was brought into cultivation and accordingly rents increased while wages and interest declined.

The increase of rent explains why wages and interest do not increase. The cause which gives to the land-holder is the cause which

[17] *Ibid.*, p. 171.
[18] *Ibid.*, p. 222.

denies to the laborer and capitalist. That wages and interest are higher in new than in old countries is not, as the standard economists say, because nature makes a greater return to the application of labor and capital, but because land is cheaper, and, therefore, as a smaller proportion of the return is taken by rent, labor and capital can keep for their share a larger proportion of what nature does return. It is not the total produce, but the net produce, after rent has been taken from it, that determines what can be divided as wages and interest. Hence, the rate of wages and interest is everywhere fixed, not so much by the productiveness of labor as by the value of land. Wherever the value of land is relatively low, wages and interest are relatively high; wherever land is relatively high, wages and interest are relatively low.[19]

Having thus separated out rent as the factor which tended to hold wages and interest to a minimum, George turned to an examination of why rent tended to increase along with material progress. Here George departed from a strictly economic approach to consider the broader social impact of advancing civilization on land values. An increase in population, one of the tangible factors in material progress, caused land values to rise as an increase in population brought poorer lands into cultivation. Still the increased population, rather than pressing against the subsistence margin of cultivation as Malthus had suggested, actually increased the productive power of the community so as to maximize the variations in land productivity. However, under his theory of rent, the increased benefits from this increased productivity would redound to the advantage of the landowner.

Furthermore, and this was one of the most important of George's insights, a community simply by its presence created value. For with a community came improvements in the arts of production and exchange, as well as improvements in knowledge, education, government, morals. It was these social values which made "poor" land in the city infinitely more valuable than "rich" land in the frontier forest. It was the presence of communities, of society, which gave value to land. For land increased in value with an increase in the community. Society, in other words, created land value; land value was thus a measure of progress and civilization. Therefore, even without an increase in population, land would increase in value when a community advanced in its scientific and cultural ideas and institutions. The rise in land values was thus the measure of the

[19] *Ibid.,* p. 223.

community's improvement either in population, productive power or art. Finally, given the above factors, rent increased, due to the speculation of landowners that the community would advance and land would become more valuable in the future. It was indeed the speculative advance in land values which decreased the earning power of labor and capital and ultimately brought on economic depressions.

Thus did Henry George develop his explanation of the association of progress with poverty. Having developed this causative theory, this explanation, the remedy was clearly indicated. If land rents absorbed the increased returns that civilization and progress brought to a community; if land value was created by society and not by the landowner; if the landowner actually contributed nothing to the processes of production beyond merely giving for a fee permission to produce, then, George argued, poverty could never be abolished as long as land was held as a private monopoly. All proposed remedies which did not deal directly with the land question, he maintained, must ultimately fail. Land must be made free for the use of all if progress was to rid itself of poverty. "The equal right of all men to the use of land is as clear as their equal right to breathe the air—it is a right proclaimed by the fact of their existence. For we cannot suppose that some men have a right to be in this world and others no right."[20]

To make possible the "equal right of all men to the use of land," George proposed to make the land common property, yet in such a fashion that the existing landownership system would not be radically disturbed. He did not wish to confiscate private property, nor even for the state to purchase back the land. On the contrary, he felt that private ownership of land might well continue if people liked to think of land as *their* land. "It is not necessary to confiscate land," George wrote, "it is only necessary to confiscate rent." Thus society, through taxation of rent, would take back that value increment which society had created. No new machinery of the state need be created, George argued; actually the private ownership of land would save the state the problem of administering the rental of land. "We already take some rent in taxation," he wrote; "we have only to make some changes in our modes of taxation to take it all."[21]

So convinced was George of the economic and ethical justification of his panacea that he believed that the rent tax need be the only

[20] *Ibid.*, p. 338.
[21] *Ibid.*, p. 405.

tax, the single tax, that would supply all the revenue needs of government. By abolishing all other forms of taxation, taxes which were not only restrictions on trade but were inequitable as they lay on earned value, the community would enjoy heretofore unknown prosperity. With progress, with prosperity, land values would increase, thus increasing the government's revenue. This revenue in turn would redound to the benefit of society through the operation of governmental functions heretofore felt to be too costly or too cumbersome for governmental control. By eliminating other forms of taxation the necessary machinery of government would be greatly simplified and complete *laissez faire* would govern all private economic activities. Under such an economic system, George felt the distribution of wealth would be channelled into the hands of those who earned it. Labor and capital would now receive their full rewards. With progress now, all would enjoy the fruits of prosperity. There seemed to be no limits to George's glowing expectations of his panacea. By appropriating rent through taxation, he believed that his "simple yet sovereign remedy" would "raise wages, increase the earnings of capital, extirpate pauperism, abolish poverty, give remunerative employment to whoever wished it, afford free scope to human powers, lessen crime, elevate morals, taste, and intelligence, purify government and carry civilization to yet nobler heights. . . ."[22] To George it was clear that his solution would bring about utopia.

George might have concluded his work at this point, for the basic problem was stated, his explanation of its causative nature clearly formulated, and his remedy was fully described. He felt, however, that it was necessary to develop a law of human progress to indicate that his solution was fully in accord with it. The current theory of progress was associated with social Darwinism, with competition between individuals and races and nations. From this competition it was asserted that the fittest survived and civilization moved forward another step in its evolutionary path. Such a theory discounted the effects of social organization and social control as it emphasized individual variation, inequality and the competitive struggle. For George's solution to be in keeping with human progress it was evident that he would have to rewrite the law of human progress. In the last book (Book X) of *Progress and Poverty* he undertook this ambitious assignment.

First, George took issue with the automatic and inevitable theory

22 *Ibid.,* pp. 405-406.

of human progress. In an age of extraordinary scientific achievement it was not unnatural to believe that progress would automatically come about through the evolutionary improvement of the racial stock. In such a view, progress was evolutionary, automatic, and necessary. Imbued with the concept of progress as a causal necessity of his condition on earth, man need fear no serious retrogressions or declines in the course of civilization. Conflicts, distress, and strife were not indications of man's decline or falling away from the path of progress but were rather the necessary goads which brought mankind to still a higher elevation in its upward climb. Thus, George noted of the current theory of progress:

> War, slavery, tyranny, superstition, famine, and pestilence, the want and misery which fester in modern civilization, are the impelling causes which drive man on, by eliminating poorer types and extending the higher; and hereditary transmission is the power by which advances are fixed, and past advances made the footing for new advances.[23]

Such a view of history, George maintained, overlooked the fact that civilizations actually did decline and die, and that the key to an understanding of a civilization was the study of its social organization. The rise and fall of civilizations, not automatic progress, marked the course of history; "what has destroyed all previous civilizations has been the conditions produced by the growth of civilization itself."[24] Indeed it was a universal rule of history that every past civilization which had been noted for its conspicuous progress had ultimately declined and fallen. Our civilization, warned George, would follow the same dismal path unless a better understanding were had of the nature of progress and how it might be perpetuated.

George, therefore, rejecting the theory of automatic progress, focused attention on the social conditions which made progress possible. He shifted the emphasis from individual heredity to social organization in order to understand the causative forces behind progress and retrogression. Indeed, George revealed a keen understanding of the nature of social organization, of the community composed of a web of interlocking little societies with their customs, languages, tastes, and knowledge. It was in such communities that "the individual is received at birth and continues until his death. This is the matrix in which mind unfolds and from which it takes its

---

23 *Ibid.*, p. 480.
24 *Ibid.*, p. 488.

stamp."[25] Progress, he argued, resulted from the transmission of knowledge and culture from the repository of the community to a new generation of individuals. But progress, like land value, represented the accumulated achievements of the community, and unless the matrix of society was properly developed, decline would take the place of progress.

Once George had developed his criticism of the existing theory of progress, he then formulated his own. The incentives to progress were the incentives characteristic of human nature itself—

> The desire to gratify the wants of the animal nature, the wants of the intellectual nature, and the wants of the sympathetic nature; the desire to be, to know, and to do—desires that short of infinity can never be satisfied, as they grow by what they feed on.[26]

This endless reaching out of man—for that which was not—required imagination and intelligence, that is, mental power. Mental power, however, might be devoted to such progressive purposes as the extension of knowledge, improved methods of activity, and social betterment. On the other hand mental power might be expended on such non-progressive purposes as maintenance and conflict. By maintenance George meant not merely physical existence but "the keeping up of the social condition and the holding of advances already gained." By conflict George meant not merely war and the preparation for war, but "all expenditure of mental power in seeking the gratification of desire at the expense of others and in resistance to such aggression."[27] Now, George argued, where mental power was not exhausted by expenditure on non-progressive purposes, it would turn to man's progressive purposes, and progress would be achieved. But where the social organization was so deficient that mental power was exhausted in its non-progressive purposes, then in the long run, decline and decay would be the result. Where the inherent conflicts in society were reduced so that man's energies might be free to work toward improvement, then one might look for an advance in civilization. Improvement was thus possible only when the major sources of conflict were removed and men lived together in peaceful association. However, one of the major sources of conflict was inequality of rights, for, George reasoned, the moral law declared that all mankind ought to possess equal rights. Inequal-

[25] *Ibid.*, p. 504.
[26] *Ibid.*, pp. 506-507.
[27] *Ibid.*, p. 506.

ity thus bred conflict, and conflict monopolized man's efforts in non-progressive purposes. "Thus association in equality is the law of progress. Association frees mental power for expenditure in improvement, and equality, or justice, or freedom—for the terms here signify the same thing, the recognition of the moral law—prevents the dissipation of this power in fruitless struggles."[28]

As opposed to a competitive struggle for the survival of the fittest, George thus postulated a law of progress which was dependent upon equality rather than inequality; on cooperation rather than competition; on association rather than individualism. He posited, in other words, a law of progress in which all might not only survive but prosper.

> Here is the law of progress, which will explain all diversities, all advances, all halts, and retrogressions. Men tend to progress just as they come closer together, and by co-operation with each other increase the mental power that may be devoted to improvement, but just as conflict is provoked, or association develops inequality of condition and power, this tendency to progression is lessened, checked and finally reversed.[29]

He likened his law of progress to the exertions of men in a boat. The progress of the boat depended not so much on the exertions of the crew as on the effort expended to propel it through the water. Energy expended in bailing, in fighting among the crew, or in pulling in different directions clearly would not accelerate the forward motion of the craft for all the expenditure of power.

His law of progress formulated, George turned back to his major thesis that private monopoly in land was inequitable in itself and promoted inequality and conflict in society. The advance of society was being hindered by conflict due to the inequities of the land system. Thus, he argued that only by accepting his remedy could the conflicting and destructive element of poverty be removed from society so that progress might continue unimpeded. The association of men in society tended to bring about and perpetuate conditions of inequality which, if not checked, would eventually destroy society itself. Furthermore, without a basic condition of equality, a democratic government could not long remain a democracy, for to put political power in the hands of men degraded with poverty was to invite destruction. The new barbarians were those condemned to

[28] *Ibid.*, p. 508.
[29] *Ibid.*

poverty in the city slums. However, George argued, such poverty, inequality and conflict were not the inevitable results of natural laws, but the results of an unenlightened social organization which failed to follow the moral law of equality for all. Equality in politics without an equal right to land was a shallow and meaningless form of equality.

> Between democratic ideas and the aristocratic adjustments of society there is an irreconcilable conflict. . . . We cannot go on permitting men to vote and forcing them to tramp. We cannot go on educating boys and girls in our public schools and then refusing them the right to earn an honest living. We cannot go on prating of the inalienable rights of man and then denying the inalienable right to the bounty of the Creator.[30]

Thus Henry George sent out his plea for a basic reconstruction of society, which would stimulate progress and bring about the "Golden Age." Here was his call to utopia.

That it was a utopian vision there can be no doubt, for George expected from his panacea, if properly tried, no less than human perfectibility. And, of course, such a vision invited criticism on grounds of impracticability; the simple panacea appeared to its critics too simple. To suggest that the cure for socio-economic conflict in a highly interdependent economy which was rapidly becoming industrialized was to be found in a simple tax measure was obviously to leap the boundaries of the assumptions of the age. Yet the increasing emphasis upon taxation as a means of social control, from George's day to the present, may well have been fostered in part by the wide acclaim eventually given to *Progress and Poverty*.

George wrote in an age when classical economics had achieved its fullest bloom and the entrepreneur had gained ascendency over the landlord. Like Ricardo before him, George saw a basic conflict in society between the landlord and the producing capitalist and laborer. In effect, George sought to eliminate this conflict by eliminating the landlord, as Karl Marx would eliminate the conflict between the bourgeoisie and the proletariat by eliminating the bourgeoisie. That is, the landlord would lose his place in the traditional sense and would receive a pecuniary return for his existence only as he became a capitalist or a worker. George expected that the elimination of the landlord in his traditional role would necessarily free funds which would make higher the returns of capitalist and worker.

[30] *Ibid.*, pp. 551-52.

But to believe that the elimination of one competing group in the productive process would necessarily bring about a reconciliation of interests between the remaining two (capitalists and workers) required an extraordinary degree of faith, for George's argument is hardly convincing on this point. Even with the interferences of the landlord eliminated, wages were, in the final analysis, still determined by the capitalist. Thus this source of conflict continued. Finally, it may be asked, why did George limit his conception of unearned increment to land? Unearned increment, like Marx's "surplus value," is an invidious term. George attacked unearned increment as a stigma on the landlord as Marx labeled surplus value a stigma on the capitalist. George was clearly aware of the impact of society on land values; by the same reasoning, however, it was evident that society had an impact on all values, and unearned increment was not restricted to land alone. He was, however, so convinced of the rightness of his panacea that he failed to broaden his conception of unearned increment even when this matter was called to his attention.

George had some difficulty in finding a publisher for *Progress and Poverty*. Political economy had always been thought of as a forbidding subject, and George's reconstruction of the "dismal science" appeared not only controversial but downright radical. Finally, however, a publisher agreed to bring out an edition of *Progress and Poverty* if the author would assume the major expense, the cost of making the original plates. Soon thereafter George's name was known across America, and beyond, as *Progress and Poverty* went into successive editions and translations. There seems to be no doubt that no other book in political economy has equaled it in sales, now estimated at around three million copies. While George never basically altered his ideas, he continued to popularize them in successive writings—*The Irish Land Question* (1881); *Social Problems* (1883), which was his rejoinder to William Graham Summer's *What Social Classes Owe to Each Other; Protection or Free Trade* (1886), in which he reaffirmed his faith in a governmental policy of *laissez faire* combined with a tax on land rent; *The Condition of Labor* (1892), in rebuttal to Pope Leo XIII's encyclical letter which implied criticism of land reform; *A Perplexed Philosopher* (1892), which attacked Herbert Spencer for his departure from his early position (in *Social Statics*, 1850) in favor of land nationalization. Finally, George set about what he considered to be his most ambitious work, a full and complete formulation of *The Science of Politi-*

cal Economy. Unfortunately, he did not live to complete this; it was edited by a son who published it in 1898.

George's fame did not rest upon his writings alone, for from his earliest days in California he had been active in politics, campaigning and lecturing for reform along the lines of his rent theory. Following the publication of *Progress and Poverty,* he went to Ireland to support the movement there for land nationalization. Altogether he made five trips to the British Isles, and he seems to have had no little influence on English politics. George Bernard Shaw and J. A. Hobson, William Morris, and H. M. Hyndman, reformers of varying political persuasions, credited George with stimulating their thinking along the lines of basic economic reform. In the United States, as a political candidate (he polled second in the New York mayoralty election of 1886; Theodore Roosevelt came in third) and as a lecturer he found a wide audience for his ideas and many leaders of the coming progressive movement were brought under his spell.

George's contribution to American thought lay primarily in his reconstruction of social theory rather than in his redesign of economics. In economics he drew heavily upon existing beliefs. He accepted Locke's labor theory of value and the right of a man to the produce of his labor, together with Locke's implied right of all men to the gifts of nature. While subsequent economists interpreted Locke's labor theory of value to bring title to the private ownership of land, there is sufficient ambiguity in Locke that he might be read in either sense. George was unacquainted with Locke at the time he wrote *Progress and Poverty.* The labor theory of value, however, was accepted by the classical economists and so was used as an ethical claim which made economic return for human effort justifiable. George accepted the Malthusian and Ricardian doctrine of rent; he reversed, however, the priorities of capital and labor as essentials to production and thus upset the wages-fund theory. And while he emphasized the importance of social concepts, he also held firmly to a belief in individual natural rights. But it was his broad humanitarianism in an age in which natural laws decreed the inevitability of poverty, panics, and industrial strife which gave hope to men. His message of equality in association gave promise that intelligence and social control might eradicate evils heretofore accepted as the necessary concomitants of the frailty of man. In a sense he took the guilt away from personal poverty as he put the emphasis upon social conditions that were beyond the control of any individual, but were subject to control by a cooperative society. In an age of diminishing public land—the public domain was being bartered or given away at an astonishing pace—in which the frontier was vanishing, George focused attention on land as the nub of the economic problem. He comforted labor without attacking capital, for in the spirit of the early classical economists he found the landholder to be the scoundrel who deprived the laborer and the capitalist of their full return for their expended efforts. Finally he brought to light the relationship of society and value, and while some socialists accused him of not carrying his reasoning far enough, he did make clear that land value was created by the community and was the increment that came with increasing civilization. He stands as one of America's few original social philosophers, and his ideas undoubtedly altered the working concepts in which subsequent political thinking was done.[31]

EDWARD BELLAMY

Utopian literature, as well as the more staid and somber treatises on politics, has since the beginning of recorded speculation occupied a substantial place in the course of political thought. The search for the New Jerusalem, the world better than the one in which we live, is apparently as old as the history of man. Plato's *Republic* (fifth century B.C.), More's *Utopia* (sixteenth century), Campanella's *City of the Sun* and Francis Bacon's *The New Atlantis* (seventeenth century) were efforts at drawing up fictional societies. It is from Sir Thomas More's *Utopia* (translated as *nowhere*) that we have taken the name for this sort of political literary endeavor. Harrington's *The Commonwealth of Oceana* (1656) was cast as a fictional utopia in which the vehicle of a story carried the author's political analysis and recommendations.

Americans, however, have been more given to attempting to achieve utopian communities than to writing about them. The ambitious experiment of the Massachusetts Puritans was a grandiose ef-

[31] Among the many tributes accorded Henry George, that of the American philosopher John Dewey is of particular interest: "It would require less than the fingers of the two hands to enumerate those who, from Plato down, rank with Henry George among the world's social philosophers." (Modern Library edition, 1929, of *Progress and Poverty*, p. vii.) Dewey also called George not only "one of the world's great social philosophers," but "certainly the greatest which this country has produced." (Foreword to George R. Geiger's *The Philosophy of Henry George*, New York: The Macmillan Company, 1933, p. xiii.)

fort to achieve a utopia in that early colony. Later, in the middle of the nineteenth century, America produced a plethora of what have been called "backwoods utopias."[32] From the first settlements of America, however, there have been occasional attempts at utopian literature, one of the earliest efforts being John Eliot's construction of a theocracy in *The Christian Commonwealth* (1659).[33] It was not, however, until Edward Bellamy wrote *Looking Backward* (1888) that an American utopia was to receive wide success in sales and influence.

The end of the nineteenth century and the early years of the twentieth saw an outburst of utopian literature both in the United States and England. Bellamy's *Looking Backward* was partly anticipated in America by lesser known utopian titles, and in turn brought forth a series of rebuttals written in the utopian vein.[34] William Dean Howells' *A Traveller from Altruria* (1894) enjoyed considerable success in America while not attaining anything comparable to the popularity of *Looking Backward*. In England, William Morris' *News from Nowhere* (1892), Samuel Butler's *Erewhon* (1872) and *Erewhon Revisited* (1901), and H. G. Wells' *A Modern Utopia* (1905) reflect the consciousness of the utopian theme at this time.

Edward Bellamy (1850-1898) had been a successful novelist for some years before he attempted his imaginary reconstruction of society. The son of a Baptist minister of Chicopee Falls, Massachusetts, Bellamy's early literary efforts were strikingly suggestive, in their use of the fantastic and the psychological, of another New England writer, Nathaniel Hawthorne. Some indication of the awakening of Bellamy's social conscience is found in one of his earliest novels, *The Duke of Stockbridge*, which appeared as a serial in 1879. In this historical novel of Shays' Rebellion, Bellamy described the plight of the debtor farmers in the Massachusetts of 1786-1787. Clearly his sympathies are on the side of the debtors, who, as one of the characters remarked, fought the Redcoats only to achieve the liberty to starve or go to jail. It was not, however, until *Looking Backward*, cast a century ahead, that Bellamy wrote a novel that pricked the conscience and offered as well a specific program of action.

Late in 1886—the year of the Haymarket riot and the collapse

---

[32] See Arthur Eugene Bestor, Jr. *Backwoods Utopias* (Philadelphia: University of Pennsylvania Press, 1950).

[33] See Vernon Louis Parrington, Jr., *American Dreams: A Study of American Utopias* (Providence, Rhode Island: Brown University Studies, vol. XI, 1947).

[34] *Ibid.*, Chapters 8 and 9.

of the Knights of Labor—Bellamy first gave serious attention to the problem of economic organization in the United States. Recalling later how he happened to write *Looking Backward,* he noted that he sought a system for the republic which might "guarantee the livelihood and material welfare of its citizens on a basis of equality corresponding to and supplementing their political equality. There was no doubt in my mind that the proposed study should be in the form of a story."[35] Yet even when he started *Looking Backward,* he had no clear idea of making a major contribution to social reform, but rather of writing a "mere literary fantasy, a fairy tale of social felicity." It was not until he hit upon the idea of an industrial army, analogous to a military army, performing the necessary chores for society, that he suddenly felt that he had found "the destined cornerstone of the new social order." This caused him to alter the character of the book completely. "Instead of a mere fairy tale of social perfection, it became the vehicle of a definite scheme of industrial reorganization."[36] Thus the novelist turned critic and social crusader.

Looking Backward depicts the story of Julian West, a wealthy Bostonian, who goes to sleep in 1887 and awakens in the year 2000 to find the world most remarkably different from the society of the nineteenth century. Under the tutelage of a Dr. Leete, his host and mentor, Julian is introduced to the principles of social organization of the new century. Gone are the squalor and poverty of the past, the avarice and cunning of the old order, the ostentatious display of personal wealth on the part of the few, the panics, ignorance and conflicts that marked the nineteenth century. Gone is capitalism and in its place is a progressive system which features equality in cooperative association.[37]

The story itself is thin and obvious and barely serves the purpose of carrying the reader along through the social criticism of the past system and its unhappy contrast with the new industrial order. But Bellamy enlivens his tale by the introduction of marvellous inventions, processes and techniques—a favorite device of utopian authors —so that the reader is struck with his anticipation of radio, shopping centers, and the airplane, among other novelties. Bellamy was well aware, as was Henry George, that the economic framework of ideas,

[35] Edward Bellamy, "How I Wrote *Looking Backward,*" *Ladies' Home Journal,* vol. II (April, 1894), pp. 1-3.
[36] *Ibid.*
[37] This, of course, was Henry George's principle governing human progress. Bellamy accepts the principle of association in equality without reference to George.

and the conceptions of morality associated with it, set the limitations on possible as well as permissible political action. That is to say, the ethic of capitalism as well as the teachings of the Manchester liberals established the political and economic norms for social organization, and to call for social control and cooperation at a time when the predominant beliefs favored individualism and competition was futile. It was first necessary to change the fundamental beliefs, the basic assumptions and values within which the economic system operated before effective social control could take place. Thus one of Bellamy's major arguments is in the direction of discrediting the old capitalistic ethic and ennobling the morality of social cooperation. Through satire and pointed criticism he attacked the prevailing conceptions of the nineteenth century.

The concept of competition and the survival of the fittest doctrine he pointed up in his famous coach simile, in which he likened the society of the nineteenth century to a prodigious coach which was dragged along a hilly and sandy road by the masses of humanity.

> The driver was hunger, and permitted no lagging, though the pace was necessarily very slow. Despite the difficulty of drawing the coach at all along so hard a road, the top was covered with passengers who never got down, even at the steepest ascents. These seats on top were very breezy and comfortable. Well up out of the dust, their occupants could enjoy the scenery at their leisure, or critically discuss the merits of the straining team. Naturally such places were in great demand and the competition for them was keen, every one seeking as the first end in life to secure a seat on the coach for himself and to leave it to his child after him. . . . For all that they were so easy, the seats were very insecure, and at every sudden jolt of the coach persons were slipping out of them and falling to the ground, where they were instantly compelled to take hold of the rope and help to drag the coach on which they had before ridden so pleasantly.[38]

Thus the coach made its weary progress, with some sitting precariously at the top, apprehensive lest they fall, and the many laboriously straining in the harness. But, as Bellamy observed, this operation took place not without feelings of compassion on the part of the riders and expressions of commiseration from those who added to the load. For when the coach became mired down or reached an especially steep ascent, "At such times," Bellamy wrote,

the desperate straining of the team, their agonized leaping and

[38] Edward Bellamy, *Looking Backward* (New York: The Modern Library, 1942), pp. 3-4.

plunging under the pitiless lashing of hunger, the many who fainted at the rope and were trampled in the mire, made a very displeasing spectacle, which often called forth highly creditable displays of feeling on the top of the coach. At such times the passengers would call down encouragingly to the toilers of the rope, exhorting them to patience, and holding out hopes of possible compensations in another world for the hardness of their lot, while others contributed to buy salves and liniments for the crippled and injured.[39]

The misery of the masses, Bellamy noted, increased the value of the seats on top of the coach, for all lived in fear of being reduced to the lot of those in the harness. That such an inhumane situation existed in the nineteenth century was partly explainable by two prevailing beliefs of the time. First, he argued, "it was firmly and sincerely believed that there was no other way in which Society could get along, except the many pulled at the rope and the few rode, and not only this, but that no very radical improvement even was possible, either in the harness, the coach, the roadway, or the distribution of the toil."[40] Such things had always existed, and such arrangements would continue to exist. Because this lot of mankind was inevitable, it was therefore better to learn to accept than to attempt to change. The second prevailing belief was the "singular hallucination which those on the top of the coach generally shared, that they were not exactly like their brothers and sisters who pulled at the rope, but of finer clay, in some way belonging to a higher order of beings who might justly expect to be drawn."[41] Thus it was that the prevailing ideas of the nineteenth century not only found the coach and harness arrangement inevitable but actually desirable. Bellamy's argument at this point is clearly in terms of an alteration of the moral climate of opinion toward a more pervasive humanitarianism.

Bellamy supported his ethical argument, however, with the contention that the capitalistic economy was faulty as a wealth producing system, for by leaving industrial production in the hands of irresponsible individuals, inevitable wastes developed. Basically he attributed four major criticisms to the inefficiency of capitalism. First, there were wastes due to mistaken undertakings, for since no one could really know what the available supply would be for any product, each new venture was a "doubtful experiment." As

[39] *Ibid.*, p. 4.
[40] *Ibid.*, p. 5.
[41] *Ibid.*, pp. 5-6.

a result there were many failures in business that were due to no fault of the entrepreneur, but rather to the system itself. Second, there was the waste that came from "the competition and mutual hostility of those engaged in industry," for the marketplace was but a battlefield in which the contestants were willing to sacrifice each other in order to achieve gain. By working for one's own rather than for society's benefit, the individual frequently gained at the expense of society. The most gain accrued to those who could control or limit supply as public demand increased. "Competition, which is the instinct of selfishness, is another word for dissipation of energy, while combination is the secret of efficient production; and not till the idea of increasing the individual hoard gives place to the idea of increasing the common stock can industrial combination be realized, and the acquisition of wealth really begin."[42] Thirdly, capitalism brought about waste "by periodical gluts and crises, with the consequent interruptions of industry." These recurring business cycles were impossible to prevent under the capitalistic system, for their elimination required planned production and direct supervision of economic resources. Furthermore, the money and credit system, which led to overexpansion of credit followed by its abrupt contraction, together with overproduction of goods, contributed to the making of economic depressions and their resulting social dislocations. Finally, capitalism was afflicted with the waste that came with idle capital and idle labor so that at all times there were vast numbers of men seeking employment and a vast aggregation of funds seeking investment. Such a system, Bellamy argued, was condemned for its irrationality and inefficiencies, as well as on moral grounds for its inhumanity. As Dr. Leete declared, referring to the nineteenth-century capitalists, "Their system of unorganized and antagonistic industries was as absurd economically as it was morally abominable."[43]

The new industrial order supplanted the old capitalistic system early in the twentieth century through a process of industrial evolution. First came the modern corporation, the beginnings of the concentration of capital. This stage took place in the nineteenth century. The modern corporation, by destroying the old employer-employee relationship that had existed under the petty proprietor, called forth the modern trade union, in which workers sought to achieve through combination a power and position commensurate

42 *Ibid.*, p. 199.
43 *Ibid.*

with that achieved by employers through a combination of wealth. The movement toward combination among both capitalists and workers indicated clearly that association and cooperation for common purposes was far more desirable than competition. The rise of the labor movement marked the decline of competition among workers and gave labor a sense of security in the new industrial order. Yet once the movement toward combination had started, it was a matter of convenience as well as necessity that it continue. "Capital," Bellamy wrote, "had been proved efficient in proportion to its consolidation."[44] In spite of the outcries against the concentration of capital, the movement toward combination and monopoly continued throughout the nineteenth century. Small businesses were driven down and often out, as syndicates, pools, and trusts assumed control of the economic order. It thus became impossible to return to the old competitive order without returning to the stagecoach era, for combinations brought efficiencies of organization and production now considered indispensable. Wealth was produced under the new system of combination at a rate undreamed of under the old competitive system. From competition and small business the economic system had evolved into an industrial order marked by big business and combinations of capital. Once the evolutionary pattern was clear, it only remained to consolidate the few remaining combinations into one great combination. Early in the twentieth century, Bellamy wrote, this final step took place. "The epoch of trusts had ended in The Great Trust."[45] The state became the one great monopoly which produced all goods and the citizens became its employees and customers.

> In a word, the people of the United States concluded to assume the conduct of their own business, just as one hundred odd years before they had assumed the conduct of their own government, organizing now for industrial purposes on precisely the same grounds that they had then organized for political purposes. At last, strangely late in the world's history, the obvious fact was perceived that no business is essentially the public business as the industry and commerce on which the people's livelihood depends, and that to entrust it to private persons to be managed for private profit is a folly similar in kind, though vastly greater in magnitude, to that of surrendering the functions of political government to kings and nobles to be conducted for their personal glorification.[46]

[44] *Ibid.*, p. 40.
[45] *Ibid.*, p. 41.
[46] *Ibid.*, pp. 41-42.

Clearly, Bellamy was primarily concerned with economic arrangements. As a result there is little in *Looking Backward* that clearly
portrays the nature of the political order. Bellamy considered the
major function of government to be the protection of society against
its enemies. The real public enemies, however, were "hunger, cold,
and nakedness." A government that could properly protect society
against these enemies would necessarily have to control the system
of production and exchange of economic goods. But this Bellamy
conceived of as primarily an administrative function, removed from
the field of politics as traditionally considered. No longer would
there be politicians or political parties, but only officers skilled
in the required techniques of production and distribution. What he
envisaged was a system of government in which the officers would
be elected by the alumni of the industrial order; that is, suffrage
was extended only to those who had retired from active work, those
forty-five years of age or older. Political considerations were so
subordinate to economic ones in Bellamy's thinking that he devoted
only one of his twenty-eight chapters to them. With perfect economic arrangements established, political problems were basically
eliminated, he believed, and thus there was not too much need for
detailed consideration of politics. Political problems, to Bellamy,
stemmed from economic problems; therefore if economic problems
were solved, political problems would disappear accordingly. He
sought a system of economic democracy, but there was little democracy in his political system. The minimum age for voting was
forty-five, and thus no active worker could vote. Most offices were
filled by appointment. Congress met only once every five years and
then only to approve or reject administrative reports and to pass
such laws as had been proposed five years earlier.

The key concept in Bellamy's new order was equality. It was in
effect a continuation of George's theme of equality in association.
All men, by virtue of their birth, possessed an equal right to life,
food, clothing, shelter, and education. All men were equally obligated, as a solemn duty, to serve the state for twenty-four years,
from the age of twenty-one to the age of forty-five. All men alike
received, regardless of the conditions of their work or office, the
same pay. Such a society, based upon a working concept of equality,
would, he believed, bring domestic peace and prosperity for all.

Bellamy applied to the new order the concepts of universal public
education as a right, and what was then common in Europe, universal military service as a duty. All were to be given an equal

opportunity in education. Then, upon reaching the age of twenty-one, a period of three years of common, unskilled service was expected of each citizen. After this period of common service, each citizen according to his choice went into trades or professional schools. After the period of apprenticeship, each pursued such employment as fitted the necessities of the state and his own desires and abilities. While the pay was the same for all types of work, the state directed the types of employment preferences by altering the hours and working conditions of jobs to encourage or discourage their choice. Thus all citizens worked for twenty-four years at jobs basically of their own choosing and for equal pay. The equal pay continued after a worker retired at forty-five as it was found that the increased, efficient and managed productivity of this society was adequate for all the citizens as long as each gave twenty-four years to work.

Money did not exist in the new industrial order. Each citizen was given an equal credit on the state, so that his purchases from the state stores involved only a subtraction from his credit. No credits were carried over into future years, as this would destroy the system of equality. The amount of the credit each was entitled to was arrived at by dividing the total estimated wealth from production for the coming year by the population of the country. Thus each received an equal share of the socially produced national product.

In this benevolent society, from which the economic sources of malevolence had been removed, there were neither criminals, nor politicians, nor lawyers, nor advertising agents. For crime was the result of inequality, except when it arose from mental disturbances which properly required hospital treatment. In a society in which falsehood had become virtually extinct, there was no need for either lawyers or law schools. Without money, criminals, private business, and real estate, there was no longer any use for a legal science that had been devoted to these matters. Nationalization, indeed, had become so complete that the state governments had been done away with, as they could only have interfered with the centralized control of the economy. Finally, so happily organized was the new industrial order in the United States that it had been copied throughout the civilized world. The United States was now a member of a loose international Federal Union. No longer were there armies or navies or customs houses or tax collectors. All civilized mankind cooperated and bartered with each other in mutual peace and good will. Such was the utopian picture Bellamy drew of the year 2000 A.D.

This Utopia was far removed from actual conditions in the United States in 1888, and *Looking Backward* became an immediate publishing success, with a circulation that ran eventually to over a million copies. This warm and gentle story with its perceptive criticisms of nineteenth-century capitalism and its promise of the millennium to come here on earth and not in some after life, brought wide renown to its author.

A new political movement was born, a movement called Nationalism, designed to popularize the Bellamy program. The frail and retiring Bellamy was hailed by his followers as the prophet of the new century. For the remaining ten years of his life, Bellamy spent every effort in study, lecturing, and writing to bring the new order to pass as soon as possible. By 1890 there were reported to be 150 Nationalist clubs spread across the nation. As a first step toward Nationalism, Bellamy called for the nationalization of the telephones, telegraphs, express business, railroads, and coal mines of the country, and the acquisition by municipalities of local public utilities.[47] The People's Party, which polled a million votes for its presidential candidate in 1892, reflected in part the wide influence of the Bellamy movement. But for all the rising temper of Populism, of which Nationalism was only a factor, the Populists lost in the election of 1896: the Republicans came to power and the old order of things continued.

In the aftermath of this heated political struggle, Bellamy turned to his final book, *Equality* (1897). This was cast as another piece of fiction, a continuation of the story in *Looking Backward*, involving the same characters. Where the plot in *Looking Backward* was flimsy, in *Equality* it was non-existent, for the entire book was occupied with an elaborate discussion and explanation of the theory and operation of the new system as contrasted with the old. Where the earlier work was as much concerned with fiction and fantasy as with basic social theory, the later work was written with full emphasis on the social and economic structure. Gone is the light, warm touch of the literary artist, and in its place is the polemical and didactic tone, often bitter and sarcastic, of the reformer who has experienced declining hopes for his reforms. Yet from the point of view of political theory, *Equality* is the more important work

---

[47] Edward Bellamy, "First Steps Toward Nationalism," *The Forum*, vol. X, October, 1890.

because it is occupied with searching and systematic criticism of the old capitalistic order and an analysis of the underlying theory of the new regime. Where *Looking Backward* was much occupied with novelties and things, *Equality* is basically concerned with ideas, with theory.

In this last work Bellamy showed that his previous ten years of study had acquainted him with the basic principles of revolutionary socialism. Now he emphasized the inevitability of the class struggle and the ultimate triumph of the proletariat in the equally inevitable, though peaceful, revolution. Bellamy does point out, however, that while his program is similar to socialism in many respects, there are two basic differences. First, socialism is not necessarily established on a national basis, while his program called for a national socialism. Second, and more fundamental, socialism need not imply full economic equality, and economic equality was the cornerstone of his system.[48]

Essentially, the message of *Equality* is that if men would only cross-examine themselves, they would agree that only under a system of fundamental equality could man be happy in his partnership and association with his fellow man. Fundamental equality in turn meant economic equality, because economic problems were the most fundamental concerns of man.

Heretofore, due to the class nature of society, the capitalists, supported by and often represented by the clergy, the professors of political economy, the lawyers, and the newspapers, had established as the prevailing point of view that it was not the function of government to regulate commerce and industry or to interfere with the production and distribution of wealth. Because of this prevailing belief in *laissez faire*, these basic functions of society were left solely in the hands of the capitalists, who were able to manipulate them to their private advantage. This, however, amounted to abdication on the part of the people of the most vital control over their lives, for it meant that their livelihood was accordingly controlled by irresponsible private governments, the various groups of capitalists. It is with amazement that Bellamy's twenty-first century heroine, Edith, receives the fact "that the people, after having abolished the rule of kings and taken the supreme power of regulating their affairs into their own hands, deliberately consented to exclude from their jurisdiction the control of the most important, and indeed the

---

[48] See Edward Bellamy, "The Programme of the Nationalists," *The Forum*, vol. XVII, March, 1894.

only really important, class of their interests."[49] That the granting of such vast power to the capitalists, to use for their private advantage rather than for the public good, was defended under the name of individual liberty, she found even more inexplicable. After some further discussion of nineteenth-century political economy and the strikes, panics, and law-enforcement problems of the period, Edith is led to remark that apparently "the main business of the people's government was to struggle with the social chaos which resulted from its failure to take hold of the economic system and regulate it on a basis of justice."[50] Thus it was argued that the old American system of government failed by default in the most crucial functions of government. The new system, Bellamy maintained, simply made more meaningful the claims in the Declaration of Independence. Since government was instituted among men to secure their equal rights to life, liberty, and happiness it was necessary that industry be nationalized and economic equality established so that these goals might be realized.

> The cornerstone of our state is economic equality, and is not that the obvious, necessary, and only adequate pledge of these three birth-rights—life, liberty, and happiness? What is life without its material basis, and what is an equal right to life but a right to an equal material basis for it? What is liberty? How can men be free who must ask the right to labor and to live from their fellow-men and seek their bread from the hands of others? How else can any government guarantee liberty to men save by providing them a means of labor and of life coupled with independence; and how could that be done unless the government conducted the economic system upon which employment and maintenance depend? Finally, what is implied in the equal right of all to the pursuit of happiness? What form of happiness, so far as it depends at all on material facts, is not bound up with economic conditions; and how shall an equal opportunity for the pursuit of happiness be guaranteed to all save by a guarantee of economic equality?[51]

Actually, Bellamy argued, the new order was but a continuation of the democratic idea in history, for "It is the democratic idea that all human beings are peers in rights and dignity, and that the sole just excuse and end of human governments is, therefore, the main-

---

[49] Edward Bellamy, *Equality* (New York: D. Appleton-Century Company, 1897), p. 7.
[50] *Ibid.*, p. 10.
[51] *Ibid.*, p. 17.

tenance and furtherance of the common welfare on equal terms."[52]
As this basic idea developed, two distinct periods marked its progress. In the first, or what Bellamy called the "negative phase of democracy," kings were replaced by the sovereign people as the legitimate rulers. This substitution of one system of government for another, while a step in the right direction, fell far short of the goal of a truly democratic social order. Yet, given the prevailing ideas and institutions, the political revolution was indeed significant, though insufficient. With the "second or positive phase" in the evolution of the democratic idea a revolution in the purposes and functions of government took place. Now it was seen that only through a system of economic equality, together with a national public system of production and distribution, could the full idea of democracy be brought to realization. Bellamy's terminology, as well as his alignment of concepts, suggests the heavy impact of orthodox socialism on his thinking since he wrote *Looking Backward*. For instance:

> The nineteenth century, during which this crop of pseudo-democracies ripened for the sickle of the great Revolution, seems to the modern view nothing but a dreary interregnum of nondescript, *faineant* government intervening between the decadence of virile monarchy in the eighteenth century and the rise of positive democracy in the twentieth.[53]

This was Bellamy's rejoinder to the pessimistic critics of late nineteenth-century democracy who, denying the legitimacy of government intervention in the economic sphere, argued that democracy should be confined to political organization. Only when democratic function was joined with democratic organization, Bellamy reasoned, could the full connotations of the democratic idea be realized. "How could intelligent men delude themselves," Bellamy has one of his characters inquire, "with the notion that the most portentous and revolutionary idea of all time had exhausted its influence and fulfilled its mission in changing the title of the executive of a nation from king to President, and the name of the national Legislature from Parliament to Congress?"[54] A political democracy which lacked control of the economic system of the nation and did not secure an equal economic base for the life,

[52] *Ibid.*, p. 18.
[53] *Ibid.*, p. 21.
[54] *Ibid.*, p. 22.

liberty, and happiness of its citizens was, he maintained, a democracy in name only.

Most of *Equality* is concerned with expounding the guiding principles associated with economic equality and pointing by way of contrast to the selfish motivation implicit in the capitalistic system. It is at once an ethical study and a study in economics. Like Henry George, Bellamy sought to elevate the "dismal science," with its pessimistic condemnation of the masses to poverty, to a science that offered promise and guaranteed prosperity for all. The style of the book, however, turns dialogue into catechism, so that it lacks in readability even as it gains in argument.

Bellamy's defense of economic equality involved several lines of argument. As has been indicated, he argued from the natural-rights proposition that every man is equal in dignity as a human being with every other man, and that this basic equality entitled everyone to equal material provisions for his life and the pursuit of happiness. The right to life necessarily implied food, clothing, shelter, and medical attention. The equal right to pursue happiness not only required the necessities of living, but an equal opportunity for education, for choice of work, and for such choice of cultural endeavors as suited one's individual taste. Without the assurance of the physical necessities of living and an equal opportunity, unrestricted by economic pressure, for work or play, the posited equal and inalienable rights of man could not be fulfilled. This argument therefore was primarily concerned with attaining an economic basis for the rights of the individual.

Another line of argument in defense of economic equality was that of community solidarity. Under the capitalistic system, he argued, the prevailing ethic was the selfish motivation of every man to get the most and give the least. Each individual and economic group sought private advantage above all else. To buy cheaply and sell dearly was not only a principle of economics but of the prevailing ethics as well. Such a society was necessarily a cutthroat society in which men, driven by fear, took advantage of their neighbors in order to advance themselves. Man competed with his fellow man, not primarily to advance society, but to achieve private gain. Thus any benefit that accrued to society under such a system was both incidental to the lust for private gain and, indeed, accidental. Riches were therefore the reward reserved for those who had been most successfully selfish. Now such a society, Bellamy argued, ennobled the basest instincts in man; it was a society plagued by fear, jealousy, and conflict. Under a system of economic equality, fear, jealousy, and conflict would vanish and in their places would be cooperation and social solidarity. For fear was motivated by want, and where each had plenty, and equally plenty, there would be no cause for fear. Jealousy arose from inequality and the resentment held by those who had less against those who had more. But where every man was equal there would be no cause for jealousy. Conflict, the result of want combined with inequality, would disappear with the elimination of want and inequality. Once man had come to see the peace and prosperity that came with cooperation in equality he would never desire to return to such a divisive system as had existed under the old order.

Bellamy's development of the principle of the cooperative community is somewhat reminiscent of Rousseau's discussion of the general will. For like Rousseau, Bellamy wished to elevate the community into something more than merely the sum of its individual parts, while at the same time making possible through the community a greater degree of individual liberty than had heretofore been the case. It was indeed this sense of citizen solidarity that made the community; it was the community consciousness of the individual citizens that made the new society more than a mere aggregation of people. By making the individual a direct contributor to the welfare of the whole society, a participant in its affairs, and an equal recipient of its blessings, the goal of the individual and the aim of the society became essentially the same. In such a system man worked for society rather than for himself against society. With the overthrow of capitalism and the institution of collective control of the economic system, Bellamy declared, "The citizen, who before had been the champion of a part against the rest, became by this change a guardian of the whole."[55]

This sense of solidarity, of the cohesive community, was further enhanced by the realization that wealth is essentially a social rather than an individual product. A man working alone produces little; but working in concert with his fellow men in an efficiently organized enterprise advances his productive output enormously. It is therefore the social organism which acts as a multiplier for an individual's productive capacity. This was true under capitalistic social organization as well, Bellamy noted. Yet under capitalism, while the social organism multiplied the productivity of the individual worker, the end product was subject to private claim or ownership. Since

55 *Ibid.*, p. 29.

society so greatly advances the productivity of any individual, the end product "can belong to no one in particular, but to nothing less than society collectively. Society collectively can be the only heir to the social inheritance of intellect and discovery, and it is society collectively which furnishes the continuous daily concourse by which alone that inheritance is made effective."[56] Society has created this value, and thus society is entitled to reap its benefits in return.[57] The social value that has enhanced the labor of each individual properly belongs therefore to the "general fund." Following this line of reasoning, Bellamy was able to argue that the basic contribution to the modern production of wealth was made by society itself and not the individual worker, and that the difference in productivity of individual workers was so slight that all workers were entitled to an equal income.

In sum, Bellamy maintained that the social organization, in a broad sense, is the major factor in the production of wealth, and individual labor the least. Therefore the labor theory of value is archaic; value is created by society through its institutions, inventions, and the uses it makes of the individual's labor. As the labor of a single individual is so slight a factor in the creation of national wealth, it is useless to compare the efforts and abilities of any two individuals as a basis for wages. Thus all who participate in the social organism help create the wealth that is the national product. As this general fund belongs to society, Bellamy would have it pro-rated on an equal basis to each citizen. Thus each year the national consumable wealth would be equally divided among all the citizens with credit cards to that amount issued accordingly. Each man received, in effect, not only his share for the work he performed, but in addition a bonus, his share of the product of "the social organism."[58] Such a system, Bellamy maintained, gave the individual assurance that his work was a genuine contribution to

[56] *Ibid.*, p. 88.

[57] Bellamy thus extended Henry George's idea that land value is socially created. The following colloquy between Julian West and Dr. Leete deals with socially created values:

" 'The idea of an unearned increment given to private properties by the social organism was talked of in my day,' I [Julian West] said, 'but only, as I remember, with reference to land values. There were reformers who held that society had the right to take in taxes all increase in value of land that resulted from social factors, such as increased population or public improvements, but they seemed to think the doctrine applicable to land only.'

" 'Yes,' said the doctor, 'and it is rather odd that, having hold of the clew, they did not follow it up.' " *Ibid.*, p. 91.

[58] *Ibid.*, p. 91.

society and his rewards a just return from the social product. This gave to the community a solid economic basis.

Bellamy's conception of the general fund as composed of more than the sum of the productivity of the individual workers, and the sense of community associated with his social organism, was bolstered by his ideas on the nature of individual liberty. For social solidarity or cohesiveness resulted partly from the individual's sense of equal participation in the work and benefits of society and, of equal importance, his sense of liberty in the new social order. Liberty, Bellamy argued, cannot be removed from economic security. Under the old order, the masses of mankind, lacking economic security, lacked genuine liberty. As long as man was dependent upon his fellow man for a livelihood, he could not know freedom. Behind the old system was an insecurity that reduced most men to a subservience bordering on vassalage. Liberty, Bellamy insisted, implies not only the right to live, "but to live in personal independence of one's fellows, owning only those common social obligations resting on all alike."[59] It was therefore one of the distinguishing features of the new system that by eradicating personal economic dependence in establishing the system of equality, individual liberty was raised to new heights. In place of the tendency for imitations and conformity that took place in the old society, "equality creates an atmosphere which kills imitation, and is pregnant with originality, for every one acts out himself, having nothing to gain by imitating any one else."[60] Thus, Bellamy argued, the new order not only made possible a close sense of community but made possible the full expression of individual liberty.

Finally, *Equality* was a direct attack upon the capitalistic system whose ethics Bellamy found barbaric and whose economics he found socially disastrous. Both in ethics and economics the emphasizing of the selfish motives led to a vast cleavage in society. His argument followed closely the theory of orthodox socialism, for he found the capitalists becoming fewer and greedier, and the masses becoming poorer and more miserable.[61] Invariably, he believed, capitalism

[59] *Ibid.*, p. 79.
[60] *Ibid.*, p. 61.
[61] Bellamy cites census and other data to indicate the degree of concentration of wealth in the United States in the 1890's. From an 1893 table prepared by a census official he found that the total estimated wealth in the United States was sixty-two billions, of which one fifth or twelve billions was owned by those in the millionaire and multi-millionaire category. Nine per cent of the population owned forty-five of the sixty-two billions while the remaining ninety-one per cent of the population owned only the remaining seventeen billion dollars. See *Ibid.*, pp. 320-322.

tended to overproduction, underconsumption and panics. One of the most biting pieces of satire on the capitalistic system is found in his "The Parable of the Water Tank."[62]

In time, Bellamy noted, the masses awakened to the injustices of the capitalistic system. Indeed, Bellamy divided American history into three phases to describe the rise and fall of capitalism. First, from 1787 to about 1840 there was a period in which there were abundant and available natural resources and private capitalism had not as yet become powerful and aggressive. Second, from about 1830 or 1840 to about 1873 there was a period in which there were stirrings of reform as men became conscious of the rapid concentration of capital and the rise of a plutocracy. But the slavery controversy demanded immediate attention, so that the nation became occupied with this issue. From 1873 until the turn of the nineteenth century occurred the last pre-revolutionary phase of capitalism. Then amid frequent panics, gross inequalities in the distribution of wealth, poverty, monopoly, and constant industrial unrest, it became evident that a new "irrepressible conflict" had come, "a conflict between the power of wealth and the democratic idea of the equal right of all to life, liberty, and happiness."[63] No ameliorative legislation, Bellamy declared, could protect the people adequately—not minimum wage nor maximum hour laws, nor cheaper currency, nor anti-trust legislation, nor cooperative movements—nothing short of the overthrow of capitalism, it was found, could bring about the equal right of all to life, liberty, and happiness. When the Revolution did come it was not one of force and violence, but the result of an election followed by a rapid transition in the economic system.

In *Equality*, as in *Looking Backward*, Bellamy was so concerned with the economic basis of society that he dismissed political considerations as of little consequence by comparison. This neglect of the central political problem in all societies—the authority of man over man—certainly left Bellamy open to the charge of social and political naïveté. For he obviously assumed that if the economic issues were settled, all other conflicts in society would disappear. By separating out the economic side of man and dealing with this aspect alone, Bellamy constructed a rational Economic Man much as the classical economists had done a century earlier. But the complexity of the motivations which lead to personal and group conflicts would seem to indicate that basic social questions cannot

---

[62] *Ibid.*, Chapter 23.
[63] *Ibid.*, p. 311.

be settled by economic solutions alone. The economic concerns of man are clearly interwoven with his psychological, social, and political concerns, to say the least. It is just as true to say that if the political and social problems of a society were settled the economic problems would disappear as it is to reverse the proposition. The perennial issues of authority and subordination are manifested in many ways—in political and social as well as in economic behavior.

Yet Bellamy made a sound contribution when, in the late nineteenth century, he focused attention on the economic system. For if he overemphasized the economic aspect of social strife, this overemphasis was a healthy antidote to the conservative tendency of the period to underemphasize or ignore it. Political equality could never be fully achieved in an economic system that created decided inequality; there was more to democracy than the requirement of a popularly elected government. Indeed, the functions of government were as consequential to democracy as its system of political organization. Curiously, Bellamy never followed through in his political reasoning. He established the welfare state with regard to governmental functions, but he disfranchised the entire working population. The result could hardly be called democracy.

Like Garrison and Channing in the antislavery discussions, Bellamy based his thinking on the natural-law assumption of equality. Just as the abolitionists had sought to eradicate chattel slavery, so Bellamy sought to eliminate wage slavery, on the same ethical grounds. It is of interest, however, that while applying the natural rights argument on the one hand, he also employed a belief in socially created values on the other. The new society would create new values; the old competitive and selfish values would pass away and new cooperative values would emerge as the social-economic structure transformed itself.

Edward Bellamy, along with Henry George, offered a basically original program in an effort to solve the deep and pervasive economic and social problems of the times, and, along with George, he did make many men think, and some believe. Both he and George realized that the realm of possible political action in the economic sphere is partially circumscribed by the prevailing beliefs concerning the operation of the economic system. There are values and assumed causative relationships implicit in all economic systems. To upset or even modify an economic system involves upsetting the existing set of values and/or the assumed causative relationships. George and Bellamy attacked Manchester liberalism by attacking both its value theory and its theory of economic causation, and in so doing they not only affected the temper of late nineteenth-century political thought but undoubtedly altered the framework of economic ideology. Manchester liberalism had denied the right of the state to interfere with economic problems, maintaining that they belonged in the category of economic questions, quite separate from political issues. George and Bellamy, through their wide appeal and persuasive styles, had considerable influence on the Progressive movement, which felt that political intervention in economic affairs was both necessary and justifiable. Thus George and Bellamy helped bring about the rise of a new liberalism.

CHAPTER 15

The Progressive Movement

THE REVISION OF LIBERALISM

THE GENERATION that came of age in 1912 found a vastly different intellectual climate in America than was found by the preceding generation during the peak of the popularity of Henry George and Edward Bellamy. The America of Theodore Roosevelt and Woodrow Wilson was not the same as that of Benjamin Harrison and Grover Cleveland, for two decades of intellectual ferment, political criticism and revision of American thought had brought about a new framework of ideas. The essential assumptions of the 1880's, the basic "givens," had been seriously modified early in the new century, and the political thought of the new age was revised accordingly. "The tight little intellectual world we were led into," the sociologist Edward A. Ross recounted of his youth, "was bounded by Presbyterianism, Republicanism, protectionism and capitalism."[1] In the new age, however, these points of reference had quite new meanings.

The gospel of wealth and the stewardship of the wealthy, which had for a time been endorsed in Protestant circles, was giving way to a new social gospel. Indeed, some theologians, W. D. P. Bliss and Walter Rauschenbusch, for example, were urging a Christian Socialism on moral and economic grounds. Rauschenbusch's *Christianity and the Social Crisis* (1907) stands in marked contrast to Russell H. Conwell's often-repeated lecture "Acres of Diamonds" in which the Baptist minister had instructed his audiences that it was their duty to get rich, and that "to make money honestly is to preach the gospel."[2] Republicanism in the new age had likewise been modified so that the party was divided between the progressive wing—

[1] Quoted in Eric F. Goldman, *Rendezvous with Destiny* (New York: Alfred A. Knopf, 1952), p. 117.
[2] Russell H. Conwell, *Acres of Diamonds* (New York: Harper & Brothers, 1915), p. 18.

the followers of Theodore Roosevelt—and the old guard followers of Taft. Protectionism as a single issue had lost much of its appeal; indeed, the logic of protection was applied to economic reform generally. Capitalism inevitably had come in for re-examination as the criticisms of George and Bellamy, the political protests of the farm and labor organizations, and the exposures of the muckrakers indicated that the assumed ethics of capitalism as well as their actual practice were pulling society off its democratic equalitarian bases. In fact, it was argued, the economic system was undermining the social and political system.

The revision of dogma that took place at the turn of the nineteenth century and shortly thereafter was quite pervasive and comprehensive. It affected a multitude of patterns of thought. It encompassed economics, politics, history, sociology, religion, literature, and, eventually, law. It established the working concepts in a number of fields which many Americans—some two generations later—still accepted as approximating final truths. In essence, the progressive movement rejected extreme individualism with its Spencerian corollary in economics, biology, and sociology; its theological emphasis upon personal responsibility and personal guilt; and its diffident assumption that political action in the economic order would upset the laws of nature and of God. In place of an emphasis upon individualism, progressives turned to the social environment and emphasized social institutions, social responsibility, and social action. In place of an ethic of competition and its accompanying assumption of inequality, progressives stressed cooperation and equality. In all, progressivism marked the arrival in America of an aroused social conscience which took as its subject the economic system, as in an earlier age the social conscience had turned upon slavery. Yet, though the instrument for action was collective, the impulse to action was a revived sense of the dignity of man and his assumed equality in rights. Just as in England much of the credit for the revision of nineteenth-century liberalism was due to the Fabian socialists, so in America the revision of liberalism was largely the work of the progressives.

Economic inequality, together with the consequent social inequality which Henry George and Edward Bellamy had so effectively portrayed, was an alarming condition to many other observers in the late nineteenth century. The new mansions on Lake Shore Drive and Fifth Avenue were monuments to inequality in cities which had teeming tenements and slums. The rise of the millionaires

—over four thousand were reported in 1892[3]—made even more distressing the plight of the millions whose lives were marked by constant economic insecurity. The rise of the pool, the trust, and still the greater trust, brought into question the moral basis for the survival of the fittest as well as the *laissez-faire* postulate of the inevitability of competition. The rich industrialist and financier stood in marked contrast to the laborer whose ranks were swollen with immigrants and the farmer whose land was burdened with mortgages. It was the fact of inequality dramatized by the conspicuous luxury of the rich and the equally conspicuous squalor of the poor that brought the class issue so strikingly into American politics; for the basic American conception of equality appeared to be challenged by each new manifestation of American economic growth. This association of poverty with progress was, as Henry George had written, the great enigma of the times. Under accepted thought, however, this condition was inevitable. The problem of inequality during the last quarter of the nineteenth century was intensified by the frequent recurrence of panics, crises, strikes, and lockouts which gave to the economic scene an appearance of conflict, division and perpetual insecurity. Each of the last three decades of the nineteenth century was marked by a panic or depression of major proportions; each of these decades was marked by a major railroad strike.

The course of radical politics gathered momentum for reform following the panic of 1873. Such monetary panaceas as Greenbackism and free coinage of silver proved to be partially effective symbols for organizing the voices of protest. Farm and labor groups gained a sense of common interest in the face of an economic system over which they felt they had little or no control. It was the organized farmers of the Midwest who spearheaded the movement for state regulation of railroads, a movement which eventually reached the national level and was enacted into law with the Interstate Commerce Act of 1887. The *Nation* dubbed this act "a piece of State socialism at variance with the real interests of the people. . . ."[4] The apparent division of interests between the Eastern bankers and industrialists on one side, and the farmers and workers on the other—between, in effect, the rich and the poor—led to two intellectual responses. First there was a tendency to call the breach more apparent

---

[3] See Harvey Wish, *Society and Thought in Modern America* (New York: Longmans, Green and Co., 1952), vol. II, p. 175.

[4] *Nation*, XXXXIV (1887), p. 93.

than real, to hold that class divisions were unnatural to America, and to maintain that where such breaches occurred the proper remedy was a deeper and more abiding sense of unity and cooperation with only minor adjustments in the economic system. The second response, quite the contrary, drawing partly upon socialist theory and partly on traditional American theory and practice, insisted that class divisions were inevitable in any society and that class struggles in fact characterized the course of American political growth. What was needed, therefore, was a comprehensive change in the economic system to modify the effects of the class struggle. The first line of reasoning was the moderate and prevailing position of many social reformers up to about 1890. It tended to give way, however, to the second line of reasoning after this period.[5]

REFORM THROUGH COOPERATION

The appeal for reform through cooperation in an age of industrial strife is found in the temper and program of Henry George, who found no cause for a conflict between the industrialist and banker on the one hand and the worker and farmer on the other. His *bête noir* was the landholder. In an industrial society, worker, farmer and capitalist were common partners who need have no quarrel with each other. But remove the landlord's private tithe upon society and the remaining productive factors would be brought together in a spirit of cooperation.

The plea for cooperation as a vague means and goal, but one which would bring together all classes of economic interests, is best found in the farm and labor programs of the 1870's and 1880's. For instance, in the *Declaration of Purpose of the National Grange,* adopted by the National Grange in 1874, it was declared that one of the specific objects of the Grange was "to foster mutual understanding and cooperation." While the Grange sought cheaper methods of transportation of crops to the market and an elimination of the middleman in farm marketing, it expressly disavowed any assumptions of inevitable conflict or antagonisms. "We wage no aggressive warfare against any other interests whatever. On the contrary, all our acts and all our efforts, so far as business is con-

[5] See Herbert W. Schneider, *A History of American Philosophy* (New York: Columbia University Press, 1946), Chapter 16, whose approach on cooperation I am following here.

cerned, are not only for the benefit of the producer and consumer, but also for all other interests that tend to bring these two parties into speedy and economical contact. . . ." It was the hope of the Grangers that a cooperative policy, practiced among farmers and reaching outward, would work advantageously in favor of all economic groups. Finally, the Grangers declared:

> We desire a proper equality, equity, and fairness; protection for the weak, restraint upon the strong; in short, justly distributed burdens and justly distributed power. These are American ideas, the very essence of American independence. . . .[6]

Thus cooperation and equality appeared in a continuing stream of reform thought. Cooperation itself took on a more specific aspect later with the rise of producer and consumer cooperatives; the equality theme, however, sparked the demand for the regulation of the strong and assistance to the weak which gave, apparently, a radical appearance to the farm politics of the Populist period.

Cooperation was emphasized in the labor movement of the 1870's and 1880's largely through the efforts of Terence V. Powderly (1849-1924), for many years head of the Noble Order of the Knights of Labor. This extraordinary individual, who looked more like a poet than a labor leader, captured and held the imagination of the American labor movement until the rise of Samuel Gompers with the American Federation of Labor. Powderly, who was three times elected Mayor of Scranton, Pennsylvania, on a Greenback-Labor ticket and who stumped for Henry George in the New York mayoralty campaign of 1886, eventually ended his political career as a McKinley Republican. While active in the labor movement, however, he stressed the necessity for tolerance and cooperation in society. Opposed to strikes except as a last-ditch necessity, opposed to the closed shop as violating his principle of voluntary cooperation, Powderly stressed the desirability of settling industrial disputes through arbitration. He carried his theory of cooperation so far that he opposed trade or craft unions because they separated the skilled from the unskilled workers, thus depriving each of the cooperative assistance of the other group. Although in Europe and in England industrialism and Marxism had brought a labor class-consciousness into the labor movements, Powderly attempted to keep the Knights of Labor on a middle-class base. It was his hope

[6] Cited in Thomas H. Greer, *American Social Reform Movements* (New York: Prentice-Hall, 1949), p. 89.

that eventually the wage system would give way to a general system of production through cooperatives. As he recalled in his autobiography, *The Path I Trod,* "cooperation is the essence of common sense not yet understood by the world's producers. . . . Cooperation is a system which will eventually make every man his own master—every man his own employer; a system which will give the laborer a fair proportion of the products of his toil."[7] Powderly was not clear as to the means or even the essential goal he wished to achieve through cooperation, for he tended to vagueness as he approached the specific.

The Knights of Labor and the Grangers were probably the two best organized national dissident groups in America in the burgeoning industrialism of the late nineteenth century; they were acutely aware of the grievances against a system which brought poverty along with progress, and they were organized in part to avoid the severities of the dislocations of rampant capitalism. In the face of the fierce competitiveness and the gross inequalities of the times it is significant that the Knights of Labor and the Grangers emphasized the essential harmony of society rather than its antagonisms and turned for remedy to a closer spirit and manifestation of cooperation.

CLASS CONFLICT AND CLASS CONSCIOUSNESS

The more radical interpretation of the American social, political and economic order came after the rise of Populism in the early 1890's. The mystical optimism surrounding the cooperative theme was now displaced by what was probably a more realistic and certainly a more cold-blooded demand for action. Spurred on by such agrarian leaders as that doughty mother of four children, Mrs. Mary Elizabeth Lease, who advised her followers to "raise less corn and more Hell," "Sockless" Jerry Simpson, the fiery Tom Watson, and the irrepressible Ignatius Donnelly, farm politics veered sharply to the left. Class consciousness and class conflict were now clearly articulated. The Georgia Populist, Tom Watson, spoke directly on the subject of class legislation to the local farmers.

What has this country ever had but class legislation? The second law Congress ever passed was aimed to build up commerce and

[7] Terence V. Powderly, *The Path I Trod* (New York: Columbia University Press, 1940), pp. 267, 269.

manufacturers at the expense of agriculture. Our statute books are filled with legislation in behalf of capital, at the expense of labor. . . . If we must have class legislation, as we have always had it and always will have it, what class is more entitled to it than the largest class—the working class?[8]

It was this new consciousness of a class division in society based on economic interests, and of an inevitable daily struggle or conflict between these economic interests, that made the pattern of post-Populist thought distinctly different from that which had directly preceded it. To some extent it represented the impact of imported socialist thought in America; to a much larger extent, however, it was a manifestation of a native humanitarian urge for reform along the lines of democracy and equality. Each great movement for economic reform in America has been accompanied by an attack upon monopolies and the economic groups which held them. The attacks of Jefferson and John Taylor upon the money powers and the First Bank of the United States, the attacks of Jackson and Bryant on Nicholas Biddle and the Second Bank of the United States, the attacks of Bryan and the Populists upon the Eastern financiers, of Theodore Roosevelt on the "malefactors of great wealth"—such attacks have typified the American contention that power does tend to corruption whether it be economic power or political power. This, after all, was the reasoning implicit in that uniquely American statute, the Sherman Anti-Trust Act of 1890. The native fear of the corruptibility of unchecked power lurked behind the suspicions of unregulated private monopoly. The association of monopoly power and private economic interest in the late nineteenth century was a fact too patent to be missed by Congress in 1890 or by subsequent critics of the American economic order.

Equally traditional in American political theory was the analysis of politics in terms of economic class conflict. John Adams, Alexander Hamilton, James Madison, Daniel Webster, and John C. Calhoun were among the illustrious names who contributed to the class theory of American politics. In turning, therefore, to a class analysis of American politics, the Populists and Progressives did not need to look abroad to Marx or the English socialists, for they were speaking in terms common to American theory and practice. The importation of English and European socialism, however, tended to bolster a position with which Americans were already familiar.

[8] Cited in Eric Goldman, *op. cit.*, p. 101.

The traditional class analysis of politics in America was, however, basically distinct from Marxian socialism in two important respects. In the first place, American theorists had assumed that classes—economic interest groups—always had existed and therefore always would exist. Class analysis in America thus assumed universal applicability; rich and poor, farmer and merchant would always vie with each other in an incessant struggle for power to improve their respective positions in society. This struggle was marked more by flux and fortuitous circumstance than by any fixed logical certainty that would assure the dominance of any one group. In Marxian theory, however, the class struggle was far more sharply defined and eventually took on the character of a rigorous and conscious struggle between those who owned the instruments of production and those without such ownership. Marxists thus narrowed the class struggle ultimately to two antagonistic groups, whereas American theorists acknowledged a diversity of groups and interest blocs. More fundamentally, however, the Marxist, while admitting the past existence of classes, envisaged a future classless society. In Marxian theory there would be a final class struggle which would result in the overthrow of the bourgeois and the triumph of the proletariat. With only one class remaining, the distinction between classes would be gone and thus the one remaining class could be called a classless society. The Marxian view of the class struggle as being fixed, determinate, and terminable, and the American view of group conflict as indeterminate, continuing, and perpetual led to a decided difference in approach and conclusions of the respective political analyses.

Thus a second basic distinction between the two analyses of the class struggle lay in the use each approach made of its class hypothesis. To the Marxist the class struggle meant exploitation of the class without economic power, the proletariat, and thus the class struggle ought to be ended as soon as possible so that the classless society might emerge. To American theorists the class struggle, classes being flexible, fluid, and involving a variety of interests, was inevitable not only now but also in the future, and thus the challenge of politics was to work out a *modus vivendi* for such diverse interest groups. John Adams, James Madison and John C. Calhoun, for example, accepted as "given" the diverse interests of groups and classes in society but sought some method—through representation and compromise—for their reconciliation and adjustment. The American ideological belief in equality, while opposed to a caste society, acknowledged the inevitability of a class society.

The class struggle thesis of the Populist and progressive periods was thus subject to a variety of interpretations and arose from rather diverse backgrounds. Socialism as it developed in the United States had been tinged with the utopianism of the French socialists until about the time of the Civil War, when the First International spread German socialism to America. Indeed the First International, meeting in London in 1864, sent a telegram of congratulations to Lincoln on his re-election. The First International, however, met with little success in the United States, even though the headquarters were moved eventually to New York City. The decided preponderance of German immigrants in the early socialist movement in America, together with its militancy, foreign vocabulary and allusions, soon branded the movement as a radical foreign "ism" rather than a possible solution to American problems. The activities and pronouncements of the Socialist Labor Party, founded in 1877, did not add to the prestige of socialism in America, for the strange assortment at this time of anarchists, syndicalists, and various sects of socialists added more to the confusions of political theory than to their solution.

Nevertheless, with the passing of the emphasis on cooperation in reform politics it was evident that a new theoretical system was required which would causatively explain the dislocations of the economic system while providing for their remedy through political action. And to a large extent socialism provided this new systematic explanation, this new frame of reference for understanding economics and politics. While it is exceedingly hazardous to attribute influence directly to any one figure, or indeed group, for altering the basic social theory of a period, it does seem evident that most of the figures associated with the progressive movement accepted in some degree some of the most basic assumptions of socialism. Manchester liberalism was being put aside in favor of a watered-down, Americanized socialistic theory which finally brought economics and politics together and sought to understand current events in terms of this union. The traditional attachment to capitalism was still too strong for socialism to achieve political success under its own name. But while political-party socialism hardly prospered, socialistic theory worked its changes in the climate of American opinion. Thus while progressivism was far removed from socialism, it was equally far removed from the economic tenets of Jacksonian democracy. Progressivism was thus a modification of traditional capitalism in the direction of socialism, generally eschewing the party labels and symbols directly associated with the socialist movement.

LAURENCE GRONLUND

Of the various writers who sought to advance socialism in America during this period, Laurence Gronlund (1846-1899) was undoubtedly one of the most influential, and his ideas may be taken as representative of theoretical socialism. In *The Coming Revolution* (1880), *The Cooperative Commonwealth* (1884), *Our Destiny, The Influence of Socialism on Morals and Religion* (1890), and *The New Economy* (1898), as well as in numerous lectures, Gronlund explained and defended the basic tenets of socialism. Toward an understanding of socialism as it appeared in its most popular American form, *The Cooperative Commonwealth in Its Outlines: An Exposition of Modern Socialism* will be considered in some detail. Written in 1884, the year in which the Fabian Society was established in England, the book has as its main purpose to make German socialism respectable in America. Gronlund was aware that socialism in the United States had previously had so foreign an orientation that it had been generally unacceptable to American public opinion; furthermore he noted that there was no systematic presentation in English of German socialism. "It is this German Socialism which is presented in the following pages," Gronlund wrote in his Introduction, "with this important modification that it has been digested by a mind, Anglo-Saxon in its dislike of all extravagancies and in its freedom from any vindictive feeling against *persons,* who are from circumstances what they are."[9]

Gronlund opened his study with an attack upon the existing

[9] Laurence Gronlund, *The Cooperative Commonwealth* (Boston: Lee and Shepard, 1884), p. 9. It is of interest that in a subsequent edition, in 1890, Gronlund noted: "The happiest effect of my book is that it has led indirectly, and probably unconsciously, to Mr. Bellamy's 'Looking Backward,' the novel which without doubt has stealthily inoculated thousands of Americans with socialism, just because it ignored that name and those who had written on the subject. It should, however, in justice to the cause, be stated, that there are three ideas in that novel for which socialism should not be held responsible. . . . These are a love of militarism, equal wages, and appointments by the retired functionaries. They are decidedly unsocialistic notions, belong exclusively to Mr. Bellamy, and will be further noticed in the course of this volume." Cited in Herbert W. Schneider, *A History of American Philosophy* (New York: Columbia University Press, 1946), p. 201.

wage and profit system through which he was able to introduce the socialists' conception of value. Referring his readers to Ricardo, Gronlund noted that *value* meant value in exchange; thus the value of an article was its value in exchange for other articles. By so defining value, Ricardo made it not a term signifying intrinsic worth or usefulness, but rather a term of the market place referring to an article's worth in exchange. The value of an article in exchange, however, was basically determined by the amount of labor which went into its production as compared with the amount of labor which went into the production of other exchangeable articles. Thus socialist thought, reaching as far back as Locke, accepted the essentials of the labor theory of value. Human labor, therefore, was at bottom the source of value. While human labor created all things of value, however, labor was not recompensed to the amount of the value created but was rather, in accordance with existing theory, paid only that amount necessary to sustain the laborer. Thus there was a great discrepancy between the amount of value which labor created and the amount of wages labor received in return. This amount of "withheld wages" socialists called *surplus value.* " 'Surplus' is the same as 'fleecings,' " Gronlund wrote, "is *the difference between the price of Labor and the price of Labor's produce,* is the latter *minus* (−) the former."[10] This conception of surplus value was, Gronlund declared, the "mother idea" of socialism. It was because of the surplus value received from articles in the market place that the laborer was doomed to perpetual poverty. For the laborer's wages held to a subsistence level while the price of the articles he had created remained high above his income. Inevitably the market would be glutted with goods which the workers could not afford to buy, and then would follow the panics and crises of overproduction. As long as the wage system continued with its accompaniment, surplus value, the interests of capitalists and laborers rather than being harmonious, must be utterly opposed, and "chronic warfare" would continue between them.

Once the theory of surplus value was established, Gronlund turned to an examination of the existing economic order, which he found to be a social anarchy dominated by the ideas of an exaggerated individualism coupled with *laissez faire.* Such a society condemned the many poor to the mercies of the powerful and cunning. Human beings became mere wares in the market place;

---

[10] Gronlund, *op. cit.,* p. 26.

small employers as well as farmers were crushed by the large capitalists, and America was becoming largely a society of wage earners.

The first result of the "Let Alone" System, thus, is that capitalists monopolize all the instruments of production, all the previous acquisitions of Society, all increase in the productivity of Labor, and, therefore, *exercise an autocratic control of all industries and over the whole working class.*[11]

The evils of the existing economic system, he maintained, were so necessarily and inevitably part of that system that no temporizing expedients could bring about an effective reform. The various proposed remedies of the times were most ineffective as they did not go to the root of the system. The extension of foreign markets to find new outlets for goods could only lead to an international rivalry which would reduce all wages to the lowest figure. Voluntary cooperation, which producers so often advocated as a benevolent solution, would not help the working class generally, but would only help some workers to raise themselves out of their class. Trade unionism offered no solution except as it served to indoctrinate workers to the inevitability of the class struggle. Likewise currency reform was only a middle-class fad which would not in the least benefit the masses. Nothing, he argued in short, less than a radical, but inevitable, change in the economic system would bring about reform. But the change, he believed, was even then in process; the inexorable logic of events was in the process of fulfillment.

Our manufacturers, our merchant "princes," our transporters, our money lenders, and, finally, our land owners will go on dwindling in numbers, as they swell in size. The millionaires *will* gobble up the Capital of the whole middle-class, and the more their own possessions grow, the wilder will be their chase after the smaller game. Our working classes, on the other hand, *will* go on being gathered into larger centres. There is no "if" at all about the matter and there is, absolutely, no patent medicine in the market that can prevent it.[12]

Thus private capitalism, even as it developed and made for greater production and larger fortunes for the few, was "at the same time digging the grave of Capital."[13] The outcome offered two alternatives to Gronlund; society would either fall back to barbarism, or move forward to the cooperative commonwealth. He expected the latter.

[11] *Ibid.*, p. 40.
[12] *Ibid.*, p. 70.
[13] *Ibid.*, p. 72.

In order to develop the socialist's idea of the cooperative commonwealth Gronlund was led into a consideration of the nature
of a state, of a commonwealth. Indeed, he noted that one of the
fundamental distinctions between individualists and socialists lay
in their understanding of the nature of the state. To the individualist
the state was synonymous with government, and society was merely
a voluntary association of men. In this view, as maintained by
Herbert Spencer in *Social Statics* (1850), the state served only as
a policeman designed to protect the natural rights of the citizens.
The socialist, however, viewed the state as an organism; the state
represented organized society. This organic view of society was
quite opposed to the view of society as a voluntary association of
men. Civil society being man's natural state, Gronlund observed,
he cannot be presupposed to have once lived outside of it. Consequently, there were no natural rights apart from society; for rights
were the product of the prevailing social conceptions. Thus Gronlund put aside all natural-rights theory, "the theory that has been
so assiduously preached to our dispossessed classes, and which has
benefited them so little!"[14] Natural-rights theory was useful in
tearing down the eighteenth-century conceptions of society, but
was quite an inadequate foundation, he believed, upon which to
construct a new system. While the prevailing American individualistic attitude toward the state promoted the conception that the
state was at best a necessary evil, Gronlund's view led quite in the
opposite direction and was indeed something of a modification of
orthodox socialism. Orthodox, or Marxian, socialism assumed that
the state—in effect identifying it with government—was an instrument of the ruling class, but would "wither away" following the
revolution and the institution of the classless society. Gronlund, to
the contrary, identified the state with organized society and made
its existence a prerequisite for progress.

> *It is Society, organized Society, the State that gives us all the rights
> we have*. To the State we owe our freedom. To it we owe our living
> and property, for outside of organized Society man's needs far sur-
> pass his means. . . . To it we owe all that we are and all that we
> have. To it we owe our civilization. It is by its help that we have
> reached such a condition as man individually never would have
> been able to attain. Progress is the struggle with Nature for mastery,
> is war with the misery and inabilities of our "natural" condition.
> The State is the organic union of us all to wage that war, to subdue

[14] *Ibid.*, p. 81.

Nature, to redress natural defects and inequalities. The State therefore, so far from being a burden to the "good," a "necessary evil," is man's greatest good.[15]

Viewing the state as an organism, its basic function becomes that of preserving the health and welfare of its constituent members. Its proper sphere of activities is to preserve and improve the general welfare. The state, therefore, if it so desires, might undertake any activity designed to promote this end. The public welfare, in the Gronlund conception, extended not only to all those living, but, in the manner of Burke, extended to the "welfare of the generations to come." For the state to serve the general welfare, however, a decided reconstruction of society would first have to come about; for under the existing system, the socialist maintained, the ruling class governed only in its own interest. That is to say, under capitalism society is divided into classes of which only those who control the industrial process control the state. "The ruling class industrially will always be the ruling class politically."[16] So long as society is divided into classes Gronlund argued, those who control the instruments of production will inevitably control the state, and governmental policy will consistently work in their favor. Thus not until the arrival of the classless society could the state truly work to the advantage of the general welfare. To describe the existing governmental policy as a "Let Alone" system, Gronlund argued, was actually quite unrealistic. For by statute and injunction and executive order, the whole machinery of government was turned to the profit-seeking advantage of the capitalist class. Yet out of the ruins of the old system Gronlund believed that the new order would evolve. The class state would evolve into a classless commonwealth, "into a State *where the whole population is incorporated into Society*," into a society of genuine equality in which one might say to another, "I am not less than a man, and thou art not more than a man."[17] Interdependence would supersede independence; duty would be predominant to rights; and the society would be such that men would "have a sense of belonging together, of being responsible for one another," in a word, a society rewarded by a feeling of "Solidarity."[18]

[15] *Ibid.*, p. 83. It should be noted that Gronlund, having denied the natural right of equality, begs the question as to why the state should redress natural inequalities.
[16] *Ibid.*, p. 92.
[17] *Ibid.*, p. 94.
[18] *Ibid.*, p. 95.

The cooperative commonwealth, brought about through the inner necessity of history which had caused capitalism to supplant feudalism, would make possible planned coordination of the instruments of production with social ownership and control, with the citizens serving as public employees having their labors rewarded according to their results. This, Gronlund argued, was not the utopianism of Fourier, but rather the result of the unfolding of history. The movement toward centralized control of industry together with the expanding functions of the state all pointed in the same direction. Socialized planning and production would, when the time was ripe, supplant private planning, and production and private labor would give way to public service. The cry of "socialism" was no longer a deterrent to the expansion of state functions. "The State will go on expanding its jurisdiction, hurry on to its destiny, without asking or caring if it is 'Socialistic.'"[19] Eschewing communism, by which he meant a common division of property, Gronlund emphasized that the socialism he advocated would bring only the instruments of production—"land, machinery, raw materials, etc."—under collective control, in contrast to communism, whose motto was, he claimed, "Everybody according to his *deeds*."[20]

In the cooperative commonwealth, Gronlund believed, everyone would be enabled to acquire private property for his own use, but not to take advantage of his fellow man. Furthermore, the natural demand for goods, augmented by a full payment to labor for the goods produced, would eliminate market gluts and assure prosperity to all. With the outlines of the new system established, Gronlund turned to a detailed explanation of the new economic arrangements as well as to a criticism of the existing political ones. He would abolish the elective term system, the three coordinate branches of government, the states, indeed the entire constitutional system of 1787. The political system was as outmoded, he argued, as its accompanying economic arrangements. Political machinery, he claimed, was but an outward symbol; behind it operated the economic system. With the destruction of the old economic system would go the old class distinctions. As class rule was abolished, so would all "rule" disappear. For the collective people, the classless society, would not need "rule" or "government" as in the past, but rather skilled administration. The traditional government therefore would be replaced by administrators, and democracy would mean

[19] *Ibid.,* p. 105.
[20] *Ibid.,* p. 107.

"Administration by the Competent."[21] These competent administrators, bound by duty to the public interest, appointed from below,
holding office during good behavior, whose rulings would be subject
to a referendum by those immediately interested, would satisfy the
political purposes of the state. Gronlund thus anticipated Bellamy's
belief that the well ordered state might be so planned and brought
into being that once in effect it would require only competent
administrators for its maintenance. Once economic conflict had been
eliminated, public and private morals would reach new heights;
education would become more purposeful; women would truly
achieve equality; and justice for all would at last be realized. Such
a change in the social order would indeed be revolutionary, though,
as Gronlund noted, the revolution need not be one of violence.
"But," Gronlund wrote in conclusion, no matter what form the
struggle and upheaval took as society evolved, "the Great Change
is coming."[22]

Gronlund thus brought the essential logic of German socialism
into American thought, couched in a language that was understandable and acceptable to many reformers and fitted with a conclusion
which, while departing from Marxism, was more applicable to the
American temper and experience. His *Cooperative Commonwealth,*
like Bellamy's *Looking Backward,* helped formulate specific criticisms of the existing socio-economic system and offered a reasonable
explanation for the ineffectiveness of earlier reform movements.
Efforts at political reform that did not effect a radical change in
the economic order were doomed to frustration and failure as long
as the ruling class—with its ethics and general intellectual framework—was retained in authority. If the class which controlled the
instruments of production actually controlled ideas and institutions,
then indeed it was futile to attempt to alter these ideas and institutions if such alterations were opposed to the interests of the ruling
group. If, indeed, the political authority only carried out the wishes
of the economic authority, if political power was subordinate to
economic power, then it would be of little use to seek through
political endeavor the reform of the economic system. This dilemma
was resolved by the socialists, however, through an appeal to the
logic of history. In an age imbued with the paramount necessity of
evolutionary development it was natural to look upon capitalism,
like feudalism before it, as an evolving system, a passing phase in

21 *Ibid.,* p. 167.
22 *Ibid.,* p. 276.

human growth. The dynamics of the idea of evolution when coupled with the class-war hypothesis resulted in a logic of history which made inevitable the triumph of the working class, the proletariat. Thus the logic of history was used to confound the inexorable logic of the rulership of the capitalist class; and it was assumed that the inevitabilities of today would vanish before the inevitabilities of tomorrow. The logic of history, historical necessity, gave a wave of the future impulse to socialism which brought a degree of assurance to believers for all their contemporary defeats. Socialism thus offered a promise of the future as well as a logical tool for understanding the present and interpreting the past.

SOCIALISM IN POLITICS

As a political movement, socialism continued to gain strength in the progressive period so that the years from 1902 to 1912 have been characterized as " 'the golden age' of American socialism."[23] Daniel DeLeon (1852-1914), a former teacher at Columbia who was indoctrinated in part by Bellamy's Nationalism, entered the Socialist Labor Party and thoroughly revitalized it in the 1890's. A strict logician and devoted follower of Marx, DeLeon clung dogmatically to Marxism and refused to compromise with opportunism or revisionism. While he kept the Socialist Labor Party on the straight and narrow path of Marxism, the continued bickering in this party, the schisms and expulsions, certainly fractionalized its efforts. It was DeLeon's contention that the trade unionism of Gompers could only eventuate in a system in which the union officials would become "labor lieutenants" of the capitalists. Marxian logic eliminated the possibility of effective ameliorative legislation or reforms on the part of the capitalists. Current reforms would always be offset, under capitalism, by the increasing gains of the capitalists. Revisionism, Fabian socialism as it was developing in England, and trade unionism were only pathetic efforts at reform which inevitably must come to nought. In place of these DeLeon offered a program which combined political and economic action toward a complete revolution or overthrow of the entire political,

[23] Daniel Bell, "Marxian Socialism in the United States," in Donald Egbert and Stowe Persons, eds., *Socialism and American Life* (Princeton: Princeton University Press, 1952), vol. I, p. 267.

economic, and social system with its attendant capitalistic ethic. He thus advocated a tight industrial unionism on a national basis.

Suppose that at some election, the class conscious political arm of labor were to sweep the field. . . . What would there be for them to do? *Simply to adjourn on the spot sine die* . . . it would be . . . a signal for social catastrophe if the political triumph did not find the working class of the land industrially organized, that is, in full possession of the plants of production and distribution, capable, accordingly, to assume the integral conduct of the productive powers of the land . . . the plants of production and distribution having remained in capitalist hands production would be immediately blocked."[24]

DeLeon thought that the revolution would be both an inevitable and a peaceful one. He was against the use of force and believed that a tight industrial unionism combined with a highly organized Socialist Labor Party could peaceably effect the change to a new order. But, like Bellamy and Gronlund, he apparently believed that once the new order was established the only basic political function would be competent administration. For once the conflicts of the capitalistic system were removed the only legislative work remaining would be the tabulation of statistics "of the wealth needed, the wealth productible, and the work required. . . ." These, he believed, "any average set of workingmen's representatives are fully able to ascertain, infinitely better than our modern rhetoricians in Congress."[25] Thus DeLeon sought to replace the political state which supported the capitalistic system with an industrial state administered by representatives of the workers.

While Daniel DeLeon, rigorously adhering to the Marxian dogma, sought with Puritanical zeal to keep socialism on the path of orthodoxy, a man of less doctrinaire temperament and inclinations rose to the leadership of the socialist movement in America. Eugene Debs (1855-1926), a man of broad humanitarian impulses, moved from the leadership of the American Railway Union, through Bryanism, into the newly formed Socialist Party and served five times as its presidential candidate. Indeed Debs, as presidential candidate for the Socialist Party while confined in the Atlanta penitentiary for his opposition to World War I, drew nearly a million

---

[24] Cited in *ibid.*, p. 247. By permission. See this article as well as the others in volume I and the bibliography in volume II for a full treatment of this subject.
[25] *Ibid.*

votes, the most any Socialist candidate has ever received in the United States. Instrumental in Debs' conversion to socialism was his reading of Gronlund and Bellamy as well as other socialist and Marxian writers. His experience in the railroad strike against the Pullman company—a strike which was put down by a sweeping injunction, the jailing of Debs and the intervention of federal troops —was indicative to the sensitive reformer of some relationship between the industrial and political power in the state. Though Debs served the cause of Populism in 1894 and 1896, he moved further to the left until he came to socialism. At first Debs was imbued with the idea that a cooperative commonwealth might be achieved in one of the western states through an energetic colonization movement. The colonization effort, reminiscent of frontier utopianism and the utopian communities of the 1840's, never fully came about. Yet so enthusiastic was Debs in the colonization movement that he even wrote John D. Rockefeller for funds to assist in the establishment of the enterprise.

> The purpose of the organization, briefly speaking, [he wrote] is to establish in place of the present cruel, immoral and decadent system, a cooperative commonwealth, ·vhere millionaires and beggars . . . will completely disappear, and human, brotherhood will be inaugurated to bless and make the world more beautiful. . . . Then the strong will help the weak, the weak will love the strong, and the Human Brotherhood will transform the days to come into a virtual Paradise.[26]

Debs was not an original thinker. He was, however, an effective speaker and writer with a distinctively American background, and his main service to the cause of socialism lay in popularizing it. Once he left the cooperative commonwealth scheme and turned his attention to the nation at large, he continually captured large audiences and attracted many followers. He brought Fabian gradualism to America by turning socialism in the direction of amelioration in the present as a step toward public ownership and control of the basic instruments of production in the future. Because he eschewed orthodoxy, he was able to make the socialist program broad enough to encompass a variety of interests and a diverse assortment of reformers. His deep sense of humanity consistently put compassion above logic, and his faith in democracy and the political process

[26] *Ibid.*, pp. 262-63.

led his mild actions to belie his most radical statements. As a socialist he believed in the inevitability of the class conflict; but as a democrat he believed that it would be settled by compromise and adjustment until the ultimate peaceful triumph of the working class. He sought an extension through propaganda and education of the peaceful purposes and program of the socialists. In order that the new order might have direction, it was necessary that the workers recognize the class nature of capitalist politics, achieve a class solidarity themselves, and put their full united weight behind the Socialist Party, the vanguard of the movement toward the new order. As he wrote in "The Growth of Socialism" (1906):

> The working class alone made the tools [of industry]; the working class alone can use them, and the working class must, therefore, own them.
>
> This is the revolutionary demand of the Socialist movement. The propaganda is one of education and is perfectly orderly and peaceable. The workers must be taught to unite and vote together as a class in support of the Socialist Party, the party that represents them as a class, and when they do this the government will pass into their hands and capitalism will fall to rise no more; private ownership will give way to social ownership, and production for profit to production for use; the wage system will disappear, and with it the ignorance and poverty, misery and crime that wage-slavery breeds; the working class will stand forth triumphant and free, and a new era will dawn in human progress and in the civilization of mankind.[27]

Socialism thus offered an interpretation of political behavior quite opposed to that given by the prevailing nineteenth-century liberalism. It assumed the preponderance of economic factors as the causative force in history; it assumed the inevitability of the class struggle culminating in the triumph of the working class. In so doing it directly assaulted the ideology of capitalism, as it took glory away from the capitalist and ennobled the wage worker. It made competition akin to savagery and greed, and gave cooperation the appearance of the final flowering of humanitarianism. Furthermore, it emphasized the traditional doctrines of liberty and equality but put them in a new economic setting. All in all, socialism challenged capitalism as an economic system whose many political corollaries led

[27] *Writings and Speeches of Eugene V. Debs* (New York: Hermitage Press, 1948), p. 267. By permission.

away from the democratic conceptions of popular, responsive government based upon the equality of men.[28]

THE REVISION OF SOCIAL THEORY

The acknowledged socialists in part reflected and in part further stimulated the revision of political and economic doctrine that was taking place in America near the close of the nineteenth century. The social legislation program in Germany and the Fabian program in England seemed portents of the new movement to bring highly industrialized economics under public control. It became increasingly evident in the United States that classical liberalism, with its bifurcation of economics and politics, was not only unrealistic as an explanation of political and economic behavior but undesirable as a program.[29]

The revision of doctrine was so encompassing that it directly affected the fields of sociology, economics, politics, and history and indirectly reached out to law, literature, and theology. The shift in sociology away from the passive political neglect of Sumner is seen in the writings of Lester F. Ward and Edward A. Ross.

Lester F. Ward (1841-1913) spent most of his life as an employee of the national government in the Treasury Department and the Geological Survey. His extraordinary intellect ranged far afield as he studied Mesozoic flora, economics, psychology, and sociology. In his *Dynamic Sociology* (1883) and in his other writings on social

[28] While inconsequential as a political movement, communist anarchism was related to the socialist criticism of the capitalistic society. Such communist anarchists as Johann Most (1846-1906) and Emma Goldman (1869-1940) emphasized, however, "propaganda of the deed" and stressed the necessity for an actual revolution to overthrow the capitalist state. Following the revolution, society would become communal and anarchistic. See Johann Most, *The Social Monster* (New York, 1890); Emma Goldman, *Anarchism and Other Essays* (New York, 1911).

[29] What was taking place, in fact, seemed clearly to be a union of economics and politics, so that a study of one field led into an understanding of another. It is perhaps ironical that at the time of the peak of prestige of classical political economy, politics and economics were thought to be two fairly unrelated systems of activity. Late in the nineteenth century, with the academic separation of the fields of study into political science and economics, the interrelationship of the two fields became better understood, and while the old term *political economy* was put aside, it was nevertheless clear that it still fairly defined the respective fields of inquiry.

organization and political behavior, Ward stressed the importance of the efficacy of social effort in overcoming the obstacles of nature. Progress consisted not so much in abiding by nature's rules as in overcoming them or adjusting them to the advantage of society. It was not, therefore, the function of the state to keep hands off economic or other forms of social activity, but to intervene in order to achieve a positive good. Wise legislation was thus a high expression of social invention. In place of political passivity in the social process Ward emphasized purposeful action. Such purposeful action would lead in the direction of social cooperation rather than toward excessive and undirected individual competition.

While Ward pointed up in numerous articles the necessity for purposeful action on the part of government to check the strong and protect the weak, another sociologist, Edward A. Ross, emphasized the high degree of interdependence of the modern industrial society and the impact of this condition on ethics. In his *Sin and Society: An Analysis of Latter-Day Iniquity* (1907), Ross noted that the concept of sin should keep pace with the new developments in social and industrial organization. Sin was no longer merely a personal matter affecting only isolated individuals, but, he believed, due to the interdependence of the new society, it gravely affected society itself. Yet the standards of sin were still those of a simple agrarian economy. "Modern sin takes its character from the mutualism of our time," Ross insisted. "Interdependence puts us, as it were, at one another's mercy, and so ushers in a multitude of new forms of wrongdoing." The new forms of sin were those by which the weak and helpless were exploited for the profit of those of easy conscience. Those who would sell adulterated foods, build fragile tenement houses, or sell fraudulent securities were as guilty of sin as those who committed murder and assault. Contemporary sinners, removed in time and distance from the objects of their evil, avoided the sense of guilt that came with personal sin, for social ethics had not yet made clear this new area of wrongdoing. Thus the impersonal sinner avoided the penalties of personal crime even though his sin was more consequential in its evil effects. Persons who were, as individuals, quite circumspect in their daily conduct to their friends and their families might in their professional lives be the greatest impersonal sinners. "The modern high-power dealer of woe wears immaculate linen, carries a silk hat and a lighted cigar, sins with a calm countenance and a serene soul, leagues or months from the evil he causes."[30] While personal sin was quickly punished, people still overlooked the unhappy effect upon society of the new impersonal sins. "They do not see that boodling is treason, that blackmail is piracy, that embezzlement is theft, that speculation is gambling, that tax-dodging is larceny, that railroad discrimination is treachery, that the factory labor of children is slavery, that deleterious adulteration is murder."[31] Ross offered no radical changes to improve society; he turned rather to a quickening of the social conscience which would bring about governmental checks upon the new kind of sin similarly as it had dealt with the old.

Clearly the old emphasis upon individualism was giving way to an emphasis upon the community, and the new social conscience demanded a positive government whose activities would keep pace with the new social ethics. This new conception of the role of government in a highly interdependent and industrialized economy found expression in each of the social disciplines. In 1885, for example, when the American Economic Association was founded, the prospectus of the new organization declared:

> We regard the state as an educational and ethical agency whose positive aid is an indispensable condition of human progress. While we recognize the necessity of individual initiative in industrial life, we hold that the doctrine of *laissez faire* is unsafe in politics and unsound in morals. . . . We believe in a progressive development of economic conditions which must be met by corresponding changes of policy.[32]

Thus did such men as Richard T. Ely, H. B. Adams, John Bates Clark, Simon Patten, and E. R. A. Seligman, among others—men whose advanced studies were influenced by German political economy—renounce the traditional "liberal" approach to public policy. Appropriate governmental intervention in the economic sphere was not only in accord with the teachings of the new economics, but was claimed to be also a necessity for good government in modern society.

The increasing demand for a positive government developed concurrently with the demand for a more popular government. The failure of the two major political parties to sponsor candidates or

---

[30] E. A. Ross, *Sin and Society: An Analysis of Latter-Day Iniquity* (Boston: Houghton Mifflin Co., 1907), p. 10.

[31] *Ibid.*, p. 15.

[32] Cited in Richard T. Ely, *Ground Under Our Feet* (New York: The Macmillan Company, 1938), p. 136.

policies that would effectuate a positive program helped stimulate the demand for a reform of the political machinery to bring government into closer accord with popular sentiment. It is significant that most of the major reforms in the democratic process were sponsored by Populists and progressives who were dissatisfied with public policies at the national, state, and municipal levels of government. To achieve a positive public policy it was thus felt necessary to make the political process more popular, more democratic. If bosses and businessmen controlled cities, the state legislatures, and the United States Senate, if judges refused to validate as constitutional popular and positive legislative programs, then the cure was to be found in circumventing the power of the bosses and businessmen and in making all public officials more responsive to the public will. The cure for the apparent evils of democracy was to be found in more democracy. The demand for the direct election of the Senate, for the direct primary, for the Australian ballot and corrupt-practices legislation, for the initiative, referendum, and recall—these were demands for a more direct form of democracy which would make government more responsive and public officials more responsible to the majority of the people.

The urge toward political reform in the political process and in public policy was heightened by the exposés of the muckrakers. The work of the muckrakers—of H. D. Lloyd, Ida Tarbell, David Graham Phillips, Upton Sinclair, Charles E. Russell, and Lincoln Steffens—brought home to Americans in a sensational manner two major observations: first, American business practice in the stockyards, in insurance companies, in the railroads, and in the Standard Oil Company operated on a dubious ethical plane; second, there was a corrupt alliance between business and government. The exalted status of the businessman was thus brought directly into question as well as the double standard of morals which assumed that political corruption stood in shady contrast to business ethics. As the *Nation* observed in 1906, "The disease which we have complacently assumed to be confined to politicians, we now see infecting businessmen."[33] Corruption in business, however, according to the muckrakers, was the source of much of the corruption in politics. Thus did David G. Phillips expose *The Treason of the Senate,* while in the big cities, Lincoln Steffens found the trail of the big businessman. "I found him buying boodlers in St. Louis, defending grafters

[33] *Nation,* LXXXII (1906), p. 440.

in Minneapolis, originating corruption in Pittsburgh, sharing with bosses in Philadelphia, deploring reform in Chicago, and beating good government with corruption funds in New York."[34]

In a sense, the muckrakers merely documented the thesis which the socialists had been maintaining all along. The exposés indicated that there was a close relationship between the economic system and the political system, and that those dominant in the economic system found ready and willing allies in the political system. Upton Sinclair and Charles E. Russell were socialists to start with; others, such as Henry D. Lloyd and Lincoln Steffens, eventually came to believe in one or another form of socialism. By showing that the dominant economic groups used the political process to their advantage, the muckrakers indicated that *laissez faire* was obsolete in theory as well as in practice. Furthermore, through their various case studies, they brought into question the entire possibility of democratic government under the prevailing economic system. For if the candidates for government and the party programs were in fact under the control of the dominant economic groups, then popular government as a meaningful political process was something of a hoax. Nevertheless, while the literaure of the muckrakers strengthened socialism, it also considerably strengthened the demand for political and economic reform short of socialism.

While muckraking proved to be spectacular and found an immediate mass response, a less spectacular, but in the long run equally influential, revision of doctrine continued in academic circles. In the fields of history and political science, the progressive ferment found expression in the work of Turner, Smith, Beard, and Parrington. In keeping with the prevailing progressive climate of opinion, the new studies consistently emphasized the relationship of economics to politics and the economic basis of attitudes on the political system. In so doing these writers "Americanized" certain basic conceptions of socialism so that some degree of economic determinism acquired a respectable aura. The burden of the arguments found in Turner, Smith, Beard, Parrington, and A. M. Simons amounted to an explanation for political attitudes and behavior in some form of economic determinism. Turner emphasized the importance of the frontier in shaping the course of American democracy. "So long as free land exists, the opportunity for a competency exists, and economic

---

[34] Lincoln Steffens, *The Shame of the Cities* (New York: McClure, Phillips and Co., 1904), p. 5.

power secures political power."[35] The economic aspect of politics, as old as Aristotle and emphasized by Harrington in seventeenth-century England, was thus given a new place in American thought. Turner had advanced the frontier thesis in 1893 in a paper before the American Historical Association, and it was to have a deep influence upon the subsequent writing of history and the subsequent understanding of politics.

Economic determinism found additional expression in J. Allen Smith's *The Spirit of American Government: A Study of the Constitution: Its Origin, Influence and Relations to Democracy* (1907). Indeed, one might characterize the work as sophisticated muckraking, for it took the muckraker's theme of the supremacy of business over politics and projected it back to the beginnings of our constitutional system. The spirit of the American constitutional system was at heart anti-democratic, Smith found. The system of checks and balances, so essential a part of the American governmental system, was "opposed to and cannot be reconciled with the theory of popular government."[36] Democracy in America was thus more of a shibboleth than a reality, for the constitutional system was designed to hold in check popular majorities while assuring that the reins of political power would be kept in the hands of the conservative economic interests. The Constitution was, in effect, a class document put over on the people by the wealthy and conservative interests who were basically distrustful of the rule of popular majorities.

> The Constitution was in form a political document, but its significance was mainly economic. It was the outcome of an organized movement on the part of a class to surround themselves with legal and constitutional guarantees which would check the tendency toward democratic legislation.[37]

Clearly, Smith was accepting the socialist interpretation with its assumptions of a class struggle and the gravitation of political power into the hands of those who held economic power. Instead of the Constitution being a charter of liberties, Smith maintained that it was rather a charter of restraints imposed by the ruling class upon

[35] Frederick Jackson Turner, *The Frontier in American History* (New York: Henry Holt and Co., 1921), p. 32. As Eric Goldman has observed in his *Rendezvous with Destiny* (New York: Alfred A. Knopf, 1952), pp. 71-72, Turner's frontier thesis was clearly anticipated by Henry George in *Progress and Poverty*, Bk. VII.

[36] J. Allen Smith, *The Spirit of American Government* (New York: The Macmillan Co., 1907), p. 9.

[37] *Ibid.*, p. 299.

the majority of the people. Smith did not follow through, however, with the logic of socialism, which held that only through a basic change in the economic system could the political system be made democratic. Instead he emphasized political reform as a method of achieving reforms in the economic area. "In the United States at the present time," Smith wrote in 1907, "we are trying to make an undemocratic Constitution the vehicle of democratic rule."[38] Implicit in Smith's argument, however, was the assumption that popular rule was possible in spite of the existing economic system and that if the people realized the conservative nature of the constitutional system they would modify it to their own advantage. Smith's primary attack was on the constitutional system, not the economic one. And though he held to the view that the Constitution had perpetuated class rule in America, he did not conclude that such inevitably would continue to be the case. His conception of economic determinism was not, therefore, entirely deterministic.

While Smith introduced the thesis that the Constitution was a class document whose spirit was undemocratic, it was Charles A. Beard who documented the thesis through careful research and gave it a genuine degree of academic respectability. Where Smith was quick to generalize, and wrote in an argumentative style, Beard wrote cautiously, and gave to his work the cast of cool objectivity. In *An Economic Interpretation of the Constitution of the United States* (1913) Beard hoped that students of history would "turn away from barren 'political' history to a study of the real economic forces which condition great movements in politics."[39] He called attention to the "political science of James Madison," and especially to the thesis of the struggle for power of competing economic factions found in Number 10 of *The Federalist*. One did not need to draw upon socialist theory for an economic interpretation of politics; one need only to draw upon the American theorist James Madison. After examining the commercial interests and the political views of the framers of the Constitution, Beard concluded that "The Constitution was essentially an economic document based upon the concept that the fundamental private rights of property are anterior to government and morally beyond the reach of popular majorities."[40]

The spirit of the progressives early in the twentieth century was

[38] *Ibid.*, p. 31.
[39] Charles A. Beard, *An Economic Interpretation of the Constitution of the United States* (New York: The Macmillan Company, 1914), p. 5.
[40] *Ibid.*, p. 325.

thus quite in contrast to the spirit of the Constitution framers in 1787. The difficulties of reforming America in the progressive period were, it was argued, better understood if one knew the class nature of the Constitution itself. Yet Beard, like Smith before him, while calling attention to the role of economics in the shaping of political attitudes, did not reach the pessimistic conclusion of the Marxian socialists that economic determinism made political reform logically impossible without a prior change in the economic system. Indeed Beard offered no guides for present action in his book. However, by stripping the framers of some of the garments of respectability, he shook the "fundamental truth" conception of the Constitution.

The revision of doctrine in the social sciences, which has only been briefly indicated here, reflected in large measure the preoccupation of the progressive era with the economic facts of life. The close relationship of political values and economic circumstance, which the progressives emphasized, made clear the fact that the most vital political issues were equally economic ones. If government had always represented economic interests, then *laissez faire* had never truly existed and a political theory based upon it was unsound. If governmental intervention in the economic sphere had been the rule rather than the exception, then the fundamental question was not whether the government should intervene in economic activity, but rather to whose advantage it should intervene. If society was a composite structure of interrelated and interdependent groups and interests, then the problem of government was how to reconcile their competing claims. By their emphasis upon the close relationship between the upper economic classes and political power, the progressive writers suggested that the socialist theory of the union of political and economic power in the ruling class was correct; but ironically, by the very act of making this statement of the case, they inspired a popular demand that the facts be altered and, in theory, proven obsolete. Thus the progressive movement led to a demand that the dominant economic forces be subject to political control, and that political control be more popular. In other words, the documented statement of economic determinism brought forth a political reaction in favor of popular political determinism. The progressive movement thus sought to keep economic power subordinate to political control, and further to keep political power in the hands of the popular majority. The demand for reform of the political process to make it more responsive to the majority was thus coupled to the demand for economic reform.

THORSTEIN VEBLEN

Undoubtedly, the most trenchant and caustic criticism of the social order of the progressive period came from the pen of Thorstein Veblen (1857-1929). Veblen, as sociologist, economist, and indirectly as political scientist, had an extraordinary influence on the thinking of subsequent generations. This strange and solitary figure seemed committed to personal iconoclasm and social heresy. He was at his superb best when he brought his scholarship and crude literary skill to bear upon the much-vaunted social institutions of the times; and few of the accepted institutions or value conceptions of his age escaped his searching criticisms and scathing observations. So successful was he in his work that many of his cumbersome but pointedly descriptive phrases passed into common parlance and became part of the useful jargon of many people who had never stopped to read his work. He was the arch-rival of the business system and the values of the business society. The natural-law approach to economics was already under attack well before Veblen wrote; Veblen's analyses, however, gave rise to a new and indigenous approach to economics in America: institutional economics. In place of universal truth, Veblen emphasized universal skepticism as a starting point for understanding economic and social behavior. By disavowing past values, prejudices, and methods, Veblen was able to approach the social order from a new angle which cut through old categories and arguments and caused speculation concerning even those issues which society had tended to regard as most certain and settled.

For all the many tangential streams in Veblen's thought, there is a strong and consistent theme that runs through all his major works —*The Theory of the Leisure Class* (1899), *The Theory of Business Enterprise* (1904), *The Instinct of Workmanship* (1914), *The Engineers and the Price System* (1921). This theme stresses the conflict between two types of interests in society: productive interests and pecuniary interests. Being far more than an economist, Veblen was able to see this conflict not alone in economic terms, but as part of the complex motivations of the human personality. The instinct of workmanship, which he prized so highly, was the instinct which led man to produce things for use, social goods having use value in themselves. It was this instinct which led man to seek relentlessly to conquer nature in order to produce more goods in every civilization. This was the occupation, in its highest sense, of the engineer and the industrial technician and the chemist and the specialist in physics and all that vast range of professional talent dedicated to converting the world of nature into distinctively useful goods for man.

Opposed to the productive interests—workmen, engineers, and technicians—were what Veblen characterized as the pecuniary or business interests. The pecuniary interests were contrasted with the industrial interests in that the former sought primarily profit while the latter sought primarily production. While the industrial engineer gloried in work and sought to increase productive skill, the pecuniary-minded man made a social fetish of leisure and sought to turn the productive system into one which would increase his personal profit. Veblen thus sought to distinguish the profit impulse from the productive impulse. In so doing, however, he ennobled the status of the engineer and diminished the prestige of the profit-minded. In a society which he characterized as a business civilization, he played havoc with the underlying pecuniary ethic. The businessman was an apostle of the pecuniary ethic; the worker and technician were subject to the productive ethic. "The ideal pecuniary man is like the ideal delinquent in his unscrupulous conversion of goods and persons to his own ends, and in a callous disregard of the feelings and wishes of others and of the remoter effects of his actions," Veblen wrote scathingly.[41] The problem of modern and, indeed, all societies was that the pecuniary class consistently undermined and turned to their own advantage the efforts of the productive class. The pecuniary-minded not only took advantage of the productive system for profit, but furthermore they ennobled an ethic which was directly opposed to productive effort. For the pecuniary-minded constituted an upper class, which was also the leisure class. The class status of its members rested in part on their claim that they were above the economic necessities of productive labor.

The Theory of the Leisure Class thus dealt with the theory that the upper classes in society established and maintained their social station by being removed from the necessities of productive toil. By devoting themselves to activities which were obviously non-productive, they were able to inspire, under the prevailing system of social

---

[41] Thorstein Veblen, *The Theory of the Leisure Class* (New York: The Modern Library, 1934), p. 237. By permission.

values, a competition in emulation in which victory passed to those who could spend the most money and do the least work. Drawing upon anthropology, Veblen argued that sports, as a non-productive activity, were a common occupation of the leisure class. As indulgence in sports increased in expense, it increased also in social prestige. Sports thus released some of the predatory impulses of the leisure class. The predatory impulses, however, were but a carry-over of barbarian traits. In maintaining that the predatory leisure class, with their pecuniary and emulative canons of taste, under-mined the creative and productive efforts of society, Veblen point-edly undermined the claim to prestige of this body.

> From what has been said, it appears that the leisure-class life and the leisure-class scheme of life should further the conservation of the barbarian temperament; chiefly of the quasi-peaceable, or bourgeois, variant, but also in some measure of the predatory variant. In the absence of disturbing factors, therefore, it should be possible to trace a difference of temperament between the classes of society. The aristocratic and the bourgeois virtues—that is to say the destruc-tive and pecuniary traits—should be found chiefly among the upper classes, and the industrial virtues—that is to say the peaceable traits—chiefly among the classes given to mechanical industry.[42]

While Veblen pointed up the contrast between the "destructive and pecuniary traits" of the ruling group and the "peaceable traits" of the working class, he admitted that the generalization as to traits was not entirely applicable since the emulative aspect of a pecuniary culture tended to affect all groups. The desire to emulate the leisure class thus had a degenerative influence on society as a whole.

Veblen's barbs at the business community and the pecuniary ethic associated with it introduced a new vocabulary into economics and sociology. The desire to prove one's social station through "con-spicuous leisure," "conspicuous consumption," and "conspicuous waste"—the function of fashion in women's apparel, for instance, in a pecuniary society—these concepts, both searching and disturb-ing, were to have a wide influence on the thinking of subsequent generations. In all, Veblen brought the business civilization under perceptive criticism at a time when most other writers were not so much concerned with its system of values as with its economic efficiency. Through his peculiar vocabulary, Veblen was able to make an accepted business trait sound shocking, or even a shocking

[42] *Ibid.*, pp. 240-41.

business practice sound normal. While his many insights were subsequently explored by a host of students, his major immediate fame rested on the limited success of his first book, *The Theory of the Leisure Class*. It was in this book that he set his initial theme—a theme that was a major part of the theory of the progressive movement—that the major difficulties facing modern society stemmed from the values and the practices of the businessman.

The revision of social theory in the work of Ward and Ross, in R. T. Ely, E. R. A. Seligman and A. M. Simons, in Turner, J. A. Smith, Beard and Veblen, for all the varying approaches, had one constant theme: the economic system conditioned the thought and action of political groups, therefore an understanding of politics required an understanding of the views and behavior of the various economic interests. In consequence, political theory that dealt solely with politics without regard for the economic basis for political action was as unreal as it was unsound. Constructive political theory could no longer ignore the economic system; furthermore, it was argued, the economic system was not something sacred and beyond the realm of political criticism. It was through this critical approach to the prevailing economic order, found in George, Bellamy, the socialists, the muckrakers, and the academic revisionists, that the progressives sought to frame a constructive political program which would achieve a certain degree of economic well-being as a prerequisite for the good society. Progressivism thus implied the progressive development of political functions to keep pace with the developing social and economic needs. It was in its fullest sense the political reaction of a democratic society to the anti-democratic tendencies of the business community at the turn of the nineteenth century.

THE NEW FREEDOM—
CROLY, WEYL, AND WILSON

It was a fundamental belief of the progressives that the democratic ideal of equal rights and responsible government was not being realized in America in the early years of the twentieth century. Indeed, much of the literature of the period characterized the United States as in fact a plutocracy, a society governed by the wealthy class. While some writers insisted that this had always been the case, virtually all progressives were in agreement that this was quite contrary to the fundamental conceptions of democracy and that if democracy was to be made truly meaningful, essential changes would have to be made in the political and economic order. It was not, however, so easy to solve the problem of developing a positive program for democracy as it was to reach agreement concerning the criticisms of the existing system.

American theory was basically committed to two often-conflicting concepts or ideologies: democracy and capitalism. The real issue before the progressives in developing a positive program, therefore, was to find a means whereby industrial capitalism could be held within the democratic framework of ideas. Thus, by and large, doctrinaire socialism was rejected at the outset, although, of course, many of its working conceptions were carried over into non-socialistic political analysis and programmatic theory. It was the programmatic, piecemeal approach to reform that was the distinctive characteristic of the progressive movement. The diverse economic reforms of the period—strengthening of railroad regulation, the eventual passage via amendment of the graduated progressive income tax, the more vigorous enforcement of the Sherman Act, the efforts at child labor laws, the Clayton and Federal Trade Commission Acts, the efforts at minimum wage and maximum hour laws, municipal ownership of public utilities—these and the various other efforts at economic reform sought to fulfill the early creed of the Grangers to effect "a proper equality, equity, and fairness; protection for the weak, restraint upon the strong; in short, justly distributed burdens and justly distributed power." Fundamental to this conception, however, was the belief in an essential equality which demanded that the strong be curbed and the weak protected from oppression. The Sherman Act and the graduated progressive income tax were expressions of two prevailing political ideas: equality and the fear of concentrated power. Both measures expressed the belief that in a pecuniary society in which wealth and power were closely associated, the rich should not become too strong, and the strong should not become too rich. The logic of free competition, carried to its ultimate conclusion in the survival-of-the-fittest theory, thus succumbed to the legal restraints imposed by society to better preserve its democratic base and fundamentally equalitarian beliefs. Furthermore, where economic power could not advantageously be fractionalized or dispersed, as in the case of public utilities, it was demanded that it be brought under public ownership or control so that concentrated power might be democratically held in check.

The political reforms—direct primaries, direct election of the senate, direct legislation, corrupt practices acts, the referendum and recall and secret ballot—these were motivated by the desire to make the government more democratic. If government had fallen prey to the plutocrats, then the cure was to design such machinery as would bring it back to the people. The progressive political reforms were clearly a resurgence of the democratic faith in popular government. The political and economic reform movements developed together, so that as government was called upon to increase its power it was also demanded that political power be kept responsible and democratic. The classical economists had assumed that competition would pit economic power against economic power and that society as a whole would benefit from the contest. The economic checks upon economic power were considered adequate to the extent that political intervention was viewed as not only unnecessary, but positively harmful. In the progressive view of political economy, where economic competition was no longer self-regulating but tended toward aggrandizement and dominance, it was necessary to counter economic power with political power. The Interstate Commerce Act, the Federal Trade Commission Act, the Sherman and Clayton Acts extended the plane of competition beyond the economic area into society as a whole. Power was still pitted against power according to the traditional check-and-balance concept, but the intended new and dominant power was popular responsible government. This was the essential theme of the constructive literature of the progressive writers who endeavored to steer between traditional capitalism and socialism.

Herbert Croly (1869-1930), author of *The Promise of American Life* (1909) and *Progressive Democracy* (1914) and editor of the *New Republic* (1914-1930), proved to be one of the most influential and constructive critics of his generation. In his first and major work, *The Promise of American Life*, he set forth a program which he called the "New Nationalism." The old days of the frontiersman and the rugged individualist were over, Croly noted, and it was well time that the American society recognize this and refurbish its ideals and institutions to bring them up to date. The distinctive fact of modern times was the socialization that had taken place in human effort. Collectivization of effort and interest characterized the new society and was in conspicuous evidence with the modern corporation and the modern labor union. Yet these groups, like many other groups in society, were constantly seeking their selfish advantage at the expense of the general welfare. Given this situation, it was public folly to appeal to the Jeffersonian-Jacksonian ideal of a public policy that avowed equal rights for all and special privileges for none. Croly, frankly stating his admiration for Hamilton and distaste for Jefferson, observed that Hamilton was the more realistic theorist in recognizing the inevitability of governmental grants of special privileges. All special-interest groups, whether labor, business or farmer associations, sought special privileges from government, and a government that did not provide such would be both unresponsive and undemocratic. A government which avowed equal rights guaranteed only those conditions which made for inequality, as the strong and cunning would soon take advantage of the weak.

In place of the old ideals of equal rights and special privileges for none, Croly countered with a mystical nationalism which was in part socialistic, but basically far removed from formal socialism. He sought, in effect, to absorb the miscellaneous local and sectional special-interest groups into a national homogeneous moral pattern which would turn groups from selfishness to altruism, from seeking their private advantage to serving the public interest. He hoped to counter the growing nationalism of the economic system with a national political system. It was again Hamiltonian nationalism against Jeffersonian localism. It was, Croly believed, the responsibility of the national government to turn private interest to public advantage through positive action. To preserve equality one could not resort to a government of equal laws; rather what was needed was adequate discriminatory legislation which curbed the strong and brought special privileges to the weak. Thus he argued in favor of a graduated inheritance tax.

In the area of business activity, Croly favored a national incorporation act, which might check the abuses of large corporations, and national recognition of labor unions. But he would repeal the Sherman Act, as it provided, he argued, a form of discrimination which favored small business without serving the public interest. While he disliked governmental regulation on the grounds that it discouraged private initiative and experimentation, he nevertheless believed that some measure of national regulation was preferable to trust-busting and futile effort to turn back economic activity into the pattern of an earlier day. Economic cooperation was inevitably supplanting the older system of rigorous competiton and, he maintained, the public was enjoying the benefits of the new stability and the new efficiencies. While it was essential that big business serve the national interest through national supervision, nothing would be gained by destroying big business, monopolies, or national utilities in favor of small competitive enterprises. Croly's "New Nationalism," therefore, called for a system of national guidance and control of the economic order with such an allocation of rights and privileges as were best calculated to serve the public interest. Such a program, Croly maintained, would "give a new meaning to popular government by endowing it with larger powers, more positive responsibilities, and a better faith in human excellence."[43] It was essentially this conception of nationalism which Theodore Roosevelt popularized in his Progressive program of 1912.

Typical of the spirit of the progressive reform era was *The New Democracy* (1912) by Walter Weyl (1873-1919). Weyl took note of the trend toward socialization in thought and institutions which so characterized the new era and sought a middle-of-the-road program that would be easily adaptable to American ideals. "The new spirit is social," Weyl wrote. "It emphasizes social rather than private ethics, social rather than individual responsibility."[44] As a result of this new socialization, consequences of individual actions had far-reaching effects. A new concept of rights and responsibilities was therefore needed to keep pace with the changing conditions. "It is this social interpretation of rights which characterizes the democracy coming into being, and makes it different in kind from the so-called individualistic democracy of Jefferson and Jackson."[45] It was necessary now to implement this socialized condition of man which Weyl noted with new protections for the welfare of society as a whole, with new restraints upon the operation of the economic system. For it was the changing economic system which necessitated the alterations in the political system. In the contemporary society, Weyl observed, "the chief restrictions upon liberty are economic, not legal, and the chief prerogatives desired are economic, not political."[46]

No longer was the conception of negative government adequate to meet the needs of a complex, interdependent society; no longer was the liberalism of an earlier day accurate in its insistence that the

[43] Herbert Croly, *The Promise of American Life* (New York: The Macmillan Co., 1911), p. 170.
[44] Walter E. Weyl, *The New Democracy* (New York: The Macmillan Co., 1912), p. 160.
[45] *Ibid.*, pp. 161-62.
[46] *Ibid.*, p. 164.

less government interfered with economic life the more freedom remained in society. Strategic governmental intervention indeed promoted and enlarged freedom.

> A law forbidding a woman to work in the textile mills at night is a law increasing rather than restricting *her* liberty, simply because it takes from the employer *his* former right to compel her through sheer economic pressure to work at night when she would prefer to work by day. So a law against adulteration of food products increases the economic liberty of food purchasers, as a tenement house law increases the liberty of tenement dwellers.[47]

As Weyl made quite clear, the basic political problem was how best to reconcile the claims of particular interest groups for liberty so as to maximize the area of liberty in society generally. To achieve this goal he suggested a departure from any fixed or dogmatic formula, whether traditional capitalism or socialism, and the development of innovations on a rather pragmatic basis. Rejecting the class struggle thesis, he assumed an inevitable contest for power between various "coalitions of classes"; but he believed that in the future "there will also be adjustments and unions for the attainment of common aims and for a succession of compromises, rendered possible by an enormous increase in the social product to be distributed."[48] Specifically, Weyl suggested a broad variety of governmental programs including government ownership and operation, general government regulation of business and labor, regulation effected through a reformed tax program, governmental competition with business, and governmental ownership with private management. The type of governmental intervention would in each instance be determined by the kind of economic activity under consideration, whether it was a monopoly, a public utility or an ordinary competitive business, and its degree of necessary social responsibility. Weyl thus hoped to achieve a public policy that moved gradually in the direction of socialism and would in any event integrate the various facets of the nation's industrial program. As the government increased its power over industrial activity Weyl sought to increase its responsibility to the people at large through instituting a more direct democracy via the initiative, the referendum and recall.

Undoubtedly the culmination of the progressive approach came

[47] *Ibid.*
[48] *Ibid.*, pp. 189-90.

with the successful candidacy for President of Woodrow Wilson. Wilson (1856-1924), with his academic background in jurisprudence, economics, history, and political science, brought into his political life a deep understanding of the traditional theoretical basis of American politics as well as of the contemporary progressive ferment which was reinterpreting traditional theory. Unlike Croly, Wilson claimed to be a follower of Jefferson rather than Hamilton; yet in his political life Wilson came close to putting Hamiltonian policy upon a Jeffersonian base. In his extraordinary political program, which included such major legislative enactments as the Federal Reserve Act, the Underwood Tariff Act, the Federal Trade Act, the Clayton Act, the LaFollette Seamen's Act, the Adamson Eight-Hour Day Act, and the Rural Post Roads Act, Wilson sought to use the broad powers of the national government to secure what he had called in his campaign speeches the "New Freedom." Whether it was called the "new nationalism," the "new democracy" or the "new freedom," Croly, Weyl, and Wilson were in agreement that the formulas of old were not applicable to the contemporary situation and that a new approach was needed.

The "New Freedom," as Wilson explained it, was a policy or system of policies which would restore to Americans that sense of freedom which was so lacking in the modern interdependent society. It was a political effort to cope with what had become, through economic change, a new form of society.

> We are facing the necessity of fitting a new social organization, as we did once fit the old organization, to the happiness and prosperity of the great body of citizens; for we are conscious that the new order of society has not been made to fit and provide the convenience or prosperity of the average man. The life of the nation has grown infinitely varied. It does not centre now upon questions of governmental structure or of the distribution of governmental powers. It centres upon questions of the very structure and operation of society itself, of which government is only the instrument.[49]

The new industrial system, Wilson pointed out, had submerged the average individual. The new society was one of employees—wage workers—rather than independent entrepreneurs. As a result, more and more people were becoming dependent upon fewer and fewer employers. The age of the corporation had displaced the older age of individual and independent business. As a result, Wilson

[49] Woodrow Wilson, *The New Freedom* (New York and Garden City: Doubleday, Page and Co., 1913), p. 4. By permission.

observed, "Your individuality is swallowed up in the individuality and purpose of a great organization."[50] Individuality, and with it personal freedom, was further hampered by the trend toward mass organizations in still another way: no longer were man's relationships with man—as employer and employee, as buyer and seller, indeed in a vast and widening circle of contact—no longer were relationships personal. "Today," Wilson noted in 1912, "the everyday relationships of men are largely with great impersonal concerns, with organizations, not with other individual men."[51] The old American concepts of freedom and responsibility had been built, by and large, upon the old system of personal relationships between men. Impersonality not only restricted the realization of individuality, but furthermore fundamentally altered the concepts of responsibility. Thus Wilson observed, in a strain similar to the reasoning of Ross, the old codes of personal conduct did not protect society against the impersonal wrongs that might be committed by an economic organization of personally responsible men. "The truth is, we are all caught in a great economic system which is heartless."[52]

In order to restore freedom and the dignity of the individual, Wilson proposed a system of legislative control and restriction upon the "heartless" economic system. Such a system would protect not just those who had reached the top and now enjoyed security, but would extend to those less favored. "What this country needs above everything else is a body of laws which will look after the men who are on the make rather than the men who are already made."[53] Wilson, arguing that "The masters of the government of the United States are the combined capitalists and manufacturers of the United States," found power to be concentrated in the hands of the men "already made." He proposed to so alter public policy that power would be restored to the middle class and to those who were still "on the make." The industrial great would thus be dislodged from the seat of power—where Hamilton would have placed them—and, following Jefferson, government would be returned to the people at large. This called for a reconstruction of economic society just as political society in America had been reconstructed before; yet, as Wilson noted, "political society may itself undergo a radical modification in the process."[54] This basic reconstruction, however,

50 *Ibid.*, p. 6.
51 *Ibid.*, p. 7.
52 *Ibid.*, p. 10.
53 *Ibid.*, p. 17.
54 *Ibid.*, p. 30.

was essential if freedom and individuality were to be restored in America. It meant revitalizing society's concern for human rights, so that where there was conflict human rights would take precedence over property rights. It meant, in effect, the end of *laissez faire* as the proper policy for freedom. "Freedom to-day is something more than being let alone," Wilson observed. "The program of a government of freedom must in these days be positive, not negative merely."[55]

The "New Freedom," in theory and in substantive political achievement, drew together many of the threads of thought that so characterized the progressive period with its humanitarian appeal. It assumed that in a highly industrialized and interdependent society political power had gravitated into the hands of those possessing economic power; that economic power did not in itself constitute fitness for political control; that increasing economic subservience was sapping the strength of personal and responsible individualism; and that popular freedom was held at bay when the most vital political and economic decisions were made by those beyond the reach of popular control. The "New Freedom" thus restated a faith in the dignity, individuality, and capacity for freedom of the average man—the democratic belief that social institutions possessing authority over men ought to be brought under social control. The solution offered by Wilson for the liberation of men differed from that offered by Croly essentially in that the latter accepted as an inevitable and desirable phenomenon of an industrialized society the concentration of economic power, while Wilson protested that such power was neither inevitable nor desirable. Where Croly would permit monopoly and the concentration of economic wealth subject to national regulation, Wilson sought a public policy which would prevent these developments.[56]

Wilson distrusted concentrated power, as had the Jeffersonian Democrats before him. He sought for the national government only such power as seemed absolutely necessary to cope with private, but national, economic power. Again, unlike Croly, he believed in state's rights rather than in nationalism. His conception of freedom

---

[55] *Ibid.*, p. 284.

[56] This conflict over the place of "big business" in American life has continued to the present day. Wilson adopted the position of Louis Brandeis that monopoly business tends toward inefficiency, and that monopolies themselves arise not from economic competitiveness, but from unfair advantages. Concentrated economic power was thus uneconomical, inefficient, and unnecessary rather than being inevitable and desirable.

consisted in keeping open as many avenues for competitive opportunity as possible. In a sense, it might be said that he turned to government regulation only to make "free competition" more fully realizable. This was his alternative to socialism or stringent public control. In this way he hoped to avoid what he feared to be the inevitable corruptibility of concentrated power, whether lodged in public or in private authorities. This was his answer in the name of democracy to the challenge of economic or political authoritarianism.

Just as Wilson sought the protection of the weak against the strong as a primary condition for a free society in domestic affairs, so he carried this basic approach into the international scene. In many respects his famous "Fourteen Points" of 1918 were an international counterpart of the "New Freedom" of 1912. The call for a general association of nations assumed that enlightened national self-interest would insure the peaceful settlement of disputes and that power in the hands of rational men would become the servant of reason. The international community was not considered to be basically different from the national community. In the tradition of the eighteenth-century rationalists, Wilson believed that man, wherever found, was essentially rational and moral. That is to say, the values of rational men were essentially the same, so that in the give and take of open and international discussion, men and nations would find that their essential interests were held in common. Self-determination was but an international application of the principles of democracy. Democracy, with its assumption of the equality of men and of nations; liberty under equitable laws, both national and international; and the universal brotherhood of man— race, creed, and nationality notwithstanding; these were the guiding norms to Wilson. Wilson thus strongly reaffirmed the American democratic faith and formulated a national and international program intended to give this faith universal meaning and applicability.

CHAPTER 16

Economic Individualism

WHEN WILSON's great crusade to make the world safe for democracy ended in 1919, the predominant strains of American political thought evidenced a search for the lost security of the nineteenth century. A wave of disillusionment with progressive causes characterized the period variously called the "age of reaction" and the "dollar decade." Political reaction, economic prosperity, and intellectual disillusionment all seemed of a piece as Americans returned from a war fought on the highest principles of idealism to the more prosaic tasks of earning a living, listening to the radio, going to the movies, or driving a Model T Ford. The progressive fervor of the New Freedom was spent, fatigued like its austere champion, and into the political vacuum came the great Red hunt, the Ku Klux Klan, fundamentalism and prohibition, state criminal-syndicalism statutes, isolationism, and the National Origins Act which authorized racial discrimination in our immigration policy. A small group of authors and artists despairing of the stultified climate of opinion at home became expatriates in order to enjoy what they perceived as the more creative and congenial atmosphere of Europe. "Here was a new generation . . . ," one young expatriate, F. Scott Fitzgerald, wrote in *This Side of Paradise* (1921), "grown up to find all Gods dead, all wars fought, all faiths in man shaken." But the protests of the novelists—as seen in Sinclair Lewis' *Main Street* (1920), *Babbitt* (1922), and *Elmer Gantry* (1927); Ernest Hemingway's *The Sun Also Rises* (1926) and *A Farewell to Arms* (1929); John Dos Passos' *Manhattan Transfer* (1925); and others—had little impact on the politics of Main Street. In the presidential election of 1920 Warren G. Harding received the greatest percentage of presidential popular vote (60.5) of any man to run for that office.[1]

---

[1] Hoover received 58.0 in 1928, Franklin Roosevelt received 57.3 in 1932 and 60.2 in 1936. Eisenhower received 57.3 in 1956. See Avery Leiserson, *Parties and Politics* (New York: Alfred A. Knopf, 1958), p. 374, Appendix I.

In 1924 the combined efforts of the Progressive Robert LaFollette, the Democrat Burton K. Wheeler, the Socialist party, and the Railroad Brotherhoods, together with the American Federation of Labor produced only about 16 percent of the popular vote and only the 13 electoral votes of LaFollette's state, Wisconsin. The overwhelming defeat, together with the death of LaFollette, marked the end of the short-lived Progressive party. In 1928, when Norman Thomas first ran for President on the Socialist ticket he came in a pitifully poor third gathering less than three hundred thousand out of a total of over thirty-six million votes. In all, the decade of the Twenties was a period of remarkable political complacency, reflected not only in the absence of popular reformist literature but in the one-sidedness of the popular political vote. Indeed, Harding no doubt well assessed the mood of the era when he pronounced it a return to "normalcy."

Implicit in the concept of "normalcy" was the assumption of business leadership in political affairs. "We want a period in America," Harding had declared in his campaign, "with less government in business and more business in government."[2] And a few years later President Coolidge echoed this refrain with his oft-quoted observation that "The business of America is business."[3] The businessman occupied so significant a role in society during this period that a popular book of the times portrayed Jesus as "the founder of modern business."[4]

To the extent that any theoretical system was worked out to explain the new relationship of business and government it appeared to be subsumed in the concepts of cooperation and service. Pre-

[2] Cited in Edward C. Kirkland, *A History of American Economic Life* (New York: F. S. Crofts and Co., 1946), p. 682.

[3] William Allen White, *A Puritan in Babylon* (New York: The Macmillan Company, 1938), p. 253. White, a Republican and close political observer noted: "In those days when the snail was on the thorn and God was in his Heaven business men crowded into the White House until the luncheon guest-list looked sometimes like a chart of interlocking directorates of high finance" (p. 335). He also noted "In the booming stock market the President and the United States Chamber of Commerce were making one big noise in the same rain-barrel" (pp. 396-397).

[4] Bruce Barton, *The Man Nobody Knows, A Discovery of the Real Jesus* (Indianapolis: The Bobbs-Merrill Company, 1924). "He picked up twelve men from the bottom ranks of business and forged them into an organization that conquered the world." In Preface, no page number.

sumably the public would be best served by business rather than by direct government services; the government in turn would co-operate and serve business. It was the promotional rather than the regulatory role of government which was usually emphasized during this period. President Hoover spoke approvingly of how "Hamilton's vision well comprehended the necessities of Federal Government activity in support of commerce and industry."[5] William E. Humphrey, a member of the Federal Trade Commission, one of the government's major regulatory agencies, portrayed this view of the politics of economics in *The Magazine of Wall Street:*[6] "The President, instead of scoffing at big business, does not hesitate to say that he proposes to protect the American investor wherever he may rightfully be. . . . Instead of passing obstructive laws for political purposes, Congress now satisfies its demagogic tendencies by ordering all sorts of investigations—which come to nothing." The antitrust laws, he noted, had been emasculated by the courts. "It is not that the courts flout statutory law, but that they interpret it in harmony with economic law." Of the independent regulatory commissions, he observed: "The Federal Trade Commission has completely reversed its attitude toward the business world. . . . The Interstate Commerce Commission has become the bulwark instead of the oppressor of railways." And of the then Secretary of Commerce, Herbert Hoover, Humphrey wrote, "far from appealing to Congress for legislation regulatory of business, [he] allies himself with the great trade associations and the powerful corporations—not to benefit them as such but to benefit the people through them. . . ."[7]

The concept of "service" with its political and economic ramifications was not unchallenged in its day. When André Siegfried, the noted French writer, visited this country in 1927 he was impressed with the American usage of the term. " 'Service' is a combination of the civic virtue of the Protestant, the materialism of Bentham, and devotion to progress," he noted. "In the end, 'service' is the doctrine of an optimistic Pharisee trying to reconcile success with

[5] William Starr Myers (ed.), *The State Papers and Other Public Writings of Herbert Hoover* (New York: Doubleday, Doran and Company, Inc., 1934), I, 69.

[6] April 5, 1927.

[7] For the subsequent consequences of his views see *Humphrey's Executor (Rathbun) vs. United States,* 295 U. S. 602.

justice."[8] One might add that if the doctrine of service, with its overtones of altruism, were seriously entertained as an economic principle it would have been contrary to the economics of Adam Smith.[9] However, in retrospect the concept of service as it was used in this period would appear to have been the product rather of an advertising than of an inquiring mind. Clearly the facts of American political and industrial behavior did not square with the conceptual formulation presented in classical economics. If the concept of service was descriptively inadequate, so also was Manchester liberalism or *laissez faire*. In the course of our political and industrial expansion we had burst the seams of our theoretical political economy. American businessmen have traditionally been loath to let economic theory interfere with tangible economic gain. Where pecuniary matters were concerned the businessman has normally been a pragmatist, and American industry has grown less in accordance with theoretical design than by day-by-day experimentation, verified by the records in the cash register.

A Lehman Brothers banker, observing the discrepancy between theory and practice in 1928 wrote:

"It may well have been that the economic conditions of Europe a century ago, or more, were determined or at least modified by the economic theses of Smith, Ricardo or Mill. But in America the forces of business have moved too fast for the building of an effective industrial philosophy upon the theories of even the best informed of our economists."[10] American prosperity, he maintained, was due to the leadership and foresight of the businessman, plus an Administration which "contributed to the kind of confidence that makes for good business. . . ."[11] With such a cooperative arrangement between business and government prosperity might well go on indefinitely. "These next ten years are to be a stirring decade in the annals of American business," he noted. And in a daring prophecy he declared: "While industry dominates the thought of America, there need be no fears—a cataclysm aside—for the future

[8] André Siegfried, *America Comes of Age* (H. H. Hemming and Doris Hemming, translators), (New York: Harcourt, Brace and Company, 1927), p. 179.

[9] "I have never known much good done by those who affected to trade for the public good. It is an affection, indeed, not very common among merchants, and very few words need be employed in dissuading them from it."—Adam Smith, *The Wealth of Nations* (New York: The Modern Library, 1937), p. 423.

[10] Paul M. Mazur, *American Prosperity* (New York: The Viking Press, 1928), p. vi.

[11] *Ibid.*, p. 76.

of American business."[12] In the following year the cataclysm commenced and business leadership was put to its severest test. It fell to Herbert Hoover, as president, to defend this leadership and what he called the American system, and to articulate a creed of liberalism which had come, until the 1930's, to symbolize for many the American way of life.

HOOVER—THE AMERICAN SYSTEM

In his last major campaign speech, at Madison Square Garden, in 1932 Herbert Hoover opened his address with a prophetic statement. "This campaign," he observed, "is more than a contest between two men. It is more than a contest between two parties. It is a contest between two philosophies of government."[13] What was indeed basically at issue was how the American people would interpret their traditional doctrine of liberalism. And even after his overwhelming defeat this was the issue which Hoover returned to in his writings and speeches for many years.

Prior to World War I, Hoover had spent some eighteen years as an administrative engineer, largely abroad, in such diverse countries as Russia, China, India, South Africa, Britain, and Mexico. As he was fond of recalling later, his life abroad brought him into intimate contact with foreign social, economic, and political systems. And always, he recalled, when he returned to the United States he was impressed by the contrast between these foreign methods of busi-

---

[12] *Ibid.*, pp. 262, 267. Until the end of the decade of prosperity businessmen eagerly championed their role of leadership in American society. See *Nation's Business*, XVIII (May, 1930), particularly "The Business Man's Responsibility," p. 52, in which a representative of the U. S. Chamber of Commerce wrote that "the American businessman is today the most influential person in the nation. Because of the wealth and manpower of our nation, the American businessman is today perhaps the most influential figure in the world." Cited in James Prothro, *The Dollar Decade: Business Ideas in the 1920's* (Baton Rouge: Louisiana State University Press, 1954), pp. 215-216. After examining the publications of the National Association of Manufacturers and the Chamber of Commerce during this period Prothro concluded that the following dogmas emerged from their literature: "The nature of man establishes the doctrine of the elite and a material standard of values; the theory of society develops the pre-eminence of economic interests and the necessity of social stability; the theory of government points to the fear of popular control and the importance of individualism" (*ibid.*, pp. 209-210).

[13] Herbert Hoover, *Addresses upon the American Road, 1933-1938* (New York: Charles Scribner's Sons, 1938), p. 1.

ness and politics and what he called the American system. Not only did his foreign experience give Hoover a sense of the vast superiority of the United States in technological, economic and political life, but furthermore it gave him a new realization of the uniqueness of the American system of liberty, for he saw an intimate relationship between the economic, political, and social lives of a country.

The holocaust of world war together with the Peace of Versailles only further convinced Hoover of the disastrous inadequacy of what he termed the Old World system.[14] Returning from Paris where he served as an economic adviser to President Wilson at the Peace Conference, Hoover supported our entry into the League of Nations. Yet withal he felt a basic incompatibility between the Old World system and the American system. Thus when the great depression came he saw it not as a failure of the American system but as primarily an international economic consequence of the war. And like the war itself it engulfed the United States as well as Europe. Thus did the Old World impinge on the New. The rise of communism in Russia, fascism in Italy, and Nazism in Germany, were also basically consequences of the dislocation of the war in which Old World systems had further degenerated into tyranny. Thus as Hoover watched the catastrophe that swept the world in the 1930's, he interpreted it as being Old World in origin and as presenting a set of ideological alternatives which were equally repugnant to our liberalism. Socialism, communism, fascism, Nazism, and national regimentation—these constituted the basic "challenge to our American System."

Removed from the heated political battles of what was an extraordinary political era, Hoover's American system is in theory strikingly similar to that of Wilson's New Freedom—twenty years too

[14] It is interesting to note that Hoover observed many years later of the British economist, John Maynard Keynes, whose *The Economic Consequences of the Peace* (1919) became justly famous: "Keynes and I agreed fully on the economic consequences of the Treaty." Herbert Hoover, *The Ordeal of Woodrow Wilson* (New York: McGraw-Hill Book Company, Inc., 1958), p. 235. Keynes in turn observed: "Mr. Hoover was the only man who emerged from the ordeal of Paris with an enhanced reputation. This complex personality, with his habitual air of weary Titan (or, as others might put it, of exhausted prize fighter), his eyes steadily fixed on the true and essential facts of the European situation, imported into the Councils of Paris, when he took part in them, precisely that atmosphere of reality, knowledge, magnanimity and disinterestedness which, if they had been found in the other quarters also, would have given us the Good Peace." Cited in Herbert Hoover, *op. cit.,* fn. p. 235.

late. Indeed, Hoover's assessment of Woodrow Wilson reads rather like a self-portrait.

> As a Jeffersonian Democrat, he was a "liberal" of the nineteenth century cast. His training in history and economics rejected every scintilla of socialism, which today connotes a liberal.
>
> His philosophy of American living was based upon free enterprise, both in social and in economic systems. He held that the economic system must be regulated to prevent monopoly and unfair practices. He believed that Federal intervention in the economic or social life of our people was justified only when the task was greater than the states or individuals could perform for themselves.[15]

The American System, Hoover repeatedly declared, "is not a system of *laissez faire*."[16] It was true that this was once thought to be a basic component of individualism. But it was only a term of invective in the 1930's for "it has been dead in America for generations—except in books of economic history."[17]

> The American economic system is hardly one of "let do" or "go as you please." Ever since the Industrial Age began we have devised and enforced thousands of regulations in prevention of economic domination or abuse of our liberties through the growing instruments of business. Furthermore, the sense of public responsibility for the general welfare has successively produced public education, public health, public works, public stimulation of scientific research, and in 1929 for the first time embraced the responsibility for public action in the battle against depression. This is hardly *laissez faire*.[18]

Like Wilson before him, Hoover placed great reliance upon the normal interplay of supply and demand and the self-regulatory aspects of competitive economic units. It was the government's function to establish the rules of the game, the framework within which competition should take place. Where the normal competitive process could not take place it was essential that government regulate in the public interest. However, Hoover preferred that wherever such regulation was necessary it be undertaken at the state

[15] Hoover, *op. cit.*, p. vii.

[16] Hoover, *Addresses upon the American Road, 1933-1938* (New York: Charles Scribner's Sons, 1938), p. 18. As early as 1922 in his little book *American Individualism,* Hoover had declared *laissez faire* obsolete (pp. 10-11).

[17] Herbert Hoover, *The Challenge to Liberty* (New York: Charles Scribner's Sons, 1934), p. 51.

[18] *Ibid.,* pp. 51-52.

rather than the national government level if at all possible. Fearful of the encroachment of the Old World system in this country, he was constantly alarmed at the dangers of excessive national power. In increased national power, he felt, lay the hidden menace of the foreign "isms"; national planning led eventually to national social-ism, and socialism was a form of tyranny. Hoover constantly opposed any additional forms of economic competition by government with business, for in his view such activity was socialistic. Thus when Congress attempted to establish what subsequently became the T.V.A., Hoover vetoed the bill. He conceded that there were many occasions in which it might be necessary for the national govern-ment to engage in business activities on an emergency basis, pro-vided that it was understood that these activities were to be con-ducted only to meet the emergency and to cease when the emergency was over.[19]

Furthermore it was quite appropriate that the Federal govern-ment construct dams, facilitate navigation, and reclaim streams where these objectives could not be met by the capital of private resources or local governments. However, Hoover vetoed the Muscle Shoals Joint Resolution because it provided not only for these legitimate objectives but also for the production and sale of electric power by an agency of the national government. "I am firmly opposed to the Government entering into any business the major purpose of which is competition with our citizens," Hoover wrote. Such an undertaking would "break down the initiative and enterprise of the American people"; it would be the "destruction of equality of opportunity amongst our people; it is the negation of the ideals upon which our civilization has been based." The problem of electric power should be solved by "Federal regulation of inter-state power in cooperation with state authorities," rather than by direct government competition. "I hesitate to contemplate the future of our country if the preoccupation of its officials is to be no longer the promotion of justice and equal opportunity but is to be devoted

[19] It is interesting to note in this connection Hoover's statement regarding Wilson's attitude on Federal intervention in the economic system. "He yielded with great reluctance to the partial and temporary abandonment of our princi-ples of life [free enterprise] during the war, because of the multitude of tasks with which the citizen or the states could not cope. But he often expressed to me the hope that our methods of doing so were such that they could be quickly reversed and free enterprise restored." Herbert Hoover, *The Ordeal of Woodrow Wilson* (New York: McGraw-Hill Book Co., 1958), p. vii.

to barter in the markets. That is not liberalism, it is degeneration."[20] Only the people of the Tennessee Valley themselves, Hoover suggested, could develop the resources of that area. "Any other course deprives them of liberty."[21]

Rejecting the extremes of socialism and *laissez faire*, Hoover's concept of liberalism centered primarily around the businessman's freedom to make decisions subject to limited regulations by the state and national governments. Within a vaguely defined framework of minimum required legislation—enacted by the legislature, administered by the executive branch in accordance with traditional procedural niceties, and adjudicated by the courts—the rugged individual pursued his profits subject to the inexorable rule of impartial economic laws. "Economic laws," Hoover wrote, "may be said to be the deduction from human experience of the average response of these varied selfish or altruistic raw materials of the human animal when applied in the mass. These cannot be repealed by official fiat."[22] The cure for the depression in the 1930's lay, therefore, not in increasing governmental expenditures, or in increasing governmental regulation, steps which could in no way affect the natural economic laws and would only destroy business confidence. Indeed, in Hoover's view the bank panic and deepening of the depression in the spring of 1933 were the result of a loss of popular confidence in the new administration. Recovery he felt, returned but slowly under the New Deal because of the unsettling effects of Roosevelt's policies. Not until the Supreme Court found much of the New Deal unconstitutional in 1935, he maintained, did confidence begin to return and timid capital venture forth. In the dark days of the depression, with the ranks of the unemployed swollen to well over ten million persons, Hoover sought to restore prosperity by restoring confidence in the American system. This system, he believed, was based upon the fundamentals of human nature itself, evolved over generations of experience. "Ours is a system of losses to the least intelligent producers as well as profits to the more intelligent, and while some individuals may at times profit unduly or may abuse Liberty, in the end it is the consumer that wins through the

[20] William Starr Myers, *The State Papers and Other Public Writings of Herbert Hoover* (New York: Doubleday, Doran and Company, Inc., 1934), vol. I, pp. 526-527.

[21] *Ibid.*, p. 528.

[22] Herbert Hoover, *The Challenge to Liberty* (New York: Charles Scribner's Sons, 1934), p. 27.

production of the plenty of goods and services. For he is the beneficiary of that increasing production at constantly lower costs which
we require to reach our social objective—in constantly increasing
standards of living."[23]

Yet in order to prevent the abuses of liberty it was necessary that
the government regulate business. "We can no more have economic
power without checks and balances," he wrote in 1936, "than we can
have political power without checks and balances. Either one leads
to tyranny."[24] To define further his conception of regulation he
enumerated a variety of categories of economic activity. Much of
business activity could be regulated by the automatic process of
competition subject to the governmental injunction that fair competition be preserved and monopolistic practices prevented. Public
utilities should be regulated "as to rates to prevent the misuse of
their privilege." Banking, finance, and public markets should be
regulated "to prevent abuse and misuse of trust." The use of our
natural resources should be regulated to prevent their wastage.
"Labor must have the right to free collective bargaining. But it
must have responsibilities as well as rights." And he accepted the
principle of income and inheritance taxes to prevent over-accumu-
lations of wealth. "I am one who believes that the only system which
will preserve liberty and hold open the doors of opportunity is gov-
ernment-regulated business."[25]

For all of Hoover's avowals of government regulation as a necessity for the maintenance of the American system, he nevertheless
saw in the New Deal only a capricious and blundering movement
down the Old World path of totalitarian dictatorship. Economic
planning was but the first faltering step away from true liberalism.
So imbued was Hoover with his businessman's philosophy of free-

[23] *Ibid.*, p. 29. John E. Edgerton, President of the National Association of
Manufacturers, observed in his annual address to the N.A.M. in 1930 (*Proceedings,* N.A.M., 1930), pp. 14-15, 16: "By no agency through which society operates can it destroy poverty outright. . . . It results not alone from involuntary
unemployment, but more often from voluntary unemployment, thriftlessness, sin
in various forms, disease, and other misfortunes." Furthermore, he noted,
"neither society nor any human power can immunize anybody against the
national consequences of the violation of law—civil, moral, spiritual, or economic. Society cannot protect against the consequences of rejected or misused
opportunity or thriftlessness." Cited in Prothro, *op. cit.*, pp. 213-214.

[24] Herbert Hoover, *Addresses upon the American Road, 1933-1938* (New
York: Charles Scribner's Sons, 1938), p. 132.

[25] *Ibid.*, p. 133.

dom that he often came suggestively close to an economic determinism. "I believe that economic freedom cannot be suppressed without suppressing also spiritual and intellectual freedom."[26] In speech after speech he reiterated his belief in the interdependence of economic and other freedoms. Not only was there an interdependence between freedoms but economic freedom was the foundation upon which other freedoms depended. The American system of liberty, he explained, "holds that the other freedoms cannot be maintained if economic freedom be impaired—not alone because the most insidious mastery of men's minds and lives is through economic domination, but because the maximum possible economic freedom is the most nearly universal field for release of the creative spirit of men."[27] And, he argued, the American economic system was the only one which would not "destroy intellectual and spiritual freedom."[28] With governmental regulations established to prevent the abuse and eventual destruction of our economic system from within, the only major source of danger to the system came from government itself. As it endangered economic freedom it endangered all other freedoms. Eventually the rise of a great bureaucracy would jeopardize all freedoms, for government would brook no criticism. Managed currency, managed economy would lead to managed opinions and managed minds. "Free speech and free press have never lived long after free industry and commerce have been repressed."[29]

Thus fearful of the fate which had fallen to Russia, Italy, and Germany, Hoover saw in what he interpreted to be our traditional liberalism our only safe course of action. Yet Hoover was faced with a basic problem in semantics, for America had clearly reached another crossroads in its interpretation of liberalism. Hoover, therefore, sought to distinguish between a true and a false liberalism.

> It is a false Liberalism that interprets itself into government dictation, or operation of commerce, industry and agriculture. Every move in that direction poisons the very springs of true Liberalism. It poisons political equality, free thought, free press, and equality of opportunity. It is the road not to liberty but to less liberty. True Liberalism

[26] *Ibid.*, p. 261.

[27] Herbert Hoover, *The Challenge to Liberty* (New York: Charles Scribner's Sons, 1934), p. 33.

[28] Herbert Hoover, *Addresses upon the American Road, 1933-1938* (New York: Charles Scribner's Sons, 1938), p. 270.

[29] Herbert Hoover, *The Challenge to Liberty* (New York: Charles Scribner's Sons, 1934), p. 136.

is found not in striving to spread bureaucracy, but in striving to set bounds to it. Liberalism is a force proceeding from the deep realization that economic freedom cannot be sacrificed if political freedom is to be preserved. True Liberalism seeks all legitimate freedom first in the confident belief that without such freedom the pursuit of other blessings is in vain.[30]

Clearly, however, the pre-emption of the term "liberal" by the New Deal had the more lasting impact upon the political beliefs of Americans. As Manchester liberalism had given way to progressivism and the New Freedom a generation earlier, so now did Hoover's liberalism, born of an earlier age, give way to the reinterpretation of the New Deal. Though Hoover continued his campaign for liberalism as he understood it, he noted in 1936 that "Today . . . the term Liberal is claimed by every sect that would limit human freedom and stagnate the human soul. . . ."[31]

In an address on the topic "True Liberalism," Hoover attempted to escape the ambiguities in contemporary political terminology by advising an adherence to the following precepts as encompassing his concept of the American system:

If an open mind, free to search for the truth and apply it in government, is liberal, then you should be liberal.

If belief in open opportunity and equal opportunity has become conservative, then you should be conservative.

If belief that this can be held only in a society of orderly individual initiative and enterprise is conservative, then you should be conservative.

If opposition to those things which abuse and limit equal opportunity, such as privilege, monopolies, exploitation, or oppression whether in business or in government, is liberal, then you should be liberal.

If opposition to managed economy whether of the Socialist, Fascist, or New Deal pattern is Tory, then you should be Tory.

If humane action to eliminate such abominations as slum squalor, child labor, and sweated labor, to give greater protection from unemployment and old age is radical, then you should be radical.

If the use of all the powers of the government to relieve our people from hunger and cold in calamity is radical, then you should be radical.

If belief in the old-fashioned virtues of self-reliance, thrift, government economy, of a balanced budget, of a stable currency, of fidelity

[30] *Ibid.*, pp. 203-204.

[31] Herbert Hoover, *Addresses upon the American Road, 1933-1938* (New York: Charles Scribner's Sons, 1938), p. 138.

of government to its obligations is reactionary, then you should be reactionary.

If holding to the Bill of Rights with its safeguards of the balance of powers and local government is Tory, then you should be Tory.

If demand that change in the Constitution be by open submission to the people and not by subterfuge constitutes reaction, then again you should be reactionary.

If demand that we have a government of laws and not of bureaucrats is conservative, then you should be conservative.

If you agree with all this, then you have shed yourselves of many "isms" or you have melted them into plain Americanism.[32]

For all of Hoover's untiring avowals of liberalism, it seemed to many during the depression to have the empty appeal of a liberalism that was past. When Wilson had campaigned for the New Freedom and talked of government regulation of business and minimum standards of protection for the weak, his thoughts were boldly challenging. In spite of the formidable opposition of the old guard, the Manchester liberals, and big business, Wilson had implemented his theory with substantive legislative accomplishments as testimony to his sincerity. On the other hand and with but few exceptions, the legislative record in the years between Wilson and the New Deal clearly evidenced a solicitude toward business which was not shown to other groups in the economy. One searches in vain through the presidential proposals of Harding, Coolidge, and Hoover to find evidence of the concern for the weaker members in society which was articulated in Hoover's liberalism. The years prior to the New Deal were marked by practically unrestricted favoritism to large business at the expense of farmers and workers. The liberalism of the American system, although in theory it sounded much like the liberalism of Wilson, was thus measured by its substantive results during the era of business control of politics. Hoover's championing of individualism, self-help, and cooperation could thus have real meaning only to those who were not basically in need of help; and his message of liberty became identified in the popular mind with freedom for business to direct the course of economic affairs. In the final analysis it was not the logic of this brand of liberalism that was at issue, but its political and economic results.

It was one of the pathetic ironies of American politics that the

32 *Ibid.,* pp. 139-140.

man who had promised prosperity should so soon find his name used as an epithet for the economics of national poverty; that the man who had deservedly won international acclaim as a humanitarian for his direction of a relief program in World War I was unable to construct an adequate relief program for his countrymen; and that the man who had personified in this century the Horatio Alger myth of the past with his astonishing rise from orphanhood to millionaire, to the Presidency, should so soon find the myth questioned and the economic system which had engendered it cast into disrepute.

Clearly, if the doctrine of the American system of free enterprise was to be politically significant, the system required resuscitation and the doctrine reformulation. Paradoxically, the New Deal provided the resuscitation of the economic system, while the most significant reformulation of doctrine came from a European, Friedrich A. Hayek.

HAYEK—THE ROAD TO SERFDOM

Friedrich A. Hayek, an Austrian economist who had left his homeland to become a British citizen and a professor at the London School of Economics,[33] published in 1944 a slender little volume entitled *The Road to Serfdom*.

As one of the significant members of the famous Austrian school of economics, Hayek was well-known among professional economists. When, however, in the dark days of World War II he stepped out of his professional role to write what he frankly called a "political book," he attracted immediate popular attention. Though written directly for an English audience, *The Road to Serfdom* in its American publication had astonishing success as a best seller. It went through numerous printings. It became one of the selections of the Book-of-the-Month Club; it was condensed in the *Reader's Digest;* it became not only a controversial and popular book but one whose profound message provoked considerable academic response.[34] For in addition to Hayek's prestige as an

[33] Since 1950 he has been on the staff of the University of Chicago.

[34] Two significant rebuttals of Hayek's thesis may be found in Barbara Wootton, *Freedom Under Planning* (Chapel Hill: University of North Carolina Press, 1945) and Herman Finer, *The Road to Reaction* (Boston: Little, Brown & Co., 1946).

economist was the fact that he was a European who had witnessed at close hand the rise of totalitarianism; thus his message was received with more than professional curiosity. Where Hoover had written on public policy as a partisan participant discussing primarily a domestic issue, Hayek appeared to be a non-partisan observer whose analysis was universal in its application. This favored position gave not only greater claim to his credentials but an added persuasiveness to what was, in the midst of the war against totalitarianism, a persuasive position. In effect Hayek's position was quite similar to Hoover's; yet in the depth of his analysis he clearly reached beyond Hoover and in so doing gave economic individualism a new champion.

In *The Road to Serfdom*, sardonically though sincerely dedicated "to the Socialists of All Parties," Hayek argued that societies which had heretofore been thought of as liberal were in the process of forging their own chains, that they were often unconsciously moving down the road which led eventually to slavery. The conquest of the system of serfdom would not be had with the winning of the war alone, for steadily over the course of a generation tyranny had been advancing at home—in both England and America. Furthermore, fascism, Nazism, communism, and socialism were not opposing and competing political systems; though different kinds they were at bottom the same: tyrannical and totalitarian. All were collectivist systems in that they had in common "the deliberate organization of the labors of society for a definite social goal."[35]

> The various kinds of collectivism, communism, fascism, etc., differ among themselves in the nature of the goal toward which they want to direct the efforts of society. But they all differ from liberalism and individualism in wanting to organize the whole of society and all its resources for this unitary end and in refusing to recognize autonomous spheres in which the ends of the individuals are supreme. In short, they are totalitarian in the true sense of this new word which we have adopted to describe the unexpected but nevertheless inseparable manifestations of what in theory we call collectivism.[36]

Paradoxically, as Hayek saw it, it was quite often the well-meaning reformers who were paving the way to totalitarianism. For the

---

[35] Friedrich A. Hayek, *The Road to Serfdom* (Chicago: University of Chicago Press, 1944), p. 56.

[36] Reprinted from *The Road to Serfdom* by Friedrich A. Hayek (1944), pp. 56-57, by permission of the University of Chicago Press.

reformers in their efforts to alleviate economic distress turned invariably to strengthening the role of government in society; and in their indoctrination of the young they preached a contempt for the old school of liberalism. But once embarked on the road to statism it was difficult if not impossible to turn back. "Few are ready to recognize," Hayek observed, "that the rise of fascism and Nazism was not a reaction against the socialist trends of the preceding period but a necessary outcome of those tendencies."[37] Modern totalitarianism was in this view not merely a by-product of the dislocations of World War I but rather the inevitable result of a basic change in public consciousness that had been developing for a generation.

The decline of nineteenth-century individualism and liberalism Hayek thought might be attributed in part, paradoxically, to their success. So successful had this liberalism been, with its ennobling view of man and society and its belief in progress, that "man became increasingly unwilling to tolerate the evils still with him which now appeared both unbearable and unnecessary."[38] Thus men became impatient with the very belief-system which had generated their expectations as well as their accomplishments. As a result, he noted, "We have progressively abandoned that freedom in economic affairs without which personal and political freedom has never existed in the past."[39] As Hoover had maintained in his speeches in the Thirties, so Hayek argued a decade later that the foundation of all freedom was economic freedom from governmental control. And again like Hoover, Hayek did not advocate a return to the *laissez faire* of the past; rather, he accepted the necessity for some degree of legislation in the economic sphere in order to maintain fair conditions of competition. But the presumption in any given case ought to be in favor of the "spontaneous forces of society" with as little resort as possible to governmental coercion.

The central question posed in *The Road to Serfdom* was whether a planned society was compatible with freedom, and to this query Hayek answered with an emphatic "No." Planning, he noted, had become something in the way of the standard panacea of the age. Indeed, it was usually argued that modern society had little choice in the matter, for planning was inevitable. Technological changes

[37] *Ibid.*, pp. 3-4.
[38] *Ibid.*, p. 19.
[39] *Ibid.*, p. 13.

had so altered the nature of the competitive system that the only realistic choice was between government control, or the economic control of private monopolies. Yet Hayek maintained that these need not be the only alternatives. Actually it was to a large extent mistaken governmental policies, rather than technological changes, which had fostered monopolies. Indeed the increasing complexity of society not only facilitated an increase in competition but made it imperative that the competitive system be retained. Modern economic society had become so complex that no one could accurately envisage the vast network of interlocking relationships. In the competitive system, decisions were inevitably made piecemeal to handle day by day problems. Yet even if national planning on a comprehensive scale were feasible, it necessarily would require an enormous concentration of power. And such a concentration of power, Hayek believed, would spell the destruction of democracy.

All collectivist systems had in common, he argued, "the deliberate organization of the labors of society for a definite social goal."[40] "The 'social goal,' or 'common purpose,' for which society is to be organized is usually vaguely described as the 'common good,' the 'general welfare,' or the 'general interest.' "[41] Clearly, however, these normative terms had no precise, definable meaning which could serve as indisputable guides to public policy. To organize the labors of society for a definite goal would not only presuppose that such a discernible goal existed but that indeed the hierarchy of values in each individual was equally determinate and evidential. "It presupposes, in short, the existence of a complete ethical code in which all the different human values are allotted their due place."[42] However, no such complete ethical code existed. "Not only do we not possess such an all-inclusive scale of values: it would be impossible for any mind to comprehend the infinite variety of different needs of different people which compete for the available resources and to attach a definite weight to each."[43] Therefore the individualist argued that each person should be permitted to formulate his own set of values and be permitted as far as possible to act upon them. There could be common action only where there were common ends in society. But even if this sphere could be precisely known and the common ends could be fulfilled through common action, society

[40] *Ibid.*, p. 56.
[41] *Ibid.*, p. 57.
[42] *Ibid.*, p. 57.
[43] *Ibid.*, p. 58.

would be threatened by another danger. For as the sphere of common action was extended it would have increasing consequences on the activities of individuals. Thus individuals would find increasingly that their private lives were subject to or dependent upon the activities undertaken by the government in the communal sphere. "We can unfortunately not indefinitely extend the sphere of common action and still leave the individual free in his own sphere. Once the communal sector, in which the state controls all the means, exceeds a certain proportion of the whole, the effects of its actions dominate the whole system."[44]

To agree on the desirability of a system of national planning, Hayek argued, was of little effect unless there was in fact agreement on the ends that such planning was to achieve. But it was precisely at this point that Hayek believed the system of planning broke down. For it was unrealistic to assume that diverse individuals with often opposing and competing interests would in fact agree on the precise ends—with all their ramifications—that planning was to fulfill.

> The effect of the people's agreeing that there must be central planning, without agreeing on the ends, will be rather as if a group of people were to commit themselves to take a journey together without agreeing where they want to go: with the result that they may all have to make a journey which most of them do not want at all. That planning creates a situation in which it is necessary for us to agree on a much larger number of topics than we have been used to, and that in a planned system we cannot confine collective action to the tasks on which we can agree but are forced to produce agreement on everything in order that any action can be taken at all, is one of the features which contributes more than most to determining the character of a planned system.[45]

Since democratic majorities would normally be unable to reach agreement on the various aspects of the planned system, the demand for planning paved the way for dictatorship. Clearly, Hayek believed, democratic assemblies could not do the planning; the very diverse nature of the interests in the legislature would preclude agreement. The demand for planning would therefore mean that somebody other than the legislature would have to do the planning and would have to have the power eventually to execute the plans. So highly interrelated and interdependent was the economic system

[44] *Ibid.*, pp. 60-61.
[45] *Ibid.*, p. 62.

that planning and control in one economic sector would be dependent, in the final analysis, on the effectiveness of planning and control in all other economic sectors. Power could not therefore be exercised on a piecemeal basis. It would have to encompass the totality of the economic system. But such comprehensive planning and control could not be achieved through existing democratic procedures. "Our point, however, is not that dictatorship must inevitably extirpate freedom but rather that planning leads to dictatorship because dictatorship is the most effective instrument of coercion and the enforcement of ideals and, as such, essential if central planning on a large scale is to be possible. The clash between planning and democracy arises simply from the fact that the latter is an obstacle to the suppression of freedom which the direction of economic activity requires."[46]

It was Hayek's contention that under a competitive capitalistic system, when the rules of the game, the laws, were broadly formulated and generally applicable, each individual might achieve the maximum amount of freedom. Under the broad rubric of what Hayek called the rule of law, as opposed to specifically directional orders and decrees, each competitor was free to take his chances in an impersonal market. Furthermore, every individual was free, within the limits of his income, to allocate his money to satisfy his needs in accordance with an order or hierarchy of values of his own choosing. Money, Hayek argued, "is one of the greatest instruments of freedom ever invented by man."[47] A man had freedom to the extent he made his own voluntary choices of means and ends. Indeed, he argued, only competitive capitalism gave man the basic freedom of individual decisions which could support democracy. Capitalism was not only democracy's economic underpinning, but with its emphasis on individual selection and choice, the fundamental ethos as well. To concentrate economic and political power would not only destroy capitalism but also democracy. Presumably, under a competitive system, "if one person refuses to satisfy our wishes, we can turn to another. But if we face a monopolist we are at his mercy. And an authority directing the whole economic system would be the most powerful monopolist conceivable."[48]

Under a competitive system power was so divided among a variety of people each acting independently of others that "nobody

---

[46] *Ibid.*, p. 70.
[47] *Ibid.*, p. 89.
[48] *Ibid.*, p. 93.

has complete power over us. . . . If all the means of production were vested in a single hand, whether it be nominally that of 'society' as a whole or that of a dictator, whoever exercises this control has complete power over us."[49] Furthermore, once discernible human direction and control replaced the impersonal forces of the market, the response of the public would undoubtedly take on a new direction, for the central question would then become who controlled whom and to what purpose. "While people will submit to suffering which may hit anyone, they will not so easily submit to suffering which is the result of the decision of authority. It may be bad to be just a cog in an impersonal machine; but it is infinitely worse if we can no longer leave it, if we are tied to our place and to the superiors who have been chosen for us."[50] The inevitable result would be that no longer would there be economic and social questions separate from political ones, for all questions would resolve themselves into political questions as all power would have to be concentrated in the hands of those who held political office.

> Once government has embarked upon planning for the sake of justice, it cannot refuse responsibility for anybody's fate or position. In a planned society we shall all know that we are better or worse off than others, not because of circumstances which nobody controls, and which it is impossible to foresee with certainty, but because some authority wills it. And all our efforts directed toward improving our position will have to aim, not at foreseeing and preparing as well as we can for the circumstances over which we have no control, but at influencing in our favor the authority which has all the power.[51]

The end of a planned "social justice" could only be served, Hayek argued, by ultimately denying the belief in individuals as ends in themselves. For as individuals, people differed as to their immediate and ultimate ends and this fact gave color and character to the free, pluralistic society. But a planned society would not only impose on others someone's conception of justice—about which others might well differ—but furthermore would view individuals as means of implementing the plan, as units in the fulfillment of the system. Individuals would thus become means in achieving somebody's conception of justice. Hayek therefore feared that a demand for a planned society would bring about not only a totalitarian dictatorship, but one in fact controlled by the worst elements in society.

49 *Ibid.*, p. 104.
50 *Ibid.*, pp. 106-107.
51 *Ibid.*, p. 107

For, he argued, the higher the intellectual level of individuals in a society the less likelihood would there be of their agreeing on a "particular hierarchy of values." The problem of agreement would thus descend to "the lowest common denominator which unites the largest number of people." The hierarchy of values that would be imposed on the rest of society would not be the values of those "with highly differentiated and developed tastes."[52] They would be mass rather than individualistic values. Also such concurrence on values would come only from the more docile and conformist members of society who would have no clear convictions themselves but were always prepared to follow the leader. Furthermore, the nature of such a value system which had a mass following would be more than likely built upon a common sense of resentment and opposition than on any constructive program. "It seems to be almost a law of human nature that it is easier for people to agree on a negative program— on the hatred of an enemy, on the envy of those better off—than on any positive task."[53] Thus the way would be ready for the most unscrupulous demagogue to take advantage of the situation and with mass support institute a totalitarian dictatorship.

Such was the disturbing and gloomy prophecy presented in Hayek's *The Road to Serfdom*. The effort to give direction to progress could only lead to retrogression; to plan for freedom was to lead inevitably to slavery; and all collectivisms—welfare planning, socialism, communism, fascism, Nazism—came ultimately to the same common end, dictatorship.

> The tragedy of collectivist thought is that, while it starts out to make reason supreme, it ends by destroying reason because it misconceives the process on which the growth of reason depends. It may indeed be said that it is the paradox of all collectivist doctrine and its demand for "conscious" control or "conscious" planning that they necessarily lead to the demand that the mind of some individual should rule supreme—while only the individualist approach to social phenomena makes us recognize the superindividual forces which guide the growth of reason. Individualism is thus an attitude of humility before this social process and of tolerance to other opinions and is the exact opposite of that intellectual *hubris* which is at the root of the demand for comprehensive direction of the social process.[54]

Hayek's thesis touched off an immediate controversy in both the

[52] *Ibid.*, p. 138.
[53] *Ibid.*, p. 139.
[54] *Ibid.*, pp. 165-166.

popular press and professional periodicals, and for a while the concept of planning became of unusual political interest. "Planned economy" and "public planning" became politically evocative expressions. For all the logical incisiveness of what appeared to be at times a rather scholastic and highly theoretical debate—both pro and con—it was no doubt not the argument but the circumstances of the times which gave to Hayek's point of view an increasingly limited following. For *The Road to Serfdom,* written during the dark days of the war against the Axis dictatorships, was being read in America at the time when such government energies as were not fully occupied with the prosecution of the war were engaged in planning for the peace. Nor was this a form of foresight and activity peculiarly restricted to public officials. Few groups in society consciously chose the passive role of permitting the future to unfold through happenstance with no effort at conscious direction. Thus, it was little wonder that whatever the theoretical deficiencies of public planning, no responsible public official was failing to engage in it. Thus, even as Hayek attacked public planning, the government planned for the United Nations, for demobilization, and the probable economic dislocations of inflation and unemployment. Indeed, the first draft of what was probably the most significant planning legislation heretofore enacted by Congress, the Employment Act of 1946, was printed in 1944 shortly after the publication of Hayek's book.[55]

Hayek's appeal to a history guided by an invisible hand rather than by the visible heads of elected officials, like Hoover's appeal to economic individualism, was readily interpreted by its critics as being a doctrine in justification of the *status quo* that had existed in America between the two world wars. It would retain in economic power those who had been in power and leave underprivileged those who had been underprivileged. And no one would be to blame for injustices or economic dislocations, for these social ills would not be the fault of visible decision-makers but of the impersonal

---

[55] The reception of the first draft of this bill in the press is indicative of the impact of *The Road to Serfdom* on American thought. A student of the Employment Act of 1946 reported that "the press was generally hostile" to the bill and that the *New York Times, Wall Street Journal,* and the *Journal of Commerce* argued editorially against it "as leading toward the type of gradual collectivism which Mr. Hayek had challenged in his *Road to Serfdom.*" Stephen K. Bailey, *Congress Makes a Law* (New York: Columbia University Press, 1950), pp. 54-55.

forces of the market. The line between nineteenth-century Manchester liberalism and twentieth-century economic individualism appeared to be exceedingly fine. For though *laissez faire* was no longer significant as an economic doctrine, the effect of the individualism of Hoover and Hayek was a political sort of *laissez faire* in which the public was expected to maintain a passive role while leaders of business made fundamental decisions. In rejecting political solutions to economic problems, the economic individualists reduced politics to the rather innocuous art of electing and unseating public officials whose talent was administration rather than public policy. The alternative to public solutions to economic problems was of course private solutions. This meant in effect turning over to the economic leaders in the country the solution to the problems which had come up under their leadership. Whatever solutions might or might not be forthcoming, it was evident that such a public policy could not disturb the existing order of economic leadership. Economic individualism thus became a modern counterpart of the survival-of-the-fittest doctrine of the nineteenth century. As the earlier doctrine had appealed to those whose economic role in society was evidence of their fitness, so did the later doctrine appeal to those whose individualism was most economically secure.

CHAPTER 17

Pragmatic Liberalism

EARLY IN September of 1929 stock market prosperity reached a new peak, confirming many of the glowing prophecies of the nation's business leaders. A month later the collapse occurred, culminating in the panic of October 29, when over sixteen million shares of stock were sold. By the middle of November over thirty billion dollars had evaporated out of the stock market, a loss which vitally affected the savings and futures of countless Americans. In 1930 the combination of a bumper harvest in one region and a severe drought in another increased the plight of the farmers, who had already seen their property values decline twenty billion dollars in the decade. In 1930 unemployment was estimated at six million; in 1931 it was estimated at ten million. In 1931 over two thousand banks closed, holding nearly two billion dollars in deposits. By 1932 no one was certain how many people were unemployed, but the official estimate was 12.7 million persons out of a total labor force of 50.9 million; nearly one out of four workers was unemployed. It was dramatically certain to many that there was something radically wrong with the system which was not to be cured by incantations of economic theory or invocations to confidence.

For millions of Americans the grim facts of the great depression pitted the reality of the Thirties against the theory of the Twenties. It was not enough to argue the logic of traditional economic or constitutional theory; what was needed was an end to the depression, and if theory did not fit the facts so much the worse for theory. What was needed was a fresh start, a new approach to problems which were daily increasing in their acuteness.

It was this search for a fresh approach to old problems which gave color and vibrancy to the New Deal era as new minds and new ideas were tested in the grim setting of breadlines, the futile efforts of leaf-rakers, and the too-often pathetic portrayals of artists struggling for a living by painting murals on post-office walls. Though economic life was sluggish, the intellectual and political scene was most certainly not. For all the false prophecies of conservatives that confidence would cure all ills, for all the crack-brained solutions of extremists with their mail-order clubs of political literature or their militant marching cadres and symbolic shirts, for all that was fearful or merely fanciful in those tempestuous days, there came much social criticism that led to constructive and lasting results. As with other major periods of reform in our history, the reform impulse took a long while to permeate deeply enough into the population to justify itself on the basis of political expediency as well as political values. Then in an extraordinarily brief space of time the spark of reform was spent as the economic necessity which gave it political urgency was removed. But embedded in law and custom for a new generation, the political accomplishments of the reform period became indeed the tenets of modern liberalism and conservatism alike.

There is no conveniently apt label which contains the various lines of thought which nourished and sustained the New Deal. Socially it marked the triumph of a new middle class swollen now with the ranks of organized labor; politically it marked, accordingly, a gravitation toward a new center with headquarters in and around the large cities, where political strength was close to the source of voter supply; economically it marked a temporary abandonment of traditional economic doctrine which had placed in effect a halo of righteousness on big business leadership. That curious pot pourri of politics and policies that led to such enactments as the N.I.R.A., F.E.R.A., A.A.A., N.L.R.A., C.C.C., and T.V.A., together with a host of other alphabetical agencies that fattened the political lexicon, is best described as pragmatic liberalism. It was pragmatic in that it evidenced a willingness to depart from doctrinaire solutions where doctrine failed to coincide with the imperatives of dilemmas. And it was liberal in that it marked a genuine concern to alleviate the distress of those who, because of the structuring of the social-economic system, were unable to help themselves. It drew indeed upon a deep heritage of American thought.

PRAGMATISM

Like most commonly accepted systems of thought, pragmatism existed in America long before it was philosophically articulated and labeled. If Americans could claim no fame as founders of intellectual systems, they nevertheless took pride in the fact that they were eminently practical men. Though they imported much of their political theory, economics, philosophy, and theology from abroad,

Americans could claim at least that their political and economic systems worked, even though this meant at times that it seemed necessary to keep theory from interfering with practice. It was, after all, the practice that counted. A political system which had endured a century and three-quarters, in spite of unforeseen expansion in territory and population; an economic system which led the world in production and standard of living—these were sufficient testimony to national prestige and character.

As the pragmatic temper reached outward, beyond merely the politics and economics of human relations, it revealed several descriptive attributes. Pragmatism rejected alike first causes and final ends, absolute systems and eternal truths. It was not confined therefore to any particular discipline, but provided a method applicable to all. As pragmatism developed in American thought, however, it became associated with a community emphasis as opposed to individualism; relationships and relativity as opposed to absolutism; inductive reasoning as opposed to rationalism; the compulsions of facts as opposed to the convictions of faith; in a word, with the scientific temper in the social field. Experiment and verification were, it was felt, surer guides to truth than the uncertain conclusions of deductive logic. Pragmatism was indeed the philosophy of experienced expediency.

The view of Americans as practical men rather than as social or political theoreticians was apparent early in the nineteenth century; following the Civil War, revolutionary economic developments gave added impetus to this point of view. Theory was the function of idle dreamers; busy men were engaged in business. The businessman was thus presumed to be a practical man, who always liked to know of an idea, will it work? Workability, within the confines of the pecuniary standard, was thus the pragmatic test of means in the business world before it was elevated to a principle for social thought and action. Indeed, so close is the association of pragmatism with business practicality that William James (1842-1910), in expounding pragmatism, found it convenient to use market-place terminology to make his ideas clear.[1]

---

[1] For all of James' use of market-place terminology he had no intention of glorifying commercialism. James attacked the "moral flabbiness born of the exclusive worship of the bitch-goddess SUCCESS" and said this worship "together with the squalid cash interpretation put upon the word success is our national disease." See John Dewey, *Characters and Events* (New York: Henry Holt and Company, 1929), vol. II, p. 543.

Although much of the credit for establishing pragmatism as a distinctive method of thought justly belongs to William James, it was the philosopher Charles Peirce who first introduced the concept.[2] William James further developed the concept and in his speeches and articles articulated it in a most lucid fashion. In his book *Pragmatism* (1907)—appropriately dedicated to the memory of John Stuart Mill—James undertook to explain the basic features of this new system of thought; in the course of his explanation he launched a broad attack upon rationalism as a method and upon *a priori* "truths" previously believed to be immutable. For James was unalterably opposed to any closed system of thought which presupposed in human affairs natural laws and final truths or truth conceived of as an abstract entity. Essentially, therefore, James was opposed to the fixity and finality of philosophical speculation derived from the heritage of rationalism. It was rationalism and intellectualism, he felt, which had led to such a wide discrepancy between theory and practice and had engendered so much metaphysical confusion. "The pragmatic method," James noted, "is primarily a method of settling metaphysical disputes that otherwise might be interminable."[3] As a method, therefore, it was concerned with the consequences of particular beliefs held to be true. "What difference would it practically make to any one if this notion rather than that notion were true?"[4] In place of interminable debate over abstractions, James urged his readers to examine the particular consequences of particular beliefs; to check beliefs in an action sense. Pragmatism thus offered not a substitute system of beliefs, or final values, but a method of examining existing ones. The pragmatist turned from the heavens of metaphysical speculation to the more earthy concerns of men.

> He turns away from abstraction and insufficiency, from verbal solutions, from bad *a priori* reasons, from fixed principles, closed systems and pretended absolutes and origins. He turns toward concreteness and adequacy, towards facts, towards action and towards power. That means the empiricist temper regnant and the rationalist temper sincerely given up. It means the open air and possibilities of nature, as against dogma, artificiality, and the pretense of finality in truth.[5]

---

[2] "How To Make Our Ideas Clear," *Popular Science Monthly*, January, 1878.
[3] William James, *Pragmatism* (New York: Longmans, Green, and Co., 1908), p. 45.
[4] *Ibid.*
[5] *Ibid.*, p. 51.

As James described pragmatism it was clear that his emphasis was not upon ends, but means of understanding ends. "It (pragmatism) has no dogmas, and no doctrines save its method," he wrote.[6] It provided a method, he believed, whereby the facts of experience might be not only related to theory, but be indeed the determinant of theory. Essentially empirical, pragmatism sought a means whereby the developing truths of everyday experience might be assimilated with the truths of previous experience. Truth, so considered, was not fixed or absolute but a variable entity determined by the total experience of the particular observer. Pragmatism thus offered a theory of truth as well as a method of ascertaining it.

Any idea is "true" James argued, "so long as to believe it is profitable to our lives."[7] An idea that was "profitable" to believe was both true and good. "The true is the name of whatever proved itself to be good in the way of belief, and good, too, for definite, assignable reasons."[8] Thus truth and goodness must always be considered in relationship to some particular purpose and not in regard to something abstract or indeterminable. James stated the pragmatic approach to truth as follows:

> Grant an idea or belief to be true . . . what concrete difference will its being true make in any one's actual life? How will the truth be realized? What experiences will be different from those which would obtain if the belief were false? What, in short, is the truth's cash-value in experiential terms?[9]

As a result, James maintained, truth was not an inherent property found in an idea; rather truth "*happens*" to an idea. It *becomes* true, is *made* true by events. Its verity *is* in fact an event, a process: the process namely of its verifying itself, its "veri-fication."[10] The test of the truth of an idea was to be had in the practical consequences which followed from the idea as an action principle. It was the consequences of an idea which demonstrated the idea's conformance with reality; and in this conformance with reality lay its verification or disproof. Truth, that is, truths in the plural, paid to the extent that they could be consequentially verified and acted upon. As opposed to rationalism, which deduced absolute truth from

[6] *Ibid.*, p. 54.
[7] *Ibid.*, p. 75.
[8] *Ibid.*, p. 76.
[9] *Ibid.*, p. 200.
[10] *Ibid.*, p. 201.

a priori principles, James countered with truths which were made *via* the process of verification. "Truth for us is simply a collective name for verification-processes, just as health, wealth, strength, etc.; are names for other processes connected with life, and also pursued because it pays to pursue them. Truth is *made*, just as health, wealth and strength are made, in the course of experience."[11] It was thus the experiences of men which led to the ascertainment of truth, as of wealth or health; and acting on experience men verified or invalidated their theory of action. It was folly to talk about the ultimate truth or falsity of propositions that had no conceivable reference to the affairs of men, which whether true or false would not alter the course of men's lives because the consequences of the propositions made no practical difference. For it was the practical difference which literally made the difference; it was the realizable difference that pragmatism was concerned with.

Truth, subjected to the pragmatic formula, took on quite a different interpretation from that usually assigned to it by the rationalists. "The true," James noted, ". . . is only the expedient in the way of our thinking, just as 'the right' is only the expedient in the way of our behaving."[12] No truth could thus be looked upon as fixed, or final, or universal; rather all truths were constantly in the process of being made, of being experienced, verified or discarded. Yet James assumed a cumulative effect to the truth-making process.

> Men's beliefs at any time are so much experience *funded*. But the beliefs are themselves parts of the sum total of the world's experience, and become matter, therefore, for the next day's funding operations. So far as reality means experienceable reality, both it and the truths men gain about it are everlastingly in process of mutation—mutation towards a definite goal, it may be—but still mutation.[13]

The very process of truth-making, however, was a forward-looking effort. Where rationalism looked back to assumed old truths, pragmatism looked forward to verifiable new truths. James thus sought to cut philosophy—and theory-makers generally—free from the absolutes and ambiguities that had stifled man in a "block-universe."

While James was engaged in expounding pragmatism, John Dewey (1859-1952), at the University of Chicago and later at Columbia,

[11] *Ibid.*, p. 218.
[12] *Ibid.*, p. 222.
[13] *Ibid.*, pp. 224-225.

developed a closely similar system of thought which he called instrumentalism. To the layman there seemed little distinction between instrumentalism and pragmatism, and outside of professional circles the label of pragmatism was accepted as a generic term that included the thought of Dewey as well as James. Dewey, however, pointed pragmatism in the direction of society and made it an instrument for social action. With James, pragmatism was a method of understanding reality, and was primarily oriented to the individual with his own subjective affirmations and beliefs. In an age of individualism, James introduced pragmatism as an individualistic philosophy. The individualistic pragmatism of the nineteenth century, however, gave way to the social pragmatism of Dewey in the twentieth. Dewey's philosophy, like James', was essentially optimistic, even opportunistic, democratic and experimental. With James, the essential referent was the individual; with Dewey there was constant reference to society. Where James emphasized the subjective judgment of the individual, the importance of the "will to believe," Dewey emphasized scientific verification. In general then the essential difference between James and Dewey was that the latter gave more emphasis to social problems and the utilization of the scientific method in their solution.

Like James, Dewey waged unremitting warfare upon all rationalists, all those who would deduce absolutist systems of thought and fixed generalizations regarding man and society. He totally rejected rationalistic generalizations regarding "human nature," "natural laws," and "natural rights," along with any form of "natural determinism" whether of the Spencerian or Marxian variety. Throughout his voluminous writings Dewey emphasized the effectiveness of intelligence in ordering change, much as Lester F. Ward had emphasized the efficacy of effort. There was no fixed or static entity in man called mind; and man was not a mere prisoner of his environment. Furthermore man was not an intellectual hermit in a social cave, a single atom living among other atomistic individuals. He was rather an organism who utilized all his organs to create a satisfying situation out of his environment. Man reacted to his environment by thinking; and thinking reconstructed man's experience which in turn became part of his environment. In other words, Dewey reasoned, wherever there is life there is activity, and man's mind does not merely react to its environment but interacts with it. Experience is thus the accumulation of interactions of an organism with its environment.

Dewey rejected simple sensationalism and materialism along with rationalism, for experience, as he used the term, connoted far more than mere sense perception. Obviously the cultural environment with its values and beliefs was an essential part of the experience of an organism. The continual interaction of individuals in society, however, led to new shared experiences and new thoughts. Thinking, like life, was process, related to activity. As experiences changed, so did the social environment.

There was no ultimate end to this process, nor ultimate truths relating to it. As a result it was mere verbiage to talk about ultimate goals for the society or for the individual. Indeed, Dewey had little use for a system which separated ends and means; there being no ends in a final or absolute sense, the means of today were in a practical way the ends of today. "We must know that the dependence of ends upon means is such that the only *ultimate* result is the result that is attained today, tomorrow, the next day, and day after day, in the succession of years and generations."[14] Dewey rejected the concept of fixed moral laws and eternal truths as being beyond the realm of man's verifiable experience, related only to some abstract notion of ends which were equally unverifiable. Rather, like James, Dewey sought to turn inquiry into the area where verification was possible and the ends or consequences were ascertainable. In place of fixed ends and fixed means and finality of belief, Dewey emphasized malleable individuals in a malleable society, with beliefs conditioned by practical consequences. In point of social consequences, Dewey's approach emphasized social experimentation in politics, education, and economics, as opposed to inherited dogma or ideology. The overthrow of the conception of a natural order with natural rights led to the conception of a socially determined order with rights derived from society. In place of the passive acceptance of socially recognized evils, Dewey sought positive governmental action to aid in their elimination. The limits of desirable governmental or private group actions were not fixed in nature but determined by the prevailing beliefs of the society. Beliefs, however, ought to be well-grounded in observable phenomena. Certainly one of the major deficiencies of rationalism as a system of thought was its manifest departure from observable phenomena in the realm of man's political and economic behavior. Only through continued social experi-

[14] John Dewey, *Freedom and Culture* (New York: G. P. Putnam's Sons, 1939), p. 176.

ment could consequences be checked against working hypotheses. "Legislation, administration and education," Dewey noted, "must be regarded as having the role of an experimentation which tests and perfects ideas rather than as a program which merely executes them."[15]

By denying that the existing social order was the product of natural laws, Dewey cut social thought free from the conservative influence of rationalism. For the argument that the given social situation was the natural product of natural forces gave to the present a deterministic fixity which denied the possibility of intelligently controlled change. What was natural was inevitable; and the natural forces that made for the present would determine the future. It was against this mystical conception of environmental determinism that Dewey rebelled. Man controlled his environment as much as the latter controlled him, Dewey replied, and the function of the social sciences was to perfect more accurate methods for the control of the social environment.

> We are living still under the dominion of a *laissez-faire* philosophy. I mean by it a philosophy which trusts the direction of human affairs to nature, or Providence, or evolution, or manifest destiny—that is to say, to accident—rather than to a contriving and constructive intelligence. To put our faith in the collective state instead of an individual activity is quite as *laissez-faire* a proceeding as to put it in the results of voluntary private enterprise. The only genuine opposite to a go-as-you-please let-alone philosophy is a philosophy which studies specific social needs and evils with a view to constructing the special social machinery for which they call.[16]

Dewey rejected all closed or completed or absolute systems of thought. He rejected alike Marx and Adam Smith; he saw no magic in either state control or private control as such. Instead he sought continued experiment whereby all means might be tested so as to determine which means in what concrete and specific situation brought about the socially desirable consequences considered as immediate ends. "The hard and fast conservative is the man who cannot conceive that existing consitutions, institutions and social arrangements are mechanisms for achieving social results. To him, *they* are the

---

[15] John Dewey, *Characters and Events* (New York: Henry Holt and Company, 1929), vol. II, p. 737.
[16] *Ibid.*, p. 837.

results; they are final."[17] To Dewey these were not ends but means, instruments for fulfilling social desires. As instruments they were merely tools for social action and their adequacy as tools could be tested, as all tools are tested, by their competency in achieving the particular goal in view.

Much of the criticism of pragmatism centers about the argument that it is merely a philosophy of means; indeed, it has often been said that pragmatism is not so much a philosophy as a method of doing without one. A philosophy, it is charged, that elevates means tends to disregard ends; if the ends are only determinable consequences, then man is limited to rather puny efforts and aspirations; further, it is argued, pragmatism and instrumentalism so slight values that one might conclude that any value system is acceptable as long as it is socially desired. In defense of Dewey it may be observed that he opposed the separation of means and ends, and certainly opposed the nihilistic argument that any means was justifiable if it achieved the desired end. It was precisely because he associated means and ends that he argued the falsity of the proposition that any means today was justifiable if it brought about the desired end in some future time. For means were but immediate ends in man's life; and life viewed as process, as activity, meant that today's ends were but means toward tomorrow's developments. Means no less than ends, therefore, were of value in the conventional sense. That a philosophy which emphasized the "workability" of concepts might degenerate into a rather naive and materialistic sort of thing Dewey was fully aware. Yet his faith in pragmatism was great enough to hope for something better.

It commits us to a supremely difficult task. Perhaps the task is too hard for human nature. The faith may demonstrate its own falsity by failure. We may be arrested on the plane of commercial "success;" we may be diverted to search for consequences easier to achieve, and may noisily acclaim superficial and even disastrous "works" and fruits as proof of genuine success instead of evidence of failure.[18]

All this was possible he conceded, yet he hoped that the leaven of pragmatism would lead to other consequences. Pragmatism was only an experiment; but then so indeed was living.

It should be evident that Dewey, in his attack upon abstract be-

17 *Ibid.*
18 *Ibid.*, p. 545.

liefs, did not reject values either as a social phenomenon or as a desirable one. Indeed much of his writing is oriented to the frame of reference of democracy and the democratic way of life. John Dewey was undoubtedly the major philosopher of democracy of the twentieth century. In his approach to politics he always sought to relate liberal democratic values with the means to their realization. Pragmatism thus, instead of overthrowing the value system of the rationalists—Locke and Jefferson—sought rather a new instrumentality for its fulfillment. Like utilitarianism, pragmatism accepted the major values of Lockean liberalism: democracy, tolerance, liberty, equality, the rationality of men, and the brotherhood of man. Rationalism, utilitarianism, and pragmatism were in essential agreement on the values associated with liberalism; each system sought, in its own age, the liberation of man. But where Locke, for instance, deduced liberal democratic values from natural law, Dewey argued on their behalf because they produced socially desirable consequences. The right of private judgment—in religion or politics— in place of being a natural right, was defended by pragmatists on the grounds that it opened more avenues to thought and action. Toleration as well was stoutly defended by pragmatists as being entirely consistent with a system of contingent belief. The difference in values between rationalist and pragmatist was not one of substance, but a difference in the method of their justification and their means of realization.

Dewey repeatedly wrote in justification of the values associated with democracy. Only in a democracy he maintained, could individuality, which he prized highly, be adequately developed. It was in a democracy that the values of fraternity, liberty, and equality could best be realized. Yet, Dewey cautioned, those concepts must be related to social life in order to be meaningful. "Fraternity, liberty and equality isolated from communal life are hopeless abstractions. Their separate assertion leads to mushy sentimentalism or else to extravagant and fanatical violence which in the end defeats its own aims."[19] Thus Dewey sought a defense of these liberal democratic values not as abstract ends but as concrete means toward the development of individual personality and the achievement of an efficiently organized and a creatively active society. Liberty, equality, and fraternity, he argued, must be interpreted in a functional

[19] John Dewey, *The Public and Its Problems* (New York: Henry Holt and Company, 1927), p. 149.

sense; as functions of the existing social conditions. To be realized, these functions must be related to an immediate time and place and social situation. And, of course, their realization brought about the consequences by which in turn they might be tested and judged. Liberty, so understood, would thus be closely related with an experimentalism in outlook and would indicate a denial of the existent as naturally necessary, of the universe as forever made and completed. A free society would thus be free from rigidity in thought and mores as well as from irresponsible rules. Equality had meaning for democracy as it opposed the view of the world as "a fixed order of species, grades or degrees. It means that every existence deserving the name has something unique and irreplaceable about it, that it does not exist to illustrate a principle, to realize a universal or to embody a kind of class."[20] It was the fact of individuality that made possible equality, and ruled out as irrelevant "consideration of greater and less, superior and inferior."

If democratic equality may be construed as individuality, there is nothing forced in understanding fraternity as continuity, that is to say, as association and interaction without limit. Equality, individuality, tends to isolation and independence. It is centrifugal. To say that what is specific and unique can be exhibited and become forceful or actual only in relationship with other like beings is merely, I take it, to give a metaphysical version to the fact that democracy is concerned not with freaks or geniuses or heroes or divine leaders but with associated individuals in which each by intercourse with others somehow makes the life of each more distinctive.[21]

Dewey gave ample testimony of the relationship of thought to action in his own system of thought by directly participating in, and often leading, reform movements. His impact on the educational system is clearly evident today; his influence on American political thought is equally pervasive. In his lifetime he sought with a crusader's zeal a multitude of social reforms that indicated clearly the nature of the social goals he held as values for society. He sought an international community organized by international action, greater economic security and educational opportunity for all, and the intelligent utilization of public power for publicly desired ends. He sought a greater degree of individuality in what he characterized

[20] John Dewey, *Characters and Events* (New York: Henry Holt and Company, 1929), vol. II, p. 854.
[21] *Ibid.*, pp. 854-855.

a corporate society. In other words his social theory always emphasized the desirability of developing more fully individuality in
what was of necessity an increasingly interdependent community.
Specifically, Dewey sought a wide measure of economic reform
as a basic step toward the development of individuality. Man lived,
he reasoned, in a collective or corporate culture, yet his moral conceptions related primarily to the prescientific age of individualism
which was past. Man's social conceptions, his ideology as it related
to political and economic views, together with his legal institutions,
related to a period little advanced beyond the age of feudalism.
Yet, Dewey argued, man was trying to fit these social institutions and
habits of thought to the realities of twentieth-century interdependent
and industrialized existence. In its present setting, Dewey noted, the
"individualism" of the past has "shrunk to a pecuniary scale and
measure."[22] What was needed to restore the individual was not a
return to the individualism of the past with its pecuniary interpretation in the present, but the development of individuality. "A stable
recovery of individuality waits upon an elimination of the older
economic and political individualism, an elimination which will
liberate imagination and endeavor for the task of making corporate
society contribute to the free culture of its members."[23]

Dewey, recognizing the increasingly collective nature of modern
industrial society, sought through experimentation and social control to enhance the position of the individual. It was a fundamental
point in the Dewey philosophy that the individual not be simply
absorbed into the collective units. He emphasized individuality with
the vigor that exponents of *laissez faire* frequently employed in exhorting men to return to individualism. Individualism, however, was
most commonly used to urge the absence of state control or direction over personal or corporate pecuniary interests. It was this
interpretation of individualism which Dewey rejected as being
inconsistent with the desires of most individuals as well as with
the economic necessities of a democratic society. Individuality and
a democratic society were necessarily related concepts in Dewey's
philosophy. In his search for the means whereby these concepts
might be more adequately made manifest Dewey turned away from
conventional capitalism and socialism as being ready-made, final

22 John Dewey, *Individualism Old and New* (New York: Minton, Balch and
Company, 1930), p. 90.
23 *Ibid.*, p. 72.

solutions, inadequate for a society that was constantly in the making. No absolute solution could be had for changing problems; each solution created new problems to be solved. But if man could divest himself of his belief in a sanctity inherent in institutions, he would take a long step forward toward designing institutions that would better suit his needs.

> There is no more an inherent sanctity in a church, trade-union, business corporation, or family institution than there is in the state. Their value is also to be measured by their consequences. The consequences vary with concrete conditions; hence at one time and place a large measure of state activity may be indicated and at another time a policy of quiescence and *laissez-faire*. . . . There is no antecedent universal proposition which can be laid down because of which the functions of a state should be limited or should be expanded. Their scope is something to be critically and experimentally determined.[24]

Pragmatism, instrumentalism, as related to political problems, thus called for a rejection of absolutism in any form and a high degree of experimentation. Recasting traditional liberal democratic values in terms of their personal and social utility, instrumentalism emphasized the importance of individuality and democracy, the liberation of man from his institutions by utilizing his institutions to effect his liberation. Thus would the social environment be brought under social control as man's physical or natural environment, because of science and technology, had been utilized to his advantage. The test of such control, or absence of it, would however be the pragmatic check upon the consequences of the action taken or withheld. In any event, intelligence, socially utilized, rather than tradition or passivity, would guide the course of social change. Dewey's thought offered man in his political capacity a challenge; and in contrast to the deterministic views of Marx or Spencer or the traditionalists of natural law, it offered optimism in place of pessimistic resignation, a genuine hope for social reconstruction.

PRAGMATIC JURISPRUDENCE

Pragmatism had existed in American politics long before it was articulated as a system of thought by James and Dewey. Indeed all

[24] John Dewey, *The Public and Its Problems* (New York: Henry Holt and Company, 1927), p. 74.

working political systems must of necessity admit of a large measure of pragmatism, for theory in operation must run the gauntlet of changing conditions and political expediency. Pure theory seldom remains pure when practiced for any sustained period of time. Theory may, however, and often does become rigid when it is venerated to the point that it becomes symbolic of absolute truth and final wisdom.

To a large measure such absolutism and rigidity had entered into American thought by the end of the nineteenth century. Because all social judgments, when put into practice, had to risk the tests of judicial decision under the rubric of the Constitution, constitutional law came to represent the manifested principles of American political, economic, indeed social thought. The final test of legitimacy was constitutionality as declared by the Supreme Court. The nature and extent of civil rights; the standards of permissible private economic transactions; the contractual relationships of groups to each other and to any unit of government; monetary standards; the legitimate extent of governmental regulation—all these were subject to scrutiny by the judiciary. Ostensibly the tests, under our system of limited government, was constitutionality; but since constitutionality took on meaning only as it was articulated by judges, decisions reflected their political and economic values couched in legal terminology. The extraordinary rise in usage of the "due process" clause in the Fourteenth Amendment in the progressive period and after, and the invention of substantive "due process," reflected the judicial attachment to the social, economic, and political principles of Manchester liberalism long after this ideology had lost popular favor. So-called "natural economic law" thus coalesced into the "higher law" of the Constitution. Constitutional law was growing rigid, and judicial decisions, guided by past cases, reflecting the ideology of an earlier day, became an effective barrier to social change.

The justices who wrote these decisions were not, however, consciously writing constitutional law. It was the judicial view that judges did not make the law though their decisions guided future courts. They "found" or "discovered" it, for the law was already there and needed only judicial revelation to give it clarity. They "found" more popular legislation unconstitutional in the years from 1910 to 1937 than they had "found" so in all the years from 1789 to 1910. Social reform was thus pitted against an absolute system of constitutional thought. This view of law, as "found" rather than "made" by judges, and as fixed and settled rather than flexible, may be illustrated by the views of two prominent Supreme Court judges, one speaking during the Populist movement, the other during the New Deal.

In an often-quoted speech before the New York Bar Association in 1893, Justice David Brewer declared of the judiciary:

> They make no laws, they establish no policy, they never enter into the domain of popular action. They do not govern. Their functions in relation to the State are limited to seeing that popular action does not trespass upon right and justice as it exists in written constitutions and natural law. So it is that the utmost power of the courts and judges works no interference with true liberty, no trespass on the fullest and highest development of government of and by the people; it only means security to personal rights—the inalienable rights, life, liberty and the pursuit of happiness; it simply nails the Declaration of Independence, like Luther's theses against indulgences, upon the doors of the Wittenberg church of human rights, and dares the anarchist, the socialist and every other assassin of liberty to blot out a single word.[25]

Two years later the Supreme Court found the Income Tax law of 1894 unconstitutional. In 1936, when the Agricultural Adjustment Act of 1933 was found to be unconstitutional, Justice Roberts noted in the course of his opinion:

> When an act of Congress is appropriately challenged in the courts as not conforming to the constitutional mandate the judicial branch of the Government has only one duty—to lay the article of the Constitution which is invoked beside the statute which is challenged and to decide whether the latter squares with the former.[26]

In opposition to this approach, the pragmatic view of the Constitution found that instrument to be, indeed, an instrument for orderly social change. Pragmatists held that judicial decisions made constitutional law, that in fact, the Constitution was what the Supreme Court declared it to be. Such law in fact did change, and ought to change, to meet new conditions. By bringing the Constitution out of the rarified atmosphere of natural law, the pragmatists weakened

[25] New York Bar Association *Proceedings*, 1893, p. 46. Cited in Ralph Gabriel, *The Course of American Democratic Thought* (New York: The Ronald Press Company, 1940), p. 233. By permission.
[26] *United States v. Butler*, 297 U. S. 1 (1936).

its symbolic rigidity. As a man-made instrument it was a man-changed instrument, viable to meet new occasions. To a large extent the credit for the articulation of the pragmatic view of law rests with the "great dissenter," Oliver Wendell Holmes. He was, however, considerably supported in this endeavor by Roscoe Pound, Dean of the Harvard Law School, Justice Louis Brandeis, and Professor Felix Frankfurter. Each of these publicists emphasized some aspect of the pragmatic point of view; each opposed mere traditionalism without regard to consequences; each opposed finality and absolutism; each defended experimental man-made law; and each defended individuality and the civil rights of minorities. As early as 1880, Holmes in his notable study of the *Common Law* declared:

> The life of the law has not been logic: it has been experience. The felt necessities of the time, the prevalent moral and political theories, intuitions of public policy, avowed or unconscious, even the prejudices which judges share with their fellow-men, have had a good deal more to do than the syllogism in determining the rules by which men should be governed.[27]

If he left, as he once wrote, absolute truth for others to discover, he also knew clearly what it was not. It was not, he once indicated, Herbert Spencer's *Social Statics*, and the Fourteenth Amendment ought not to be interpreted as though it were. In his famous dissent in *Lochner v. New York* he observed: "A constitution is not intended to embody a particular economic theory, whether of paternalism and the organic relation of the citizen to the state or of *laissez-faire*."[28] The Constitution was made for "people of fundamentally differing views," and judges ought not to equate their views with what was permissible under the Constitution. In still another famous dissent Holmes wrote, in defence of freedom of speech:

> But when men have realized that time has upset many fighting faiths, they may come to believe even more than they believe the very foundations of their own conduct that the ultimate good desired is better reached by free trade in ideas,—that the best test of truth is the power of the thought to get itself accepted in the competition of the market; and that truth is the only ground upon which their wishes safely can be carried out.[29]

[27] Oliver Wendell Holmes, Jr., *The Common Law* (Boston: Little, Brown and Company, 1944), p. 1.
[28] 198 U. S. 45 (1905).
[29] *Abrams v. United States*, 250 U. S. 616 (1919).

It was the pragmatic Holmes who noted of the Constitution that "It is an experiment, as all life is an experiment," and who set up the pragmatic standard of "clear and present danger" in cases involving free speech.[30]

The new approach to law was called by Roscoe Pound "sociological jurisprudence." Yet, as Pound made clear, this was essentially pragmatism as applied to law. Indeed, he maintained there was a definite pragmatic element in modern law. "In the whole development of modern law, courts and lawmakers and law teachers, very likely with no theory of what they were doing but guided by a clear instinct of practical purpose, have been at work finding practical adjustments and reconcilings and, if nothing more was possible, practical compromises, of conflicting and overlapping interests."[31] Law reflected, generally, the prevailing social values, the ethics of the community where it was called upon as an instrument of social control. Where law became detached from the interests and desires of the community, it tended toward abstraction, and a rigidity that favored the *status quo*. Thus Pound maintained, "the conception of law as a means toward social ends, the doctrine that law exists to secure interests, social, public and individual, requires the jurist to keep in touch with life."[32]

Sociological jurisprudence was like the pragmatism of James and Dewey, a part of the ferment of the progressive era in America. Like pragmatism, the new jurisprudence stressed intelligent experimentation tested by social consequences in place of assumed final principles and the absolutism of logic. In the preface to his lectures on *The Spirit of the Common Law* (1921), Pound noted that "they show the faith in the efficacy of effort and belief that the administration of justice may be improved by conscious intelligent action" which characterized the progressive era. And, he noted further, "The real danger to administration of justice according to law is in timid resistance to rational improvement and obstinate persistence in legal paths which have become impossible in the heterogeneous, urban, industrial America of today."[33] Pound's jurisprudence, like Holmes'

---

[30] *Schenck v. United States*, 249 U. S. 47 (1919).

[31] Roscoe Pound, *Social Control Through Law* (New Haven: Yale University Press, 1942), p. 111.

[32] Roscoe Pound, *The Spirit of the Common Law* (Boston: Marshall Jones Company, 1921), p. 205.

[33] *Ibid.*, pp. xi, xii.

decisions, tended to upset the established legal frames of reference as it looked into the social implications of judicial decisions.

The emphasis upon intelligent experimentation and social consequences was continued in the judicial work of Louis Brandeis and Felix Frankfurter. Justice Brandeis, turning away from abstractions and logical order, looked primarily at economic and sociological facts, while Justice Frankfurter became the champion of the state legislatures in their efforts to solve public problems through experimental methods. More recently, pragmatic jurisprudence has been clearly illustrated in the notable Supreme Court decisions which have found racial segregation in public school systems incompatible with the Constitution. For years the Supreme Court had accepted the ruling in *Plessy v. Ferguson*[34] that "separate but equal" accommodations for whites and Negroes met the injunction of the Fourteenth Amendment that no state might deny a person the equal protection of the laws. The acceptance of this legal fiction permitted for half a century the continued discrimination against Negroes in states which chose to give this discrimination the sanction of law. It was not until the Supreme Court examined the *Plessy v. Ferguson* ruling in the light of the facts of the Negroes' experiences, in effect the consequences, in states which sanctioned racial segregation, that the "separate but equal" doctrine was successfully challenged and eventually overruled. In the government's brief in *Henderson v. United States*,[35] in which the Court prohibited segregation in dining cars of interstate trains, it was argued, in part:

> It is a question of fact what the community at large understands to be the meaning of singling out the members of the colored race for separation from all other citizens, whether it is in purchasing a bus ticket at the same ticket window, riding on the same street car or railroad coach, or going to the same restaurant, theatre or school. In the *Plessy* case the Court concluded that this minority race is not stigmatized as inferior, as constituting a lower social caste, when law decrees that it shall ride apart, eat apart, or stand in line for tickets apart. We submit that the Court's a priori conclusion cannot stand today in the face of a wealth of evidence flatly contradicting it.[36]

[34] 163 U. S. 537 (1896).

[35] 339 U. S. 816 (1950).

[36] Cited in Wallace Mendelson, *The Constitution and the Supreme Court* (New York: Dodd, Mead and Company, Inc., 1959), p. 450.

A few years later, in *Brown v. Topeka*,[37] the Supreme Court directly overruled the "separate but equal" doctrine as it applied to public education. Drawing heavily upon sociological and psychological testimony, the Court observed that it was not sufficient to compare the tangible evidence of equal facilities, such as school buildings, curricula, teachers' salaries and qualifications, in segregated schools. "We must look instead," Chief Justice Earl Warren wrote, "to the effect of segregation itself on public education." In the course of his opinion, Chief Justice Warren noted of education, using the language of the social-psychologists, "Today it is a principal instrument in awakening the child to cultural values, in preparing him for later professional training, and in helping him to adjust normally to his environment." Thus the consequences of a segregated school system were of vital concern to the nation. The consequences of a compulsorily segregated school system were such, the Court held, that even though all tangible evidences of equality were present, Negro children would feel a sense of inferiority which would in turn diminish their motivation to learn. "We conclude," the Chief Justice wrote, "that in the field of public education the doctrine of 'separate but equal' has no place. Separate educational facilities are inherently unequal."

The Warren Court in its handling of the segregation cases, both in terms of its substantive decisions and its method of implementation of these decisions, gave evidence of an approach to politics which may best be described as pragmatic liberalism. The search for the sociological facts behind legal formulas, the concern for the consequences of authoritative rulings in society, be they those of state legislatures or the Supreme Court, and the ultimate concern for the individual, for the development of personality of all peoples in a highly interdependent and interacting society—these considerations were in the finest traditions of William James and John Dewey. In the area of racial equality recent constitutional law has become revitalized because it has been informed, to paraphrase the words of Holmes, less by logic than by experience.

FRANKLIN D. ROOSEVELT

The pragmatic and the liberal streams of American thought were clearly imbedded in the personality and merged in the politics of

[37] 347 U. S. 483 (1954).

Franklin D. Roosevelt. Once, as president, Roosevelt declared: "There is a mysterious cycle in human events. To some generations much is given. Of other generations much is expected. This generation of Americans has a rendezvous with destiny."[38] These words might have been spoken of himself. For Roosevelt, bringing certain optimism, in a time of depression, hope in a time of despair, combining political ability with dedication, gave charismatic leadership to the nation and channelled, pragmatically, the widespread feeling of discontent into liberal and humanitarian reform. Through all of his many years in public service, as New York State Senator, as Assistant Secretary of the Navy under Wilson, as Governor of New York—there were clear indications that Roosevelt was personally dedicated to humanitarian reform.[39] But it was equally clear that in his liberalism Roosevelt was generally ahead of his party. Even as late as 1932 Senator James A. Reed of Missouri declared to the National Democratic Convention which had nominated Roosevelt for the presidency:

> It is the highest duty of the Democratic Party to get back the old principles and old methods. There has been no improvement on the policies of George Washington in regard to international affairs, and there never will be an improvement. There has been no improvement on the philosophy of Thomas Jefferson, and there never will be an improvement. There has been no improvement on the philosophy— the economic philosophy—of John Stuart Mill and there never will be an improvement.[40]

Here was a succinct statement of that traditional dogmatism which refused to see in changed conditions the need for new approaches. The day after Reed spoke Roosevelt flew to Chicago to accept the nomination. In observing that in the past candidates had not appeared before the Convention to accept their nomination, Roosevelt

---

[38] *The Public Papers and Addresses of Franklin D. Roosevelt.* Special Introduction and Explanatory Notes by President Roosevelt (New York: Random House, Inc., 1938), vol. V, p. 235.

[39] See Arthur M. Schlesinger, Jr., *The Crisis of the Old Order* (Boston: Houghton Mifflin Co., 1957). It is of interest to note, in view of subsequent political developments, that in 1919 Roosevelt wrote of Herbert Hoover, whose humanitarian accomplishments gave him a national reputation: "He is certainly a wonder and I wish we could make him President of the United States. There could not be a better one." Roosevelt was thinking of Hoover as a Democratic candidate. See Schlesinger, *op. cit.*, p. 82.

[40] Cited in Schlesinger, *op. cit.*, p. 311.

declared, "Let it . . . be symbolic that in so doing I broke traditions. Let it be from now on the task of our Party to break foolish tradi- tions." Furthermore, he told his fellow Democrats, "Ours must be a Party of Liberal thought, of planned action, of enlightened inter- national outlook, and of the greatest good to the greatest number of our citizens."[41] True, he did promise to reduce taxes and "elimi- nate actual functions of government," but clearly he would not be bound by received economic doctrines. The opposition, he charged, "tell us economic laws—sacred, inviolable, unchangeable—that these laws cause panics which no one could prevent. But while they prate of economic laws, men and women are starving. We must lay hold of the fact that economic laws are not made by nature. They are made by human beings."[42] In place of old doctrine therefore, Roose- velt promised a "new deal for the American people."[43]

Just how the "new deal" would be brought about was left unclear, for Roosevelt did not present any doctrinaire solutions. But it was the very nature of pragmatic liberalism not to be doctrinaire but rather to be experimental in its approaches to problems to which no doctrine had proven solutions, and Roosevelt, throughout his speeches prior to his nomination, had emphasized experimentation as the proper approach to public problems. In an often-quoted speech he had declared early in 1932, "The country needs and, unless I mistake its temper, the country demands bold, persistent experi- mentation. It is common sense to take a method and try it: if it fails, admit it frankly and try another. But above all, try some- thing."[44] Thus as the New Deal opened its first fabulous "one hun- dred days," the legislative mills were swamped with executive pro- posals, many of which had originated among that small body of advisors who had become known as the "brain[s] trust." "This Na- tion asks for action, and action now," Roosevelt had declared in his inaugural address of 1933. "We must act and act quickly," he empha- sized. And Congress responded with incredible speed with a flood of legislation.

If action and experimentation were essential ingredients of the New Deal, so also was the concept of intelligent planning. "In the

41 *The Public Papers and Addresses of Franklin D. Roosevelt.* Special Intro- ductions and Explanatory Notes by President Roosevelt (New York: Random House, Inc., 1938), vol. I, pp. 648, 650.
42 *Ibid.*, p. 657.
43 *Ibid.*, p. 659.
44 *Ibid.*, p. 646.

long run, state and national planning is an essential to the future prosperity, happiness and the very existence of the American people," Roosevelt had declared at the annual Governor's Conference in 1931.[45] Now as president, he proposed to Congress the creation of the Tennessee Valley Authority. "Many hard lessons have taught us the human waste that results from lack of planning," his message to Congress read. "Here and there a few wise cities and counties have looked ahead and planned. But our Nation has 'just grown.' It is time to extend planning to a wider field, in this instance comprehending in one great project many States directly concerned with the basin of one of our greatest rivers."[46]

Where the pragmatic aspect of the Roosevelt era was borne out in planning, experimentation, and almost exhausting activity, the liberal aspect centered around the greater distribution of social, economic, and political benefits to those far down in the economic pyramid. "The real truth of the matter is, as you and I know," Roosevelt wrote in a personal letter in 1933 to Colonel Edward M. House, one of Wilson's advisors, "that a financial element in the larger centers has owned the Government ever since the days of Andrew Jackson—and I am not wholly excepting the Administration of W. W. The country is going through a repetition of Jackson's fight with the Bank of the United States—only on a far bigger and broader basis."[47] It was Roosevelt's belief that big business jeopardized the economic life of the rest of the American public and that, as Berle and Means had documented in *The Modern Corporation and Private Property* (1932), more than half of the wealth of the United States was under the control of less than two hundred large corporations. In his acceptance speech for his nomination to a second term, Roosevelt likened the struggle in 1936 to that which the country had gone through in 1776. In the American Revolution the battle had been against political tyranny; now it was against the "economic royalists." Calling up the clichés of the Progressive era, he attacked those who had created a "new despotism" built on "other people's money."

"For too many of us the political equality we once had won was

---

[45] *Ibid.*, p. 495.

[46] *Op. cit.*, vol. 2, p. 122.

[47] *Franklin D. Roosevelt: Selected Speeches, Messages, Press Conferences, and Letters,* edited by Basil Rauch (New York: Rinehart and Co., Inc., 1957), p. 121.

meaningless in the face of economic inequality. A small group had concentrated into their own hands an almost complete control over other people's property, other people's money, other people's labor —other people's lives. For too many of us life was no longer free; liberty no longer real; men could no longer follow the pursuit of happiness."[48] The "economic royalists," Roosevelt argued, had accepted the principle of political freedom, that is the right of every man to vote. But they had denied the right of equal opportunity in the market place, maintaining instead that "economic slavery was nobody's business." "These economic royalists complain that we seek to overthrow the institutions of America. What they really complain of is that we seek to take away their power."[49]

Roosevelt's opponents charged him with undermining the free enterprise system, of sapping the strength of American individualism. To these criticisms Roosevelt replied in a campaign speech in Chicago in 1936 with the record of the New Deal. It was, he contended, the New Deal which had saved the economic system when it was on the brink of ruin. "I believe," he emphasized, "I have always believed, and I always will believe in private enterprise as the backbone of economic well-being in the United States."[50] But he argued, the concentration of economic power in the hands of a few large corporations was in fact destroying the free enterprise system by turning private corporations into private governments with vast control over all aspects of America's life. The freedom of a few thus led to the regimentation of many. And the effort to preserve individualism for many required some restriction on the rampant individualism of the few.

"I believe in individualism. I believe in it in the arts, the sciences and professions. I believe in it in business. I believe in individualism in all these things—up to the point where the individualist starts to operate at the expense of society. The overwhelming majority of American business men do not believe in it beyond that point. We have all suffered in the past from individualism run wild. Society has suffered and business has suffered."[51]

The test of Roosevelt's beliefs was not in his public pronounce-

[48] *The Public Papers and Addresses of Franklin D. Roosevelt.* Special Introductions and Explanatory Notes by President Roosevelt (New York: Random House, Inc., 1938), vol. V, p. 233.

[49] *Ibid.,* p. 234.

[50] *Ibid.,* p. 487.

[51] *Ibid.,* p. 488.

ments alone but in the long record of New Deal public policies—policies in health, in housing, in education, in the broad area of social security; in the area of the producer groupings of farmers, laborers, and businessmen—which sought to promote individualism by aiding the weak and curbing the strong. Not since the Wilson era had America witnessed such a program of reform. Yet tragically, as with Wilson, the catastrophe of a world war interfered with the completion of reform, and much was left for another generation. As post-war guideposts Roosevelt left his famous Four Freedoms—freedom of speech, freedom of religion, freedom from want, and freedom from fear—to be achieved everywhere in the world. But for all of the efforts of the Fair Deal to continue the Roosevelt legacy, much of the crusading spirit of liberalism had departed with the conclusion of the war. Yet the pragmatic spirit of politics, which had epitomized the philosophy of Roosevelt, remained, for it had a heritage older than the New Deal and drew deeply upon a wide segment of American experience.

CHAPTER 18

Protest Ideologies

THE GREAT DEPRESSION which engulfed America in the Thirties
while Stalin consolidated power in Russia, Mussolini rode triumphant
in Italy, Hitler fashioned his Nazi legions, and Spain was torn with
civil strife caused Americans to reassess their political beliefs more
critically than ever before in the twentieth century. Though the dominant lines of political thought seemed to run between economic
individualism and pragmatic liberalism or progressivism, America
was not lacking a host of critics who offered more radical solutions
to the crisis than were contained in the mild and often confusing
patch-work patterns of the New Deal. Some sought to turn the desperate state of the country to their private advantage, seeking personal power or wealth; some more altruistic souls spent all, health
and wealth, in their effort to aid their fellow-man; some were militant, vituperative, and vindictive; some were kindly, charitable, and
compassionate. Some, in these confusing times, wrote simple panaceas only to find that such were the needs of the country that suddenly they were looked upon as messiahs, and urged to lead the
helpless, insecure, and unemployed out of the wilderness. Such a
one was Upton Sinclair, the Socialist writer whose novel *The Jungle*
(1906), with its lurid description of health hazards and inhumane
working conditions in the meat-packing industry, had left its mark
on American thought. Now, in 1933, Sinclair joined the Democratic
party and wrote a political pamphlet entitled *How I Ended Poverty
in California.* Suddenly E.P.I.C. (End Poverty in California) became a political symbol of great significance and Sinclair barely
missed being elected Democratic governor of California. These
were the days of Huey Long and his "Share-the-Wealth" program,
of Father Coughlin with his inflammatory *Social Justice;* of Senator
"Bob" Reynolds, with his Silver Shirts and *American Vindicator,* as
well as the days of the benign Dr. Townsend with his old-age pension plan. In these unhappy days there was a certain abundance of

food for thought, for all the uncertainty of nourishment for the body. While the main stream of American thought moved with the elections a little left of center, or rather more to the center from the right, there were voices of dissent and protest which radically challenged the basic preconceptions of a capitalistic democracy. With an ideological struggle soon to engulf the world, it was inevitable that some measure of this struggle be mirrored in the philosophical controversies over domestic politics. The many varieties of Marxism in America had all their devotees in frequent and ferocious eschatological dispute, closely infighting with the extraordinary zeal known only by the sectarian devout. Stalinists, Trotskyites, and various Socialist sects waged mortal combat with each other, and with endless fission reduced themselves to insignificant proportions, thereby dissipating the energy which they might have been expected to expend on their common enemy, capitalism. Meanwhile, into the confusion, dressed in various patriotic garbs, came the exponents of fascism. Out of this curious and often bewildering mélange of dissident voices, three—Lawrence Dennis, Norman Thomas, and Paul Sweezy—are especially worthy of mention here in that they departed in some measure from the trodden paths of American thought and sought to turn the thinking of their countrymen in new political directions.

AMERICAN FASCISM: LAWRENCE DENNIS

When, in 1935, Sinclair Lewis's best-seller *It Can't Happen Here* was published, portraying the coming of fascism to the United States, there were those who felt that it could indeed happen here. Huey Long (until assassinated in 1935) ruled Louisiana with virtually dictatorial power. Father Coughlin preached anti-Semitism; Senator Reynolds' Silver Shirts seemed to have a similarity to Mussolini's Black Shirts; and Nazi Bund meetings were on the rise. It was, in all, plausible to believe that the historic hour of democracy had passed and a new wave of the future was coming into being. The insecurity, frustration, and fear that swept across the land in those dark days severely challenged the benevolent conceptions of man inherent in democratic values. Toleration was challenged by movements dedicated to intolerance; equality was met with sinister suspicion when not the outward violence of racial battles; liberty was countered with such a crude economic interpretation as to deny its traditional moral meaning. It was in this setting that American fascism rose as a sporadic political movement and as a system of political thought.

The identification of capitalism with democracy, and the subsuming of each under the term liberalism, was characteristic of fascism along with other anti-democratic thought of this period. The obvious historic parallel of capitalism and democracy gave to each system an intriguing suggestion of dependency upon the other. For capitalism, like democracy and Protestantism, was an outgrowth of the medieval period; indeed, in the subsequent centuries these three value systems or ideologies were often found together. The relationship of the religious ethic and the spirit of capitalism has often been remarked on.[1] America, like England, was predominantly Protestant, capitalistic, and democratic. It was the relationship of capitalism and democracy, however, which received most attention in the writings of modern American political theorists. Were they in fact conflicting systems of thought, as seemed implicit in the writings of the Populist and progressive reformers, as well as in the opinions of the staunchest defenders of judicial review of economic legislation? Or were they mutually supporting ideologies, as was implicitly maintained by such proponents of a natural aristocracy as More, Babbitt, and Cram (concerning whom, see Chapter 19)?

The assumption that liberalism—capitalism and democracy—had reached its peak in the nineteenth century and was now collapsing before the march of a new order was common to fascists and communists alike. Both held that democracy in a capitalist country was not only actually impossible but undesirable. Both thus sought the overthrow of capitalistic-democracy and the institution of a totalitarian dictatorship. The fascist sought the dictatorship of the elite while the communist sought the dictatorship of the proletariat; proponents of each system thought of it, however, as the inevitable new order.

While there were many minor fascistic movements in America during the Thirties, there were few coherent spokesmen for fascism. Lawrence Dennis (1894-   ) was undoubtedly the most articulate and intellectual defender of American fascism as a system of thought.

[1] See R. H. Tawney, *Religion and the Rise of Capitalism* (London: J. Murray, 1926); Max Weber, *The Protestant Ethic and the Spirit of Capitalism* (London: G. Allen, 1930); Ernst Troeltsch, *The Social Teachings of the Christian Churches,* 2 vols. (New York: The Macmillan Co., 1931).

In his three major works, *Is Capitalism Doomed?* (1932), *The Coming American Fascism* (1936), and *The Dynamics of War and Revolution* (1940), as well as in his numerous articles in the *American Mercury*, Dennis made clear the major features of fascism for America. Fascism, as Dennis developed it, was basically an attack upon liberalism—capitalism and democracy—which he found to be obsolete as an ideology and impractical as a scheme of social organization. The major burden of the fascist criticism, however, was upon *laissez faire* capitalism, not democracy; democracy came under attack largely because it permitted the follies of business leadership. Tracing the rise of capitalism through nineteenth-century America, Dennis found that capitalism prospered as long as there was an expanding frontier, an expanding population, and easy wars of conquest. With the twentieth century, however, these major props for capitalism were gone. Capitalism thus approached a senility marked by inflation and bust, the depression of the Thirties which could only be alleviated by war. To a large extent Dennis blamed the international bankers for modern wars and depressions. Yet, he charged, capitalistic leadership, such as usually existed in a democracy, was generally incapable of effective social programming and control.

> Business is a competitive game of profit-seeking and not a cooperative way of promoting human welfare. Love of the game, love of activity, love of power and love of lucre are the dominant motives in business enterprises. The driving force is human greed. The technique is human cunning. Such a system calls for moderation and practice under the effective play of strong factors of social impulse, guidance and restraint.
>
> The charm of capitalism is that it may be practiced in a way to allow of a varied and balanced civilization. When business leadership becomes dominant, balance is lost.[2]

The business ethic, Dennis argued, was contrary to the normal requirements for social order, let alone growth and development. Furthermore, such an ethic was totally lacking in those vague and mystical qualities that gave cohesiveness to the community. As a result the urge to profits could have only limited appeal and therefore only limited social utility.

[2] Lawrence Dennis, *Is Capitalism Doomed?* (New York: Harper and Brothers, 1932), p. 7. By permission.

The problem of society is the pursuit of happiness according to some scheme of values. The problem of business can only be the competitive pursuit of profits through the satisfaction of human wants and the exploitation of human weaknesses. The pursuit of these conflicting objectives must always involve a conflict between society and profit seekers.[3]

The profit motive had proven satisfactory in the past only because it had not been the primary motivating force in capitalism. The expansion of capitalism had been a part of the "militant nationalism" of the nineteenth century which thus gave a spiritual or "noncommercial" impulse to the social order. Something beyond the search for profits was needed if a society wished to prevent stagnation. "The success of communism or fascism and the futility of liberalism are explained largely by the fact that communism and fascism are living religions and that man is an emotional being."[4] Capitalism was thus subjected to the fascist criticism that it was unable to provide the sort of leadership necessary to a people who desired more than the mere satisfaction of the pecuniary desires. Military leadership was preferable to business leadership, Dennis argued, in that the soldier-leader recognized a sense of obligation to his subordinates, whereas the business leader looked only to his own advantage. "Profit makers cannot lead a people. Profit makers are against and never with the people."[5]

Thus, in 1932, Lawrence Dennis maintained that capitalism was doomed for two main reasons: first, the conditions which made the rise and flourishing of capitalism possible no longer existed; second, the type of social leadership which capitalism brought forth was socially destructive rather than constructive and because of its emphasis on the profit motive denied to society the mystical or spiritual values that gave impetus to social growth and development. Even in the field of economics, Dennis maintained, business leadership had failed.

States of feeling, not knowledge of facts or technique, determine choices, generate activity and, in short, shape human destiny, in economics quite as much as in love or in war. Value and demand, the two most fundamental economic concepts, are the products of the emotions. If the capitalistic machine, as it is now functioning, inhibits

[3] *Ibid.*, p. 14.
[4] *Ibid.*, p. 85.
[5] *Ibid.*, p. 256.

such leadership as is essential to the creation of the right states of feeling for a satisfactory quantity and quality of activity for the biological survival and the spiritual growth of the human race, it would seem that the machine is doomed. . . . Possibly frequent wars, which will bring into play strong spiritual leadership, will continue to provide the requisite solutions at appropriate intervals. But, then, can capitalism survive many modern wars? Russia suggests grave doubt.[6]

Dennis had predicted the end of capitalism, and with it the end of liberalism as an ideology, well before the full effects of the depression were felt. By 1936, in the depths of the depression, he believed that the collapse of capitalism had been adequately demonstrated. In *The Coming American Fascism* he continued his attack upon capitalistic-democracy with the evidence of the depression fresh at hand. The charge that the system had failed, he maintained, was supported by the fear, frustration, and unemployment throughout the land. Only war, he argued, could temporarily salvage the system. Viewing capitalistic-democratic society much as Hobbes had viewed the state of nature, Dennis argued that life in a profit system was a war of every man against every man, of minority groups against minority groups, with each and every contestant indifferent or opposed to the national welfare. Yet under the logic of *laissez faire* capitalism, government ought not to intervene; in fact government in a constitutional democracy, as interpreted by the courts, was powerless to intervene. When intervention in the economy was considered permissible it was only because some minority group had temporarily succeeded in gaining power to the disadvantage of opposing groups and interests. Such a system—which Dennis called liberalism—was obviously irrational as it assumed that out of this struggle of selfish forces would come a beneficial social order. To the contrary, Dennis maintained, out of this struggle could come only temporary victories for selfish groups which were usually contrary to the best or more general interests of society.

This continual combat, this chaos, was carried on under the framework of a legal system which was supposed to make this country a government of laws and not of men. This fiction, as Dennis called it, led to two misconceptions. First, it led to the belief that the constitutional and legal systems were impartial expressions of the people's will, as was usually stated in defense of judicial review.

[6] *Ibid.*, p. 317.

Second, it overlooked the crucial and partial role of the administrator and interpreter of the laws. The struggle for advantage, Dennis insisted, reached its highest point in the making and interpreting of the laws which controlled men. The conception of law and its administration as impartial justice expressing the general popular will was a vestigial remnant in theory from the eighteenth century, clearly fallacious in any realistic view of politics. Neither the laws nor their administration was either general in source or impartial in application. Indeed, Dennis countered, laws in America were generally the achievement of the capitalist elite; and these laws were then interpreted by the partisans of this elite.

Thus far Dennis attacked capitalistic-democracy as being not a system of order but a state of chaos whose laws were rules which worked to the advantage of the powerful. Like Hobbes, Dennis rejected moral restraints upon human behavior as being nothing more than platitudes which limited no one not otherwise restrained. The terms of peace in this war of each against all were determined by force and power, not platitudes nor law. Law was an instrument of force which might only be employed by those already possessing force. Dennis thus rejected the assumptions of an ultimate harmony of interests between competing groups or individuals, a moral code actually governing human behavior, and impartial justice administered by a disinterested government. Government, indeed society, under the liberal ideology, was to Dennis a storehouse which each tried to rob to his private advantage, the spoils of which went to the most ruthless and cunning robber.

Capitalistic-democratic thought, Dennis noted, attributed to itself as one of its virtues the claim that wide areas of freedom existed within the law. That is to say, freedom existed where governmental restraint was absent. This view, too, Dennis attacked as a misconception. There was little difference to him between the force employed by the police, or a large corporation, or a labor union. Economic coercion was an instrument of force; the policeman's club was an instrument of force. Force was found wherever conflict existed in society; and the heart of liberalism was competition and conflict. Freedom was thus a shibboleth in a complex, highly interdependent society. Beyond such normative expressions as freedom, justice, truth, etc. was always the ulterior value which was sought by the user of the expression. If one sought employment and there were no jobs available, he was as coerced into unemployment as though there were a law against employment. Coercion, or force, permeated society; governmental repression was simply a tool which some of the victors employed when it served their convenience. "The much vaunted freedom of modern capitalism is largely a matter of the freedom of property owners from social responsibility for the consequences of their economic choices."[7]

Dennis's use of Hobbesian assumptions regarding human nature led him directly to Hobbesian conclusions regarding the social order. The great Fascist Leviathan, to be brought forth from the chaos of liberalism, would establish a sovereign leader, or committee of the elite, with absolute power over all within the national boundaries. Out of the depression, or the next war, he maintained, the frustrated elite would come into power. Who were the elite? "The elite may be defined roughly and arbitrarily as including capitalists deriving most of their income from property, business enterprisers and farmers, the professional classes, and, generally, the employed whose salaries are considerably above the average."[8] In other words, the upper-income groups constituted the elite. Yet these were the very groups who Dennis claimed control the country anyway. By Dennis's own argument, leaders were those with a will to power who possessed power; therefore a change in leadership would represent a change in the locii of power; were power to remain in the hands of those already possessing it, it is difficult to see how there would be either a change in leadership or a change in political ethic. Nevertheless he argued that when fascism came about—and he assumed that its coming was inevitable—there would be a complete change in our political system as well as in our political thought. The change in political values and the thought associated with them would be extremely consequential.

> Two simple but profound and fundamental notions are essential to any understanding of planning, or fascism, or communism as well as to the formulation of any new social system. The first notion is that any social system represents a given scheme or hierarchy of ultimate values, or group and personal objectives, the upholding of which is one of the chief duties of man, the State, and social institutions generally. The second notion is that these ultimate values cannot be validated by the processes of logic or by reason.[9]

[7] Lawrence Dennis, *The Coming American Fascism* (New York: Harper & Brothers, 1936), p. 23. By permission.

[8] *Ibid.*, p. 229.

[9] *Ibid.*, p. 107. The brief quoted passages in the text following are from pages 105 and 106.

It was this emphasis upon ends rather than means which gave to fascism no little of its Machiavellian appearance, for the criterion for judging the means employed was the degree of success in accomplishing the desired end. In other words, there was no question of the morality of any means which might be indicated to reach the ulterior value or end. Furthermore, rather than being bound by any given scheme of values, fascism employed a flexible approach, based on the assumption that there were no absolute values or absolute truths. "The fascist scheme of things is an expression of human will which creates its own truths and values from day to day to suit its changing purposes." Fascism then "is essentially an expression of the human will reacting to the changing situations of life in the eternal struggle for existence." Fascism was not however "anti-intellectual or anti-rational"; it only rejected the rationalism of the eighteenth century which assumed that reason was normative "instead of being merely instrumental, or the tool of the will and of our emotional drives." The ultimate values of fascism—while not specifically defined—were thus not absolute ones.

The elite of the fascist state would select the ultimate values, the ends of the social order, and would establish the means for their fulfillment. Conscious planning and control would supplant the older system of economic anarchy. Since coercion existed under any system, the introduction of social control would not necessarily increase coercion but simply shift the location and subjects of power. "We cannot demonstrate scientifically that there is more or less freedom or coercion under any one of the three systems, capitalism, fascism, and communism, than there is under the other."[10] Planning, however, would emphasize social order rather than "individual or group self-expression." Toleration, however, would exist to the extent that such a policy was socially useful. There could be, of course, no place for a right of an individual or minority against the government, or against society. Utility rather than righteousness was the heart of fascist policy. Or to state the matter another way, righteousness was the standard established by the strong, which in fascist theory meant the government could do no wrong. Judged by political consequences, the government might act ineffectually but never wrongly. "It is a favorite and basic axiom of liberalism that might does not make right. It is a self-evident fact that under the liberal, as under every other, regime, might does make right and always has made

[10] *Ibid.*, p. 118.

right."[11] Since the victors made the rules, Dennis argued, it was impossible for justice to be otherwise.

As superior power was to be found in the hands of the elite controlling the fascist government, superior virtue was to be found there accordingly. All institutional checks upon the government would be abolished. Government officials would have permanent terms. As did Hobbes, Dennis argued that the absolute ruler would be most inclined to promote the public interest. "The art of insuring a desired standard of performance by public officials is to be found in making it their professional pride and self-interest under the system created so to perform—not in creating a system of checks, restraints, and interferences, the principal results of which will be irresponsibility in administration, frustration of efficient government, and the fostering of rackets, rather than protection of the weak or curbing of the mighty."[12]

Fascism, by exploiting the driving emotional force of patriotism, or nationalism, would achieve a social solidarity lacking in the individualistic ethic of liberalism. In its economic program, there would be state planning and control over the more vital areas of the economy. All economic institutions would be considered as means to the national ends, rather than as ends in themselves. The techniques of social control would be varied; most small private enterprises would be permitted to exist. "It is necessary only to nationalize large financial institutions and monopolistic industries, as well as all corporations whose services are indispensable but whose management has become completely divorced from ownership, and to discipline adequately all private enterprise."[13] Some amount of "free market" would be permitted to help establish economic values. Generally, private property would continue in private hands but again not as a right but as long as it was a convenient means to a socially desired national end.

The specific political arrangements of fascism were not made clear by Dennis. One political party would exist, but only one, for its function was primarily that of a channel of communication between the people and the government. When Dennis speaks of representation, he defines it as "the process through which the government is

11 *Ibid.*, p. 139.
12 *Ibid.*, p. 162.
13 *Ibid.*, pp. 175-176.

kept apprised of the popular will and through which government makes the popular will understand and will the means and ends of public administration."[14] Federalism, the separation of powers, and the rigid Constitution would of course be eliminated. Education would be rigidly controlled in order to make of the pupils "good citizens."

> In the fascist view of things, all institutional formation of character, mind, social attitudes, and opinions with a social purpose, must harmonize with, and not be antagonistic to, the larger purposes of the national plan. This means that fascism holds that no institution forming people's minds, characters, and attitudes should have among its purposes or effects the unfitting of people for good citizenship as the State defines good citizenship.[15]

There could be no academic freedom in the fascist state, for education served a crucial function of indoctrinating students with the correct political and social values. To leave this to chance would be even more disastrous to the state than to permit an equal amount of freedom in the economic sphere. It must be understood, of course, that Dennis's denial of objective truth in the realm of values led him to argue that values represented the advantageous claims of strong groups or interests. Conflicting values represented conflicting groups or interests. Thus in the realm of values or attitudes it was always a question of whose values and to what purpose. Or, as he posed the question:

> Who shall manipulate the opinions, feelings, and attitudes of the masses?—for manipulated they must and will be in a civilization as complex and highly organized as ours. Is it preferable to have mass opinions, feelings, and social attitudes manipulated by powerful private interests for personal or minority group ends, or to have mass opinions guided by a national State in the pursuit of some idealized plan of social well-being and order?[16]

It was thus a function of the elite in the fascist state to know clearly what they wanted as national ends; to accomplish these national ends; and to make the people feel these national ends were exactly what they really wanted. Through the manipulation of public opinion the will of the people thus coincided with the will of the elite

14 *Ibid.*, p. 197.
15 *Ibid.*, pp. 211-212.
16 *Ibid.*, pp. 213-214.

who ruled them. Since the masses wanted what they got, they got what they wanted and thus their will was satisfied; so they enjoyed perfect freedom. Through the accomplishment of the national will, fascism in effect forced people to be free.

The fascist concept of the elite assumed that there were in every society a few individuals who were distinguished from the rest of the people by their excessive will to power. Unlike the "natural aristocracy" line of thought, fascism did not attribute to the elite superior wisdom or virtue or any ethical qualification. The elite possessed superior power, or such an obvious will to power that their claims were recognized in society. Ethical standards in society simply reflected the decisions of the elite. All societies were in fact governed by minorities; in democratic societies the various elites gave the masses issues to vote on and manipulated public opinion so as to control the outcome. However, in democratic societies there were conflicting and competing elite groups which led to schisms in public opinion and irrational political behavior as power shifted from one minority group to another. Under fascism, it was argued, the perpetual character of the triumphant elite would eliminate the conflicts inherent in democratic government and give order and consistency to the policies that furthered the national interest.

This conception of the role of the elite, however, introduced some difficulties into fascist thought. First, it may be observed that if elites inevitably do rule, and if the social attitudes are what the elite in power have manipulated the public to accept and desire, how could Dennis and others come to a contrary political attitude? Second, if the pragmatic test of elitism is the possession of power, how could the fascists out of power lay claim to elitism? Obviously Dennis's objection to what he called liberalism was—given the assumption that elites always ruled—that the wrong elites were in power, and motivated by the wrong ethic, they were doing the wrong things. In other words, after having reduced political values to nothing more than the codes of the stronger, fascism failed to follow its own logic but challenged liberalism precisely on ethical grounds. Liberalism was bad, Dennis had argued, because there were so many unemployed, because the courts favored the rich, because America engaged in world wars, because the big corporations had their own way, because property was favored over humanity, and because political and economic power were irresponsible. To criticize the "is" as what ought not to be is completely contrary to the fascist logic that the victors make the rules and the people accept them as moral standards.

Fascists were inclined to refer all matters to the supposed standard of the national interest. Thus they criticized liberalism for neglecting the national interest or acting contrary to the national will. But since, by the logic of fascism, the national interest is what the rulers say it is, it would appear to be impossible for any ruler to neglect the national interest or oppose the national will. The fascist use of such terms as the national interest, the national will, and the responsibility of leadership is clearly a resort to a supposed ethical standard quite beyond the bounds of fascist thought. It is indeed a return to the normative approach of the eighteenth century which Dennis castigated liberalism for accepting. Fascism, Dennis wrote, "proposes a formula of national interest and national discipline under which power is exercised with responsibility to the State for the social consequences of its exercise and with a view to realizing the national plan."[17] To introduce the concept of responsibility in this fashion would seem to indicate that power does not necessarily set the standards of political conduct. That is, it introduces a reference point as to how power ought to be exercised.

"A powerful State guided by a capable elite loyal to some scheme of national interest is far more expressive of the popular will than a weak liberal State, because the powerful State can do more than a weak State to shape social events of importance, and also chiefly because the powerful State can make the people genuinely like or assent to what it does."[18] Beyond the elite, it would appear, there was a national interest which was not just what the elite declared it to be. There would seem, however, to be no special virtue in the elite's expression of the popular will which they created; thus fascism rejected the popular will as a normative factor even as it claimed for fascism the virtue of being that system which best expressed it. "The great contribution of fascism to mass welfare is that of providing a formula of national solidarity within the spiritual bonds and iron discipline of which the elite and the masses of any given nation, every one in the measure of his capacity, can operate for the common good."[19] The common good, like the national interest, is of course a normative proposition.

17 *Ibid.*, p. 234.
18 *Ibid.*, p. 241.
19 *Ibid.*, p. 252.

There being no institutional checks upon the elite, the only restraint upon their authority was their own sense of responsibility to the national interest. Fascism, in Dennis's theory, would introduce responsibility into elite leadership, in place of the irresponsible leadership which he charged against liberalism. Responsibility so used, however, reduces that term to sheer mysticism. Fascism rejects responsibility to the judgment of others not in power as being both impossible and undesirable. Responsibility is impossible because the elite always rule according to their own standards; it is undesirable because the masses are incompetent to rule. Responsibility to the national interest is therefore not responsibility to people but to an ideal, a value, as interpreted by the elite. Responsibility thus is a matter of the leader's loyalty to his own judgment; which is not political responsibility at all but the total rejection of it.

Fascism offered an elitist system based upon no clear principle of responsibility, and, in fact, no clear definition of the elite. Dennis's elite was a mystical notion which defied identification in practice as it did definition in theory. Rejecting liberalism, fascism looked to a golden age of inequality in the future in which the frustrations, insecurities, and materialistic ambitions of man would either be eliminated or checked in favor of a "higher order" of life. Social duties would be emphasized in place of private rights; and the rights of man would always be subordinate to the interest of the right man. Indeed, in the final sentence of his bitter *The Dynamics of War and Revolution* (1940), Dennis declared, "One will hear less about the rights of man and more about the duties of man and the rights of the American people."[20] In fascism, patriotism, nationalism, and Americanism were put to service in a mystical system in which authority was imposed from above and the masses were condemned to a political impotence commensurate with their alleged incompetence.

Fascism in America never achieved much in the way of a popular following. For a time, just before World War II, there was a motley assortment of racists, super-patriots, and isolationists who, under the label of America First, were ominously suggestive of a nascent fascist movement, but the movement died with the coming of the war.

The significance of Lawrence Dennis lay in the fact that he gave philosophical respectability to one of the major ideologies of the

[20] Lawrence Dennis, *The Dynamics of War and Revolution* (The Weekly Foreign Letter, 1940), p. 250.

decade. While other supporters of fascism in America were frequently rabble-rousers, eager to incite and inflame crowd grievances to no apparent end other than personal power, Dennis performed the less spectacular role of fascist theoretician. He thus gave substance to a line of argument more usually conveyed by shouted slogans. Should the course of world politics give rise to the spectre of fascism again, one may assume that in America the writings of Lawrence Dennis would be called again into service.

NORMAN THOMAS: SOCIALISM

For all of the efforts of the Socialist Party to enlarge the following of Karl Marx in America early in the twentieth century, the efforts proved largely unsuccessful. Eugene Debs attracted a large personal following, but this undoubtedly was as much in spite of his socialism as because of it. Deb's appeal no doubt lay as much in his old fashioned Populism as in his socialism; indeed there is no evidence that there was any great conversion of people to socialism for all of the limited popularity of Debs. Although Socialists had won over a few cities—Milwaukee, Pittsburgh, Reading—early in the twentieth century, there was no great intellectual or political following of socialism on a national basis. Faced with seemingly endless internal dispute and fractionalization, together with the declining health and prestige of Debs, the Socialist Party failed to run a presidential candidate in 1924, choosing instead to support the candidacy of Robert LaFollette on the Progressive ticket. Thus had the fortunes of socialism declined since the peak of membership and influence in 1912. By the time of Debs' death in 1926, many former socialists had left the party while others were writing of the passing of socialism in the United States.

Although socialism seemed dead in the prosperous Twenties, the depression of the Thirties temporarily revitalized the movement. The instrument of this brief revitalization was Norman Thomas (1884-). A perennial candidate for President on the Socialist ticket, like his predecessor Eugene Debs—(Thomas ran 6 times, Debs 5)—Thomas gave leadership to Socialist Party thought for over three decades. The son of a minister, Thomas also became a minister, but hardly before the religion of humanity had come into competition in his mind with more orthodox theology. Inspired by

Woodrow Wilson and Walter Rauschenbusch, the advocate of Christian Socialism, Thomas's early years in the ministry were spent largely in social work in New York. His experiences as a social worker, his keen sense of social injustice, and his complete abhorrence of cruelty and war brought him early in his career increasingly close to socialism. The militant anti-war stand of the Socialist Party in World War I completed Thomas's conversion, and in 1918 he formally became, and has since remained, a Socialist.

While Norman Thomas lacked the personal warmth and magnetism that had attracted so many people to Eugene Debs, if not precisely to socialism, Thomas nevertheless worked for the cause of socialism with evangelical enthusiasm strengthened by an almost Puritan sense of dedication and conviction. One feels, in Thomas's writings and speeches, the early ministerial training coming through, the sense of mission of a man exhorting his people to come forward out of darkness into the promised land of "plenty, peace and freedom." Dreadfully aware of the catastrophe of war, Thomas called for disarmament, pacifism, and internationalism and believed that socialism would more surely lead the world to peace than imperialistic capitalism. But this same abhorrence of war led him equally to reject the Marxian notion of a class war. The modern revolutionary, he counselled, should model himself on the example of Mr. Gandhi of India. "There are times," he wrote in 1932, echoing Thoreau, "when honest men must explain why they are not in jail, and when a willingness to endure without flinching is more effective than the will to fight. The final and most difficult revolution will not be in the ends men seek but in the means they use."[21]

Thomas attempted to give socialism in America a new program based upon a broad philosophy. He was more successful in the former endeavor than in the latter. For as a socialist he never advocated thorough-going socialization. Admiring Marx, he rejected much of Marxism; respecting the accomplishments of the Russian Revolution, he rejected the tyranny and brutality of Soviet communism; rejecting all dogma as stultifying to man's creativity and inventiveness, he was a socialist without a distinct philosophy of history or a clear-cut doctrine of social change. Eschewing, apparently, communism more firmly than capitalism, he was a pragmatic socialist, a liberal who was a little to the left of and in advance of

[21] Norman Thomas, *As I See It* (New York: The Macmillan Company, 1932), p. 60.

the New Deal. Indeed, numerous New Deal reforms, such as social security, unemployment insurance, collective bargaining, etc., were long advocated by Thomas before they were incorporated into law. But it was not the specific reform measures advocated by Thomas that made him significant, for those were days when the land was full of reformers of all persuasions. Rather, his significance lay in the direction he helped guide reform; the temper, attitude, or spirit of his program; and the class he appealed to in his speeches and writings.

To be sure, Thomas pushed for socialism, if by socialism is meant a large degree of state ownership of the major basic industries. However, he saw no easy panacea to social and economic problems in state or national ownership per se, and thus the extent of his socialism was inevitably displeasing to orthodox Marxist and other more doctrinaire socialists. Furthermore, though he indicated some degree of socialization of economic life as a major step toward reform, his tolerance and open-mindedness kept him from mere dogmatism, so that in the end his pragmatism was just as apparent as that of most pragmatic New Dealers. Finally, such appeal as he had lay mainly in the middle class, and he was no doubt a more familiar figure on college campuses than in the coal fields. A son of the middle class, he spoke the language of the middle class, and though his sympathies were with the underprivileged he quite rejected the prospect of a worker's rebellion. He remained indeed a socialist minister, who counselled his middle class parishioners on the need for a social and intellectual awakening that would bring in its wake a new degree of harmony, a better realization of the theological precept of universal brotherly love. Yet there is no doubt some truth in the observation of some of his critics that his moderation and urbanity probably converted more voters to the New Deal than to socialism. Thomas endeavored to employ Marx in the service of socialism without making socialism dependent upon Marx. Writing in *As I See It* (1932) in defense of his attitude toward Marxism and his degree of disagreement with it, Thomas gave due credit to Marx in the historical development of socialism. "The Marxian theory of crisis finds immense confirmation in the present depression," he observed, "and the Marxian prophecy of the destruction of capitalism, when its work was done, by the doom it carried within it, is being fulfilled before our eyes."[22] Yet even so, Thomas inquired,

[22] *Ibid.*, p. 16.

when the inevitable doom came would it be merely the result of economic laws as Marx expected or would it not rather be "due to the stupid and blind psychology of an acquisitive society and to its nationalistic follies"?

The economic interpretation of history Thomas held to be "the most useful single theory we have for historical interpretation and forecast. Yet again Thomas inquired how useful was it when one spoke in terms of scientific precision? "Still less can we make it, in these times of revolutionary change in science, psychology and philosophy, a satisfactory metaphysics."[23]

Marx's theory of the class struggle Thomas found to be extremely valid as a description of the inevitable conflict that exists among groups with different economic interests and especially between "an owning and a working class." The concept of the class struggle was also a valid ethical idea which might serve to unite workers all over the world. Furthermore, an understanding of the class struggle would perform a service in saving one "from merely Utopian appeals to a general goodwill and in driving us to a proper organization and education of the class on which we must depend." Yet having conceded this much to the concept of the class struggle Thomas still rejected it as absolute and infallible dogma with its logical culmination in class war. "The socialist ideal," he wrote, "as distinguished from the communist, is social salvation *without* catastrophe, and with a minimum of confusion and disorder."[24] Apparently Thomas drew a line between the class struggle as a philosophical conception and the class war as a political principle conducive to bloodshed and violence. The socialists, he counselled, ought not to compete with the communists on the question as to who had the greatest " 'revolutionary' devotion to class *war*," for in this question the communists, backed by Russia, were sure to win. "Practically the road of exclusive insistence on class war as the first and last commandment of Marx in our day and in our country will lead to communism, not to some militant new labor movement. It will lead to war and dictatorship; not to peace and a wiser democracy."[25]

Not only was a rigid belief in a class war offensive to Thomas, but equally repugnant was the prospect of alienating the middle class to whom he made his widest appeal. The Marxian division of society

23 *Ibid.*, p. 17.
24 *Ibid.*, p. 18.
25 *Ibid.*, pp. 21-22.

into workers and owners anticipated the eventual dissolution of the middle class; therefore, it followed, political effort should be devoted to awakening the political self-consciousness of the proletariat. In this conception the middle class, as a class, was not politically significant, except as it might be viewed as essentially hostile to the proletarian revolution, because of its bourgeois ideology. To a Marxist the middle class, while it existed, was the bourgeois enemy. But to Norman Thomas this was most certainly not the case.

Not vengeance on a middle class but absorption of it into a classless world of prosperous workers for the common good is our socialist hope. In trying times like these not only that part of the middle class which is struggling with increasing difficulty to maintain its precarious foothold, but those in its ranks still economically secure, may have more than an esthetic or ethical interest in the crusade for peace and economic security and freedom. Their help is not to be despised or needlessly alienated. The plain fact is that in the curious American scene to-day with its peculiarly backward labor organization, the socialist and working class movement gets a valuable degree of help, intellectual, moral and financial, from within the middle class. We shall not more speedily win the workers by rejecting that help.[26]

It is little wonder that among his supporters in various elections were included such diverse persons as John Dewey, Paul H. Douglas, C. Wright Mills, Franz Boas, Max Eastman, Dorothy Thompson, Max Lerner, Harry Emerson Fosdick, Reinhold Niebuhr, Stephen Wise, and Walter Reuther.[27]

Thomas's revisionism had so modified the Marxian analysis that socialism in America became not so much a blueprint for the reorganization of society as a broadly humanitarian way of life. Gone or emasculated were the Marxian concepts of surplus value, economic determinism, historical materialism, and class war; instead socialism came to symbolize a pragmatically planned society. The greatest achievement of Russia, Thomas observed, was that it "taught the lesson that has been implicit in the specialization and interdependence of the machine age—plan or perish."[28] No longer in our complex economy could we expect the good society to be the inevitable result of individualistic and uncoordinated effort pursued

[26] Quoted from Norman Thomas, *As I See It* (New York, 1932), p. 19, by permission of the publisher, The Macmillan Company.
[27] Murray Seidler, "The Social Theory of Norman Thomas," *The Southwestern Social Science Quarterly* (March, 1958), p. 361, fn.
[28] Norman Thomas, *op. cit.*, p. 86.

for private advantage. "Before society can plan for general use rather than for private profit," Thomas wrote, "it must own or at least control the vital economic enterprises for which it plans. All of which is a way of saying that socialism is the essential condition of planning even as planning is the essential tool of successful socialism."[29] Thus in 1931, before the advent of the New Deal, Norman Thomas was emphasizing the importance of economic planning as the pathway to the good society.

The inevitable association of planning with socialism raised certain fundamental questions in Thomas's mind which anticipated several of the more basic arguments against planning advanced by the critics of socialism. For example, to what extent, Thomas inquired, was planning compatible with political democracy? Furthermore, would planning on such a vast scale as would eliminate mass unemployment, also tend to eliminate freedom of choice for consumers? Was planning compatible with consumer freedom, "or must we all be rationed, fed, clothed, housed and entertained much as any army is fed, clothed, housed and entertained, with the inevitable corollary that we shall be assigned jobs much as soldiers are assigned jobs"[30]? Surely these were curious, if fundamental, questions to be raised by a dedicated socialist; yet one senses that Thomas's liberal humanitarianism was always a deeper belief system with him than his socialism. He hoped that planning could be made compatible with political democracy and a wide degree of consumer choice, but he saw no magic in planning that these high goals would necessarily be realized. Writing in 1951, he observed that while democratic socialism required public ownership of what he called the "commanding heights of the modern economic order," he saw no necessity nor desirability for a "monolithic type of ownership and control."[31] "There is a wholesome stimulus in competition, or emulation, and in diversity of functional apparatus," he noted. In effect what Thomas advocated was a mixed economy with public corporations, private ownership and a "large place for cooperatives" functioning to the best advantage of the common good. It was indeed a pragmatic approach to socialism.

As early as 1931 Thomas had written: "Socialism is not a com-

[29] *Ibid.,* p. 91.

[30] *Ibid.,* p. 92.

[31] Norman Thomas, *A Socialist's Faith* (New York: W. W. Norton and Company, 1951), p. 186.

pletely fixed and rigid scheme even of economic relations. . . . It must avoid if it is true to its mission abstractions about humanity, the working class, the masses, which make it forget men and women and children. It is not a nation or a class or a mass but individuals who know happiness or misery, freedom or bondage, hope or despair."[32] In a rapidly changing world, democratic socialism had to be experimental. "It must not degenerate into dogmatic creedalism."[33] Some twenty years later, in 1951, in his testament of faith Thomas reiterated this theme. If democratic socialism was to emerge victorious in the world, it "must unite the social actions of men of varying beliefs on the common denominator of a conviction that through cooperation men may win plenty, peace, and freedom. Inspired by this faith, socialism must be experimental rather than rigidly doctrinaire."[34]

For some two decades and in the six elections in which he was a candidate for President, from 1928 through 1948, Norman Thomas served as the spokesman for American democratic socialism. He was a champion of pacifism in an era of global strife, of plenty in a period of mass unemployment and economic depression, and of freedom when others had despaired for the future of democratic liberty in the face of the threat of dictatorships abroad. While it would be difficult if not impossible to know the influence of this gentle crusader upon the minds of his countrymen, it is certain that his influence was far greater than his voter support would indicate. For in turning socialism in America increasingly away from Marxism, and keeping it quite separate from Communism, he gave its goals a measure of middle-class respectability. And though his pragmatic program might not have been politically attainable under his own party's label, nevertheless his plea for peace, plenty, and freedom undoubtedly gave encouragement to those who sought these objectives under other terminology and political symbols. Socialism under Norman Thomas thus bolstered the cause of pragmatic liberalism.

As a footnote to a discussion of Norman Thomas, it might be added that in 1954, after President Eisenhower's State of the Union

[32] Norman Thomas, *America's Way Out* (New York: The Macmillan Company, 1931), p. 147.

[33] *Ibid.*, p. 150.

[34] Norman Thomas, *A Socialist's Faith* (New York: W. W. Norton and Company, 1951), p. 300.

message to Congress, Thomas observed: "After twenty years of Republican denunciation of the New Deal and Fair Deal, the first Republican President since Herbert Hoover accepts completely the duty of the federal government to act as and when necessary to prevent or check depression; to look after farm prices; to extend the scope of social security; to regulate labor relations equitably; and to accept a large measure of responsibility for public health and better housing."[35] Thus far had we accepted the concept of the "Welfare State." Yet unfortunately our public theory was woefully obsolete, so that we paraded before the world as the stronghold of capitalism, gaining little credit for our many achievements in socio-economic planning and control. Socialism had also experienced a transformation in practice. "Almost everywhere abroad, notably in Asia, American propaganda has convinced people that we hate socialism and are the capitalist country *par excellence*. Now both socialism and capitalism have rather different meanings and very different emotional overtones for Americans than for our foreign friends. The latter usually are persuaded that if our America is capitalist, then it must be imperialist, too."[36] Our failure to reconcile our theory and practice thus worked to the advantage of the Communists in the cold war as they equated our self-proclaimed capitalism with imperialism, and equated our self-proclaimed rejection of socialism in theory as a universal rejection of socialism in practice. In the light of the Communist threat, Thomas wrote, "the outstanding immediate issue is not socialism versus capitalism, both concepts being in a state of transformation, but democracy versus totalitarianism." It was the socialists' hope and belief that democracy would fulfill itself in socialism; totalitarianism, however, was the denial of the socialists' aspirations, for "it destroys liberty without bringing peace or material equality, much less abundance, to its slaves."[37]

PAUL SWEEZY: MARXIAN ECONOMICS

As protest movements, fascism, socialism, and communism found their most congenial environment in the economic dislocation of the

[35] Norman Thomas, "Our Welfare State and Our Political Parties," *Commentary* (Vol. XVII, No. 4, April, 1954).
[36] *Ibid.*
[37] *Ibid.*

1930's. The magnetic personality of Roosevelt, the substantive reforms of the New Deal, the threat to national security together with increasing prosperity under the preparedness program, rapidly brought about the demise of these competing "isms" as significant political alternatives in America. Fascism had never gained sufficient strength to maintain a national political organization. Socialism, under Norman Thomas, had moved from its early position of being in the vanguard of revolution to being more closely identified with the vanguard of liberalism, a more progressive New Deal. Communism's limited following of the "popular front" days barely survived the trauma of the Nazi-Soviet pact. Only the Socialists continued to run a candidate for President and in 1944 Thomas's pitiful showing amounted to only 80,000 votes.

While, politically, World War II and its cold-war aftermath marked the end of over a decade of radical movements in American politics, a few voices of radicalism continued nevertheless to be heard. Such a voice belonged to Paul Sweezy (1910-   ) who the noted Harvard economist, Seymour Harris, has described as "the leading Marxian in the United States."[38]

The teachings of Marx and Engels, in part or in toto, are not of course the peculiar preserve of their politically active disciples; they belong as do the writings of other nineteenth-century giants, such as Darwin and Freud, to all who seek to understand themselves and their environment. Thus, at the outset, one must make a distinction between intellectual Marxists and Communist Party Marxists. The discussion which follows is concerned only with the former category.

For many years various aspects of Marxian analysis have contributed greatly to the thinking of social scientists in Europe. Max Weber, Karl Mannheim, Roberto Michels, to mention but a few of the significant recent European social scientists who were influenced by the Marxian analysis, had in turn considerable impact on the structuring of social science in America. Indeed it would be hardly an exaggeration to state that modern social science is more heavily indebted to Marx than to any other precursory figure. Yet aside from highly political tracts and presentations, there has been in America relatively little literature, such as has existed in Europe, which has sympathetically and searchingly expounded Marxian political economy. It was to fill this gap that Paul Sweezy wrote

[38] Introduction by Seymour E. Harris to *Socialism* by Paul M. Sweezy (New York: McGraw-Hill Book Company, Inc., 1949), p. xii.

The Theory of Capitalist Development (1942), the book which soon established his reputation as a formidable expounder of Marxism. Sweezy, whose scholarly and philosophical attainments were matched to a remarkable degree by his facility of expression (a most unusual attribute among Marxian scholars), maintained that capitalism was doomed to collapse because of its own inherent contradictions, and would eventually be supplanted by socialism. It must be remembered that in 1942 American war production was reaching toward its extraordinary height, the depression was over, and most thinkers were anticipating a post-war resurgence of capitalism, liberally guided by Keynesian economics. Indeed the New Deal, it was argued, was Keynesian economics in action. The levers of taxation, public spending, and directed investment were thought by many to be the checks which would level off inflation or depression and breathe new vitality into capitalism. Sweezy could not accept this view. "The Keynesians tear the economic system out of its social context and treat it as though it were a machine to be sent to the repair shop there to be overhauled by an engineer state."[39] Such an overhaul was impossible, he argued, for the government was not an agent of the whole society, as was maintained in liberal thought, but rather was the government, or the state in a capitalist society, explicitly the "guarantor of capitalist property relations." The fundamental fault with Keynesian economics was thus not in its economics but in its politics. If it were possible to assume that the state in a capitalist society would act contrary to the interests of the capitalists, then one might give credence to the Keynesian formula. But throughout the history of capitalism, Sweezy argued, the state "has been unmistakably the instrument of capitalist class rule; its personnel—bureaucratic, executive, and legislative—has been drawn from strata of the population which accept the values and objectives of capitalism unquestioningly and as a matter of course."[40] The capitalist, motivated as he was by the urge to accumulate, would never accept voluntarily a program designed to diminish his capacity to accumulate. The fallacy of traditional liberal reform movements was that of necessity they stopped short of basic reform, for they were unable actually to change the system. In a capitalist society all strategic positions were held by capitalists; they had power and prestige,

[39] Paul M. Sweezy, *The Theory of Capitalist Development* (New York: Monthly Review Press, 1956), p. 349.
[40] *Ibid.*

they controlled the purse, the press, and the police. "Movements of reform are born into and grow up in a society dominated materially and ideologically by capital," in which in the final analysis principles were exchanged for votes.[41] As a result, "the outcome is not the reform of capitalism, but the bankruptcy of reform. This is neither an accident nor a sign of the immorality of human nature; it is a law of capitalist politics."[42]

If meaningful reform, Keynesian or otherwise, was impossible under capitalism because of the internal logic of the system, there was to the Marxist no need for despair, for the logic of the system ultimately caused its own collapse. To understand this logic however it was necessary to turn to the broader field of Marxian analysis. To the Marxist, Marx was not alone an economist, historian, philosopher, and political scientist. He combined all these eminent qualities into a single system to become above all else a social scientist. His rare combination of scholarship, observation, and insight led him not only to a comprehensive and synthetic understanding of much of the past, but also to the ability, by employing the proper tools of analysis, to foretell the future. Since the ultimate test of a science rests in its capacity to predict, Marx is viewed by his more dedicated intellectual disciples as a social scientist *par excellence*.[43]

In the Marxian analysis the relationship men have with each other is ultimately determined by the economic system they find themselves in. Every economic system has its concomitant social and political order. As throughout history the economic system, characterized essentially by the method of production, has changed, so has the social order existing within it. Slavery, feudalism, capitalism—each distinctive economic system has had a distinctive social order based upon it. Because of the structuring of society into classes, whether of masters and slaves, lords and serfs, or owners and workers, each social system is dependent upon the economic system which gives rise to it, and the vision, values or perspective of each social class is restricted by the role it has in the productive

[41] *Ibid.*, p. 352.

[42] *Ibid.*

[43] "Marxists hold that ever since the *Communist Manifesto* events have amply confirmed the diagnosis which it contains, and they believe that the history of the Socialist movement in the last hundred years provides innumerable proofs of the reliability of historical materialism as a guide to action." Paul M. Sweezy, *Socialism* (New York: McGraw-Hill Book Company, Inc., 1949), p. 123.

process. The record of history is the record of the struggle between classes. In the Marxian view the singular function of the state is, by holding a legal monopoly of force, to preserve the *status quo;* that is "to safeguard the existing economic and social order in the interest of the class or classes which dominate it and benefit from it."[44] Which is to say that every political system seeks the social order, the class relationships, that are derivative from its economic system, its system of production. Economics, seen in its dynamic historical setting, was thus the key to political understanding, and it was in these terms that Sweezy articulated the Marxian view that capitalism would dig its own grave.[45]

Capitalism, seen as a system of production, was marked by two major classes: capitalists, who owned the instruments of production, and workers who owned only their own labor which they sold to the capitalist in accordance with the market demand for wages. The capitalist sought not merely to consume but to accumulate wealth, with its social by-products of power and prestige. The laborer, limited by his wages, was merely able in varying degrees to consume. At the outset this provides to the Marxist a basic contradiction in capitalism for it is viewed as a production system which at the same time as it produces restricts consumption. This paradox is explained under the concept of surplus value.

In Marxian economics, the value of a product is equal to the amount of labor that goes into its production. In a general sense all commodities possess a value which is equivalent to the amount of labor required to produce them—or to put the matter in another way, to reproduce them. Labor is thus (as also in classical economics) the source of all value. An equal exchange of goods is thus an exchange of equal labor components. But, labor is also a commodity which is bought and sold. To use Sweezy's words: "If we now apply the labor theory of value to the value of the laborer, we see that the quantity of labor required to produce the laborer is but another way of saying the quantity of labor required to produce the laborer's means of subsistence. Thus, finally, we conclude that the value of the special commodity, labor power, can be reduced to the value of

[44] *Ibid.,* p. 127.

[45] Note the similarity between the *Communist Manifesto's* pronouncement: "What the bourgeoisie therefore produces, above all, are its own gravediggers. Its fall and the victory of the proletariat are equally inevitable," and the interpretation by Khrushchev before the National Press Club of his phrase "We will bury you." (See *New York Times,* Sept. 17, 1959, p. 18.)

a certain number of ordinary commodities."[46] All of which was to say that labor was paid in wages which were at merely a subsistence level of living.

It would be pointless however for the capitalist, bent upon accumulation, to receive from the worker only that amount of labor necessary to sustain him, for no accumulation on the part of the capitalist would be possible. Thus the capitalist, while paying the worker only that amount in wages necessary to his subsistence, received from the worker labor beyond this amount. This additional increment of labor Marx called "surplus labor"; it created what Marx called surplus value. It was indeed this surplus value which made possible the accumulation of the capitalist.

The increasing use of modern technology which the capitalist may employ to his advantage reduces his dependence on human labor, adding to unemployment. In the Marxian analysis the presence of an "industrial reserve army" (unemployed workers) serves as a check on a rise in wages, while a reduction in capitalist accumulation would bring about a reduction in employment, that is a depression. A depression would tend to concentrate wealth in the hands of the strongest accumulators. Thus it was expected that as capitalism developed the number of accumulators (capitalists) would diminish due to the concentration of wealth into the hands of the few, while the ability of the worker to consume would diminish, thus increasing the misery of the many. Theoretically therefore this basic contradiction in capitalism would cause its collapse.

The fact that capitalism, even in industrially advanced nations, did not collapse was explained by Marxists in accordance with Lenin's view of imperialism. Imperialism, it was argued, by opening new markets for exploitation and stimulating the semblance of national unity, bought time for capitalism by turning temporarily the scope of the conflict from an internal to an international one. Yet this does not solve the contradictions of capitalism, for according to Sweezy, "In the period of imperialism all the national and international contradictions of capitalism plunge toward the one supreme contradiction—that war and preparation for war become the only purposes capable of sustaining the system: that death becomes the only possible means of life. It is this condition which marks imperialism as the final stage of capitalism."[47]

[46] Paul M. Sweezy, *Socialism* (New York: McGraw-Hill Book Company, Inc., 1949), pp. 141-142.
[47] *Ibid.*, p. 153.

If America had been guilty of imperialism in the past, some argued, this past had been not only renounced but even somewhat atoned for with the inauguration of the Point Four program of aid to underdeveloped areas. Paul Sweezy, however, would not accept this position. "The relations now existing between the United States and backward countries are typically imperialist," he wrote in 1953.[48] "Point Four, to the extent that it succeeds, will extend and intensify, not alter, these relations." To support his position, Sweezy quoted from President Truman's message to Congress of June 24, 1949, in which Truman had declared that a purpose of Point Four was "to create conditions in which capital investment can be fruitful," and further that "private sources of funds must be encouraged to provide a major part of the capital required."[49] The object of Point Four, Sweezy noted, "is pretty clearly the encouragement and protection of American foreign investment, not the balanced development of backward countries." Why, Sweezy inquired, should the overseas investments of the present be any more successful in promoting the balanced development of backward countries than the investments of the past when they fell into the hands of "corrupt and reactionary regimes"? "And has the United States or any of the other imperialist countries ever done anything to help the backward countries get rid of regimes of this kind?"[50] The international role of capitalism in the age of imperialism thus sought to maintain abroad in the colonial areas as it sought to maintain at home the existing power structure. Only a thoroughgoing socialism of the variety sponsored by Russia offered to the masses, whether in backward areas or advanced capitalistic countries, a meaningful alternative to capital-ism, for only by uprooting the economic system could one alter the political system so as to put genuine political control into the hands of the workers. In Sweezy's view this was as desirable as it was inevitable. Capitalism survived today, he argued, only because of its vast preparedness program which absorbed so much of the national budget and sustained an atmosphere of uncritical patriotism discouraging protest and dissent. Modern capitalism thus led inev-itably to Armageddon. "According to the Marxian view," Sweezy wrote, "the alternatives before mankind are not socialism or capital-

[48] Paul M. Sweezy, *The Present as History* (New York: Monthly Review Press, 1953), p. 92.

[49] *Ibid.*, pp. 89-90.

[50] *Ibid.*, p. 91.

ism, but socialism now or socialism later—when even greater devastation and bloodshed have finally driven home the lesson that capitalism has completed its historic function of building up man's productive forces and lingers on only to destroy its own achievements."[51]

Thus did Paul Sweezy articulate Marxism and prophesy the collapse of capitalism in the days of the cold war. There has been such a vast amount of literature critical of the Marxian position (speaking of it as a theoretical system rather than as a political movement) that it is unnecessary here to repeat these criticisms. It would seem sufficient to observe that, generally, as a social science system it has proved inadequate to predict political behavior. For all the fruitfulness of such concepts as economic determinism, ideology, and class conflict, the precise uses of these concepts and their degree of applicability remain a century later, subjects of academic dispute. For all of Marx's insights into economic behavior it is usually argued that the labor theory of value, formulated by Locke and accepted by the classical economists, was a frail reed to serve Marx as a major prop in his economic system and has been in the view of orthodox economists discredited for a century. For all of Marx's suggestiveness in his analysis of history, his limited system of causality led him to conclusions which have not been verified by history, at least not in terms of his system. The type of socialism advocated by Marx has simply not come about by revolution where it was predicted (in the most advanced capitalistic countries) but rather in those countries more clearly identified with feudalism than capitalism. In capitalistic countries the workers have not become poorer and more numerous nor has the middle class diminished in size but rather the converse has taken place. Nor has the abolition of capitalism achieved the elimination of the class problem in society.[52] Yet in spite of these criticisms no thoughtful student can dismiss the vitality of Marx in the modern world nor fail to observe how exceedingly inaccurate in their economic predictions were the capitalistic critics of the Soviet system. For all the critics' predictions of economic collapse and mass discontent, Soviet Russia astonished the world in World War II with its capacity to produce military might and the loyalty

[51] Paul M. Sweezy, *Socialism* (New York: McGraw-Hill Book Company, Inc., 1949), p. 153.
[52] See Milovan Djilas, *The New Class* (New York: Praeger, Inc., 1957).

of its armed forces. If, as Sweezy observed, "It is the Soviet Union's military success in the war against Germany which more than anything else has convinced the world that socialism really works,"[53] its spectacular scientific achievements following the war were no less a convincing demonstration that the organization of knowledge, goods, and services was not the singular monopoly of capitalistic societies. Clearly the appeal of Marxism in the less-developed areas of the modern world was not the result of the activities of the various Communist parties alone but stemmed from a basic discontent, which Communism has been able to channel to its advantage.

In 1942 when Sweezy wrote *The Theory of Capitalist Development* he predicted the decline of world capitalism and the rise, side by side with imperialism, of socialism. Rather than socialism being only an "island in an ocean of imperialism," he believed that imperialism would fall back in the face of a rising tide of socialism. He predicted that capitalism would collapse in Europe after the war and that Europe and Asia would both turn to socialism. "The United States would therefore become the center of a much shrunken imperialist system which, according to our assumptions, would include Britain, the dominions, and probably Latin America and parts of Africa."[54] "The question now arises whether the world socialist system based on Europe and Russia and the world imperialist system based on North America would inevitably clash in a struggle for supremacy."[55] Sweezy, while accepting the possibility of an open clash between the opposing power systems, felt that it was not a certainty. The successes of socialism would be so compellingly attractive and the decline of capitalism so certain that there might be a peaceful transition, even in the citadels of capitalism, to socialism. Sweezy concluded his prophecy of 1942 with the observation that "the great majority of readers will no doubt feel that our analysis is far-fetched and unreal, to use no stronger terms. . . . But the issue need not be debated here; we gladly leave it to the future to decide."[56] One might only add that the cold war is evidence that history is in the process of making a decision.

[53] Paul M. Sweezy, *Socialism* (New York: McGraw-Hill Book Company, Inc., 1949), p. 29.

[54] Paul Sweezy, *The Theory of Capitalist Development* (New York: Monthly Review Press, 1956), p. 360.

[55] *Ibid.*

[56] *Ibid.*, p. 363.

THE POLITICS OF AMERICAN MARXISM

American interpreters of Marx clearly disagreed on the crucial political question as to whether Marx sought to fulfill democracy or to destroy it. It was, for instance, never entirely clear whether the classless society might come about peacefully through the use of ballots or whether the revolution would have to be one of force and violence. For if capitalistic-democracy contained the seeds of its own destruction then a transition in ideologies—given a materialistic interpretation of history—would follow in the course of capitalistic decadence and a majority of voters would choose the new order. On the other hand, if the prevailing ideology could only be that advanced by the owners of the instruments of production, and if the class struggle would inevitably increase in severity, then nothing short of armed mass uprising could effect the change in social orders. In America, both the Socialist Party and Socialist Labor Party tended to the former view that the revolution might be peaceably accomplished through the democratic use of the ballot while the Communist Party assumed the inevitability of violence.

A further difficulty in interpreting Marx centered around the political aspects of the new society once the revolution had taken place. Marx spoke of a transitional period, following the revolution, in which there would have to be a "dictatorship of the proletariat" prior to the "withering away of the state." Was the dictatorship of the proletariat a fulfilling of democracy or its antithesis? Was a stateless society democratic? Or did democracy demand such a politically ordered behavior that it could not exist without the institutional framework provided by the state? In America the Socialist Party consistently revised Marx to the point where the stateless society became merely a theoretical flight of fancy, unimaginable in the forseeable future, while the dictatorship of the proletariat was interpreted in such a way as to constitute the fulfillment of democracy. The Socialist Labor Party, however, accepted the end of the stateless society—society to be managed by the Industrial Union—but rejected the notion of the dictatorship of the proletariat. Political activity would presumably cease with the accomplishment of the revolution.

On one point however the followers of Marx in America were in complete agreement: in a capitalistic society, democracy was either incomplete at best, or an outright sham at worst. Indeed the inescapable conclusion of Marxian logic was that democracy was impossible under capitalism; to an orthodox Marxist, American democracy was in reality the dictatorship of the bourgeois. Wherever Marxism was fully accepted, with its assumptions of economic determinism, the class struggle, and political ideology as a rationalization of dominant class interest, democracy was rejected as impossible in a capitalistic state. Thus, before democracy was possible, capitalism would have to be destroyed; yet before capitalism could be destroyed there would first have to be a class war culminating in the victory of the proletariat. American Socialists, however, shied away from this logical dilemma through modifying Marxism. Economic determinism was found to be more suggestive than absolute as a guiding principal of political behavior; the class war was found not to be as bitter and intense as Marx had believed; indeed class collaboration or cooperation on many issues was found to be both normal and desirable; furthermore, it was argued, democracy did exist under capitalism and was preferable to any form of dictatorship. The successive platforms of the Socialist Party, together with the writings of the Socialist presidential candidate Norman Thomas, reveal the revision of Marx in America to keep it within the framework of democratic conceptions.

The Communist Party program, however, brought Marx to America revised by Lenin rather than by American conditions or American theoreticians. The association of the American Communist Party with the Third International gave to the American Communist movement an immediate identification with Bolshevik policies as such were stated by Lenin, and later, Stalin. Communism in America thus became merely an outpost of the Soviet Communist Party and thus limited, it offered little in the way of American political theory. What was offered by the Communist Party prior to the change in "front" of the Comintern in the mid-nineteen thirties, was distinctively in the class of anti-democratic thought. For the Communists maintained that the revolution could not be accomplished peacefully through democratic methods; the dictatorship of the proletariat would in fact have to be a dictatorship; and the proletariat would have to be led by an elite group who were the leaders of the Communist Party, which was in turn a body with restricted membership. Like all elitist systems of thought, Communism rejected the competency of the masses to make valid political judgments. Only the elite in the party could cut through the obfuscations of bourgeois ideology to grasp the truth of scientific materialism. Only the elite were competent to guide; the masses could only add disciplined force and weight to the decisions of the elite.

At its first convention, in 1919, the Communist Party laid down the following program:

> The Communist party shall keep in the foreground its consistent appeal for proletarian revolution, the overthrow of capitalism, and the establishment of a dictatorship of the proletariat. . . . Participation in parliamentary campaigns, which, in the general struggle of the proletariat, is of secondary importance, is for the purpose of revolutionary propaganda only. Parliamentary representatives of the Communist party shall not introduce or support reform measures. Parliaments and political democracy shall be utilized to assist in organizing the working class against capitalism, and the state parliamentary representatives shall consistently expose the oppressive class character of the capitalist state, using the legislative forum to interpret and emphasize the class struggle; they shall make clear how parliamentarism and parliamentary democracy deceive the workers. . . . The uncompromising character of the class struggle must be maintained under all circumstances.[57]

Communism in the United States was less concerned with the perfecting of existing democracy than the annihilating of capitalism. Thus it had no use for ameliorative legislation, or political cooperation with the bourgeois state, which might prolong the life of capitalism. The democratic methods of persuasion, compromise and gradual reform, which the Socialists adopted, were rejected by the Communists. William Z. Foster, perennial Communist presidential candidate, declared that "in all its parliamentary activities the communist party makes it clear to the workers that the capitalist democracy is a sham and that there must be no illusions about peacefully capturing the state for the working class."[58] A doctrine known as "American exceptionalism" was developed in the late Twenties by Jay Lovestone and Benjamin Gitlow, which, contrary to Foster's position, held that capitalism developed unevenly and that the tenets of Lenin were not fully applicable in America. For such right-wing

[57] *The American Labor Year Book, 1919-1920* (New York: Rand School of Social Science), p. 418. By permission.

[58] William Z. Foster, *Toward Soviet America* (New York: Coward-McCann, Inc., 1932), p. 255.

deviation, however, these leaders were expelled from the Communist Party.

Following the rise of Hitler and Mussolini, the Comintern shifted its policies, and the shift was reflected in the policies of the Communist Party, U.S.A. The growth of fascism and Nazism now called for a "united front" against these new political menaces. For a few years, prior to the German-Russian non-aggression pact of 1939, Communists advocated cooperation with progressives and Socialists and a program of economic amelioration within the framework of bourgeois democracy. With the signing of the non-aggression pact, the Nazi invasion of Russia in 1941, and the defeat of the Axis powers in 1945, the radical shifts in the Communist Party line departed from even the slightest suggestion of political theory. From the invasion of Russia by Germany in 1941 until the end of the war in 1945, during most of which period America and Russia were allies, American Communists favored cooperation with the bourgeois government to win the war. With the defeat of the Axis however the Party line returned to the Marx-Lenin-Stalin formula and Earl Browder, who had led the Communist collaboration with the bourgeoisie in America, was expelled from the Communist Party. Clearly now Communist parties in America and elsewhere sought as their major objective the triumph of the Russian nation and its satellites.[59]

While the early years of the Communist party in the United States manifested its fundamentally anti-democratic nature, and placed its pronouncements within the category of authoritarian thought, it based its major appeals on the grounds of humanitarianism when not relying simply on Marxist-Leninist theory. It sought to appeal broadly to the masses. However, it advocated a dictatorial system, even though the dictatorship claimed to be one of and for the proletariat. It is ironical, though nevertheless a tribute to the vitality of the democratic ideology, that the accomplishment of Communist dictatorships in several countries following World War II should find the label "dictatorship of the proletariat" rejected in favor of the label "People's Democracy." The Marxian interpretation of history denies the absoluteness or eternal validity of the democratic ideology as a norm, for democracy must be considered in its historical relationship to the demise of feudalism and the rise of capital-

[59] Irving Howe and Lewis Coser, *The American Communist Party* (Boston: Beacon Press, 1957) state: "For all intents and purposes, as these lines are being written in late 1957, the American Communist Party is dead" (p. 498).

ism. Since political institutions are, according to Marx, particular manifestations of contemporary economic arrangements, it would appear that of necessity the political ideology of a people would change with their change of economic systems. The continued use of the term "democracy" by the Communists would indicate that to them the term possessed a value as an ideology independent of the economic system in which it claimed to be applicable. That the phrase "dictatorship of the Communist Party elite," even though accurately descriptive, was not successfully employed as a slogan to move the masses is some indication that even where dictatorship exists in fact its appeal as an ideology is slight beside the ideological appeal of the term "democracy."

CHAPTER 19

Conservatism

"EVERY WAR BRINGS after it a period of materialism and conservatism; people tire quickly of ideals and we are now repeating history."[1] Thus had Franklin D. Roosevelt characterized the immediate era after World War I. The characterization might have applied with equal weight to the era which succeeded World War II, particularly the decade of the Fifties. Here and there the goals of pragmatic liberalism continued to be achieved: the G.I. Bill, the Employment Act of 1946, the Vinson and Warren Supreme Court's decisions in the field of civil rights. An age, however, which saw the Supreme Court as the greatest champion of liberalism might truly be called a conservative age.

This new age possessed an atmosphere startlingly different from that of the Thirties. It was as though the political and intellectual heterogeneity of the previous era had been pressed by the weight of war and the subsequent international tensions into a single mold that now passed for the American culture. Our Russian ally of World War II became our awesome enemy in the cold war; former enemies, Italy, Germany, and Japan became our new allies in the new international alignment that formed soon after the mushroom-shaped cloud of Hiroshima had blown away. At home old friends became new enemies, old enemies new friends as Americans searched for security in an increasingly anxious world. The loyalty oaths of the era and the security checks, down to the lowest level of public employment, were at once cause and effect of the search for security. Probably not since Pearl Harbor had Americans been as shaken as they were by the disclosures of Whittaker Chambers against Alger Hiss. Like the famous nineteenth-century French *affaire* Dreyfus, it left its scar on the political scene. And certainly few television programs had the terrifying hypnotic appeal that the

[1] Franklin D. Roosevelt as quoted in Arthur M. Schlesinger, Jr., *The Crisis of the Old Order* (Boston: Houghton Mifflin Company, 1957), p. 366.

Army-McCarthy hearings had before a dismayed national audience. Now, invidious terms came into the political vocabulary as normally well-meaning individuals released their fears and tensions with such epithets as "Fifth Amendment Communists," and "McCarthyite." In the anxious days of the depression it had generally been thought that there were few major problems which economic well-being could not solve; now in the prosperous post-war era the inadequacy of economic solutions alone was readily apparent. Indeed purely economic issues themselves receded into the background as the paramount issue of survival in an increasingly hostile world in the age of the hydrogen bomb, inter-continental missiles, and nuclear radiation became of the most immediate and pressing importance. No longer were domestic issues of domestic importance alone, for Americans became aware that as a great power seeking the political support of people throughout the world their behavior was subject to the examination of a larger public. Achievements and failures were questioned at home in the light of a hypothetical world opinion. What was the effect of the Supreme Court's decision on desegregation in public schools on world opinion? Or, subsequently, of the incidents at Little Rock? Or the achievements of the Salk vaccine? Or the comparative failure, compared to Russia, in the conquest of space? Such considerations were certainly symptoms of a heightened degree of tension in an insecure society.

The search for peace and security which so characterized international politics mirrored, albeit grotesquely, the insistent personal dilemmas of the post-war period. The unprecedented popularity of such works as Norman Vincent Peale's best-selling *The Power of Positive Thinking* (1952), or Joshua Liebman's *Peace of Mind* (1946), or Fulton J. Sheen's *Peace of Soul* (1949) was evidence of an extraordinary demand for individual security. For many, though the cold war and fear engulfed the world, there was still the promise of peace and security for the individual within the tenets of his faith. Whether the revival of religion in America was caused by the cold war, domestic prosperity, or the tendency toward conformity, or none of these factors, was a matter of debate; but it was generally agreed that religious ties were strengthening and that this was related to an inward need for peace.

It had been a point of Marx's criticism of capitalistic culture that under it a man experienced a sense of "alienation," a sense of purposelessness, a loss of the sense of belonging. The critical literature of the post-war period seemed to indicate that Marx's prediction in this matter had come true and that man indeed had become lost in the complex world of his own making. Erich Fromm in his popular and suggestive *Escape From Freedom* (1941) seemed indeed to confirm Marx. The much vaunted freedom of Western society did not inevitably lead to the peace and security of the individual, as had been tacitly hypothesized in liberal thought, but frequently led to a terrifying sense of helplessness and inadequacy from which there was no escape other than a firm reliance on authority. Freedom was not only a goal but a challenge and many indeed were unable to meet it. Thus, bringing his knowledge of psychology to bear on his cultural analysis, Fromm found that man turned outside of himself for guidance and direction as he found his ego inadequate to cope with the multitudinous and multifarious problems with which he lived. He literally sought escape from freedom either into the arms of a dictator, as in Hitler's Germany, or into the middle-class conformity that characterized so much of Western democratic culture. Of what value is freedom, Fromm inquired, to the man who looks outside of himself to find what he should like and dislike, how he should behave, what he should do—who has in effect transferred all his crucial decisions to others so that in the final analysis he has to look elsewhere to find out who he is. Fromm continued this theme some years later in *The Sane Society* (1955). In modern society man had become a prisoner of the institutions he had created to free him. He had lost his sense of direction. The worker expended his daily efforts in creating a piece of a product he might never see, to be sold to a customer he would never know. Where was the ego satisfaction in a daily impersonal routine in which creativity was stifled under a cultural blanket of standardization and personal effort produced monotonously for an impersonal market? Modern man exhausts himself in endless occupation, his creativity cast into a mold, his accomplishments lost in an endless chain of anonymous products. Little wonder that his so-called freedom proves frequently unbearable; nor little wonder that man becomes as standardized as his products, merely a digit in a numerical mass, a willing victim of mass manipulators; and, indeed, little wonder that even the normal man must struggle for sanity in such a situation.

Fromm's psychological analysis of modern society was indirectly bolstered by the work of an obscure west coast longshoreman whose insightful epigrammatic prose was frequently quoted in academic circles. In *The True Believer* (1951), Eric Hoffer observed that mass movements were the refuge of frustrated individuals. "Faith in a holy cause is to a considerable extent a substitute for the lost faith in ourselves," Hoffer noted. "The less justified a man is in claiming excellence for his own self, the more ready is he to claim all excellence for his nation, his religion, his race or his holy cause.[2]

An abject conformity, it appeared, might well be the symptom of the sick society. Yet the critical literature of the post-war period seemed to point to an extraordinary degree of conformity in all phases of American life. David Riesman commented on it in his highly suggestive study of the American character, *The Lonely Crowd* (1950). The "inner-directed" American of the past had given way to a conforming "other-directed" type. In his plea for a revival of individuality Riesman wrote, "If the other-directed people should discover how much needless work they do, discover that their own thoughts and their own lives are quite as interesting as other people's, that, indeed, they no more assuage their loneliness in a crowd of peers than one can assuage one's thirst by drinking sea water, then we might expect them to become more attentive to their own feelings and aspirations."[3] At the time that statement was made, Riesman admitted that such a possibility seemed remote. But he concluded, "The idea that men are created free and equal is both true and misleading: men are created different; they lose their social freedom and their individual autonomy in seeking to become like each other."[4]

The passing of the individualistic ethic into a "social ethic" was also pointed up by William H. Whyte, Jr. in his popular study *The Organization Man* (1956). "By social ethic," Whyte wrote, "I mean that contemporary body of thought which makes morally legitimate the pressures of society against the individual."[5] Whyte found the new social ethic to contain three propositions: "a belief in the group as the source of creativity; a belief in 'belongingness' as the ultimate need of the individual; and a belief in the application of science to

[2] Eric Hoffer, *The True Believer* (New York: Harper & Brothers, 1951), p. 14.

[3] David Riesman, with Nathan Glazer and Reuel Denney, *The Lonely Crowd* (New York: Doubleday & Company, 1953), p. 349.

[4] *Ibid.*

[5] William H. Whyte, Jr., *The Organization Man* (New York: Doubleday & Company, 1956), p. 7.

achieve the belongingness."[6] It was not the mere fact of conformity which concerned Whyte but the underlying scale of values which legitimatized it. The organization man "is not only other-directed, to borrow David Riesman's concept, he is articulating a philosophy which tells him it is right to be that way."[7] In his attack upon the social ethic Whyte observed: "It is hard enough to learn to live with our inadequacies, and we need not make ourselves more miserable by a spurious ideal of middle-class adjustment. Adjustment to what? Nobody really knows—and the tragedy is that they don't realize that the so-confident-seeming other people don't know either."[8]

It was against this background of international tension, domestic prosperity and individual anxiety and discontent that the call for a return to the principles of conservatism was sounded. Coinciding as it did with the electoral victories of President Eisenhower, who called himself a conservative, the decade of the Fifties may be called the era of modern conservatism. Indeed it was presaged in 1949 by the publication of Peter Viereck's historico-philosophical recapitulation of the Metternich era entitled *Conservatism Revisited*. Viereck, writing soon after the start of the cold war, caught with prophetic insight the coming political temper of the West. "What justifies the western union and gives it moral cohesion is the common desire to conserve a common heritage: our free institutions," Viereck stated in his foreword. It was this motif that characterized the new conservative temper and made it in fact so awkward to define. For much that proved to be part of modern conservatism was the liberalism of the recent past; while other parts, the more controversial aspects, reached further back into an era that only echoed indistinctly with memory. Viereck, however, clearly caught the temper of American thought. Americans of necessity had finally rejected isolation as a political principle of international relations and had in part returned to the home of their fathers, and in part invited their fathers into a new enterprise called collectively the West. Conservatism, Viereck noted, for all its impressive heritage was not a popular doctrine in America. In fact few political candidates chose to style themselves as "conservative," for, unfortunately, too often conservatism had become associated with the preservation of the economic privileges of the few rather than with the larger and more bona fide problem

[6] *Ibid.*
[7] *Ibid.*, p. 439.
[8] *Ibid.*, p. 441.

of conserving "the humane and ethical values of the West." Clearly, Viereck's paramount concern was the preservation of the values of the West in a world threatened by the Soviet Union. Likening the modern era to the post-Napoleonic period in which Metternich's ambitious Concert of Europe foreshadowed the modern western alliance, he saw the need for giving to the West a sounder philosophical base for unity than had existed in the Metternich era. In doing so however he was led inevitably into consideration of the distinction between "liberals" and "conservatives." "Most liberals are not the fellow travelers of Joseph Stalin; most conservatives are not clamoring for a man on horseback," he observed with his characteristic urbanity and toleration.

> Frequently the real difference between liberal and conservative is in their reaction to such problems as: tempo of social change; need for tradition; confidence in modern technics; faith in the masses and in the natural goodness of man; feasibility of changing human nature; importance of utilitarian motives (economics vs. 'ideas' in history); risk of extending full democratic privileges even to those engaged in forcibly destroying democracy; conflict between liberty and a leveling equality; absoluteness or relativeness of existing restraints and standards.[9]

In the decade of debate which followed, these distinctions were severally reconsidered, but the reconsiderations only appeared to confirm the accuracy of Viereck's delineation. The conservatism of Viereck was a warm and ennobling doctrine which could hardly give offense to even the most dogmatic liberals. "The core and fire-center of conservatism, its emotional élan, is a humanist reverence for the dignity of the individual soul," he noted.[10]

> The conservative principles *par excellence* are proportion and measure; self-expression through self restraint; preservation through reform; humanism and classical balance; a fruitful nostalgia for the permanent beneath the flux; and a fruitful obsession for unbroken historic continuity. These principles together create freedom, a freedom built not on the quicksand of adolescent defiance but on the bedrock of ethics and law.[11]

A professor of history as well as a poet, Peter Viereck sought to

---

[9] Peter Viereck, *Conservatism Revisited* (New York: Charles Scribner's Sons, 1949), p. xiv. By permission.

[10] *Ibid.*, p. 6.

[11] *Ibid.*

conserve the humane values of the West as these had evolved through history. Human freedom was not the antithesis of order, but dependent on order for its realization. The modern world, threatened as it was by a "totalitarian mass-man," whether of the Hitler or Stalin variety, urgently needed to reconsider its scheme of values and to espouse fervently those values which had made possible the progress of the past. The lessons from the era of Metternich—though of course not all his politics—were applicable therefore to the problems of today as once again man waged his ceaseless combat to preserve freedom. "Upon the United States of America," Viereck concluded, "upon the heirs of the American Conservation of 1776, falls the task of conserving the western heritage today."[12]

The increasingly conservative temper of the post-war era gained momentum in the early years of the Fifties. In 1950 *Life* magazine editorialized on "The Conservative Revival";[13] in 1951 Francis Wilson wrote *The Case for Conservatism;*[14] in 1953 Russell Kirk wrote *The Conservative Mind*[15] and Peter Viereck *The Shame and Glory of the Intellectuals;*[16] in 1954 Clinton Rossiter won the Charles A. Beard Memorial Prize for his *Conservatism in America.*[17] The above books, written by academicians, were but a typical sample of the vast literature in academic journals debating and defining the nature of the "new conservatism" which it was generally agreed permeated the political atmosphere.[18]

The scope of modern conservatism was so broad that most of its adherents found difficulty in defining it, or even in reducing it to

[12] *Ibid.*, p. 135. In a later work, *The Shame and Glory of the Intellectuals* (Boston: The Beacon Press, 1953), Viereck reiterated the theme that genuine freedom can only exist in an orderly setting. The truly free man was he whose life was guided by an "ethical inner check," the heritage of classical philosophy and religion, rather than being dependent upon the coercive restraints of society.

[13] "The Conservative Revival," *Life* (May 15, 1950), p. 38.

[14] Francis G. Wilson, *The Case for Conservatism* (Seattle: University of Washington Press, 1951).

[15] Russell Kirk, *The Conservative Mind* (Chicago: Henry Regnery Company, 1953).

[16] Peter Viereck, *The Shame and Glory of the Intellectuals* (Boston: The Beacon Press, 1953).

[17] Clinton Rossiter, *Conservatism in America* (New York: Alfred A. Knopf, 1955). See also Gordon Harrison, *Road to the Right, The Tradition and Hope of American Conservatism* (New York: William Morrow and Company, 1954).

[18] Of particular merit is Daniel Bell and others, *The New American Right* (New York: Criterion Books, 1955).

its most basic propositions. Kirk, however, did try to reduce the principles of conservatism to six major canons which may serve here as something of a guide to the conservative approach.

1. Belief that a divine intent rules society as well as conscience, forging an eternal chain of right and duty which links great and obscure, living and dead. Political problems, at bottom, are religious and moral problems.

2. Affection for the proliferating variety and mystery of traditional life, as distinguished from the narrowing uniformity and equalitarianism and utilitarian aims of most radical systems.

3. Conviction that civilized society requires orders and classes. The only true equality is moral equality.

4. Persuasion that property and freedom are inseparably connected, and that economic levelling is not economic progress.

5. Faith in prescription and distrust of "sophisters and calculators." Man must put a control upon his will and his appetite, for conservatives know man to be governed more by emotion than by reason.

6. Recognition that change and reform are not identical, and that innovation is a devouring conflagration more often than it is a torch of progress.[19]

Though not all conservatives would agree exactly with Kirk's formulation of the tenets of conservatism, and indeed Kirk came to represent the right wing of modern conservatism, there was nevertheless considerable agreement on which writers ought properly to be admitted to the conservative camp. In virtually all of the literature the principles of the great conservative Edmund Burke, critic of the French Revolution, were reexamined in an effort to demonstrate their applicability to the current revolutionary era. A conservatism that frankly made its appeal to the heart as well as the mind could not do justice to itself by the mere enunciation of abstract principles. Thus the richness, variety, and values of the historic past were called upon to support the conservatism of the uncertain present. A new interest was thus awakened in the history of our political thought and coincidentally, if unrelatedly, new interpretations of our past were forthcoming. Robert Brown demonstrated persuasively that in Massachusetts, at least, the Revolution was no more than a war of independence and not the great political-social revolt usually por-

[19] Russell Kirk, *The Conservative Mind* (Chicago: Henry Regnery, 1953), pp. 7-8. By permission.

trayed in the history books of the past.[20] Charles A. Beard, who by an earlier generation was practically considered the historian of America, was to have many of his liberal-oriented interpretations challenged in the light of new research.[21] Richard Hofstadter was to call attention to some of the neglected and less savory aspects of the populist and progressive movements which had helped set the direction of modern liberalism.[22] Indeed it would not be too strong a statement to say that in the light of the new history both the American Revolution in Massachusetts and the Populist Revolt of the Midwest a century later were essentially conservative reactions to what in each case was perceived to be a rapidly and adversely changing environment. In any case historians seemed in general agreement that the liberal dynamic was absent from the American culture of the Fifties and the major focus of debate was whether the new era was predominantly one of "radicalism from the right," "pseudoconservatism," or bona fide conservatism.

PRECURSORS OF MODERN CONSERVATISM

If it was difficult to define precisely just what a genuine conservatism was, it was nevertheless possible to point to previous conservative theoreticians.[23] John Adams, sometimes Alexander Hamil-

[20] Robert E. Brown, *Middle-Class Democracy and the Revolution in Massachusetts, 1691-1780* (Ithaca: Cornell University Press, 1955).

[21] Robert E. Brown, *Charles Beard and the Constitution: A Critical Analysis of "An Economic Interpretation of the Constitution."* (Princeton: Princeton University Press, 1956).

[22] Richard Hofstadter, *The Age of Reform* (New York: Alfred A. Knopf, 1956).

[23] Some of the difficulty of definition and identification of conservatism is indicated by Friedrich A. Hayek in the foreword to the 1957 publication of *The Road to Serfdom.* Hayek, who calls himself a liberal, observes: "Conservatism, though a necessary element in any stable government, is not a social program; in its paternalistic, nationalistic, and power-adoring tendencies it is often closer to socialism than true liberalism; and with its traditionalistic, anti-intellectual, and often mystical propensities it will never, except in short periods of disillusionment, appeal to the young and all those others who believe that some changes are desirable if this world is to become a better place. A conservative movement, by its very nature, is bound to be a defender of established privilege and to lean on the power of government for the protection of privilege. The essence of the liberal position, however, is the denial of all privilege, if privilege is understood in its proper and original meaning of the state granting and protecting the rights to some which are not available on equal terms to others." Friedrich A. Hayek, *The Road to Serfdom* (Chicago: The University of Chicago Press, 1957), pp. xi-xii. By permission.

ton, John C. Calhoun, Edwin L. Godkin, William Graham Sumner, Henry and sometimes Brooks Adams, Paul Elmer More, Irving Babbitt, and Ralph Adams Cram were found to be the major formulators of conservatism in American thought. Because the first five figures have been dealt with previously in this book, the following discussion will deal only with the latter five. These writers, it might be noted at the onset, were elitist critics of the American culture, that curious conjunction of capitalism and democracy, which seemed to them to reduce all standards to the lowest mass denominator. In place of such a system they turned instead to the romantic vision which has haunted mankind since the days of Plato, of a society governed by philosopher-kings.

In the land of philosopher-kings there is good and evil, superiority and subordination. In this land of ordered hierarchy the higher governs the lower, good overrules evil, the few control the many. Here aristocracy rules over the popular passions: the higher few control the base many; the intellect controls the animal. Each man knows his place; each fulfills his station. Things of the spirit take precedence over things of the flesh, and the crass materialism of getting and spending are not considered the primary aims of life.

The theory of inequality and its corollary, a demand for an aristocratic governance of society, is much older than the theory of equality and majority rule in American thought. The Puritan assumption of an elect and its authority to govern; the colonial claims of the rich and well-born; the theories of Hamilton and John Adams, of Calhoun and the pro-slavery writers—they constitute a substantial segment of our political thought. Up until the Civil War, however, the doctrine of inequality was clearly enunciated by political theorists who were also public officials appealing for public support. After the Civil War the doctrine of inequality was seldom voiced openly by politicians. When it appeared it was usually expressed not by politicians or public officials, but primarily by literary critics and a handful of academicians.

In the late nineteenth century, Charles Eliot Norton, James Russell Lowell, and Edwin Lawrence Godkin were voicing criticisms of democracy and equality not unlike the views held in England by such writers as William Lecky, Henry Sumner Maine, and J. K. Stephen. The high, optimistic expectations for democracy held by many Northern liberals at the conclusion of the Civil War had passed into pessimism near the end of the century. Another generation moved from this questioning pessimism into rejection of democracy. The progress of disenchantment is suggested in a few titles of criticism of democracy: Godkin's *Unforeseen Tendencies of Democracy* (1898), Henry Adams' *The Degradation of the Democratic Dogma* (1919). Ralph Adams Cram's *The End of Democracy* (1937). The line of criticism throughout these works however is essentially the same: democracy and capitalism brought forth the twin evils of plutocracy and demagogic mob rule. Each of these evils sapped the strength and spirit of modern society; together they spelled the doom of civilization.

After a century of experience in American democracy, James Russell Lowell inquired, "Is Democracy doomed by its very nature to a dead level of commonplace?" while Charles Eliot Norton complained that the rise of democracy was the "rise of the uncivilized, whom no school education can suffice to provide with intelligence and reason."[24] In an enthusiastic review of Lecky's *Democracy and Liberty*, Godkin's *Nation* observed:

> Ignorance, so far as it is vested with power, tends to drive out intelligence, just as a debased currency tends to drive out gold. . . . No American of mature years can read Mr. Lecky's book without feeling that the experience of his own country furnishes a great deal of the strongest proof in it.[25]

The deep forebodings of the intellectual critics of democracy were not relieved but only intensified with the rise of Populism, progressivism, and imperialism. Faithful to the tenets of Manchester liberalism they rejected all political efforts at economic reform as follies propounded by demagogues and subscribed to by fools. That such follies received increasing popular support only heightened the apprehension of the critics that the average man was ignorant and had no ethical restraints upon his inordinate lust for bread and circuses. Social justice was specious justice, if indeed, it was justice at all. On the other hand the governance of the country by the plutocracy was equally anathema to the critics. The elevation of the gospel of success into a social ethic, the amoral search for wealth, made for a completely materialized morality contrary to the tradi-

---

[24] Charles Eliot Norton (ed.), *Letters of James Russell Lowell* (New York: Harper & Brothers, 1894), vol. II, p. 173. Charles Eliot Norton, *Letters of Charles Eliot Norton* (Boston: Houghton Mifflin Company, 1913), vol. II, p. 237.

[25] *The Nation*, LXII (1896), p. 381.

tional spiritual values of civilization. The plutocrats were no more worthy of esteem than were the popular demagogues they opposed. The rich were thus as guilty as the poor in their corruption of the traditional standards of society. The critics who rejected Bryan's Populism had little patience with Mark Hanna's plutocracy.[26] The plutocracy and populism that seemed the inevitable counterparts of a democratic, capitalistic society were alike rejected by the literary critics who turned instead to an aristocratic order in which men would rule not because they were rich or many but because, in some indefinable way, they were virtuous. Thus out of the gloomy pessimism of Godkin, Norton, and Lowell there came in the twentieth century a little coterie of elitists who sought a fundamental rejection of the democratic ideology as it had been accepted in capitalistic America.

THE DEGRADATION OF THE DEMOCRATIC DOGMA

Henry Adams (1838-1918), who had watched with increasing gloom the transitions in American society from pre-Civil War days to the end of World War I, finally concluded that civilization itself had been declining since the Middle Ages. In place of the optimism inspired by the science of evolution, he countered with the pessimism of the second law of thermodynamics—that energy is constantly being dissipated, not to be replaced. Society, instead of progressing upward as the evolutionists had believed, was actually degenerating downward according to a law of degradation. In his popular *The Education of Henry Adams* (1918), he vividly portrayed man's quest for order in a chaotic universe. *The Degradation of the Democratic Dogma* (1919)—the title which Brooks Adams gave to his collection of Henry's essays—reveals the extent of his pessimism regarding contemporary society and his belief that a tragic future

[26] "To invest money in politics as in a mine or railroad, and, to look as confidently for the pecuniary return; to appeal for votes on the basis of sheer material advantage; to cry up prosperity as the be-all and end-all of government; to vulgarize politics by making its watchwords the cries of the market and the slang of the gambler; to make of the electoral struggles of a free people an exciting game with huge and glittering money stakes—in a word, to put mercantile methods in the place of forensic, and to hold the best title to office to be the fact that it has been bought and paid for—this was the great political distinction of Mr. Hanna." *The Nation*, LXXVIII (1904), pp. 122-123.

of oblivion lay ahead. The gloomy determinism which Henry Adams accepted lacked any spark of faith in humanity, and thus his diagnosis and prognosis of the ills of society were characterized by an unrelieved pessimism. Having no faith in modern man it was not unnatural that he should have no faith in democracy as a political system. The elevation of the system of society into a gigantic force, or combination of forces, beyond the power of men to control cut him loose from the democratic belief that institutions might be purposively directed and controlled and left him no recourse but to seek in history the chaotic course of impersonal forces. As Spencer had read the laws of zoology and botany into social growth and development, so now did Henry Adams accept Lord Kelvin's physics. The price of such questionable determinism however was pessimism, for neither system left much for man to make of man except to assist him in resignedly accepting the course of the inevitable. Adams' secular Calvinism thus accepted, fully, predestination in a damned universe unrelieved by any possibility of salvation in the here or hereafter.

Henry Adams' belief in the degradation of democracy was fully supported by his brother Brooks Adams (1824-1927). Brooks Adams lived under the dark shadow of imminent social catastrophe. An anxiety for the future of America, of civilization, indeed of the human race, underlies all his writings.

Like Henry, Brooks assumed that the dismal end was not far off and he sought through intense scholarship to understand why. In *The Law of Civilization and Decay* (1895) he first brought together the basic generalizations from history which remained with him as his theory of historical development. As he interpreted history, Brooks Adams believed that the movement from barbarism to civilization was essentially a movement from dispersion to concentration and centralization. Without effective social concentration and centralization, civilization collapsed and barbarism returned. Like Henry, however, Brooks Adams related social movements to expenditures of energy.

In the early stages of civilization energy found expression in fear, and thus primitive communities produced religious, military, and artistic mental types. However, "As consolidation advances, fear yields to greed, and the economic organism tends to supersede the emotional and martial." With the advance in consolidation, there was an increasing accumulation of wealth, which in turn accelerated the movement toward centralization. Capital then becomes the dominant force in the community and "energy vents itself through those organisms best fitted to give expression to the power of capital."[27] It was during this stage that the economic and scientific intellect propagated, while the imaginative and artistic types of manhood decayed.

> As the social movement of a race is accelerated, more of its energetic material is consumed, and ultimately, societies appear to attain a velocity at which they are unable to make good the waste. In high stages of civilization, when unrestricted economic competition prevails, this loss of energy is manifested by a gradual dissipation of capital, which, at last, ends in disintegration.

Thus the course of energy expenditure which gave rise to civilization brought about its dispersion and decay. The economic motive, so essential in the movement from savagery to civilization, would according to Brooks Adams, if allowed to run its course return mankind to barbarism.

In 1914 Brooks Adams brought out a collection of his essays, under the title of *The Theory of Social Revolutions,* in which he elaborated on his law of civilization and applied it directly to America. Civilization was, he wrote, essentially centralization brought about through inventions and scientific knowledge. Such social consolidations, however, if they were to survive, required an extraordinary degree of competent administration.

> I take it to be an axiom, that perfection in administration must be commensurate to the bulk and momentum of the mass to be administered, otherwise the centrifugal will overcome the centripetal force, and the mass will disintegrate. In other words, civilization will dissolve.[28]

This was the fear that had plagued Alexander Hamilton, the fear that without a strong centralizing force in society law and order would give way to chaos and anarchy. Thus Hamilton had argued for a strong centralized government which united in its personnel and its policies economic and political power. However, where Hamilton looked to the wealthy merchants and capitalists for leader-

[27] Brooks Adams, *The Law of Civilization and Decay* (New York: The Macmillan Co., 1897), pp. ix, x.

[28] Brooks Adams, *The Theory of Social Revolutions* (New York: The Macmillan Co., 1914), p. 204.

ship in society, Brooks Adams saw in such leadership only further cause for despair. It was the capitalist, Adams contended, who was destroying the American social order and leading it on the downward path.

Brooks Adams maintained that advances in civilization represented the advances in administration engineered by the governing class. New inventions, discoveries, new social situations demanded new administrative skills to turn them to the advantage of society. As society increased in complexity, the demands upon the administrators increased accordingly so that a society which did not develop new leadership and administrative talent commensurate with its problems was doomed to decline and failure. In the past, social changes in America had effected social revolutions which had brought forth new governing classes, readjustments of wealth, and new administrative skills. The colonial aristocracy was supplanted by the planter aristocracy, which in turn was succeeded by the industrial aristocracy of the North. Leaders who misjudged the temper of the new environment lost not only their leadership but frequently their property as well. This was the warning Brooks Adams sounded to the industrial leadership which had dominated America for about two generations. "If this class, like its predecessors, has in its turn mistaken its environment, a redistribution of property must occur, distressing, as previous redistributions have been in proportion to the inflexibility of the sufferers."[29]

Yet Brooks Adams had little faith that the governing class in America would exercise any greater foresight than had the previous governing class which they had replaced. Thus he expected that the capitalists would prove deficient in the very skill—administration—which not only held society together but carried it forward. Administration, Adams noted, "is the capacity of co-ordinating many, and often conflicting, social energies in a single organism, so adroitly that they shall operate as a unity." Administration thus required an extraordinary scope of knowledge, sensitivity, and sharp intellectual perception. It required a keen capacity for generalization. The modern age, however, he believed, had placed a premium upon specialization rather than generalization, so that the capacity for adroit generalization was not a distinctive characteristic of contemporary America. Modern capitalism had evolved "under the

29 *Ibid.*, p. 207.

stress of an environment which demanded excessive specialization in the direction of genius adapted to money-making under highly complex industrial conditions."[30] Money-making as a specialization was thus the characteristic feature of American capitalism to such a degree that other skills had become subordinate to it. The broad administrative talent for organizing society had succumbed to the personal demand for self-enrichment. Thus the capitalist exploited the institutions of social order—law, government, education—for his own enrichment. In so doing, Brooks Adams maintained, the capitalist was destroying the very social order which had brought him to a position of dominance and control.

The Adams brothers, Henry and Brooks, found in their studies of history laws which they believed proved that civilization was declining. The idea of progress was thus supplanted in their thought by the idea of regression. Both writers held an aristocratic contempt for the bourgeois leaders of the industrial civilization; yet both men were elitists at heart. America had clearly entered upon an industrial age of new frontiers in politics and economics at home and across the seas. Admitting the necessity for intelligent leadership in such a complex social and economic culture, the Adams brothers nevertheless rejected the possibility that such leadership might develop within a capitalistic democracy.[31] Rejecting democratic leadership, and disliking what they saw of industrial and commercial leadership, the Adams brothers rejected the society in which they lived. They were aristocrats who turned away from the common and the commercial in favor of a cultured and educated elite. They

[30] *Ibid.*, p. 208.

[31] Note the contempt and bewilderment in Brooks Adams' letter to Henry Cabot Lodge, of January 18, 1920: "Poor Roosevelt. He never could become reconciled. He went on to the end actually believing in 'democracy.' That was what gave him strength. He actually believed in the 'common people.' Like Lincoln. And he believed in Democracy. It was strange." Cited in Thornton Anderson, *Brooks Adams, Constructive Conservative* (Ithaca: Cornell University Press, 1951), p. 180.

The third brother, Charles Francis Adams, Jr., was equally contemptuous of capitalism and democracy. Of the plutocrats he noted, "Not one that I have ever known would I care to meet again, either in this world or the next; nor is one of them associated in my mind with the idea of humor, thought or refinement." Of the democratic tendency toward social legislation he wrote, "For myself, I don't believe in it. I never have believed in it; and for this reason, perhaps, have failed to be in sympathy with the sturdy champions of the 'Dear Peepul.'" Charles Francis Adams, Jr., *An Autobiography: 1835-1915* (Boston: Houghton Mifflin Company, 1916), pp. 190, 175.

were neither democrats nor capitalists, and in an era that sought to reconcile these two value systems they pessimistically saw about them only symptoms of declining civilization.

ARISTOCRACY AND SOCIAL JUSTICE

Paul Elmer More (1867-1937), Irving Babbitt (1865-1933), and Ralph Adams Cram (1863-1942) were intellectual leaders who rejected alike plutocracy and populism and turned searchingly toward an aristocratic, class-structured society. Paul Elmer More, scholar, biographer, essayist, and editor was an outspoken critic of democracy. As a neo-humanist he sought to place spiritual values above material ones and to emphasize the individual rather than society. He rejected the social consciousness of the progressive period in favor of the conscience of the individual. A predominantly theological tone runs throughout More's writings, as indeed it does in the works of Babbitt and Cram. Man is depraved and prone to sin and no mere institutional arrangements can entirely avoid the consequences of this alleged fact. Character is thus far more important than environment, and it is to the strengthening of character rather than the tampering with social conventions that reformers ought to turn their energies. The efforts at social reform, of economic amelioration, were misguided efforts as they sought to achieve the wrong objectives. Any philosophy, More argued, based upon an assumed goodness of man, on the idea of perpetual and inevitable human progress, upon the validity and trustworthiness of human emotions—in a word Jeffersonian democracy—was bound to lead man only to catastrophe, for such a philosophy was built upon false assumptions. Man was at bottom depraved; in every meaningful sense unequal; and man's emotions were of value only when they were properly channelled and curbed by a superior authority, namely reason.

In order that reason might check passion, that the better might control the worse, More believed that it was first necessary to rid society of the democratic cant that had so long held sway in American thought. Every society was in actuality ruled by leaders; what was now needed was a higher type of leadership. Majority rule was no formula for a moral system of government for it only declared that numerical might meant right. To elevate right in place of might it was necessary to establish the right kind of leadership, which in turn required the frank recognition of the place of the natural aristocracy. Such an aristocracy, More maintained, ought not to rest upon prescriptive claims or on money; "it is not synonymous with oligarchy or plutocracy."[32] Rather it would arise from the recognition on the part of the natural aristocrats of a duty to lead, and of a willingness on the part of the masses to be led. Like Calvin's predestination, More's concept of the elect was extremely nebulous and mystical, and he offered no certain criterion for its selection. "Why should there not be an outspoken class consciousness among those who are in the advance of civilization as well as among those who are in the rear?" More asked, echoing the thought of John C. Calhoun.

Before the aristocratic state might come about, certain contemporary social conceptions would have to be eliminated. Writing in the aftermath of the progressive movement, More was bitterly opposed to the prevailing attitudes toward humanitarianism and social justice, for these views emphasized emotional sentimentality and a levelling equalitarianism contrary to the spirit of his aristocratic society. "Before anything else is done we must purge our minds of the current cant of humanitarianism."[33] Just subordination rather than pity was the primary need of society. Social justice came about neither through the rulership of power, in the Nietzschean sense, nor through the social realization of the equalitarian ethic. "It is such a distribution of power and privilege, and of property as the symbol and instrument of these, as at once will satisfy the distinctions of reason among the superior, and will not outrage the feelings of the inferior."[34] Social justice, like personal justice, consisted in a proper proportion of reason and passion, in which reason acted as guide and check upon the self-destroying impulses. By reversing the analogy of Plato, More thus sought through an understanding of personal justice to find it "writ large" in the state itself. Only through a rational proportion of the factors in man's nature could one achieve personal justice; and only through an extension of such a proportion to the governance of man could social justice be achieved.

[32] Paul Elmer More, *Aristocracy and Justice, Shelburne Esseys Ninth Series* (Boston: Houghton Mifflin Company, 1915), p. 30. By permission.

[33] *Ibid.*, p. 31.

[34] *Ibid.*, p. 120.

No little of More's concern for social justice, however, emanated from his concern for the rights of property in the face of social reform legislation. Property, he believed, lay at the root of civilization; and interpreting social reform as an attack upon property, he found in the progressive movement an effort to destroy civilization itself. It was the possession of property as much as the possession of reason that distinguished man from the beasts. Thus More maintained that "To the civilized man *the rights of property are more important than the right to life.*"[35] To diminish the influence of property in society would so loosen the already flimsy social fabric that only chaos followed by despotism would be its aftermath. In spite of the misguided humanitarianism and soft sentimentality of the age, More exhorted his readers to stand firm on the question of property; for, he noted, "we need to remind ourselves that laws which would render capital insecure and, by a heavy income tax or other discrimination in favor of labor, would deprive property of its power of easy self-perpetuation, though they speak loudly in the name of humanity, will in the end be subversive of those conditions under which alone any true values of human life can be realized."[36] Where property was secure, more spiritual, or rather less material, ends might be sought; but where property was insecure it would be sought as an end in itself. That property to many, during the late stages of the progressive movement, seemed either insecure or unattainable, More failed to notice. Yet his approach was consistent, for his primary interest was in the development of a narrow number of aristocrats, not in the broader concern of social justice as it was considered at that time.

In his conclusion to *Aristocracy and Justice*, More offered a convenient summary of his beliefs.

We need to be less swayed by our sympathies and more guided by the discriminations of reason; to put a harsh stop to the feminism that is undermining the sober virility of our minds; to control our equalitarian relaxation, of which recent legislation has been over full, by a stricter idea of the distinctions of value in human achievement; to be less ready to throw upon society the guilt of the individual, and to be firmer in our recognition of personal duty and responsibility; to revise our philosophy of emotional expansion, with its tendency to glorify extremes, for a saner perception of the virtue

35 *Ibid.,* p. 136.
36 *Ibid.,* p. 147.

that lies in limits and for a keener search after the truth that dwells in mediation.

The whole matter can be summed up in a single word—justice.[37]

The anti-democratic theory of the intellectual critics of the first quarter of the twentieth century undoubtedly reached its finest expression in the writings of Irving Babbitt (1865-1933). Babbitt, like More, an editor, scholar, and critic, was a leader of the neo-humanist movement. Of his several works critical of democracy, Babbitt devoted only one book exclusively to his political and social theory. In his *Democracy and Leadership* (1924), Babbitt explained his antagonism to equalitarianism, humanitarianism, and democratic government. Yet Babbitt went well beyond More in the depth of his criticism and the range of his scholarship. It was his purpose, Babbitt wrote in *Democracy and Leadership,* to write "a defense of the veto power."[38] By the "veto power" Babbitt meant the restraining check of conscience upon impulse. All about him Babbitt believed men were succumbing to their baser passions; rich men seeking more riches, poor men seeking to be rich, society itself rushing madly forth in the cause of materialism. Society was unrestrained because individuals had lost their sense of self-restraint. It was therefore Babbitt's mission, as a secular Puritan, to remind Americans of the personal and political need for restrictive living if a proper social order was to be maintained.

Babbitt, along with More, held that leadership was inevitable in any society, democratic or otherwise. Majorities had leaders as well as minorities; thus to talk vaguely of majority rule without recognizing that in front of the majority were leaders of men was a "pernicious conceit" without basis in fact. Since people were led, for good or bad, the significant problem in politics was the achieving of the right leadership. The right leadership, to Babbitt, consisted not only in the employing of vision and imagination to the solution of current problems, but in the employing of restraint and inhibitions to curb popular efforts at social panaceas. The Supreme Court in the United States was one such fundamental restraining device; but further, what was needed, was an aristocracy which would guide as well as restrain. "In the final analysis," Babbitt observed, "the

37 *Ibid.,* pp. 241-242.

38 Irving Babbitt, *Democracy and Leadership* (Boston: Houghton Mifflin Company, 1924), p. 5. By permission.

only check to the evils of an unlimited democracy will be found to be the recognition in some form of the aristocratic principle."[39]

It was Babbitt's contention that one of the serious deficiencies of Locke as a political theorist was that he omitted the problem of leadership, restraint, and subordination. "The very logic of natural rights," Babbitt noted of Lockean theory, "runs counter to the idea of deference and subordination, at least on any other basis than that of force."[40] For majority rule, by vesting all political power in the hands of those possessing numerical might, denied any ethical standard for rulership beyond that of numerical power, or force. And Locke's equalitarianism, in turn, denied the fundamental political fact of the inevitability of leadership. It was against Rousseau, however, that Babbitt launched his heaviest attack. Indeed, Babbitt believed that since the eighteenth century the great conflict in political theory had been primarily one between the spirit of Rousseau and the spirit of Burke. An intellectual follower of Burke, Babbitt was as bitterly opposed to Rousseau as had been that illustrious eighteenth-century conservative.

Rousseau, Babbitt argued, had substituted the religion of naturalism for traditional theology. In the crucial period of history when traditional outer forms of authority were in decline, Rousseau initiated and popularized a new set of myths which in turn became generally accepted to the detriment of civilization. For Rousseau superimposed upon the existing political concepts of natural law and a state of nature a secularistic interpretation of the fall from Grace and the coming of sin. "Just as in the old theology everything hinged on man's fall from God, so in Rousseau everything hinges on man's fall from nature."[41] Man moved, according to Rousseau, from an idyllic and equalitarian Eden into a miserable state of subordination because of the invention of private property. With the institution of private property, Rousseau had held, equality had disappeared and work and slavery had become necessary. Rousseau had thus substituted a new dualism for the old theology. "The old dualism put the conflict between good and evil in the breast of the individual, with evil so predominant since the Fall that it behooves man to be humble; with Rousseau this conflict is transferred from

[39] *Ibid.*, p. 61.
[40] *Ibid.*
[41] *Ibid.*, p. 75.

the individual to society."[42] It was Eden therefore that was corrupted and not man; fault lay not in man but in the institutions which controlled him; what had been called depravity was thus only the result of social disorganization. The Rousseau myth, Babbitt argued, thus continued the concept of equality in the face of subordination, and natural or innate goodness in spite of the existence of depravity. Especially did the concept flatter those who were poor and oppressed at the bottom of society. "Christianity at its best has sought to make the rich man humble, whereas the inevitable effect of the Rousseauistic evangel is to make the poor man proud, and at the same time to make him feel that he is the victim of a conspiracy."[43] The shift of burden of responsibility from the individual to society, Babbitt argued, sapped the strength of individual conscience at the same time that it aroused in the masses of men an intense sense of social injustice. With the Rousseau assumption of the natural goodness of mankind in general, any project of social reform desired by the masses was legitimate. Majority desire was thus, in this conception, social justice. In place of the historic doctrine that the king can do no wrong, Rousseau had therefore substituted the belief that the people could do no wrong. Yet, Babbitt observed, "The king, if not responsible to what is below him, is at least responsible to what is above him—to God. But the sovereign people is responsible to no one. It *is* God."[44] Thus Babbitt found in Rousseau the basic philosophy which he believed to be undermining western civilization.

In place of Rousseau, Babbitt offered the conservatism of Burke plus a stern, Puritanical call to duty—self-restraint, inhibition, and containment. Let every man find his place in a rigidly subordinated hierarchy. Then let him work as a duty as well as necessity, mindful of his own responsibilities, undistracted by sentimental humanitarianism and misguided pleas for social justice. Let every man observe his own conscience and not the "social conscience that operates . . . through a megaphone. . . . We are in fact, as some one remarked, living in the Meddle Ages."[45] If every man attended to his own work, Babbitt argued, the quality of his work would determine his place in society; this arrangement would achieve true

[42] *Ibid.*, p. 76.
[43] *Ibid.*, p. 77.
[44] *Ibid.*, p. 89.
[45] *Ibid.*, p. 200.

justice in which every man received in accordance with his due. Thus Babbitt assumed a natural standard of excellence to define the qualifications of the natural aristocracy; yet Babbitt, like More, never made clear just how this standard of work performance could be made a meaningful criterion for political judgments.

Babbitt's call to true excellence, and competition, as a method of social classification may sound very similar to Manchester liberalism. Yet Babbitt had little use for pure commercialism, or the whetting of the pecuniary appetite. He inveighed against materialism as he did against the romanticism of Rousseau. Neither system led to the creation or acceptance of an aristocracy or strengthened the impulse or will to self-restraint. Pure selfish competition for material goods was as repugnant to him as unselfish humanitarianism. "People will not consent in the long run to look up to those who are not themselves looking up to something higher than their ordinary selves."[46] Thus he argued that while the possession of property was a means to a higher end it ought not to be confused with the end itself. And the same was true of personal enrichment. "Commercialism is laying its great greasy paw upon everything."[47] Babbitt rejected alike plutocracy, which he saw as the outgrowth of the commercial system, and populism, which he believed to be the outgrowth of democracy. The true solution, he believed, lay in the development of aristocratic leadership and general self-restraint. One should, he argued, "seek to substitute the doctrine of the right man for the doctrine of the rights of man."[48] Only with such an emphasis, he maintained, could self-control supplant the contemporary efforts at social control.

> Our present drift away from constitutional freedom can be understood only with reference to the progressive crumbling of traditional standards and the rise of a naturalistic philosophy that, in its treatment of specifically human problems, has been either sentimental or utilitarian. The significant changes in our own national temper in particular are finally due to the fact that Protestant Christianity, especially in the Puritanic form, has been giving way to humanitarianism.[49]

Babbitt sought a return from Rousseau, from the natural-rights

[46] *Ibid.*, p. 204.
[47] *Ibid.*, p. 242.
[48] *Ibid.*, p. 246.
[49] *Ibid.*, p. 250.

philosophy of the eighteenth century with its emphasis upon equality, majority rule, and humanitarianism; and the erection in its place of the historic philosophy of authority, hierarchy, and inequality. This would, he believed, restore the conflict of good and evil to its source in the man as an individual and place a premium upon character and self-restraint. "A State that is controlled by men who have become just as the result of minding their own business in the Platonic sense will be a just State that will also mind its own business."[50] Babbitt, however, was as vague as More as to how these just men might be known and selected. One thing was clear however: neo-humanism as it was portrayed by Paul Elmer More and Irving Babbitt was as a political theory essentially neo-Platonism.

While More and Babbitt sought a revival of classicism in politics, modelled along Platonic lines, another searcher for an aristocratic pattern found a haven, as had Henry Adams, in the Middle Ages. Ralph Adams Cram (1863-1942), architect and social critic, rejected nearly all political and social theory that did not lie within the compass of the medieval period. He yearned for the grandeur, order, and symmetry expressed in Gothic architecture and he sought to carry over into politics medieval social and political ideas. The modern temper characterized the democracy that had come with the Renaissance, the Reformation, and eighteenth-century rationalism; modern democratic society he found to be an amorphous mass, drifting into chaos.

> Now as always the great mass of men look for the master-man who can form in definite shape the aspirations and the instincts that in them are formless and amorphous; who can lead when they are more than willing to follow, but themselves cannot mark the way; who can act as a centripetal force and gather into potent units the diffuse atoms of like will but without coordinating ability. So great is this central human instinct (which was not only the foundation of feudalism but harks back to the very beginnings of society) that when the great leader is not revealed he is invented out of the more impudent element of any potential group, assurance taking the place of competence.[51]

Yet, Cram argued in *The Nemesis of Mediocrity* (1917), democracy had reduced mankind to a "dead level of incapacity" in which

[50] *Ibid.*, p. 309.
[51] Ralph Adams Cram, *The Nemesis of Mediocrity* (Boston: Marshall Jones Company, 1917), p. 6. By permission.

good leaders were neither available nor desired. Social order demanded leadership; yet the social temper of the democratic age militated against the creation and perpetuation of an aristocracy to lead. So pessimistic was Cram in his view of democracy that he believed it was "now not a blessing but a menace."[52] For democracy, he argued, had enthroned mediocrity, and mediocrity in power tended to degenerate into outright inferiority. Democracy, by mingling races, created a "mongrel" population in place of one with "pure blood."[53] Democracy led to the "political survival of the unfit."[54] Without an aristocratic leadership, democracy was doomed to move from failure to catastrophe. "Men and nations have been what they have been, either for good or evil, not by the will of a numerical majority but by the supreme leadership of the few—seers, prophets, captains of men; and so it always will be."[55]

Twenty years later, in his last published work, Cram restated his gloomy political expectations in *The End of Democracy* (1937). In the dark days of the depression Cram believed that his early political predictions had come to pass and that democracy was now paying for its loss of good leadership. Business leadership, however, rather than the politicians, had brought on the depression, he felt. Indeed, he found that the "captains of industry, masters of 'big business,' the bankers and the lords of high finance are precisely the least well informed, the most easily deluded, the most unreliable as leaders and managers, of all the factors in society."[56] The politician, he argued, however, would not have been able to avoid the catastrophe, for the spirit of modern philosophy, religion, politics, and economics led consistently in the direction of retrogression. The high point of man's political achievement, Cram believed, lay back in the medieval period and he curiously called this achievement "High Democracy," as opposed to the present system which he called "Low Democracy." "High Democracy" was, to Cram, the same as "Monarchical Feudalism," in which religious values were predominant and authoritatively announced, and man's secular life was fully ordered under a rigidly stratified social system. The vices of private judg-

[52] *Ibid.*, p. 22.
[53] *Ibid.*, p. 35.
[54] *Ibid.*, p. 43.
[55] *Ibid.*, p. 46.
[56] Ralph Adams Cram, *The End of Democracy* (Boston: Marshall Jones Company, 1937), pp. 9-10.

ment, equality and humanitarianism had not made themselves felt in the world; thus every man knew his place as well as what to believe. Here there was no problem of universal suffrage and majority rule, or commercialism, or pragmatism, or relativism in any form. "High Democracy" was thus truly the antithesis of modern "Low Democracy." Yet, Cram maintained, "High Democracy" sought to assure man of life, liberty, and the pursuit of happiness and was far more successful in achieving these goals than was "Low Democracy." By the simple expedient of definition Cram found greater freedom within the "law" in the Middle Ages and therefore more happiness, than at any subsequent time; for the "law" was certain and known, in church and state, as had not been the case since. Status, at whatever social level, carried with it known rights and obligations. "In theory, and not infrequently in practice, honor, faithfulness, loyalty, and devotion were inseparable from social and political actions and relationships."[57] The Protestant revolution, however, destroyed this happy social unity and brought in an emphasis on "individual authority, private judgment and rugged individualism."

> The peasantry became enslaved, independent craftsmen were forced into the position of wage earners, and society found itself again sharply divided into two classes: the omnipotent rich, the oppressed and degraded poor.[58]

The sequel to this unhappy state of affairs was the proletarian revolution, which, Cram found, commenced in the seventeenth century and was still in progress. For the ruthless leadership of the entrepreneurial class was constantly challenged by the majority of the people who were poor. With the extension of the franchise, the proletarian class finally achieved political control in democratic states. Thus the much-talked-of dictatorship of the proletariat, Cram declared, "has been in existence, socially, politically, and economically," for the past century.[59]

Society, torn between plutocratic aristocracy and proletarian democracy had, Cram believed, chosen the latter as the lesser of two evils. Yet civilization could only deteriorate under such a system. "The majority of mankind are of the mass, or tabloid type.

[57] *Ibid.*, p. 45.
[58] *Ibid.*, p. 46.
[59] *Ibid.*, p. 56.

Before God and the Law they are the equals of their fellows of a more advanced stage of development, but here their parity ceases. In the social fabric they are not entitled to obtain equal rights, privileges, or duties. The radical slogan, now current, is based on fundamental reality. 'From each according to his ability. To each according to his needs.' "[60] Not until society acknowledged the fundamental inequality of men, and placed superiors in political authority, could the course of retrogression be halted.

Cram, like Babbitt and More, was, however, quite vague when he came to formulating a positive program rather than attacking democracy. He advocated that the United States adopt a system of constitutional monarchy, and place in political power the natural aristocracy, as well as create "a number of Orders of Knighthood, membership in which would carry the proper and official title of 'Sir.' "[61] Primarily, however, he hoped that a gradual change in public opinion would lead to the acceptance of a class society, and upper-class control. With the inclination to a class society present, Cram believed that the natural aristocracy would develop accordingly and accept its responsibility to rule over lesser man.

A remodelling of the state was necessary, however, to foster the rise of the aristocratic regime.

> The Organic Law of this Republic must then be recast in order that it may accomplish the following end: *First*, set salutary bounds to the exercise of personal liberty by the individual; *second*, guarantee more perfectly life, liberty and the pursuit of happiness to the citizens; *third*, make more possible the development of men of character, capacity, and intelligence through the establishment of a creative form of social, economic and political life; *fourth*, the placing of such men, *and such men only*, in all positions of power and responsibility.[62]

Just how the limitation on liberty espoused in the first proposition was to be reconciled with the more perfect guaranteeing of liberty in proposition two was not made clear. But since liberty, as Cram used the term, was liberty under the "law" and quite removed from private judgment, it would appear that the term lacked generally meaningful specific content. Cram's third point would appear to be at odds with his continued opposition to the various legislative efforts to achieve a greater degree of social justice. His fourth point

[60] *Ibid.*, p. 64.
[61] *Ibid.*, p. 211.
[62] *Ibid.*, p. 240.

however is clear: the placing, not electing, of the aristocracy into "all positions of power and responsibility."

More, Babbitt, and Cram were spokesmen for an age that was centuries past and was fondly remembered by only a handful of men of letters. The fall from Grace, which Rousseau had found in the invention of private property, Babbitt found in Rousseau, and Cram found in the Protestant revolution. Each found a happier time in some preceding age, and each was ready with his devil. More, Babbitt, and Cram rejected alike plutocratic and proletarian government and society. They were unalterably opposed to commercialism and materialistic standards, even though they stoutly defended the private property system. They sought to escape from both the existing economic and political systems through a return to the values and practices of an age when neither system had existed. They sought thus to escape the problem rather than to solve it; and their appeals for an aristocracy which is not clearly defined for politically cognitive purposes amounted to little more than sheer mysticism.

THE PUBLIC PHILOSOPHY

Although it was difficult for many to see where the guidance of such conservatives of the past might prove helpful in the troubled world of the present, it might generally be agreed that in over-all import the renaissance of conservative thought was marked less by the lulling sermons of complacency than by the sounding of a warning, an alerting to the dangers of complacency and conformity. If what was being conserved was in the views of many some of the best features of the liberal tradition in America, it was equally an effort to break away from the rigidities of what many feared was a repressive "totalitarian-liberalism." If the age may be characterized as one of international tension, domestic prosperity, and personal insecurity, the conservative formula was hardly an insistence upon a faith in the past heritage to carry one through, with the help of Divine guidance, into the future. Rather was it a call to a new austerity in a time of materialism, a new individualism in an age of conformity, indeed, a new inequality in an age marked both globally and nationally by the increasing equalizations of the opportunities and functions of men.

The ambiguities and confusions surrounding the contemporary usages of the terms "liberal" and "conservative" were conspicuously delineated with the publication of a book viewed by most reviewers as a significant contribution to modern conservatism by an author who proclaimed himself a liberal. For many years Walter Lippmann (1889-   ) had stimulated the public consciousness with his thought-provoking commentaries on the American scene. When only twenty-three years of age, and fresh out of Harvard, he wrote one of his many notable books on American politics, entitled A Preface to Politics (1912). In this early work he was concerned with the general public apathy to the political process and sought through the newly discovered techniques of psychology to understand more thoroughly the relationships of politics and personality. It was in a sense the beginnings of Lippmann's long search for some element of permanence and certainty in political values. A decade later, in 1922, Lippmann published Public Opinion, in which he challenged the validity of traditional democratic conceptions of self-government in an age of mass communications, when people dealt not so much with facts as with political stereotypes, when the complexity of the modern world necessitated generalization, and stereotyping these phenomena could hardly speak well for the future of popular consent. For a mass public easily manipulated by slogans and symbols was a far cry from the early conception of democratic decision as the result of conscious and intelligent choices made by informed individuals. It was therefore incumbent upon the knowing student of politics to re-evaluate democratic theory and practice in the light of the new knowledge of advertising and propaganda, the unconscious mind and the uses of crowd psychology. These portentous problems provided a basic theme in Lippmann's writing, and were clearly evident in his recent best-seller The Public Philosophy (1955).

Lippmann, writing as a fervent and dedicated advocate of liberal democracy, felt compelled to write The Public Philosophy to alert his countrymen to the fact that "there is a deep disorder in our society which comes not from the machinations of our enemies and from the adversities of the human condition but from within ourselves."[63] Twice within a generation had the western democracies entered upon a world war in a struggle for their survival; twice they

[63] Walter Lippmann, Essays in the Public Philosophy (Boston: Little, Brown and Company, 1955), p. 5.

had won the war; yet tragically, twice had they failed to win the peace. "Could it be denied that they were sick with some kind of incapacity to cope with reality, to govern their affairs, to defend their vital interests and, it might be, to insure their survival as free and democratic states?"[64] The democratic malady, as Lippmann defined it, was the increasing tendency to democratize government to make it increasingly sensitive to the least shift of mass opinion. By appealing to the mass mind, democratic governments not only lost their essential power to govern in their own right, but they committed their peoples to popular though irrational goals. Such was the case with those who sought "total victory" and promised "total peace." The decline of western democracies was marked by the declining ability of democratic governments to govern. The pattern of democratic dissolution was marked by the cession of executive powers to representative assemblies, which transmitted them to the voters "who, though unable also to exercise them, passed them on to the party bosses, the agents of pressure groups, and the magnates of the new media of mass communication." The fundamental question of the present, Lippmann wrote as a liberal democrat, was whether "both liberty and democracy can be preserved before the one destroys the other."[65]

In order to return vitality to democratic governments Lippmann proposed a broad two-fold program. The first part had to do with the structure and function of democratic government; the second with its ethic.

To cure the "derangement of the functions" of democratic governments, Lippmann proposed in effect a strengthening of the executive power.[66] It was the proper function of the executive to initiate and propose measures and of the legislature to accept or reject measures. It was the proper function of the voter to elect or reject his government. But in no fashion was he to govern directly through public opinion. Indeed Lippmann distinguished between the people as voters and the *people* "as a community of the entire living popula-

---

[64] *Ibid.*, p. 6.

[65] *Ibid.*, p. 13.

[66] Not all conservatives supported this position. James Burnham, author of the popular *The Managerial Revolution* (1941), wrote that conservatives "are specifically opposed to the concentration of power in the executive to which the nearly exclusive presidential control of foreign policy contributes." James Burnham, *Congress and the American Tradition* (Chicago: Henry Regnery Company, 1959), pp. 218-219. See especially his arguments in Part Three.

tion, with their predecessors and successors."[67] As voters, the people were entitled to elect public officials; but "the voters cannot be relied upon to represent *The People*. The opinions of voters in elections are not to be accepted unquestioningly as true judgments of the vital interests of the community."[68] Citing Burke for authority, Lippmann clearly distinguished between the contemporary voting population and the larger community of the living, dead, and unborn. Indeed, he observed in an extraordinary statement, "Because of the discrepancy between The People as voters and *The People* as the corporate nation, the voters have no title to consider themselves the proprietors of the commonwealth and to claim that their interests are identical with the public interest."[69] In Lippmann's view, however, it was the felt presence of this largely "invisible, inaudible, and so largely nonexistent community" which made problems of government of the most fundamental concern and bound the conscientious man to work toward the future of posterity as well as his own concern. If the public interest was not to be known from the latest election figures or public opinion poll, what was it? In Lippmann's view the public interest was "what men would choose if they saw clearly, thought rationally, acted disinterestedly and benevolently."[70] Admittedly only a few, not the many, would meet these specifications. In the final analysis it was therefore necessary to protect the elected from the importunities of the electors.

To effect in part this protection and thereby strengthen the executive role in decision making, Lippmann called into service the second aspect of his program, the ethic of the public philosophy. Returning to the theme of an earlier book, *Public Opinion,* Lippmann noted that men react in life "to the pictures in their heads." This was their intellectual environment. What was needed today was the recreation of the historic intellectual environment of a public philosophy, a conception of the larger public interest which transcended any given age or place. To reformulate this public philosophy, which he equated with "natural law," Lippmann retraced history to extract from the classics of religion and philosophy those precepts which he felt to have universal significance and applicability. If the public philosophy, the "tradition of civility," con-

[67] Walter Lippmann, *op. cit.,* p. 32.

[68] *Ibid.,* p. 32.

[69] *Ibid.,* p. 33.

[70] *Ibid.,* p. 42.

stituted the basis of democracy and free institutions, then he hoped that a new understanding of its relevance would revitalize modern democracy. The revitalization of the tradition of natural law was thus in his view essential to the future of democracy. If the struggle with totalitarian communism were waged without a conscious philosophical basis it was quite likely to fail. For, he wrote, "There is not much doubt how the struggle is likely to end if it lies between those who, believing, care very much—and those who, lacking belief, cannot care very much."[71] Yet paradoxically the public philosophy, by its very nature, could not become popular, "For it aims to resist and to regulate those very desires and opinions which are most popular." "The public philosophy is addressed to the government of our appetites and passions by the reasons of a second, civilized, and, therefore, acquired nature."[72] Nevertheless, Lippmann hoped if the philosophers and intellectuals would reinstate the public philosophy as a precept for public guidance, in time its wisdom might permeate to the larger public and serve as a restraint upon their appetites and passions.

Lippmann's *The Public Philosophy* was quite clearly in the conservative tradition that had reached from the Englishman Edmund Burke to the American Irving Babbitt and was basically in agreement with the canons of conservatism laid down by Russell Kirk. The search for a higher morality beyond the conformity of public opinion, the emphasis on a Divinely inspired and guided morality known especially by the few, a sense of faith or mystical reverence for an order in the universe which might not readily be apparent, a de-emphasis when not outright rejection of the concept of equality with all its concomitant connotations, and emphasis on the relationship of private property and personal freedom, a stress upon restraint and the "inner check" of conscience, a respect for leadership, preferably when unpopular, coupled with a distrust for the competency and sagacity of those led—all of these elements tended to constitute a recurring theme in the literature of conservatism. While domestic factors, such as the general level of prosperity, the tendency toward mass conformity, and the centralization of authority in government, business, and labor—indeed the destruction of individuality through over-organization—all played a part in con-

[71] *Ibid.*, p. 161.
[72] *Ibid.*, p. 162.

tributing to the revitalization of conservatism, in the final analysis it was the cold war which provided the favorable atmosphere for it to flourish. For this conservatism was less an effective criticism of our domestic liberalism than a reflection of the role of the United States in world politics as America sought to conserve the values of the West against the challenge of the new totalitarianism.

Bibliography

GENERAL

A SELECTED bibliography for each chapter follows, listing mainly secondary and interpretive studies of the ideas and figures discussed in the chapter. Since the major primary sources which I have used are noted in the text or in the footnotes, they are not repeated in the bibliography.

My indebtedness to all who have previously written in this field is, of course, very heavy. In one way or another my own interpretations have been affected by theirs. The pioneering work in the history of American political thought was Charles E. Merriam's *A History of American Political Theories* (New York, 1903). He also wrote *American Political Ideas, 1865-1917* (New York, 1920). Then followed Raymond G. Gettell's *History of American Political Thought* (New York, 1938) and William S. Carpenter's *The Development of American Political Thought* (Princeton, 1930). J. Mark Jacobson's *The Development of American Political Thought* (New York, 1932) combined text and readings. Edward R. Lewis' *A History of American Political Thought from the Civil War to the World War* (New York, 1937) and Francis G. Wilson's *The American Political Mind* (New York, 1949) complete the list of previous texts on the subject. Of special help to the student are the readings in American political thought. In addition to Jacobson's work there are Benjamin F. Wright's *A Source Book of American Political Theory* (New York, 1929); Francis W. Coker's *Democracy, Liberty and Property* (New York, 1942); Perry Miller's *American Thought: Civil War to World War I* (New York, 1954); Alpheus T. Mason's *Free Government in the Making* (New York, 1956); and Andrew M. Scott's *Political Thought in America* (New York, 1959).

The intellectual environment of which American political thought has been but a part has been treated in a number of general intellectual histories. The monumental *Main Currents of American Thought* (New York, 3 vols., 1930) of Vernon L. Parrington, though cut short by the author's death, is still the most comprehensive work on American letters from the colonial period to the late nineteenth century. Ralph H. Gabriel's *The Course of American Democratic Thought* (New York, 1956) traces American intellectual history since 1815 with considerable emphasis on political thought. Merle Curti's *The Growth of American Thought* (New York, 1943) is the most complete one-volume intellectual history, and ranges over a wide field of social thought. Harvey Wish's *Society and Thought in Modern America* (New York, 2 vols., 1952) is very useful as background material for understanding political thought. Broad and suggestive interpretations of American politics are found in Daniel Boorstin's *The Genius of American Politics* (Chicago, 1953), and Richard Hofstadter's *The Age of Reform: From Bryan to F. D. R.* (New York, 1956). Of special interest is Louis Hartz's *The Liberal Tradition in America* (New York, 1955). Recent political thought is found in Richard Hofstadter's *Social Darwinism in American Thought, 1860-1915* (Philadelphia, 1945); Henry Steele Commager's *The American Mind* (New Haven, 1950); and Eric Goldman's *Rendezvous with Destiny* (New York, 1956). Brief biographical and interpretive essays on political thinkers are in Charles A. Madison's *Critics and Crusaders: A Century of American Protest* (New York, 1947); Richard Hofstadter's *The American Political Tradition and the Men Who Made It* (New York, 1948); and Daniel Aaron, *Men of Good Hope* (New York, 1951).

For a general background in Western thought I have found most helpful John H. Randall's *The Making of the Modern Mind* (New York, 1940) and Bertrand Russell's *A History of Western Philosophy* (New York, 1945). In European political theory I have been guided by George H. Sabine's *A History of Political Theory* (New York, 1950) and have found useful Francis W. Coker's *Recent Political Thought* (New York, 1934) and John H. Hallowell's *Main Currents in Modern Political Thought* (New York, 1950).

The course of American philosophic thought may be found in Harvey G. Townshend's *Philosophical Ideas in the United States* (New York, 1934), I. Woodbridge Riley's *American Thought From Puritanism to Pragmatism and Beyond* (New York, 1941), and Herbert W. Schneider's *A History of American Philosophy* (New York, 1946). Joseph Dorfman's monumental *The Economic Mind in American Civilization* (New York, 3 vols., 1949) is the standard guide to economic thought in America. For constitutional thought I have turned to Carl B. Swisher's *American Constitutional Development* (New York, 1943) and to *The American Constitution* (New York, 1948) by Alfred H. Kelly and Winfred A. Harbison. Finally, for a general background in American history I have used *The Growth of the American Republic* (New York, 2 vols., 1942), by Samuel E. Morison and Henry S. Commager.

Chapter 1

THE RISE OF PROTESTANTISM

There is an abundance of material on the political thought of the Reformation. For a general historical background see Preserved Smith, *The Age of the Reformation* (New York, 1920). The most complete study of the Medieval period is the six-volume study by R. W. Carlyle and A. J. Carlyle, *A History of Medieval Political Theory in the West* (London, 1936). John N. Figgis' *Studies of Political Thought from Gerson to Grotius, 1414-1625* (Cambridge, 1923), J. W. Allen's *A History of Political Thought in the Sixteenth Century* (London, 1928), and Robert H. Murray's *The Political Consequences of the Reformation; Studies in Sixteenth-Century Political Thought* (London, 1926) cover the Reformation in detail. Also see F. J. C. Hearnshaw (ed.), *The Social and Political Ideas of Some Great Thinkers of the Renaissance and the Reformation* (New York, 1949), and James Mackinnon's *Calvin and the Reformation* (London, 1936). For interpretations of the interaction of religious and social thought see R. H. Tawney, *Religion and the Rise of Capitalism* (New York, 1926), Max Weber, *The Protestant Ethic and the Spirit of Capitalism* (London, 1930), and Ernst Troeltsch, *The Social Teaching of the Christian Churches* (2 vols., London, 1931).

Chapter 2

PURITAN POLITICAL THOUGHT

Perry Miller is the authority on Puritan Massachusetts. Of especial importance here are his *The New England Mind; The Seventeenth*

Century (New York, 1939), and its sequel *The New England Mind; From Colony to Province* (Cambridge, 1953). The readings and commentary in *The Puritans* (New York, 1938), by Perry Miller and Thomas H. Johnson, are of great help in understanding the period. Thomas J. Wertenbaker's *The Puritan Oligarchy: The Founding of American Civilization* (New York, 1947) is rich with historical material and interpretations. Herbert W. Schneider's *The Puritan Mind* (New York, 1930) and Ralph Barton Perry's *Puritanism and Democracy* (New York, 1944) are highly rewarding in their philosophical treatment of what was implicit in Puritanism. Of a more general nature, see Evarts B. Greene's *Religion and the State: The Making and Testing of an American Tradition* (New York, 1941) and William Haller's *The Rise of Puritanism* (New York, 1938).

Roger Williams has been studied in James E. Ernst's *The Political Thought of Roger Williams* (Seattle, 1929) and Samuel H. Brockunier's *The Irrespressible Democrat: Roger Williams* (New York, 1940). Perry Miller's *Roger Williams* (Indianapolis, 1953) contains excellent selections of Williams' writings with commentary by Perry Miller. See also H. B. Parks' "John Cotton and Roger Williams Debate Toleration," *New England Quarterly*, October 1931, and F. B. Wiener's "Roger Williams' Contribution to Modern Thought," *Rhode Island Historical Society Collections*, XXVIII, 1935, pp. 1-20.

Stanley Gray's "The Political Thought of John Winthrop," *New England Quarterly*, October 1930, and E. A. J. Johnson's "Economic Ideas of John Winthrop," *New England Quarterly*, April 1930, treat two related aspects of Winthrop's thought. Clinton Rossiter's "Thomas Hooker" in the *New England Quarterly*, December 1953, is of especial interest to political theorists. Of a more general nature see Herbert L. Osgood's "The Political Ideas of the Puritans," *Political Science Quarterly*, March 1891, and George L. Mosse, "Puritanism and Reason of State in Old New England," *William and Mary Quarterly*, January 1952.

Chapter 3

The English Revolution

Like the Reformation, the English Revolution has received considerable scholarly attention, and there is an abundance of material on the subject. J. W. Allen's *English Political Thought, 1603-1660* (London, 1938) and G. P. Gooch's *English Democratic Ideas in the Seventeenth Century* (Cambridge, 1929) are particularly good studies of the period. Also see F. J. C. Hearnshaw (ed.), *The Social and Political Ideas of Some English Thinkers of the Augustan Age, A.D. 1650-1750* (London, 1928). A fuller orientation to the period is found in G. P. Gooch's *Political Thought in England from Bacon to Halifax* (London, 1946). While space did not permit a fuller discussion of the English Revolution, students will find rewarding studies of the political ideas associated with some of the lesser figures of the period. See Theodore C. Pease's *The Leveller Movement: A Study in the History and Political Theory of the English Great Civil War* (Washington, 1916), and Don M. Wolfe (ed.), *Leveller Manifestoes of the Puritan Revolution* (New York, 1944). A. S. P. Woodhouse has edited the Clarke manuscripts under the title *Puritanism and Liberty, Being the Army Debates (1647-9) from the Clarke Manuscripts* (Chicago, 1951). John Milton is studied in Don M. Wolfe's *Milton in the Puritan Revolution* (New York, 1941) and in Arthur Barker's *Milton and the Puritan Dilemma, 1641-1660* (Toronto, 1942). The more radical movement is discussed in Edward Bernstein's *Cromwell and Communism; Socialism and Democracy in the Great English Revolution* (London, 1930).

The most profound study of Hobbes is Leo Strauss' *The Political Philosophy of Hobbes: Its Basis and Its Genesis* (Chicago, 1952). Also see John Bowle's *Hobbes and His Critics; A Study in Seventeenth Century Constitutionalism* (New York, 1952), and George E. Catlin's *Thomas Hobbes as Philosopher, Publicist, and Man of Letters* (Oxford, 1922). Interpretive essays on Hobbes include the study in F. J. C. Hearnshaw (ed.), *The Social and Political Ideas of Some Great Thinkers of the Sixteenth and Seventeenth Centuries* (London, 1928) and S. P. Lamprecht's article, "Hobbes and Hobbism," in the *American Political Science Review*, February 1940.

For material on Harrington see H. F. R. Smith, *Harrington and His Oceana: A Study of a 17th Century Utopia and Its Influence in America* (Cambridge, 1914). Also see Theodore D. Dwight, "Harrington and His Influence Upon American Political Institutions and Political Thought," *Political Science Quarterly*, March 1887, and J. W. Gough, "Harrington and Contemporary Thought," *Political Science Quarterly*, September 1930; and Judith N. Shklar, "Ideology

Hunting: The Case of James Harrington," *American Political Science Review*, September 1959.

There is considerable material on Locke. Most relevant here are: S. P. Lamprecht's *The Moral and Political Philosophy of John Locke* (New York, 1918); Paschal Larkin's *Property in the Eighteenth Century with Special Reference to England and Locke* (London, 1930); Willmoore Kendall's *John Locke and the Doctrine of Majority Rule* (Urbana, 1941); C. J. Czajkowski's *The Theory of Private Property in John Locke's Political Philosophy* (South Bend, 1941); J. W. Gough's *John Locke's Political Philosophy* (Oxford, 1950). For the issue of natural rights, see Leo Strauss' "On Locke's Doctrine of Natural Rights," *Philosophical Review*, October 1952, and especially his *Natural Right and History* (Chicago, 1953). And for Locke's influence in America, see Merle Curti's "The Great Mr. Locke: America's Philosopher, 1783-1861," *The Huntington Library Bulletin*, April 1937.

Chapter 4

The American Revolution

The eighteenth-century English background of the American Revolution is covered in Leslie Stephen's *History of English Thought in the Eighteenth Century* (London, 1881). For eighteenth-century France see Kingsley Martin's *French Liberal Thought in the Eighteenth Century* (Boston, 1929), and F. J. C. Hearnshaw (ed.), *The Social and Political Ideas of Some Great French Thinkers of the Age of Reason* (London, 1930). Also see Carl Becker's *The Heavenly City of the Eighteenth-Century Philosophers* (New Haven, 1932) and J. B. Bury's *The Idea of Progress* (New York, 1932).

There have been many interpretive studies of American Revolutionary thought. See Clinton Rossiter's *Seedtime of the Republic* (New York, 1953), and Moses Coit Tyler's pioneering study, *The Literary History of the American Revolution* (New York, 1897). For a general historical background of the Revolution see J. F. Jameson's *The American Revolution Considered as a Social Movement* (Princeton, 1926), and Elisha P. Douglass' *Rebels and Democrats: The Struggle for Equal Political Rights and Majority Rule During the*

American Revolution (Chapel Hill, 1955); however, compare these with Robert E. Brown's *Middle-Class Democracy: the Revolution in Massachusetts, 1691-1780* (Ithaca, 1955), and see Edmund S. Morgan's "The American Revolution: Revisions in Need of Revising," *William and Mary Quarterly*, January 1957. Also see E. B. Greene's *The Revolutionary Generation, 1763-1790* (New York, 1943); John C. Miller's *Origins of the American Revolution* (Boston, 1943); Helen and Edmund S. Morgan's *The Stamp Act Crisis* (Chapel Hill, 1953); Alice Baldwin's *The New England Clergy and the American Revolution* (Durham, N. C., 1928); and Philip Davidson's *Propaganda and the American Revolution 1763-1783* (Chapel Hill, 1941).

The political thought of the Revolution is interpreted in R. G. Adams' *Political Ideas of the American Revolution* (New York, 1939); C. H. McIlwain's *The American Revolution: A Constitutional Interpretation* (New York, 1923); G. A. Koch's *Republican Religion: The American Revolution and the Cult of Reason* (New York, 1933). Also see Louis Hartz' "American Political Thought and the American Revolution," *American Political Science Review*, June 1952, and Clinton Rossiter's "The Political Theory of the American Revolution," *Review of Politics*, January 1953.

On the eighteenth-century conception of natural law and the Declaration of Independence, see Benjamin F. Wright's *American Interpretations of Natural Law* (Cambridge, Mass., 1931); C. F. Mullett's *Fundamental Law and the American Revolution, 1760-1776* (New York, 1933); Florence Pooke's *Fountain-Sources of American Political Theory* (New York, 1930); Carl Becker's *The Declaration of Independence: A Study in the History of Political Ideas* (New York, 1922); Edward Dumbauld's *The Declaration of Independence and What It Means Today* (Norman, Okla., 1950); Julian P. Boyd's *The Declaration of Independence: The Evolution of the Text as Shown in Facsimiles of Various Drafts by Its Author, Thomas Jefferson* (Princeton, 1945); and W. F. Dana's "The Declaration of Independence as Justification for Revolution," *Harvard Law Review*, January 1900.

Much of a biographical nature has been written regarding the major political figures in the Revolution. Of special interest to students of political theory are the following articles by Clinton L. Rossiter: "John Wise: Colonial Democrat," *New England Quarterly*, March 1949; "The Life and Mind of Jonathan Mayhew," *William and Mary Quarterly,* October 1950; "The Political Theory of Benjamin Franklin," *Pennsylvania Magazine,* July 1952; and "Richard Bland: The Whig in America," *William and Mary Quarterly,* January 1953. See also Malcolm R. Eiselen's *Franklin's Political Theories* (Garden City, 1928) and Gerald Stourzh, "Reason and Power in Benjamin Franklin's Political Thought," *American Political Science Review,* December 1952. On Paine, see F. J. C. Hearnshaw (ed.), *The Social and Political Ideas of Some Representative Thinkers of the Revolutionary Era* (London, 1931) and Charles E. Merriam's "Thomas Paine's Political Theories," *Political Science Quarterly,* September 1899. Material on John Adams and Alexander Hamilton will be found in the bibliography for Chapter 6, while material for Thomas Jefferson will be found in the bibliography for Chapter 7. However, of particular relevance here is Dumas Malone's *Jefferson the Virginian* (Boston, 1948), the first volume of the projected four-volume biography entitled *Jefferson and His Time.* This first volume deals with Jefferson during the Revolution.

Chapter 5

American Constitutionalism

On the concept of constitutionalism see Francis D. Wormuth's *The Origins of Modern Constitutionalism* (New York, 1949); C. H. McIlwain's *Constitutionalism, Ancient and Modern* (Ithaca, 1947); C. Perry Patterson's "The Evolution of Constitutionalism," *Minnesota Law Review,* April 1948; Edward S. Corwin's "The Debt of American Constitutional Law to Natural Law Concepts," *Notre Dame Lawyer,* Winter 1950.

For a historical background of the period see Allan Nevins' *The American States During and After the Revolution, 1775-1789* (New York, 1924). An analysis of constitutional thought is found in Conyers Read (ed.), *The Constitution Reconsidered* (New York, 1938); Merrill Jensen's *The Articles of Confederation: An Interpretation of the Social-Constitutional History of the American Revolution, 1774-1781* (Madison, 1940) and his *The New Nation: A History of the United States During the Confederation, 1781-1789* (New York, 1950). Also see Edward S. Corwin, "Progress of Constitutional Theory between the Declaration of Independence and the Meeting of the Philadelphia Convention," *American Historical Review*, April 1925.

The original sources on the Constitution are Max Farrand (ed.), *The Records of the Federal Convention of 1787* (New Haven, 1937, 4 vols.); Paul L. Ford (ed.), *Pamphlets on the Constitution of the United States, Published During Its Discussion by the People, 1787-1788* (Brooklyn, 1888); Paul L. Ford (ed.), *Essays on The Constitution of the United States, Published During Its Discussion by the People, 1787-1788* (Brooklyn, 1892); Jonathan Elliot's *The Debates in the Several State Conventions on the Adoption of the Federal Constitutions* (Philadelphia, 1861, 5 vols.); and, of course, *The Federalist*, now available in the Modern Library edition. For commentary on this material see Max Farrand's *The Framing of the Constitution of the United States* (New Haven, 1913); A. T. Prescott's *Drafting the Federal Constitution* (University, La., 1941); and Carl Van Doren's *The Great Rehearsal: The Story of the Making and Ratifying of the Constitution of the United States* (New York, 1948). For a new and radically different interpretation see William Winslow Crosskey's *Politics and the Constitution in the History of the United States* (Chicago, 1953, 2 vols.).

Economic considerations affecting the framing of the Constitution are found in J. Allen Smith's *The Spirit of American Government* (New York, 1907) and Charles A. Beard's *An Economic Interpretation of the Constitution of the United States* (New York, 1913). However, see Richard Hofstadter's "Beard and the Constitution: The History of an Idea," *American Quarterly*, Fall 1950; Robert E. Brown's *Charles Beard and the Constitution: A Critical Analysis of 'An Economic Interpretation of the Constitution'* (Princeton, 1956); Douglass Adair's "The Tenth Federalist Revisited," *William and Mary Quarterly*, January 1951; and Martin Diamond, "Democracy and *The Federalist*: A Reconsideration of the Framers' Intent," *American Political Science Review*, March 1959.

On judicial power see Edward S. Corwin's *The Doctrine of Judicial Review, Its Legal and Historical Basis* (Princeton, 1914), as well as C. Perry Patterson, "James Madison and Judicial Review," *California Law Review*, XXVIII (1939). There has been a considerable amount of writing on James Madison recently. Irving Brant's *James Madison* (New York, 1956, 5 vols.) is the most complete biography; also see E. M. Burns' *James Madison, Philosopher of the Constitution* (New Brunswick, 1938); and the following articles: Neal Riemer, "The Republicanism of James Madison," *Political Science Quarterly,* March 1954; Neal Riemer, "Two Conceptions of the Genius of American Politics," *Journal of Politics,* November 1958; Ralph L. Ketcham, "Notes on James Madison's Sources for the Tenth *Federalist* Paper," *Midwest Journal of Political Science,* May 1957; and Edward S. Corwin's "James Madison: Layman, Publicist and Exegete," *New York University Law Review,* April 1952; Edmond N. Cahn's "Madison and the Pursuit of Happiness," *New York University Law Review,* April 1952; Saul K. Padover, "Madison as a Political Thinker," *Social Research,* Spring 1953. On *The Federalist,* see Douglass Adair's "The Authorship of the Disputed *Federalist* Papers," *William and Mary Quarterly,* 3rd Series, April 1944; Benjamin F. Wright's "*The Federalist* on the Nature of Man," *Ethics,* January 1949; and Alpheus T. Mason's "*The Federalist*—A Split Personality," *American Historical Review,* April 1952.

On federalism and the separation of powers, see Benjamin F. Wright's "The Origins of the Separation of Powers in America," *Economica,* May 1913; Francis G. Wilson's "Mixed Constitution and the Separation of Powers," *Southwestern Social Science Quarterly,* June 1934; Walter H. Bennett's "Early American Theories of Federalism," *The Journal of Politics,* August 1942; John C. Ranney's "The Bases of American Federalism," *William and Mary Quarterly,* January 1946; and William S. Livingston's "The Legal and Political Determinants of American Federalism," *Southwestern Social Science Quarterly,* June 1953. Material on John Adams and Alexander Hamilton will be found in the bibliography for Chapter 6.

Chapter 6

The Federalists: Power, Property, and Law

For an interesting discussion of this period and the nascent conflict between capitalism and democracy, see Louis Hartz' "The Whig Tradition in America and Europe," *American Political Science Review,* December 1952. The conflict between the ideas of Hamilton and those of the democratic opposition is pointed up in Claude G.

Bowers' *Jefferson and Hamilton; The Struggle for Democracy in America* (New York, 1925). A thorough discussion of the Federalist party in power, their politics, policies, and administrative accomplishments, is found in Leonard D. White's *The Federalists: A Study in Administrative History* (New York, 1948). For interpretations of Hamilton see Frederick Scott Oliver's *Alexander Hamilton, An Essay on American Union* (New York, 1906); and Rexford Guy Tugwell and Joseph Dorfman's "Alexander Hamilton: Nation-Maker," *Columbia University Quarterly*, XXIX (1937); XXX (1938). Also compare the interpretations of Hamilton in Louis Hacker's *Alexander Hamilton in the American Tradition* (New York, 1957) and Broadus Mitchell's *Alexander Hamilton* (New York, 1957), and his *Heritage from Hamilton* (New York, 1957).

John Adams' political thought is studied in C. M. Walsh's *The Political Science of John Adams: A Study in the Theory of Mixed Government and the Bicameral System* (New York, 1915), Zoltan Haraszti's *John Adams and the Prophets of Progress* (Cambridge, 1952), and Manning J. Dauer's *The Adams Federalists* (Baltimore, 1953). For a briefer and very sympathetic treatment of Adams, see Russell Kirk, *The Conservative Mind: From Burke to Santayana* (Chicago, 1953).

Federalist political thought may be studied further in the ideas of John Marshall, James Kent, and John Quincy Adams. See Edward S. Corwin's *John Marshall and the Constitution* (New Haven, 1919); the monumental *Life of John Marshall* (New York, 1919) in 4 volumes, by A. J. Beveridge; and David Loth's *Chief Justice John Marshall and the Growth of the Republic* (New York, 1949). Also see J. T. Horton's *James Kent, a Study in Conservatism, 1763-1847* (New York, 1939), and George A. Lipsky's *John Quincy Adams, His Theory and Ideas* (New York, 1950).

Chapter 7

JEFFERSONIAN DEMOCRACY

In contrast to the limited amount of commentary on the Federalists, there is an abundance of literature dealing with Jeffersonian democracy. Fortunately, Jefferson's vast writings are currently being brought together and edited by Julian P. Boyd under the title of *The Papers of Thomas Jefferson* (Princeton, N. J., 1950-   ). Fifteen volumes are available at this writing, bringing his papers up to 1789. The fullest biographical treatment of Jefferson is in Dumas Malone's *Jefferson and His Time* (Boston, 1948, 1951), two volumes of which are now available, dealing with his life up to Washington's second administration. Claude Bowers' *Jefferson and Hamilton* (New York, 1925) draws a clear contrast between the two men and their systems of thought. Also see Bowers' *Jefferson in Power* (Boston, 1936) and Leonard D. White's *The Jeffersonians: A Study in Administrative History, 1801-1829* (New York, 1951).

For treatment of Jefferson as a political theorist, see particularly: Adrienne Koch's *The Philosophy of Thomas Jefferson* (New York, 1943); Gilbert Chinard's *Thomas Jefferson, the Apostle of Americanism* (Boston, 1929); Henry W. Foote's *Thomas Jefferson, Champion of Religious Freedom, Advocate of Christian Morals* (Boston, 1947); and Max Beloff's *Thomas Jefferson and American Democracy* (New York, 1949). Charles M. Wiltse deals with both Jefferson and John Taylor in *The Jeffersonian Tradition in American Democracy* (Chapel Hill, N. C., 1935). Charles A. Beard's interpretation of this movement is found in his *Economic Origins of Jeffersonian Democracy* (New York, 1915). For the relationship of church and state in Jeffersonian thought, see Hamilton J. Eckenrode's *Separation of Church and State in Virginia; A Study in the Development of the Revolution* (Richmond, Va., 1910), and Evarts B. Greene's *Religion and the State* (New York, 1941). A general symposium on Jefferson is found in *Ethics*, July 1943.

There has been a host of articles on Jefferson and Jeffersonian democracy, of which the most relevant are the following: Joseph Dorfman's "The Economic Philosophy of Thomas Jefferson," *Political Science Quarterly*, March 1940; Charles M. Wiltse's "Jeffersonian Democracy: A Dual Tradition," *American Political Science Review*, October 1934; Francis G. Wilson's "On Jeffersonian Tradition," *Review of Politics*, July 1943; Clement Eaton's "The Jeffersonian Tradition of Liberalism in America," *South Atlantic Quarterly*, January 1944; A. Whitney Griswold's "The Agrarian Democracy of Thomas Jefferson," *American Political Science Review*, August 1946. In addition, see Julian P. Boyd's "Thomas Jefferson's 'Empire of Liberty,'" *Virginia Quarterly Review*, Autumn 1948, and his "The

Relevance of Thomas Jefferson for the Twentieth Century," *American Scholar*, Winter 1952-53.

For John Taylor's political thought, see Eugene T. Mudge's *The Social Philosophy of John Taylor of Caroline* (New York, 1939). The most useful articles on Taylor are William E. Dodd's "John Taylor of Caroline, Prophet of Secession," *John P. Branch Historical Papers of Randolph-Macon College* (Ashland, Va., 1908), vol. 2, pp. 214-52; Benjamin F. Wright's "The Philosopher of Jeffersonian Democracy," *American Political Science Review*, November 1928; Manning J. Dauer and Hans Hammond's "John Taylor: Democrat or Aristocrat?" *Journal of Politics*, November 1944; and Grant McConnell's "John Taylor and the Democratic Tradition," *Western Political Quarterly*, March 1951.

Chapter 8

THE CONCEPT OF THE COMMON MAN

The basic ideas of Jacksonian democracy are discerningly treated in the classic *Democracy in America* by Alexis de Tocqueville (New York, 1843, 2 vols.). For the historical background, see William McDonald's *Jacksonian Democracy, 1829-1837* (New York, 1906), and especially Arthur M. Schlesinger, Jr., *The Age of Jackson* (Boston, 1945). Also see C. R. Fish, *The Rise of the Common Man, 1830-1850* (New York, 1927). An excellent compilation of original source material, together with an introductory essay, is found in Joseph L. Blau (ed.), *Social Theories of Jacksonian Democracy* (New York, 1947). For a general background of ideas for this period, see Arthur A. Ekirch's *The Idea of Progress in America, 1815-1860* (New York, 1944), and Marvin Meyers' *The Jacksonian Persuasion: Politics and Beliefs* (Stanford, 1957), and Merle Curti's "The Age of Reason and Morality, 1750-1860," *Political Science Quarterly*, September 1953. Also see R. A. Billington's *The Protestant Crusade, 1800-1860* (New York, 1938), and Ernest Sutherland Bates' *American Faith, Its Religious, Political and Economic Foundations* (New York, 1940). The role of the frontier as an environmental factor conditioning Jacksonian democracy is discussed in Frederic Jackson Turner's *The Frontier in American History* (New York, 1920) and in Benjamin F. Wright's "American Democracy and the Frontier," *Yale Review*, December 1930; compare with Schlesinger, cited above. Some economic aspects of the Jacksonian period are dealt with in Joseph Dorfman's "The Jackson Wage-Earner Thesis," *American Historical Review*, January 1949, and Louis Hartz' *Economic Policy and Democratic Thought: Pennsylvania, 1776-1860* (Cambridge, 1948); the spread of Jacksonian democracy is noted in Gerald Ashford's "Jacksonian Liberalism and Spanish Law in Early Texas," *Southwestern Historical Quarterly*, June 1953.

Andrew Jackson has been reappraised by Harold C. Syrett in *Andrew Jackson: His Contribution to the American Tradition* (Indianapolis, 1953). Also see Marquis James' *Andrew Jackson, Portrait of a President* (Indianapolis, 1937). The role of Bryant and Leggett is discussed in Schlesinger, cited above. Also see Allan Nevins' *The Evening Post* (New York, 1922). There is good background material in Carl B. Swisher's *Roger B. Taney* (New York, 1935). The social views of the controversial Cooper are presented in R. E. Spiller's *Fenimore Cooper, Critic of His Times* (New York, 1931), and James Grossman's "James Fenimore Cooper: An Uneasy American," *Yale Review*, Summer 1951. For Brownson, see Arthur M. Schlesinger, Jr., *Orestes A. Brownson: A Pilgrim's Progress* (Boston, 1939), and Theodore Maynard's *Orestes Brownson: Yankee, Radical, Catholic* (New York, 1943). Bancroft's belief in progress and democracy, together with the climate of opinion of the period, is developed in Russell B. Nye's *George Bancroft: Brahmin Rebel* (New York, 1944).

Walt Whitman commentary continues to grow. Van Wyck Brooks' *The Times of Melville and Whitman* (New York, 1947) discusses Whitman's social criticism as well as his place in *belles-lettres*. Floyd Stovall's *Walt Whitman: Representative Selections* (New York, 1934) discusses Whitman's conception of democracy in his introductory essay. For fuller biographical and political treatment, see Newton Arvin's *Whitman* (New York, 1938). A brief comparison of ideas is found in Gregory Paine's "The Literary Relations of Whitman and Carlyle with Especial Reference to their Contrasting Views on Democracy," *Studies in Philology*, July 1939. A greater emphasis on political thought, however, may be found in Frederick Mayer's "Whitman's Social Philosophy," *Sociology and Social Research*, March-April 1949, and in Richmond C. Beatty's "Whitman's Political Thought," *The South Atlantic Quarterly*, January 1947.

Chapter 9

THE NEW SOCIETY: INDIVIDUALISTS AND UTOPIANS

New England transcendentalism has been a popular field for philosophical research. A general orientation to the literary movements of this period is found in Van Wyck Brooks' *The Flowering of New England, 1815-1865* (New York, 1936). The social history is best portrayed in Alice Felt Tyler's *Freedom's Ferment* (Minneapolis, 1944), which covers both the transcendentalist thought and the utopian communities. For studies of transcendentalism, with its Western and Eastern influences, see: Octavius B. Frothingham's *Transcendentalism in New England* (Boston, 1876); Henry David Gray's *Emerson: A Statement of New England Transcendentalism as Expressed in the Philosophy of Its Chief Exponent* (Palo Alto, California, 1917); Arthur Christy's *The Orient in American Transcendentalism* (New York, 1932); and the full commentary in Kenneth W. Cameron's *Emerson the Essayist; An Outline of His Philosophical Development Through 1836* (Raleigh, N. C., 1945, 2 vols.).

Of the many articles dealing with Emerson, the most relevant to students of political thought are Perry Miller's "Jonathan Edwards to Emerson," *New England Quarterly*, December 1940, and Miller's recent "Emersonian Genius and the American Democracy," *New England Quarterly*, March 1953. Other aspects of Emerson's philosophy are dealt with in: René Wellek's "Emerson and German Philosophy," *New England Quarterly*, March 1943; Edward C. Lindeman's "Emerson's Pragmatic Mood," *American Scholar*, Winter 1946-47; John C. Gerber's "Emerson and the Political Economists," *New England Quarterly*, September 1949; and Steward G. Brown's "Emerson's Platonism," *New England Quarterly*, September 1945.

Interpretations and commentary on Thoreau are found in Charles A. Madison's "Henry David Thoreau: Transcendental Individualist," *Ethics*, January 1944; Wendell P. Glick's "Thoreau and the 'Herald of Freedom,'" *New England Quarterly*, June 1949; and Charles H. Nichols, Jr., "Thoreau on the Citizen and His Government," *Phylon*, First Quarter 1952. Also see F. G. Bratton's *The Legacy of the Lib-*

eral Spirit; Men and Movements in the Making of Modern Thought (New York, 1943), and Francis G. Wilson's "Intellectuals and the American Tradition," *Education,* March 1943, for commentary on this period. While Hawthorne is not discussed in the text, students will find L. S. Hall's *Hawthorne: Critic of Society* (New Haven, 1944) of interest and relevant to the general topic.

There has been considerable writing done on utopian communities, mostly on those with denominational backing. Ernest Sutherland Bates' *American Faith, Its Religious, Political, and Economic Foundations* (New York, 1940) deals with these. Arthur Eugene Bestor, Jr., in *Backwoods Utopias* (Philadelphia, 1950), gives the best treatment of the utopian settlements, especially of the Owenite movement. Harry W. Laidler's *Socio-Economic Movements* (New York, 1945) devotes a few chapters to Owen and Fourier, who are also discussed in J. O. Hertzler's *The History of Utopian Thought* (New York, 1923). Also see V. F. Calverton's *Where Angels Dared to Tread* (New York, 1941).

For specialized studies of the era of utopias see: Carl Wittke's *The Utopian Communist; A Biography of Wilhelm Weitling, Nineteenth-Century Reformer* (Baton Rouge, La., 1950); Katherine Burton's *Paradise Planters: The Story of Brook Farm* (New York, 1939); the venerable G. B. Lockwood's *The New Harmony Movement* (New York, 1905); and Redalia Brisbane's *Albert Brisbane, A Mental Biography* (Boston, 1893). For the American literature of utopias see Vernon L. Parrington, Jr., *American Dreams; A Study of American Utopias* (Providence, 1947).

Chapter 10

SLAVERY AND THE RIGHTS OF MAN: ANTISLAVERY THOUGHT

The general historical background of slavery and the Civil War is thoroughly explored in A. C. Cole's *The Irrepressible Conflict, 1850-1865* (New York, 1934); Avery O. Craven's *The Coming of the Civil War* (New York, 1942); and Allan Nevins' *Ordeal of the Union* (New York, 1947). For the slavery aspect of the issue see Arthur Y. Lloyd's *The Slavery Controversy, 1831-1860* (Chapel Hill, N. C., 1939). Also see Madeleine Rice's *American Catholic Opinion in the Slavery Controversy* (New York, 1944); A. B. Hart's *Slavery and Abolition, 1831-41* (New York, 1906); and Alice Dana Adams' *The Neglected Period of Anti-Slavery in America, 1808-1831* (Boston, 1908).

The fullest discussion of the challenge to personal freedom that arose during the slavery conflict is found in Russell Nye's *Fettered Freedom; Civil Liberties, and the Slavery Controversy, 1830-1860* (East Lansing, Michigan, 1949); also see his *William Lloyd Garrison and the Humanitarian Reformers* (East Lansing, Michigan, 1955), and Alice F. Tyler's *Freedom's Ferment* (Minneapolis, 1944) gives brief attention to this aspect. Zechariah Chafee's *Freedom of Speech* (New York, 1920) and Howard K. Beale's *A History of the Freedom of Teaching in American Schools* (New York, 1941) deal, as the titles indicate, with specific aspects of freedom including the discussion of slavery.

Abolitionism is covered in a number of books, notably John F. Hume's *The Abolitionists* (New York, 1905); Hilary Herbert's *The Abolition Crusade and Its Consequences* (New York, 1912); Jesse Macy's *The Anti-Slavery Crusade* (New Haven, 1919); and the more recent work by G. H. Barnes, *The Antislavery Impulse* (New York, 1933). Of special interest is Hazel Catherine Wolf's *On Freedom's Altar; The Martyr Complex in the Abolition Movement* (Madison, Wisconsin, 1952), and Harry F. Jaffa's *Crisis of the House Divided: an Interpretation of the Issues in the Lincoln-Douglas Debates* (New York, 1959).

For antislavery argument, together with an interpretation of the importance of the abolitionists, see Dwight Lowell Dumond's *Antislavery Origins of the Civil War in the United States* (Ann Arbor, Michigan, 1939). For the political thought of the abolitionists, see Benjamin F. Wright's *American Interpretations of Natural Law* (New York, 1931); T. V. Smith's "Slavery and the American Doctrine of Equality," *Southwestern Political and Social Quarterly*, March 1927; C. L. Shanks' "The Biblical Antislavery Argument of the Decade 1830-40," *Journal of Negro History*, April 1931; and T. Harry Williams' "Abraham Lincoln: Principles and Pragmatism in Politics," *Mississippi Valley Historical Review*, June 1953. Finally, abolitionist theory is related to the Fourteenth Amendment in Jacobus Ten Broek's *The Antislavery Origins of the Fourteenth Amendment* (Berkeley, California, 1951).

Chapter 11

SLAVERY AND THE RIGHTS OF MAN: PRO-SLAVERY THOUGHT

Most of the historical works cited in the bibliography to Chapter 10, dealing with the general background of the issue of slavery and the Civil War, apply as well here. There have been, in addition, several excellent works which deal with the South, including its social and political thought. Of particular relevance are J. T. Carpenter's *The South as a Conscious Minority, 1789-1861* (New York, 1930); R. S. Cotterill's *The Old South* (Glendale, California, 1936); and W. B. Hesseltine's *A History of the South* (New York, 1943). The intellectual aspects are stressed in Virginius Dabney's *Liberalism in the South* (Chapel Hill, N. C., 1932) and Clement Eaton's *Freedom of Thought in the Old South* (Durham, N. C., 1940). See especially Book I of the brilliant and suggestive work of W. J. Cash, *The Mind of the South* (New York, 1941). There is also a wealth of monograph material and biographical material dealing with various aspects of the ante-bellum South, too abundant to specify here.

The abortive efforts at colonizing Negroes is covered in Early Lee Fox, *The American Colonization Society, 1817-1840* (Baltimore, 1919). The early economic aspects of Britain's slave trade are treated in Eric Williams' *Capitalism and Slavery* (Chapel Hill, 1944), and the later economic aspects in America in Philip S. Foner's *Business and Slavery* (Chapel Hill, N. C., 1941).

William S. Jenkins' *Pro-Slavery Thought in the Old South* (Chapel Hill, N. C., 1935) is the most comprehensive study of the subject. Highly suggestive is the interpretation given by Louis Hartz in "The Reactionary Enlightenment: Southern Political Thought Before the Civil War," *Western Political Quarterly*, March 1952. For Calhoun, see the three-volume biography, *John C. Calhoun* (Indianapolis, 1944-51) by Charles M. Wiltse, as well as August O. Spain's *The Political Theory of John C. Calhoun* (New York, 1951). Also see Wilfred Carsel, "The Slaveholders' Indictment of Northern Wage Slavery," *Journal of Southern History*, November 1940. For Fitzhugh, see Harvey Wish's *George Fitzhugh: Propagandist of the Old South* (Baton Rouge, La., 1943) and "George Fitzhugh and the

Theory of American Conservatism" by Arnaud Leavelle and Thomas I. Cook, *Journal of Politics*, May 1945.

Chapter 12

THE NATIONAL CONCEPT OF SOVEREIGNTY

The historical background of conflicting interpretations of the nature of the Union is described in Henry H. Simms' *A Decade of Sectional Controversy, 1851-1861* (Chapel Hill, N. C., 1942). The most comprehensive treatment of the general concept of sovereignty is found in Charles E. Merriam's *History of the Theory of Sovereignty since Rousseau* (New York, 1900), while the general concept of nationalism is covered in Hans Kohn's *The Idea of Nationalism: A Study in Its Origins and Background* (New York, 1944). For a fuller historical study of American interpretations of the nature of the Union after the Civil War see Charles E. Merriam's *A History of American Political Theories* (New York, 1903). More recent interpretations are found in Alpheus T. Mason's "The Nature of our Federal Union Reconsidered," *Political Science Quarterly*, December 1950; M. D. Boland's *Reinterpreting History; or, The Fight for Democracy* [the Southern Confederacy] (Tacoma, 1947); and Thomas I. Cook and A. B. Leavelle's "German Idealism and American Theories of the Democratic Community," *The Journal of Politics*, August 1943.

For Calhoun, see especially Volume III of Charles M. Wiltse's biography, *John C. Calhoun* (Indianapolis, 1951) and August O. Spain's *The Political Theory of John C. Calhoun* (New York, 1951). In addition see Gunnar Heckscher's "Calhoun's Idea of 'Concurrent Majority' and the Constitutional Theory of Hegel," *American Political Science Review*, August 1939; Peter F. Drucker's "A Key to American Politics; Calhoun's Pluralism," *Review of Politics*, October 1948; and Margaret Coit's "Calhoun and the Downfall of States Rights," *Virginia Quarterly Review*, Spring 1952.

The best commentary on the position of the nationalist is associated with the thought of Francis Lieber. See L. R. Harley, *Francis Lieber: His Life and Political Philosophy* (New York, 1899); Frank Freidel, *Francis Lieber: Nineteenth-Century Liberal* (Baton Rouge,

La., 1947); Merle Curti, "Francis Lieber and Nationalism," *Huntington Library Quarterly*, April 1941. However, compare the latter with Charles B. Robson's "Francis Lieber's Theories of Society, Government and Liberty," *Journal of Politics*, May 1942, and especially his "Francis Lieber's Nationalism," *Journal of Politics*, February 1946. Finally, see Bernard Edward Brown's *American Conservatives; The Political Thought of Francis Lieber and John W. Burgess* (New York, 1951).

Chapter 13

MANCHESTER LIBERALISM IN AMERICA

Although there have been many excellent studies of nineteenth-century liberalism in England and Europe, only a few studies deal with its American counterpart. The best treatment by far of the general background and nature of this liberalism abroad is found in Elie Halévy's *The Growth of Philosophic Radicalism*, translated by Mary Morris (New York, 1928). For further background material, see Guido de Ruggiero's *The History of European Liberalism*, translated by R. G. Collingwood (Oxford, 1927), and Harold Laski's *The Rise of European Liberalism* (London, 1936). As most of this doctrine of liberalism arose out of English political thought, one should consult Leslie Stephen's *The English Utilitarians* (London, 1900, 3 vols.); William L. Davidson's *Political Thought in England, The Utilitarians from Bentham to J. S. Mill* (New York, 1916); and Crane Brinton's *English Political Thought in the Nineteenth Century* (Cambridge, 1949).

For the method of the Utilitarians, see Fred Kort's "The Issue of a Science of Politics in Utilitarian Thought," *American Political Science Review*, December 1952. Also see David Baumgardt's *Bentham and the Ethics of Today* (Princeton, N. J., 1952), and the following articles: P. A. Palmer, "Benthamism in England and America," *American Political Science Review*, October 1941; K. M. Adams, "How the Benthamites Became Democrats," *Journal of Social Philosophy and Jurisprudence*, January 1942; and Jacob Viner, "Bentham and J. S. Mill: The Utilitarian Background," *American Economic Review*, March 1949. In addition see A. W. Leir, *A Study in the Social Philosophy of John Stuart Mill* (Chicago, 1940) and R. P. Anschutz, *The Philosophy of J. S. Mill* (New York, 1953).

The economic ideas of this liberalism are found in Charles Gide and Charles Rist's *A History of Economic Doctrines* (Boston, 1948), and in Jacob Viner's "Adam Smith and Laissez Faire," *Journal of Political Economy*, April 1927. Also see William D. Grampp's "On the Politics of the Classical Economists," *Quarterly Journal of Economics*, November 1948, and Eli Ginzberg's *The House of Adam Smith* (New York, 1934). For the reception of this economic thought in America see Arthur M. Schlesinger, Jr., *The Age of Jackson* (Boston, 1945).

The economic history of late nineteenth-century America is found in T. C. Cochran and W. Miller's *The Age of Enterprise* (New York, 1942). Two excellent interpretations of American thought of this period, with considerable emphasis on political ideas, are Henry Steele Commager's *The American Mind* (New Haven, 1950) and Eric F. Goldman's *Rendezvous With Destiny* (New York, 1952). Both of these works carry America's intellectual and social history from the post-Civil War period to the present. James Bryce's *The American Commonwealth* (London, 1891, 2 vols.) provides an interesting and suggestive commentary on this period by an English liberal of the Godkin variety. Also see Edwin Lawrence Godkin's books: *Reflections and Comments, 1865-95* (New York, 1895); *Problems of Modern Democracy: Political and Economic Essays* (New York, 1896); *Unforeseen Tendencies of Democracy* (New York, 1898). The political ideas of Godkin's *Nation* are traced in Alan P. Grimes' *The Political Liberalism of the New York Nation, 1865-1932* (Chapel Hill, N. C., 1953), which should be supplemented with Daniel C. Haskell's *The Nation, Vols. 1-105 (1865-1917) Indexes of Titles and Contributors* (New York, 1951-53). For the impact of this liberalism on the judicial mind, see Benjamin R. Twist's *Lawyers and the Constitution; How Laissez-faire Came to the Supreme Court* (Princeton, N. J., 1942), and Carl B. Swisher's *Stephen J. Field, Craftsman of the Law* (Washington, 1930). Also see Chester M. Destler's "The Opposition of American Businessmen to Social Control During the 'Gilded Age,'" *Mississippi Valley Historical Review*, March 1953, and Sidney Fine's *Laissez Faire and the General-Welfare State: A Study of Conflict in American Thought, 1865-1901* (Ann Arbor, Michigan, 1956).

The conservative temper of Manchester liberalism in late nineteenth-century England, and its confluence with social Darwinism, is evidenced in F. J. C. Hearnshaw (ed.), *The Social and Political Ideas of Some Representative Thinkers of the Victorian Age* (London, 1932); D. G. Ritchie, *Darwinism and Politics* (New York, 1889); Ernest Barker, *Political Thought in England, 1848-1914* (New York, 1950); and Benjamin E. Lippincott, *Victorian Critics of Democracy* (Minneapolis, 1938). Also see John H. Hallowell's *The Decline of Liberalism as an Ideology, with Particular Reference to German Politico-Legal Thought* (Berkeley, 1943); and Thomas P. Neill, *The Rise and Decline of Liberalism* (Milwaukee, 1953).

The conservatism of Manchester liberalism in America, and its conjunction with social Darwinism, is discussed in Ralph H. Gabriel's *The Course of American Democratic Thought* (New York, 1940), Part III; Robert Green McCloskey's *American Conservatism in the Age of Enterprise; A Study of William Graham Sumner, Stephen J. Field and Andrew Carnegie* (Cambridge, Mass., 1951); and Richard Hofstadter's *Social Darwinism in American Thought, 1860-1915* (Philadelphia, 1944). Also see George Nasmyth's *Social Progress and The Darwinism Theory* (New York, 1916). On the issue of imperialism see Julius W. Pratt's *Expansionists of 1898* (Baltimore, 1936) and Fred H. Harrington's "The Anti-Imperialist Movement in the United States, 1898-1900," *Mississippi Valley Historical Review*, XXII (1935), 211-230.

Additional primary sources, not included in the text or footnotes, are: Truxton Beale (ed.), *The Man Versus the State: A Collection of Essays by Herbert Spencer* (New York, 1916); and Maurice R. Davie (ed.), *Sumner Today* (New Haven, 1940). Also see Andrew Carnegie's *Triumphant Democracy* (New York, 1893); *The Gospel of Wealth and Other Timely Essays* (New York, 1900); *The Empire of Business* (New York, 1902). More material on Social Darwinism is found in Edward Livingston Youmans (ed.), *Herbert Spencer on the Americans and the American on Herbert Spencer* (New York, 1883), and in the writings of John Fiske, of which the most relevant here are: *American Political Ideas* (New York, 1885); *Darwinism and Other Essays* (New York, 1885); *Excursions of an Evolutionist* (New York, 1884); and *The Destiny of Man, Viewed in the Light of His Origin* (New York, 1898). Also see John Fiske's *Civil Governmen in the United States* (Boston, 1890) and *Edward Livingston Youmans* (New York, 1894). For commentary on Fiske see Henry

Steele Commager, "John Fiske," *Proceedings of the Massachusetts Historical Society,* LXVI (1942).

Chapter 14

AMERICAN UTOPIAN REFORMERS: GEORGE AND BELLAMY

The most comprehensive study of Henry George is George R. Geiger's *The Philosophy of Henry George* (New York, 1933). In addition see the biography by Charles A. Barker, *Henry George* (New York, 1955). Further biographical studies are found in *The Life of Henry George* (Toronto, 1900) by his son, Henry George, Jr., *Henry George: Citizen of the World* (Chapel Hill, 1950) by his daughter, Anna George DeMille, and Louis F. Post's *The Prophet of San Francisco* (New York, 1930). For George's influence on English thought see Elwood P. Lawrence's *Henry George in the British Isles* (East Lansing, Michigan, 1957).

For the development of the George tax program see Arthur N. Young, *The Single Tax Movement in the United States* (Princeton, N. J., 1916). Also see the catalogue of the collection of George material in the New York Public Library compiled by R. A. Sawyer under the title of *Henry George and the Single Tax* (New York, 1926).

Interest in George continues, as is attested by numerous recent articles. See especially Charles A. Barker's "Henry George and the California Background of *Progress and Poverty,*" *California Historical Society Quarterly,* June, 1945; J. H. Holmes' "Henry George and Karl Marx," *American Journal of Economics and Sociology,* October 1951; and R. E. Noble, Jr., "Henry George and the Progressive Movement," *American Journal of Economics and Sociology,* April 1949.

The commentary on Bellamy is quite limited. Arthur E. Morgan has made the most thorough study of Bellamy, and has brought together Bellamy manuscripts not otherwise available. See Morgan's *Edward Bellamy* (New York, 1944) and *The Philosophy of Edward Bellamy* (New York, 1945). Briefer commentary on Bellamy is found in Lewis Mumford, *The Story of Utopias* (New York, 1922); J. O. Hertzler, *The History of Utopian Thought* (New York, 1933);

Allan Seager, *They Worked for a Better World* (New York, 1939); and Charles Madison, *Critics and Crusaders* (New York, 1947).

In addition to Bellamy's *Looking Backward* and *Equality,* one should also consult his articles, written during the rise of Nationalism: "To Whom This May Come," *Harper's Monthly,* February 1889; "Looking Backward Again," *North American Review,* March 1890; "What Nationalism Means," *The Contemporary Review,* July 1890; "First Steps toward Nationalism," *The Forum,* October 1890; "Progress of Nationalism in the United States," *North American Review,* June 1892; and "Programme of the Nationalists," *The Forum,* March 1894.

Chapter 15

THE PROGRESSIVE MOVEMENT

The intellectual and historical background of this period, with its basic change in ideology, is found in Henry Steele Commager's *The American Mind* (New Haven, 1950), Eric F. Goldman's *Rendezvous with Destiny* (New York, 1952), and Richard Hofstadter's *Social Darwinism in American Thought, 1860-1915* (Philadelphia, 1944), and especially his insightful *The Age of Reform: From Bryan to F. D. R.* (New York, 1956). Also see H. B. Parkes' *The American Experience* (New York, 1947); Daniel Aaron's *Men of Good Hope; A Story of American Progressives* (New York, 1951); and Horace Samuel Merrill's *Bourbon Democracy of the Middle West: 1865-1896* (Baton Rouge, 1953).

The change in viewpoint on social problems of Protestant theology is best portrayed in the work of Walter Rauschenbusch. See his *Christianity and the Social Crisis* (New York, 1907); *A Theology for the Social Gospel* (New York, 1917); and *Christianizing the Social Order* (New York, 1919). For commentary on his work and the movement he represented see J. A. Dombrowski, *The Early Days of Christian Socialism in America* (New York, 1936); Charles H. Hopkins, *The Rise of the Social Gospel in American Protestantism, 1865-1915* (New Haven, 1940); and Vernon R. Bodein, *The Social Gospel of Walter Rauschenbusch* (New Haven, 1944).

There is considerable material on the politics of the progressive ferment. See Solon J. Buck's *The Granger Movement* (Cambridge, 1913) and *The Agrarian Crusade* (New Haven, 1921) and Frank L. McVey's *The Populist Movement* (New York, 1896) and John D. Hicks' *The Populist Revolt* (Minneapolis, 1931); and Fred E. Haynes' *Third Party Movements Since the Civil War* (Iowa City, 1916). Also see Harold Faulkner's *The Quest for Social Justice, 1898-1914* (New York, 1931); Cornelius C. Regier, *The Era of the Muckrakers* (Chapel Hill, N. C., 1932); Louis Filler, *Crusaders for American Liberalism* (New York, 1939) and Arthur Mann, "British Social Thought and American Reformers of the Progressive Era," *The Mississippi Valley Historical Review*, March, 1956.

For more detailed interpretation and analysis of the politics of this period, see Chester McArthur Destler, *American Radicalism, 1865-1901: Essays and Documents* (New London, 1946); Russell B. Nye, *Midwestern Progressive Politics; A Historical Study of Its Origins and Development, 1870-1950* (East Lansing, Mich., 1951). Also see David Noble, "The Paradox of Progressive Thought," *American Quarterly*, Fall 1953; Alan F. Estin, "The Supreme Court, The Populist Movement, and the Campaign of 1896," *Journal of Politics*, February 1953; Harvey Goldberg (ed.) *American Radicals: Some Problems and Personalities* (New York, 1957); and Victor Ferkiss, "Populist Influences on American Fascism," *Western Political Quarterly*, June 1957. The impact of progressive politics on particular regions—South, Midwest, West—is found, respectively, in Comer Vann Woodward's *Tom Watson: Agrarian Rebel* (New York, 1938); Claude Bowers' *Beveridge and the Progressive Era* (Boston, 1932); and George E. Mowry's *The California Progressives* (Berkeley and Los Angeles, 1951). Finally, see John Chamberlain's *Farewell to Reform: Being a History of the Rise, Life and Decay of the Progressive Mind in America* (New York, 1932).

Socialism in America is traced and analyzed in Donald D. Egbert and Stow Persons (ed.), *Socialism and American Life* (Princeton, 1952, 2 vols.). Volume II contains the most complete bibliography on the subject available. For briefer studies see Morris Hillquist, *History of Socialism in the United States* (New York, 1910) and Harry W. Laidler, *A History of Socialist Thought* (New York, 1927). Also see Lillian Symes and Travers Clement, *Rebel America; The Story of Social Revolt in the United States* (New York, 1934). Of special merit are three recent studies: Ira Kipnis, *The American Socialist Movement, 1897-1912* (New York, 1952); Howard H. Quint, *The Forging of American Socialism: Origins of the Modern Movement* (Columbia, S. C., 1953); and David A. Shannon, *The Socialist Party of America* (New York, 1955) which covers the history of the party from 1901 to 1954. Also see Ray Ginger's *The Bending Cross: A Biography of Eugene Victor Debs* (New Brunswick, N. J., 1949), and his *Altgeld's America: The Lincoln Ideal versus Changing Realities* (New York, 1958). On the I. W. W. see John G. Brooks, *American Syndicalism: The I. W. W.* (New York, 1913), Paul F. Brissenden, *The I. W. W.: A Study of American Syndicalism* (New York, 1920), and Ralph Chaplin's *Wobbly: The Rough and Tumble Story of an American Radical* (Chicago, 1948).

The revision of social theory is found in Commager, Goldman and Hofstadter, cited above. There is an abundance of original sources. In addition to the titles cited in the text, see: H. C. Adams, *Relations of the State to Industrial Action* (Baltimore, 1887); Lester Ward, *The Psychic Factors of Civilization* (Boston, 1893); John Bates Clark, *The Philosophy of Wealth* (Boston, 1894); Richard T. Ely, *Socialism and Social Reform* (New York, 1894); Henry D. Lloyd, *Wealth Against Commonwealth* (New York, 1894); W. D. P. Bliss, *The Encyclopedia of Social Reforms* (New York, 1898); Jane Addams, *Democracy and Social Ethics* (New York, 1902); William J. Ghent, *Our Benevolent Feudalism* (New York, 1902); James Mackaye, *The Economy of Happiness* (Boston, 1906); Simon N. Patten, *The New Basis of Civilization* (New York, 1907); Arthur F. Bentley, *The Process of Government: A Study of Social Pressures* (Chicago, 1908); Lyman Abbott, *The Spirit of Democracy* (New York, 1910); E. R. A. Seligman, *The Economic Interpretation of History* (New York, 1912, 2nd ed. rev.); and Walter Lippmann, *A Preface To Politics* (New York, 1914), and his *Drift and Mastery* (New York, 1914).

For commentary and analysis of the new socio-economic thought, see Allan G. Grunchy's *Modern Economic Thought* (New York, 1947); Malcolm Cowley and Bernard Smith (eds.), *Books that Changed Our Minds* (New York, 1939). In the latter see especially the sections on Beard and Veblen. Additional commentary on the academic spokesmen of progressivism is found in Howard E. Dean, "J. Allen Smith: Jeffersonian Critic of the Federalist State," *American*

Political Science Review, December 1956; Max Lerner, " The Political Theory of Charles A. Beard," *American Quarterly,* Winter 1950; Robert E. Thomas, "A Reappraisal of Charles A. Beard's *An Economic Interpretation of the Constitution,*" *American Historical Review,* January 1952; and Robert E. Brown, *Charles Beard and the Constitution: A Critical Analysis of "An Economic Interpretation of the Constitution"* (Princeton, 1956); Richard W. Taylor, "Arthur F. Bentley's Political Science," *Western Political Quarterly,* June, 1952; and Sidney Fine, "Richard T. Ely, Forerunner of Progressivism, 1880-1901," *Mississippi Valley Historical Review,* March 1951. Analysis of Veblen is found in Daniel Aaron, "Thorstein Veblen—Moralist," *Antioch Review,* Fall 1947; Bernard Rosenberg, "Veblen and Marx," *Social Research,* March 1948; Abram L. Harris, "Veblen as Social Philosopher: A Reappraisal," *Ethics,* April 1953; and Lewis Feuer, "Thorstein Veblen: The Metaphysics of the Interned Immigrant," *American Quarterly,* Summer 1953. The fullest discussion of Veblen's thought is found in Joseph Dorfman, *Thorstein Veblen and His America* (New York, 1934). Also see the introduction by Max Lerner to *The Portable Veblen* (New York, 1948), and David Riesman's *Thorstein Veblen, A Critical Interpretation* (New York, 1953).

Herbert Croly and his relationship with Roosevelt is discussed in Goldman, *op. cit.* Also see Theodore Roosevelt, *The New Nationalism* (New York, 1911). The fullest discussion of this aspect of Roosevelt's career is in George E. Mowry, *Theodore Roosevelt and the Progressive Movement* (Madison, 1946). For Wilson's political ideas, in addition to the campaign speeches called *The New Freedom* (New York, 1913), see his *The State* (Boston, 1889); *Congressional Government* (Boston, 1890); and *An Old Master, and Other Political Essays* (New York, 1893). See Arthur S. Link's *Wilson, the Road to the White House* (Princeton, 1947); his *Woodrow Wilson and the Progressive Era, 1910-1917* (New York, 1954); and *Woodrow Wilson, The New Freedom* (Princeton, 1956); and Earl Latham (ed.) *The Philosophy and Policies of Woodrow Wilson* (Chicago, 1958). Also see Byron Dexter, "Wilsonian Idealism," *Confluence,* June 1953. A further expression of progressivism is found in Ellen Lorelle (ed.), *The Political Philosophy of Robert M. LaFollette as Revealed in His Speeches and Writings* (Madison, 1920), and in E. N. Doan's *The LaFollettes and the Wisconsin Idea* (New York, 1947). Also see Charles A. Madison, "Robert M. LaFollette: Prophet of the New Deal," *Chicago Jewish Forum,* Winter 1951-52.

Chapter 16

ECONOMIC INDIVIDUALISM

For general background material see James T. Adams, *Our Business Civilization* (New York, 1929); Adolf A. Berle and Gardiner C. Means, *The Modern Corporation and Private Property* (New York, 1932); James W. Prothro, *The Dollar Decade: Business Ideas in the 1920's* (Baton Rouge, La., 1954); George Soule, *Prosperity Decade: A Chapter from American Economic History, 1917-1929* (London, 1947); Karl Schriftgiesser, *This Was Normalcy: An Account of Party Politics during Twelve Republican Years: 1920-1932* (Boston, 1948); Frederick Lewis Allen, *Only Yesterday: An Informal History of the Nineteen-Twenties* (New York, 1931), and his *Since Yesterday: The Nineteen-Thirties in America* (New York, 1939); see especially Arthur M. Schlesinger, Jr., *The Crisis of the Old Order* (Boston, 1957).

Critical interpretations of the prosperity era by contemporaries may be found in André Siegfried, *America Comes of Age* (New York, 1927); Lincoln Steffens, *The Autobiography of Lincoln Steffens* (New York, 1931); John Chamberlain, *Farewell to Reform: The Rise, Life and Decay of the Progressive Mind in America* (New York, 1933); William Allen White, *A Puritan in Babylon: The Story of Calvin Coolidge* (New York, 1938), and *The Autobiography of William Allen White* (New York, 1946).

Economic individualism and the business mind may be found in Bruce Barton, *The Man Nobody Knows: A Discovery of the Real Jesus* (Indianapolis, 1924); Jacob H. Hollander, *Economic Liberalism* (New York, 1925); Paul M. Mazur, *American Prosperity: Its Causes and Consequences* (New York, 1928); Earnest E. Calkins, 'Business the Civilizer," *Atlantic Monthly,* February 1928; *Report On The Constitutionality of the National Labor Relations Act* by the National Lawyers Committee of the American Liberty League (Pittsburgh, 1935); Ogden L. Mills, *Liberalism Fights On* (New York, 1936); Raoul E. Desvernine, *Democratic Despotism* (New York, 1936); Thomas J. Norton, *Undermining the Constitution: A History of Lawless Government* (New York, 1950); Russell W. Davenport, *U.S.A.: The Permanent Revolution* (New York, 1951); Crawford H. Greenewalt, *The Uncommon Man: The Individual in the Organization* (New York, 1959); for an historical view sympathetic to this persuasion see Arthur A. Ekirch, *The Decline of American Liberalism* (New York, 1955).

For studies of the political values of business groups see Benjamin Twiss, *Lawyers and the Constitution: How Laissez-Faire Came to the Supreme Court* (Princeton, 1942); Frederick Rudolph, "The American Liberty League, 1934-1940," *American Historical Review*, October 1950; Thomas P. Jenkin, *Reactions of Major Groups to Positive Government in the United States, 1930-1940* (Los Angeles, 1945); John H. Bunzel, "The General Ideology of American Small Business," *Political Science Quarterly*, LXX (1955); and John H. Bunzel, "Comparative Attitudes of Big Business and Small Business," *Western Political Quarterly*, September, 1956.

For recent interpretations of the changing role of business in society see James Burnham, *The Managerial Revolution* (New York, 1941); Peter Drucker, *Concept of the Corporation* (New York, 1946); Robert A. Brady, *Business as a System of Power* (New York, 1947); Alpheus T. Mason, "Business Organized as Power: The New Imperium in Imperio," *American Political Science Review*, June 1950; and his "Welfare Capitalism: Opportunity or Delusion?" *Virginia Quarterly Review*, Autumn 1950; Thurman Arnold, *The Future of American Capitalism* (Philadelphia, 1950); Robert L. Hale, "Economic Liberty and the State," *Political Science Quarterly*, September 1951; Alpheus T. Mason, "American Individualism: Fact and Fiction," *American Political Science Review*, March 1952; David E. Lilienthal, *Big Business: A New Era* (New York, 1952); J. K. Galbraith, *American Capitalism: Concept of Countervailing Power* (Boston, 1952); Adolf Berle, Jr., *The 20th Century Capitalist Revolution* (New York, 1954); and William H. Whyte, *The Organization Man* (New York, 1956).

Chapter 17

PRAGMATIC LIBERALISM

For the intellectual and historical background of this period see the interpretations found in Henry Steele Commager's *The American*

Mind (New Haven, 1950), Eric Goldman's *Rendezvous with Destiny* (New York, 1952), and Richard Hofstadter's *The Age of Reform: From Bryan to F. D. R.* (New York, 1955).

In addition to William James' *Pragmatism* (New York, 1908), one should also see his *A Pluralistic Universe* (New York, 1909) and *The Will To Believe* (New York, 1912). The best commentary on James is Ralph Barton Perry's two-volume *The Thought and Character of William James* (Boston, 1935-36). In addition to the John Dewey titles cited in the text, see his *Democracy and Education* (New York, 1916); *Reconstruction in Philosophy* (New York, 1920); *Human Nature and Conduct* (New York, 1922); *The Public and Its Problems* (New York, 1927); *The Quest for Certainty* (New York, 1929); and *Liberalism and Social Action* (New York, 1935). Also see Paul A. Schlipp (ed.), *The Philosophy of John Dewey* (Evanston and Chicago, 1939). Brief, relevant commentary is found in George R. Geiger, "Dewey and the Experimental Attitude in American Culture," *American Journal of Economics and Sociology*, January 1953, and Robert E. Fitch, "John Dewey—The Last Protestant," *Pacific Spectator*, Spring 1953; and Howard White, "The Political Faith of John Dewey," *Journal of Politics*, May 1958. For an attack on pragmatism, see William Y. Elliott, *The Pragmatic Revolt in Politics* (New York, 1928). However, see also G. H. Sabine, "The Pragmatic Approach to Politics," *The American Political Science Review*, November 1930.

The change in American jurisprudence from traditionalism, with emphasis on natural law, to pragmatism, with emphasis on sociological facts, may be found by comparing the views of Justice Field with those of Justice Brandeis. See Carl B. Swisher's *Stephen J. Field, Craftsman of the Law* (Washington, D. C., 1930) and Alpheus T. Mason's *Brandeis: A Free Man's Life* (New York, 1946). Also compare Joel Francis Paschal's *Mr. Justice Sutherland; A Man Against the State* (Princeton, 1951) with Max Lerner's *The Mind and Faith of Justice Holmes* (Boston, 1943). The literature on Holmes is rapidly growing. See Felix Frankfurter (ed.), *Mr. Justice Holmes* (New York, 1931); Mark DeWolfe Howe (ed.), *The Holmes-Pollock Correspondence* (Cambridge, Mass., 1946) and *The Holmes-Laski Letters* (Cambridge, Mass., 1953, 2 vols.); and Samuel J. Konefsky, *The Legacy of Holmes and Brandeis: A Study in the Influence of Ideas* (New York, 1956). For brief commentary, see Francis E. Lucey, "Holmes—Liberal, Humanitarian, Believer in Democracy?"

Georgetown Law Journal, May 1951; Wallace Mendelson, "Mr. Justice Holmes—Humility, Skepticism and Democracy," *Minnesota Law Review,* March 1952; and "Mr. Justice Holmes: A Reappraisal," *Western Political Quarterly,* March 1952.

Roscoe Pound has written extensively on the revision of legal theory in America. See particularly his *The Spirit of the Common Law* (Boston, 1921) and the early articles on "The Scope and Purpose of Sociological Jurisprudence," *Harvard Law Review,* June 1911; December 1911; April 1912. Analysis of judicial values in the spirit of sociological jurisprudence is found in the studies of C. Herman Pritchett. See his *The Roosevelt Court* (New York, 1948), and *Civil Liberties and the Vinson Court* (Chicago, 1954). Also see Herbert Garfinkel, "Social Science Evidence and the School Segregation Cases," *Journal of Politics,* February 1959. The changing nature of judicial values is also evidenced in the attacks on traditionalists during the past two decades. See especially Charles G. Haines' *The Revival of Natural Law Concepts* (Cambridge, Mass., 1930) and his *The American Doctrine of Judicial Supremacy* (Berkeley, Calif., 1932); Louis B. Boudin's *Government by Judiciary* (New York, 1932, 2 vols.); Edward S. Corwin's *The Twilight of the Supreme Court* (New Haven, 1932) and his *Constitutional Revolution, Ltd.* (Claremont, Calif., 1941); Robert H. Jackson's *The Struggle for Judicial Supremacy: A Study of a Crisis in American Power Politics* (New York, 1941); and Alpheus T. Mason's "The Conservative World of Mr. Justice Sutherland," *American Political Science Review,* June 1938, and his "The Supreme Court: Instrument of Power or Revealed Truth, 1930-1937," *Boston University Law Review,* June 1953.

Most of the enormous literature on the New Deal is concerned more with politics than with political thought. For a succinct analysis of New Deal policies see Basil Rauch, *The History of the New Deal* (New York, 1944). Samuel I. Rosenman (ed.), *The Public Papers and Addresses of Franklin D. Roosevelt* (New York, 1938-1950, 13 vols.) provides the source material for Roosevelt's political thought. For commentary see Clinton L. Rossiter, "The Political Philosophy of F. D. Roosevelt," *Review of Politics,* January 1949, and the interpretations by Rexford G. Tugwell in a series of articles in *Western Political Quarterly:* "The Preparation of a President," June 1948; "The New Deal in Retrospect," December 1948; "The New Deal: The Available Instruments of Governmental Power," December

1949; "The New Deal: The Progressive Tradition," September 1950; "The New Deal: The Decline of Government, Part I," June 1951; "The New Deal: The Decline of Government, Part II," September 1951; "The Two Great Roosevelts,". March 1952; "The New Deal: The Rise of Business, Part I," June 1952; "The New Deal: The Rise of Business, Part II," September 1952; as well as in his *The Democratic Roosevelt: A Biography of Franklin D. Roosevelt* (New York, 1957).

The most comprehensive study of the politics of the period is found in Arthur M. Schlesinger, Jr., *The Age of Roosevelt*, two volumes of which have thus far been published under the titles *The Crisis of the Old Order* (Boston, 1957), and *The Coming of the New Deal* (Boston, 1958). For a comprehensive, brief biography see James MacGregor Burns, *Roosevelt: The Lion and the Fox* (New York, 1956). For a brief analysis of Roosevelt's political thought see Thomas H. Greer, *What Roosevelt Thought: The Social and Political Ideas of Franklin D. Roosevelt* (East Lansing, Michigan, 1958).

For further background see Adolf A. Berle, Jr., and Gardiner C. Means, *The Modern Corporation and Private Property* (New York, 1932); Thurman W. Arnold, *The Folklore of Capitalism* (New Haven, 1937); David E. Lilienthal, *TVA: Democracy on the March* (New York, 1944); Max Lerner, *It Is Later Than You Think* (New York, 1938), and *Ideas for the Ice Age* (New York, 1941); Frederick Lewis Allen, *Since Yesterday* (New York, 1939); Dixon Wecter, *The Age of the Great Depression: 1929-1941* (New York, 1948); Broadus Mitchell, *Depression Decade: From New Era through New Deal, 1929-1941* (New York, 1947); Thomas P. Jenkin, *Reactions of Major Groups to Positive Government in the United States, 1930-1940* (Los Angeles, 1945); and Harry K. Girvetz, *From Wealth to Welfare: The Evolution of Liberalism* (Stanford, 1950). For further interpretations see Irving DeWitt Talmadge (ed.), *Whose Revolution: A Study of the Future Course of Liberalism in the United States* (1941); T. V. Smith and Eduard C. Lindeman, *The Democratic Way of Life* (New York, 1951); Morris Cohen, *The Faith of a Liberal* (New York, 1946); Alpheus T. Mason, "Liberalism: Dilemma," *Journal of Social Philosophy*, April 1938; Alan P. Grimes, "The Pragmatic Course of Liberalism," *Western Political Quarterly*, September 1956; and Currin Shields, "The American Tradition of Empirical Collectivism," *American Political Science Review*, March 1952.

Chapter 18

THE PROTEST IDEOLOGIES

For the historical context of these idealogies see the bibliography for the preceding chapter. A critical analysis of elitist thought is found in David Spitz, *Patterns of Anti-Democratic Thought* (New York, 1949). Additional views on international affairs of Lawrence Dennis are in his articles in the *American Mercury:* "What Price Good Neighbor," XLV (1938); "After the Peace of Munich," XLVI (1939); and "Propaganda for War: Model 1938," XLIV (1938). For the politics of fascism see Raymond Gram Swing, *Forerunners of American Fascism* (New York, 1935); Dwight MacDonald, *Fascism and the American Scene* (New York: Pioneer Publishers, n.d.); John Roy Carlson, *Under Cover* (New York, 1943), and *The Plotters* (New York, 1946).

There is a growing literature linking fascism with populism in America. See Oscar Handlin, "How U. S. Anti-Semitism Really Began," *Commentary,* XI (1951); Richard Hofstadter, *The Age of Reform* (New York, 1955); Peter Viereck, "The Revolt Against the Elite," in Daniel Bell (ed.), *The New American Right* (New York, 1955); and particularly Victor C. Ferkiss, "Populist Influences on American Fascism," *Western Political Quarterly,* June, 1957. Also see Victor C. Ferkiss, "Ezra Pound and American Fascism," *Journal of Politics,* XVII (1955).

For socialism see Donald D. Egbert and Stow Persons (eds.), *Socialism and American Life* (Princeton, 1952, 2 vols.), particularly the long study by Daniel Bell in volume one entitled "The Background and Development of Marxian Socialism in the United States." Further material on the background of the Socialist Party is found in Ira Kipnis, *The American Socialist Movement, 1897-1912* (New York, 1952), and Howard H. Quint, *The Forging of American Socialism: Origins of the Modern Movement* (Columbia, S. C., 1953). David A. Shannon's *The Socialist Party of America* is a particularly readable and thoughtful study covering the history of the Party from its beginnings to its "decline and death" in the 1950's. Norman Thomas is a prolific writer and continues to publish in current periodicals. For an assessment of him see Murry Seidler, "The Social Theory of Norman Thomas," *Southwestern Social Science Quarterly,* March 1958.

For further exposition of Marxism in America see Egbert and Persons cited above, and particularly the essays by Paul M. Sweezy, "The Influence of Marxian Economics on American Thought and Practice," and by Will Herberg, "American Marxist Political Theory." For a critical analysis of Marxian economics see Joseph A. Schumpeter, *Capitalism, Socialism and Democracy* (New York, 1942). Also see Alfred G. Meyer, "Marxism and Contemporary Social Science," *Centennial Review,* Fall 1959. For an exposition and critique of Marx see Alfred G. Meyer, *Marxism* (Cambridge, Mass., 1954).

For the formative years of the Communist Party, U.S.A. see Theodore Draper, *Roots of American Communism* (New York, 1957); the best one-volume study thus far of American communism is found in Irving Howe and Lewis Coser, *The American Communist Party: A Critical History, 1919-1957* (Boston, 1958). Also see Herbert Krugman, "The Appeal of Communism to the American Middle Class Intellectuals and Trade Unionists," *Public Opinion Quarterly,* Fall 1952. For a communist's point of view see William Z. Foster, *History of the Communist Party of the United States* (New York, 1952).

Chapter 19

CONSERVATISM

American conservatism is developed historically, and defended, in Russell Kirk, *The Conservative Mind: From Burke to Santayana* (Chicago, 1953), and Clinton Rossiter, *Conservatism In America* (New York, 1955). Also see Gordon Harrison, *Road to the Right: The Tradition and Hope of American Conservatism.* Further statements of conservatism may be found in Russell Kirk, *A Program For Conservatives* (Chicago, 1954), and *The American Cause* (Chicago, 1957); Peter Viereck, *The Shame and Glory of the Intellectuals* (Boston, 1953), and *Conservatism From John Adams To Churchill* (New York, 1956); Francis G. Wilson, *The Case For Conservatism* (Seattle, Washington, 1951). Also see Wilson's "A Theory of Conservatism," *American Political Science Review,* February 1941, and

"Ethics of Political Conservatism," *Ethics*, October 1942. In addition see James Burnham, *Congress and the American Tradition* (New York, 1959); William F. Buckley, *Up from Liberalism* (New York, 1959), and any issue of the *National Review*.

For the background of contemporary conservatism see Erich Fromm, *Escape from Freedom* (New York, 1941), and *The Sane Society* (New York, 1954); David Riesman, *The Lonely Crowd* (New Haven, 1951) and *Individualism Reconsidered* (Glencoe, Illinois, 1954); Samuel Lubell, *The Future of American Politics* (New York, 1952), and *Revolt of the Moderates* (New York, 1956); Daniel Bell (ed.), *The New American Right* (New York, 1955); William H. Whyte, *The Organization Man* (New York, 1956); and Reinhold Niebuhr, *The Nature and Destiny of Man* (New York, 1949, 2 vols.), and *The Structure of Nations and Empires* (New York, 1959).

For fuller discussion of individual conservatives see William H. Jordy, *Henry Adams: Scientific Historian* (New Haven, 1952); Henry Wasser, "The Thought of Henry Adams," *New England Quarterly*, December 1951; Thornton Anderson, *Brooks Adams; Constructive Conservative* (Ithaca, 1951); Daniel Aaron, "The Unusable Man; An Essay On The Mind of Brooks Adams," *New England Quarterly*, March 1948; and W. A. Williams, "Brooks Adams and American Expansion," *New England Quarterly*, June 1952.

The Neo-Humanistic criticism of democracy is sympathetically discussed in Robert Shafer's *Paul Elmer More and American Criticism* (New Haven, 1935). Also see Frederick Manchester and Odell Shepard (eds.), *Irving Babbitt, Man and Teacher* (New York, 1941). For commentary and criticism see Henry S. Kariel, "Democracy Limited: Irving Babbitt's Classicism," *Review of Politics*, October 1951, and David Spitz, *Patterns of Anti-Democratic Thought* (New York, 1949).

For critical interpretations of contemporary conservatism see Gordon K. Lewis, "The Metaphysics of Conservatism," *Western Political Quarterly*, December 1953; Arthur Schlesinger, Jr., "The New Conservatism in America: A Liberal Comment," *Confluence*, II (1953), and "The New Conservatism: Politics of Nostalgia," *The Reporter*, June 16, 1955; Herbert McClosky, "Conservatism and Personality," *American Political Science Review*, March 1958; and the articles by Reinhold Niebuhr and Arthur Schlesinger, Jr., in M. W. Childs and J. B. Reston, *Walter Lippmann and His Times* (New York, 1959).

Index

Abolitionist of Channing, 227
Abolitionists, ch. 10, 260, 261; and civil rights, 228-229
"Acres of Diamonds" of Conwell, 303, 354
Acts of Supremacy and Uniformity, 15
Adams, Brooks, 487, 489, 490-494
Adams, Charles Francis, Jr., 493 *n*
Adams, H. B., 376
Adams, Henry, 487, 488, 489-490, 493
Adams, John, 52, 75, 150, 157, 167, 168, 169, 276, 288, 360, 486; and American Revolution, 83-85, 88, 94; and aristocracy, 143-149, 170, 171, 273; and mixed constitution, 108-113, 116, 126, 160, 177, 361
Adamson Eight-Hour Day Acts, 391
Agrarian Crusade, 313
Albany Plan of union, 76, 77
Alien and Sedition Acts of 1798, 165
American Anti-Slavery Society, 224, 235, 244
American Democrat of Cooper, 180, 183
American Economic Association, 376
American Federation of Labor, 314, 358
American Historical Association, 379
American Mercury, 446
American Political Economy of Bowen, 301
American Railway Union, 371
American Republic of Brownson, 285
American Scholar of Emerson, 203
American Society for the Colonization of the Free People of Color in the United States, 244
Ames, Fisher, 129
Ames, William, 18, 19
Anarchism, communist, 374 *n*, philosophical, 300 *n*
Anarchism and Other Essays of Goldman, 374 *n*
Andrews, Stephen Pearl, 300 *n*
Andros, Governor, 67
Anglicanism, 5, 14, 15, 16, 18, 19
Anti-imperialism, 309-311
Areopagitica of Milton, 41

Aristocracy, and John Adams, 143-147; and Jacksonian democracy, 186-187; and social justice, 494-497; and John Taylor, 169-171, 173
Aristocracy and Justice of More, 496
Aristotle, 51, 145, 245, 379
Articles of Association of 1774, 284
Articles of Confederation, 98, 103, 106, 113, 114, 115, 116, 119, 263, 284, 298
As I See It of Thomas, 459
Australian ballot, 377
Autobiography of Jefferson, 155

Babbitt, Irving, 220, 302, 445, 487, 494, 497, 501, 504, 509
Babylonian Captivity, 3
Bacon, Francis, 334
Bancroft, George, 192-194, 195, 201
Bank of the United States, 137, 175, 185, 186, 360
Barton, Bruce, 396 *n*
Beard, Charles A., 378, 380, 381, 385, 486
Becker, Carl, 66
Bellamy, Edward, 221, 313, 314, 334-353, 354, 355, 363 *n*, 369, 370, 371, 372, 385
Bentham, Jeremy, 185, 289, 290, 292, 293, 294, 295, 296, 298, 299, 302
Biddle, Nicholas, 360
Bill of Rights, American, 64, 117, 118, 156, 163
Bill of Rights of 1689, 46, 64, 99
Blackstone, Sir William, 81, 112, 113, 289
Bledsoe, Albert, 245, 250
Bliss, W. P. D., 354
Bloody Tenets of Persecution, for Cause of Conscience of Williams, 41
Boas, Franz, 461
Boleyn, Anne, 14
Boniface VIII, Pope, 2
Boston Quarterly Review, 188
Boucher, Jonathan, 92, 93, 95
Bowen, Francis, 301
Brandeis, Louis, 393 *n*, 434, 436

Brewer, David, 433
Brewster, William, 17
Bright, John, 289
Brisbane, Albert, 216-219
Brook Farm, 212, 216
Brooklyn Daily Eagle, 194
Browder, Earl, 476
Brown v. Topeka, 437
Brown, John, 227
Brown, Robert, 485
Browne, Robert, 16, 17, 18, 19
Brownson, Orestes A., 187-191, 285
Brownson's Quarterly Review, 188
Bryan, William Jennings, 360
Bryant, William Cullen, 185, 186, 201, 223, 289, 360
Burgess, John W., 285
Burke, Edmund, 282, 284, 367, 485, 508, 509
Burr, Aaron, 146
Butler, Samuel, 335

Calhoun, John C., 245, 246-250, 261, 267-276, 277, 280, 281, 288, 304, 360, 361, 487
Calvin, John, 6-17, 27, 41, 47, 68
Calvinism, 5-13; in England, 14-21; in Massachusetts, ch. 2
Cannibals All of Fitzhugh, 246
Capitalism, 20, 23, 57, 64, 136, 173, 187, 261, 288; criticized by Bellamy, 335-353, 355; and democracy, 386, ch. 16; and Gronlund, 365, 367; and industrial concentration, 308, 340; in Manchester liberalism, ch. 13; mentioned by Ross, 354; and Marxism, ch. 18; and socialism, 362, 373, ch. 18
Carlyle, Thomas, 188, 189, 256
Carnegie, Andrew, 307
Cartwright, S. A., 245
Catholic Church, 8, 14, 15, 16
Cause of God and His People in New England of Higginson, 35
"Challenge of Facts" of Sumner, 306
Chambers, Whittaker, 478
Channing, William Ellery, 202, 216, 227-235, 238, 242, 243, 261, 289, 352
Charles I of England, 19, 20, 46, 48, 72
Charles II of England, 102
Chartism of Carlyle, 188
Chartist movement, 188, 257
Chase, Salmon P., 284
Child labor laws, 386
Christian Commonwealth of Eliot, 335
Christian socialism, 354
Christianity and Social Crisis of Rauschenbusch, 354
Christy, David, 245
Church and state, in Calvinism, 9-13; in

England, 14-19; in Lutheranism, 6; in Medieval period, 2-5; in Puritan Massachusetts, ch. 2; in Virginia, 155-156
Churches Quarrel Espoused of Wise, 68
Cicero, 72, 99
City of the Sun of Campanella, 334
Civil disobedience, 206, 208-209
"Civil Disobedience" of Thoreau, 206
Civil service reform, 294, 297, 309, 312
Civil War, 261, 263, 277, 280, 284, 285, 287, 288, 291, 292, 310, 313, 314, 362
Clark, John Bates, 376
Class legislation, 359, 360
Class struggle, in Calhoun, 249-250; in Gronlund, 365; in J. A. Smith, 379; in Marxian theory, 361, ch. 18; in progressive movement, 357, 362; in Weyl, 390
Clayton Act, 386, 387, 391
Cleveland, Grover, 301, 302, 310, 354
Cobden, Richard, 289
Coke, Sir Edward, 39, 47, 81, 99
Coleridge, Samuel Taylor, 202
Colonial Charters, 100-102
Coming American Fascism of Dennis, 446, 448
Coming Revolution of Gronlund, 363
Comintern, 476
Commentaries on the Laws of England of Blackstone, 112
Committees on Correspondence, 85
Common Law of Holmes, 434
Common Sense of Paine, 86
Communism, 409, 415, ch. 18
Communist Manifesto of Marx and Engels, 188, 467 n
Communist Party of the United States, 465, 473-477
Conciliar movement, 3
Concurrent majority, 272-273
Condition of Labor of George, 332
Congregationalism, 17
Conservatism Revisited of Viereck, 482
Considerations of the Nature and Extent of the Legislative Authority of the British Parliament of Wilson, 81
Constitution of the United States, and nature of the Union, ch. 12; and pragmatic jurisprudence, 431-437; as class document, 379, 380, 381; and bill of rights, 118, 126, 127, 259, 163; criticism of, 118; framing of, 113-117; and Garrison, 226; ratification of, 117
Constitutional Law of Pomeroy, 285
Constitutional View of the Late War Between the States of Stephens, 285
Constitutionalism, in America, ch. 5; in Calhoun, 268-276; English constitution, ch. 4, 112-113, 150-151

Constitutions Construed and Constitutions Vindicated of Taylor, 172, 266

Contract theory, and nature of the Union, 263, 264; demise of, 280-283; in American Revolution, 75, 85, 96, 97; in Boucher, 95; in Calhoun, 247-248; in constitutionalism, 100; in Fitzhugh, 255-256; in Hamilton, 83; in Hobbes, 47-51; in Locke, 56-57, 60-63; in Paine, 86; in Puritanism, 18, 24, 25, 26, 29; in Separatism, 16-17; in Virginia constitution, 107; in Wise, 69, 70, 73

Conwell, Russell H., 303, 354

Coolidge, Calvin, 396, 407

Cooper, James Fenimore, 180-184, 201

Cooperation, reform through, in progressive movement, 357-359, 362, 365

Cooperative Commonwealth of Gronlund, 363, 369

Corrupt-practices legislation, 377, 387

Cotton, John, 18, 32-38, 39, 41, 61, 73, 105, 157

Coughlin, Charles E., 443, 444

Cousin, Victor, 216

Cram, Ralph Adams, 445, 487, 488, 494, 501-505

Cramer, John, 184

Croly, Herbert, 386, 387-389, 391, 393

Cromwell, Oliver, 46, 48

Curtis, George William, 292

Dana, Charles A., 216

Dangers of American Liberty of Ames, 129

Danton, 146

Darwin, Charles, 282, 304

Debs, Eugene, 371-373, 457, 458

Declaration of Independence, 64, 88-92, 154, 155, 174, 222, 225, 227, 234, 236, 237, 238, 243, 247, 253, 254, 261, 284, 311, 345

Declaration of Purpose of the National Grange of 1874 357

Declaration of Sentiment of the American Antislavery Convention, 225, 226

Declaration of Sentiments of Mott and Stanton, 200

Defence of the Constitutions of Government of the United States of America of John Adams, 109, 143, 147, 150

Degradation of the Democratic Dogma of Henry Adams, 489

De Jure Naturae et Gentium of Pufendorf, 68 *n*

DeLeon, Daniel, 370

Democracy, 20, 288; and Bellamy, 345, 346, 347, 352; and capitalism, 386, ch. 16; and George, 330; and nineteenth-century liberalism, 297, 310; and the progressive movement, 377; and Woodrow Wilson,

394; Norton on, 296; Dewey on, 427-428; Lowell on, 292, 296; Jacksonian democracy, ch. 8; Jeffersonian democracy, ch. 7; in framers of U.S. Constitution, 116; in Locke, 63, 64; in Puritan Massachusetts, 23, 25, 28, 29, 30, 33; in Williams, 41, 43, 44; in state constitutions, 106; in Wise, 70, 71

Democracy and Leadership of Babbitt, 497

Democracy and Liberty of Lecky, 488

Democracy in America of de Tocqueville, 178 *n*

Democratic Party, 181, 185, 186, 192, 195, 438, 439

Dennis, Lawrence, 444-457

Dewey, John, 334 *n*, 423-431, 435, 437, 461

Dial, 204 *n*

Dickinson, John, 79-81, 84, 85

Direct election of Senate, 377, 387

Direct primary, 377, 387

Discourse on the Constitution and Government of the United States of Calhoun, 268, 273

Discourses on Davila of John Adams, 143

Disquisition on Government of Calhoun, 268

Dix, Dorothea, 200

Domestic and Agricultural Association of Fourier, 216

Donnelly, Ignatius, 359

Dorr's Rebellion, 102

Dos Passos, John, 395

Douglas, Paul, 461

Douglas, Stephen A., 237

Dred Scott Case, 236, 237

Duke of Stockbridge of Bellamy, 335

Duty of the Free States of Channing, 227

Dynamics of War and Revolution of Dennis, 446, 456

Dynamic Sociology of Ward, 374

Eastman, Max, 461

Economic Consequences of the Peace of Keynes, 400 *n*

Economic influence on politics, and muckrakers, 378; in Gronlund, 367, 369; in Hamilton, 129, 136-143, 148; in Harrington, 51-54, 65; in John Adams, 110-112; in Marxian theory, 361, ch. 18; in progressive movement, 378-381, 385; in *The Federalist*, 124-125

Economic Interpretation of the Constitution of Beard, 380

Edict of Nantes, 13

Education of Henry Adams of Henry Adams, 489

Edward VI of England, 14

Eisenhower, Dwight D., 395 *n*, 463

Eliot, John, 335

Elizabeth I of England, 15, 52

Ely, Richard T., 376, 385
Emancipation of Channing, 227
Emerson, Ralph Waldo, 196, 202-205, 206, 210, 211, 213, 216, 220, 223, 227, 289
End of Democracy of Cram, 502
Engels, Friedrich, 188
Engineers and the Price System of Veblen, 382
Equality of Bellamy, 343-351
Equal rights, and Croly, 388; in Jacksonian democracy, ch. 8; in progressive movement, 385; Lincoln on, 238
Erewhon of Butler, 335
Erewhon Revisited of Butler, 335
Escape From Freedom of Fromm, 480
Essay Concerning Human Understanding of Locke, 64 n
"Essay on Population" of Malthus, 321
Essay on Slavery of Channing, 227, 229

Fabian socialism, 355, 370, 363, 374
Farmer Refuted of Hamilton, 83, 130 n
Federal Reserve Act, 391
Federal Trade Commission Act, 386, 387, 391
Federalism, and nature of the Union, ch. 12; in Jefferson, 162; in Taylor, 168; in *The Federalist*, 121; in U.S. Constitution, 117, 127
Federalist of Hamilton, Madison, and Jay, 119-127, 131, 132, 134, 263, 266, 270, 380
Federalists, 128, 129, 130, 131, 132, 139, 143, 144, 148, 150, 165, 166, 167, 168, 169, 172, 173, 174, 175, 176, 193
Field, Stephen J., 297, 298
Fifteenth Amendment, 295
Filmer, Sir Robert, 56, 95, 96
First Amendment, 165
First Continental Congress, 75, 76, 85, 114
First Inaugural Address of Jefferson, 157
First Inaugural Address of Lincoln, 284
First International, 362
First Report on the Public Credit of Hamilton, 136
Fiske, James, 297
Fitzgerald, F. Scott, 395
Fitzhugh, George, 245, 246, 254-261
Foote Resolution, 277
Forty-Two Articles of Anglican faith, 14
Fosdick, Harry Emerson, 461
Foster, William Z., 475
Fourier, Charles, 202, 212, 215-219, 223, 368
Fourierists in America, 257, 313
Fourteen Points of Wilson, 394
Fourteenth Amendment, 261, 308, 432, 434
Frankfurter, Felix, 434, 436
Franklin, Benjamin, 75-77, 78, 79, 88
French Revolution, 144
Fromm, Erich, 480
Fugitive Slave Law of 1850, 235

Full Vindication of Hamilton, 83
Fuller, Margaret, 200
Fundamental Constitutions for the Government of Carolina of Locke, 54
"Fundamental Orders of Connecticut," 100

Gandhi, Mahatma, 209, 458
Garrison, Wendell Phillips, 292
Garrison, William Lloyd, 224-227, 228, 234, 235, 238, 242, 243, 261, 352
Gelasius I, Pope, 2
General Court of Massachusetts Bay, 23, 24, 29
General Court of Rhode Island, 40, 101
George, Henry, 313, 314-334, 336, 349 n, 352, 353, 354, 355, 356, 357, 358, 379 n, 385
George III of England, 74, 108, 155
German socialism, 363, 369
Gitlow, Benjamin, 475
Glorious Revolution of 1688-89, 46, 54, 56
Godkin, Edwin Lawrence, 292-294, 295, 310, 311, 314, 487, 488, 489
Godwin, Parke, 216
Godwin, William, 227
Goldman, Emma, 374 n
Goldman, Eric, 379 n
Gompers, Samuel, 358, 370
Gospel of wealth, 354
Gould, Jay, 297
Granger movement, 313, 314 n, 386
Greeley, Horace, 216
Greenbackism, 356
Gronlund, Lawrence, 363-370, 371, 372
Grote, George, 292
"Growth of Socialism" of Debs, 373

Hamilton, Alexander, 51, 260, 288, 360, 388, 391, 392, 487; and American Revolution, 83, 84, 85, 93, 94; and *The Federalist*, 119, 120, 122, 123; and the national government, ch. 6, 150, 151, 163, 164, 167, 168, 172-173, 175, 184, 193, 195
Hammond, J. H., 245, 246
Hanna, Mark, 489 n
Harding, Warren G., 395, 396, 397
Harper, William, 245, 250-254
Harrington, James, 47, 51-53, 54, 57, 64, 65, 136, 177, 289, 334, 379
Harrison, Benjamin, 354
Hawthorne, Nathaniel, 201, 216, 335
Hayek, Friedrich, 407-417
Haymarket Riot, 298, 335
Hayne, Robert, 277, 278
Hegel, G. W. F., 216, 282, 285
Helper, Hinton R., 239-243
Helvetius, Claude Adrian, 154 n
Hemingway, Ernest, 395
Henderson v. United States, 436
Henry VII of England, 52

Henry VIII of England, 14, 52
Henry, Patrick, 75
Higginson, John, 35
Hiss, Alger, 478
History of the United States of Bancroft, 192
Hitler, Adolph,
Hobbes, Thomas, 153, 247, 255, 290; and Declaration of Independence, 90, 91; and Federalists, 129, 130, 142, 151; and Harrington, 52, 53, 54, 64, 65; and Locke, 53, 56, 57, 60, 64; and Loyalists, 93, 94, 96; and Wise, 68-70, 73; political thought of, 47-51
Hobson, J. A., 333
Hodge, Charles, 245
Hoffer, Eric, 481
Hofstadter, Richard, 486
Holmes, Oliver Wendell, 308, 434, 435, 437
Hooker, Thomas, 32, 39
Hoover, Herbert, 395 *n*, 397, 399-407, 409, 410, 417
Howells, William Dean, 335
Hume, David, 63 *n*
Humphrey, William E., 397
Hurd, John C., 285
Hus, John, 4, 5
Hutchinson, Anne, 9
Hyndman, H. M., 333

Impending Crisis of the South: How to Meet It of Helper, 239
Implied powers, 136-138
Income tax, 386
Individualism, 203, 204, 220, 221, 317, 330; and capitalism, ch. 16, 419-431; and progressive movement, 355, 376
Initiative, 377
Inquiry Into the Principles and Policy of the Government of the United States of Taylor, 168
Instead of a Book; A Fragmentary Exposition of Philosophical Anarchism of Tucker, 300 *n*
Instinct of Workmanship of Veblen, 382
Institutes of the Christian Religion of Calvin, 6, 10
Instrument of Government of the Protectorate, 46
Interest groups, and economics; 361; in Croly, 388; in *The Federalist*, 124-126
Interstate Commerce Commission Act of 1887, 301, 356, 387
Intolerable Acts, 74
Irish Land Question of George, 332
Is Capitalism Doomed? of Dennis, 446

Jackson, Andrew, 184, 185, 199, 289, 360, 389
Jacksonian democracy, ch. 8, 289, 311, 362

James I of England, 15, 18, 19
James, William, 420-425, 431, 435, 437
Jameson, John A., 285
Jay, John, 119
Jefferson, Thomas, 88, 91, 92, 116, 122, 130, 137, 138, 144, 145, 146, ch. 7, 198, 199, 203, 229, 244, 260, 287, 288, 360, 388, 389, 391, 392
Jeffersonian democracy, ch. 7, 174, 198, 261, 311, 392
Judicial review, and pragmatic jurisprudence, 431-437; Jefferson on, 166; in *The Federalist*, 123-124, 132-135; Taylor on, 168
Judiciary Act of 1789, 132

Kansas-Nebraska Act of 1854, 236
Kant, Immanuel, 202
Keaine, Robert, 35
Kent, James, 176, 178, 179
Kentucky Resolutions, 159, 165, 168, 266
Kercheval, Samuel, 164
Keynes, John Maynard, 400 *n*
Kirk, Russell, 484, 485, 509
Knights of Labor, 314, 336, 358, 359
Knox, John, 13, 15
Ku Klux Klan, 395

"Laboring Classes" of Brownson, 188
Labor movement, in progressive movement, 358
Labor theory of value, and Bellamy, 349; in George, 333; in Gronlund, 364; in Locke, 57, 58, 59, 60, 63, 333; in Marx, 468, 469
LaFollette, Robert, 396, 457
LaFollette Seaman's Act, 391
Laissez-faire, 23, 86, 136; American Economic Association on, 376; and Bellamy, 344; and fascism, 446, 448; and Gronlund, 364; and George, 327; and muckrakers, 378; and progressive movement, 356, 381, 393; Dewey on, 426; Holmes on, 434; in Fitzhugh, 256, 260; in Jacksonian democracy, 175, 184-186, 187, 191, 192, 195, 196, 220, 223; in Jefferson, 163, 164, 166; in Taylor, 172; in Manchester liberalism, 294, 299, 300, 301, 302, 305, 306, 307, 309, 310; *also see* ch. 16
Laud, William, 19, 32, 46
Law of Civilization and Decay of Brooks Adams, 490
Lease, Mrs. Mary Elizabeth, 359
Leaves of Grass of Whitman, 198
Lecky, William, 487, 488
Lee, Richard Henry, 88
Leggett, William, 185, 186, 194, 223, 289
Leo XIII, Pope, 332
Leonard, Daniel, 47, 51, 92, 93, 94
Lerner, Max, 461

Letter Concerning Toleration of Locke, 54
Letter to the Town of Providence of Williams, 44
Letters from a Farmer in Pennsylvania of Dickinson, 79, 80, 81
Letters of a Westchester Farmer of Seabury, 93
Leviathan of Hobbes, 48, 129
Lewis, Sinclair, 395, 444
Liberator, 224
Lieber, Francis, 283, 292
Liebman, Joshua, 479
Lincoln, Abraham, 227, 235-238, 284, 288, 362
Lincoln, Thomas, 180
Lippmann, Walter, 506-510
"Little speech" of Winthrop, 30, 33
Livingston, Robert, 88
Lloyd, H. D., 377, 378
Lochner v. New York, 434
Locke, John, 47, 68, 70, 72, 99, 129, 229, 247, 255, 256, 264, 287, 289, 364; and American Revolution, 77, 90, 91, 95, 96, 97; and Constitutionalism, 105, 106, 133, 160; and Jefferson, 151, 152, 153, 154, 198; and political thought of, 53-65; and right to property, 57-60, 119, 154, 231, 303, 333
Lodge, Henry Cabot, 493 *n*
Lollards, 4
Lonely Crowd of Riesman, 481
Long, Huey, 443, 444
Looking Backward of Bellamy, 221, 335-344, 346, 351, 369
Lovestone, Jay, 475
Lowell, James Russell, 216, 292, 296, 487, 488, 489
Loyalists in American Revolution, 92-96
Luther, Martin, 4, 5, 6, 45, 47
Lutheranism, 5, 8, 14, 15, 45

Madison, James, 116, 119, 120, 121, 122, 125, 126, 141, 146, 157, 162, 163, 270, 288, 360, 361, 380
Magna Carta, 22, 99
Magnalia Christi Americana of Mather, 23 *n*
Maine, Henry Sumner, 487
Malthus, T. R., 145, 303, 320, 321, 322, 323
Mannheim, Karl, 465
Man Versus the State of Spencer, 304
Marbury v. Madison, 123, 132, 177
Marshall, John, 99, 123, 132, 135, 138, 148, 166, 167, 175, 176, 177, 266, 279
Marsilio of Padua, 3
Marx, Karl, 52, 188, 282, 331, 332, 360, 370, 426; Norman Thomas on, 457, 458, 459, 460; Paul Sweezy on, 465, 467, 471
Marxian socialism, 361, 366, 369, 370, 381;

also see Norman Thomas and Paul Sweezy
Mary of England, 15
Mary of Scotland, 13
"Massachusettensis" letters of Leonard, 94
Massachusetts Bay Co., 19, 20, 27, 32
Massachusetts *Body of Liberties* of N. Ward, 38
Massachusetts constitution of 1780, 108
Massachusetts Convention of 1820, 176
Mather, Cotton, 68
Mather, Increase, 68
Mayflower Compact, 17, 100
Mayhew, Jonathan, 71-73, 74
Melville, Herman, 201
Memorial to the Legislature of Massachusetts of Dix, 200
Michels, Roberto, 465
Mill, James, 289, 296
Mill, John Stuart, 289, 290, 292, 294, 296, 300, 302, 398, 421
Mills, C. Wright, 461
Milton, John, 41, 47, 72, 229
Missouri Compromise of 1820, 235, 236, 237
Mixed government, in Blackstone, 112-113; in Calhoun, 273; in John Adams, 84, 108-113, 147; in Leonard, 94; in Massachusetts constitution of 1780, 109; in Seabury, 93; Taylor on, 169-170; in Webster, 176-178
Modell of Christian Charity of Winthrop, 28
Modern Utopia of Wells, 335
Monopolies, attacked by progressives, 360
Montesquieu, C. L. de Secondat de, 61, 105, 106, 112, 160
More, Paul Elmer, 220, 302, 445, 487, 494-497, 500, 501, 504
More, Sir Thomas, 334
Morris, William, 333, 335
Motley, J. L., 201
Mott, Lucretia, 200
Muckrakers, 355, 377, 378, 379, 385
Mulford, Elisha, 285

Napoleon, 146, 200
Nation, 292-294, 295, 296, 297, 300, 301, 302, 311, 313 *n*, 314 *n*, 356, 377
Nation of Mulford, 285
National Grange, 357, 358, 359
National Labor Union, 314
Nationalism, in the colonies, 74-75; of Croly, 387, 388, 389, 391; of Dennis, 452; political movement, 343, 370; in the Union, 276-280, 282, 283-286
Natural Law, in American Revolution, 96; and Bellamy, 352; in constitutionalism, 98; Constitution as symbol of, 127, 133, 148, 298; in Declaration of Independence,

89; and Dewey, 426, 431; in economics, 300-301, 303, 305; in eighteenth century, 73; in Hobbes, 48; in Locke, 57, 60, 63; and Manchester liberalism, 291; and pragmatic jurisprudence, 428; and slavery, 238, 259; in Wise, 68, 69, 70, 71
Natural rights, in American Revolution, 85; in antislavery thought, ch. 10; and Babbitt, 409; and Bellamy, 352; in constitutionalism, 99, 107; in Declaration of Independence, 90, 91; and Dewey, 425; in eighteenth century, 73; and George, 333; and Gronlund, 366; in Hamilton, 83, 142; in Hobbes, 49-50; in Jefferson, 156-157; in Locke, 54, 57, 60-63; in Otis, 77; in Paine, 86; and pre-Civil War thought, 287; and proslavery thought, ch. 11; and Utilitarianism, 293
Nature of Emerson, 202, 204 n
Navigation Acts, 74
Nemesis of Mediocrity of Cram, 501
Neutrality Proclamation of 1793, 131
New Atlantis of Bacon, 334
New Deal, 136, 141, 418, 419, 433, 443, 465; and Hoover, 403, 404, 439, 441, 442; and Thomas, 458, 459, 464
New Democracy of Weyl, 389
New Economy of Gronlund, 363
New England Company, 19
New Freedom of Wilson, 391, 393, 395, 400, 407
New Harmony, 212, 213, 215
New Nationalism of Croly, 387, 389
New Nationalism of Theodore Roosevelt, 389
New Republic, 387
New View of Society of Owen, 213
New Views of the Constitution of the United States of Taylor, 168, 172, 267
New York Evening Post, 185, 186, 216
New York Sun, 216
New York Tribune, 216
News from Nowhere of Morris, 335
Newton, Sir Isaac, 145, 151
Nicholas of Cusa, 3
Niebuhr, Reinhold, 461
Ninety-Five Theses, 5
Northampton Church Covenant, 25 n
Northwest Ordinance of 1787, 114
Norton, Charles Eliot, 296, 310, 487, 488, 489
Notes on Virginia of Jefferson, 156, 158, 159, 161
Notions of the Americans Picked Up By a Travelling Bachelor of Cooper, 181
Nott, Josiah Clark, 245
Novanglus of John Adams, 84, 94
Nullification, 275, 278

Oceana of Harrington, 51, 65, 177, 334

"Office of the People In Art, Government and Religion" of Bancroft, 192
Opinion of the Constitutionality of the Bank of the United States of Hamilton, 137
Organization Man of Whyte, 481
Origin of Species of Darwin, 304
Otis, James, 77-79, 99
Our Destiny of Gronlund, 363
Our Land and Land Policy of George, 317
Owen, Robert, 212-215, 223
Owenites, 313

Pacificus articles of Hamilton, 131
Paine, Thomas, 85-88, 92, 225, 287
Panic of 1873, 314, 356
Parkman, Francis, 201
Parrington, Vernon A., 378
Paterson, William, 116
Path I Trod of Powderly, 359
Patrons of Husbandry, 313
Patten, Simon, 376
Peace of Augsburg, 6
Peale, Norman Vincent, 479
Pendleton Act of 1883, 297
Peoria speech of Lincoln, 236
Perplexed Philosopher of George, 332
Petition of Rights, 19, 23, 99
Philadelphia Convention of 1787, 113, 114, 115, 116, 117, 123, 131, 132
Philip the Fair of France, 3
Phillips, David Graham, 377
Pierce, Charles, 421
"Plantation Agreement at Providence," 101
Platform of Church Discipline, 23, 26
Plato, 51, 72, 334
Plessy v. Ferguson, 436
Political Science and Comparative Constitutional Law of Burgess, 285
Politics of Emerson, 205
Pomeroy, J. N., 285
Populism, 359, 372
Populists, 343, 358, 360, 362, 377
Pound, Roscoe, 434, 435
Powderly, Terence V., 314, 358, 359
Pragmatic jurisprudence, 431-437
Pragmatism of James, 421
Prescott, W. H., 201
Progress and Poverty of George, 318-334
Progressive Democracy of Croly, 387
Progressive Party, 396
Progressive program of 1912, 389
Progressives, 360
Promise of American Life of Croly, 387
Property, and aristocracy, 494-496; cause of aristocracy, 145; cause of faction, 125; Channing on, 230-233; in Dickinson, 81; Fitzhugh on, 258, 259; and the Federalists, 148; Harper on, 251; in Harrington, 52-53; and Jefferson, 154-155; in John

Adams, *see* Mixed government, Aristocracy; in Locke, 57, 58, 59, 60, 62, 97, 119; and ninetenth-century liberalism, 302, 303, 308, 311; qualifications for suffrage in state constitutions, 106, 108-109, 176-184; and rent, *see* Henry George
Proportional representation, 294, 297
Protection or Free Trade of George, 332
Protestantism, 20, 64
Protestant Reformation, ch. 1, 45, 47, 62, 66
Providence Plantations, 41
Public Philosophy of Lippmann, 505-509
Pufendorf, Samuel, 68
Pullman Strike, 372
Puritan Parliament, 41
Puritans, in England, 18, 19, 20, 46; in Massachusetts, 20, 21, ch. 2, 66, 68, 313

Quatre Mouvements of Fourier, 216

Railroad regulation, 386
Randolph, Edmund, 116, 137, 145
Rauschenbusch, Walter, 354, 458
Recall, 377, 387
Reed, James A., 438
Referendum, 377, 387
Reflections on the Revolution in France of Burke, 282
Religious toleration; in Calvinism, 9-13; in eighteenth century, 73; in England, 14; in Jefferson, 155-156; in Locke, 54-56, 61, 62; in Puritan Massachusetts, ch. 2; in *Report on Manufactures*, 140; in Williams, 40-45
Report on Manufactures of Hamilton, 140
Republic of Plato, 334
Republican-Democrats, Jeffersonian, 129, 130, 143, 144, 149, 150, 167
Reuther, Walter, 461
Reynolds, Senator "Bob," 443, 444
Ricardo, David, 289, 290, 294, 300, 302, 303, 305, 322, 323, 331, 363
Riesman, David, 481, 482
Rights of the British Colonies Asserted and Proved of Otis, 77
Ripley, George, 216
Road to Serfdom of Hayek, 408, 409, 410, 415, 416
Roberts, Owen J., 433
Robespierre, Maximilian, 146
Robinson, John, 17
Rockefeller, John D., 307, 372
Roosevelt, Franklin Delano, 395 *n*, 437-442
Roosevelt, Theodore, 333, 354, 355, 389, 493 *n*
Ross, Edward A., 354, 374, 375-376
Rossier, Clinton, 484
Rousseau, Jean Jacques, 56, 227, 348, 498, 499, 500

Rush, Benjamin, 150
Russell, Charles E., 377, 378

Saint-Simon, Henri de, 216
Sane Society of Fromm, 480
Saye and Sele, Lord, 32, 33, 34
Science of Political Economy of George, 332-333
Seabury, Samuel, 83, 92-94, 130 *n*
Secession, 275, 284
Second Book of Common Prayer, 14, 18
Second Continental Congress, 85, 88, 103
Security Council of the United Nations, 272, 273
Self-Reliance of Emerson, 203
Seligman, E. R. A., 376, 385
"Separate but equal," 436, 437
Separation of powers, in Blackstone, 112-113; in Harrington, 53; in John Adams, 112, 148; in Locke, 61; in *Notes on Virginia*, 160-161; in state constitutions, 104-106, 108, 109; in *The Federalist*, 121-122; in U. S. Constitution, 117, 118, 127; in Webster, 177
Separatism, 16, 17, 18
Separatists, 17, 18, 19, 20
Seven Years War, 72, 74
Shaw, George Bernard, 333
Shays' Rebellion, 119, 125, 144, 335
Sheen, Fulton J., 479
Sherman Anti-Trust Act, 302, 360, 386, 387, 388
Sherman, Roger, 88
Sidney, Algernon, 47, 72
Siegfried, André, 397
Silver Shirts, 443, 444
Simmons, A. M., 378, 385
Simpson, Jerry, 359
Sin and Society: An Analysis of Latter-Day Iniquity of Ross, 375
Sinclair, Upton, 377, 378, 443
Single tax, 327
Slavery, antislavery thought, ch. 10; in Brownson, 189; Jefferson on, 155; and Jeffersonians, 173; proslavery thought, ch. 11; Thoreau on, 206, 208; Whitman on, 197
Slavery in the Light of Social Ethics of Harper, 250
Smith, Adam, 289, 290, 294, 299, 300, 302, 309, 398, 426
Smith, J. Allen, 378, 379-380, 381, 385
Social Darwinism, 304, 305, 310, 314, 327, 330
Social Darwinists, and Calhoun, 248, 261, 313
Social Destiny of Man of Brisbane, 216
Social gospel, 354
Social legislation; and social Darwinism, 305, 306

Social Monster of Most, 374 *n*
Social Problems of George, 332
Social Statics of Spencer, 304, 308, 332, 366
Socialism, in America, 362; Debs on, 372-374; DeLeon on, 370-372; in Fitzhugh, 257; German, 362, 363; Gronlund on, 363-370; Marxian, 361, 366 and ch. 18; and muckrakers, 378; in politics, 370-374; and progressive movement, 360; and Sumner, 306; and Sweezy, 464-472; and Thomas, 457-465
Socialist Labor Party, 362, 370, 371, 473
Socialist Party, 371, 373, 396, 457, 458, 473, 474
Society for Christian Union and Progress, 187
Sociological jurisprudence, 435
Sociology for the South, or the Failure of Free Society of Fitzhugh, 255
Sovereignty, and the nature of the Union, ch. 12
Spencer, Herbert, 302, 304, 305, 308, 332, 366, 434
Spirit of American Government: A Study of the Constitution: Its Origin, Influence and Relations to Democracy of J. Allen Smith, 379
Spirit of the Common Law of Pound, 435
Spirit of the Laws of Montesquieu, 105
State constitutions, post-Revolutionary, 103-109
Stamp Act, 74, 77, 80, 85
Stamp Act Congress, 78, 79, 114
Standard Oil Company, 307, 377
Stanton, Elizabeth Cady, 200
States rights; in Calhoun, 246-247; in Jeffersonian democracy, ch. 7; and nature of the Union, ch. 12
Steffens, Lincoln, 377, 378
Stephen, J. K., 487
Stephen, Leslie, 296
Stephens, Alexander H., 285
Stephens, Uriah S., 314
Steward Machine Company v. Davis, 141
Stoics, 89, 90
Story, Joseph, 141, 176
Stowe, Harriet Beecher, 236
Stringfellow, Thornton, 245
Strong, Josiah, 310
Suffrage, Calhoun on, 270-271; Cooper on, 180-184; and emancipated Negroes, 294-296; in Massachusetts constitution of 1780, 108-109; and nineteenth-century liberalism, 293, 294; in *Notes on Virginia,* 159, 161; and property qualifications, 176-180, 223; Whitman on, 195, 198; woman, 296
Sugar Act, 74, 75, 77
Summary View of the Rights of British America of Jefferson, 154

Sumner, William Graham, 292, 302-309, 310, 311, 314, 332, 374, 487
Survival of the fittest, 304, 306, 307, 308, 310, 317, 321, 330, 356, 386
Sweezy, Paul, 444, 464-472

Taft, William Howard, 355
Taney, Roger B., 237
Tarbell, Ida M., 377
Tariff, Hamilton on, 140, 141; Jefferson on, 164-165; Jackson on, 185; and nineteenth-century liberalism, 301; Taylor on, 167
Tariff Act of 1832, 250
Taylor, John, 144, 145, 163 *n*, 167-173, 180, 181, 186, 191, 195, 199, 266, 267, 360
Taylor, William C., 240 *n*
Tenth Amendment, 118
Texas v. White, 284, 287
Theory of Business Enterprise of Veblen, 382
Theory of Capitalist Development of Sweezy, 466, 472
Theory of Our National Existence of Hurd, 285
Theory of the Leisure Class of Veblen, 382, 383, 385
Theory of Social Revolutions of Brooks Adams, 491
Thirty-Nine Articles of Anglican faith, 15
Thomas Aquinas, 99
Thomas, Norman, 396, 444, 457-465, 474
Thompson, Dorothy, 461
Thoreau, Henry David, 202, 206-210, 211, 213, 216, 220, 223, 224, 227, 289
Tilden, Samuel J., 318
Tocqueville, Alexis de, 174, 178 *n*
Townshend Acts, 74
Transcendentalism, 202, 204
Transcendentalist of Emerson, 204
Traveller from Altruria of Howells, 335
Treason of the Senate of Phillips, 377
Treatise on Constitutional Convention of Jameson, 285
Treatise of Reformation Without Tarying for Anie of Browne, 16
True Believer of Hoffer, 481
True Civilization of Warren, 300 *n*
True Constitution of Government in the Sovereignty of the Individual of Andrews, 300 *n*
Truman, Harry S., 470
Tucker, Benjamin R., 300 *n*
Turgot, Anne Robert Jacques, 109
Turner, Frederick Jackson, 378, 379, 385
T.V.A., 402, 419, 440
Twain, Mark, 297
Two Swords, Doctrine of, 2, 11
Two Treatises of Government of Locke, 54, 56-65
Tyranny Unmasked of Taylor, 172

Uncle Tom's Cabin of Stowe, 236
Underground Railroad, 235
Underwood Tariff Act, 391
Unforeseen Tendencies of Democracy of Godkin, 488
Union, preservation of, ch. 12; Lincoln on, 238
Unitarianism, 202
United States v. Butler, 141
Unlimited Submission and Non-Resistance to the Higher Powers of Mayhew, 72
Utilitarianism, in Manchester liberalism, 289-291, 293; and pragmatism, 428
Utopia of Sir Thomas More, 334
Utopian settlements, 211, 212; *also see* Owen, Fourier

Vanderbilt, Commodore, 297
Veblen, Thorstein, 382-385
Viereck, Peter, 482-484
View of the Causes and Consequences of the American Revolution of Boucher, 95
Vindication of the Government of the New England Churches of Wise, 68, 69
Virginia Bill of Rights of 1776, 107
Virginia Resolutions, 168

Walpole, Robert, 72
Ward, Lester F., 374-375, 385, 424
Ward, Nathaniel, 38
Warren, Earl, 437
Warren, Josiah, 300 *n*
Washington, George, 131, 137, 163
Watson, Tom, 359
Wealth of Nations of Adam Smith, 309

Weber, Max, 465
Webster, Daniel, 52, 176, 177, 178, 277, 278, 279, 280, 360
Wells, H. G., 335
Westminster Review, 292
Weyl, Walter, 386, 389-390, 391
What Social Classes Owe to Each Other of Sumner, 306, 332
"What the Railroad Will Bring Us" of George, 316
Wheeler, Burton K., 396
Whig Party, 195
Whiskey Rebellion, 139
White, John, 19
Whitman, Walt, 194-198, 201
Whittier, John Greenleaf, 216
Whyte, William H., Jr., 481, 482
William and Mary of England, 46, 54, 56
William of Occam, 3, 4
William the Conqueror, 87
Williams, Roger, 32, 38-45, 54, 55, 56, 101, 155, 187, 229
Wilson, Francis, 484
Wilson, James, 81-83, 84, 85
Wilson, Woodrow, 354, 386, 391-394, 401, 442, 458
Winthrop, John, 19, 27-31, 33
Wise, John, 67-73
Wise, Stephen, 461
Wollstonecraft, Mary, 227
Woman of the Nineteenth Century of Fuller, 200
Wright, Frances, 200
Wycliffe, John, 4, 5